THE ROYAL HORTICULTURAL S

# FRUIT &
# VEGETABLE
# GARDENING IN
# AUSTRALIA

Dear Beth + Mark,
Many congratulations
on the beginning of
your new life together!
xoxo
Aliese

Denni + BLIXA
June, 2012

THE ROYAL HORTICULTURAL SOCIETY

# FRUIT &
# VEGETABLE
# GARDENING IN
# AUSTRALIA

MICHAEL POLLOCK  EDITOR-IN-CHIEF

PETER ANDERSON  PHOTOGRAPHER

ALLEN GILBERT, LAURIE COSGROVE AND JENNIFER WILKINSON
AUSTRALIAN CONSULTANTS

# LONDON, NEW YORK, MUNICH,
# MELBOURNE, DELHI

## CONTRIBUTORS

| | |
|---|---|
| Jim Arbury | Tree Fruits, Grape Vines |
| Guy Barter | Vegetables, Crops |
| John Edgeley | Soft Fruits |
| Jim England | Vegetables, General and Crops |
| Michael Pollock | Growing Fruit and Vegetables, Culinary Herbs |

## AUSTRALIAN CONTRIBUTORS

| | |
|---|---|
| Allen Gilbert | Tree and Soft Fruits, Grape Vines |
| Laurie Cosgrove | Tree and Soft Fruits, Grape Vines |
| Jennifer Wilkinson | Vegetables, General and Crops, Culinary Herbs |

| | |
|---|---|
| Senior editor | Annelise Evans |
| Project art editor | Murdo Culver |
| Editors | Louise Abbott, Alison Copland, Helen Fewster, Candida Frith-Macdonald, Linden Hawthorne, Jane Simmonds |
| Designer | Alison Lotinga |
| Managing editor | Anna Kruger |
| Managing art editor | Lee Griffiths |
| DTP design | Louise Waller |
| Media resources | Romaine Werblow |
| Picture research | Samantha Nunn |
| Production controller | Mandy Inness |
| Australian managing editor | Rosie Adams |

First published in Australia in 2004 by
Dorling Kindersley Australasia Pty Ltd

This edition published in 2006 by
Dorling Kindersley Australasia Pty Ltd
250 Camberwell Road, Camberwell, Victoria 3124
A division of Pearson Australia Group Pty Ltd

Published in association with
The Royal Horticultural Society

Copyright © 2002, 2004
Dorling Kindersley Limited, London

National Library of Australia Cataloguing-in-Publication data:
Fruit and vegetable gardening in Australia.
Rev. ed.
Includes index.
ISBN-13: 978-1-74033-570-6

1. Fruit-culture - Handbooks, manuals, etc. 2. Vegetable gardening -
Handbooks, manuals, etc. I. Pollock, Michael. II. Anderson, Peter.
III. Royal Horticultural Society (Great Britain).

Colour reproduction by GRB Editrice Slr. Italy
Printed and bound by Star Standard, Singapore

See our complete catalogue at
## www.dk.com.au

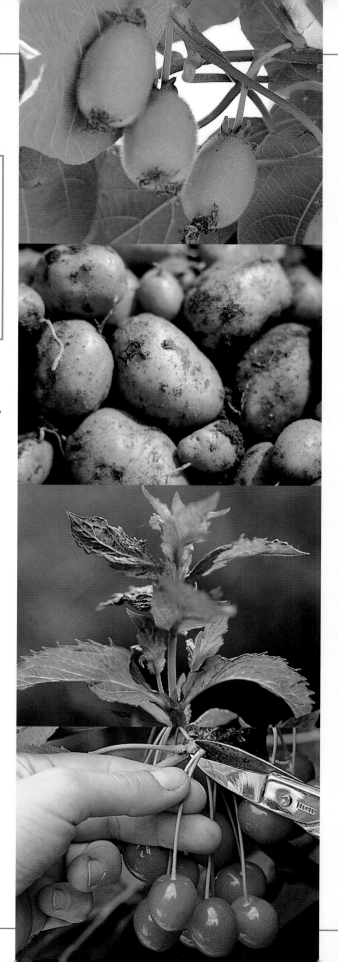

# CONTENTS

## The Australian gardening year

Throughout this book, the gardening year is assumed to consist of 12 seasons, or part-seasons. These correspond to calendar months, as shown below.

| | |
|---|---|
| early spring: September | early autumn: March |
| mid-spring: October | mid-autumn: April |
| late spring: November | late autumn: May |
| early summer: December | early winter: June |
| midsummer: January | midwinter: July |
| late summer: February | late winter: August |

# INTRODUCTION

GROWING YOUR OWN vegetables, culinary herbs, and fruit brings a very special satisfaction to gardening. There are, of course, substantial savings to be made in turning a small investment on seed or plants into a regular supply of food for the table, whether you grow only a selection of choice seasonal crops, such as asparagus, or strive for self-sufficiency. For those concerned about additives in commercially produced food, there is the security of knowing exactly how your produce has been grown. The exceptional pleasure of kitchen gardening lies, however, in the subtlety and freshness of flavour of crops gathered straight from your garden – a flavour that has not been diminished by long transport, storage, or special packaging.

**Fruits of your labours**
*Enjoy the intensity and subtlety of flavour that is possible only with produce freshly picked from the plant.*

amateur allotment holders have built up an impressive body of expertise and knowledge over the years. This volume sets out to continue the tradition by distilling that experience into an accessible format for the modern gardener.

The cultivation of food crops, more than any other form of gardening, demands commitment from the gardener. Knowledge of basic principles, thoughtful planning, good preparation, and, above all, time spent in regular care of growing crops, are crucial to success. Failure in any of this leads to disappointing results, and wasted time and money.

The decorative qualities of edible crops, whether grown in a dedicated plot or among conventional ornamental plants, are too little appreciated. Colourful blossom smothers fruit trees in spring, handsome foliage such as the ferny fronds of carrots or crinkly leaves of lettuces adorn the summer garden, and evergreen herbs and overwintering vegetables are enhanced by frost. Tree and soft fruits trained along walls and fences or over archways can be very attractive as well as productive.

Those new to kitchen gardening would be wise to start on a modest scale, but to plan the garden so that the area given over to food crops can expand with your experience. There is no ideal size for a kitchen garden because it depends on many variable factors such as family demand, the garden site, and personal abilities and preferences. The good news is that no garden is too small: crops can be grown in all sorts of containers, including windowboxes.

## LEARNING FROM EXPERIENCE

It is not surprising then that interest in growing fruit and vegetables is on the increase. Generations of professional gardeners from private estates and

## IN HARMONY WITH NATURE

Most gardeners have a particular affinity with the natural environment and fully appreciate the good sense of maintaining a natural balance of living organisms within the garden and of conserving natural resources. Many take the opportunity to run their kitchen garden entirely on organic lines. It is not necessary to grow produce that is totally free of blemishes or to extract the maximum possible yield from every plant – as is the case with commercial cultivation. A reasonable level

**Potager garden, Tintinhull**
*Orderly lines of well-managed vegetables and flowers for cutting, abundant and full of promise, have their own special beauty.*

of pests and diseases can be tolerated in the garden, and there are means of recycling organic waste and of using water wisely. This philosophy is followed throughout the book and you may be inspired to examine further aspects of gardening organically. Chemical treatments are available for those who wish to use them, but there is no doubt that the range is diminishing because of safety regulations and commercial considerations.

## INCREASING CHOICE

The wide range of fruit, vegetables, and culinary herbs described in this book reflects the modern gardener's interest in growing an increasing variety of crops. Most of the crops can be reliably grown outdoors in temperate climates, although some, such as peppers and peaches, produce better quality crops for a longer season under cover. The prospect of climate change, and the popularity of the conservatory, however, raise new possibilities; so tender fruits such as citrus and pineapples are covered – to fire the imagination.

The introduction of new cultivars (garden varieties), often with improved quality or genetic resistance to a pest or disease, is a great boon to the kitchen gardener. To help you choose from the bewildering number of cultivars now available, each crop covered in the text includes a core list of recommended cultivars. Many have received the Award of Garden Merit after extensive trials by the Royal Horticultural Society. Your own experience will eventually be the best guide.

The comprehensive information in this text will provide a good grounding for you to develop your own style of kitchen gardening. Never forget the principles, keep abreast of new developments, and, above all, take time to enjoy your garden.

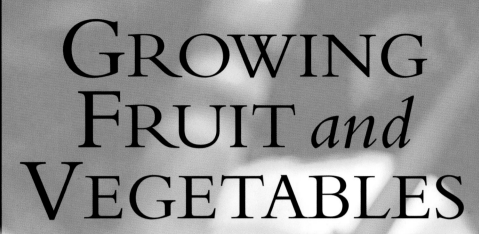

# GROWING FRUIT *and* VEGETABLES

PLANTS GROWN FOR FOOD differ from ornamentals in one key respect — that in harvesting their crops, full of goodness and nourishment, we continually take something from the plants and from the soil. It is critical, therefore, that we repay this debt with care — choosing the best site possible for our crops, understanding and nurturing the soil, recycling where we can (for example, by making garden compost), and tending the plants as they grow — protecting them from competition from weeds, attack by pests and diseases, and harsh conditions.

Growing fruits and vegetables can be demanding, and does require commitment, but brings with it an enormous amount of satisfaction — the excitement of planning which crop, and which cultivar, to grow and how to grow it; control over how the food we eat is produced; a sense of expectation and work and patience rewarded as crops in their turn come into season; and, of course, plentiful harvests.

# Climate and location

For most of us the choice of where we live is governed by considerations other than the ideal conditions for gardening. In many cases one has to make do with a challenging site, but a great deal can be achieved by careful planning, imaginative design, and choosing suitable crops and cultivars.

The characteristics of your location are even more significant for fruit and vegetables than for ornamental plants, because the range of plants is narrower, with less scope for selecting to suit the climate. It is essential to understand the basic needs for healthy plant growth: light, suitable temperature, water, air, and nutrients. Each is influenced to varying degrees by the conditions in the area, which we cannot change; but through respecting, maintaining, or improving the physical characteristics of a garden within such constraints, we can still help meet these needs.

## The importance of light

Direct sunshine provides the quantity and quality of light needed to maximize photosynthesis – the process by which plants use light to convert water and carbon dioxide into energy for plant activity. This is vital for healthy growth, producing bulk in leafy vegetable crops and sturdy development of flowers and fruits. The importance of sunshine can be seen in the weak, unproductive growth of plants that are shaded by buildings or hedges. Summer sunshine

**Breeze**
*Warmth of wall counters cooling effects of any breeze*

**Warm spot**
*In a sheltered garden, a wall facing the sun absorbs heat during the day and then releases it again at night when the air temperature falls. It also concentrates the power of the sun by reflecting some warmth back immediately. Breezes will be deflected, but a solid wall is not suitable as a windbreak in an exposed position.*

ripens the shoots of woody fruit plants, improving flowering and consequent fruiting in the following season.

Average daily hours of sunshine vary from place to place, but in all areas the aim should be to ensure that any shade to the kitchen garden is kept to a minimum by avoiding, or removing wherever possible, any trees or other obstructions that create shade cover. Cane fruits, brassicas, and perennial vegetables will all tolerate moderate shade where a site is only partly in sun.

There are a few situations where it may be necessary to provide temporary artificial shade. Prolonged exposure to strong sun can cause scorch or, more often, wilting in newly transplanted crops; this is associated mainly with the sun's warmth, which is primarily of benefit to the gardener.

## The effects of temperature

The way in which sunshine raises air temperature is almost entirely beneficial to the gardener. It encourages all stages of plant growth, from the sowing of vegetables or bud burst in woody fruit plants through to crop maturity. It raises the soil temperature, promoting seed germination and also enhancing root growth. Bright, warm days increase insect activity, essential for satisfactory pollination of fruiting crops. Areas that enjoy high levels of sunshine and resulting warm air usually have a relatively long local growing season. Growth starts early and finishes late, so cropping may be extended, especially in vegetable gardens.

The adverse effects of low temperatures are considerable. Cold air and soil lead to slower germination, growth, and bud burst; frost can be devastating. Tender vegetables, such as tomatoes or cucurbits, will be destroyed, and frost brings the threat of very serious damage to the blossom of fruit plants, resulting in loss of the crop.

The restrictions on fruit and vegetable growing in areas with a high risk of frost can be reduced by choosing hardier crops and cultivars. For instance, the brassica group of vegetables includes very hardy crops compared with the generally more tender pea and bean group, and among the fruit crops peaches are more tender than apples. There are lettuces bred to survive winter outdoors, and relatively late-flowering fruit plant cultivars are less likely to be damaged by spring frosts.

## WHAT IS A MICROCLIMATE?

Whatever the general climate of an area, variations due to topography, such as the sunny or shaded sides of a hill, will create differences within it, producing microclimates. The structures and plants around and in a garden create their own microclimates, making one garden, or even one area within a garden, markedly different from another. Levels of shade and shelter will almost certainly vary; some corners may be more prone to frost, and moisture levels are likely to differ across a site. It is important to be aware of these variations and use them to their best advantage when planning your fruit and vegetable garden, as plants that thrive in one area can do poorly in another.

- **Open areas** of the garden that face into the sun, particularly if they slope down towards it, warm up quickly in spring and are ideal for early crops.
- **Walls and buildings** can provide added warmth and protection for fruit trees if they face the sun, but can also create turbulence by blocking or funnelling winds.
- **Sheltering hedges** will provide a better microclimate for all crops, but the areas of the garden closest to them may be relatively dry and receive less light.
- **Low-lying areas** may be sheltered from wind, but are potential frost pockets and are also likely to have colder, wetter soil than higher areas in winter.

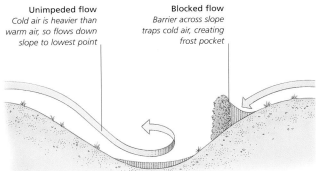

**Unimpeded flow**
*Cold air is heavier than warm air, so flows down slope to lowest point*

**Blocked flow**
*Barrier across slope traps cold air, creating frost pocket*

◁ **Winter freeze**
*Some crops, such as these Savoy and ornamental cabbages, are hardy enough to withstand even a freezing blanket of snow in winter.*

△ **How frost pockets form**
*Cold air may accumulate in certain areas of the garden, making them prone to frost – these areas are known as frost pockets. They can occur in hollows in the ground or behind a barrier, such as a hedge; thinning the lower branches of hedging plants will improve the situation by allowing some cold air to flow through and away.*

Protection with glass or plastic is a well-tried method of growing fruit and vegetables in a frost-prone climate (*see pp. 43–48*), and tender fruits may be nurtured in the shelter of a relatively warm wall (*see facing page*).

Frost does provide some benefits to gardeners. It helps in the shattering of clods on clay soils (*see pp. 14–15*), and will also help to destroy or reduce overwintering pests and diseases.

Cold air accumulates in hollows, so be alert to the potential effects of frost pockets (*see above right*). Sometimes such reservoirs of cold air can be removed by opening up gaps in barriers, such as hedges, to allow air current to flow to a lower level. A slightly sloping garden site is therefore less likely to be prone to frost, provided that the air flow is not obstructed. Gardens in coastal areas are much less likely to be subject to frost, although this is inevitably at the expense of exposure to the damaging effects of high winds.

## Levels of rainfall

Rainfall is a major influence on the success of fruit and vegetable gardening. Levels of rainfall across Australia are often highly variable, due to the size of the continent and its geology and topography. A hillside facing the prevailing wind experiences relatively high rainfall, as the rising air cools, causing precipitation; the leeward side of the hill is its rain shadow, with lower rainfall, as the falling air warms. In areas of low rainfall there is risk of drought, the effects ranging in severity from checked plant growth to crop loss. Leafy vegetables, like lettuces, require a steady supply of water to develop into an edible product, and water is similarly essential for fruit to swell. Conservation of natural water resources is very important, and gardeners need to ensure that the soil holds moisture well and to reduce surface evaporation by the use of mulches (*see pp. 41–42*).

A high-rainfall climate brings its own challenges: the greatest of these is the likelihood of waterlogged soil. Good soil drainage is important for kitchen gardens anywhere, but it is a prime consideration in such localities. Young vegetable plants are particularly vulnerable in saturated soils that are cold and airless: growth is inhibited, and vital nutrients, such as lime and nitrogen, may also become depleted.

High rainfall encourages some pests and diseases, such as slugs and snails and damping off (*see* Plant problems, *pp. 246–264*). Fruit crops are more prone to disease in areas of high rainfall and high humidity: trees suffer shoot, leaf, and fruit infections, and soft fruits, such as strawberries and raspberries, are affected by fruit soft rot and show root growth restriction. Fruit crop management in areas receiving more than 100cm (39in) of rainfall in an average year will be very demanding.

Fungicides can be effective in controlling diseases, but care needs to be taken and organic approaches are preferable to the use of harsh chemicals. Fungicides can be less effective in high-rainfall areas. Where the gardener sensibly wishes to keep fungicide spraying to a minimum, it becomes essential to discourage diseases by excellent plant care. Some fruit and vegetable cultivars with natural resistance to disease are also available, but the general choice will inevitably be reduced in a high-rainfall climate.

## Altitude and exposure

Strong winds are predominantly a feature of exposed sites. Gardens at high altitudes will usually be more prone to strong winds, as will coastal sites, where salt deposits on leaves can be an additional problem. Strong winds can also be created where air is funnelled between buildings or natural features.

The most obvious effects of wind are physical damage and loss of stability; other adverse effects, less immediately apparent, include increased water loss and a reduction in the pollinating activity of flying insects.

Shelter, in the form of well-placed windbreaks (*see pp. 12–13*), is necessary for the gardener to achieve success in cropping in these conditions. Fortunately, of all the elements of natural climate, the effects of wind can perhaps most readily be modified.

# Shelter from wind

There is no doubt that the provision of shelter around a fruit and vegetable garden is vital to successful production. It has been shown to raise temperatures by up to 3°C (5°F), encouraging the opening and pollination of flowers and the ripening of wood and fruit. In any site, no matter how suitable the soil and climate, carefully selected shelter will increase yields. In some cases, shelter will be essential for any kind of success, and the earlier it is in place the better.

## The effects of wind

Wind has both immediately apparent and unseen influences on crops. The most obvious effects result from high winds. Branches of fruit trees and bushes are broken, and trees on rootstocks that are shallow-rooting can be blown over in gales. There may be blossom damage in springtime, and loss of fruit as crops reach maturity. Physical damage to vegetables is most likely to be seen in taller crops, such as Brussels sprouts and broad beans, keeling over. Pea and bean supports may be loosened or destroyed, and high winds can damage or even destroy glass or plastic structures, such as tunnel cloches, used to protect crops like strawberries and many vegetables. More tender foliage, such as that of lettuces, beans, and cucurbits, may be damaged. Near the sea, wind often also carries damaging salt deposits.

Apart from these clearly visible effects of wind, horticultural experiments have shown significant depression in the growth and cropping of fruits and vegetables on open sites. The most likely causes are higher water loss

**Sheltered garden**
*The mature hedge that surrounds this garden affords ideal protection from wind. Its semi-permeable nature has the effect of breaking up and slowing the wind, without giving rise to damaging turbulence. In the settled conditions that are created within such shelter, crops flourish.*

from plants and lower average air and soil temperatures. Winds increase water loss from plants, especially those newly planted out, because air moving over the leaves causes evaporation. This drying slows growth, as plants reduce activity to conserve moisture. The effect is heightened during hot, dry summer months and is aggravated by the drying effects of wind on the soil surface.

On exposed, flat or elevated sites, wind can erode very light or peaty soils. The pollinating activity of insects is likely to be reduced, and, if pesticide sprays are used, their operation can be much less effective as they are blown off-target.

## Planning shelter

There is a wide range of potential benefits to be gained from shelter, both in gardens with some level of existing shelter within a developed urban setting, and in country gardens, but the advantages do need to be weighed against the possible disadvantages.

Establishing shelter incurs financial expense and physical effort. There is often a risk of creating a frost pocket by enclosing an area where very cold air can accumulate (*see p. 11*). Shelter features can cause shade and impede the even distribution of rainfall. The enhanced temperature and relatively still air of the microclimate (*see p. 10*) may create favourable conditions for plant pests and diseases. Where living plants are used to establish shelter, they may compete for moisture. In any situation, bear in mind all of these considerations at the planning stage.

Shelter is clearly most valuable in protecting crops from the prevailing wind, but there can be damage from cold winds from other directions, and the best practice is to establish shelter around all sides of the fruit and vegetable garden. A good windbreak will provide 10m (30ft) of protection on the leeward side for every 1m (3ft) of height, so a large garden will need

**Action of wind**
*Solid windbreak barriers are actually counter-productive. Oncoming air is forced up over the barrier, then drawn down on the other side by the low pressure behind the barrier. Turbulence is created both on the leeward side and to a lesser extent on the windward side.*

**Negative pressure**
*Air passing over top of barrier creates negative pressure on lee side*

**Height of turbulence**
*Air will be disturbed for up to twice height of barrier*

**Extent of turbulence**
*Effects may extend over whole garden site*

**Windward side**
*Turbulence created as air is forced upwards*

## PLANTS FOR SHELTER HEDGES

**Coastal rosemary (*Westringia fructicosa*)** *This hardy plant has foliage like the herb rosemary. It grows to 2–3m and produces attractive white/purple flowers throughout the year. Can take regular pruning.*

**Flowering currant (*Ribes sanguineum*)** *Makes a decorative hedge with pink flowers in spring if grown in full sun, and does well on most soils. Trim after flowering.*

**Grevillea (*Grevillea spp.*)** *Of the many grevilleas, some grow as bushes, others as ground covers or shrubs. G. 'Robyn Gordon' is an example of a good hedging form.*

**Hawthorn (*Crataegus monogyna*)** *Tolerates strong winds. Trim after flowering or in autumn.*

**Hazel (*Corylus avellana*)** *Multi-stemmed, with strong shoots, attractive catkins in spring if lightly trimmed, and yellow leaves in autumn.*

**Hop bush (*Dodonea sinuolata*)** *Has attractive red foliage and attractive pink seed pods. It is drought tolerant and can take regular pruning.*

**Spiraea 'Arguta'** *Grows on most soils in full sun and bears dense clusters of white flowers in spring. Trim after flowering.*

**Tea tree (*Leptospermum spp.*)** *Many of the tea trees can be used as hedging plants. They take well to pruning and shaping.*

*Spiraea 'Arguta'*

some internal windbreaks if the perimeter shelter is not to be too high and cause possible shading problems.

Avoid solid barriers, which can create turbulent eddies and cause damage on the leeward side. If gusting wind is filtered through a roughly 50 per cent penetrable shelter barrier there is little risk of this. Many hedges naturally give this sort of shelter; with artificial barriers, solid parts should be separated by their own width or slightly less.

### Shelter hedges

Hedges will be the first choice for most gardeners, because they are attractive and have a natural association with fruit and vegetables. They require careful planning to ensure that they do not block sunlight and rainfall, and regular trimming to keep them tidy and within bounds. The garden needs to be large enough to allow for an uncropped area at least 2m (6ft) wide along the hedge, due to the moisture and nutrient needs of the hedging plants; in many sites this area can be used as an access pathway.

Almost any woody ornamental plant can be trained as a hedge (*see box above*) and many evergreens are traditionally grown as excellent barriers. However, it is best to choose a deciduous subject for enclosing a kitchen garden, because it is more likely to filter the wind acceptably: native species will do well. A mix of shelter hedges provides a greater range of seasonal interest, and espalier- and cordon-trained apples and pears (*see pp. 174–184*) make attractive shelter barriers within the garden.

Autumn planting allows trees or shrubs to establish over winter and grow well in the following spring. Set out plants at 60–90cm (24–36in) spacings, and plan to restrict shelter hedges to a maximum height of 2.5m (8ft). After planting, always add a mulch of rotted manure or compost (*see pp. 41–42*) along the line.

### Artificial barriers

Shelter barriers made from fencing provide instant protection and require less annual maintenance than hedges. They do not encroach, and in many cases can more readily be moved, but initial outlay in cost and effort are generally greater than with planting a hedge, and the effect is less decorative.

Artificial shelter screens are suitable for erection at the exposed boundaries of a garden or as internal dividers, and they should be no more than 2m (6ft) high. Make the fence with strong support posts, spaced at a distance equivalent to the screen height, and always attach the cladding to the windward side of the posts.

There are several purpose-made materials available, such as plastic net, or more durable and expensive plastic strap cladding; black is the least intrusive colour. Instant decorative cover can be achieved with post and wire fences planted with blackberries or rambler roses. Permeable wooden lath panels and tea tree panels are also suitable.

## Artificial shelter barriers

**Plastic strap cladding**
*This heavyweight windbreak is suitable for an exposed site. The initial cost is high, and it is not the most visually appealing solution, but it will stand up to strong winds and last for years. Relatively lightweight uprights must be closely spaced, as here.*

**Woven mesh fence**
*This lightweight plastic mesh makes an effective and relatively inexpensive windbreak. It can also be used to provide quick temporary shelter while hedging plants become established to provide a more permanent solution.*

# Soil types and structure

Just as we cannot alter features such as climatic conditions and aspect, so we have to accept the soil that comes with a garden or allotment. One may be fortunate enough to have a garden site with soil naturally quite suitable for producing excellent crops, or one that has been made so through a history of careful cultivation; the ideal soil would be a fertile, well-drained loam 45cm (18in) deep. Often, however, we have to contend with cold, heavy, poorly drained clay soil or light, sandy soil prone to rapid drying and loss of fertility. Luckily these less than ideal soils can almost always be improved; even where this cannot be done, at least some fruit and vegetables can be grown in raised beds (*see pp.32–34*) or in containers (*see pp.35–36*).

Soil supports and sustains plants, providing anchorage and a source of nutrients and water. It is highly variable according to location, even between sites in close proximity. Soils differ in their physical characteristics, their levels of organic matter, and their depth and condition. All soils are a mixture of weathered rock and rotted plant and animal remains or waste, naturally supporting myriad organisms, whose life cycles make the soil into a living medium. It is organic matter and this soil fauna that give the surface layers their range of brown colouring.

## Soil texture

The average gardener does not need to learn or understand soil science in depth, but it is necessary to be able to identify the essential type of the soil on which a kitchen garden is to be established. This is because the different soil types have different attributes, which affect plant growth and call for different ways of cultivating and maintaining the site. With a few specific preferences, most fruits and vegetables will grow reasonably well on a wide range of soils.

Soil texture is broadly classified into five main types: clay, silt, sandy, chalky, and peat (*see chart below left*). The term "loam" is widely used to suggest fertility and soil of all round excellence for growing, as in the recommendation to choose "a good medium loam". The term really needs qualification, for there is clay loam, silt loam, or sandy loam depending on the basic soil type; clay, silt, and sand describe soil textures based on the proportions of different-sized mineral particles found in them. Although the basic mineral content of soil is fixed by its origin, the structural nature is affected by the occurrence of stones or gravel and also by the addition of lime (*see pp.18–19*) and organic matter (*see pp.24–26*).

## Soil fertility and structure

The organic matter and fauna in the soil give it both its fertility and its structure; these two are closely linked.

One essential component of a fertile soil is humus. The term is usually taken to refer to the actual organic content of soil, but this is a simplification. Humus is a complex mix of compounds that derive from the decay of that organic matter to form a dark-coloured, sticky substance. It has a crucial influence on the retention and release of nutrients, the formation of good soil structure, and the soil's ability to hold water.

Also essential to soil fertility are the wide range of living organisms that populate it, which we often take for granted. These include beneficial bacteria and fungi, and a range of microscopic worms and mites, besides the visible centipedes, earthworms, and beetles. All rely on organic matter, variously incorporated and applied annually in mulches, which they break down into humus.

## BASIC SOIL TYPES

*Clay*

Particles below 0.002mm in size are defined as clay. Clay soil is often described as heavy, and sometimes regarded as difficult, but it has very useful qualities. Clay naturally holds certain nutrients in chemical combination, so that they are not easily leached out and instead become available to plant roots gradually. It binds together better than sandy soil and is more water-retentive. Disadvantages are that it is relatively slow to warm and is susceptible to waterlogging in winter and baking in summer, problems reduced by adding bulky manures. Timing of cultivation requires care, but in many respects a clay soil is very desirable in the kitchen garden. Blackcurrants, plums, Brussels sprouts, and cabbages often do well on clay.

*Silt*

Particles between 0.002mm and 0.05mm in size are classified as silt. The silt soil is intermediate between clay and sandy soil, and has a smooth or silky texture. Silty soil is more retentive of nutrients and water than sandy soil, but it is liable to compaction, especially when it is dry. Plentiful organic matter will make this a good soil, especially for early sowings.

*Sandy*

Particles between 0.05mm and 2.0mm in size are sand; a sandy soil is commonly termed light. It does not hold together well, so is prone to erosion on exposed or sloping sites, and its ability to retain water and nutrients is poor because of its open nature. These properties can be corrected by the incorporation of generous amounts of bulky organic manures. Advantages are that it is relatively easy to cultivate and also early in warming, a trait useful for strawberries, salad crops, young root crops, and legumes.

*Chalky*

Chalky or limestone soil is abundant in some areas. It is invariably shallow and well drained, but the high lime content can pose problems, particularly in the cultivation of fruits. This kind of soil is moderately fertile, with organic matter being broken down quickly, and should be regularly dressed with acidic organic matter such as farmyard manure (see pp.22–23).

*Peat*

Peat soil is encountered on basically wetland sites where sedges and mosses naturally thrive. Where it is drained and dressed with fertilizer this type of soil can be made highly fertile, as it is both moisture-retentive and high in organic matter. Peat soils are usually acidic, and they can be prone to being blown away by wind when they are dry.

# Visual assessment of soil

### Clay soil
*A clay soil is one containing more than 25 per cent clay particles. It is sticky after rainfall, sets into hard clods when dry, and is heavy to dig (see above left). Test the soil by handling it. When moist, a clay soil feels tacky, is shiny if smoothed, and can be formed into a ball that holds together (see above right).*

### Sandy and silt soils
*Sandy soil has less than 8 per cent clay and is mainly sand particles. It is very easy to dig (see above left), feels gritty when rubbed between the fingers, and does not hold together when squeezed (see above right). Silt soils are intermediate between clay and sand: they feel silky and show imprints when pressed, but do not form a cohesive ball.*

A soil must have good structure if plants are to thrive. Soil structure is measured by its tendency to form crumbs of mineral particles and organic matter held together by humus. Well-structured soil is easy to cultivate and has evenly distributed air spaces. This aeration allows plant roots to extend through the soil easily and facilitates movement of water and nutrients. It also has the effect of warming the soil and so promoting plant growth. Soil structure is influenced by the activities of soil organisms in creating humus and by the levels of organic matter present. Also important are the nutrients that the organisms need to form humus, and lime (*see pp. 18–19*), which is vital to crumb formation.

Other factors helping the development of good soil structure include the action of frost and alternating wet and dry conditions. Ensure that the soil structure is not damaged by being cultivated in wet conditions or by excessive traffic over the dug surface. Walking or moving wheeled implements across the surface can compact soil at any time, but especially in wet conditions. Aeration can even be damaged by continual winter rain. This damage can be reduced by leaving a covering of organic matter (*see pp. 41–42*) on the surface during winter, which can be dug in to maintain soil fertility, or by planting an overwintering green manure or crop cover (*see p. 23*).

## Soil profile
The horizontal bands that can be seen when digging down into a soil make up the profile. The most easily identifiable profile in gardens is topsoil, subsoil, and the parent rock material below them. Topsoil is the layer of most activity, because this contains organic matter and organisms that live on it. The subsoil is usually paler in colour, and is formed from weathered rock. The depth of topsoil and subsoil through which roots can penetrate has great importance to the growth of plants. It is worth digging a small test hole on your site to ascertain the profile.

Fruit trees (*see pp. 174–205*) do best where the total depth of well-drained, weathered soil is at least 60cm (24in); cherries and citrus ideally prefer at least 90cm (3ft). Soft fruits (*see pp. 211–233*) require a soil depth of at least 45cm (18in), except for strawberries, which can succeed in a depth of 38cm (15in), as can vegetable crops. These are general limits and are based on the success of crops grown commercially; what is of paramount importance is that water can drain freely through any depth of profile.

### △ The gardener's friend
*Among the most beneficial inhabitants of fertile soil, earthworms burrow extensively, improving soil aeration and pulling organic matter down from the surface and assisting in its breakdown by digesting it.*

### ▷ Soil profile
*Almost all soils are made up of distinct layers of topsoil, subsoil, and material weathered from the parent rock. The depth of all of these layers can vary depending on the soil's history.*

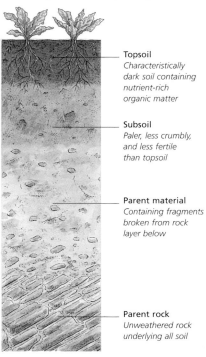

**Topsoil**
*Characteristically dark soil containing nutrient-rich organic matter*

**Subsoil**
*Paler, less crumbly, and less fertile than topsoil*

**Parent material**
*Containing fragments broken from rock layer below*

**Parent rock**
*Unweathered rock underlying all soil*

## Drainage of the soil

Roots require air to grow and to absorb nutrients and water. Waterlogged soil becomes cold and airless. This prevents nutrient uptake and leads to plant roots becoming diseased or even dying.

There are clues that indicate a poorly drained garden site. The most obvious is evidence of persistent puddling after rain. Others are the presence of plants that thrive in wet conditions, such as sedges, rushes, or moss, and poor growth of perennial plants.

Poor drainage arises in several ways. It can occur if the topsoil is infertile through poor cultivation or lack of humus: careful cultivation and dressing with organic matter (*see pp. 22–23*) will improve structure. The soil profile may naturally include an impervious layer known as a pan, which is often only 2.5–5cm (1–2in) thick. A pan can occur in the subsoil as a result of accumulated minerals, especially iron. Alternatively, there may be a barrier in the subsoil or the topsoil caused by compaction. Free drainage is important, so it is worth

### A soil pan

*Digging an inspection pit to a depth of 90cm (3ft) should reveal the cause of any poor drainage. Here, the problem is a densely compacted layer or pan that has formed between the topsoil and the subsoil. This is preventing water from draining freely into the subsoil, and needs breaking up. Compaction like this can be avoided by minimizing traffic over the soil.*

**Topsoil**
*Open and crumbly soil can become temporarily waterlogged if drainage is impeded*

**Compacted layer**
*Dense, hard layer of compacted soil impedes flow of water*

**Subsoil**
*Once compaction is broken up, water should drain well through subsoil structure*

digging a narrow inspection pit on suspect sites to examine the soil profile. A natural hard pan is easily identified, as is compaction, which is often marked by a dark horizontal band (*see above*). Deep double digging (*see pp. 38–39*) will break up compacted layers, and a natural hard pan can be breached with a pickaxe. Other problems are more

intractable: it may be that the garden lies in a hollow of natural drainage from surrounding land, or that the area has a naturally high water table. Both of these situations would be very difficult to remedy, and in such conditions it may be necessary to grow crops in raised beds (*see pp. 32–34*) or in containers (*see pp. 35–36*).

---

# Constructing drains

Where cultivation methods will not solve the problem, it can be worth installing a drainage system, but only the most difficult sites justify the expense and work. At their simplest, such a system consists of surface ditches (*see below*) leading into a soakaway – a large pit at a low point filled with rubble. Water will seep into the drains and be carried to the soakaway. The drains can be either left open or filled with gravel and topped with upturned turves. A more elaborate system is to lay a herringbone grid of buried pipes (*see right*).

**Topsoil**
*May be laid to give level surface*

**Brushwood**
*Prevents soil from clogging gravel below*

**Gravel or stones**
*Provides free-draining base to trench*

### Traditional French drain

*This version of a land drain is simply a ditch with sloping sides, up to 90cm (3ft) deep, filled first with a layer of gravel or rubble, then brushwood, finally covered over with topsoil to give a level and natural surface.*

**Pipe trenches**
*Pipes should be at least 60cm (2ft) and up to 90cm (3ft) below ground level*

**Spacing pipes**
*Lines of plastic or clay pipes should be laid approximately 3.5m (11ft) apart*

**Joining pipes**
*Pipes are laid end to end – at junctions, pipe ends are roughly shaped to fit together, then covered by flat tiles to stop soil silting up inside*

**Upturned turves**

**Gravel bed**
*Coarse rubble graded to fine sand ensures water flows smoothly into drainage pipes*

**Drainage material**
*Soakaway is filled with rubble, then coarse sand or gravel and topped with upturned turves*

**Soakaway**
*Brick-lined pit, about 2m (6ft) square and up to 2m (6ft) deep*

### Simple herringbone drainage system with soakaway

*A permanent system of 10–15cm (4–6in) diameter perforated plastic drain pipes can be laid, herringbone-fashion, across the site.*

*On a flat site, the pipes must be laid sloping down towards the soakaway; on a sloping site, they can be laid parallel to the surface.*

# Essential nutrients

All fruit and vegetable crops need a constant adequate supply of nutrients to sustain growth and yield a worthwhile harvest. Good nutrition is ensured by attention at the time of preparing the garden and then continual maintenance.

Soil nutrients come from several sources – weathering of minerals, the breakdown of organic matter, chemical reaction in the soil, and absorption from the atmosphere. The gardener can also influence nutrient levels by applying additional fertilizers and organic matter (*see pp.20–23*).

## Major and minor nutrients
The essential plant nutrients required in the greatest quantity are nitrogen, phosphorus, and potassium. Nitrogen is absorbed in quantity by plants to promote growth; leafy vegetables (*see pp.123–128*) use a great deal, as do blackcurrants, plums, and pears among the fruit crops (*see pp.146–237*). Phosphorus is necessary for chemical reactions within the plant and is vital for cell division and consequently the development of shoots and roots. Potassium is essential in plant metabolism, giving hardiness, steady growth, disease resistance, and colour and flavour in vegetables and fruit.

Magnesium, calcium, and sulphur also have essential roles, but are required in smaller amounts. Magnesium is a constituent of chlorophyll, needed to convert light into energy for growth, and has a role in the transport of phosphorus within plants. Calcium facilitates growth. Sulphur is a central constituent of the protein in living cells, and is usually in short supply.

There are also essential trace elements or micronutrients, required in much smaller quantities. The most important of these are iron, manganese, copper, molybdenum, boron, chlorine, and zinc.

## Determining nutrient levels
Total absence of a nutrient from the soil is rare; low nutrient levels as a result of leaching by rainfall or flooding, or through depletion by successive crops over time are more common. Another significant cause of deficiency is reserves in the soil becoming unavailable due to

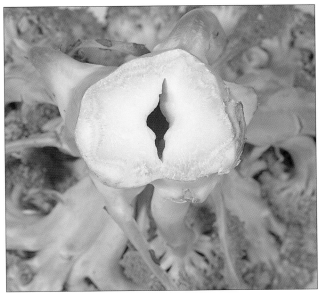

**Boron deficiency**
*Plants of the brassica family may occasionally be affected by boron deficiency in garden soil. The most common symptom is the appearance of hollow stems in the plants. This is likely to be the result of a naturally alkaline soil, a deficiency or excessive applications of lime, as a high pH causes boron to be locked up and so unavailable to plants.*

the effects of acidity (*see p.18*), excessive amounts of another nutrient, or poor root growth as a result of waterlogging (*see facing page*) or disease.

Measuring levels of nutrients such as nitrogen, phosphorus, and potassium in a garden soil is not easy – especially nitrogen because of its mobility. Proprietary kits are available, but, for accuracy, laboratory testing and professional analysis are best; this is inevitably less straightforward, and expensive. Once initial testing of the kitchen garden soil has taken place, annual testing thereafter is not necessary provided the soil is well maintained.

## Levels of the major nutrients
Nitrogen is used in quantity and is also highly prone to washing out in rain. Make regular supplementary dressings, but avoid excessive amounts, which can lead to rank growth and unfruitfulness, and also lead to the pollution of water courses. Follow directions on proprietary fertilizers (*see pp.20–21*).

Phosphorus is retained quite well, and sufficient levels are present in most soils, an exception being old, grazed pastures converted to garden. Supplements are probably needed only every two or three years in a well-maintained garden.

Potassium is usually held in clay soils by a chemical reaction, but is easily lost to leaching on sandy, free-draining and acidic soils. Dressings of potassium are needed annually in the kitchen garden; it should always be included in dressings that are applied prior to planting, in order to balance the effects of nitrogen.

## Levels of micronutrients
Although plant growth requires very low levels of micronutrients, deficiency symptoms are often seen on plants growing in soils that are strongly acidic or alkaline, sandy or naturally deficient in elements such as zinc or copper.

Plants on alkaline soils frequently show symptoms of iron deficiency, such as severe yellowing of the growing tips, with the mature leaves also yellowed except around the small veins. Often seen in fruit crops, this is known as lime-induced chlorosis. Manganese deficiency occurs on acidic and alkaline soils, causing yellowing of the older leaves, starting at the edges; on acid soils levels of manganese toxic to plants can occur. Boron deficiency may arise on poor soils or after heavy liming, and is often seen in hollow stems in brassicas; zinc deficiency can occur in similar conditions, stunting shoots and leaves. Molybdenum can be made unavailable on acid soils, causing damaged growing points and whiptail in cauliflowers, in which the leaf blade does not develop. Controlling the pH of the soil will help to prevent these problems (*see pp.18–19*).

# Lime and soil acidity

Lime is a vital soil ingredient in the kitchen garden because it affects the fertility of the soil in several ways. Lime is itself a source of calcium, an essential major element for healthy plant growth, and is also vital to the production of a good soil structure.

## The effects of lime

The presence of lime governs the acidity of the soil: the more lime is present, the less acidic is the soil. This affects the micro-organisms that break down organic matter, which mostly cannot survive in a soil that is very acidic. Soil acidity is also important in the uptake of nutrients, because some of them, such as potassium compounds, become unavailable to plants in soils that are very acid, while others may accumulate to concentrations that are toxic to plants (*see p. 17*). The incidence of some diseases is influenced by soil acidity; clubroot in cabbages thrives on acid soils and scab in potatoes on alkaline ones (*see* Plant Problems, *pp. 246–264*).

Lime has a valuable beneficial effect on the structure of clay soils, because its presence initiates a chemical process that aggregates soil particles into stable crumbs, which are clusters of mineral and organic matter. A good crumb structure is important both for proper aeration of the soil and for effective water and nutrient retention (*see p. 15*).

The level of lime also influences the living inhabitants of soil. The activity of earthworms and the micro-organisms, especially bacteria, that reduce bulky organic matter to a constituent of humus (*see p. 14*), decreases as the acidity of the soil increases.

## Knowing your soil pH

To gain the maximum benefits of lime in soil and avoid the problems resulting from its absence or excess, it is necessary to understand firstly how to measure the acidity of the soil, and secondly how to adjust the level. The degree of acidity of a substance is measured on a graduated system known as the pH scale. At the middle of this scale, pH 7 represents the neutral condition: values lower than this, down to pH 0, indicate increasing acidity, and

values above it, up to pH 14, indicate increasing alkalinity. Garden soils usually have a pH between 4.5 and 7.5, and most of the crops to be grown in a fruit and vegetable garden will do best on soils of around pH 6.5. This standard remains constant, and is the level for which you should aim in treating your soil; the pH level directly or indirectly affects everything else that you do.

There are accessible and inexpensive means for the gardener to determine the level of soil acidity and the need for lime. Simple pH measurement kits are available from good garden centres and mail-order retailers; their results are easy to read and sufficiently reliable. Use a kit in the first stages of planning, and rectify any imbalance before planting. It is also advisable to use them for checking every few seasons, as levels will change, and it may be necessary to make adjustments.

On a large site, take small samples from across the area, then mix them before testing a small quantity as a representative sample. Alternatively, carry out several tests at various points.

## Extreme pH problems

The acidity of the soil affects the availability of nutrients (*see p. 17*), and modifying soil acidity by applying lime is an effective means of influencing nutrient availability. Some liming products can also be sources of the main nutrients; for example, ammonium nitrate formulated with lime contributes nitrogen, and dolomitic limestone also contains magnesium.

A soil with an excessively high lime content is just as unsatisfactory for fruit and vegetable growing as a soil with too little. In very alkaline conditions, most of the essential nutrients that are

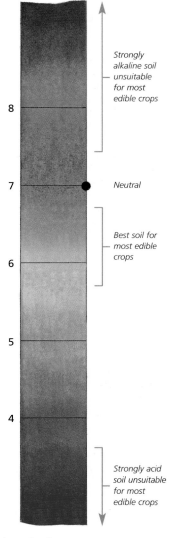

**pH scale and values**
*This section of the pH scale shows the range most likely to be found in garden situations. The best soil testing kits assess a suspension of soil in distilled water; the pH level is indicated by the colour of the suspension after mixing.*

| | GUIDE TO LIME APPLICATION | | |
|---|---|---|---|
| Original pH | Amount of ground limestone per sq m (sq yd) to adjust to pH 6.5 | | |
| | Sandy or gravelly soil | Medium loam soil | Peat or clay soil |
| 4.5 | 640g (1lb 3oz) | 920g (1lb 10oz) | 1150g (2lb 2oz) |
| 5.0 | 400g (12oz) | 650g (1lb 3oz) | 790g (1lb 7oz) |
| 5.5 | 225g (7oz) | 375g (11oz) | 470g (14oz) |
| 6.0 | 135g (4oz) | 190g (5oz) | 400g (12oz) |
| 6.5 | 0 | 0 | 0 |

Image labels (pH scale):
8
7 — Neutral
6
5
4

Strongly alkaline soil unsuitable for most edible crops

Best soil for most edible crops

Strongly acid soil unsuitable for most edible crops

# Liming the soil

1 **Weigh out enough lime** to treat 1sq m (1sq yd) of your plot. Put it into a pot and mark the level, so that you can measure out the rest of the lime using the pot. Mark out your site into a square metre (square yard) grid.

2 **Put the lime on** the blade of a shovel and scatter it gently and evenly over your marked-out square of soil. It is important that liming is done on a still day, so that the lime is not blown onto other areas of the garden, causing scorching of plants.

3 **Work across the plot** treating each square of the grid in the same way. Rake over the surface to distribute the lime evenly and incorporate it into the soil, or dig it in to a depth of 15cm (6in).

required in only small quantities – trace elements such as iron, manganese, and copper – cannot be readily absorbed by the plant (*see p.17*). On overly lime-rich soil, apples and pears often show marked yellowing (chlorosis) between the leaf veins, due to iron or manganese having become unavailable, and similar chlorosis is found in some vegetables, for example beetroot.

## Applying lime

It is much easier to reduce soil acidity than to raise it, so take care in deciding how to apply lime. Three forms of lime are generally available: quicklime, which is caustic and dangerous, hydrated lime, which is faster acting but can damage foliage, and crushed chalk or ground limestone, the least hazardous and usually the least expensive form of lime for garden use.

Rates of application to bring an acidic soil to pH 6.5 vary not only according to the existing pH value but also to the soil type: the chemistry of a clay soil makes it far more resistant to the effects of liming than a sandy soil. A general guide to application rates is shown in the table (*see left*). The pH of very acidic soil can be raised only

gradually, so regular pH checking is needed in the early development of the garden. Dressing requirements of more than 400g per sq m (12oz per sq yd) need to be applied over several seasons.

Whatever the quantity, best effects will be obtained where the application is made well before planting, ideally on two or more occasions in autumn and winter; this will allow the lime to initiate changes in the soil gradually and more effectively. Apply lime after incorporating animal manures, but not less than three or four weeks later, to avoid chemical reactions that will release ammonia and allow nitrogen to escape, and aim to work in the dressing to a depth of 15cm (6in).

## Reducing alkalinity

Rainfall, continuous cultivation, and cropping will gradually increase soil acidity. Application of flowers of sulphur also has an effect, but this is slow, and dependent on relatively warm soil for bacterial activity. For general guidance, apply 270g per sq m (8oz per sq yd) on clay soils and half this quantity on sandy soils. Repeat pH testing and application as necessary; the process is only worth considering in extreme conditions.

## SAFETY TIPS

- **Store with care,** keeping lime or sulphur in a clearly labelled, closed container, securely placed out of reach of children.
- **Choose your time** and only ever apply lime or sulphur on a still day.
- **Cover your eyes** with protective goggles that offer protection around the sides and fit closely to the face.
- **Protect your skin** by wearing trousers, long sleeves, and close-fitting gloves.
- **Wear a simple cloth mask** over your mouth and nose, as lime is easily inhaled.
- **Be sensible:** the operation of liming is a perfectly safe practice if these simple precautions are followed.

*Protective mask*

*Latex gloves*          *Eye protectors*

# Fertilizers and manures

Most previously cultivated garden sites have adequate levels of nutrients (*see p.17*), with the most likely exception of lime (*see pp.18–19*); old grassland converted to garden use is often low in phosphorus. Cropping makes heavy demands on soil, however, and a fruit and vegetable garden requires more feeding than an ornamental garden. As an insurance, incorporate fertilizers and manures (*detailed below and on p.22*) containing nitrogen, phosphorus, and potassium as a base dressing before planting. After good site preparation (*see pp.37–40*), maintain fertility by annual, light applications of fertilizer to areas dug over for cropping, and by top-dressing or surface application to growing crops.

## Understanding terminology

The terms "manure" and "fertilizer" are commonly used interchangeably, but it is worth distinguishing them. Manure best describes bulky material that is derived directly from animal and plant wastes, while fertilizer is any material that provides more concentrated nutrients than bulky manure, and can be in powder, granular, or liquid forms.

Manure inevitably comes from organic sources; fertilizers may be from organic or inorganic sources. Organic substances are those derived from decomposed plant and animal remains and the waste products of animals; inorganic fertilizers are derived from non-living, carbon-free sources, including rock. Many gardeners, committed to the principles of organic growing, prefer to use organic products to the total or near exclusion of inorganic fertilizers, regarding their use as unacceptable for a variety of reasons. There is a view that organic derivatives are much less likely to pollute the environment, and that edible crops grown organically are more wholesome and of better flavour than those grown using other products.

## Chemical constituents

The letters N, P, and K on fertilizer packaging are the chemical symbols standing for nitrogen, phosphorus, and potassium respectively.

Phosphorus and potassium are included in fertilizers as more stable or accessible chemical compounds: phosphorus as phosphate ($P_2O_5$) and potassium as potash ($K_2O$). The shorter chemical symbols are most used for convenience, but all the different descriptions are met with in general gardening parlance.

There is a recognized notation for the nutrient content of compounds, which is always printed on the fertilizer packaging. This gives the percentage content of each nutrient, always in the order N:P:K, so a compound fertilizer that is described as 20:10:10 will contain 20 per cent nitrogen, 10 per cent phosphate, and 10 per cent potash (*see also chart, below*).

| Commonly available forms of fertilizer | Average nutrient content (per cent) | | | Approximate rate of application | Characteristics and uses |
|---|---|---|---|---|---|
| | Nitrogen | Phosphate | Potash | | |
| Sulphate of ammonia | 21 | 0 | 0 | 35–70g per sq m (1–2oz per sq yd) or 1½ times this for the higher-demand crops | Also called ammonium sulphate, this is a fast-acting, crystalline source of nitrogen, particularly suitable for top-dressing. Nitrogen is used in quantity, especially by cabbages, main-crop potatoes, celery, leeks, beetroot, pears, plums, blackcurrants, and rhubarb. |
| Sulphate of potash | 0 | 0 | 50 | 20–35g per sq m (½–1oz per sq yd) | Also called potassium sulphate. Potassium chloride has a higher potash content and is cheaper but can be toxic in excess, especially on tomatoes, gooseberries, and redcurrants. Potassium nitrate is expensive and used in liquid feeds. Potash is important for crop quality, balanced growth, and disease resistance. |
| Triple superphosphate | 0 | 47 | 0 | 35–70g per sq m (1–2oz per sq yd) | A concentrated form of phosphate, best added to a depth of 20cm (8in). Phosphate, vital for cell division and root growth, is relatively immobile and quite small annual dressings are needed. Farmyard manure and garden compost maintain suitable levels. Superphosphate is less concentrated, at about 18–21 per cent. |
| General compound | 7 | 7 | 7 | 135–210g per sq m (4–6oz per sq yd) | The widely available Growmore formulation is a general compound fertilizer suitable for the maintenance of nutrients in a well-prepared fruit and vegetable garden, ensuring adequate supplies of all three essential nutrients. |
| High-nitrogen compound | 20 | 10 | 10 | 35–70g per sq m (1–2oz per sq yd) | Artificial fertilizers that are incorporated as a base dressing at preparation time should be scattered evenly over the surface of the soil to avoid pockets of infertility: this is easiest to achieve with granulated formulations. This 20:10:10 compound is suitable for leafy crops. |

**Top-dressing crops**
*Weigh out fertilizer for 1sq m (1sq yd) and use a small container to judge the volume. Wearing protective gloves, tip out the fertilizer into one hand and scatter it evenly over the crop rooting area. Take care not to drop any onto the plants – it could scorch the foliage.*

## Applying fertilizers

Wear gloves and take precautions against inhaling airborne particles when handling any kind of fertilizer or manure.

When applying base dressings before planting, ideally mark out the area in a grid; at least measure out one square to help you to estimate the area. Weigh out the appropriate quantity, mark its volume in a pot, and then use this to distribute. Incorporate the fertilizer down to a depth of 10cm (4in) by forking in or raking. This guidance applies to ground preparations for most planting or sowing. All fertilizers need moisture to be effective; wait until just before rainfall before applying it, or if this is not practicable, water in any dressings made to dry ground.

Liquid fertilizers may be applied by watering a solution along crop rows or around individual plants; always water onto moist soil for even distribution. Alternatively, liquids can be applied as foliar feeds through a watering can or sprayer. Cover the leaves thoroughly, and never apply foliar feeds in full sunshine, as the leaves may be scorched.

## Inorganic fertilizers

Inorganic fertilizers are often known as artificials. These fertilizers are usually fast-acting, and often more efficient than organics weight-for-weight, with quite consistent content. In most cases, however, they lack trace elements and have relatively short-term effects. Their beneficial effects are directed primarily at the plant, rather than the soil in which it grows.

Two types of inorganic fertilizer are available. Those formulated to supply mainly just one of the three principal nutrients of nitrogen, phosphate, or potash are referred to as straight

fertilizers. The average nutrient content is printed on the packaging (*see also chart, facing page*). Combinations of the elements are known as compound fertilizers. Straight fertilizers may be formulated as crystals, powder, or granules, while compounds are almost always sold in granular form, which is easier to apply. Inorganic fertilizers are also available in liquid form, suitable for watering in or using as a foliar feed to boost growth or supplement nutrition in developing crops.

Where straight inorganic fertilizers are used as base dressings, remember that both phosphorus and potassium take longer than nitrogen to become available to plants, and the ideal times for incorporation of these nutrients are autumn and spring respectively. These timings are not critical, however, and a base dressing of compound fertilizer can be applied when most convenient.

Inorganic fertilizers are suitable for nitrogen top-dressing around individual plants or along crop rows. Take care not to let the fertilizer touch the stems or leaves, which could be scorched. Work the top-dressing into the soil surface using a push hoe or a rake. The insurance dressings suggested in the chart (*see facing page*) are likely to be excessive on fertile soils. In the interests of economy and avoiding harm to the garden environment, always limit applications. Much can be learnt about your crops' annual requirements through careful observation.

## Organic fertilizers

In all situations concentrated organic fertilizers have a unique role, and their use in the kitchen garden can certainly be complementary to the use of inorganic fertilizers.

Processed organic fertilizers (*see chart, p.22*) are usually relatively expensive per unit of nutrient due to their manufacturing process, and weight-for-weight they contain less of the major nutrients than inorganic fertilizers. They have the advantage, however, of containing trace elements that are usually lacking in artificials, and are also useful for their slow release of nutrients as the substance decomposes in the soil. This release is governed by soil temperature, because the soil organisms involved need warmth for activity.

Soil of any texture also benefits from the presence of organic matter, which increases humus content and encourages worm activity, improving the soil structure and in turn its capacity to hold water and air, its temperature, and its drainage (*see pp.14–16*).

Seaweed meal, bone meal, hoof and horn, fish meal, and fish, blood, and bone meal are all widely available forms of concentrated organic fertilizer that have long been recommended for inclusion in base dressings.

For top-dressing growing crops, dried blood has excellent effects, and many organic growers also advocate the use of liquid feeds containing extracts of comfrey or seaweed, both of which are rich in minerals. Some animal carcass derivatives are likely to be withdrawn from sale because of associated risks to health, however remote these may be: take precautions when using to avoid any skin contact, accidental ingestion, or inhalation. Store these substances in sturdy, sealed containers, as they can attract vermin and flies.

**Raking in fertilizer**
*Measure out the fertilizer and scatter over the surface, here a seedbed. Draw a wide rake lightly and evenly over the surface so that the fertilizer is worked into the soil.*

## Bulky manures

Bulky organic manures contribute far more to good soil structure than any of the concentrated organic fertilizers. They are mainly used as a soil additive, but also have an important use as a surface mulch (*see pp. 41–42*). Manures are often more difficult to find and transport, and are much more laborious to apply, but these challenges are well worth facing up to. Homemade garden compost has the advantages of being free and made on site (*see pp. 24–26*).

The most commonly quoted form of bulky organic is farmyard manure. This term describes a variable mix of dung, urine, and some kind of litter, usually straw; the main constituent is cattle manure, but pig and poultry dung may be added. Nutrient levels are low and variable (*see chart, below*). Horse manure is often more readily available, and usually has a relatively high straw content and higher nutrient levels; it is excellent for improving soil structure.

Use only well-rotted farmyard or stable manure, in which the litter is already substantially broken down.

Fresh manure is likely to generate ammonia as it breaks down, which can damage plants. If your supply has not been weathered outside, leave it in a covered stack in the garden for at least six months before use.

Spent mushroom compost is another possible source of bulky organic matter. It consists of straw well-composted with horse manure or a high-nitrogen fertilizer, together with the spawning layer, usually a mixture of peat and chalk or ground limestone. The nutrient value of mushroom compost is normally similar to that of farmyard manure.

In coastal areas it may be legal and practicable to collect seaweed; check with the relevant authorities before doing so. Seaweed is relatively rich in potassium, with 0.5 per cent nitrogen and one per cent potassium; it contains significant amounts of iron, magnesium, and manganese, too. To avoid subjecting young crops to unacceptable levels of common salt, leave seaweed out in heavy rain before incorporation. Seaweed is also excellent for mixing with farmyard manure in a stack to be rotted down.

There are environmental reasons for considering the use of treated sewage sludge and municipal waste as bulky soil additives, but theoretically these substances can contain heavy metal contaminants and are best avoided in the domestic garden.

## Applying manures

Bulky organic manures are most often incorporated into soil during autumn or winter digging (*see pp. 37–40*). For most crops, it is best to mix the manure evenly throughout the soil down to the depth of a spade blade (*see p. 37*).

An alternative system is to overwinter the material as a deep layer spread over the surface of the soil and then dig in the residue during early spring. Much of a layer of manure overwintered this way will be pulled into the top layers of soil by the action of earthworms. This natural action does not allow for incorporation to much depth, but it is a suitable method for sandy soils. These benefit from protection against severe weather during the winter, and are quite amenable to spring digging,

### TYPES OF ORGANIC FERTILIZER AND MANURE

| Fertilizer | Typical nutrient content (per cent) | | | Approximate rate of application | Characteristics and uses |
|---|---|---|---|---|---|
| | Nitrogen | Phosphate | Potash | | |
| Dried blood | 10–12 | 0 | 0 | 70g per sq m (2oz per sq yd) dry or in 1 litre (1¾pt) water | Dried blood has excellent effects on boosting growth when used as a top-dressing, and it may also be used as a base dressing. It can be applied either as a powder or as a liquid suspension. |
| Blood, fish, and bone meal | 3.5 | 8 | 5 | 135g per sq m (4oz per sq yd) | Use as a base dressing applied several weeks before planting or sowing, and as a top-dressing. |
| Hoof and horn | 7–15 | 1–10 | 0 | 135g per sq m (4oz per sq yd) | A slow-release fertilizer of varying nutrient levels, suitable for base dressing. Hoof and horn also raises the level of calcium in the soil. |
| Pelleted chicken manure | 2–5 | 1–4 | 1–2.5 | 135g per sq m (4oz per sq yd) | Pelleted chicken manure is often available. This processed form is easier to spread than bulky, unprocessed manures. Chicken manure has a higher nitrogen and phosphate content than farmyard manure. Use as a base dressing. |
| Rotted animal manures | 0.5 | 0.25 | 0.5 | 5kg per sq m (10lb per sq yd) | The most commonly available bulky organic manure. NPK content varies with methods of stock rearing, straw content, and time stored; horse manure usually has higher levels. Of special benefit in improving soil structure. |
| Spent mushroom compost | 0.7 | 0.3 | 0.3 | 5kg per sq m (10lb per sq yd) | A bulky organic material with physical properties that vary with age. Its main value is as a soil structure improver with low nutrient content. Because of its lime content, regular dressings of mushroom compost can raise the soil pH. |

**Neglected soil**
*Soil devoid of organic matter is likely to have poor structure. Water absorption can be a particular problem on poorly structured light soil, as shown here. Bulky manure improves absorption and retention on all soils.*

**Spreading manure**
*On light soil the structure can be protected from winter rain by spreading a 5–8cm (2–3in) layer of well-rotted manure over the surface. Much of the manure will be drawn into the soil by worms; dig or fork in the rest in spring.*

when the residues can be turned in. Generally speaking, the more well-rotted bulky organic matter that can be worked into the fruit and vegetable garden soil at preparation time the better. Plan to add at least 5kg per sq m (10lb per sq yd).

## Green manures

Green manuring involves sowing a suitable fast-maturing crop, either broadcast or in very closely spaced rows, cutting it down while still young, and incorporating the bulky living plant material into the soil by digging. Here it will decay fast, quickly releasing its constituent nutrients and aiding the production of humus.

When a kitchen garden has been well established, with close attention to soil condition, there is no doubt at all that green manures are a useful means of improving and maintaining fertility. Well-managed green manuring practice is helpful in the production of humus and the maintenance of soil structure, although it is unlikely to be sufficient on its own.

Careful management, however, is crucial to the success of any green manuring. The choice of plants, the planning of their place in the cropping calendar, and their maturity at the time of incorporation into the soil are all important considerations. The soil type, as well as its existing state of fertility, will have a strong influence on the usefulness of green manuring. Green manuring is particularly relevant to the management of light-textured soils, especially where the green manure can

be left to grow over winter. It will help to stabilize the soil and also allow for the steady absorption of soluble nutrients that might otherwise be washed out in heavy winter rainfall.

Remember that in dry seasons green manures can actually deplete the soil of moisture reserves. Before digging in green manure plants, chop them to aid decomposition.

## Planning green manures

Unless one is totally committed to this style of soil management, it is most sensible to see green manuring as a technique supplementary to the use of other types of organic manuring and fertilizer application, rather than a replacement for them. The system will

fit more easily into the plan of short-term vegetable crops than into the growing of perennial fruit crops.

The greatest nutrient contribution from green manuring is nitrogen. To gain the most benefit from this, plan for the shortest interval between incorporation and cropping. Usually the best time to dig in a green manure crop is as it nears flowering time; do not allow it to be in the ground so long that it becomes woody; this contributes less nitrogen and will temporarily take nitrogen from the soil on decomposition.

## Green manure crops

A suitable green manure crop needs to establish well from sowing and grow quickly to produce lush bulk. Suitable annuals for garden use are peas and annual lupins (*Lupinus*), both of which have root nodules capable of absorbing atmospheric nitrogen. Also suitable are rape (*Brassica napus*) and white mustard (*Sinapis alba*), both of which will grow rapidly and break down quickly to release nitrogen.

Of the perennial candidates, comfrey (*Symphytum officinale*) is well tried, as is borage (*Borago officinale*). Rye grass (*Lolium perenne*) is useful because of its searching root growth. The tops of all the perennial green manures will need cutting down before digging; where tops have become very mature, consign them to the compost heap rather than digging them in.

## Digging in a green manure

1 **Cut green manure** crops to the ground when they reach about 15–20cm (6–8in) in height and are still green and soft. Leave them to lie and wilt on the surface for a day or two.

2 **Skim off** the wilted residue of the green manure plants into a trench as deep as a spade blade (spit) as single digging proceeds across the plot (*see p.38*).

# Making compost

Rotted plant refuse is a valuable source of organic matter for improving and maintaining the fertility of soil, and making garden compost from plant remains and kitchen waste has a place in even the smallest of gardens.

The practice also makes a positive contribution to recycling. When we compost household and garden waste materials we reduce the need for collection and dumping of refuse, and also avoid using wasteful and potentially polluting bonfires to dispose of plant remains. All these factors are in the interests of our natural environment.

Composting is a practical alternative to the use of animal manures (*see p.22*), which may be difficult for the kitchen gardener to obtain. Garden compost is low in nutrients, but is a rich source of humus (*see p.14*). It has most of the advantages of other forms of bulky organic matter, without the possible disadvantages, such as difficulty of transportation or unacceptable odour.

Any heap of plant waste will gradually decay and reduce to yield a useful soil additive, but careful management of a compost heap will pay dividends. The aim is to produce a dark-coloured,

friable material of even consistency that is agreeable to handle and not too wet. This is best achieved by what is called aerobic composting, which involves ensuring that air can get into the bulk of waste material, accelerating decay.

## Compost bins

Place compost bins in a screened area, perhaps conveniently near the kitchen; they can be in shade. Depending on the productive garden size and the space available, plan for at least two bins side by side, each about 1–1.5m (3–5ft) square. The purpose of having more than one bin is to allow the rotting compost to be turned and moved from one bin to another. This exacting process is well worth the effort for aeration.

Bins need to be established either on a 20cm (8in) layer of thin, woody prunings laid on soil base, or with a floor of strong wire mesh laid over bricks. Both methods allow air to circulate at ground level. You can make your own bins (*see left*) with walls of strong, treated timber, builders' pallets, concrete blocks, or even straw bales. Ideally, construct the front walls with removable boards that slot in, allowing the height of the front to be raised as the bin is filled. A removable cover is essential to avoid the heap becoming too wet, but fit it so that some air circulation is possible over the surface of the compost.

Proprietary composting containers made from strong, rigid plastic are available, and these are suitable for use in the smaller garden.

## Composting materials

Any bulky matter of plant origin is suitable for composting. Nitrogen-rich material, in the form of leaves and nitrogen-rich additives such as animal manures, will accelerate decomposition. There must be a good balance of material in a heap in order to ensure the movement of air. Mixing in a proportion of semi-woody material helps this by preventing the heap from becoming compacted.

It is quite easy to ensure a supply of lush, leafy waste during the warm days of summer, but as the growing season

## Constructing a compost bin

**1 Lay 2 uprights** on the ground. Nail planks to them using 2 nails each end. Start 8cm (3in) from the bottom and keep the planks 1cm (½in) apart. Make 2 sides in this way.

**2 Stand the sides** up and tack 2 strips of wood across the tops to hold them the correct distance apart. Attach the planks for the back to the uprights, as for the sides.

**3 Nail a plank** across the front of the bin at the bottom, so that it is in line with the bottom boards of the sides and back. Remove the stabilizing strips from the top of the bin.

**4 Attach 2 battens** to the front uprights with nails, leaving a gap to allow planks to slide down between them. Nail a piece of wood in the bottom of this channel as a stop.

**5 Try sliding each** of the planks for the front of the bin down between the battens to make sure that they fit correctly. If necessary, trim the ends to the correct length.

**6 Paint the bin** with a water-based preservative, with particular attention to cut edges. Tie a strong nylon cord around the front posts to prevent the sides from bowing as the bin is filled.

draws to a close, the nature of material available for composting is relatively low in nitrogen. Temperatures also fall, slowing the composting process. At this time rotting can be encouraged by adding nitrogen in the form of a 5cm (2in) layer of animal manures, including litter from poultry or pets such as rabbits. Alternatively, add dried blood at a rate of 250g per sq m (8oz per sq yd) or a proprietary compost activator.

Lawn clippings, fallen leaves, and cleared plant debris from ornamental borders will all decay suitably, as will trimmings made from vegetables on harvesting and waste from fruit and vegetable preparation in the kitchen. Brassica leaves and stems can be added; the stems are best chopped up. Pea and bean plants, including the pulled roots, will compost. Unused root crops can be added, chopped into fragments, provided they are pest and disease free. Doubts are often raised about adding rhubarb leaves to compost, but this is quite acceptable. Blight-diseased potato haulms can be composted in a well-made heap that reaches a high temperature. Annual and perennial weeds are usually relatively high in nitrogen and the tops will compost well.

Hedge clippings and thin woody prunings will decompose if reduced to small fragments, and for this purpose it

may be worth investing in a small shredding machine. Other less obvious materials can also be composted, as long as they are made from natural substances. Newspaper and card can be added if they are shredded first; even cotton and woollen items that have been cut up can be composted, although they will inevitably take a much longer time to break down than other waste.

## Materials to avoid

Although the heat generated in a well-managed compost heap will destroy many plant pests and diseases (*see* Plant Problems, *pp. 246–264*), exclude any material carrying persistent infections, such as clubroot in brassicas, black spot in roses, canker in apples, and white rot in onions. It is best not to add brassica roots, which may be diseased; similarly, potato tubers may perpetuate disease and can also be troublesome in re-sprouting.

Take care not to carry over weed populations in the form of seeds, roots, bulbs, corms, and fleshy parts that may survive composting. All the underground parts of grasses, docks, nettles, and oxalis, for example, should be excluded from compost; it is also best not to put in abundantly seeding annual weeds. Check that grass clippings and straw added to the heap have not recently been treated with selective (or hormone)

**Using a compost activator**
*Specially formulated compost activators that accelerate rotting are available, and are useful when leafy green material is scarce. Sulphate of ammonia is a good activator.*

weedkillers, for there is a small risk of contaminating the crops grown on ground to which these composted remains are added.

It is also important not to put any plastics in a compost heap, nor any waste food products, such as meat, that might attract rats to it.

## Making the heap

Build the compost heap up in layers of about 15cm (6in) depth, aiming to mix the type of material added where possible. It is best, if possible, to have a space beside the bins to store heaps of different materials until there is enough to make a proper layer, ensuring a good variety of material through the heap. Add chopped, moist straw to a similar depth over each layer to maintain aeration. Do not allow compacted layers of a single type of plant waste, such as lawn clippings, to lie in the heap, because they will form a slimy mass and create airless conditions that slow the rotting process.

The heap must not be allowed to become waterlogged, which will exclude air and lower the temperature. Keep it covered at all times to keep off rain and maintain warmth and internal moisture. Conversely, the heap should not be too dry, as this similarly slows decay; in warm summer weather you may need to water it.

**Layered material**
*Straw separates 15–23cm (6–9in) deep layers of preferably differently textured material*

**Rotting down**
*As compost rots, it will reduce in volume and sink down*

**Twin compost bin system**
*Fill the first bin with alternating layers of different types of organic material. Keep the heap covered with black plastic or carpet to keep it moist and warm. When the bin is full and partly rotted, turn the contents into the empty second bin and start refilling the first bin. Once the first load of compost is black and friable (above right), it can be removed and used. You can then turn the contents of the other bin (above left) into it, and repeat the process over again.*

Rotting waste generates heat through the activity of micro-organisms, and a well-made compost heap can reach around 70°C (158°F) within three or four weeks. It is most beneficial to turn the heap from time to time, ideally by forking rotting material out of a full bin into an empty one. Move less rotted material from the sides of the bin to the centre of the new load, where it will rot faster. Do this at least once per full loading and preferably more often.

The speed of decay is determined by the nature of the waste, but above all by the management of the heap. A heap that is carefully loaded, regularly turned, and has suitable additives can produce useable compost within six months, although it is wiser to plan for a year.

## Anaerobic composting

It is not always possible or convenient to make compost in the ideal manner. There is still value in producing bulky organic manure simply by stacking plant waste to rot in the open or in plastic sacks, mixing types as much as possible as for a standard heap. This method allows less air to penetrate, and is known as anaerobic composting. Complete rotting takes much longer, at least one year and up to two years. Burying waste in a large trench and digging it up once it has rotted down is also suitable on a small scale.

## Leaf mould

Tree leaves collected in autumn can form compacted layers if not mixed with other materials before adding to a compost heap. They are best composted in a separate container of similar size to compost bins, but with mesh or netting sides. They rot slowly, taking at least a year to produce leaf mould. This has an excellent friable texture, and is very suitable for mulching and as an ingredient of potting composts. Oak and beech leaves in particular are a great bonus to a leaf mould mix.

**Forking out finished compost**
*Compost is ready for use when it has decayed to a crumbly, dark mass that has few large particles and runs easily through the hands. Use it for digging into beds or mulching.*

## Worm composting

Worm composting is a relatively small-scale process, of particular use where space is limited or for dealing with kitchen waste. Dried samples of this small-scale nutrient-rich compost are especially suitable for adding to potting mixes. There are various sizes and styles of proprietary wormery; alternatively, a plastic bin, wooden box, or any large, rigid container can be adapted. The bin needs to have a lid and good drainage, and to be kept frost-free in a sheltered place. Suitable worms, known as muck or compost worms or brandlings, resemble small earthworms but are darker red. They can be found in rotting manure or plant waste, or be purchased from a specialist supplier. Managing the bin requires experience: only small quantities of kitchen waste should be added at a time. To harvest the waste, spread it on a plastic sheet and place wet newspaper over part of it: the worms will collect under the paper and can be returned to the bin.

## The role of compost

Any of these types of compost is beneficial: they all make an excellent mulch (*see pp. 41–42*) for fruit canes, bushes, and trees, and for perennial vegetables and runner beans. Although a surprising amount of compost can be made in many gardens, it is likely that it will need to be supplemental to other means of improving the soil's organic content because of limited production.

# Making compost in a worm bin

Brandling worms will turn kitchen waste into fine worm casts in about 10 weeks. Avoid onions and leeks, and citrus fruits, which can make the mix too acidic; crushed eggshells help counteract acidity. Meat and dairy products can attract flies and vermin if the bin is not securely lidded. Waste should be added in thin layers: compost worms can eat up to their own weight each day, but it is best to add at half this rate.

*Brandling worms*

**Kitchen waste**
*Chop waste into small pieces and mix well*

**Composted material**
*Worms work upwards leaving casts below*

**Drainage material**
*Liquid drains through layer of boards or permeable membrane into gravel or crocks*

**Covering**
*Layer of newspaper helps to keep bin moist and warm*

**Active layer**
*Worms thrive and work best in warm, dark conditions*

**Initial bedding**
*Dampened straw or shredded newspaper, or rotted manure*

**Drain tap**
*Excess liquid should be drained regularly to avoid flooding*

# Planning your garden

The content and layout of a garden is determined by many factors. Although practical considerations are paramount in growing fruit and vegetables, try to make the most of these plants as an extension of the ornamental qualities of a garden. They may not offer the same breadth of interest as ornamental plants, but they certainly have their attractions.

## Crops in the garden

Garden sites come in all aspects, shapes, and sizes. On the reasonable assumption that the majority of garden sites can be made suitable for fruit and vegetables, consideration of how they are to be laid out is to do with personal preference and the practical limitations of the site. Take some time to learn and think about the style of garden you want.

One of the most basic considerations in planning a garden is the structural form. Here, single specimens of fruit trees and bushes can be used to good effect; the structure of carefully trained trees will provide strong interest throughout the year. Bold architectural form is also found in perennial crops, such as tall artichokes and sweetcorn, and the dramatic leaves of rhubarb.

Climbing plants, such as peas, beans, squashes, and melons contribute height and structure from the supports needed to grow them. These may be timber or steel poles, or more ornate wooden or metal structures, and can make pleasing features themselves. The way in which plants are grown also has an effect: where fruit and vegetable plants are arranged in beds and straight rows, the geometric layouts can make a strong visual impact.

Once the form of a garden has been established, texture and colour can be considered. Many vegetable plants have striking leaves and stems. In the beet group, for example, are plants with corrugated, deeply coloured leaves, and chards with glowing, coloured stems. Carrots have graceful, finely cut foliage, the leaves of brassicas are both bold in shape and glaucous, and lettuces mostly have a soft, crinkled texture. The great range of culinary herb plants includes many that could be grown as much for ornament as for usefulness. These include sage, with its felty leaves, ruffled parsley, and thymes, which contribute both aroma and flowers in addition to their carpeting foliage.

For most people, flowers and fruit are essential in any garden. Fruit trees, canes, and bushes produce beautiful blossom and brightly coloured fruits.

Taking all these considerations into account, there are three basic points to decide on at the outset. Do you wish to grow crops separately, or mixed with ornamental plants? If separately, should they be integrated within the overall garden design or in a separate plot? How large an area should be devoted to crops?

## Borders and potagers

There are two main possibilities for integrating fruit and vegetables in the ornamental garden. They can be grown within the mixture of plants in a herbaceous or mixed border, or they can be grown alongside ornamental features in formal beds, a system usually described as potager gardening.

Growing crops within the ornamental borders of a garden is particularly suitable where space is limited, or where only small supplies are wanted. There are disadvantages: the gaps left as annual vegetables are progressively harvested are not attractive, and it is

**Pretty potager**
*Even a small space can be planted with vegetables and herbs to create an attractive and functional potager plot. Here squares separated by box hedging allow for planned crop rotation, while crops of contrasting forms and colour are planted in simple patterns. As crops mature, the gaps will be filled with succeeding crops.*

more difficult to keep successional supplies going; raising plants in modules that can be transplanted to replace plants as they are harvested will alleviate these problems.

Fruit and vegetables grown with ornamentals require particularly close attention. Additional watering or feeding may be necessary, as it is very easy for them to be starved of nutrients or moisture by neighbouring plants, and intervention may be needed to prevent crowding by more vigorous species. It is also easier for pest and disease attacks to be overlooked, so extra vigilance is vital. For gardeners who wish to use garden chemicals on ornamentals but not on crops, mixing the two types will be impossible.

The potager is a more traditional approach for incorporating crops into your garden, with fruit and vegetables contained in formal beds. These are surrounded by permanent, trimmed edging of plants such as box (*Buxus*), lavender (*Lavandula*), or cotton lavender (*Santolina*). The crops within the beds are laid out in carefully planned proportions to maximize visual impact. A more relaxed variation is to use small island beds of a size and position to suit your particular garden. These could even be of a curved shape, making them suitable for an informal garden.

Another productive and potentially attractive way of including vegetables, herbs, and fruit in smaller gardens is by growing them in containers, such as tubs or pots, or even hanging baskets (*see pp. 35–36*).

**Temporary screen**
*A row of runner beans supported on canes provides a quick and colourful divide, whether between crops or between a kitchen garden and flowering plants. There are beans with red, white, or bicoloured flowers – try mixing cultivars to create a decorative effect.*

## The kitchen garden

The traditional approach to growing fruit and vegetables is to use a separate section of the garden. Making a special enclosed area will not only provide beneficial shelter (*see p. 12*) but also create a "garden room" leading on from the ornamental areas, adding interest to the garden. An attractive entrance can be made with an archway of trained fruit, such as thornless blackberry, or a climbing vegetable, such as runner beans.

On a large garden plot the kitchen garden area can be enclosed with hedges or permeable fencing (*see p. 13*). Hedging is attractive, but for small gardens the shade and the competition for water and nutrients from hedging plants makes fencing more advisable. Post-and-wire fences or trellis used to support ornamental climbers and ramblers or espalier- or cordon-trained apples, pear, gooseberries, or redcurrants

are also both attractive and productive options, as long as they are not exposed to severe winds.

## Location and size

There are good reasons for siting a kitchen garden in close proximity to the house. Easy accessibility is especially desirable in wet weather, but there are likely to be frequent demands throughout the growing season if a wide range of produce is grown; this is particularly true for a herb garden. The shortest possible walk encourages both regular inspection of the wellbeing of crops and frequent use of compost bins (*see pp. 24–26*). Moreover, having the kitchen garden close to the house could help to deter some animal pests.

The size of the area allocated to fruit and vegetables will depend on what you wish to grow, how much you wish to grow, and the overall size of the garden. Availability of water is also an important factor to consider where water is scarce. It is not meaningful to make definite recommendations as to the size of a kitchen garden because of these variable factors, the most limiting of which is the area of ground available. Outlined below are the considerations that should be dealt with in planning your space.

There really must be room for some compost bins. You may wish to include a small glass or plastic-clad greenhouse (*see pp. 43–48*) in which to raise young plants, mature tender ones, or extend the cropping season by providing protection for an early start or late cropping. Such protection can increase the range and yields from a kitchen

### Ornamental beds
*In this kitchen garden, changes of level, decorative supports of woven willow, and close planting of colourful crops such as lettuce 'Red Oak Leaf', peas, red cabbage, and nasturtiums, create an exuberant display.*

garden, and so will amply justify the time, effort, and garden space devoted to it.

Remember to allow for pathways, with a continuous one running around the perimeter of the kitchen garden and an internal network of paths dividing the growing areas into suitable permanent plots. Plan for widths of 60cm (24in), and remember the need for wheelbarrow access may require wider pathways of up to 90cm (36in).

Once any such features are allowed for, it is most realistic to think in terms of containing the range of what will be grown. If the available space and your enthusiasm are great enough, an area of 150 sq m (175 sq yd) will accommodate a good range of fruit and vegetables.

## Using space efficiently

It will be helpful in planning your garden to have some idea of the likely yield of individual crops. Estimates vary greatly, being dependent on many factors. The productivity of fruit plants varies with their age; vegetables may yield a small, succulent early harvest or a larger crop if harvested later, and different cultivars of the same crop can show considerable variation. On top of these factors, the time and length of the local growing season, the site, and the feeding and watering regime also all have considerable effects. Average yields (*see p.242*) are useful in planning initial plantings, but, with so many variables affecting yield, these estimates always have to be refined through individual trial and error. In the long run, this is the only realistic means of planning the quantities to be grown.

In using the available space efficiently, take account of how long a crop will occupy the soil: a plot that produces a great deal if several fast-maturing crops are grown in succession will yield much less if one slow-growing crop occupies the ground all season. Intercropping is a practical way to increase output, in which rapidly maturing catch crops like lettuce and radish are planted between slower crops (*see p.71*). Also consider the alternative purchase price of what you grow. For instance, potatoes, Brussels sprouts, and cabbages not only take up a great deal of space for a long time, but are also fairly cheap to buy and so may not be worth growing in a small plot, whereas beans, lettuces, and peppers are relatively expensive and are frequently in great demand when they are in season. Rotation of crops is also a consideration at this point, because you will need to plan your groups of plants carefully (*see p.31*).

To some extent the freezing and storage qualities of crops are relevant to the quantities grown. Peas, broccoli, raspberries and blackcurrants freeze well, and onions and potatoes can be dry stored (*see p.73*). Other crops, such as carrots and leeks, hold in the garden and can be harvested as required.

It is quite easy to overproduce fruit and vegetables; a little beetroot or radish, for example, goes a long way. You can avoid a glut by planning to make successional sowings (*see p.69*) of these, and of lettuces and French and runner beans. Some crops are demanding to grow successfully, so might not be a good choice for the less experienced; for example, cauliflowers require close attention to cultivation, and are then very likely to mature all together in greater quantity than can reasonably be used at one time.

## Crop sites

Once you have chosen your crops and decided on the space you have available, you need to decide how they should be arranged within the allocated space.

The position of non-perennial crops should ideally be governed by rotation (*see p.31*). One consideration when planning crop sites is shade. Fruit and vegetable crops will not thrive in the

**Work and pleasure**
*In this kitchen garden ornamental lavatera, calendulas, and sweet peas (Lathyrus) grow alongside crops of brassicas, sweetcorn, and leeks. Some gardeners claim that additional flowering plants can attract more pollinating insects and improve the yields of fruiting crops; they certainly help to create an attractive setting to sit and enjoy.*

dense shade of fences or overhanging trees. You should also ensure that there is a minimum of shading from one crop over another. This can be achieved by planting fruit trees at the south end of the plot and low crops such as strawberries at the north. Very tall vegetables, such as sweetcorn, Jerusalem artichokes, or trained runner beans, are also best not arranged in east-to-west rows that will reduce the light available to shorter crops, but this is unlikely to be critical.

Take full advantage of relatively warm spots (*see* What is a microclimate?, *p. 10*). Areas that slope towards the sun, and those backed by fences, or possibly walls facing the sun, are valuable for growing more tender plants such as tomatoes, melons, eggplants and peppers. Wherever possible, arrange rows to run north to south, so that sunlight is evenly distributed among the plants – but this is a bonus rather than an essential.

Another way of maximizing the sun and reducing wind is to use solid panels for part of the kitchen garden boundary or as internal dividers. Position such panels carefully to minimize shading (*see p. 12*). Cordons and espaliers or vine fruits trained on posts and wire make effective and attractive boundaries or dividers, while bush and cane fruits should be planted in blocks separate from those for tree fruits. Soft fruits, peaches, and cherries need protection from birds, and the same is true of most vegetables, especially when newly emerged or planted. The most effective solution is netting, usually in the form of a cage (*see p. 51*), and you should allow for removing and replacing the netting where appropriate, and for working around the plants inside it.

## Designing your kitchen garden

Settling down with a sheet of squared paper to plan the layout of a fruit and vegetable garden is a worthwhile contribution to good results.

Start by measuring the area, working from fixed points such as house corners for accuracy. Draw an outline plan with permanent features such as beds, trees,

**Rough plan**
*Start by drawing a rough, relatively small-scale plan of the kitchen garden area within the whole site. This will give you an idea of the space you are going to devote to it and the impact that it will have on your garden.*

perennial vegetables, or compost bins: you can cut these out of paper so you can easily try them in different positions before reaching a decision. When the layout is set, you can plan planting of crops in detail: this last part is essential whether you have a kitchen garden, a potager, or informal island beds.

**Detailed plan**
*A larger-scale plan of the layout within the kitchen garden allows for proper calculation of how much you can expect to fit into each area. This is the time to adjust the design: decide just how important each element is and balance the plants' requirements of space, orientation, and shelter to find the best solution. Every plan involves compromises.*

**Compost bins**
Allow for at least two bins, about 1.2m (4ft) wide

**Mini greenhouse**
Useful for propagating

**Cordon-trained fruit**
Cordon apples and espalier apples and pears can line the boundary, while loganberries and blackberries can be trained over arches to make entrances into garden

**Greenhouse**
2 x 2.5m (6 x 8ft) greenhouse should be sufficient for most gardens: collect run-off from roof as supplementary water supply

**Fan-trained fruit**
Allow 4m (12ft) between specimens for fan-trained trees

**Rotation beds**
Annual vegetables can be rotated in bed system, with temporary protection such as fleece or tunnel cloches if needed

**Fruit cage**
Must be big enough to allow access to all sides of fruit bushes – bushes will need to be 2m (6ft) apart for ease of management and optimum yield

**Raspberry canes**
You must be able to pick from both sides

**Strawberry tunnel**
Strawberries should be spaced at least 30cm (12in) apart in beds and can be protected by tunnel cloches

**Climbing beans**
Trained on cane wigwams

**Dimensions:**
17 x 12m (56 x 40ft)

# Crop rotation

Generations of experience have shown that growth and yield can be reduced if crops are grown in the same ground year after year. Rotating crops in sequence is a long-established practice to prevent this. There are three main reasons for using rotation: to combat pests and diseases, to maintain soil fertility, and to keep the soil well cultivated.

## The advantages of rotation

The greatest advantage in leaving a gap of at least three or four years before growing the same crop in a site again is in interrupting conditions that favour particular pests or diseases. Several fruit and vegetable problems (*see pp. 246–264*), like eelworms in vegetables such as potatoes and tomatoes, root rots in carrots, peas and beans, clubroot in brassicas, white rot in onions, and parsnip canker, are carried in the soil. Continually growing related or similar crops on the same site will only nurture the pests and pathogens.

Strawberries are highly susceptible to virus diseases, some of which are carried by eelworms; plant new stock where large populations of eelworms are less likely to have built up. It is also best to avoid replanting fruit bushes, canes, or trees on sites from which old ones have been removed. A condition known as replant disease

can cause reduced or even stunted growth. Nutrient exhaustion, virus transmission from eelworms, and fungal diseases may all be implicated.

A second reason for using rotation is to meet differing nutritional needs. Well-planned rotation can help to maintain fertility, taking account of the different preferences of crop groups. Legumes, especially broad beans, can extract nitrogen from the atmosphere (*see p. 95*), while brassicas need plenty of nitrogen to produce edible leaves and flowerheads; therefore it makes sense to plant brassicas where legumes have recently grown. Root crops, which require low levels of nitrogen, can be grown after brassicas.

Alternating crops also sets up a regular pattern for maintaining ideal soil pH (*see pp. 18–19*). Legumes benefit from ground dressed with organic matter, which lowers pH, while brassicas do best in soil with a higher pH, which discourages clubroot: alternating manuring and liming with these rotating crops ensures that the soil never becomes either too acid or too alkaline.

The third benefit of rotation is that it helps to control weeds and maintain good soil structure. This is where the third group is particularly beneficial: the cultivation of the soil for potatoes and other root vegetables helps to break up the ground and keep it open.

## The limitations of rotation

There are practical problems in strictly following rotation. Crops in the groups may be required in different proportions, or their seasons may overlap. Close proximity of crops enables diseases or pests to spread readily to new areas; a few diseases, like clubroot and white rot, can remain viable in the soil for many years beyond a reasonable rotation period.

Rotation is an aid to pest and disease suppression, not a total prevention or cure. Some gardeners hold that in small areas it is better continually to grow one crop on the same ground, and then avoid it altogether for susceptible crops when infestation reaches an unacceptable level.

## Planning rotation

It is difficult to adhere strictly to a three plot rotation in a small garden, but the principles are sound and it is a practice to be aimed at. The plantings suggested here are reasonably flexible: as long as the main plant groups of legumes, brassicas, and potatoes and root crops are kept separate, the other crops that are included with them may be placed in one group or another to suit other planting considerations. The crucial rule is to have two complete cropping seasons without repeating a vegetable group if at all possible. Keeping a record of operations in the fruit and vegetable garden is always time well spent, and a diary of each year's planting is especially valuable for planning rotations.

## Rotation plan

*This crop rotation plan suitable for kitchen gardens is based on dividing the vegetables that are grown into three groups. Some crops are grouped not with the plants to which they are most closely related, but with those that share their cultivation needs. Tomatoes, for example, are related to potatoes, but as they are not a root crop they would neither break up the soil nor benefit from the low levels of nitrogen left by brassicas, and so they are placed with the legumes instead.*

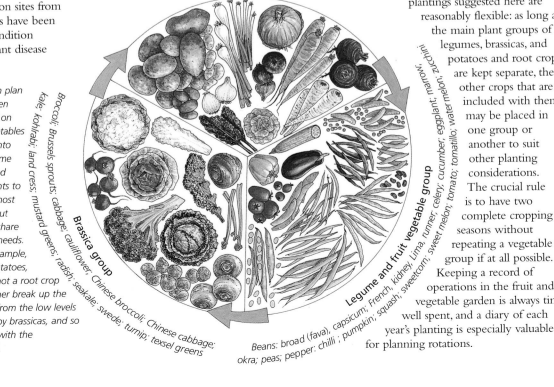

Beetroot; carrot; leek; lettuce; onion; parsnip; potato; salsify; scorzonera; spinach; Swiss chard
**Root vegetable group**

Broccoli; Brussels sprouts; cabbage; cauliflower; Chinese broccoli; Chinese cabbage; kale; kohlrabi; land cress; mustard greens; radish; seakale; swede; turnip; texsel greens
**Brassica group**

Beans: broad (fava), French, kidney, Lima, runner; capsicum; celery; cucumber; eggplant; marrow; okra; peas; pepper: chilli ; pumpkin; squash; sweetcorn; sweet melon; tomato; tomatillo; watermelon; zucchini
**Legume and fruit vegetable group**

# The bed system

Fruit and vegetables are best grown in open ground, either on the flat or in raised beds. In these situations the soil benefits from rainfall and weathering, and the plants have a free root run.

Although it is quite possible to mix edible crops with ornamental plantings (*see pp.27–28*), it is more usual to set aside a particular garden area specifically for fruit and vegetables. This area can be a wide, open plot, but an excellent alternative is to set out the vegetable garden as a series of narrow beds divided by pathways.

## The traditional vegetable patch

A common arrangement for a kitchen garden is to have long rows of vegetables across the plot. A packet of lettuce seed, for example, will advise sowing in rows 30cm (12in) apart, and thinning seedlings to 20cm (8in). This is a perfectly good way to grow produce, including strawberries, allowing all of the ground to be used with maximum flexibility and large areas to be machine cultivated.

Growing crops, however, requires constant access for sowing, thinning, planting out, watering, top-dressing, pest and disease control, weeding, harvesting, and clearing. Where long rows cover the whole plot, each of these tasks brings the need to tread on the ground alongside the growing plants, and every

**High raised beds**
*This version of raised beds is suitable for a wheelchair user, but it could provide moveable beds in a courtyard. There needs to be at least 15cm (6in) depth of growing medium.*

visit results in compression of the soil. Compaction reduces the air in the soil, resulting in poor growth (*see pp.14–16*). Look at the rows of vegetables beside heavily trafficked pathways, and you will invariably find that they are less vigorous than the rest. The adverse effects of compaction can be avoided or reduced by taking care not to tread on wet soil and by walking on planks to spread the weight; narrow beds avoid the need to walk on cropped areas. Gardens beds abutting grassed areas require constant edge trimming to remove encroaching weeds. Solid edging prevents this.

## Using beds

In a bed system, the kitchen garden is

**Large bed**
*Large beds like this one can be planted with several crops in longer rows, but have the disadvantage that the crops can be reached only by walking on the soil.*

△ **Standard raised bed**
*The soil in raised beds remains uncompacted, providing better conditions for plant growth, in this case, celeriac and carrots.*

◁ **Narrow flat bed**
*Narrow beds that are easily reached from the surrounding paths are particularly suitable for crops that are frequently harvested, such as these cut-and-come-again vegetables.*

divided into semi–permanent or fixed beds. All the cultivation tasks can be carried out from the dividing pathways, without needing to step onto the soil. This avoids soil compaction, and one important benefit is that harvesting and other jobs can be done soon after rain without risk of damaging soil structure. There is less need to dig beds once they are established and fertile, and what cultivation is necessary is greatly reduced because of the smaller cropped area. Another advantage of using beds is that, because bulky organic manures are concentrated on a smaller area, it is easier to build up high levels of fertility: this encourages better soil aeration and drainage, which in turn leads to stronger root growth.

The number of plants per square metre (or square yard) can generally be increased in a bed system, because there is no need for access along crop rows, so it is possible to grow the plants equidistant from each other. In a bed system, the lettuces of the example above might be arranged 20cm (8in) apart in all directions in staggered rows. This arrangement will allow the maximum root space for each plant in the smallest area, making the best use of the soil available and increasing the total yield of the area.

The close spacing of plants in beds has further indirect benefits. Irrigation using low-level distribution systems such as seep hoses (*see p.54*) will be more manageable, due to the smaller areas that are to be served.

Close spacing of plants in fixed beds also results in the smothering of annual weed growth, so there is usually less weeding to be done. Using a bed system can also make crop rotation (*see p.31*) much easier, as each crop group can be allocated a bed and then planted in a different bed each year according to the rotation.

## Planning bed layouts

Beds may be rectangular, square, or curved if that suits your garden best. An ideal width is 1.2m (4ft); this can be increased to 1.5m (5ft) if this makes better use of available space, or reduced to 1m (3ft). Narrow strips are particularly suitable for strawberries, for ease of mulching and harvesting. The length of a bed is governed only by how far one has to walk to get around to the opposite side without treading on the bed, although it is, of course, possible to bridge the bed with a plank resting on raised edging. The orientation of the beds is not of vital importance, but running them from north to south generally ensures the most even distibution of sunlight.

The width of the paths between beds is also important: they will need to be at least 45cm (18in) wide in order to allow for easy foot and wheelbarrow access.

## Making a flat or semi-flat bed

1 **Measure and mark** out the beds and paths to the dimensions you require (here, 1.2m/4ft beds with 45cm/ 18in paths), bearing in mind access and convenient use.

2 **Rake the soil** from the path area over to the adjoining bed area, so that the beds are raised slightly above the surrounding paths. Incorporating organic matter into the growing area will also slightly raise the level to make a semi-flat bed.

3 **Tread down** the paths to firm them and define the edge of the beds more clearly. The paths can simply be left as soil or given another surface covering (*see p.34*).

## Types of beds

There are many terms that are used to describe beds, but for most purposes it is simplest to distinguish between flat or semi-flat beds and raised beds.

A flat or semi-flat bed is simply marked out from the surrounding garden and cultivated (*see above*). With repeated annual cultivation and the addition of bulky organic dressings, the surface of such a bed will gradually become raised above the path level.

Raised beds are constructed by similarly marking out beds and then building sides up to 30cm (12in) high from timber, such as railway sleepers, or even bricks or cement blocks (*see below*). It is possible to dispense with the walls,

## Making a raised bed

1 **Measure and mark out** beds. Edge with 15 x 2.5cm (6 x 1in) boards, sunk into a 5cm (2in) slit trench and supported by timber pegs driven into the ground every 1.2–1.5m (4–5ft).

2 **Fill the bed** with good-quality topsoil that has been enriched with organic matter such as well-rotted manure (*see pp.22–23*) or garden compost (*see pp.24–26*).

3 **Spread the soil** using a rake. Break up any lumps, aiming to achieve an even, firm texture and bring the surface roughly level with the top of the boards.

4 **Level the soil** with the back of the rake to leave a smooth finish. Top up with more soil as necessary in later weeks when the filled bed settles and the level of the soil falls.

# Making a mulched path

Pathways between beds can be formed simply of trodden soil, but it is worth making a semi-permanent path, as shown here, to avoid unsightly and invasive weeds and to provide a firm, all-weather surface. Use preservative-treated 10 x 2.5cm (4 x 1in) planks as edging and make sure that they are proud of the bed surfaces. Once the base of the path has been constructed, it can be finished with any of a variety of surfacing materials (*see box below*), such as the bark chips shown here.

**1** **Mark out a path** 45–60cm (18–24in) wide. Cut a length of landscape fabric 15–20cm (6–8in) wider than the path. Level and tread down the path, then cut a 2.5cm (1in) slit trench along each edge.

**2** **Fold the landscape fabric edge** into the slit trench on one side, then lay the wood edging into the trench on top of it and knock down with a hammer until it is level. Repeat on the other edge, making sure that the fabric is taut.

**3** **Using a sharp knife,** cut crosses in opposing pairs in the landscape fabric close to the plank at 1.5–2m (5–6ft) intervals. Knock in a wooden peg through each cross, to at least 2.5cm (1in) below the top of the plank, to support the board.

**4** **Pour in the mulch** (here of bark). Rake it level and tamp down with the rake, so that the mulch surface is flush with the top of the boards and the supporting pegs are completely covered.

but in that case the base of the bed should be about 30cm (12in) wider than the finished top for stability; this shaping is most suitable for narrower beds, such as for strawberries. Making the top of any bed rounded rather than flat aids drainage and increases the surface cropping area.

## The advantages of raised beds

Raised beds bring all the advantages of flat beds, but have improved drainage, are separated from surrounding grass and the soil warms up faster in spring. Raised beds provide a means of gardening successfully on the most unpromising ground, such as where a site is naturally very badly drained (*see p.16*) or perhaps even concreted over.

Higher raised beds can also extend the pleasure of gardening to people who are less mobile; this is a more expensive undertaking, but worthwhile. Higher beds can be made by constructing walls to a height of 60–90cm (24–36in). The base of the bed should be filled with rubble, which is then topped with 30–45cm (12–18in) of fertile soil.

## Making paths

At their simplest, paths between beds can be maintained as soil areas and weed growth is regularly skimmed off.

A mulched path is an alternative that requires more initial effort, but which should reduce maintenance in the longer term. The path should first be covered with a weed-suppressing landscape fabric, which is then topped with mulch of bark or gravel (*see above*) to make a hard-wearing and attractive garden feature.

Grass pathways are also a possibility, provided that a durable edging, for example rigid plastic or concrete blocks, is constructed around the beds; the grass surface must stand proud of the edging to allow for unobstructed mowing. Tufted grasses are recommended. Avoid rhizomatous grasses such as couch, which are too widespreading for paths.

# Types of path surfacing

**Landscape fabric**
*Available by the roll and can be cut to measure; water-permeable.*

**Bark mulch**
*Relatively inexpensive, blends well with surroundings, and soft to walk on.*

**Granite screenings**
*Easily obtained and long-lasting; use with landscape fabric base.*

**Stone mulch**
*An attractive option, available in blue or green hues, but relatively expensive.*

**Fine gravel**
*Soft surface material that needs regular raking.*

**Turf**
*Fairly inexpensive and easy to establish, but requires regular maintenance.*

# Using containers

Not all gardens are suitable for growing crops in the open ground. The soil may have intractable drainage problems (*see p.16*), or contain persistent soil-borne pests or diseases, or just be paved or otherwise sealed over. In these situations many crops can be grown in containers.

This is a technique much used with flowering plants, allowing every area of a garden to be fully exploited. Growing in containers has its benefits: crops can be grown immediately outside the kitchen door, especially herbs, or small containers moved to a prominent spot when most attractive, and containers can be filled with soil or compost of better structure than exists in the open garden site. When plants are grown in containers, they can be moved to the site that best suits the season i.e. sun or shade. In many tropical gardens growing vegetables and herbs in containers is the only way to grow crops that rot or succumb to fungal disease due to excessively damp conditions.

Container growing also makes demands. There will be expenditure on containers. Above all, there is the need for constant attention to watering and feeding.

## Choosing containers

There are various types of container to choose from: pots of all shapes and sizes made in earthenware, concrete, plastic, galvanized metal, or terracotta; wooden tubs, either specially made or adapted from barrels; or units temporarily built up from blocks, bricks, or timber. Even small containers like windowboxes and hanging baskets can be used, and there is scope for all sorts of ingenuity in adapting various used containers of all sizes for growing vegetables or fruit – stacks of used tyres or sections of very wide drainpipe.

When choosing containers, make sure they will be large enough for the crop you intend to grow. The greater the volume of a container, the more likely it is that the growing conditions of open ground can be matched, and this is most important with regard to maintaining water supplies. Some specially made plastic containers for tree and bush fruits or most vegetable crops may be as

**Herbs on display**
*Many fruits and vegetables are as decorative as flowers, and in containers can make very attractive garden features. This range of herbs* including purple sage, rosemary, mint, and flowering thyme, make a bright and aromatic feature in a sunny corner.

much as 90cm (36in) wide and 60cm (24in) deep. Smaller versions for annual vegetables or strawberries should have a depth of at least 15cm (6in); the deeper they are, the better. A trough approximately 60cm (24in) long by 20cm (8in) wide and deep or a polystyrene fruit box can hold a useful selection of salad vegetables or herbs, and a 40–45cm (16–18in) basket can hold herbs, strawberries, or a trailing tomato plant.

Whatever type of container is used, think carefully about its position. Avoid shade but at the same time aim to site containers away from full summer sun and wind exposure, where they are likely to heat or dry out quickly. The largest sorts should be correctly placed before filling, because they can be very heavy to move after. Always raise containers on pot feet or shallow blocks about 5cm (2in) high to aid drainage. Make sure that pots for woody plants or tall crops on climbing supports will not become top-heavy when the crop is fully grown; they must be large and of

heavy construction. Lightweight containers can be weighted with ballast in the bottom. Place hanging baskets conveniently for watering and to avoid troublesome drips.

## Suitable crops for containers

Apple and pear trees raised on semi-dwarfing rootstocks (*see pp.174 and 181*) can be grown in large containers, as can many bush fruits; even blueberries can be grown in a lime-free mix. Strawberries can be grown in pots or tall planters with holes for several plants. Special care in watering, feeding, and pest and disease monitoring is necessary for these mostly long-term crops.

Almost any vegetable crop can be raised in containers. Successional sowing will keep supplies constant, and transplanted seedlings are recommended for all container-grown vegetables (*see p.65*). There are tomatoes suitable for any of the types described, including hanging baskets; other fruiting vegetables and legumes will also succeed. Salad crops are an excellent use of containers, and herbs lend themselves to growing in windowboxes or other small containers. Root vegetables are possibilities; these particularly benefit from transplanting as multiblock-sown plants. Perennial vegetables are the least worthy of space in containers.

## Planting containers

All containers must be well drained; waterlogging leads to crop failure. This can be ensured by the existence of several drainage holes in the base; if there is only one and more cannot be made, put plenty of pieces of broken pots in the bottom to provide a drainage layer.

Proprietary soilless or soil-based potting mixes are best for filling the smallest of the containers, including windowboxes and hanging baskets. Soil-based products will give more stability and are likely to hold moisture better. Adding 'water crystals' to the potting mix aids moisture retention and adding up to 20 per cent sand or grit by volume will aid drainage, add weight, and probably make the overall purchase less expensive. For the largest of rigid containers the best course is to resort to filling with fertile garden soil, specially prepared by mixing in well-rotted manure or garden compost and a good measure of grit. In addition, apply a

## Growing vegetables in boxes

Vegetables can be grown in polystyrene boxes filled with potting mix. Here vine tomatoes are growing hydroponically in a greenhouse. The boxes of moisture-retentive sawdust are watered and fertilized automatically via a dripper installed in each box. Vegetables and herbs can also be grown in boxes that are watered and liquid fertilized via the watering can.

compound fertilizer to the soil surface at 50g per sq m (1oz per sq yd) and work it in to a depth of 5–8cm (2–3in).

## Watering and feeding

Where porous materials are used, such as terracotta, it is helpful to line the sides with thin plastic sheet or paint the inside with a waterproof coating, which will effectively reduce water loss. Surface evaporation can be reduced by applying a mulch of well-rotted organic matter or even composted bark or pebbles (*see below*). In all cases, watering crops in containers requires close attention to the plant and weather conditions, and the feel of the soil. Always water copiously and not in dribbles; in hot or windy weather this may be necessary twice a day or more. Never assume that natural rainfall has done the job for you.

Nutrients are also used up rapidly in free-standing containers. The roots will be restricted when growing in

containers, and have to obtain all the necessary nutrients from a smaller volume of soil than they would have naturally, so the soil needs to be enriched by adding a slow-release fertilizer. Supplementary feeds (*see pp.20–23*) can be added as growth proceeds. This can be done by top-dressing with a dry compound fertilizer, but liquid fertilizers are most effective and convenient. For annual crops, it is best to start each season with fresh potting mix, but the growing medium in large, well-fed and watered containers can be left in place for more than one season. Most packaged potting mixes are ready-mixed with fertilizer but this may be insufficient for hungry vegetables.

The need for constant attention to crops grown in containers cannot be over-emphasized. Plants growing in containers are living in fundamentally stressful conditions, and it is all too easy for much enthusiastic investment to go to waste, because of a little neglect.

### Scaling the heights
*Peas and beans can be grown in containers, and the largest pots will accommodate brushwood or bamboo-cane wigwams or proprietary kinds of support.*

Gravel mulch
*1cm (½in) layer to conserve moisture*

Potting mix
*Soil-based or soilless mix can be used*

Leaf mulch
*5–8cm (2–3in) deep prevents soil mix from clogging drainage layer*

Drainage layer
*Broken pots or stones*

Pot feet
*Hold base off ground so water drains through holes*

### Filling a container
*A layer of porous ballast in the base, such as broken pots or stones, will help drainage. This should be 10cm (4in) deep in large containers and 2.5cm (1in) deep in the smallest. Cover this with leaf mulch or twigs before adding growing medium to 2.5cm (1in) below the rim to allow for watering.*

# Soil preparation

The time and care that are invested in soil management will be repaid in the successful growth and productivity of fruit and vegetable crops. Seasonal weather is an inevitable challenge, but soil conditions can be governed to a large extent by improvement and good maintenance. Thorough preparation and continuing care serve to keep the soil free-draining yet suitably retentive of moisture, well aerated, and satisfactorily supplied with nutrients: characteristics that all encourage root growth and the supply of essential elements for healthy plant development (see pp. 14–17).

Most vegetable crops are annuals or otherwise short-term crops, and basic soil preparation is therefore a seasonal operation. Most fruit crops are perennials, and the considerations of soil preparation are occasional, but all the more important.

Garden soil that has been managed well for several years can be prepared shortly before planting, but previously uncultivated ground should be dug in advance, removing perennial weeds, breaking up any compaction, and improving soil fertility with the addition of lime and organic matter (see pp. 18–23).

## Digging the soil

Most gardeners find that the best soil preparation is digging. A prime reason for digging is that it provides immediate clearance of annual and perennial weed cover by burying or removing the upper layer, leaving a neat surface exposed to weathering. Digging can also break up compacted layers within the soil profile (see p. 15), ensuring free drainage and allowing the roots of plants to explore to their maximum range. Turning the soil over allows rotted organic matter to be incorporated rapidly throughout the top layers – although do not underestimate the capacity of earthworms to do the same on undug sites – and at the same time exposes some soil-inhabiting insect pests to the attention of birds.

Certainly digging is laborious, but if it is tackled in limited sections, at the most suitable time, and using the best technique, it can in fact be a very satisfying activity.

**Forking sandy soil**
*Light, sandy soils may be prepared with a fork. Spread a good layer, 5–8cm (2–3in) deep, of well-rotted manure or compost over the surface at the time of cultivating. Keeping the fork as upright as possible, push it into the soil to its full depth and twist to turn over the soil, so that the manure is well worked in.*

Never attempt digging when the soil is saturated from heavy rain, as this risks compaction and damage to the existing structure. Most importantly, the task is made much harder because of the extra weight and stickiness of the turned-up soil, and it will be difficult to achieve a satisfying result.

### Dealing with different soils

Relatively heavy soils are best dug when moist but not wet or dry. Turning over portions of topsoil in cold weather exposes them to the beneficial effects of winter frost. Water in the soil freezes and expands, so that the soil clods are naturally shattered to provide the basis of good structure. Together with liming (see pp. 18–19), this is the most effective way of handling soils of high clay content.

Light, sandy or silt soils are best dug a week or two before planting, because otherwise weathering may destroy what natural structure there is. With such soils it is a good plan to cover the surface with well-rotted organic matter well before planting (see p. 22 and pp. 41–42).

Both types of soil can be dug with a spade, but the garden fork is an essential partner tool. It provides the best means of removing perennial weeds without breaking the roots before you dig, and of moving and spreading organic matter. It is just as suitable as the spade for digging light soils.

### Preparing to dig

Plan the digging in an orderly way. The best approach is to have or mark out a rectangular plot. Large plots can be divided into more conveniently sized segments by running a line down the middle: in this situation the ground is effectively dug as two plots side by side. Beds (see pp. 32–34) are dug from end to end, following the same procedure as for a wide plot.

The length of a spade blade or fork prongs is 25–30cm (10–12in). This is referred to as the spit, and it is the most usual cultivated depth of soil. In some circumstances it is beneficial to cultivate to two spits depth, but this will really

### DIGGING TIPS

- **Fix the principles** of the method in your mind at the outset, and work methodically and rhythmically.
- **Adopt a comfortable** and relaxed body posture when digging into and lifting soil; this will help you to work for longer periods without strain.
- **Keep your shoulders** down and use the weight of your body, not your arms, to drive the spade or fork into the soil.
- **Know your limits** and never attempt to do too much at one time.
- **Don't overload the spade** – it is quicker and less stressful to lift smaller amounts.
- **Keep the wall** of the digging trench vertical, so that the full spade's depth of soil is cultivated.
- **Use the best tools** you can afford; if you are tall, it may be worth seeking out long-handled tools for greater comfort when working.
- **Keep your tools** clean and sharp for ease of working.

# Single digging the soil

1 **Mark out the plot** and dig out the first trench to a depth of one spit and a width of 30–40cm (12–15in). Place the spoil in a wheelbarrow to be taken to the other end of the plot, where it will be used to fill the last trench.

2 **Scatter well-rotted manure** or compost over the base of the trench to a depth of 2.5–5cm (1–2in) and over the ground that is to be dug next.

3 **Mark out the next area** to be dug. Insert the spade blade at right angles to the digging trench, nicking the soil surface in order to mark out manageable portions that can be turned over neatly without overloading your spade.

4 **Moving along the trench**, thrust the spade blade vertically into the soil to its full depth to loosen each section.

5 **Press the handle downwards** while levering it back. Lean forwards and downwards and twist the spade blade to turn the portion of soil over into the trench. Take care to bend at the knees, and hold the shaft of the spade near the blade, to reduce the strain on your back.

6 **At each progressive run** of digging across the plot, scatter some organic matter over the floor of the new trench, along the face of the turned-over soil, and on the ground to be dug next. Spreading it in this way results in a good mix through the top spit of soil.

7 **Continue down the plot**, turning each trench into the previous one. Fill the last trench with the spoil from the first. Do not chop or beat the surface of the soil; leave it roughly dug so that weathering will break it down.

only be necessary on compacted soils when first preparing the kitchen garden, and only occasionally thereafter.

There are a number of systems of digging, but for general purposes soil preparation can be covered by two: single digging and double digging. Both procedures follow the same pattern of digging and suit most kitchen garden situations. For widely spaced fruit trees or row planting, the principles can be adapted to preparing either individual planting holes or trenches.

## Single digging the soil

This is the most common annual treatment, in which the ground is cultivated to the depth of a single spit. The operation requires moving methodically backwards down the plot, digging trenches from right to left and left to right on alternate runs.

Take out a trench about 30–40cm (12–16in) wide to a spit depth across the width of the plot. Remove the soil from this trench by wheelbarrow to the opposite end of the plot and deposit it in an even line outside the plot boundary. This transported soil will be used to fill in the last trench at the end of the dug site.

Start by digging the soil into the first trench, which in turn creates a second trench (*see above*). If organic matter has previously been spread over the surface it will automatically be incorporated. Manure may also be added at the base of each trench or, much better, scattered in forkfuls over the full profile. Scattering in this way is generally a preferable system to burying manure at the bottom of the trench, because the matter will break down faster.

Skimmed-off grass and annual weeds can be buried (*see facing page, top*), but perennial weeds are best removed manually, teasing out the underground runners of weeds like couch grass, dock, and nettles with a fork.

The operation is repeated down the plot, and the last trench is filled with the soil from the first. In the case of a large split plot, the second plot is dug in the opposite direction to the first, and the last trench will be adjacent to the first. This removes the need to transport the soil removed from the first trench; it can be deposited outside the plot boundary right next to where digging the first plot began.

## Double digging the soil

This is a system for first opening up a site and for occasional use thereafter if necessary. Double digging follows the same pattern as single digging, but the ground is cultivated to two spits depth. The working trench is 60–75cm (24–30in) wide; this allows the base of a much more clearly defined succeeding trench to be forked to a second spit depth. Because the trench is wider, it is necessary to turn over two parallel furrows into the previous trench, instead of one (*see below*).

In all digging operations be sure not to bring the subsoil to the surface; this is most likely to be a problem when double digging a plot.

## The no-digging system

Some gardeners hold that digging is not essential and point to disadvantages in treating the soil in this way. The most obvious disadvantage of digging is that it is hard work – although the energy required can make it a healthy exercise. It is possible to damage soil structure by digging, and there may be disadvantages in disturbing the balance of beneficial soil-inhabiting organisms. Buried weed seeds are brought to the surface by the procedure, and digging is also likely to result in the soil losing moisture as it is exposed to the air.

Management of a no-digging system is based on minimum disturbance of the surface, which is regularly dressed with a thick mulch of rotted organic matter

(*see pp. 41–42*). This needs to be applied well in advance of cropping, to allow for worms to pull the material down into the surface layers, improving soil structure and enhancing fertility.

On soils that have a good structure, the no-digging regime is a good way of dealing with the areas between crop rows or between widely spaced trees.

It is vital initially to remove perennial weeds like couch grass, nettle, and dock from a site that is to be managed without digging. This can be done by meticulous forking out of clumps of weeds, or by laying a covering of sheet mulch over the infested area; this latter treatment will be successful only if left in place for many months (*see p. 49*).

## Skimming weeds

1 **If the ground** to be dug is covered with weeds, remove any established perennial weeds with a fork. You can then skim off the annual weeds and bury them.

2 **Before you dig** each trench, use the spade to cut the soil into sections about the size of a spade blade, then slide the blade just under the surface of the soil and lift the weeds off.

3 **Turn the skimmings** into the base of the previous trench, so that the weeds lie upside-down. Once they are covered by soil they will die down and enrich the soil.

## Double digging the soil

1 **Mark out the plot;** with a large area, as here, divide the plot lengthways into 2 halves. At one end, dig out a trench 60–90cm (2–3ft) wide to the depth of a spit, as for single digging. Place all the removed soil in a long heap, next to the end of the adjoining section.

2 **Cover the base** of the trench with a 5–8cm (2–3in) layer of well-rotted manure or compost. Fork it into the soil to another full spit depth, so that the manure is worked into the subsoil.

3 **Mark out** a second trench to the same width. Dig the trench in 2 halves, or strips. Take out the soil from the strip furthest from the first

trench, placing it against the wall of the trench. This will keep the shape of the trenches clearly defined.

4 **Fill the first trench** with the soil from the remaining strip to be dug. A new, second, trench has now been created. Repeat the process, working down the plot to the other end.

Fill the last trench of a half-plot with soil dug from the first trench of the second half-plot. Continue to the end, filling the final trench of the second half-plot with the soil that was placed off the plot at the very outset.

The weedkiller glyphosate is also an effective treatment for removing perennial weeds in gardens that are not committed to organic principles.

Include the possibility of a no-digging policy when planning the kitchen garden (*see pp.27–30*), but do not regard it simply as an easier solution. It is crucial to pay close attention to soil preparation by this means. Incorrectly managed, it can result in a very weedy patch carrying poor crops.

## Surface preparation

How the soil surface is prepared after digging is dependent on the cropping intention.

Where fruit plants and robust transplanted vegetable plants, such as brassicas (*see pp.78–81*) and leeks (*see p.93*), are to be grown, all that is necessary is to level the surface with a wide wooden rake. On light soils, the ground may also need to be firmed by gentle treading as levelling proceeds.

For seed-raised crops and the smaller vegetable transplants, it is necessary to prepare a tilth: a surface layer with a fine, crumbly structure. This is easiest on light, sandy and silt soils, where it can be achieved by cultivating the surface in different directions with a wide rake.

Stones and plant remains are most easily pulled off by holding the rake near to upright, whereas levelling and tilth-making are more readily achieved

**Avoiding soil compaction**
*When preparing the surface of beds for planting or sowing, stand on planks laid across the bed to avoid compacting the soil. Mark the intervals for drills (here with canes), and line one of the planks up with these. Stand on the planks and draw out a straight drill along the plank edge with a hoe or cane.*

by holding the tool with its handle as close as is comfortable to the ground.

Heavy soils are effectively cultivated with a multi-tined cultivator, followed by raking – all in various directions. Treading with your feet is helpful on heavy soils for breaking down clods and on light soils for firming soft ground. Treading must never be done on wet soil, no matter what the soil texture: a suitable test is that the soil should not stick to your boots – it should instead disintegrate quite easily when crushed in a hand grip.

The process of creating a tilth can include the incorporation of granular fertilizer dressing (*see pp.20–21*). When the top 5–8cm (2–3in) of surface is suitably friable, seed drills can be drawn

out or the area marked out with shallowly drawn drills for transplant lines (*see pp.66–67*).

In a no-digging situation, preparation beyond the surface mulching stage entails simply pulling aside remaining organic matter to expose the soil, with possibly the need for shallow hoeing off of any established annual weeds. This operation can be done either at spaced planting stations, as appropriate to fruit plants or well-spaced vegetable plants, or along marked out rows for smaller transplants or sowing seed. The vital mulch dressing will have improved the surface texture of the soil, and taking out planting holes and drawing drills will be no problem: in many instances it is perfectly suitable to plant through the mulch remnants.

# Preparing soil for planting and sowing

**Multi-tined cultivator**
*A three- or five-tined cultivator is an effective tool for preparing roughly dug ground. Draw the tines through the soil to break down large clods and loosen the surface.*

**Wooden rake**
*Use a wide wooden rake to level the surface and remove large stones. To achieve a good level, hold the rake low and guide it through one hand so that it glides through the surface.*

**Metal-headed rake**
*Use a metal rake with a head at least 30cm (12in) wide to create a fine tilth suitable for sowing. Rake the entire surface first in one direction, then at 90° to this.*

# Mulching

Mulching is the process of covering the soil surface with a layer of organic or inorganic material. It is one of the most useful gardening practices, which can bring significant improvements in cultivation of fruits and vegetables. The benefits of mulching cannot be over-emphasized, and it is a technique not sufficiently appreciated and used.

Mulching should feature in the plans and maintenance of any size of kitchen garden; it will save labour and result in better quality and yield. There is a wide choice of methods, so mulches can be used by anyone, in any size of garden.

## The benefits of mulching

All crops require continuous supplies of water, and mulching helps this in two ways. Any type of mulch provides a seal, reducing evaporation from the soil: this is particularly beneficial during warm or windy weather when large quantities of water are lost in this way. Organic mulches also help moisture retention by improving soil structure and fertility (*see pp.14–17*) as they are drawn down into the surface layer by earthworms. A mulch can also protect soil structure from being damaged by heavy rain.

Mulches can enhance or maintain soil temperature. In winter mulch reduces heat loss as air temperature falls: this can keep plant growth active and in frosty weather prevent physical damage to parts below ground, such as mature carrot roots.

In cool weather clear plastic sheet mulch applied before sowing raises soil temperature, encouraging germination

## Using organic mulches

▽ **Choose well-rotted manure**
*All animal manures should be well weathered before use, to avoid the emission of ammonia, which can be damaging to plants. After a period of stacking, coarse-textured, strawy manure takes on a darker colour and becomes more friable.*

*Fine, crumbly texture*

*Well-rotted manure*

*Straw still prominent*

*Fresh manure*

△ **Applying organic mulch**
*Apply well-rotted manure or garden compost to a depth of 2–3in (5–8cm) while the ground is moist. Take care not to heap the mulch up around the stems of the plants (here runner beans), as this encourages rot.*

and early growth. Another important benefit of mulch is that it keeps the ground relatively cool during summer: this reduces water loss and also maintains good conditions for the growing roots and beneficial soil-inhabiting organisms.

These advantages apply to fruit plants as much as vegetables. Mulching around fruit trees and bushes can have a dramatic effect on growth, easily confirmed by leaving a plant or two untreated.

Covering the soil with a mulch of almost any sort will reduce germinating weeds by depriving them of light. Short-term coverings suppress annual weeds; to control perennial weeds, mulches such as heavy gauge black film plastic or thick carpet (*see p.49*) should be put in place for a long time, well in advance of cropping. If annual weeds do grow through mulches they are invariably weak-rooted and easily pulled out.

## Organic mulches

Most bulky organic manures (*see pp.22–23*) can be used for mulching, providing they are well decomposed. Garden compost and leaf mould (*see pp.24–26*) are ideal, as well as spent mushroom compost. Shredded prunings, bark and wood chips, and weathered sawdust are effective, but add supplementary dressings of nitrogen-rich fertilizer (*see pp.20–21*), for the soil may become deficient in this as the products are broken down. Straw is especially good around strawberries or over vegetable and rhubarb beds. In coastal areas seaweed may be available, but

## Straw mulch
*Mulching is useful to keep developing fruits clean of soil on surface or trailing plants such as strawberries, melons, marrows, and pumpkins (as here). Straw is particularly suitable for this.*

check that gathering it is permitted. Organic mulches must be kept aerated and free-draining: for this reason do not put thick layers of lawn clippings around plants as a mulch, because they become slimy and compacted. Some gardeners use old carpet and cardboard or newspapers for mulching. These are most useful around fruit trees and between rows in the vegetable garden but they are unsightly unless well covered with straw or another natural-looking material. However, do not consider newspaper as an under-mulch if black birds or other scratching birds are present as it will result in a mess of scattered paper.

Old carpet, cardboard or newspaper several pages thick can also be used to smother annual weeds. However, they are not an effective control for perennial weeds.

## Inorganic mulches

Film plastic is sometimes used as an inorganic mulching material. Clear film plastic is most effective for raising soil temperatures, but because it lets light through it not only allows but also actually encourages weed growth. Use black film plastic for longer-term cover. It suppresses weeds, conserves moisture, and is useful for keeping fruits, particularly strawberries, and vegetables off the soil surface. Heavier grades of plastic sheet are less likely to tear and will last for more than one season, especially when made with a sunlight-inhibiting ingredient. Old fertilizer or compost sacks can be cut to form covers for use around trees.

Film plastics that are white or silver on one side and black on the other are used in commercial plots: with the black side downwards they reflect light up into the plants. All-white plastic gives similar benefits.

Some heavy-gauge woven weed matting can be used for long-term mulching such as around fruit bushes and trees or for pathways, where they are an economic investment.

Decorative pebble mulch is a possible candidate for some situations.

## Disadvantages of mulching

Mulching has a few potential pitfalls. Organic kinds can encourage disease if layered heavily right up to the necks

**Landscape fabric mulches**
*Various fabrics such as weed matting that are permeable to water and air are available for long-term mulching, or as a membrane on which loose mulching material can be laid.*

of plants. Fresh animal wastes can cause damage to plants through high levels of ammonia. More inert organic materials, like wood derivatives, can deplete the soil of nitrogen as they decompose. Some materials such as newspaper are unsightly when scattered by foraging birds. All mulches provide refuge for slugs and some types similarly for snails and even small animal pests. Most film plastics are impervious to rain or irrigation and require watering lines (*see p.54*) laid beneath. None of these problems cannot be dealt with. The important thing is be aware of them and be watchful about methods of mulch application and of methods of pest control where appropriate.

## Applying mulches

Apply all mulches to soil that is neither very wet nor very dry: a mulch will only serve to exacerbate both these conditions. Spring application is valuable because the conservation of soil moisture encourages early growth and suppresses the first flushes of annual weeds. Mulch fruit plants immediately after planting, and put straw around strawberries just as young fruit trusses are enlarging. Mulch vegetable rows as soon as the plants are well established. Mulch in autumn to top up earlier applications as a soil improver or provide frost protection to root crops. Mulches of garden compost, leaf mould, or manure must be of friable texture. Apply to a depth of 2.5–8cm (1–3in). Straw and hay around robust plants may be twice as deep, allowing for settlement.

Fix all plastic sheet mulches as tightly as possible, and lay during a warm, sunny period, when the material will be flexible. The soil surface should be flat, so that water will not collect in puddles on the sheet. Push the edges of the sheet into the ground with a spade, making a deep slit in the soil beforehand. Ensure the sheet is removed as soon as its useful life is over, as it can shatter on degrading. Organic mulches are absorbed into the soil so do not need removing.

Mulching has a practical place for covering pathways, too, not only to control weed growth but also to give a safe, clean walking surface (*see p.34*).

△ **Black plastic sheet mulch**
*Thin film plastic can be used as a mulch in cool climates. Lay it as tightly as possible to stop wind lifting it or puddles forming on top.*

◁ **Plastic mulch is ideal for strawberries**
*Before covering the bed with plastic, install a drip irrigation line along the bed. The black plastic warms the soil and keeps the fruit clean.*

# Crop protection

Crops are vulnerable to many hazards that can reduce the harvest or destroy the crop entirely. One of these hazards in Australia is the weather. Gardens in southern and mountain areas may experience frost that destroys young seedlings or flowers before fruit set. In hot climates excessive heat may be hazardous or in the 'tropical wet' it may be excessive wind and rain. Other hazards that can damage crops include birds, rabbits and other pests. The greatest difficulty with all these hazards is that their timing is unpredictable. The best solution therefore is crop protection.

Several factors govern the range and harvest period of fruits and vegetables that we can grow in the garden. Natural season and site are important, but the greatest influences are temperature and humidity. Also, where the water supply is not available, water availability influences the size of the garden and the type of crop grown. Many popular fruit and vegetable crops struggle to grow satisfactorily where there are temperature extremes.

## Protecting crops from cold
The range of produce grown in the kitchen garden can be widened quite

△ **Sun protection**
*Young seedlings here are protected from the hot sun under shade cloth. Tender leafy vegetables, berries and summer fruits also benefit from sun protection in hot climates.*

◁ **Frost protection**
*Some fruit trees are tender to frost when young, but can withstand a degree of frost when established e.g. macadamias. Cover them with hessian or shadecloth during winter.*

considerably by using various forms of protection: that is, raising the soil and air temperature above that of the surroundings by covering crops with some sort of protective layer.

There are many ways of protecting crops from the cold. A greenhouse is probably the most ambitious and demanding possibility, but it provides the greatest opportunity in cool

climates for growing variety over the longest possible period. Similar benefits can be obtained to some extent with mini-greenhouses, cloches and floating mulches (*see pp. 45–46*).

## Greenhouses
In cool climates a greenhouse is invaluable for raising vegetables (*see pp. 62–65*) such as brassicas, capsicum, tomatoes and eggplant. Crops can be started early, sown and established in containers in warmer air temperatures than those outside; they can be set out as sturdy plants when frost is less likely and soil temperature is rising (*see pp. 70–71*). Quicker germination and better planning of succession are also possible, and establishing crops can be kept under close scrutiny. Module-raised plants are less dependent on high-quality tilth than those sown directly in the garden.

The harvest season can be extended for fruiting crops (*see pp. 108–119*), such as tomatoes, sweet peppers, cucumbers, and melons when they are grown in a greenhouse. Strawberries are suited to greenhouses and are often grown hydroponically. The largest greenhouses are suitable for tree fruits (*see pp. 149–205*) such as lemons and avocados and for vines (*see pp. 227–233*). However, a greenhouse is not necessary

**Vine tomatoes in a greenhouse bed**
*In temperate climates, tomatoes and other warm climate vegetables can be grown through the cooler months in a greenhouse.*

**Hydroponic vegetables**
*Hydroponic systems produce quick crops in a greenhouse. Here lettuces are grown without soil and the roots are constantly moist in a flow of recycled hydroponic solution.*

# Greenhouse ventilation

Good ventilation is essential in a greenhouse. Warm air rises to the ridge of the greenhouse, and is dispersed by operating ridge ventilators. As a guide, the roof area that can be opened should be equal to 20 per cent of the floor area of the greenhouse. Side ventilators are needed to replenish the flow of air into the greenhouse; these should be plentiful, sited on both sides of the structure, and positioned as low as possible for maximum benefit. Hand operated ventilators are the least expensive option, but automatic controllers are available. Louvres provide effective side ventilation, and are opened or closed by means of a simple lever.

*Louvre vents*

*Top vents*

*Side vents*

for vegetables if the right varieties are planted at the right time. Seed-raised plants can be bought from garden centres to gain the seasonal advantages, and can be grown in the garden, albeit with a more restricted season.

At all costs, do not underestimate the care and attention required to get good results: regular greenhouse maintenance will include ventilating, watering, and shading, over and above the specific care of the crops grown.

## Choosing a greenhouse
Glass is the best material for light transmission and heat retention, and it is the most durable cladding if carefully maintained, but it is relatively expensive, heavy, and fragile. Plastic requires less

### Extending the season
*While a polytunnel would not be an efficient choice for use as a heated greenhouse, it can extend the growing season considerably. Here a range of winter greens, including mizuna and pak choi, are being grown together with winter radish and beetroot.*

robust load-bearing structures than glass; units are therefore generally cheaper and easier to repair. Rigid plastic is available as acrylic or acrylic-coated polycarbonate sheet; sheets coated on both sides offer improved insulation.

Walk-in polytunnels are the cheapest greenhouse choice, in terms of covered surface and load-bearing structure. The flexible film plastic is stretched over regularly spaced tubular metal hoops and held in place by a timber beam or by burying the edges along the sides of the structure. Film plastic containing an ultraviolet-light inhibitor gives up to five seasons' use.

Glass- or rigid-plastic-clad greenhouses come in many shapes and qualities: even polygonal shapes are available, and can

make attractive garden features. They may be free-standing or abutted to a building as a lean-to structure, ideal for growing out of season tomatoes. They may be made of wood, which needs the most maintenance, aluminium, or polyvinyl chloride plastic (PVC). Older or more traditional, glass-clad greenhouses may have brick wall supports up to half the side wall, or may be glass- or plastic-clad to ground level.

## Equipping the greenhouse
Where tomatoes and other warm-climate crops are to be grown through winter in temperate regions supplementary heating is required. The higher the temperature desired, the more expensive it is to maintain. Because film plastic does not retain heat as well as rigid plastics or glass, heating is much less worthwhile in a polytunnel. However, for propagating purposes it is feasible to build a small, enclosed frame or other unit within these structures. Heat loss from rigid-clad greenhouses can be reduced by fixing insulation during winter and early spring. Bubble-wrap products are particularly effective, and the light loss will not be crucial.

All greenhouses must have built-in systems for ventilation through air movement. In polytunnels it is most convenient to rely on air movement through the structure from large doors constructed at each end, operated by rolling up or down sheet covers strengthened with horizontal wooden battens. End-door ventilation is equally valuable for temperature control in glass and rigid-plastic clad structures, but here vents are also used (*see above left*).

In order to avoid crop damage from overheating in summer, you will need to provide shading facility for greenhouses. This can be a moveable cover in the form of a roller blind; more economical, and suitable for all types of structure, is the application of a white wash in early summer, removed in the autumn. Be sure to have a continuous water supply connected to the greenhouse.

Benching, preferably removable for convenience, is invaluable in a greenhouse. It is also worthwhile investing in a soil-warming mat to provide bottom-heat to germinating seed and developing plants; the ideal situation is to have this within a frame sitting on the benching. All heating equipment should be controlled by a thermostat, and the electrical installation should be made by a qualified person.

Vine tomatoes and other climbing plants grown in a greenhouse need support, and this is best done by fixing wires and strings to the structural roof members of the greenhouse.

## A mini-greenhouse

A mini-greenhouse is sometimes called a cold frame and is a simple alternative to a greenhouse for plant raising, especially where it is possible to fit a soil-warming mat. As seedlings grow, progressively more air is admitted to the mini-greenhouse every few days, until the plants are completely exposed.

Site the mini-greenhouse in an accessible position that is prone to neither wind nor shade. For raising young plants, it may be stood on a hard surface area, but where the structure is portable, it can be placed over the bed of sown seed and removed when seedlings are established.

The most efficient mini-greenhouse is constructed with the rear wall higher than that at the front, in most cases with a fall of no more than 5cm (2in). This sheds rain and, when suitably orientated, captures the maximum sunlight.

## Hydroponics in the greenhouse

Many vegetable crops and strawberries grow well hydroponically and to achieve optimum results the hydroponic system is best installed in a greenhouse. Hydroponics is a system where plants are grown in water in which nutrients have been dissolved. This nutrient solution supports plant growth but it provides no physical support for the plant.

There are different methods of growing plants hydroponically but the two most popular are the recirculating system and the aggregate system. In the recirculating system young plants growing in a plug of rockwool or a small tube pot are suspended in a container of hydroponic solution so that the growing roots are bathed in the recirculating nutrient solution. This is an expensive system to install and

**Mini-greenhouse**
*The most durable is constructed with brick walls, which retain heat better than all-glass or plastic frames.*

requires automatic pumps to ensure the roots are constantly bathed in solution. In the aggregate system young plants are planted in containers filled with a coarse soilless aggregate such as sawdust, perlite or sand. The containers can be large pots, bags or polystyrene boxes and each is supplied with an irrigation dripper through which nutrient solution is fed. The aggregate system is less expensive to install and produces excellent results, especially with greenhouse tomatoes.

All hydroponic growing methods require daily attention to be sure the plant is receiving adequate amounts of solution and the solution contains an adequate amount of nutrients. Hydroponic nutrients are completely soluble in water and relatively expensive.

## Cloches

Cloches are another long-established means of protecting and advancing edible crops. They are very useful for

seedlings and strawberries, and they can also be successfully used to grow early lettuce, melons, and zucchini.

The term cloche derives from the use of bell glasses placed over individual plants to hasten maturity. There are variations in design of individual cloches and most consist of panes of horticultural glass clamped together on a wire framework. Large jars and 2 litre clear plastic bottles that have had the base cut out, make inexpensive but effective covers for seedlings. Simply place the bottle over the newly planted seedling, and it will be safe from cold wind and birds and other pests. Remove the bottle cover when the seedling is established and the weather warms.

Glass cloches do have their disadvantages. However, they are prone to breakage because of the necessary pattern of regularly moving them within the garden. The glass requires cleaning every season to remove soil and particularly tenacious algal growth.

For economy, safety, and relative ease

**Tunnel and tent cloches**
*This kitchen garden is exploiting a range of crop protection methods, from large frames in the background to tunnel cloches over large crops and barn cloches over the smaller plants.*

**Access to tunnel cloches**
*To ventilate tunnel cloches push the film plastic up from ground level between the metal hoop and the retaining string. This also gives access for watering and harvesting.*

of handling, consider cloches made from materials other than glass, such as rigid plastic.

The main disadvantages are that these cladding materials usually transmit less light than glass and do not retain heat as well. Furthermore, they are light and more vulnerable to wind. Whereas glass is durable when carefully handled, plastics are subject to degeneration through the action of sunlight, unless a light-inhibiting chemical is added to the material at the time of manufacture.

## Tunnel and tent cloches

Tunnel and tent cloches can be made to fit a garden bed. One method is to stretch sheet plastic over hoops of wire (*see below*). An extension of this method is to secure a second hoop of wire over the plastic so that the plastic can be gathered up between the wires. This allows for the amount of covering to be adjusted according to the weather. Similarly a length of shadecloth can be used instead of plastic in hot weather to protect plants from hot sun. This form of cloche is relatively inexpensive and easy to make. The plastic covering should last for at least two seasons.

To get maximum use out of cloches, plan to grow crops in long, narrow strips. While not exactly portable, tunnel cloches can be moved from one bed to another as the need arises. The plastic sheet can also be changed to shadecloth as the need arises.

As with using a greenhouse, watering

**Throw-over bird netcovers**
*Crops such as these raspberries, can be protected from birds by covering with a fabric netting. To minimize branch tangling, the net should be removed once the crop is harvested.*

the covered crop is crucial. It is possible to benefit from rainfall by moving or opening the cloches, but for the best insurance handwater or lay inexpensive irrigation lines (*see p.54*) along the crop rows. Consider using a straw mulch under cloches to conserve soil moisture; seedlings can be planted through this mulch.

Choose a sheltered site wherever possible, but carefully fitted cloches can withstand quite strong winds. Tunnel cloches must be constructed carefully so that the sheet is taut and the ends are tied or firmly buried in the soil.

## Floating mulches

Crops may also be protected from frost (or hot sun) with the use of floating mulches. The fabric used for floating mulches is very lightweight spun or woven fabric and is often called 'fleece'. The system is quite compatible with a vegetable garden laid out in 1.2m (4ft) wide beds (*see pp.32–34*).

Floating mulches are effective in raising soil temperature and protecting developing seedlings and young growing crops from wind, light frost and pounding rainfall. Another advantage is that some types of cover form a physical barrier to protect certain crops from damaging pests such as aphids and cabbage white butterfly (*see Plant Problems, pp.246–264*). Horticultural fleece is a soft, lightweight material manufactured from spun and bonded acrylic fibres and is the most popular floating mulch. It is usually white and is permeable to air and to some rainfall.

## Protecting crops from hot sun

In very hot weather, tender leafy vegetables and most types of fruit exposed to the sun are prone to "sunburn". This results in withered leaves and exposed fruit may bleach or turn black and rot. Even in temperate gardens tomatoes and capsicums are

---

## Making a tunnel cloche

**1** **Use a former** made from a plank with coach bolts to make eyelets and 23cm (9in) legs in lengths of galvanized wire.

**2** **Bend the wires** into hoops about 60cm (2ft) wide. A second former, with the hoop shape outlined in nails driven into a thick sheet of wood, will be helpful for this.

**3** **Press the legs of the hoops** into the ground at intervals in a straight line. Drive wooden stakes into the ground at an angle of 45° beyond the last hoops. Secure one end of a roll of 150 gauge clear film plastic to the stake. Unwind the roll over the hoops as tightly as possible; this is easier if the roll is warm. Secure the other end to the second stake. Use polypropylene twine tied to the eyelets to hold the sheet taut.

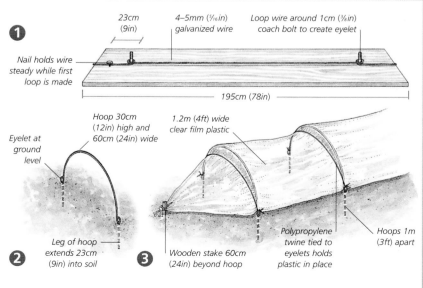

**1**
23cm (9in)
4–5mm (³⁄₁₆in) galvanized wire
Loop wire around 1cm (³⁄₈in) coach bolt to create eyelet
Nail holds wire steady while first loop is made
195cm (78in)

**2**
Eyelet at ground level
Hoop 30cm (12in) high and 60cm (24in) wide
Leg of hoop extends 23cm (9in) into soil

**3**
1.2m (4ft) wide clear film plastic
Wooden stake 60cm (24in) beyond hoop
Polypropylene twine tied to eyelets holds plastic in place
Hoops 1m (3ft) apart

prone to sunburn as are berries and apples, pears and stone fruits. Keeping the water up to crops in hot, dry weather helps reduce damage but shading susceptible crops from the sun may be neccessary too.

Where shading is neccessary, sun covers can be made to protect crops. Shadecloth is ideal but the fabric is weighty and may be too heavy for leafy vegetables and non-woody plants unless the fabric is supported over a frame such as tunnel cloche hoops. Lightweight hessian and horticultural fleece *(see* Floating mulches *p.46)* is more suitable for throw-over covers. Fruiting crops are less exposed if the foliage is dense and the ripening fruit is shaded by leaves. Therefore, it is important not to prune off foliage before harvest.

Heat damage is worst on north and west sides of a crop and where hot sun is a problem a screen of tall plants, such as corn, could be grown to protect a crop or the crop could be planted where it is shaded from a fence or wall. Another solution for small gardens is to grow susceptible crops in containers and move them into the shade when the need arises.

## Protecting crops from wind

Crops exposed to persistent wind do not grow and fruit as well as those grown in a sheltered position. Where

### Scarecrows
*For a fun and attractive bird deterrent, make a scarecrow for your garden. This friendly figure is made with a wooden frame in the shape of a cross over which old clothes are draped.*

wind is troublesome, windbreaks of dense hedging or solid fencing will improve the growing environment and crop yields *(see p.12)* .

## Protecting crops from humidity and excessive rain

In tropical gardens many crops can not be grown through the "wet" season because the high temperature, coupled with high humidity and heavy rain, causes disease and physical damage to crops. Where vegetables can be grown in containers, they can be moved to a verandah or other dry position. The best potting mix to use is a free-draining coarse mix containing stone or pebbles and organic compost. Perennial crops can also be planted on a mound of free-draining mix to improve drainage and reduce humidity.

Think of weather protection as a desirable development, a means of extending the productive range, season, and quality of crops.

## Protecting crops from birds

By far the most destructive pest in fruit and berry crops is birds. Birds can also be very destructive to vegetables scratching out newly sown seed or newly planted seedlings or nipping off young seedlings. Large birds are particularly destructive in some country regions, defoliating leafy crops and

eating fruit and even root crops. Fruit bats also devour soft fruits such as berries, tomatoes and stone fruits. Where these pests are troublesome, crop protection is essential. Not only is the protection essential from a yield aspect, but the worry and disappointment when crops have been damaged makes crop protection a worthwhile investment. Providing a physical barrier is the most successful protection in the home garden. Visual deterrents can also be effective in some situations.

Where many types of birds are troublesome, the most effective barrier is to cover the whole orchard, berry patch and vegetable garden in bird netting. This can be an expensive exercise where the area to be covered is large. Where fruit trees are to be covered, the height required is at least 3m (10ft).

The strongest and most durable orchard cover is a frame constructed from timber or galvanized piping with a net cover of galvanized wire netting.

A simpler orchard cover can be constructed from a lightweight timber or plastic piping frame with a lightweight synthetic netting cover. One example of a lightweight orchard cover is to construct piping hoops similar to those of a polytunnel, and stretch the netting over the hoops.

Perhaps the most important factor in designing an orchard cover comes before any construction is planned. In planning a bird-proof orchard it is wise to plant the trees intensely and keep them pruned low to minimize the size of the structure required. Another important factor is to be sure the cover

### Bird-proof orchard
*Where birds are very troublesome to fruit and vegetables, the ideal solution is to cover the whole area in bird net. Here the vegetable garden, berry patch, and orchard are covered.*

is situated away from large trees because it is almost impossible to remove fallen leaves and branches from the netting roof.

Where a small bird-proof structure is to be made over a vegetable garden or berry patch, it may be possible to attach a lean-to frame onto an existing wall or fence and cover the frame with bird netting. Head height is desirable in all bird covers to ensure easy management. Where small portable bird covers are chosen for vegetable beds or strawberries, these can be made tunnel cloche-style using hoops of wire or plastic piping covered with synthetic bird netting.

Synthetic bird netting can also be draped over individual fruit trees when the fruit is ripening, but this is seldom successful because it becomes tangled in the branches. Another disadvantage is that the birds usually find their way in and become entangled. Portable tree-size covers made with lightweight frames can be the answer where trees are small but moving the covers from tree to tree becomes tedious.

## Choice of bird cover materials

The materials used are dependent on the size of the structure. While a large bird cover may be constructed from heavy galvanized piping or timber

**Fine woven mesh**
*This fine-grade, insect-proof woven mesh is carefully laid to allow the lettuce plants beneath to develop with protection against insect pests.*

# Mechanical barriers and deterrents

△ **Using a cage**
*Protect crops from birds with a cage of nylon netting, supported on metal or timber posts. You can make one yourself or buy a kit like this one, here protecting winter Savoy cabbages and Brussels sprouts.*

▷ **Netting on cabbages**
*Low-level netting can be fitted to home-made structures made from canes to exclude bird pests. Fine-mesh netting will also protect the crop from egg-laying insects, such as cabbage white butterflies.*

△ **Bird scarers**
*A plastic bird of prey suspended on a line from a cane bobs and twists in the breeze to scare off birds. Bird scarers may need to be moved regularly to remain effective.*

poles concreted into the ground, smaller structures may only require light metal or plastic tubing. The second factor that affects the size of the frame is the weight of the netting covering the frame. Wire netting is heavy in large amounts while synthetic netting is lightweight. There are several sizes and weights of wire netting. The most effective is aviary netting, which will keep out all types of birds, but this may not be desirable where small birds are not troublesome and actually assist with insect control. The width of the roll of netting may also affect the choice of netting due to the difficulty of installation.

Synthetic netting is approximately half the cost of wire netting, a fraction of the weight of wire netting and comes in a roll many metres wide which simplifies installation. Access doorways can be made curtain-style. However, synthetic netting melts if it comes in contact with a spark from a fire and the material is affected by ultra violet light. Some types of

synthetic netting are guaranteed for more than ten years and others come with no guarantee. Synthetic netting is available in black and white, with different hole sizes. The type of manufacture of synthetic netting includes extruded plastic and knitted and woven netting.

## Protection from other pests

Where rabbits, wallabies or grazing livestock are present a strong netting fence is essential. Rabbit netting must be at least 50cm (18in) high and secured onto the ground. A normal wire stock-proof fence fitted with rabbit netting at the bottom is perfectly adequate. Timber and brick fences are also suitable and provide wind protection also.

Mesh fabric covers over a crop can be useful where European wasps are troublesome on ripening fruit such as grapes. Insect-proof covers can also be used to protect susceptible crops from cabbage white butterfly, fruit fly or whitefly.

# Weed control

Weeds are plants growing where they are not wanted. Sometimes they are native plants that grow successfully in the wild, but quite often they may be introduced plants.

Some weeds are not only attractive but may also have beneficial effects. Scarlet pimpernel (*Anagallis arvensis*) and wild pansy (*Viola tricolor*) bear attractive flowers, wild carrot (*Daucus carota*) supports beneficial hoverflies, and cape weed (*Artotheca calendula*) attracts bees.

Crops will be adversely affected by weed competition, and for most people a weed-free garden is more attractive than one left to its natural development. Weeds can be divided into two groups for the purposes of control: perennial weeds and annual weeds.

## How weeds affect crops

By far the worst effects of weeds lie in competition. Weeds absorb water and nutrients from the soil, depriving crop plants and so restricting their growth. They compete for light, and vigorous weed growth can seriously shade young developing plants. They also compete for space, which may result in restricted or stunted growth of cultivated plants.

Weeds can also affect pest and disease incidence (*see* Plant Problems, *pp.246–264*). Some weeds may harbour pests such as eelworm and diseases such as clubroot of brassicas or rusts, these being found in weed plants closely related to cultivated crop species. Dense weed growth may become soaked by rain, reducing air movement and increasing humidity around plants, providing ideal conditions for diseases such as botrytis (*see p.252*), which affects the fruits of strawberries.

Heavy weed growth looks unsightly and can make harvesting more difficult; pulling vegetables that are surrounded by nettle growth can be painful. Another effect worth noting, although of very limited importance, is that some weeds may exude chemical substances at root level that have the effect of restricting the growth of non-related plants.

## Perennial weeds

The potentially most troublesome weeds are those perennials that increase

## Controlling weeds by light deprivation

**Using black film plastic**
*Annual and perennial weeds can be suppressed by covering the area with thick black film plastic buried at the edges. Cover for a whole season if possible.*

**Using old carpet**
*Any durable, light-excluding material can be used to control weeds. Even where some perennials are not killed, they are markedly weakened and much easier to fork out.*

primarily by vegetative means, such as spreading roots or runners or rooting stem tips, rather than by seed production. These weeds are of particular concern on uncropped sites where they become well established; they are also potentially troublesome where they spring up among newly sown or planted fruit and vegetable crops and are then very difficult to eradicate without disturbing the crop.

Notorious perennials are docks (*Rumex* species), dandelions (*Taraxacum officinale*), stinging nettle (*Urtica dioica*),

**Forking out perennial weeds**
*Established perennial weeds may have deep tap roots or spreading roots, like these nettles. Take care to loosen and tease out as much of the root as possible.*

creeping buttercup (*Ranunculus repens*), kikuyu (*Pennisetum clandestinum*), couch grass (*Agropyron repens*), blackberries (*Rubus* species) and soursob (*Oxalis pescaprae*).

A new site in which such weeds are well established can be daunting, but it is essential to clear out any of these inhabitants and destroy early any small colonies within already cultivated plots.

## Mechanical control

Non-woody perennials can be controlled by long-term covering with heavy-gauge black film plastic or other durable, light-excluding material such as old carpet. To be most effective it will need to be in place for at least a whole growing season, so forward planning is essential. Lift the cover occasionally and carefully dig out any struggling weeds.

The more usual method is to cultivate the ground with a spade or fork. Break open the ground to a spit depth, and shake or pick out by hand tuberous or woody roots or underground runners. This is best done on hot days, leaving weeds exposed for a while to be desiccated and killed; then dispose of them off-site. It is unlikely that one session will clear the land, because many of the weeds will regenerate from even the smallest fragment, so be prepared to repeat the task.

Using a mechanical rotary cultivator to chop up the existing ground cover is less advisable. It is effective only with many repeat operations, because underground weed parts are chopped into pieces, each of which will regenerate. Worst of all, it can destroy the soil structure and produce an impermeable soil pan (*see p. 16*) at the depth of the spinning blades.

The persistence of perennial weeds varies. Docks, dandelions, and creeping buttercup soon succumb to careful cultivation, but couch grass and stinging nettles require careful and repeated lifting. Worst of all is kikuyu, which may be very deep-rooted and impossible to eradicate. The armed stems of blackberry are formidable, but they can be successfully removed with methodical use of secateurs and a spade.

Bulbous perennials, such as a few *Oxalis* species or montbretia (*Crocosmia crocosmiiflora*), call for meticulous lifting or constant removal of leaves to weaken the plant. In high density these bulbous plants can smother other plants.

## Using weedkillers

Chemical weedkillers can be a great help in preparing new ground, in controlling persistent or deeply established perennial weeds, and where weeds invade from adjoining land. Their use is a matter of imposed as well as personal choice, as the range is narrowed due to legal restrictions on their manufacture.

There is no real risk to personal safety if the instructions are followed to the letter, but valued plants are vulnerable to drift or careless use of weedkiller. Important rules are: keep a marked watering can or sprayer solely for weedkiller; choose the appropriate material; mix and apply it with great care, preferably on a still day – a dribble bar (*see p. 53*) can be useful; and place physical barriers around any crop plants in the immediate area.

The chemical glyphosate is highly effective; it will be absorbed into actively growing plants. There are also chemicals specifically for perennial grasses and hormone weedkillers for persistent weeds like blackberries and lantana (*Lantana montevidensis*). The latter can be painted on to aerial parts of plants. Inspect the shelves of a well-stocked garden centre and spend a while making a careful selection. Bear in mind that many perennial weeds are also prolific seeders, including dock and dandelion.

## Annual weeds

Annual weeds complete their life cycle in one season; there may even be more than one life cycle per season. There are a few biennial weed plants, which make growth in one season and flower in the following one, and these may be regarded as annuals.

By and large, annuals are more readily controlled than perennials. The group

**Planting through a plastic sheet mulch**
*Avoid weeding by laying a sheet mulch (here landscape fabric) over the bed and secure at the sides by pushing into a slit trench. Cut crosses in the sheet and plant through them.*

includes chickweed (*Stellaria media*), annual winter grass (*Poa annua*), fat hen (*Chenopodium album*), hairy bittercress (*Cardamine hirsuta*), thistles (*Cirsium* species), common purslane (*Portulaca oleraceae*), and annual nettle (*Urtica urens*). These weeds reproduce through the prolific production of seeds, making up a large part of the estimated 100,000 seeds in each square metre (square yard) of soil. Many seeds are lost to the predations of birds and soil-inhabiting creatures, while others fail to develop after germination. Cultivating will destroy many, but moves dormant seeds to conditions favourable to germination.

Destroy all flowering weeds before they have chance to set seed. Regular hoeing is the most effective means of controlling annuals, as severed parts do not regenerate. Hoe as soon as the crop rows can be identified, and repeat frequently. Work shallowly to avoid bringing more seeds to the surface and to minimize soil moisture loss. It is most important to hoe between crop rows.

Hand-weeding is a quite satisfying pastime in the control of annual weeds. A flame gun can be used on pathways, but it is a specialist tool rather than an essential. A valuable technique for suppressing seeding weeds is the stale seedbed practice of allowing a flush of weeds to grow on a prepared bed, and then destroying them by shallow hoeing or with a flame gun before sowing.

## Spraying weeds with weedkiller

**1 Herbicides** such as those containing glyphosate are an effective aid for destroying perennial weeds. Take care not to use them on a windy day; the spray may drift onto valued plants and kill them.

**2 Over two weeks** the treated weeds progressively die back and are more readily removed. Glyphosate does not persist in the soil, so you can plant very soon after the weeds are cleared.

# Keeping your garden healthy

Neglected crops of fruit and vegetables may fail due to factors such as weather (*see pp. 10–13*), nutrition (*see pp. 14–17*), weeds (*see pp. 49–50*), lack of water (*see pp. 53–54*), and from pests and diseases (*see Plant Problems, pp. 246–264*).

Animals, fungi, bacteria, viruses, and other organisms can destroy, disfigure, or debilitate crops, wasting the time, effort, money, and garden space devoted to them. It is vital to be aware of what problems may occur with each crop, and think ahead about how to combat them. Above all, inspect crops regularly and closely, so that you can deal with problems before they become serious.

## Natural strategies

Plants have remarkable mechanisms for repelling pests. Some produce chemicals that discourage feeding by their scent or taste. Some insects, such as the caterpillars (*see p. 253*) of the cabbage white butterfly, can tolerate chemicals produced by brassicas and find a niche as specific predators; other pests feed on a range of plants. Plants also emit scents that attract predators or parasites of their attackers. In nature, diversity in a plant community minimizes the effects of pests and diseases; in a kitchen garden, we tend to grow blocks of a single crop, advertising its existence and increasing the chances of attack. Keeping the area weed-free also reduces the habitat for beneficial predators and parasites.

## Growing healthy plants

Weak or weed-choked crop plants will be most vulnerable to attack by disease, so prepare and maintain your garden well. Accumulated plant litter perpetuates diseases, as does infected wood, such as cankers (*see p. 253*), left in fruit trees and bushes. Practise good garden hygiene.

Plant problems are encouraged by waterlogging and drought, so prepare and manage the soil well (*see pp. 37–40*).

**Keeping equipment clean**
*Dirty equipment and containers can harbour diseases and minute pests. Clean your tools regularly and wash all containers between uses, scrubbing them out with a stiff brush and horticultural disinfectant.*

Plants with unbalanced nutrient levels, especially where large amounts of nitrogen-rich fertilizers (*see pp. 20–21*) are applied, can be far more susceptible to aphid attack (*see p. 251*) or botrytis disease (*see p. 252*). Liquid conditioners, including those made from plant extracts such as comfrey or seaweed (*see p. 21*), keep crops in good health and probably stimulate the plants' natural defences.

Plants repeatedly grown on the same site are likely to suffer from a build-up of pests, such as onion white rot (*see p. 258*). Rotation (*see p. 31*) is therefore a good practice. A basic knowledge of life cycles assists in knowing how to prevent diseases from carrying over in the soil from season to season.

Buy only healthy stock. Clubroot of brassicas (*see p. 254*) can easily be imported on purchased plants. Always look for certificated strawberries and other fruit plants. Remember also that there are degrees of resistance available in vegetable and fruit cultivars.

## Protective mechanisms

Plants can be effectively protected from birds (*see pp. 48 and 251*), rabbits (*see pp. 48, 261*), and wallabies by netting or individual tree guards. Many insect pests can also be controlled by mechanical means: on a garden scale it is possible to remove caterpillars (*see p. 253*) or slugs and snails (*see p. 262*) by

## Natural pest control

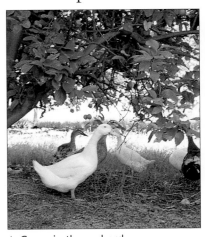

△ **Geese in the orchard**
*Running a few geese, hens or ducks in the orchard is a natural way to keep grubs and other pests under control. They also provide valuable manure.*

▷ **Companion planting**
*Research has shown that sweet basil deters thrips. These sap-sucking insects can spread virus disease.*

△ **Companion planting**
*Marigolds are reputed to inhibit pests including nematodes and wireworms.*

# Natural allies in the garden

It is worth thinking of ways to encourage the activities of natural predators in and around the kitchen garden. This can be as simple as choosing to use hedges, which provide cover for birds, rather than fencing, or incorporating a pond for frogs and toads. Useful insects such as hoverflies need a range of flowering plants on which to feed. Reserve areas of uncultivated land on the margins of the kitchen garden for the food and cover of useful creatures wherever it is practical to do so. Bear in mind the wellbeing of friendly wildlife at all times, especially when applying any chemical treatments which might harm them.

*Hoverfly*

*Ladybirds*

*Frog*

*Ladybird larva eating blackfly*

*Lacewing*

hand, or to squeeze clusters of aphids on shoot tips. Apples can be protected from codling moth (*see p.254*) by fixing hessian or corrugated cardboard around tree trunks. Sticky traps impregnated with attractant chemicals also help to reduce infestations of codling moth (*see below*). It is also possible to avoid the effects of a pest by planting practices, for example by not growing cabbages in summer when cabbage white butterfly is most troublesome.

Another protective mechanism is companion planting. Companion plants make good companions for many reasons: they may be attractive to predators of crops, or they may expel a chemical substance that deters a pest such as the effect marigolds have on nematodes, or they may deter a pest that spreads disease, for instance sweet basil deters thrips around tomatoes.

## Using predators

Besides the natural predations of birds, small animals, and insects (*see above*), it is possible to introduce parasites or predators artificially. This is most effective under the protection of a greenhouse, where the atmosphere can be controlled, and a successful example is the use of *Encarsia* wasps to parasitize the young stages of whitefly (*see p.264*). For outdoor use, a bacterial preparation called Bt is available for the infection of caterpillars. All of these biological controls require careful understanding and management, but the range of such pest and disease control measures makes it clear that the choice is much wider than simply resorting to chemical sprays.

## Chemical weapons

It is possible to maintain an armoury of chemicals to eradicate or protect against pests and diseases. Because of increased regulation on the use of these substances, however, the range of treatments that is available will be much reduced in the future, and the use of alternative control methods will become essential.

It should be remembered that, unlike the commercial producer, the gardener usually has no need for maximum crop yield or unblemished produce. Many pest- or disease-induced defects can be cut out of harvested fruit and vegetables.

Chemical treatments are expensive in both purchase price and the time taken in applying them, and need to be applied at defined times for effectiveness. While quite safe for humans if applied strictly according to the instructions, chemical substances may have harmful effects on natural pest predators or other friendly insects like bees. Regard spraying and dusting as a last resort and other methods as the first line of attack or defence. The reasonable approach is to try to keep pests and diseases at an acceptably low level; attempting to eliminate them altogether is impractical and rarely vital.

## Biological controls
*These pest controls take many forms, from predators to traps or parasites. Biological controls are released into the environment (usually in the greenhouse), or watered into the soil or compost as appropriate. Some must be applied at a particular time or temperature to be effective.*

**Whitefly control**
*Encarsia larvae in test tube ready for release*

**Flying insect control**
*Brightly coloured sticky traps lure insects such as aphids*

**Codling moth monitors**
*By attracting codling moths to a sticky trap, the degree of infestation can be monitored. These traps are impregnated with a pheromone that attracts the moth to the sticky surface. When several moths are found in the trap, it is time to spray. Traps to attract codling moth can be placed in an apple tree during spring and summer.*

# Watering and irrigation

Good growth and yields depend on continuous adequate supplies of water. This is much influenced by the soil type and condition (*see pp. 14–16*). Clay soils hold more water than sandy ones, because there are more spaces in the soil to hold it, but plants are able to extract water from sandy soils more easily, because the spaces are larger. The water-holding capacity of any soil is improved by the addition of organic matter (*see pp. 22–23*), and water retention by the use of mulches (*see pp. 41–42*).

The best source of water is rain, but due to seasonal fluctuations in rainfall and high temperatures in summer, soils often become dry during periods of crucial plant growth, and added water from stored sources or mains supply is needed. Many garden centres and stores stock a good choice of watering and irrigation equipment for this purpose.

## Watering crops

Water thoroughly, so that the amount applied is absorbed down to a useful depth. This can be achieved by gentle and repeated applications of a fine, rain-like spray or continuous droplets applied around the base of plants. High-pressure or rapid, swamping applications lead to the water running off, resulting in waste and in erosion of the soil around roots.

## Watering can attachments

An oval, flat rose with the face upwards produces a fine spray for watering seedlings or damping down foliage. Face downwards, it provides a fine drenching flow. A round, conical rose with the face downwards will give a drenching spray of greater volume for watering established plants or settling in robust transplants.

Small holes give fine spray

Large holes give fast flow

Oval rose

Round rose

**Dribble bar**
*A dribble bar attachment is very useful for watering crops or applying liquid feed. It provides an even, steady spray, ensuring good coverage of the crop.*

As a very general guide to application rate, whether by watering can, spray gun, or sprinkler, aim at not less than 10 litres per sq m (2¼ gallons per sq yd).

A good way of ensuring that water benefits the crop is to make mini-reservoirs around widely spaced plants or along planted rows such as peas and beans: pull the soil into shallow walls to form basins or troughs. Similarly useful are plastic pots – or cut-down plastic bottles – sunk up to their rims, close to individual plants such as tomatoes.

## Watering cans

A common way of watering is with a plastic or galvanized watering can. Models with a long spout are most useful, and they can be fitted with various interchangeable roses, which are normally made of brass (*see above*). Round roses have large holes, ideal for settling in newly planted crops or heavy watering of established crops on a well-structured soil. Oval roses with smaller holes deliver a fine spray of water onto tender plants or newly sown areas.

Large droplets can be gently applied with a dribble bar fitted to the spout of the watering can (*see above*). This is most usually used for applying liquid feed, or weedkiller, for which a separate, marked can and bar will be needed.

## Spray guns and sprinklers

A hand-held spray gun attached to a hose supply can provide the same distribution effects as a watering can. Spray guns may or may not have a solid lance (*see left*) to which the head is fitted. The flow and pattern of water can be adjusted by turning controls at the spray head, and with some models the flow can be locked on manually.

Low-level sprinklers, fed from a hose attachment, can also be used (*see far left*). Some models have heads that move under water pressure to distribute the flow, but for the kitchen garden the cheaper models made with a push-in spike are quite adequate.

△ **Rotating sprinkler**
*Sprinklers are fixed to the end of a hose to water one area at a time. The simplest types have fixed heads; the rotating types often cover a slightly larger area, but their spray may be coarser.*

▷ **Hose attachment**
*A spray-gun attachment on a rigid lance fitted to the end of a hose allows you to reach crops without treading on beds. Because it can be manoeuvred between plants, water can be delivered more efficiently close to the soil.*

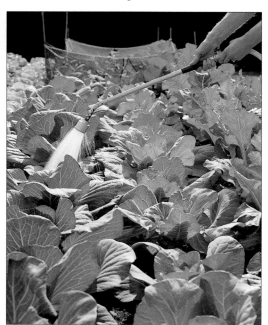

Sprinklers have the advantage of watering unattended – but it is essential to check them frequently to ensure that the pressure and distribution of flow are not causing flooding. Even sprinklers with moving heads can distribute water unevenly, so do check regularly and move them when necessary.

### Low-pressure irrigation systems

A range of low-pressure watering systems made from plastic are available. They are an excellent choice for effective distribution in the kitchen garden, ensuring that water is delivered close to the plants, in readily absorbed quantities and with a minimum of wastage.

The simplest form is a thin-walled plastic tube called a drip hose, which lies flat and is connected to a water supply. It emits thin arching sprays of water from pinholes 30–50cm (12–20in) apart (*see right*). A variation on this is a porous-walled hose of 1–2.5cm (½–1in) diameter formed from porous rubber, or sometimes plastic, from which water weeps in small droplets. Both of these flexible systems work with very low water pressure. They are prone to blockage over time, however, so regular maintenance is advisable; squeezing, rolling or otherwise flexing the pipe along its entire length and then flushing it through with a strong flow of water should clear any build-up.

A useful, more durable low-pressure system is mini-sprinkler irrigation. Here small plastic sprinklers are fitted to narrow plastic tubing which is connected to low-pressure plastic pipe. Mini-sprinklers can be secured away

**Drip hose used among strawberry plants**
*This irrigation system uses a perforated hose connected to a tap. The hose can be laid close to the crops, with the water dripping out directly near the roots, avoiding wasteful evaporation. The system can be controlled either manually or with a timer.*

from the supply pipe and have a spray coverage of 1–3m (3–10ft). Perhaps the most water-efficient irrigation is drip irrigation, where low-pressure pipe is fitted with dripper nozzles or micro-tubing. Drip irrigation is ideal for berries and fruit trees, and 4–6 drippers may be required to supply established trees. Both mini-sprinkler and drip irrigation can deliver water right to the base of individual plants.

Check the output of all of these irrigation systems regularly, at each station where appropriate, to ensure that no plants are deprived because of blocked outlets; dig down with a trowel near plants to ensure that water has penetrated to a useful depth. Fit a timed switching device to the main supply line for maximum efficiency.

### Using water wisely

Whatever watering and irrigation systems you use, remember that water is a valuable resource: use it effectively and economically. Priorities for irrigation are newly established plants and all fruits that are beginning to swell, such as strawberries, raspberries, peas, and beans, as well as leafy summer vegetables such as lettuce. Water at the start or end of a day; in the middle of the day, much will be wasted in evaporation. Collect rainwater wherever possible.

Household waste water, or grey water, usually contains residues that are best not used on edible crops, and should be reserved for watering trees, shrubs and woody ornamental plants. Keep an eye on the weather and the state of the soil, so that you can predict when plants are likely to be stressed due to inadequate water, and top up supplies before your crops show the obvious visual symptom, which is wilting and fruit drop.

**Seep hose**
*Hoses made from reconstituted rubber ooze water droplets along their entire length to provide a steady supply. Wind them among plants for even distribution.*

**Mini-sprinkler on hose**
*These small attachments can be strategically placed close to particular plants to direct the water to where it is most needed. They are available in a variety of spray patterns, watering to one or both sides of the hose.*

# Tools and equipment

A set of tools is necessary from the start in preparing and maintaining a kitchen garden. It is worth investing in the best-quality tools that you can afford; they will repay the expense and last a lifetime if they are properly used and cared for. A good-quality tool should be well-designed, strong, and, if appropriate, lightweight; such quality is guaranteed in well-known branded products.

Stainless steel is worth the expense, as it is both strong and durable, and handles of wood or aluminium are the best choice. When selecting new or second-hand tools make sure that the heads and handles are securely joined to the shafts. Test the weight of the tool and be sure that it feels comfortable to hold. Try out a range of sizes and designs to find a model that feels right for you.

## Choosing a range of tools

A few basic tools are essential, especially a spade, fork, hoe, trowel, hand fork, and secateurs. There are many variations on all of these implements.

A lesser-known but recommended tool is the arrow-headed hand cultivator, which is very effective for breaking down roughly structured soil after digging or overwintering. It is also

## Spades and forks

These are essential tools for digging, trenching, and skimming weeds (*see pp.37–40*) and for planting and moving soil. The handles of standard spades and forks are about 60cm (2ft) long, although longer ones are available to suit individual needs.

▽ **Choosing a spade**
*A standard digging spade has a 28 x 20cm (11 x 8in) blade; a border or lady's spade, with a blade usually of 23 x 15cm (9 x 6in), is lighter to use and is especially helpful for digging in confined spaces. There are other specialized spades for specific tasks.*

Standard spade

Border spade

*Handles may be of wood or metal*

*Narrow metal strips make digging more comfortable*

*Tines are usually square in section*

*Head of border fork is shorter and narrower*

Digging fork

Border fork

△ **Choosing a fork**
*A standard fork has a head of four tines, or prongs, each 30cm (12in) long; there is also a border or lady's version, which is ideal for working between perennial plants.*

▽ **Handle grips for spades and forks**
*Handle grips may be shaped in one of several ways; a D- or Y-shaped grip is found to be comfortable by most gardeners.*

T-shaped

Y-shaped

D-shaped

## Rakes

Rakes are needed for making seedbeds, especially in levelling and preparing tilth. They are also useful for pulling off litter, tamping seed rows after sowing, and pressing out seed drills on soft ground.

*Metal prongs ideal for preparing a tilth*

△ **Metal rake**
*Choose a metal rake with a head 30–38cm (12–15in) wide and prongs 6cm (2½in) long, spaced about 2.5cm (1in) apart. The handle should be about 1.5m (5ft) long.*

▽ **Wooden rake**
*Look for a head about 75cm (30in) wide, holding wooden peg teeth 8cm (3in) long, and fixed to a handle up to 2m (6ft) long, to allow for wide, sweeping strokes in various directions.*

*Wide head of wooden rake is best for clearing and levelling soil*

useful for loosening a compacted surface between fruit plantings, and on paths. Also worth considering at an early stage is a spading or potato fork; this has flat tines, which come in various widths, and is particularly suitable for digging heavy-textured soils.

Other, more specialized tools can be added as the kitchen garden develops and as your preference and budget will allow: loppers and saws, for example, are really only needed in the cultivation of fruit trees. Tools such as dibbers and seed sowers make gardening tasks easier but are not essential.

## Maintaining your tools

Whatever tools you buy, it is vital to maintain them properly, keeping them clean, rust-free, and, where appropriate, properly sharpened. If you neglect this, the tools will be harder to use and less efficient, and will have a shorter life.

After using a tool, clean off all earth, plant matter, or other debris promptly. For stainless steel tools, this is all that is necessary for day-to-day maintenance. Tools made from carbon steel will rust if they are left damp, however, so these should also be wiped over with an oily rag after use. Always store tools in a dry place; never leave them outside.

All tools with cutting edges, such as secateurs and hoes, will need regular sharpening with an oilstone or steel to give the best possible performance.

If tools will not be used for a month or two, clean them very thoroughly and oil them well before putting them away.

## Cultivators and hoes

Cultivators are excellent tools for breaking down newly dug ground and working in top-dressings. The push hoe is used to slice off weeds with a push-pull action and must be kept sharp; conversely, the draw hoe is used in a chopping motion, which entails walking forwards on the hoed ground. A draw hoe can also be used for marking out drills or earthing up crops. An onion hoe is most suitable for cultivating along vegetable rows and for thinning.

### Types of cultivating implements
*A cultivator usually has 3 or 5 prongs; it is possible to buy models with interchangeable heads. A push hoe has a flat, oblong blade, while a draw hoe has a blade mounted at a right angle to the handle; an onion hoe is a smaller, hand-held version of the draw hoe.*

Cultivator with interchangeable five-pronged head

Narrow three-pronged head

Swan-necked draw hoe

Push, Dutch, or scuffle hoe

Onion hoe

## Planting tools

There are two essential tools for planting: the trowel and the hand fork. The trowel is ideal for making planting holes and firming soil around transplants, such as module-raised vegetables and strawberry plants. Forks are necessary for hand weeding and for loosening soil along rows and around plants.

### Trowels and hand forks
*The trowel has a scoop-shaped, tapered blade about 15cm (6in) long, attached to a short, rounded handle. Forks have 3 or 4 prongs and a similar handle. There are long-handled versions of both tools available.*

Trowel    Narrow trowel    Fork

Lid can be rotated to adjust size of opening

### Seed sowers
*These release one seed at a time, and so make it easier to make thin or spaced sowings. The outlet can be adjusted to suit small- to large-sized seeds.*

### Dibbers
*Tray dibbers are pointed, pencil-like tools of wood, metal, or plastic, used to make planting holes or for pricking out seedlings at the propagating stage. Larger planting dibbers are used to sow bean seeds or to transplant vegetable plants in open ground.*

Plastic tray dibber    Metal tray dibber    Steel-tipped planting dibber

# Cutting tools

Secateurs and loppers may be anvil or parrot-bill types. Anvil types have a single sharp blade that cuts against a flat anvil, and can cut thick wood; parrot-bill types act more like scissors, and make a cleaner cut without crushing. Saws are required for pruning large branches, and knives for a range of essential tasks.

### ▽ Secateurs
*Secateurs should be strong and able to cut woody stems up to 1.5cm (½in) thick. Look for hardened steel blades with reasonably long handles and a comfortable grip, replaceable parts, and a simple safety catch.*

Blade closes down onto flat anvil

*Anvil secateurs*

Blade slices against bar

*Parrot-bill secateurs*

Look for comfortable cushioned grips

Curved handle gives an easier grip for more effective action

Handles may be fixed, or telescopic for greater reach

### ◁ Loppers
*Loppers are suitable for reaching into fruit trees and bushes and exerting powerful leverage; they can be used on branches of up to about 4cm (1½in) diameter.*

### ▽ Pruning saws
*Folding saws are easily carried around, but a Grecian saw, with a curved blade and teeth set for use in a single pulling action, makes cutting easier and should be the first choice.*

Blade folds into handle for safe carrying

*Folding saw*

*Grecian saw*

### ▽ Knives
*A good multi-purpose knife has a straight blade 9cm (3½in) long; a budding knife has a fine blade and relatively long handle to make precise cuts. Sharpen with an oilstone, then keep an edge with a diamond steel.*

*Budding knife*

*Pocket diamond steel*

# Watering and spraying

Watering cans will be essential for maintaining plants both in pots and in the garden, and they need to have detachable roses to deliver coarse or fine droplets. Long-necked watering cans are ideal, but there is a wide choice of other sturdy cans. It is vital to have separate and clearly labelled cans or sprayers for applying weedkillers, to avoid accidents.

Hand pump plunger

Garden pressure spray

Trigger on nozzle controls spray

Useful capacity is 10 litres (2¼ gallons)

Long neck gives well-balanced can

*High-quality metal watering can*

# Measuring tools

Some measuring and marking tools are essential for spacing crops properly. A folding measure is easily portable, but you can make your own measuring stick by marking out a length of light timber at 15cm (6in) intervals. Marker line is used in sowing and planting outdoors, pegged taut at either end. Brightly coloured string is easily seen.

Home-made measuring rod

*Marker line*

*Folding measuring stick*

# VEGETABLES

THE RANGE OF VEGETABLES that can be grown
in any garden is enormous, and there are many
factors that may influence your choice. Certain
basic principles and techniques – for example,
sowing seed – are common to the majority of
vegetable crops, involving skills that are easy and
satisfying to master. In fact, for some gardeners
the vegetable plot is the only area in which they
practise raising and nurturing their plants
from tiny seeds to maturity.

The crops in this section have been arranged in
conventional groupings – the onion family, for
example, or salad plants. The members of each
group share a number of characteristics, such as
soil preferences or vulnerability to certain
problems, that make it convenient to grow them
together. This also makes it easier to follow a
crop rotation, vital for healthy plants and good
harvests. Even within the groups, the wealth and
variety of produce to be had – leaves, stems,
roots, flower buds, and fruits – will provide good
food, fresh or from store, in every season.

# Vegetable seed

Most vegetables are grown from seed, of which there are two basic kinds. The first is open-pollinated seed, which, whether bought or home-saved, is produced naturally and derived from a mix of parent lines – although good open-pollinated seed from a reliable seed merchant will have been subject to careful selection of breeding material. The second is F1 hybrid seed, which is produced by crossing two inbred, stable parent lines; the resulting plants are more uniform and vigorous. This type can only be bought – seed saved from F1 hybrids will produce variable and often inferior plants – and is more expensive than open-pollinated seed. Hybrid seed is usually treated to prevent pest damage while open-pollinated seed is usually untreated (*see chart, below*).

## Should I buy or save seeds?

Packeted vegetable seeds, widely available in great variety, are subject to legal requirements on "trueness" (where the offspring plant conforms to a described type) and viability – a guarantee, in practice, that a statutory minimum percentage of the seed will germinate and produce healthy seedlings with the expected characteristics of the named cultivar. The expertise and reputation of established seed merchants usually ensures good quality and reliability. Buying seed is convenient and packets usually carry helpful advice.

Many gardeners also like to save seed from the garden, to keep costs down and for the satisfaction involved in raising their own plants. There are two main problems, however, with amateur seed-saving: extracting and storing the seeds in such a way as to keep them viable, and maintaining trueness to type. Any vegetables allowed to set seed in the open garden are likely to be cross-pollinated – fertilized by pollen from different cultivars – and their offspring will therefore show variation. An additional problem in cool climates is that it may be difficult to ripen home-saved seed sufficiently.

## Heritage seed

Seed merchants are only allowed to sell vegetable cultivars that appear on approved official lists. These inevitably tend to feature only those cultivars that are commercially viable to produce, and so many older cultivars suitable for the amateur garden have disappeared from retailers' catalogues. Organizations have been set up to conserve such cultivars both for interest and to maintain the gene pool. Contact details appear in gardening magazines. There are many fine traditional cultivars worth seeking out in this way.

## Choosing vegetable seed

Many factors may influence the type of seed that you buy. Organically raised seed may be of particular interest to you, for example. The various seed treatments available (*see chart, left*) can help in the control of particular pests and diseases. Pelleted seeds, being larger, are easier to handle and sow, and are easier to see, enabling more accurate spacing and thus reducing the need for thinning, which saves money. The cultivars you choose will largely be determined by what will succeed in

## TYPES OF VEGETABLE SEEDS

*Natural (parsnip)*

**Natural/untreated seeds** have been saved, cleaned, and not coated in any way. They may be home-saved, conventionally produced for sale, organic, or heritage seeds. Organic seed is produced on land that has been certified as free from chemicals and added fertilizers.

*Coated (cauliflower)*

**Treated seeds** have been coated with fungicides or insecticides or soaked in hot water in order to produce disease-free seedlings. Chemical coatings will not rub off and are usually brightly coloured. Wear latex gloves when sowing these and wash your hands afterwards. They should be sown soon after purchase.

*Hot water (carrot)*

**Hot water treated seeds** are heated in hot water to a temperature sufficient to disinfect the seeds. They are then dried before storage. This treatment is seldom used today but was popular before chemical treatments were available.

*Multigerm (beetroot)*

**Multigerm seeds,** such as beetroot and chard, are rough clusters of seeds, rather than individual ones, each of which may produce a few seedlings. These may be thinned or left to grow into a cluster of baby vegetables as in the multiblock sowing technique (*see p.65*).

*Pelleted seeds*

**Pelleted seeds** (usually of lettuce) are coated, for ease of handling and germination, in a moisture-absorbing substance which disintegrates in the soil.

*Chitted (sugar pea)*

**Chitted or pregerminated seeds**
You can also help some seeds, such as peas or beans, to chit by soaking them for a short time (up to 24 hours); this speeds up germination when sown.

*Tape (spring onion)*

**Seed tapes** are available for a limited range of vegetables to enable evenly spaced sowings. These biodegradable paper tapes have seeds embedded at regular spacings and can simply be laid at the bottom of a seed drill (*see p.66*), enabling long rows of vegetables that will not need thinning to be sown very quickly and easily.

**Drying pea and bean pods**
*In damp conditions, it is a good idea to pull up whole stems (here beans), with their pods still attached, and hang them upside down by their roots in a dry, airy, frost-free place. When dry, crush the pods and shake out the seeds.*

your region and by personal preference. If you have little practical experience, look around local gardens, or ask local gardeners, to discover cultivars that do particularly well in your area, or show good disease resistance. But be adventurous too: try out different cultivars to compare with your old favourites, and experiment with new introductions and novel plants such as differently coloured sweetcorn.

## Buying vegetable seed

Seed can be purchased either from retail outlets such as garden centres or by mail order from seed merchants. The latter usually stock a wider range of cultivars. If using a seed merchant, send your order in early to secure your chosen cultivars; otherwise, unsuitable substitutions may be made. Well before sowing, read all the information

# Preparing seeds from pulpy fruits

**1** **Scoop pulpy seeds** (here of sweet melon) from very ripe fruits with a spoon, and place in a household sieve. Rinse them in running water, making sure that all the pulp is removed; if left, it will hinder germination.

**2** **Spread the seeds** out on a layer of kitchen paper in a shallow container, and leave them to dry in a warm and airy place for at least a week. When they have dried out, store them in a cool, dry place for sowing in the following spring.

on the packets. Be particularly careful to sow at the recommended time, or you could face problems such as poor germination, or bolting of mature plants. Bolting is especially troublesome with cabbages, cauliflowers, broccoli and Brussels sprouts and these vegetables may be best grown from commercial seedlings (*see also individual crops, pp. 74–135*).

## How to save seed

Choose only strong, healthy plants to save seed from. Remember that you cannot save seed from F1 hybrids, and that some crops, such as carrots, are biennial and will need to be over-

wintered in order to flower in the second season. Always allow the seeds, or the fruits that contain them, such as tomatoes and sweet melons (*above*), to ripen or mature fully before you collect them. Leave pea and French bean pods on the plants until they have dried and just split, and then extract the seeds; in damp weather, you can remove entire stems and dry them out under cover (*see above left*). With broad beans and runner beans, grow one type of cultivar only in one location to reduce the risk of cross-pollination, and select the best pods from which to collect the seeds.

## Storing vegetable seed

Seed loses viability and vigour with age, and this process is accelerated if seed is kept in moist, warm conditions. Some crops, such as parsley, carrots, and parsnips, are best sown fresh each year. Seed of peas, beans, and brassicas will last for several years if kept correctly.

Seed should be stored in a cool, dry, dark place, at 1–5°C (34–41°F) with even moisture and temperature levels. Sheds and kitchen drawers are not suitable. Unopened vacuum-packed seeds store best; reseal opened packets securely with sticky tape, or tape home-saved seeds into small paper packets. Keep packets in an airtight tin or jar, surrounded by silica gel to absorb any moisture. If you open a packet to sow only some of the seeds, do not let the rest get damp before resealing. Before sowing seed stored for more than a year, test its viability (*see left*).

# How to test seed for viability

When seed has been stored long-term, test its viability before sowing. Put 50 or 100 seeds on damp absorbent paper on a saucer, and keep it moist and in a warm, dark place. The seeds should germinate within 2–3 weeks, producing roots and first seed leaves. Count the seedlings and work out the percentage of germination.

Do not count seeds that have merely swollen; all seeds swell when wet, whether viable or not. Sixty per cent germination (30 out of 50 seeds, for example) is the minimum required for you to consider sowing that batch of seed, for when sown outside, the percentage will be lower. In the examples shown here, using cabbage seed, one set (*left*) shows 60% viability and the other (*right*) 100%. The growth of the seedlings on the right is also more even and vigorous, indicating that the seed will produce stronger, healthier seedlings.

*Low viability*

*High viability*

# Sowing seed in pots and punnets

In most regions in most seasons, vegetables can be sown directly into the garden. However, in cool weather it may be an advantage to start some crops by sowing seed under cover, in a greenhouse or cold frame (*see pp. 43–48*), or in the house. You can control the environment – temperature, compost moisture and air humidity, and nutrient supply – to provide optimum conditions for germination and for the seedlings to establish. Seed of frost-tender plants can be germinated in favourable conditions, and the seedlings grown on until all risk of frost outdoors is past. Seed can also be sown earlier for a longer cropping season. Even seed that will germinate outdoors in very low temperatures, like peas and broad beans, can benefit from being sown under cover, where the risk of seed and seedlings rotting in cold, wet soil is reduced.

If you have only a small garden, you may not have room for the outdoor seedbed that some crops, such as many brassicas, require. Young punnet- or module-raised brassica plants suffer less transplant shock and resist some plant problems better than seedlings raised in and transplanted from open ground.

## Temperature requirements

Seed of many crops will germinate in an unheated greenhouse or cold frame, although extra warmth will speed up germination. However, seed of plants indigenous to warm climates – for example tomatoes, cucumbers, eggplants, sweetcorn, capsicums, and zucchini, – will only germinate at constant temperatures in the range, usually, of 15–24°C (59–75°F).

At this stage the soil temperature matters more than that of the air. The most energy-efficient way of raising soil temperature is to warm it from below; hence the expression bottom heat. Bottom heat can be provided by putting pots and trays on a bed of grit or sand containing soil-warming cables or on a heated blanket. The heating system may be built into the base of a specialized propagator (*see facing page*), the lid also helping to retain heat and moisture in the air.

Once seeds have germinated and the seedlings are growing they generally require lower temperatures. Many crops can, once hardened off (*see p. 65*) be planted directly outside,

provided that conditions are favourable. Other crops need continued warmth; capsicums and eggplants, for example, need to be kept at 21°C (70°F) until planting. This can be achieved by maintaining bottom heat, if convenient, but also by growing on the young plants in a warm room.

## Seed-raising systems

Traditionally, most vegetable seed sown under cover is sown into pots or trays filled with seed raising mix. Once the seeds germinate and the seedlings need more room to develop, they are transplanted, spaced more widely apart, into larger trays or into their own small pots. This is known as pricking out.

The advantage of this system is that it minimizes the amount of space in a heated propagator needed at the first, critical period during which the seeds germinate – especially useful with slow germinators, such as celery and parsley. It is also an easy way to sow fine seed. The disadvantage is that pricking out the delicate seedlings can cause root damage and a check to growth.

*Flexible modular strip*

*Half seed tray*

*13mm module tray*

*Rigid modular insert*

*20mm module tray*

*9cm (3in) pot*

*30mm module tray*

*Standard seed tray*

*13cm (5in) pot*

*13cm (5in) pan*

*Treated paper tube pots*

*37mm module tray*

## Types of containers
*A variety of containers may be used for sowing. Make sure that pots have holes at the base for drainage. Modular inserts and trays have a hole at the bottom of each cell. Tube pots are biodegradable, so can be planted without the need to disturb roots.*

To avoid this pricking-out stage, seed can be raised in modules – individual, self-contained cells within a tray – until ready for planting out. This modular method gives very good results. Each seedling can grow without competition, and is transplanted with its own well-established rootball, minimizing any check to growth. The disadvantages are that more seed raising mix is used, and that the trays take up more room in a propagator.

If propagator space is at a premium, you can sow seed into pots and trays and then prick out the seedlings into modules. This works particularly well for seed of tomatoes and capsicums, which can be sown in small pots in a heated propagator and then transplanted into large-celled trays (*see p.64*).

## Containers

Any small pots can be used to sow seed; punnets or squat pots are also ideal for most crops. It is advisable to choose plastic over terracotta; plastic can be kept cleaner, and makes it easier to control soil moisture. If only a few plants are required, say 10–12, a 9cm (3½in) pot will suffice. If 30 or more, sow in 13cm (5in) pots, or in a punnet or tray.

Some plants, for example sweetcorn, must be encouraged to form a long

**Seedlings in an unheated propagator**
*Propagators keep seeds warm and moist, and encourage them to germinate. Here, tomato and celery seedlings are developing well. Use the vent in the lid to control condensation.*

root from an early stage. For these, long, narrow pots known as tube pots are ideal. If made from treated paper they can be planted directly into the soil, as can compressed fibre pots.

Module trays are graded by the size and number of their individual cells. Those with 13mm cells produce small plug plants that will quickly need transplanting; they are ideal when soil conditions will soon be good for planting out. The large, 37mm cells are suitable for plants with large seeds that need time and space to develop before transplanting. When ready, the young plants can be pushed out from below.

## Propagators

A propagator provides a warm and humid microclimate, aiding the rapid and successful germination of seeds. In its simplest form, a propagator can be a sheet of glass or clear plastic, or even plastic film or fleece, placed over a pot or tray of seeds until they germinate. To develop further, however, seedlings need more headroom; purpose-built propagators consist of a moulded plastic tray with a box-like, clear lid (*see left*), with vent holes to allow air to circulate.

Small unheated propagators are fine for windowsills. Large, heated ones are ideal for unheated greenhouses. The heating element should provide a minimum soil temperature of 15°C (59°F). An adjustable thermostat regulates how much heat is generated. In frosty weather, cover propagators at night with bubble wrap.

## Seed and potting mixes

Proprietary seed raising mixes tend to be a more even product than home-made mixes; they will also be free of pests and diseases. It is important to use fresh mixes every year; they undergo detrimental chemical changes in store.

Proprietary seed raising and potting mixes are usually soilless, consisting of a sieved bulky material such as pine bark mixed with fine sand to ensure good

---

# Broadcast sowing in a half seed tray or punnet

**1 Fill the tray** past the rim with a special seed raising mix. Moisten it with water if dry. Tap the tray on a bench in order to settle the mix, and then remove any excess by drawing a piece of wood carefully across the surface.

**2 Firm the mix** to remove air pockets using the base of another tray or a presser board, which can be easily made at home. With peat-based mixes, only minimum firming is necessary, or you risk compaction. Water the mix lightly and leave it until any excess has drained off.

**3 Carefully scatter the seeds** onto the surface of the mix, direct from the seed packet. The seeds should be sown evenly and not too thickly, to avoid overcrowded seedlings later.

**4 Sieve a fine layer of mix** over the seeds, and lightly firm it down. Keep the mix moist, but not wet, to encourage successful germination.

## Sowing in pots

**1** **For just a few plants,** scatter the seeds (here of cabbage) thinly and evenly in a 9cm (3½in) pot of moist seed raising mix. Sprinkle with a layer of mix equal to the seed depth, water, and label.

**2** **When 2 seed leaves** have developed, transplant the seedlings into individual modules of standard potting mix, discarding any that are damaged or diseased.

**Using vermiculite to cover seed**
*Vermiculite can be used instead of compost to cover some seed; it allows air to reach the seeds, while keeping them moist.*

drainage. Seed raising mixes are low in nutrients, which germinating seeds do not need. Multi-purpose or home-mixed soils can be used, with added sand to open them up, but avoid products and ingredients that are high in nutrients.

For transplanting seedlings into larger containers, use a potting mix that contains a higher level of nutrients to help the young plants develop. Adding moisture-retaining materials, such as peat or water crystals, to the potting mix helps to keep the mix moist, while adding a slow-release fertilizer helps maintain nutrition. Materials such as leaf mould and worm composts are also good ingredients in potting mixes.

### The importance of hygiene
Conditions under cover – warmer, and with still, humid air – increase the risk of disease, and plants are most vulnerable at the seed and seedling stage. Soil mixes, water, containers, propagators, and all other items used must be scrupulously clean to avoid

contamination that might cause disease, especially damping off (*see also* Plant Problems, *pp. 246–264*). Do not use brackish or salty water.

### Sowing seed in pots or trays
Large seeds to be sown in pots or seed trays can be pushed into the mix individually. Fine seed can be sown broadcast – scattered randomly – and then spaced out more evenly at the pricking out stage. To sow fine seeds in pots (*see above*) or trays (*see p. 63*), shake them straight from the packet, or sprinkle pinches from between finger and thumb. Cover thinly with sifted mix, sand, or vermiculite (*see above right*), and lightly firm. The smaller the seeds, the lighter the covering should be. Water lightly; at this stage you could water in a copper-based fungicide to protect against damping off.

Place the container in a propagator, or cover with a sheet of glass or plastic film. Remove covers as soon as germination occurs to avoid disease.

In the early stages, ensure the

seedlings are kept warm and moist. It is helpful to stand seeded containers on water-absorbent matting. Avoid exposure to strong sun; a temporary covering of newspaper is a useful device. Plants on a windowsill will grow towards the light, so turn the container regularly. Check regularly for signs of disease, as this can rapidly spread. Once the seed leaves have fully developed, prick out the seedlings.

### Pricking out seedlings
Always prick out seedlings promptly, or they will become crowded and grow weak and leggy. Water the seedlings, and fill the new container with moistened potting mix. Hold each seedling gently by a leaf; never touch the stalk or roots. Using a dibber or a pencil, lift out the seedlings in groups, and separate them carefully so as not to damage the delicate root hairs. Discard any unhealthy-looking seedlings.

Transplant them into fresh potting mix, either regularly spaced, 2.5–5cm (1–2in) apart, in a large seed tray, or one plant per module cell (*see left*), with the seed leaves just above the compost. To avoid scorching, keep the seedlings out of full sun for a couple of days. Grow the seedlings on and harden off (*see facing page*) ready for planting outside.

### Pricking out into individual pots
This is ideal in cool regions for frost-tender crops such as tomatoes and capsicums that are to be grown on in the greenhouse before being planted out when the weather warms. Prick out each seedling into a 10cm (4in)

**Pricking out into modules**
*To avoid too much damage to the roots, as soon as the seed leaves are fully open (here celery), prick out the seedlings into modules or small pots. Gently ease out the seedlings from the soil mix using a dibber or pencil. Hold each seedling by its leaves, because the stems bruise very easily. Dibble a hole in each cell and drop in a seedling. Then use the tip of the tool to push and gently firm the soil mix around it. Water and label.*

pot. Place the pots close together initially, and then move them apart as the plants develop and their leaves begin to touch.

## Sowing directly into modules

Large seeds are easy to sow individually in modules. Small seeds can be carefully pushed off a piece of board, glass, or paper, or lifted individually on a damp artist's paintbrush. Fill the cells with seed raising mix in the same way as described for pots and seed trays. Either sow one seed per module, just pushing it into the surface or, for seed of doubtful viability (for example, old seed), sow three to a cell and thin to one strong seedling as soon as the seed leaves are fully developed.

Module trays sown with cool-season crops can be placed in an unheated greenhouse or cold frame. Cover the trays with clear plastic or glass to keep the seeds relatively warm and moist until they have germinated, especially if sowing early in the season when temperatures are low. When the seedlings start to emerge, uncover them, and grow them on in good light until large enough to plant out.

## Multiblock sowing

This sowing technique (*see above right*), in which clusters of plants are grown rather than individual ones, is very useful if you have limited space. It

# Multiblock sowing

1 **Fill a module tray** with moist potting compost. Make a slight depression in each cell with your finger, and sow 3–5 seeds in it. One module tray could be used for a mixture of crops to avoid gluts. Cover the seeds with a 5mm (¼in) layer of grit, and water and label. Put the tray in a position with good light.

2 **When the seedlings** have grown further and developed 1–2 true leaves, carefully plant out each group, without thinning, at an appropriate spacing for the vegetable (here turnips).

3 **Allow the unthinned** plants to grow on to form a group of mature baby vegetables. This method enables you to grow many plants in a small space, and is especially suitable for root, bulb, and stem vegetables.

produces a larger number of smaller, or baby, vegetables, and is suitable for turnips, beetroot, round carrots, spring and bulb onions, chives, leeks, and parsley. Multiblock seedlings should be raised in a greenhouse or a cold frame, where there is good overhead light that will reach all of the seedlings in the cluster, and be planted out before they become leggy. It is important to give them enough space for the whole cluster to grow to maturity.

## Feeding young plants

If young plants have to be left in pots or modules for long periods because adverse weather conditions prevent planting out, add a slow-release fertilizer to the mix or liquid fertilize regularly (*see p.21*) to maintain health and vigour. As soon as the plant's roots fill the pot or module cell, pot up into larger containers of potting mix.

## Hardening off

Young plants raised from seed under cover need to be gradually acclimatized to the outside temperature before they are permanently planted out. This is known as hardening off. Put the plants in a sheltered spot and gradually increase the ventilation each day until the plants are eventually completely uncovered. Leave them for a few days close together to protect each other; this helps them to establish when finally planted out singly.

## GROWING SALAD SEEDLINGS

You can grow mustard, rape, or cress (*see p.106*) in 2–3cm (¾–1¼in) of compost in small pots, punnets, or shallow pans. Scatter the seeds thickly on the surface and leave to germinate. Keep moist but not over-wet. This will produce a mass of seedlings ready to eat in 7–10 days. Cress must be sown three days before mustard or rape to obtain a mixture for salad. Alternatively, line a saucer, 13cm (5in) in diameter, with absorbent paper, add water to soak the paper, and drain off any excess before sowing the seeds thickly (*see below*). Cover with a plastic bag to retain moisture, and place on a windowsill, at a maximum temperature of 15°C (59°F).

*Scatter cress seeds thickly*

*Cress seedlings ready to eat*

# Sowing seed in the garden

Successful vegetable cropping from seed sown directly in the garden is dependent on a satisfactory seedbed and the care with which the sowing is carried out. The seed is usually sown in rows known as drills (*see below*). Most crops are sown where they will be harvested. Vegetables that have large seeds, such as peas, beans, corn, squash and cucumber, are easy to grow from seed sown directly into the garden bed. Vegetables that have medium-sized seeds, such as spinach, beetroot, lettuce and radish, also grow easily from seed sown *in situ*. Root crops such as carrot and parsnip are always sown *in situ* because transplanting these seedlings causes forked or deformed roots. After germination the seedlings are thinned to create the right spacing. Vegetables that are slow to grow such as Brussels sprouts, are best started in pots under cover.

## When to sow

The site where seed is to be sown must always be well prepared in advance. The soil should be moist enough for the seeds to take up water, and also sufficiently warm for the crop being sown (*see p. 62 and individual crops, pp. 74–135*).

## Preparing the soil

Before sowing, dig over the site of the seedbed thoroughly, incorporating organic matter (*see pp. 37–40*), and allow it to settle. If the soil of the seedbed contains a high population of annual weed seeds, prepare it in advance: allow a flush of weeds to develop, then hoe or pull these out. Dig the ground with a fork or cultivator, and level it with a wooden rake. Apply a base dressing of fertilizer if appropriate (*see individual crops, pp. 74–135*). For large areas, if the soil is very lumpy or soft, carefully tread over the whole area evenly, but never

do this when the soil is wet, or it will become compacted and airless. For small areas, stand off the bed and use the back of a rake head to tamp down lumps gently to break them up.

## Producing a fine tilth

If the soil is dry, water it before working it. Rake the seedbed until the texture of the soil is quite crumbly and friable, with small particles – this is known as a fine tilth. Soils with a high organic matter content are usually easier to work than others. It is essential to use long sweeps of the rake and to pull and push the soil in different directions to ensure a level, even seedbed. Keep the rake handle low for the best results. The surface tilth should be deep enough to draw out a drill without going into undisturbed soil. Seed is best sown in a straight line or drill because this makes it easier to weed around the growing seedlings.

## Sowing seed in single drills

1 **Stretch a marker line** of strong cord over the seedbed around pegs marking the end of each drill line. Use the corner of a hoe to draw out an even drill along the line to the depth required for the seed. Stand on the line to keep it taut and straight.

2 **If the seeds are large,** such as these parsnip seeds, sow 3 of them per station at the required interval, here every 15cm (6in), using a measuring stick to ensure the stations are regularly spaced.

3 **For seeds in tape form,** which are supplied ready-spaced, simply cut a length of tape to the length of the drill and lay it along the bottom.

4 **For small seeds,** such as carrots, sow thinly along a drill. Rub the seeds between your fingers to scatter them evenly, or use a seed sower.

5 **Cover the drill** promptly, by raking the soil back over it evenly, holding the rake at 90° to the drill. You can also use the back of the rake head.

## Single drills

Small seeds such as lettuce should be sown thinly in regularly spaced, single rows about 30cm (1ft) apart. Using a garden line and hoe, form a drill (*see facing page*), making sure that the line is as tight as possible in order to get an even, straight depression. It is most important to achieve a uniform depth along the drill. Sow pelleted seeds shallowly at a depth of about twice their diameter, and keep the soil moist to aid germination.

Where a system of narrow beds is being used (*see pp.32–34*), drills can be made by drawing a hoe or stout stake along the edge of a straddling plank. Alternatively, it is possible to make drills by pressing a pre-measured length of timber into the tilth.

An adjustable marking tool (*see p.68*) can be useful, saving walking up and down. Draw out the first drill along a fixed line, then draw the tool down this drill to pull out subsequent ones.

## Wide drills

Wide drills are suitable for sowing peas (*see below*), and for broadcast sowing strips of carrots, radishes, and cut-and-come-again seedling crops such as spinach, cress, and some types of lettuce. Such strips can be very close together, making good use of land, although they are less easily weeded than single rows. To make a wide drill, draw out a shallow trench 15–20cm (6–8in) wide using a line and a wide draw hoe (*see below*), or carefully shovel out the soil to the width of a narrow spade. Make sure that the depth of the drill is uniform.

---

# Sowing in wet or dry conditions

**Sowing in wet conditions**
*If the soil is wet, or very heavy and slow to drain, place a layer of sand in the base of the drill before sowing any seed. This will improve conditions for germination.*

**Sowing in dry conditions**
*If the soil is particularly dry, give the drill a good watering first, and then sow the seed immediately. Use a fine spray to maintain soil moisture until the seedlings emerge.*

---

## Wet or dry conditions

You may not be able to wait for ideal weather conditions before sowing. It is possible to compensate for too much or too little soil moisture by adding sand or watering drills before sowing (*see above*). Use a fine spray to water, and only water after sowing if the weather conditions will cause soil drying. Soil may become crusted if over-watered.

## Depth of sowing

The depth at which you should sow seeds varies according to their size. Seedlings depend on their own reserves for nutrients in the first few days after germinating, until they pierce the soil surface and reach the light. Then they can start to make their own food. Large seeds have more reserves than small ones, and can therefore be sown more deeply. Very fine seed should be sown

**Hand-held seed sower**
*This useful device is designed to release seeds gradually. It can be set for the flow of differently sized seed, from thin sowings of fine seed to space sowing of large seed, as here with pelleted seed.*

nearer the surface. Check the seed packet for recommended sowing depths (*see also individual crops, pp.74–135*).

## Sowing methods

When sowing, try to choose a still day; great care will be needed if it is windy, especially with light seeds like parsnips. Sowing seed evenly takes plenty of practice. For all the methods described, practise first by sowing seed into a piece of guttering about 90cm (3ft) long and adjusting the amounts until you achieve the correct density.

Seeds large enough to be handled individually can be sown (*see p.69*) in drills at regular intervals. Use a measuring stick until you are practised and can judge the correct spacing. A hand-held plastic sower (*see above*) with adjustable settings will help. The sower must be shaken evenly and steadily as you go.

For small, fine seed, sowing direct from the packet works well with paper or rigid-plastic packets, if they have a clean-cut edge and a narrow opening. Shake evenly, holding the packet nearly horizontal to regulate the fall of seeds.

---

# Sowing in wide drills

**1 Draw out a drill** with the blade of a suitable hoe, flicking the soil to one side as you go. Make the drill as deep as required for the crop (here 5cm/2in).

**2 Sow pea seeds in 2 rows** along the drill. Here, they are sown at 5cm (2in) intervals in rows 10cm (4in) apart. Cover over gently, and protect from birds.

You can also sow small seeds from your palm. Hold a small quantity and move your hand horizontally and steadily over the prepared area, tapping it gently with your other hand so that seeds drop off. This is a very good means of broadcast sowing.

Another method is to put some seed in the palm of one hand and take a few between first finger and thumb of the other hand, rubbing them together to disperse the seed. The thinner the sowing required, the fewer seeds should be picked up at a time.

## Covering seed in drills

Once you have sown seed in drills, use a rake to cover the seeds. Gently rake the surface along the covered drill to ensure firmness. Never rake across the lines as this will disturb the seeds and could remove them from the drill. Cultivating carefully between drills with a fork or hand cultivator will loosen any heavily compacted soil.

## Spacing of plants

Space is needed between rows of crops for air circulation, thinning, and for weeding. The spacing of crops sown directly in the garden, or planted out, is determined by the ultimate height and spread of the crop. Parsnips grow to about 30cm (12in) high, and butterhead lettuces up to 30cm (12in) wide, and therefore with both, the rows of plants should be 30cm (12in) apart to allow in

light to produce good crops. Peas may grow to 90cm (3ft), so allow 90cm (3ft) between rows. Carrot and radish rows can be as close as 10cm (4in) apart. Within the rows, thin root crops so that the vegetables will be just touching when mature.

To calculate the space required between rows of different crops, as a general rule of thumb you can add the recommended row spacing for each crop together and divide the total by two. For example, if growing parsnips and peas in rows next to each other at the spacings given above, add the row spacing for parsnips – 30cm (12in) – to the row spacing of peas – 90cm (3ft) – and halve it to give a between-row spacing of 60cm (2ft).

## Thinning seedlings

Thinning – removing surplus seedlings – is essential to obtain a satisfactory final spacing for each plant to grow to maturity. These distances vary with the crop. It should be carried out early, before competition for light and water occurs and the plants become stressed. Because thinning disturbs the roots of plants growing close by, and can attract pests, try to reduce the necessity for thinning by sowing seeds thinly or by sowing seeds at well-spaced intervals this is called station sowing (*see below*).

When the seedlings have reached the first true leaf stage, either pull or pinch out weaker seedlings (*see below*

**Adjustable marking tool**
*These have adjustable tines that can be set at different spacings. Useful tools for marking out planting rows and stations, they can also be handy for marking out shallow seed drills.*

*left*) to leave the strongest and best. Pinching is better for carrots and onions because the soil is disturbed when the seedling is pulled out by its roots, and the foliage bruised, causing odours which attract onion flies which may then lay their eggs in the loosened soil. Remove all thinnings, to avoid the risk of disease and of attracting pests.

## Station or space sowing

This method is used to conserve seeds that are expensive, and to reduce the amount of thinning required later. Large seeds such as spinach may be sown 5cm (2in) apart and left to mature *in situ*. For crops like sweetcorn, which must be grown in a block rather than a row, mark out an area of a bed in a grid pattern, using a marking tool (*see above*). At each station where the rows cross, sow two seeds. These should later be thinned to one strong seedling.

## Broadcast sowing

Random broadcasting of seed is suitable for growing patches of radishes, early carrots, or turnips. It is also used for cut-and-come-again seedling crops, such as mustard and cress. Prepare the seedbed and scatter the seed evenly over the surface. Rake the seed into the surface. The method is easy but there can be a wide variation in size among the seedlings, and sowing in drills better allows for hoeing and weeding. Crops suitable for broadcasting can just as easily be sown in very closely spaced, wide drills (*see p. 67*).

---

# How to thin seedlings

**Pulling**
*Once seedlings are large enough to handle, gently pull them out to leave single, strong specimens at the appropriate spacings.*

**Pinching out**
*With some crops it is best to thin by pinching seedlings off between thumb and forefinger at ground level, to avoid disturbing the soil.*

## Sowing large seeds using a dibber

This means of space sowing is ideal for crops with very large seeds, such as broad, French, and runner beans, sweetcorn, and marrows. First rake over the seedbed to ensure that the soil is loose. Then make a series of holes with a dibber (*see below right*). Drop one or more seeds into the bottom of each hole and cover with soil.

For beans, a single seed per hole is usual; for sweetcorn, three seeds; for marrows, two. Thin the seedlings (*see facing page*) to one per site when they are large enough. It is wise to sow some spares, to fill any gaps that may appear due to poor germination. You can cover the sites of marrow and sweetcorn seeds with jam jars – individual cloches – to keep the soil warm and moist to encourage germination.

## Intersowing

Intersowing involves sowing seed of two different vegetables in the same drill. One crop is quick to mature and therefore does not compete with the other, which is slow growing or slow to germinate. Parsnips and radishes make a good combination for this method (*see above right*). The faster-growing radishes will show up the line of the drill long before the parsnips emerge, enabling earlier hoeing for weed control, and they are harvested before they represent competition to the slower crop.

## Successional sowings

To avoid harvesting gluts and to ensure continuity of supplies, especially of salad vegetables, sow just a few seeds at a time, following with a few more at regular intervals thereafter. This method is suitable for lettuces, radishes, turnips, beetroot, and salad onions. Sow the next batch when seedlings from the previous one have just come up; for example, sow a few lettuce seeds every 10–14 days for a succession of crops.

## Catch crops

To save space, especially in a small garden, plan to grow fast-maturing crops, such as radishes or spinach, before or between other crops, such as tomatoes, sweetcorn, and winter brassicas.

# Intersowing parsnip and radish seed

1 **Station sow the parsnip seeds,** 3 to a station, every 10cm (4in). Then sow radish seeds at 2.5cm (1in) intervals in between the parsnip seeds. The radish seedlings will come up very quickly, indicating the line of the drill to guide early hoeing of any weeds.

2 **Harvest the radishes** when ready so that they do not crowd the parsnip seedlings. Pinch out the parsnip seedlings to thin them when they have 4 leaves.

## Rates of germination

The percentage of seed you sow that will actually germinate depends on a variety of factors, not all of which can be controlled by good gardening practice. Natural germination rate varies with crop groups: for example, brassicas generally have a germination rate of 90 per cent, whereas with leeks it is usually no more than 70 per cent. Large seeds are usually more viable than fine seeds, which are more prone to desiccation. In many cases, seed sown soon after harvest performs better than stored seed. Parsnip and parsley seed is naturally very slow to germinate compared with that of radish and turnip. Dormancy of seed is affected by temperature – for instance, French bean germination is inhibited below 12°C (54°F) and that of lettuce above 25°C (77°F).

All these factors may affect how many plants you get compared with the amount of seed you sow, but given careful seed harvest and storage, they are unlikely to greatly affect success in the garden, provided they are understood. In practice, poor germination is more often due to problems with the condition of the seedbed, such as moisture content, temperature and air, or in the method of sowing. The ground rules for success: use quality seed and give careful attention to all aspects of sowing it.

## Using protection covers

Fleece or other sheet covers (*see p. 48*), tucked into the soil or held down at the edges with bricks, can help to warm the soil before sowing in cool climates. After sowing, they encourage early establishment, help retain soil moisture, and keep off birds and some insect pests. Shade covers can be used to protect plants from hot sun. Remove covers before the seedlings grow tall enough to be restricted. Where scratching birds are troublesome, cover new seedlings with netting.

**Station sowing large seed**
*Large seeds may be sown into well-spaced holes made with a dibber. For broad beans, as here, make holes 5cm (2in) deep, 10cm (4in) apart in rows 15cm (6in) apart, and drop the seeds into them. Cover with soil, water, and label.*

# Planting

Young vegetable plants that are raised in pots to be planted out, or raised in an outdoor seedbed and then transplanted to their final growing site, are known as transplants.

The main point to remember when transplanting is to cause as little damage to the young plant and its roots as possible; handle them carefully and no more than is necessary, and never allow roots to dry out. Water the young plants well in advance so that they are turgid – plump with water – on transplanting, to reduce the risk of wilting. Do not take transplants out of containers or lift them from seedbeds until the planting site is ready.

## When to plant out crops

Young plants of some crops, like the capsicums shown opposite, are raised in pots in greenhouses (*see pp. 43–44*). They can be planted in their permanent homes as soon as their rootballs fill the container.

If planting transplants into beds outside, exactly when to plant out will be dictated by the development of the seedlings and the weather, since it affects the condition of the soil. Ideally, choose a mild, dull day to plant out. Seedlings should be well established, with four to six true leaves and a good root system. Do not let them become tall and stressed; if necessary, pot on the

**Nursery seedlings**
*Ready-to-plant seedlings save weeks of growing time. Most types of vegetables and annual herbs are available. They usually come in punnets of 8 seedlings. Separate the seedlings carefully to avoid root and stem damage and water well after planting.*

plants until conditions are right.

The soil should be moist but not sodden, and relatively warm – for many crops there should be no further danger of frost. The young plants must also be adequately hardened off (*see p. 65*).

For specific planting times, refer to individual crop entries (*see pp. 74–135*).

## Buying seedlings in punnets

Most types of vegetables are available from nurseries in seedling punnets. The main advantage of buying commercially-raised seedlings is that it saves weeks of growing time, which is ideal for gardeners with limited time and space. It also eliminates the need

for propagation facilities. Another advantage of buying seedlings is that gardeners can be sure they are planting the right variety at the right time because local nurseries stock the appropriate variety for the season in that locality. Buying brassica seedlings in punnets is highly recommended because it is essential to plant the right variety at the right time to avoid bolting.

In cool southern regions summer vegetables such as tomatoes are available in early spring before the weather is warm enough for planting out and these seedlings can be grown on in pots under cover and then planted out when the weather permits. Unfortunately, the number of varieties of seedlings available is limited. The range of seed available is much wider and so raising your own seedlings from seed is the only way to grow heritage varieties and other lesser known varieties.

Commercially-raised seedlings are mechanically sown and punnets usually contain exactly eight seedlings. More advanced single plant punnets are available of some varieties such as eggplant and tomato. Sometimes punnets of parsley or basil are sown with numerous seeds and it is difficult to separate the crowded seedlings without damage. In this situation, seedling separation may be easiest by

## Transplanting seedlings from a seedbed

**1 Water the entire row** thoroughly to make the young plants (here cabbages) easy to lift without damage and to retain soil around the roots. Hold them by their leaves, not stems. Put them in a bucket with a little water to prevent wilting.

**2 Mark out planting stations** (here, 45cm/18in) in a prepared bed. Make a planting hole for each transplant and water each hole well. Hold the plant at the correct depth and firm by pushing the dibber sideways towards the roots.

**Planting out seedlings**
*Young lettuces are here planted at equidistant spacing, following a grid marked out across the bed surface. Hold plants by the rootball, not the leaves.*

# Interplanting climbing beans and sweetcorn

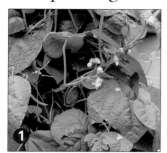

1 **Climbing beans** and sweet corn are grown through summer in temperate gardens and through winter in the tropics. The two vegetables grow well together because the corn is tall and sturdy and the beans require a tall and sturdy support. All varieties of climbing beans are suitable for interplanting with corn.

2 **Sow one or two** bean seeds beside each corn plant when the corn is approximately half grown. This allows the corn to be harvested before it is covered in bean foliage.

washing the soil from the rootball. When selecting seedlings, choose strong, healthy plants of good colour and plant them out as soon as possible.

## Transplanting seedlings grown in punnets or containers

Before planting out (*see below right*), water plants well. Knock plants out of pots by tapping the rim on a hard surface until the rootball becomes free. Remove plants from punnets either by squeezing the base gently, or by poking them up and out through the drainage hole with a dibber or similar. If necessary to avoid damage to roots, cut the punnet off the plants.

Plant out carefully into prepared soil with the surface of the rootball just below the soil surface. Firm around the plant, remove any dead foliage, stake if necessary, water to settle the plants in, and label. If the sun is hot and strong, shade the young plants with sheets or cones of newspaper, or fleece draped lightly over them, and keep well watered. A moisture-conserving mulch (*see p.41*) can be applied around sturdy transplants such as brassicas and beans, but do not let it touch the stems.

## Transplanting in the garden

When seedlings raised in a drill or seedbed reach a height of 10–13cm (4–5in), they are ready for transplanting. To minimize wilting after replanting, choose a dull, damp day, or transplant in the evening, and water the seedlings thoroughly before lifting. Loosen the soil around the seedlings with a trowel or small hand fork. Lift the plants and carefully tease them apart if necessary, trying to keep the roots intact (*see far left*). Select evenly sized plants, and discard any that are bent, damaged, weak, or showing signs of disease. Put the plants in the cool shade to prevent them from drying out. Do not delay replanting. Holding each plant by its leaves make a hole, then set the plant in the hole, holding it upright while you fill and firm in gently around the roots. Water in and label the plants.

## Spacing

When raising transplants at home, keep the seed packets so that you have the information on spacing that they carry when you need it. Advice on crop spacings is also given in the A–Z listings of individual crops later in this section (*see pp.74–135*).

Distance between plants will also vary according to whether you are planting in a conventional row arrangement or using equidistant or block spacing.

## Intercropping

Provided that you get the timing right, you can plant transplants in the space between rows of maturing crops, ready to grow and fill the space left when those crops are harvested. This inter-cropping is an efficient use of space. You can also use the space between slow-growing transplants, such as brassicas, to sow catch crops (*see also p.69*) of fast-growing crops such as salads to harvest before the slower crops fill out the plot.

Transplants are also useful in potager or edible landscape gardening where vegetable plants are grown among established ornamental plants; they will grow away more successfully than plants that are raised from seed.

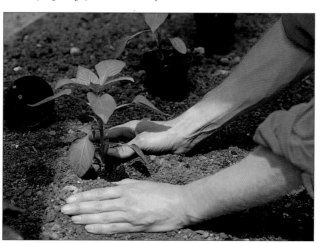

### Planting out

*Here young capsicum transplants have been raised in 9cm (3½in) pots for planting out in a garden bed. Water the plants thoroughly a little time before removing the pot. Dig a planting hole with a trowel and plant firmly with the top of the rootball just below the planting bed surface.*

# Routine care

All vegetables need attention as they grow to produce a good crop. However, you can do much to anticipate and prevent problems and extra work with good planning and preparation. A well-nurtured soil to which plenty of organic matter is added every year, for example, reduces the need for extra watering and feeding during the growing season. Regular, early attention to routine tasks such as weeding can lessen the incidence of some pest and disease problems. For all the topics mentioned below, specific advice on the requirements of individual crops is given on pp.74–135. *See also* Plant Problems (*pp.246–264*) for help with diagnosing and controlling specific pest and disease problems.

## Plants that need support

Providing adequate supports for plants that need it, and checking ties regularly, can prevent unnecessary damage. Short, wire cages or strong stakes and twine are needed for tomatoes, and smaller fruiting vegetables can be supported with individual canes or with canes and twine (*see p.109*). Peas generally require only light support but vigorous climbing beans (*see p.96*) and cucurbits (*see p.115*) need more robust frames or nets.

## Watering

How much and how often you need to water (*see p.53–54*) will depend largely on weather conditions and also on the nature of your soil. The lighter the soil (*see p.14*), the less water it can hold, so plants in sandy soils need much more watering than those in heavy ones. A high organic content in the soil helps retain water. If crops are shaded for part of the day, this will also help reduce water loss. Bear in mind that the roots of nearby trees and shrubs, hedges or other tall crops will take water from a wide area around them.

A mulch (*see pp.41–42*), whether organic or inorganic, also conserves moisture. Hoe mulching (*see above right*) is a traditional way of creating a loose surface layer that protects the lower levels of soil against evaporation.

Propagation and transplanting are critical times for watering, but, once

established, plants usually need no more than one good watering a week in cool weather and daily in hot weather. Water heavily to ensure good penetration down to the roots. Frequent light sprinklings are wasteful and less effective. Leafy crops usually need more plentiful, regular watering than root crops. Other vegetables may need more water at critical stages of development; for example pod set in beans, and when tomato fruits are swelling.

Plants growing in containers (*see pp.35–36*) and greenhouses (*see pp.43–45*) need more frequent watering than those in the garden. Use a moisture-retentive potting mix, and mulch containers if possible to minimize evaporation. Water containers daily for best results. In hot weather, they can need watering three times a day. Also, just as wind has a drying effect outdoors, over-ventilation can have a similar effect in a greenhouse. Damping down – sprinkling water on the greenhouse floor – increases air humidity and discourages some pests.

## Feeding

If you have fertile soil to which you regularly add organic matter and general fertilizers when beds are prepared, plants are less likely to go short of essential nutrients (*see p.17*).

**Hoe mulching**
*Lessen the need for watering by hoeing regularly to keep the top 1cm (½in) of soil loose, creating air spaces that reduce evaporation.*

**Providing supports**
*Make sure that supports are sturdy enough for the weight and number of plants they are to hold, and that the bases of poles and canes are firmly embedded in the soil.*

Supplementary feeding may be necessary on impoverished soil, however, or desirable to boost yields. As nitrogen is constantly leached out of the soil, it is the nutrient most likely to need replacing during the growing season, through the addition of organic manures or high-nitrogen fertilizers. Fast-acting liquid feeds can be useful. High-nitrogen feeds promote lush, leafy growth in crops such as spinach, but are not advisable for root crops. High-potash fertilizers, such as tomato feeds, are suitable for fruiting vegetables.

Deficiencies of the minor nutrients or trace elements are uncommon in well-managed soil, but can be caused by other cultural problems – drought, for example, can impede the availability of calcium to plants. Details of symptoms and remedies for the more common nutrient deficiencies can be found in Plant Problems (*see pp.246–264*).

## Weeding

Good weed control, by hand or by light, regular hoeing, lessens competition for water and nutrients, and also removes potential hosts for some garden pests and diseases. Both organic and inorganic mulches (*see pp.41–42*) are extremely effective means of suppressing weeds.

# Storage

Given adequate moisture and good planning, Australian gardeners are able to grow a series of vegetables for harvest throughout the year. However, the range of these vegetables may be limited at certain times of the year, particularly during summer in the tropics and during winter in temperate regions . Therefore it is worthwhile to store good-keeping varieties for out-of-season use.

The storage requirements of vegetables vary according to the type of vegetable and the climatic conditions. In cool southern regions, winter storage of some vegetables is possible in a cool shed or cellar, while in warmer northern regions, refrigeration or controlled atmosphere coolroom storage is usually required in order to keep these vegetables. Most vegetables will keep fresh in a refrigerator for a week; others freeze well. Preserving and pickling also provides out-of-season supplies. There are other storage methods, however, that can extend the season of availability of crops that quickly become over-mature or where it is necessary to harvest all of a crop to clear the ground. For more detail on storage of individual crops, *see pp. 74–135*.

## Storing in situ

In well-drained cool situations, parsnips, swedes, and carrots can be left in the ground and lifted as required. However, roots can deteriorate when the ground is sodden or frozen, especially on heavy soil. Hard frosts will also damage turnips and beetroot.

Pumpkins, marrows, and squashes can be left out on the ground after harvest, where in favourable weather conditions the sun will complete the hardening of the skins that is essential for good keeping properties. If the ground is wet, a plank or straw placed under the fruits will reduce the risk of rotting or they can be placed on a sunny verandah. Once the weather deteriorates, bring the crop indoors.

## Storing crops indoors

A cool but frost-free, dry place, such as a cellar or shed, is perfect in cool regions for storing many crops after harvest. Some must not dry out if they are to stay in good condition for eating; others must be thoroughly dried, but in both cases cool temperatures, good ventilation and low humidity are essential. Slatted wooden shelves, trays, or racks are ideal, allowing good air circulation. Do not use plastic or cardboard boxes; they increase humidity and encourage rots. Be careful, too, that the food is safe from vermin.

Large, shallow, wooden boxes can be used to store lifted root crops, within layers of sand. Potatoes left in the ground are very vulnerable to pest damage; once mature, crops are also best lifted and stored. Potatoes exposed to light produce poisonous alkaloids, indicated by the greening of tubers, so must be stored in complete darkness. Paper sacks (*see below*) are ideal; plastic bags will encourage condensation and rots.

Onions, shallots, and garlic, once well ripened and dried, can be stored in single layers in stacked slatted boxes, or strung up in plaited ropes (*see below*), or hung in nets or even old nylon tights – anything that allows air to circulate freely around the bulbs. Whole plants of capsicums and chillies can also be hung up for use as required, as can bean and pea plants to complete the ripening of drying pods. Alternatively, dry off the pods in slatted boxes before shelling and storing the beans or peas in jars. Dry pumpkins on an airy dry shelf.

While leafy, loose-headed cabbages do not store well, the densely hearted winter and red cabbages can be stored on wooden slatted racks in a cool cellar or coolroom. They keep best at an even temperature just above freezing. Store only good-quality, undamaged produce. Check all stored crops regularly and remove any that show signs of disease or deterioration.

## Storing vegetables

**Storing potatoes**
*Keep only undamaged potatoes in a double-layered paper sack in a clean, dry place. Fold the top of the sack over loosely after access to exclude light.*

**Storing pumpkins**
*Long-keeping varieties of pumpkin such as 'Golden Nugget', 'Butternut' and 'Queensland Blue', store well in an airy, dry, vermin-proof shed.*

◁ **Drying chillies**
*Pick chillies when fully mature and thread them onto a piece of raffia or string.*

▷ **Plaiting onions**
*To form a rope of onions, suspend one from a string hung from a beam or the ceiling, and then either use the long necks of the onions, or a second string, to secure successive bulbs above it, working from the bottom upwards.*

# Visual index of vegetables

Use this index to locate details of individual vegetable crops. Each section will have a table detailing sowing, planting, and harvest times. The times given are for crops in temperate climates.

*Abelmoschus esculentus* p.112 — **Okra**

*Allium cepa* p.92 — **Onion**

*Allium cepa* Aggregatum Group p.94 — **Shallot**

*Allium cepa* p.94 — **Spring onion**

*Allium fistulosum* p.94 — **Welsh onion**

*Allium porrum* p.93 — **Leek**

*Allium sativum* p.92 — **Garlic**

*Amaranthus* species p.125 — **Amaranth**

*Apium graveolens* var. *dulce* p.121 — **Celery**

*Apium graveolens* var. *secslinum* p.121 — **Leaf celery, cut celery**

*Apium graveolens* var. *rapaceum* p.121 — **Celeriac**

*Asparagus officinalis* p.133 — **Asparagus**

*Barbarea verna* p.104 — **Land, American cress**

*Beta vulgaris* subsp. *cicla* var. *flavescens* p.128 — **Silver beet**

*Beta vulgaris* subsp. *vulgaris* p.85 — **Beetroot**

*Brassica juncea* p.127 — **Mustard greens**

*Brassica napus* Napobrassica Group p.88 — **Swede**

*Brassica oleracea* Acephala Group p.81 — **Kale, curly kale**

*Brassica oleracea* Botrytis Group p.80 — **Cauliflower**

*Brassica oleracea* Capitata Group p.79 — **Cabbage**

*Brassica oleracea* Gemmifera Group p.79 — **Brussels sprouts**

*Brassica oleracea* Gongylodes Group p.81 — **Kohlrabi**

*Brassica oleracea* Italica Group p.78 — **Broccoli**

*Brassica oleracea* Italica Group p.78 — **Sprouting broccoli**

*Brassica rapa* Rapifera Group p.88 — **Turnip, turnip top**

*Brassica olenaceae* var. *alboglabra* p.126 — **Chinese broccoli, Chinese kale**

*Brassica rapa* var. *chinensis* p.127 — **Pak choi**

*Brassica rapa* var. *nipposinica* p.106 — **Mizuna greens**

*Brassica rapa* var. *pekinensis* p.126 — **Chinese cabbage**

*Brassica rapa* var. *perviridis* p.104 — **Komatsuna**

*Capsicum annuum* p.111 — **Capsicum and chilli**

*Cichorium endivia* p.104 — **Endive**

*Cichorium intybus* p.103 — **Chicory**

*Cucumis melo* p.118 — **Rock melon**

*Cucumis sativus* p.117 — **Cucumber and gherkin**

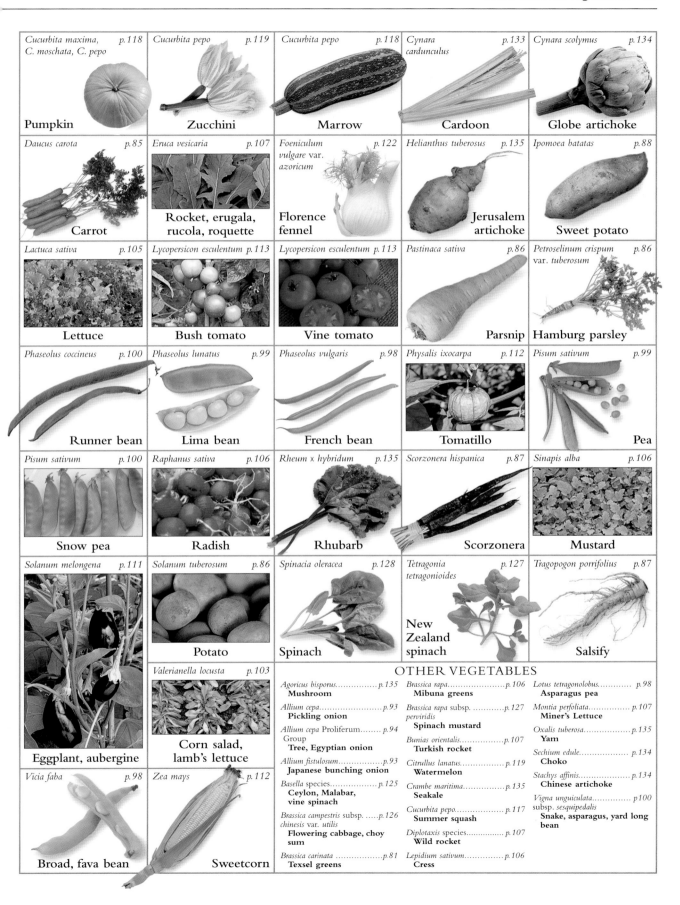

*Cucurbita maxima,* p.118
*C. moschata, C. pepo*

Pumpkin

*Cucurbita pepo* p.119

Zucchini

*Cucurbita pepo* p.118

Marrow

*Cynara* p.133
*cardunculus*

Cardoon

*Cynara scolymus* p.134

Globe artichoke

*Daucus carota* p.85

Carrot

*Eruca vesicaria* p.107

Rocket, erugala,
rucola, roquette

*Foeniculum* p.122
*vulgare* var.
*azoricum*

Florence
fennel

*Helianthus tuberosus* p.135

Jerusalem
artichoke

*Ipomoea batatas* p.88

Sweet potato

*Lactuca sativa* p.105

Lettuce

*Lycopersicon esculentum* p.113

Bush tomato

*Lycopersicon esculentum* p.113

Vine tomato

*Pastinaca sativa* p.86

Parsnip

*Petroselinum crispum* p.86
var. *tuberosum*

Hamburg parsley

*Phaseolus coccineus* p.100

Runner bean

*Phaseolus lunatus* p.99

Lima bean

*Phaseolus vulgaris* p.98

French bean

*Physalis ixocarpa* p.112

Tomatillo

*Pisum sativum* p.99

Pea

*Pisum sativum* p.100

Snow pea

*Raphanus sativa* p.106

Radish

*Rheum x hybridum* p.135

Rhubarb

*Scorzonera hispanica* p.87

Scorzonera

*Sinapis alba* p.106

Mustard

*Solanum melongena* p.111

Eggplant, aubergine

*Solanum tuberosum* p.86

Potato

*Spinacia oleracea* p.128

Spinach

*Tetragonia* p.127
*tetragonioides*

New
Zealand
spinach

*Tragopogon porrifolius* p.87

Salsify

*Valerianella locusta* p.103

Corn salad,
lamb's lettuce

*Vicia faba* p.98

Broad, fava bean

*Zea mays* p.112

Sweetcorn

## OTHER VEGETABLES

*Agoricus bisporus*................ p.135
**Mushroom**

*Allium cepa*......................... p.93
**Pickling onion**

*Allium cepa* Proliferum........ p.94
Group
**Tree, Egyptian onion**

*Allium fistulosum*.................. p.93
**Japanese bunching onion**

*Basella* species................... p.125
**Ceylon, Malabar,
vine spinach**

*Brassica campestris* subsp. ......p.126
*chinesis* var. *utilis*
**Flowering cabbage, choy
sum**

*Brassica carinata* ..................p.81
**Texsel greens**

*Brassica rapa*.......................p.106
**Mibuna greens**

*Brassica rapa* subsp. ............p.127
*perviridis*
**Spinach mustard**

*Bunias orientalis*..................p.107
**Turkish rocket**

*Citrullus lanatus*.................p.119
**Watermelon**

*Crambe maritima*.................p.135
**Seakale**

*Cucurbita pepo*...................p.117
**Summer squash**

*Diplotaxis* species................p.107
**Wild rocket**

*Lepidium sativum*................p.106
**Cress**

*Lotus tetragonolobus*............. p.98
**Asparagus pea**

*Montia perfoliata*..................p.107
**Miner's Lettuce**

*Oxalis tuberosa*..................p.135
**Yam**

*Sechium edule*....................p.134
**Choko**

*Stachys affinis*.....................p.134
**Chinese artichoke**

*Vigna unguiculata*............... p100
subsp. *sesquipedalis*
**Snake, asparagus, yard long
bean**

# Growing brassicas

The botanical family Brassicaceae is the largest in the vegetable garden, including not only those members of the genus *Brassica* covered in these pages, sometimes called the Western brassicas – Brussels sprouts, cabbage, broccoli, cauliflower, kale, kohlrabi, sprouting broccoli, and texsel greens – but also leafy Oriental vegetables such as Chinese cabbage (*see p. 126*) komatsuna and mizuna greens (*see Salad crops, pp.101–107*) and root crops such as swede and radish (*see pp.82–88*).

The brassicas in this section are cool-climate crops, many of them occupying growing space for a long time; for these, careful planning is needed as well as continued care. In tropical regions some brassicas can be grown through winter but hearting types, particularly cabbages, are prone to rot. Most brassicas can be grown throughout the year in cool southern and alpine regions. Many are attractive plants, several having striking cultivars – kales with vividly coloured leaf stems, for example, or the deep violet heads of the purple sprouting broccoli.

A minimum crop rotation of three years (*see p.31*) is extremely important for brassicas, as they are very susceptible to the persistent soil-borne disease clubroot (*see box, facing page*). Pests such as caterpillars must also be controlled.

## Site and soil
Although brassicas tolerate partial shade, choose a sunny site if possible. Their tough leaves stand up well to wind, but some shelter and staking may be necessary for tall-stemmed crops such as sprouting broccoli, Brussels sprouts, and some kales, to stop them being blown over. Cabbage and cauliflower plants are relatively stable. The best soil for most brassicas is fertile, well-drained yet moisture-retentive, and firm. Brassicas need to get a good roothold, especially those that must withstand winter weather, so incorporate plenty of organic matter into light, sandy soils (*see pp.22–23*). Most brassicas benefit from a base dressing of a general fertilizer (*see pp.20–21*). Top-dress overwintered crops such as spring cabbage with fertilizer in spring.

Although brassicas grow well on neutral to slightly acid soil, a higher pH, of 6.8 or above, is desirable because it helps to discourage clubroot. If the pH of your soil is below this level, apply lime to raise it (*see pp.18–19*). If you lime heavily, it is best not to follow brassicas with potatoes, because alkaline conditions favour potato scab.

## Continuity of cropping
Successional sowing (*see p.69*) is a simple means of extending supplies of spring cabbage, broccoli, and kohlrabi. Some brassicas are divided into distinct groups for planting and cropping at different times of year; there are specific groups of cabbages and cauliflowers, for example, for spring, summer, autumn, and winter, sown and planted in different seasons. Within each of these seasonal cropping periods there are cultivars that mature at slightly different times. F1 hybrids reach maturity simultaneously, ideal for the commercial grower but usually not for the gardener; open-pollinated cultivars (*see p.60*) may be a better choice. Planting commercially grown seedlings is the easiest way to ensure the right variety is grown at the right time. While the particular cultivar or hybrid name is seldom displayed on the punnet label, the seedlings sold under a general name such as "Cauliflower", are actually different cultivars or hybrids chosen for the particular season.

## Sowing seed
Some brassicas are direct-sown where they are to crop in conventional drills. These include the leafier crops such as kale and texsel greens, often grown as cut-and-come-again plants. However, most brassicas, especially longer-term crops that need time to form substantial, dense heads, are planted as seedlings purchased from the nursery or raised either in seedbeds or in pots. They are then transplanted into their final cropping positions.

Raising plants in containers in a greenhouse not only saves space but also advances crops and helps to guard against clubroot: strong roots undisturbed on transplanting help the plant to grow away quickly. Sow seed directly into module trays, or sow in pots or punnets and prick out into larger pots or modules (*see p.64*). Harden off and plant out once seedlings are growing strongly.

Transplants that are raised in a seedbed in the garden do not need

### Brassica transplants
*These seedlings are both ready to be transplanted – they have 4 true leaves in addition to their seed leaves. Take care when handling the seedlings, especially if bare-root (left), rather than pushed out of a module cell (right). Roots can be easily damaged.*

### Earthing up
*On very light, sandy soils (left), draw a drill 10cm (4in) deep and plant into it. Once plants have grown clear of the soil surface, gradually fill in the drill. On heavy clay soils (right) where deep planting would risk water-logging, plant at soil level; then earth up as the plants grow.*

*Drill gives shelter from wind and directs water to roots*

*Soil mounded up by about 5cm (2in) once the plant has established*

Light sandy soil

Heavy clay soil

**Planting through landscape fabric**
*Lay the sheet over the bed and secure the edges. Make holes at each planting station by cutting two cross slits about 2.5cm (1in) long with a garden knife. Use a large dibber to make holes, drop the seedlings in, and firm.*

**Protect from cabbage white butterfly**
*These butterflies lay their eggs on the leaves of brassicas and soon the grubs hatch and devour the foliage. Dust young plants with derris dust, spray with a Bt spray or squash grubs by hand.*

protection or hardening off. Such plants are also often more robust, which can be an advantage. Once soil conditions in the seedbed are suitable for the crop, sow in drills (*see pp. 66–67*), and transplant the bare root seedlings to the cropping site once it is vacant. Although the young plants must not be left too long to become drawn and leggy, there is less urgency in moving them to their cropping site compared to seedlings in pots and modules, which soon become root-bound. Bare-root transplants take longer to grow away because of the greater planting check to growth, and require even more careful attention than module-raised plants until established.

## Transplanting seedlings
Transplanting is best carried out on a dull, ideally showery day; in warm summer weather, wait until the cool of the evening to minimize overheating and wilting. Brassicas can normally be planted to the same depth at which they were previously growing. Once commercial seedlings and module-raised and bare-root plants have established, they may be earthed up (by drawing up a little soil around each plant's stem) to aid stability. On light soils, planting into a shallow drill aids establishment before earthing up in a

similar fashion (*see facing page*). The drill provides some protection to young transplants and also helps retain water applied to the plants.

## Common pests
The most common pest to trouble all brassicas is cabbage white butterflies. These butterflies lay their tiny eggs on the leaves and very soon green caterpillars emerge and devour the leaves. Protect young seedlings with

Derris dust or a Bt spray. Caterpillars can also be removed by hand. Brassica plants are seldom troubled by these caterpillars in cool weather. Brassicas are often attacked by cabbage aphids. These can be controlled with cabbage dust insecticide on young plants. When mature plants are infested, the vegetables are best washed in salt water to remove the pest.

## Routine care
Adequate water is crucial for good brassica crops. In dry spells, water seedlings and new transplants daily until well established. Thereafter, water well once or twice a week if conditions are dry during the growing season. Mulching helps to conserve moisture and suppress weeds.

Garden hygiene (*see p. 51*) and correct feeding appropriate to the individual crop (*see pp. 78–81*) do much to help prevent diseases. Check plants regularly for signs of disease, removing any dead or dying leaves. Follow the advice below (*see box*) to reduce the risk of clubroot.

## Harvesting and storing
Crops maturing in the warmer months are best harvested when ready and eaten fresh, but winter and spring crops will stand well in the garden. Many brassicas grow away again after harvest, even in cold weather, to produce useful secondary crops of sideshoots or leafy "tops".

## CLUBROOT AND HOW TO AVOID IT

Clubroot is a fungal disease that causes brassica roots to develop gross swellings, which in turn decay to release disease spores into the soil. Infected plants become stunted, discoloured and wilted, eventually dying. The spores can remain active in the soil for up to 20 years, so it is essential to use every means possible in order to prevent infection.

- **Rotate crops** (*see p.31*). Continuous brassica cropping can lead to a build-up of clubroot in the soil.
- **Lime soil** if necessary (*see pp.18–19*).
- **Avoid importing clubroot** on bought-in plants by raising your own transplants.
- **Control weeds**. Some common weeds, such as shepherd's purse, belong to the brassica family and can harbour clubroot.
- **Clean hoes** and other tools to avoid bringing in disease from other garden areas.

If your soil is infected with clubroot, remember that it is young brassica plants that are most vulnerable.

- **Burn all affected material** after digging it up complete with roots; never compost it.
- **Start all plants off in modules,** in clean compost, and grow larger, sturdier transplants than usual; they will be less vulnerable than small seedlings. A larger planting hole filled with clean soil also helps transplants establish in safety.
- **Foliar feeding** (*see p.21*) can help young plants to establish quickly and well on infected sites.
- **Choose fast-growing crops** such as texsel greens. They may reach maturity before being affected.
- **Avoid using the green manures** fodder radish and mustard, which are brassicas.

# A–Z of brassicas

## Broccoli

*Brassica oleracea* Italica Group

There are three types of broccoli. The common broccoli is also called calabrese or green sprouting broccoli, and produces a large head followed by numerous smaller side shoots. The second type is Romanesco, which produces an attractive pale lime green, pointed head, and the third type is called sprouting broccoli. Varieties of sprouting broccoli produce purple or white smallish heads over a long period.

### Broccoli

| Season | Spring | Summer | Autumn | Winter |
|---|---|---|---|---|
| Sow | • • • | • • • | • • | |
| Transplant | • • • | • • • | • • | • • |
| Harvest | • • • | • • • | • • • | • • • |

Also known as American, Italian, or green sprouting broccoli, or calabrese, broccoli is a fast-growing brassica that has become very popular. Broccoli grows up to 60cm (2ft) tall, and produces bluish-green heads, up to 15cm (6in) in diameter and 110–225g (4–8oz) in weight, as well as further, smaller heads borne on sideshoots that appear after the main head has been cut. It can be sown throughout the year in cool climates. Best heads are produced in cool weather; in hot conditions the heads – immature flower buds – develop and run to seed quickly. Some cultivars resist this tendency better. While the flowers look pretty and bees enjoy them, the stems become tough and woody. Plants are removed when they go to flower. Cabbage white butterflies are also troublesome in warm weather unless plants are covered with fleece or insect netting. It is therefore best to grow broccoli through the cooler months only. Broccoli is a nutritious vegetable and is a good source of vitamins A, C, E and folate. Broccoli freezes well.

**Site and soil**  A fertile, well-drained, moisture-retentive, firm soil (*see p.76*) is best, but broccoli will grow well on less fertile soils than other brassicas, so a base dressing of fertilizer is not usually necessary. Lime the soil if necessary to raise the pH and thus deter clubroot (*see p.77*).

**Sowing and planting**  Broccoli does not transplant well in warm weather, resulting in premature production of tiny heads. Plant out nursery-grown seedlings, or if propagating seed, it is best station-sown (*see p.68*) where it is to crop, and thinned to one plant per site. Closer spacing encourages smaller shoots.

| Sowing depth | 2cm (¾in), three seeds per station |
|---|---|
| Seed spacing | 30cm (12in) |
| Row spacing | 45cm (18in) |

**Routine care**  Keep evenly moist throughout the growing season, watering at a rate of about 20 litres per sq m (4 gallons per sq yd) every week. After the main head has been harvested, apply a top-dressing of a complete fertilizer or organic liquid feed to encourage sideshoots to form.

**Harvesting**  Cut the central head while it is still firm, and before any flowers open. This stimulates the production of sideshoots.

**Common problems**  As for Brussels sprouts.

## Romanesco

Gardeners in northern Italy have been growing Romanesco for generations. Consequently it is often called Italian broccoli. Romanesco has become more popular in Australian gardens in recent years. The head is pale lime green in colour and looks slightly like a pointed cauliflower when immature but develops smaller pointed shoots as it matures. In the garden the plants grow in an open vase shape.

**Site and soil**  As for broccoli.

**Sowing and planting**  Romanesco needs cool weather when the heads are developing otherwise it may bolt to seed. In temperate regions the seed is sown in late summer or early autumn to crop through winter. Sow seed 1 cm (half an inch) deep in a tray or punnet. Transplant seedlings into moist garden soil at a spacing of 50cm (18 in) when they have 2–4 true leaves and when the weather is cool. Romanesco is a hungry vegetable and the growing plant should be side-dressed with a general purpose fertilizer.

**Harvesting**  The head should be picked before the tight buds elongate and flower.

**Common problems**  As for Brussels sprouts.

## Sprouting broccoli

Sprouting broccoli is not commonly grown in Australia but it is productive over a long period. There are both purple and white forms of sprouting broccoli, the purple ones being much hardier and producing many more edible shoots. In cool climates these crops are in the ground for a long time, taking up a lot of space, but give useful produce from late winter to late spring when other fresh garden vegetables are in short supply. Picked regularly, ten plants can yield 3kg (around 7lb) over the season. In good, rich soils, plants can grow to 90cm (3ft) across and up to 90cm (3ft) tall, and are liable to become top-heavy. Most cultivars can be sown over a long period for harvest in the same season.

**Site and soil**  This crop needs a fertile soil that is very well-drained in order to avoid waterlogging. It also needs shelter from wind to reduce rocking. Lime soil if necessary (*see p.18*) to raise the pH and deter clubroot.

**Sowing and planting**  Sow seed in late summer, either in modules or in a seedbed (*see pp.66–68*), to transplant to their final site.

| | |
|---|---|
| Sowing depth | 2cm (¾in) |
| Plant spacing | 60cm (24in) |
| Row spacing | 60cm (24in) |

**Routine care** Keep weed-free, and water in dry spells until established. Plants must be securely supported with stakes (*see p.72*) to avoid windrock. Earth up stems to increase stability.

**Harvesting** When the flowering shoots are about 15–20cm (6–8in) long, but before the flower buds open, snap off around 8–10cm (3–4in) of their length. New sideshoots will be produced; harvest these as they are ready.

**Common problems** As for Brussels sprouts.

**Recommended cultivars**

BROCCOLI
'Di Cocco Early' – an old Italian variety.
'Greenbelt' - hybrid with tight heads and many sideshoots.
'Green Sprouting Calabrese' – variety with good head followed by prolific sideshoots. Plant for winter harvest.
'Marathon' – a hybrid with a tight head followed by many sideshoots over a long period.
'Pirate' – hybrid that resists bolting.
'Small Miracle' – small, quick-growing variety suited to small gardens.

ROMANESCO
'Romanesco' – Italian broccoli with a minaret-like pointed head of pale lime green; suited to cool climates.

SPROUTING BROCCOLI
'Purple Sprouting' – vigorous sprouting broccoli that produces masses of colourful purple sideshoots over winter and spring.
'Red Spear' – a sprouting type that produces numerous smallish claret-red heads.

# Brussels sprouts

*Brassica oleracea* Gemmifera Group

| Season | Spring | Summer | Autumn | Winter |
|---|---|---|---|---|
| Sow | • • • • | • | | |
| Transplant | • • | • • • | | |
| Harvest | | | • • | • • • • • |

These traditional winter vegetables can be picked fresh for most of the year; the plants are strong and can survive severe winters. Most modern cultivars are F1 hybrids (*see p.60*), producing uniform plants and compact sprouts. Plants grown to full height can produce 60–70 sprouts each; weight depends on the size they are allowed to reach. The small buttons are excellent for freezing. There is also a small crop of leafy tops. Sprouts are suitable for intercropping (*see p.71*), for example with fast-growing salads.

**Site and soil** Brussels sprouts do well in temperate zones in firm, fertile soils, with plenty of organic matter incorporated well in advance. Lime if necessary (*see p.18*) to raise the soil pH to deter clubroot. Before sowing or planting, apply a base dressing of fertilizer (*see pp.20–23*), except on highly fertile soil –

too much nitrogen produces loose, leafy sprouts.

**Sowing and planting** Brussels sprouts are slow to grow, taking up to six months from sowing to harvest. Sow seed under cover (*see p.62*) in late winter for an early crop in late summer and early autumn. For winter crops, sow from early to mid-spring, outdoors in a seedbed (*see p.67*) or under cover in modules (*see p.64*), and transplant to the cropping site in early to midsummer. Close planting (less than 60cm/2ft each way), for example on narrow beds (*see pp.32–33*), will produce smaller sprouts of uniform maturity, while wider spacing will yield larger sprouts to be picked in succession over a longer period. Sowing different cultivars to mature at varying times will ensure a long cropping period. Keep seedlings and new transplants well watered.

| | |
|---|---|
| Sowing depth | 2cm (¾in) |
| Plant spacing | 60cm (2ft) |
| Row spacing | 60cm (2ft) |

**Routine care** To produce small, evenly sized sprouts that will mature simultaneously, for example for freezing, pinch out the growing tips of the plants when the lower sprouts are 1cm (½in) in diameter. To encourage the sprouts to fill out, top-dress in midsummer with sulphate of ammonia at a rate of 25–50g per sq m (1–2oz per sq yd). Water after top-dressing. Once established, plants should grow away without further watering unless there is a period of drought. Overwintering plants need supporting with stakes, especially on light, sandy soils.

**Harvesting** Starting from the bottom of the plant, pick when the sprouts reach 2–3cm (¾–1¼in) in diameter for the sweetest taste; snap them off with a downward motion. At the same time, remove any yellow leaves and discard any loose or yellow sprouts. Whole stems or sticks of sprouts keep well standing in a little water in a bucket in a cool place. Later in the season, the leafy tops of the plants can also be picked as greens.

**Common problems** Caterpillars (*see p.253*), especially those of the cabbage white butterfly, can cause extensive crop damage. Large colonies of mealy cabbage aphids (*see p.257*), can quickly establish, causing distorted foliage. Do not mistake them for whitefly (*see p.264*); although this can be a conspicuous pest, it rarely causes significant damage, although in mild winters whitefly can persist on brassicas to affect other young plants in spring. It is also difficult to wash off sprouts before cooking. Other pests include cutworm (*see p.254*), and slugs and snails (*see p.262*).

In addition to clubroot (*see pp.77, and also p.254*), brassicas are susceptible to leaf diseases such as downy mildew (*see p.255*), and powdery mildew (*see p.260*).

Plants grown well and fed correctly rarely suffer nutrient deficiencies. Hollow stems may indicate boron deficiency (*see p.252*). Poor seedling growth can be the result of molybdenum deficiency (*see p.258*).

**Recommended cultivars**
'Long Island Improved' – short plant with compact sprouts.
'Long Island' – old variety that is sown early.
'Roger' – adaptable hybrid with tight sprouts.
'Rubine' – produces unusual beetroot-red sprouts with a nutty flavour.
'Ruby' – attractive lavender blue foliage with ruby sprouts.

# Cabbage

*Brassica oleracea* Capitata Group

By growing cultivar groups that mature in different seasons, cabbages can be harvested and eaten fresh throughout the year in temperate zones. Spring cabbages are usually small, and may be either pointed or round-headed. Early summer cabbages are normally pointed or round, and late-summer or autumn ones rounded or oval, and more compact. The leaves of some spring and autumn cabbages may also be eaten as greens, before they form a heart. Winter cabbages include the Dutch white types, the purple-tinged types, and the crinkly-leaved Savoy types, as well as some hybrids between these. Yields vary according to the type of cabbage being grown (*see* Average crop yields, *p.242*).

| Season | Spring | Summer | Autumn | Winter |
|---|---|---|---|---|
| **SPRING CABBAGE** | | | | |
| Sow | | | • • • | |
| Transplant | | | • • • | |
| Harvest | • • • | | | |
| **EARLY SUMMER CABBAGE** | | | | |
| Sow | • • | | | • |
| Transplant | • • • | | | |
| Harvest | | • • • | | |
| **SUMMER/AUTUMN CABBAGE** | | | | |
| Sow | • • • • | | | |
| Transplant | | • • • | | |
| Harvest | | | • • • • | |
| **WINTER CABBAGE** | | • • • • | | |
| Transplant | | • • • • | | |
| Harvest | • | | • • • • | |
| **RED CABBAGE** | | | | |
| Sow | • • | | | |
| Transplant | | • • | | |
| Harvest | | | • • | • |

**Site and soil** Cabbages prefer fertile, well-drained, moisture-retentive, but firm soil (*see p.76*). Apply a base dressing of a general fertilizer (*see pp.20–21*) when sowing or planting in spring and summer. Lime soil if necessary to raise the pH to deter clubroot (*see also p.18*).

**Sowing and planting** Plant out commercial seedlings or sow seed either in a seedbed or in modules (*see p.76*) at the correct time of year for the type. To produce both spring greens and cabbages in the same bed, space the plants 10cm (4in) apart in rows 30cm (12in) apart. Use two out of each three for greens, and leave the third to heart up. Sow summer cabbages in succession for a continuous crop.

The earliest transplants raised under cover should be hardened off carefully (*see p.65*), or they may bolt. Covering them with fleece after planting out will reduce this risk and advance crops by 10–14 days. Winter cabbages should be sown in succession. Protect all seedlings and young transplants from cabbage white butterfly (*see p.77*).

| Sowing depth | 2cm (¾in) | |
|---|---|---|
| SPRING CABBAGE/SPRING GREENS | | |
| Plant spacing | 25cm (10in) for hearted cabbages | |
| | 15cm (6in) for greens | |
| Row spacing | 30cm (12in) | |
| EARLY SUMMER CABBAGE | | |
| Plant spacing | 38cm (15in) | |
| Row spacing | 38cm (15in) | |
| SUMMER/AUTUMN CABBAGE | | |
| Plant spacing | 45cm (18in) | |
| Row spacing | 45cm (18in) | |
| WINTER CABBAGE | | |
| Plant spacing | 45cm (18in) | |
| Row spacing | 60cm (24in) | |
| RED CABBAGE | | |
| Plant spacing | 23–38cm (9–15in) | |
| Row spacing | 45cm (18in) | |

**Routine care** Practise good weed control. Keep young plants well watered if necessary until they are established, then water only in very dry weather. Earth up the stems of spring and winter cabbages during the winter, and remove dead leaves regularly. Top-dress with a high-nitrogen fertilizer or organic liquid feed before the leaves touch across the rows.
**Harvesting** For greens, harvest young leaves as soon as they are large enough. Cut spring and summer hearting cabbages when the hearts are solid throughout. Stumps left in the ground may resprout to provide a small crop of greens, especially if a cross-cut is made across the surface of the cut stem. The hardier winter cabbages can be left to stand in the ground for one or two months, to harvest as needed.
**Common problems** As for Brussels sprouts.
**Recommended cultivars**
GREEN VARIETIES
'Green Coronet' – hybrid cabbage that holds well and can be autumn sown in warm climates.
'Golden Acre' – quick-maturing mini-cabbage with round heads. Sow in early summer.
'Gourmet' – large, pale cabbage that holds well in the garden.
'January King' – handsome variety with pink-tinged leaves; holds well in summer.
'Mini' – quick-growing variety with small heads.
'Puma' – small hybrid cabbage that produces a small head.
'Savoy King' – hybrid cabbage with decorative crinkled leaves and good solid heads.
'Sugarloaf' – a small, cone-shaped cabbage that is quick to mature.
'Vertus' – old savoy type with large heads.
RED VARIETIES
'Mammoth Red Rock' – an open-pollinated

cultivar. Sow in early summer.
'Red Drum Head' – variety with large, handsome, deep purple leaves surrounding the rich red head.
'Red Dutch' – large red heads.
'Red Ranger' – hybrid with tight head; best sown in winter.
'Rookie' – an early-maturing hybrid that holds well in the garden.
'Super Red Hybrid' – mini red cabbage with small head but good flavour.

# Cauliflower

## *Brassica oleracea* Botrytis Group

The typical cauliflower has a cream or white curd, or head, but there are also green- and purple-headed cultivars. Cauliflowers make large plants, and those that overwinter will occupy the ground for about six months. They are quite difficult to grow because they need a lot of water and fertile soil. Cultivars maturing before midsummer are therefore the easiest to raise successfully. At a conventional wide spacing, only 5–6 cauliflowers can be grown in a 3m (10ft) row. Mini cauliflowers are produced by plants grown much closer together (up to 20 in a 3m/10ft) row, taking 13–18 weeks to produce heads 4–8cm (1½–3in) in diameter.
**Site and soil** To produce large, well-formed curds, cauliflowers need a fairly rich soil with plenty of nitrogen-rich fertilizer applied as a base dressing before planting (*see p.76*).

| Season | Spring | Summer | Autumn | Winter |
|---|---|---|---|---|
| EARLY SUMMER CAULIFLOWER | | | | |
| Sow | | | ● | ● ● |
| Transplant | ● ● | ● | | |
| Harvest | | ● ● | | |
| SUMMER CAULIFLOWER | | | | |
| Sow | ● ● | | | |
| Transplant | | ● | | |
| Harvest | | | ● ● | |
| AUTUMN CAULIFLOWER | | | | |
| Sow | ● ● ● | | | |
| Transplant | | ● ● ● | | |
| Harvest | | | ● ● ● ● | |
| WINTER-HEADING CAULIFLOWER | | | | |
| Sow | | ● ● | | |
| Transplant | | | ● ● | |
| Harvest | | | | ● ● ● |
| SPRING-HEADING CAULIFLOWER | | | | |
| Sow | | ● ● | | |
| Transplant | | | ● ● | |
| Harvest | ● ● ● ● | | | |
| MINI CAULIFLOWER | | | | |
| Sow | | ● ● ● ● | | |
| Transplant | | ● ● ● ● | | |
| Harvest | | | ● ● ● ● ● | |

**Sowing and planting** Most varieties of cauliflower are grown from summer onwards for harvest in winter and spring. Seed is sown in summer for autumn planting or in early autumn for late autumn planting. Cauliflowers take from 3 to 6 months to mature, depending on the variety and the weather. Summer

seedlings will need protection from cabbage white butterfly. They need a sheltered site and protection from severe frost, which can damage the curds. All cauliflowers need to be planted firmly, and should be transplanted as young as possible since they suffer if their growth is checked. For mini cauliflowers, sow in succession, or sow several different cultivars, to ensure a prolonged harvesting season.

| Sowing depth | 2cm (¾in) | |
|---|---|---|
| EARLY SUMMER CAULIFLOWER | | |
| Plant spacing | 45cm (18in) | |
| Row spacing | 60cm (24in) | |
| SUMMER CAULIFLOWER | | |
| Plant spacing | 45cm (18in) | |
| Row spacing | 60cm (24in) | |
| AUTUMN CAULIFLOWER | | |
| Plant spacing | 60cm (24in) | |
| Row spacing | 60cm (24in) | |
| WINTER- AND SPRING-HEADING CAULIFLOWER | | |
| Plant spacing | 70cm (28in) | |
| Row spacing | 70cm (28in) | |
| MINI CAULIFLOWER | | |
| Seed or plant spacing | 15cm (6in) | |
| Row spacing | 15cm (6in) | |

**Routine care** It is essential to control weeds and keep the soil moist throughout the growing period, or small, deformed heads will form prematurely. In summer, snap and fold in leaves to protect the curd from strong sun. In winter, bunch and tie leaves together over the curd to protect it from frost. Top-dress (*see p.76*) spring-heading types in late winter or in early spring to stimulate new growth.
**Harvesting** Harvest curds while they are still firm and dense; they are in effect immature flower buds and will open up and deteriorate in time. Cut with enough leaf attached to protect the curd. Harvest mini cauliflowers promptly, as they readily deteriorate.
**Common problems** As for Brussels sprouts (*see p.79*). Downy mildew (*see p.255*) is a particular problem with cauliflowers; they are also especially vulnerable to problems caused by nutrient deficiencies, such as whiptail (*see molybdenum deficiency, p.258*). Boron deficiency (*see p.252*) may cause brown rings in the stalk. *See also* frost damage, *p.255*.
**Recommended cultivars**
'Allegro' – easy to grow, early-maturing variety with white head.
'Green Crown' – a decorative, lime green head that grows well in cool climates.
'Green Macerata' – quick-maturing variety with a rounded, lime green head.
'Hawksbury' – hybrid with pure white head; bred for warm conditions.
'Melody' – a hybrid, very reliable producer. Sow summer and autumn.
'Mini White' – a small variety suited to small gardens.
'Orange Bouquet' – hybrid with rusty orange colouring that is retained during cooking.
'Paleface' – produces firm white head and can be planted throughout the year in cool climates.
'Phenomenal Early' – produces white heads

and is suited to warm conditions.
'Selection 174' – an adaptable variety that shows heat and cold tolerance.
'Sicilian Purple' – produces large purple heads.
'Snowball' – quick-growing early variety with small heads; suited to warm regions.
'Violet Queen' – pinkish-purple head that turns green when cooked.
'White Rock' – a late variety that can be grown through summer for autumn harvest.

# Kale

*Brassica oleracea* Acephala Group

| Season | Spring | | Summer | Autumn | Winter |
|---|---|---|---|---|---|
| Sow | | • • | • • | | |
| Transplant | | | • • | • | |
| Harvest | • • | | | • | • • • |

Kale is not commonly grown in Australia but it has lush colourful foliage that withstands the coldest winters. It is also known as Scotch kale and borecole. As few as six plants picked regularly can provide 1.8–2.25kg (4–5lb) of greens over the season. Modern curly kale cultivars are sweeter and more tender than the older broad-leaved types, of which only the young shoots are eaten. Kale can grow to a height of 90cm (3ft), but the dwarf types reach only about 30cm (1ft), and are therefore more suitable for small gardens. All make ornamental plants for a winter garden. Some kales can be grown as a cut-and-come-again crop of salad leaves (*see p.102*).

**Site and soil** Kale grown as a winter crop needs well-drained, rich soil that will not become waterlogged.

**Sowing and planting** Sow either in a seedbed or in containers in summer or autumn (*see p.76*). Transplant 6–8 weeks after sowing, planting them firmly. Dwarf cultivars may be spaced closer together than tall ones. If growing a seedling salad crop, cut the seedlings when they are 5–8cm (2–3in) tall, or thin them to 8–10cm (3–4in) apart and cut them when 15cm (6in) tall.

| Sowing depth | 2cm (¾in) |
|---|---|
| Plant spacing | 60cm (24in) |
| Row spacing | 45cm (18in) |

**Routine care** Control weeds, and water after planting if necessary until the plants are well established. Thereafter avoid overwatering, because this will produce lush, soft growth less able to survive the winter. If the crop shows sign of yellowing in early autumn, top-dress with a nitrogenous fertilizer or organic liquid feed (*see pp.20–23*) to maintain good colour. Remove any yellow leaves.

**Harvesting** Harvest young leaves regularly from all plants to encourage more growth. Remove any flower shoots that appear. Continue to harvest until the plants go to seed, when they will become bitter.

**Common problems** As for Brussels sprouts (*see p.79*). Whitefly (*see p.264*) can be a problem, because it infests the edible parts. However, leaf diseases do not normally occur if plants are harvested regularly, and clubroot is less of a problem than for other brassicas.

**Recommended cultivars**
'Dwarf Green' – light green, curled leaves on short stems.
'Half Tall Scotch' – curled, dark green variety; easy to grow.
'Red Bor' – a hybrid with decorative frilled, wine-coloured leaves.
'Red Russian' – dwarf variety with purple-stalked greyish leaves.
'Toscano' – long dark green leaves; tolerates heat.
'Tuscan Black' – variety with narrow slate-blue leaves.
'Winter Bor' – vigorous hybrid with curled leaves.

# Kohlrabi

*Brassica oleracea* Gongylodes Group

| Season | Spring | | Summer | Autumn | Winter |
|---|---|---|---|---|---|
| Sow | • | • • | • • | | |
| Transplant | • | • | • | | |
| Harvest | | • | • • | • • | • • |

This often underrated, tasty brassica has an unusual-looking swollen stem that is eaten like a turnip, or shredded for use in salads. There is a gap of 2.5–4cm (1–1½in) between the soil and the base of the swollen stem. Young, tender leaves are also useful as greens. Green and purple cultivars are available. Kohlrabi can also be grown as a catch crop (*see p.69*), because it is fast-growing.

**Site and soil** Kohlrabi needs less nitrogen than other brassicas, and will thrive in a rich, light, sandy soil, although it will also grow in heavy soil. It is essential to lime the soil if necessary to raise the pH and thus guard against clubroot (*see p.77*).

**Sowing and planting** Kohlrabi seed is sown directly into the garden bed because transplanted seedlings tend to bolt. In cool climates, seed is sown in summer and early autumn for winter harvest. In warm climates, seed can be sown in autumn/winter for spring harvest. Thin at an early stage to avoid unnecessary root disturbance to the plants that remain. Succession sow every two weeks for continuity.

| Season | Spring | | Summer | Autumn | Winter |
|---|---|---|---|---|---|
| Sow | • | • • | • • | • | |
| Harvest | | • | • • | • • | • |

**Routine care** It is essential to keep plants well watered throughout the growing period, in order to avoid a check in growth which will lead to unpalatable, woody flesh being produced. Control weeds promptly.

**Harvesting** When the stems are between golf- and tennis-ball size, usually 7–8 weeks after sowing, cut off at the root and trim off the outer leaves to 2cm (¾in), leaving the central leaves on the stem to help maintain its freshness. Newer cultivars grow rapidly, and can still be tender when larger. Kohlrabi has a milder flavour than turnip and can be added to stir-fry dishes, salads, soups and casseroles.

**Common problems** As for Brussels sprouts (*p.79*). Some leaf damage can be tolerated as leaves are not edible. Clubroot can be severe.

**Recommended cultivars**
'Early Vienna White' – early-maturing with green skin and white flesh.
'Purple Globe' – purple skin and white flesh; slightly later to mature.
'Purple Vienna' – hybrid with purple skin and white flesh.
'White Vienna' – hybrid with white skin and flesh.

# Texsel greens

*Brassica carinata*

| Sowing depth | 2cm (¾in) |
|---|---|
| Seed spacing | 23cm (9in), 3 seeds per station |
| Row spacing | 30cm (12in) |

Also known as Tamu-Texsel, this leafy vegetable is rare in Australia but is becoming better known. It has been bred from Ethiopian mustard. Fast-growing, maturing in as little as seven weeks, it makes a useful catch crop. Texsel greens have shiny leaves, high in nutritional value and with a flavour slightly reminiscent of spinach. Young leaves are used for salads, and older plants for cooking. The flavour and texture is best in winter and spring. When grown as a cut-and-come-again salad crop (*see p.102*), a 3m (10ft) row of texel greens yields 6–9kg (13–20lb) over the season, depending on the size of the leaves harvested. There are no named cultivars of texsel greens.

**Site and soil** As for all brassicas, texsel greens prefer a fertile, well-drained soil, but, because they crop so quickly, they often succeed even on clubroot-infected soils.

**Sowing and planting** Broadcast sow (*see p.68*) in succession every 2–3 weeks. Thin the seedlings to 2.5cm (1in) apart. If growing them as a seedling crop, there is no need to thin.

| Sowing depth | 1cm (½in) |
|---|---|
| Seed spacing | broadcast; thin to 2.5cm (1in) |
| Row spacing | 30cm (12in) |

**Routine care** Keep evenly moist for steady growth and to prevent bolting.

**Harvesting** For salad crops, harvest the shoots and leaves when young. Once they are mature, harvesting a few leaves from each plant rather than picking them all from one or two will keep plants cropping steadily.

**Common problems** As for Brussels sprouts (*see p.79*).

# Growing root crops

This group of vegetables encompasses beetroot, carrots, parsnip, and the very similar Hamburg parsley, potatoes, salsify, scorzonera, swedes, sweet potatoes, and turnips, all of which produce edible crops below ground or at soil level. Potatoes and sweet potatoes have underground tubers whereas the others all have swollen roots. Salsify and scorzonera also have edible flowering shoots and buds.

Root crops are prone to several major soil-borne pests and diseases, and in some cases this influences methods of cultivation. Root crops are susceptible to root rot where soil is permanently damp and few root crops grow in tropical gardens for this reason. Since root crops represent a wide range of species there are various cultural requirements to be considered, especially with regard to soil conditions.

## Soil pH
To grow a particular crop successfully, check the acidity level of your soil with a testing kit to ascertain whether liming will be necessary (*see pp. 18–19*).

Potatoes do best on a slightly acid soil of pH 5–6; on soils that are rich in lime, the skin disease potato powdery scab (*see p. 260*) will thrive to attack many cultivars.

Parsnips prefer slightly acid soils of pH 6.5. Beetroot, carrots, salsify, and scorzonera have a broader range of

**Using fleece**
*You can warm the soil, protect from hot sun and retain moisture by covering the bed with a double layer of fleece (as here and see p.48). Remove the covering when the seed has germinated.*

**Quality roots**
*Root crops require deep, friable soil to develop well-formed roots. Carrots, in particular, are often forked and twisted at harvest and although this does not alter the flavour, they are difficult to wash and prepare. To ensure straight carrots, prepare the soil to a good spade depth making sure it is free from stones and undecomposed material, then sow the seed in situ and thin the seedlings when they are at the two-leaf stage.*

tolerance and will grow well on soils with a pH 6.5–7.5.

Turnips and swedes grow best in slightly acid soil. However, like other members of the brassica family, they are vulnerable to the persistent soil-borne disease clubroot (*see p.254*), which is less prevalent on neutral to alkaline soil with a pH 7 or more.

## Soil fertility
It is important to take account of the nutrient requirements of each crop, which are various. Parsnips, salsify, scorzonera, swedes, and turnips have low nitrogen needs, and those of carrots and beetroot are very low. Potatoes and beet have high nitrogen requirements. All root crops do best on soils with a high content of organic matter, which is best incorporated into the soil a month or more prior to cropping. (*See also individual crops, pp.85–88.*)

## Soil texture
Crops with long roots that grow down into the soil, such as carrots, parsnips, salsify, scorzonera, and some beetroot types, do best on light, sandy soils where the roots can penetrate easily, making vegetables of good shape and length. All the root crops, however, can be grown on heavy soils, provided that

they are well-drained, deeply cultivated, and free of stones. Short rooting varieties of carrot are the best varieties for heavy soils.

## Rotation
It is essential to rotate root crops (*see p.31*) in order to reduce infestation by pests and especially disease infections, to keep the soil nutrient levels suitably balanced, and to keep weeds in check. A minimum of a three-year rotation lessens the risk of a build-up of pests such as eelworm (*see p.255*) and diseases such as carrot root rot (*see p.261*) and parsnip canker (*see p.259*).

Rotation helps to maintain fertility by permitting one crop to benefit from nutrient levels that were appropriate to the previous crop – a classic example is planning to grow nitrogen-hungry brassicas after nitrogen-fixing legumes. Following legumes with root crops, which need less nitrogen, can result in their developing excessive foliage growth at the expense of roots.

Rotation assists in controlling weeds. For example, in the cultivation of potatoes the ground is well dug and disturbed because the crop is earthed up regularly – a process that suppresses weed growth. The crop also has a good canopy of leaves to smother annual weeds. Subsequent crops benefit by resulting reduction in weed population, particularly because there is invariably no need for further deep cultivation that would bring even more weed seeds to the surface.

## Short- or long-term crops?

If you have only limited growing space, short-term crops of beetroot, carrots, early potatoes, and turnips are helpful in allowing at least two crops per year to be obtained from the same piece of land. Clearing crops quickly in this way also reduces the likelihood of pests and diseases building up in the area. Harvest crops as soon as they are ready, to enjoy them at their best and to avoid any deterioration through splitting and development of pests and diseases.

Long-term crops such as parsnips and maincrop potatoes are suitable where space is not at a premium, but in order to ensure good quality they must not be subjected to a check in growth through lack of water. You should also be vigilant for signs of pests or disease and take appropriate action as soon as possible (*see also* Plant Problems, *pp. 246–264*).

## Sowing

Root vegetables are grown from seed, with the exception of potatoes, which may be grown from tubers (*see below*). Root crops are best sown direct in the garden where they are to crop to minimize disturbance to their edible roots, but multiblock sowing (*see p. 65*) is also possible. It is essential to produce a fine tilth (*see p. 66*) and a good depth of soil in the seedbed so that the roots can penetrate unhindered. Improve heavy soils by digging in plenty of well-rotted organic matter. Some root crops prefer soil that has not been freshly dug (*see individual crops, pp. 85–88*).

In most cases, sowing is carried out from early spring (*see individual crops, pp. 85–88*). Large seeds, such as those of parsnips, can be station sown (*see p. 68*). Small seeds, such as those of carrots and turnips, should be sown thinly in single drills (*see p. 66*) and thinned at the seedling stage (*see p. 68*). Turnips and beetroot may be sown in successive batches (*see p. 69*). Parsnips are suitable for intersowing with fast-maturing salad crops such as radishes (*see p. 69*).

## Planting tubers

Potatoes are normally raised by planting out small sprouted or "chitted" tubers referred to as seed potatoes (*see box*) direct in the ground. True potato seeds are unreliable, less convenient, and unsuitable for garden use.

Seed potatoes are usually planted in a

## Chitting seed potatoes

Seed potatoes are small tubers grown in areas of low virus infection, often obtained by mail order. "Chitting", or sprouting, aids early growth. As soon as tubers are obtained, place them upright in trays, with the most eyes or dormant sprouts – at the "rose" end – uppermost, in a cool, dry, light place. They will send out healthy, short, green shoots or chits (*see below, right*), ideally 12mm (½in) long. Kept in a warm, dark place, chits will be pale, weak, and become too long (*see below, left*).

*Weak, pale chits*     *Strong, dark chits*

deep drill or individual planting holes and earthed up as they grow.

## No-dig potatoes

Seed potatoes can also be planted in a no-dig bed where they are covered with layers of straw and manure or compost. Make sure the straw is deep and that the manure is not fresh or the heat from decomposition will "cook" the potatoes. A capping layer of compost or sawdust may be needed to exclude light from the developing tubers. Water and fertilize as required. No-dig potatoes are clean at harvest and need little washing (*see p. 84*).

## Growing root crops in containers

Where garden space is limited or there are persistent problems with pests or diseases, container growing is an alternative method of cultivating early beetroot, carrots, potatoes, and turnips.

Pots should be at least 25cm (10in) deep and wide, filled with a mixture of rotted compost or manure and good garden soil. Tubs and windowboxes are other options. Always keep containers well watered.

## Protecting against pests and diseases

Despite adhering to good management practices such as maintaining soil

## Planting seed potatoes in a drill

1 **Draw out a drill** 8–15cm (3–6in) deep – sufficient to cover the chits with at least 2.5cm (1in) of soil. Press a tuber with chits uppermost into the soil every 30–38cm (12–15in) along the drill.

2 **Push or pull the soil** back gently over the tubers with the back of a rake. Lightly rake over the soil surface to level it, and mark the drill. Fertilizer can be added along the drill before planting (*see p. 87*).

fertility and crop rotation mentioned above, infestations of pests and diseases occur in root crops from time to time. Pests include the sap-sucking insects whitefly, thrips, and aphids that can spread virus diseases, and root damage can occur through infestations of weevils and nematodes cause deformed roots. Rotten patches on the roots are caused by bacterial soft rots (*see p.251*).

Potatoes are susceptible to potato common scab (*see p.260*), particularly in alkaline soil or soil that has been recently limed or had wood ashes added. Scab causes rough patches on the skin of the tubers. Potato moth larvae also reduce potato quality and infestations result in tunnelling and rotting of tubers. However, the most serious cause of rotten tubers is a fungal disease called potato blight. This causes spots on the leaves in the early stages and, if left untreated, the disease will spread to the tubers. Spores of potato blight are washed down onto the soil from the leaves and if leaf spotting is evident, the growing plants should immediately be sprayed with a copper-based fungicide. If symptoms continue repeat sprays will be necessary. Blight is more common in damp conditions and where there is overhead watering. Chances of infestation are reduced when the seed potatoes are certified disease-free and when potatoes are grown in new ground.

## Planting potatoes in a no-dig bed

1 **Place the seed** potatoes on the soil with a deep layer of straw and manure. Repeat the layers and as the plants grow add more manure or fertilizer and cover with sawdust or compost to exclude the light.

2 **Varieties of potato** vary in size, shape, colour and flavour. Some have white flesh and some have yellow flesh. All taste best fresh from the garden.

Companion planting – planting possibly beneficial plant combinations – may be successful in deterring root crop pests. Remove any infested crops as soon as possible off site. Storing or composting infested crops will assist in maintaining the life cycle of the pest so it can return the following year.

### Harvesting and storing

Where pests are a problem, harvest carrots and parsnips as soon as they are ready. Where root crops are free from pests and diseases and the soil is well drained, carrots and parsnips can be left in the garden and harvested as required. So too can beetroot, swede, and turnips. In temperate regions, these crops are sown in spring, roots grow through summer and harvest begins in late summer and continues through autumn and winter, until the plants go up to seed in spring. Lift potatoes by early or mid-autumn; the later you leave them the greater the possible damage from slugs and rot. Leave to dry outside for 2–3 hours before storing. Potatoes can be left in the ground where conditions permit. Check regularly to ensure tubers are not rotting or greening. Lift scorzonera and salsify as needed, and use fresh. Sweet potatoes will need to be cured (*see p.88*). Most root crops are suitable for storing (*see p.73*). Store only undamaged roots or tubers, which are least prone to rot.

## Practising crop rotation reduces pests and diseases

It is essential to rotate root crops with other types of vegetables (*see p.31*). Root crops include vegetables such as carrots, parsnips, beetroot, and potatoes (*right*) and also swedes, sweet potatoes, and turnips. Practising crop rotation reduces the build-up of pathogens in the soil and breaks the life cycle of pests. Thus the cycle is broken because there is no root crop host for that period. Crop rotation can be managed easily when crops are grown in separate beds (*far right*) and rotated from one bed to another.

# A–Z of root crops

## Beetroot

*Beta vulgaris* subsp. *vulgaris*

| Season | Spring | Summer | Autumn | Winter |
|---|---|---|---|---|
| Sow | • • • • • | | | |
| Harvest | | • • • • | • • • | • |

Beetroot is easy to grow and the swollen roots can be harvested from early summer onwards. It can be stored or pickled for use in salads or steamed as a sweet vegetable. It may be round, long, or oval in shape and comes in a range of outer colours, from purple or deep red to yellow or white. The inner flesh may be purple, red, yellow, white, or even red with white rings. All the colour forms are similar in flavour. Most beetroot types are short-term crops, suitable for catch cropping (*see p.69*), and they are easier to cook and are sweeter-tasting when harvested young; long-rooted types hold in the ground longer and are well-flavoured. The young leaves may be eaten like spinach or in salads.

Beetroot may also be grown in containers (*see p.83*). Early sowings may be prone to bolt and run to seed, but resistant cultivars are usually available. Mature beetroot normally yields 30 roots, each weighing 450g–1kg (1–2lb), per 3m (10ft) row.

**Site and soil** Beetroot needs an open, sunny site, with fertile, light, sandy soil, preferably one that has been manured in the previous season. Long-rooted cultivars need a good depth of soil. A pH of 6.5–7 is ideal.

**Sowing** Make successional sowings direct in the garden bed (*see p.69*) every few weeks in spring and summer. Space seeds 5cm (2in) apart, then thin the seedlings for standard-sized beets. Leave unthinned for pickling beets about 5cm (2in) in diameter. Beetroot seed looks like a woody crumb and it is actually a cluster of two or more seeds. Each cluster therefore produces more than one seedling.

| Sowing depth | 2.5cm (1in) |
|---|---|
| Plant spacing | Standard: 10cm (4in) |
| | Pickling: 5cm (2in) |
| Row spacing | Standard: 23–30cm (9–12in) |
| | Pickling: 15cm (6in) |

**Routine care** Keep the soil moist, and when the roots start to swell after about 8–9 weeks give the plants a good watering. In a dry spell, use 11 litres per sq m (2 gallons per sq yd) at intervals of 1–2 weeks. Too frequent or light watering leads to a lot of leafy growth and no roots. Light, sandy soils of high pH may be low in manganese and possibly boron (*see p.17*), so spray once or twice with a foliar, seaweed-based fertilizer (*see p.22*) that has a range of trace elements.

**Harvesting and storing** Start harvesting roots once they are about 5cm (2in) in diameter; spring sowings will be ready in summer and summer ones in autumn. Lift the beets as they are needed; this thins out the crop, leaving other roots to achieve a larger size. Harvest by pulling up the beets and twisting off their tops about 2.5cm (1in) above the root. Roots can be overwintered *in situ*.

**Common problems** Cutworm (*see p.254*), damping off (*p.254*), and fungal leaf spot (*p.257*) may all be troublesome, as well as occasional deficiencies of boron (*p.252*) and manganese (*see p.257*).

**Recommended cultivars**
'Bulls Blood' – an American heirloom variety with red leaves and striped roots.
'Chioggia' – globes display colourful pink and white stripes when cut in half.
'Cylindrica' – long, tender, cylindrical roots of sweet flavour; holds well in the ground.
'Derwent Globe' – old variety with good flavour.
'Detroit Dark Red' – deep red globular roots.
'Early Wonder' – flattened globes and tall tender leaves.
'Golden Beet' – tender leaves and decorative golden orange roots.
'Kestrel' – vigorous hybrid and early maturer.
'Melbourne Early Slowbolt' – also called 'Boltardy'; uniform red roots; good picked early as mini beet.
'Mini Gourmet' – small and sweet and delicious served whole.
'White' – stain-free white globes and tender leaves.

## Carrot

*Daucus carota*

| Season | Spring | Summer | Autumn | Winter |
|---|---|---|---|---|
| Sow | • • • • • | | | |
| Transplant | | | | |
| Harvest | • • | | • • • | • • • • |

Carrots are classified according to shape, maturity, and size, although root shape and also colour are influenced by soil type and growing conditions.

The earliest crops are obtained with Amsterdam-type cultivars: narrow, cylindrical, stump-ended roots with smooth skins and of small size. Nantes types are of similar shape, but broader and longer. Chantenay cultivars are short, broad, and more conical, and are suitable for summer and autumn harvest. Berlicum types produce long, large roots; the long-season, tapering Autumn King types produce the longest roots of all.

These types have been used as parents to breed new F1 hybrid cultivars with mixed characteristics and of high quality. Small, round-rooted, "baby" cultivars are also available and are suitable for container raising where garden space is restricted. Short-rooted varieties are the best varieties to grow in heavy or shallow soils.

**Site and soil** The preferred pH range is 6.5–7.5. Carrots do best on light soils, and a relatively dry site produces a sweeter flavour; heavy soils can carry satisfactory crops if they are not waterlogged or compacted. All benefit from well-rotted organic matter incorporated in the previous season. A low-nitrogen base dressing should be added. Prepare a fine tilth several weeks in advance and destroy any germinated weeds just before sowing.

**Sowing** Carrots are often difficult to grow because the seed dries out quickly in the shallow drill. To avoid drying be sure to water the soil before sowing and sow at a time when the weather is not hot. For best germination, use fresh seed and sow in spring. Sprinkle seed thinly along the shallow drill and cover with soil. The newly sown seed can be covered with damp hessian or a wooden board to reduce soil drying. This is removed as soon as the seed germinates. Thin seedlings to a spacing of 4cm (2in), nipping the stems to prevent root disturbance.

By sowing different varieties of carrot that mature at different rates, in temperate regions it is possible to harvest fresh roots from summer through to late winter. Carrots stay in good condition in the ground in well-drained soil.

Early summer harvest can be obtained by sowing in early spring or mid-spring to midsummer. Round, Amsterdam, and Nantes types are all suitable for early sowings. Successional sowings in mid- and late spring of Chantenay and Berlicum types crop from late summer.

| Sowing depth | 1–2cm (½–¾in) |
|---|---|
| Seed spacing | sow thinly; thin to 10cm (4in) |
| Row spacing | 30cm (12in) in open garden |
| | 15cm (6in) under cover |

**Routine care** Keep weed-free by hand weeding until the leaf canopy suppresses any competition. Water in dry spells, but do not overwater carrots because this encourages leaf growth. Supplementary feeding should not be necessary on well-prepared sites.

**Harvesting and storing** Pull the first roots when 12–15mm (½–⅝in) thick, remembering that the roots will grow continuously as the seasonal temperature rises. On heavier soils, it is necessary to ease roots out of the ground with a fork. In cool gardens where the soil is well-drained, carrots can be left in the ground and harvested as required in summer, autumn and winter. By mid-spring, the plants go to seed and the carrots become woody and inedible. Alternatively, roots can be harvested and stored (_see p.73_).

**Common problems** Aphids can be troublesome. Downy and powdery mildews (_see p.255 and p.260_) and bacterial soft rot (_see p.251_) can cause problems.

**Recommended cultivars**
'All Seasons' – Virus-resistant with long roots;

suits a range of climates.
'Amsterdam Forcing' – baby carrot harvested at finger-size.
'Chantenay Long' – long, smooth roots; can be harvested early as baby carrot.
'Chantenay Red Cored' – short, tapered roots.
'Collosus' – very large, long roots.
'Flame Hybrid – Nantes type; sweet, tender, colourful root with small core; suits a range of climates.
'French Round' – almost globular roots. Ideal for shallow soils.
'Kuroda' – Chantenay type popular in Japan; deep orange-red in colour.
'Lady Finger' – short finger-sized roots; rich colour and sweet flavour.
'Manchester Table' – Nantes type with sweet flavour and crisp texture.
'Thumbelina' – almost globular, stubby roots; ideal for shallow soil.
'Tip Top' – Nantes type with sweet flavour and crisp texture.
'Western Red' – old variety with very long roots.
'Yellowstone' – hybrid carrot with yellow roots.

# Hamburg parsley

_Petroselinum crispum_ var. _tuberosum_

| Season | Spring | Summer | Autumn | Winter |
|---|---|---|---|---|
| Sow | • • • | | | |
| Harvest | • | | • • • | • • • |

Hamburg parsley has roots similar in taste and appearance to parsnips, although smaller. The plant has parsley-like leaves that remain green through winter, and can be used instead of the more tender herb parsley (_see p.144_). Root yield is 3kg per 3m (6½lb per 10ft) row.

**Site and soil** As for parsnip (_see below_).

**Sowing** Sow thinly in rows and thin seedlings when they have two true leaves.

| Sowing depth | 2cm (¾in) |
|---|---|
| Seed spacing | thin to 15–20cm (6–8in) |
| Row spacing | 30cm (12in) |

**Routine care** As for parsnip (_see below_).

**Harvesting and storing** As for parsnip (_see below_). Pick the leaves as required.

**Common problems** As for parsnip (_see below_).

**Recommended cultivar**
'Hamburg Turnip Rooted' – strong flavour.

# Parsnip

_Pastinaca sativa_

| Season | Spring | Summer | Autumn | Winter |
|---|---|---|---|---|
| Sow | • • • | | | |
| Harvest | • • | | • • • | • • • |

This long-term root crop is valuable for its hardiness and distinct flavour. All types taste similar; the quicker the growth, the sweeter

the taste. The roots can be 13–25cm (5–10in) long, and of various shapes – some long and narrow, some bulbous – depending on cultivar as well as soil and conditions. In shallow soils, a cultivar with a shorter root is best. Parsnips yield about 4kg per 3m (9lb per 10ft) row.

**Site and soil** For best results, parsnips need an open, sunny site, and a deep, light, sandy soil, although good crops can be obtained from heavy soils. The ideal pH is 6.5. Parsnips have a low nitrogen requirement.

**Sowing** Seed sown direct in mid- to late spring is more likely to germinate than seed sown earlier. Germination is slow.

Sow thinly or station sow with 2–4 seeds per station (_see p.68_). Use 10–15cm (4–6in) spacing for medium-sized roots up to 5cm (2in) in diameter and a wider spacing for later, stored roots. Parsnips can be intersown (_see p.69_) with radishes to mark the rows.

| Sowing depth | 2cm (¾in) |
|---|---|
| Seed spacing | Medium: 10–14cm (4–6in) |
| | Large: 20cm (8in) |
| Row spacing | 30cm (12in) |

**Routine care** Control weeds. Water only in very dry conditions, at a rate of 11 litres per sq m (2 gallons per 10sq ft) every 1–2 weeks. If left too dry, the roots are liable to split after watering. Most late-sown seeds need more regular watering to aid germination. Feeding is not usually needed, but if growth is poor, apply a liquid feed according to manufacturer's instructions.

**Harvesting and storing** Parsnips are ready for lifting from late summer but may be left in the soil until needed, although there may be a risk of carrot fly (_see p.84_). Alternatively, lift and store in sand in boxes (_see p.73_).

**Common problems** Parsnip canker (_see p.259_) can be a major problem if resistant cultivars are not used. Downy mildew (_see p.255_) can be serious in dry weather as well as powdery mildew in damp conditions (_see p.260_).

**Recommended cultivars**
'Champion Hollow Crown' – long, smooth roots.
'Cobram' – wedge-shaped with good flavour.
'Melbourne Whiteskin' – large, wedge-shaped roots.

# Potato

_Solanum tuberosum_

| Season | Spring | Summer | Autumn | Winter |
|---|---|---|---|---|
| Plant | • • • | | | |
| Harvest | | • • • • • | • | |

The potato is a staple vegetable that stores well in cool climates and may be eaten all year round. Tubers vary in size, colour, texture, and taste. Early-harvested potatoes, often referred to as new potatoes, are small and are cooked whole for hot dishes and salads. Late-harvested potatoes are large tubers that can be cooked in many ways.

Plants can be raised in containers (*see p.83*). To thrive, potatoes need to grow where they are unchecked by frost or lack of moisture; excess wet early in the season can produce leaf growth at the expense of tubers. It can also cause potato blight.

Potatoes are most conveniently grown from seed potatoes that are sprouted, or chitted (*see p.83*) before planting; use seed tubers raised in isolation and certified free of virus diseases. Some suppliers offer pre-chitted seed tubers but avoid old, soft tubers.

Potatoes normally yield around 10kg per 3m (22lb per 10ft) row; container crops yield much less.

**Site and soil**  Potatoes prefer an open site, which must not be a frost pocket (*see p.11*), and deep, fertile soil with a pH of 5–6. Rotate crops (*see p.31*) and incorporate plenty of organic matter such as well-rotted manure before planting. Apply a general fertilizer (*see pp.20–23*), either on the soil surface and worked into the soil shortly before planting, or spread along the sides of prepared drills at the time of planting.

**Planting**  There are two methods of planting seed tubers in the garden, either in a drill (*see p.83*) or in individual holes. Potatoes that are planted in a no-dig bed (*see pp.83–84*) are placed on the prepared soil or layer of straw and are covered with deep straw and manure and compost. The covering must be thick to provide growing space for tubers and exclude light to prevent greening.

To grow potatoes in a container (*see p.83*), rest two chitted tubers on 10–13cm (4–5in) of soil or compost in a large pot or tub that is least 30cm (12in) deep. Cover the tubers with 10cm (4in) of soil or compost, water in, and stand the container in a light, sheltered spot.

| Planting depth | 8–15cm (3–6in) |
|---|---|
| Seed potato spacing | 30–38cm (12–15in) |
| Row spacing | 38–50cm (15–20in) |

Potatoes are best grown in temperate gardens in fertile, well-drained soil. They are seldom successful in tropical gardens because the tubers rot due to the high humidity. Some tropical gardeners have had success by planting the tubers in a container or a raised garden bed in autumn. Potato tubers are planted in spring in temperate gardens after the frosts are past.

**Routine care**  Protect early crops from frost (*see pp.82–83*). If the skins of the newly formed tubers are exposed to light when they are pushed to the surface, they will become green and poisonous, and should not be eaten. To prevent this happening, plantings should be earthed up, by drawing soil around the stems with a draw hoe or spade. This is best done when the stems are about 23cm (9in) tall; draw the soil up to about 10cm (4in) so as to leave sufficient foliage for good growth. To make earthing up easier, fork the soil between the rows beforehand. It will be necessary to earth up in two stages, especially for small, early plants that have been protected against frost.

For plants in containers, add a 10cm (4in) layer of soil or compost when the stems are 15cm (6in) tall. Repeat until the plants have grown to 5cm (2in) of the top of the pot.

Keep growing plants moist by giving them a good soaking of 16–22 litres per sq m (3–4 gallons per 10sq ft) every 10–14 days in dry spells. To get the best yield, water at the same rate only when the tubers are starting to swell, and are around the size of marbles; this usually coincides with flowering, but not all cultivars flower.

Do not water mature potatoes after the tubers reach full size or they may rot. Apply a top-dressing of a nitrogenous fertilizer (*see pp.20–23*) when earthing up. In late summer, or earlier if signs of potato blight (*see p.260*) appear, cut down the dying top-growth to 5cm (2in) above soil level. This should be done around two weeks before harvest to help "set" the skins for better storing quality.

**Harvesting and storing**  Lift "new" potatoes carefully with a fork as soon as they are ready, often indicated by the plant flowering. Check that tubers are ready by pulling aside the soil.

As long as they are healthy, leave plants until late summer or autumn to bulk up, but remember that the longer the tubers are left in the ground, the more prone they are to grub or rot damage. Lift on a dry day, and leave the tubers on the ground for 2–3 hours. Store in boxes, paper sacks, or hessian bags. When the area has been cleared, fork it over to ensure all small tubers have been removed, as these can carry disease into the next year.

**Common problems**  Pests that may cause damage are cutworm (*see p.254*), slugs (*see p.262*) and potato moth (*see p.260*). Frost can damage crops (*see p.255*). Potato blight (*see p.260*) thrives in warm, humid conditions. Other common diseases are potato common scab (*see p.260*), bacterial soft rot (*see p.251*) and potato viruses (*see p.260*).

**Recommended cultivars**
'Desiree' – waxy, yellow flesh; smooth, pink skin; good keeper.
'Kennebec' – smooth, white skin and white flesh; good keeper.
'King Edward' – pear-shaped with cream flesh.
'Kipfler' – small, stubby tubers with yellow flesh; excellent salad potato.
'Nicola' – small, oval tubers with buttery yellow flesh and skin.
'Pink Eye' – waxy, cream flesh with purple blush on the skin.
'Pontiac' – large, round tuber with pink skin and white flesh.
'Sebago' – white skin and white flesh; popular all-rounder.
'Sequoia' – cream skin and white flesh; vigorous, adaptable grower.
'Toolangi Delight' – purple skin and white flesh; versatile in cooking.

# Salsify

*Tragopogon porrifolius*

| Season | Spring | Summer | Autumn | Winter |
|---|---|---|---|---|
| Sow | • • • | | | |
| Harvest | • | | • • | • • • |

Salsify is an unusual root vegetable similar to scorzonera. It is a hardy biennial with long, thin, creamy white roots that are used as a winter vegetable. It is sometimes called the oyster plant, because of its taste. It is usually grown as an annual, but crops can be overwintered in order to produce the edible young shoots, known as chards, and edible flower buds. Salsify is a long-term crop, taking six months to mature, and the roots should be eaten fresh or they may shrivel. Salsify normally yields about 1.5kg (3lb) of roots per 3m (10ft) row.

**Site and soil**  A cool climate in an open, sunny site with deep, light, stone-free soil, that has been manured for a previous crop, is best. The preferred soil pH is 6.8.

**Sowing**  Seed quickly deteriorates; sow fresh seed thinly in drills (*see p.66*) in spring. Thin once seedlings have two true leaves (*see p.68*).

| Sowing depth | 1cm (½in) |
|---|---|
| Seed spacing | sow thinly; thin to 10cm (4in) |
| Row spacing | 15–30cm (6–12in) |

**Routine care**  Control weeds, and water in dry spells at a rate of 16–22 litres per sq m (3–5 gallons per 10sq ft). Supplementary feeding is unnecessary. If chards and flower buds are required, cut off the old leaves to 2.5cm (1in) above ground level in autumn and earth up the roots with 13cm (5in) of soil. Alternatively, when growth starts in spring, cover the tops of the leaves with a 13cm (5in) layer of straw or bracken.

**Harvesting and storing**  Roots may be left in the ground all winter; lift them carefully when needed, from mid-autumn to early spring, and use at once to avoid shrivelling. Cut chards in early spring when 15cm (6in) tall. Pick flower buds in early spring before they open, along with 10cm (4in) of stem.

**Common problems**  There are no problems.
**Recommended cultivars**
'Improved Mammoth' – thick, creamy white roots.
'Mammoth Sandwich Island' – long, tapered root.

# Scorzonera

*Scorzonera hispanica*

| Season | Spring | Summer | Autumn | Winter |
|---|---|---|---|---|
| Sow | • • • | | | |
| Harvest | • | | • • | • • |

Scorzonera, or black salsify, is an unusual root vegetable and is similar to salsify but is perennial and has broader leaves and black-skinned roots. These are 20cm (8in) long or more, and have an unusual flavour. To prevent bleeding, wash them just before boiling them in salted water. Young shoots and flower buds are also edible. Scorzonera may repel carrot flies, and can be planted near susceptible crops. It yields about 1.5kg per 3m (3lb per 10ft) row.

**Site and soil**  As for salsify (*see p.87*).

**Sowing**  As for salsify (*see p.87*), and also in late summer to grow on for a second season and harvest in the following autumn.

| Sowing depth | 1cm (½in) |
|---|---|
| Seed spacing | sow thinly; thin to 10cm (4in) |
| Row spacing | 15–30cm (6–12in) |

**Routine care**  Control weeds, but do not disturb the roots or they may fork. Treat young shoots and flower buds as for salsify.

**Harvesting**  Take utmost care when lifting roots, as they are prone to bleed. If growth is poor in the first year, leave plants for another year for bigger roots. Harvest young shoots and flower buds as for salsify.

**Common problems**  As for salsify (*see p.87*).

# Swede

## *Brassica napus* Napobrassica Group

| Season | Spring | Summer | Autumn | Winter |
|---|---|---|---|---|
| Sow | • • • | | | |
| Harvest | | | • • • • | • |

Swede is a winter root crop, belonging to the brassica family (*see pp.76–81*), with similar cultivation needs. A long-season crop, it takes 20–26 weeks to mature, and is not easy to grow. The flesh is normally yellow, but skin colour varies from purple to green. The roots range in shape from thin and narrow to the more popular bulbous, influenced by seed quality; newer cultivars are more reliable. The sweet-tasting roots are cooked as a winter vegetable. Swedes yield 6kg per 3m (13lb per 10ft) row, depending on the stage of cutting.

**Site and soil**  Swedes do best in cool climates on an open, sunny site, with light, fertile soil, low in nitrogen, with a pH of at least 6.8, that suffers neither from drought nor waterlogging and has been manured for a previous crop.

**Sowing**  Sow direct in drills (*see p.66*) in late spring and thin (*see p.68*).

| Sowing depth | 2cm (¾in) |
|---|---|
| Seed spacing | sow thinly; thin to 23cm (9in) |
| Row spacing | 38cm (15in) |

**Routine care**  Keep well watered and free of weeds and pests.

**Harvesting and storing**  When roots are 10–15cm (4–6in) in diameter, in autumn to early winter, lift carefully and store (*see p.73*).

**Common problems**  Mealy cabbage aphid (*p.257*) and cabbage white butterfly (*see p.253*) attack seedlings. Swedes are prone to clubroot (*p.254*), boron deficiency (*see*

*p.252*), downy and powdery mildews (*p.254, p.260*).

**Recommended cultivars**
'Champion Purple Top' – purple-topped, white root with yellow flesh.
'Hunters Butter' – white skin and white flesh.
'Laurentian' – rosy-pink flushed top of roots, with fine flavour.

# Sweet potato

## *Ipomoea batatas*

| Season | Spring | Summer | Autumn | Winter |
|---|---|---|---|---|
| Sow/plant | • • | | | |
| Transplant | | • • | | |
| Harvest | | | • | |

The sweet potato is a frost-tender perennial grown as an annual for its sweet-tasting tubers, which are eaten cooked. The leaves may also be eaten like spinach. In cooler regions, grow sweet potatoes in a greenhouse. Sweet potatoes thrive in tropical gardens, spreading far and wide like a weed. However, they make a welcome substitute for potatoes in the tropics and can be harvested as required. They normally yield 1.5kg per 3m (3lb per 10ft) row.

**Site and soil**  Sweet potatoes require highly fertile, sandy soil with a high nitrogen level and a pH of 5.5–6.5. They must be grown in temperatures of 24–28°C (75–82°F) and prefer high humidity.

**Sowing and planting**  In temperate gardens, tubers are stored over winter and in early summer they are placed in a box and covered with sand and allowed to shoot. When the shoots are about 150mm (6in) high, the shoots are pulled off and planted 30cm (1ft) apart in a raised bed. Orange-fleshed varieties mature earlier than white-fleshed varieties.

| Sowing depth | 2.5cm (1in) |
|---|---|
| Planting depth | 5–8cm (2–3in) in ridge |
| Plant spacing | 25–30cm (10–12in) |
| Row/ridge spacing | 75cm (30in) |

**Routine care**  Keep well watered; feed with a general-purpose fertilizer (*see pp.20–21*) every 2–3 weeks until tubers have formed.

**Harvesting and storing**  Carefully lift tubers and cure in sun for 4–7 days. Store at 10–15°C (50–59°F). Pick leaves as required.

**Recommended cultivars**
'Abundance' – purplish skin and white flesh.
'Beerwah Gold' – orange flesh.
'Centennial' – orange flesh.
'Resisto' – orange flesh.
'White Maltese' – white flesh.

**Common problems**  Aphids (*see p.251*), whitefly (*see p.264*), and red spider mite (*see p.261*) may be troublesome. Sweet potato weevil is a serious problem in tropical gardens, turning the tubers to mush.

# Turnip, turnip tops

## *Brassica campestris* Rapifera Group

| Season | Spring | Summer | Autumn | Winter |
|---|---|---|---|---|
| TURNIP | | | | |
| Sow | • • • • | | | • |
| Harvest | | | • • • | • • • • • |
| TURNIP TOPS | | | | |
| Sow | • | | • • | |
| Harvest | • | | | • • • |

Turnips belong to the brassica family (*see pp.76–81*). They are biennials, usually grown as annuals. The roots may be flat, round, or long; the flesh is white or yellow. They are best eaten fresh and young but can be stored as a winter vegetable. Turnips take 6–10 weeks to mature, and may be intercropped (*see p.71*). They normally yield ten 500–750g (1–1½lb) roots per 3m (10ft) row. The young leaves, or turnip tops, can be used as spring greens, and make a good catch crop (*see p.69*).

**Site and soil**  Cool, moist conditions are preferred, with a soil high in nitrogen and a pH of at least 6.8. Turnips need plenty of organic matter worked into the soil.

**Sowing**  Sow thinly in succession (*see p.69*) every 2–3 weeks from late winter and thin (*see p.68*) seedlings. Protect very early sowings (*see pp.82–83*). Late-spring or summer sowings may not germinate in very hot, dry weather, unless the seedbed is moist and shaded. For turnip tops, sow as for turnips in late summer, early autumn, or early spring.

| Sowing depth | 2cm (¾in) |
|---|---|
| Seed spacing | thin to 10–15cm (4–6in) |
| Row spacing | roots: 23–30cm (9–12in) |
| | tops: 15cm (6in) |

**Routine care**  Control weeds and keep well watered. In dry periods, water weekly at a rate of 11 litres per sq m (2 gallons per 10sq ft). Supplementary feeding is not necessary.

**Harvesting**  Pull early roots when 4–5cm (1½–2in) in diameter and use fresh. Later crops may be pulled until early winter and stored in boxes. When turnip tops are 13–15cm (5–6in) tall, cut them 2.5cm (1in) above ground level. If kept moist, further cuttings will be possible but the leaves will be tough if allowed to mature.

**Common problems**  Cabbage white butterfly (*see p.253*), cutworm (*p.254*), mealy cabbage aphid (*p.257*), downy and powdery mildews (*p.255, p.260*) may occur.

**Recommended cultivars**
'Laurentian' – rosy-purple on the top of the root and excellent flavour.
'Presto' – small, white, quick-growing turnip.
'Purple Top' – old favourite with tasty flesh.
'Scarlet Queen' – hybrid with red skin and mild flavour.
'Tokyo Cross' – hybrid with tender crunchy white roots.

# Growing the onion family

The onion family includes all edible crops within the genus *Allium* – ranging from bulb onions through garlic and shallots to leeks. Spring onions are harvested for use when the bulbs are very small and the white stems and leaves are still tender. Welsh onions are evergreen perennials grown for their leaves, which may be eaten in salads. Japanese bunching onions are a type of Welsh onion. Most alliums have similar cultivation requirements, and with careful choice of cultivars and sowing times you can harvest them almost all year round. Some onions may also be lifted and stored for winter use. Bulb onions may be raised either from seed or by planting "sets", which are tiny bulbs, with good food reserves, that have been specially produced. Leeks need different treatment (*see p.93*) from other alliums, because they are grown for their blanched stem-like shanks.

**Seed or sets?**
*In this bed, shallots have been grown in two ways – from seed and using sets, or bulbs. The seeds* (main picture) *have germinated well and have produced a good crop of large shallots. The sets* (inset) *have produced a healthy, but slightly smaller crop in a much shorter time.*

## Site and soil

Members of the onion family need an open site in order to avoid the high humidity that can encourage diseases. While quick-growing salad onions and shallots grow well in tropical gardens, slow-growing bulb onions rot in damp conditions. The soil must be fertile and well-drained, especially for early sowings and overwintered crops. Onions will not tolerate soil acidity, and lime dressing should be done where the pH level is below 6.5 (*see pp.18–19*). To prevent build-up of soil pests or diseases, rotate onions around the garden on at least a three-year cycle (*see p.31*). The ground should be dug in advance, incorporating plenty of well-rotted organic matter; do not sow on freshly manured ground because the plants are likely to grow too "soft" and will be more susceptible to disease. Alliums generally have low nitrogen requirements, but there are exceptions (*see individual crops, pp.92–94*). Top-dress overwintered onions in spring.

## Why use sets?

There are advantages and disadvantages to raising onions from sets, or bulbs. Sets are invariably more expensive than seed and only a limited range of cultivars is available. Some varieties of brown onion are available as sets but the usual method of growing brown, white, and salad onions is from seed. Shallots are available as both seed and sets. Multiplying onions, such as tree onions and potato onions and garlic, are grown by planting bulbs. These are available commercially or can be saved from the previous crop. It is usually much easier to buy sets and plant them out than to grow from seed (*see above*), and many gardeners choose from among available sets in order to get good-sized mature onions in a shorter time. Sets are less prone to disease, easier to manage, and earlier to mature. They will tolerate poorer soils.

Plants grown from sets are more likely to bolt (produce a flower stem early and go to seed prematurely). This results in small, poor-quality crops. To reduce the risk of bolting, choose smaller or heat-treated sets. The latter have been stored at a high temperature for a few months, which kills the embryos that form flower stems.

## Sowing seed

Seed of brown, red, and white bulb onions can be sown directly in seed drills only when the soil temperature starts to rise and it begins to dry (*see p.66*); if the soil is too cold or damp, germination will be slow and poor. Sow from late autumn to early spring in cool climates, depending on the crop (*see individual crops, pp.92–94*). When the seedlings are big enough, thin according to the desired size of the final bulb (*see left*).

Successional sowings (*see p.69*) about every two weeks are required for salad onions such as spring onions, which mature in about ten weeks. They will only stand for a couple of weeks. Wet weather increases their susceptibility to downy mildew (*see p.91*).

**Thinning onions**
*Seedlings in drills should be thinned according to the desired size of bulb – the closer the spacing the smaller the bulb. These were thinned to 10cm (4in), 5cm (2in), and 2.5cm (1in), respectively.*

## Planting

For commercial seedlings and seedlings raised in a propagator or in an outdoor seedbed, and for sets, planting should be carried out from late winter to mid-spring. For heat-treated sets, you should wait until mid-spring. Before planting, decide on the final size of onion bulbs you want. All sizes are equally good in cooking and salads, although small onions ripen better and generally last longer when lifted. Plant in rows 25–30cm (10–12in) apart.

To produce a high yield of small onions, plant 2.5cm (1in) apart; for medium-sized bulbs plant 5cm (2in) apart; and for larger bulbs space 10cm (4in) apart. For very big onions, plant 15cm (6in) apart in 30cm (12in) rows. Wide spacing allows good air movement, which reduces the likelihood of mildew (*see p.91*). To grow a good crop of multiblock onions (*see p.65*), plant the clusters 30cm (12in) apart each way.

Use a trowel when transplanting seed-raised seedlings (*see pp.70–71*) into their final positions in well-prepared ground. For planting sets, rake the soil (*see p.40*) so that it is loose enough to push the sets into shallow drills without compacting the ground beneath the set. The roots, when they emerge, should be able to penetrate the soil and not push the set out of the ground.

If a good tilth is made, the sets can be pushed into the soil without effort. After placing each set, cover it with soil and lightly firm the soil around it, leaving just the tip exposed (*see above*). If sets are planted any shallower than this, birds may take a dustbath in the

### Planting sets

1 **When soil conditions** are workable, lightly press each of the sets into the bottom of a shallow drill. Space about 10cm (4in) apart, or less if you require smaller bulbs (*see p.89*).

2 **Using your fingers,** gently bring the soil up around the sets and firm it so that the tips can still be seen. Remove any dead leaves or stems. Watering the sets is only necessary if the soil is very dry when you are planting.

area and pull them out of the ground. Garlic cloves need experience of cold to develop and are planted directly into soil. Where soil is heavy and wet, plant the cloves in module trays (*see below*) in autumn, and place in a sheltered spot outdoors over winter. In this way they experience low temperatures but are not at risk of becoming waterlogged.

### Planting leeks

Leeks differ from onions in that the white stem, or shank, at the base of the leaves is eaten. Although they are sown initially as other seed, in seedbeds or under cover, leeks are transplanted in a different way from other alliums (for sowing methods and transplanting times, *see p.93*). Each seedling is planted quite deeply in a narrow hole, which produces a long, blanched stem without having to earth up the plant. If the seedlings have been raised in a seedbed,

carefully lift and separate them after 8–10 weeks, when they are about 20cm (8in) tall (*see facing page*). Discard any diseased or damaged plants. Collect a group of similar size together, lay the bundle on the soil, and cut the roots back to about 2.5cm (1in) in length.

The leaves should be 15–20cm (6–8in) long; if they are longer, trim the tops to this length. Some gardeners argue that trimming leeks reduces yield, but if they are planted untrimmed it is more difficult to get the plants into the bottom of the holes.

If the seedlings have been raised in modules, gently push out the rootballs from below to remove them. Make a row of holes 15cm (6in) deep and 15cm (6in) apart with a dibber (*see facing page*). Drop one plant into each hole, making sure it sits on the bottom. Water in along the row using a fine-rosed can; fill the holes right to the top to settle in the plants. Ensure that the heart tip of the plant is at or just above soil level; the seedling should not be completely buried.

After planting, water the young leeks daily, especially during dry spells, until the plants are established, which usually takes about a week. You could also protect them with fleece (*see p.69*) for a few days to keep them moist. As the plants expand, and with hoeing, watering, and rainfall, the planting holes will fill up completely.

### Intercropping

Garlic, shallots and onion sets are suitable for intercropping (*see p.71*) with quick-maturing vegetables such as lettuce.

## Planting garlic cloves in modules

1 **In autumn, prepare** garlic cloves by separating them from the bulb. Do not use any that show signs of disease. Remove the papery tunic, but keep a piece of basal plate (*see inset*).

2 **Insert each clove** into a module-tray cell that is part-filled with compost. Cover with compost and keep in a cool place over winter. In spring, transplant cloves which have sprouted into their final positions.

# Planting out young leeks

1 **In mid-spring** for early leeks, or early to midsummer for late leeks, lift seedlings from the seedbed drill about 8 weeks after sowing, before they are of about pencil thickness. Water the soil first if it is dry. Use a hand fork to loosen the soil beneath the roots, then gently pull the seedlings.

2 **Select bundles** of about ten seedlings of equal thickness and trim with a sharp knife. Cut the roots to about 2.5cm (1in) and the leaves to 15–20cm (6–8in).

3 **Draw out a drill** in the planting bed and make planting holes with a large dibber, here 15cm (6in) apart and deep. Place one seedling into each hole, so that the heart, or growing point, is at or only just below the soil surface.

4 **Water the seedlings** well to settle their roots. It is not necessary to fill in the holes; this will occur naturally as the leeks grow.

## Harvesting onions

Allow the foliage to die down naturally before lifting the bulbs; folding down the leaves to help ripening can affect storage quality. Any thick-necked bulbs should be used fresh, as they will not store well. Lift carefully, so as not to bruise the bulbs, and place them in a single layer on a drying rack made from chicken wire (*see right*), sacking, netting, or inverted wooden slatted trays. This keeps them off the ground and allows plenty of air to flow around them. They will ripen best in full sun, but should be covered in rainy weather. Turn the bulbs regularly to achieve even ripening.

Bulbs should not be stored until the green parts and the papery skins are "rustling" dry. When fully dried, clean off any loose skins and plait the tops into ropes (*see p.73*) or hang the bulbs in bunches. Alternatively, trim off the tops and store in nets or in single layers in trays (*see p.73*). Do not store onions in the dark, as this encourages sprouting.

## Bolting

Like some leafy salads, alliums are prone to premature flowering, or bolting. Planting in spring can protect them from exposure to cold soil and waterlogging, which may check growth and initiate bolting. Use heat-treated sets and bolt-resistant cultivars to avoid this problem.

## Common problems

Most crops in the onion family are susceptible to the same problems. To minimize the effects, grow some of the cultivars that have inbred resistance, and use preventative measures such as crop rotation (*see p.31*) and air circulation.

Onion white rot (*see p.258*) is a soil-borne disease and can stay in the soil for 20 years or more – if your onions have it, stop growing them and remove and destroy affected plants. A more expensive solution is to replace the affected soil with clean soil. Be careful not to spread the disease around on tools and footwear. Downy mildew (*see p.255*) appears when wet, humid conditions are causing soft growth, which increases the plants' susceptibility to infection. Onions should be kept as dry and hard as possible, so only water in very dry conditions. As soon as you see the tips of the leaves becoming grey and dying back, remove infected parts and burn them. Onion neck rot (*see p.258*) and fusarium, which rots the basal plates of the bulbs (*see p.256*), affect overwintered crops. Viruses (*see p.264*) are occasionally troublesome, especially with garlic, so always buy certified stock to get the best yields.

Onion fly (*see p.258*) is a particular problem in dry soils, and is active from late spring to late summer. When sowing seed at these times, use dressed seed, treat the drills, or cover the drills with fleece to keep out the flies until the crop has germinated. Be careful, however, as allium leaves will grow through the fleece fabric, and they can then be damaged when the fleece is removed. Onion thrips (*see p.259*) and stem and bulb eelworm (*see p.263*) are both quite common pests.

**Drying shallots**
*Create a drying rack by attaching a piece of chicken wire to four short posts to raise the wire off the ground. Place the bulbs on top, where air can circulate around them.*

# A–Z of the onion family

## Bulb onion

### *Allium cepa*

| Season | Spring | | Summer | Autumn | Winter |
|---|---|---|---|---|---|
| Sow/plant | • • | | | • • • | • • |
| Transplant | • • | | | | • • |
| Harvest | | | • • • • | | |

Bulb onions are either lifted at time of use or stored for winter use. Small bulbs are usually preferred. Most cultivars are yellow- or brown-skinned with white flesh, but there are also red-skinned ones, some of which have red-and-white striped layers inside. A long season of growth is needed, and the final size of the bulb is determined by spacing (*see pp. 89–90*). A 3m (10ft) row will yield 60 small, 30 large, or 15 very large onions, or 1–3kg (2¼–6½lb). Onion sets are suitable for intercropping.

**Site and soil** Bulb onions require an open, fertile, non-acid soil (*see p. 89*). Good drainage is needed, especially for long-keeping varieties.

**Sowing and planting** Brown onions and some varieties of red onions are good keeping onions, and if stored correctly provide year-round supplies. Seed of these varieties is sown in late autumn or early winter, and seedlings are transplanted in late winter or early spring. Onion varieties to be used fresh are sown from autumn to spring, depending on variety. Seedlings of these varieties can be transplanted in winter and spring and are harvested as required in summer. Treated seed is available that protects against fungal diseases. From late autumn, sow seed in punnets or multiblocks (*see p. 89*); as soon as conditions are warm and dry enough sow thinly outdoors in rows (*see p. 67*), and thin the seedlings according to the desired size (*see p. 89*). Plant sets (*see p. 90*) from late winter to early spring, and heat-treated ones in mid-spring. Some seedlings may be lost during the winter, so you can afford to plant or sow a little more closely.

| Sowing depth | 2cm (¾in) |
|---|---|
| Plant/set spacing | 2.5–10cm (1–4in) as desired |
| Row spacing | 30cm (12in) |

**Routine care** Keep the crop well weeded, especially in the first month or so after sowing or planting. Water only until the plants are established; if spring-sown or planted onions are over-watered after midsummer, they take longer to mature and may keep less well. Check regularly for signs of disease.

**Harvesting and storing** Lift onions in early to mid-summer. Harvest spring-sown or planted onions in late summer and dry them (*see p. 91*). Store some bulbs for winter use (*see p. 73 and p. 91*).

**Common problems** *See p. 91* (for symptoms and controls, *see* Plant Problems, *pp. 246–264*).

**Recommended cultivars**
BROWN
'Creamgold' ('Pukekohe') – the best keeping onion, with golden skin and strong flavour.
'Gladalan' – early onion with firm bulb, suited to warm climates.
'Kiwi Gold' – firm, good-keeping onion with strong flavour.
'Odourless Vividleaf' – very mild onion but not a good keeper.
WHITE
'Early Flat White' – best harvested in spring when still green; use fresh.
'Gladalan White' – early onion with firm bulb, suited to warm climates.
'White Sweet Spanish' – pick early as spring onions or later as a small bulb; good for pickling.
RED
'Red Brunswick' – dark red skin and good keeper.
'Red Cal' – large, flattened bulb; sweet salad onion.
'Red Italian Torpedo' – very mild salad onion with long bulbs.
'Red Odourless Globe' – mild salad onion with sweet, mild flavour.

## Garlic

### *Allium sativum*

| Season | Spring | | Summer | Autumn | Winter |
|---|---|---|---|---|---|
| Plant | | | | • • • | • • |
| Harvest | | | • • • | | |

Garlic has a strong flavour and distinctive aroma, and is used extensively. A range of cultivars is available, some of which are virus- and nematode-free. Garlic also has medicinal properties and is often recommended for use in a healthy diet. Each bulb consists of a number of individual cloves, which are used in cooking. Even if the plants bolt to flower, they will still produce reasonable bulbs.

To grow well, garlic requires a cold period of 1–2 months at 0–10°C (32–50°F), and is usually therefore planted in autumn or early winter. Late-planted garlic may not mature well. Expect a yield of 17 bulbs per 3m (10ft) row. Garlic is also suitable for intercropping (*see p. 71*). A very large 'garlic' that is popular in cottage gardens is called Jumbo, Elephant, Russian or Field Garlic; however, this plant is actually a type of leek (*Allium ampeloprasum*). Elephant Garlic has a very mild flavour and keeps extremely well.

**Site and soil** An open, sunny site and a well-drained, light, alkaline soil are best (*see* p.89); heavy soils should be lightened with horticultural sharp sand. Give the soil a good dressing of well-rotted organic matter. Avoid using fresh manure for the dressing.

**Planting** From autumn to mid-winter, split into cloves, ideally 1.5cm (½in) in diameter, and plant upright either outdoors or in modules, depending on the suitability of your soil (*see p.90*). Ensure that the basal plate is facing downwards. Planting 10cm (4in) deep on light soils gives the best yields.

| Planting depth | 2.5–10cm (1–4in) |
| Clove spacing | 18cm (7in) |
| Row spacing | 30cm (12in) |

**Routine care** Keep weed-free and moist throughout, to avoid any check in growth.

**Harvesting and storing** Lift autumn- or winter-planted bulbs in early summer, as soon as the leaves start to fade and turn yellow; if harvesting is delayed, the bulbs may resprout, causing a greater risk of rotting in storage. Dry well (*see p.91*), taking care to avoid bruising them. Store in a dry place (*see p.73*) at 5–10°C (41–50°F); if stored correctly, the bulbs will keep for up to ten months.

**Common problems** As for bulb onions (*see p.91*); viruses are troublesome. For symptoms and controls, *see* Plant Problems, *pp.246–264*.

**Recommended cultivars**
'Elephant Garlic' – (*Allium ampeloprasum* var.) – a type of leek with huge, multiplying bulbs of garlic flavour. Excellent keeper.
'Italian White' – white skin and good flavour.
'New Zealand Purple' – purplish skin with good flavour.

# Japanese bunching onion

## *Allium fistulosum*

| Season | Spring | | Summer | | Autumn | | Winter | |
|---|---|---|---|---|---|---|---|---|
| Sow | | • | • | • | • | | | |
| Transplant | | • | • | • | • | | | |
| Harvest | | | | | • | • | • | • |

Japanese bunching onions, or Nebuka, are selections of Welsh onions (*see p.94*). They are perennial but best grown as annuals in cold climates; forms vary from small salad onion types to large-leaved types like leeks. The clusters of stems, used in salads, are more pungent than spring onions. Plants mature in two seasons, growing up to 60cm (2ft). A 3m (10ft) row yields 250–300 salad onions, or 40–50 large ones.

**Site and soil** Japanese bunching onions will tolerate less fertile soil conditions than most of the onion family (*see p.89*).

**Sowing and planting** For salad use, sow seed in drills in autumn, winter, or spring in warm climates, and from mid-spring to mid-summer in cool climates; thin in stages to 8cm (3in) apart. For larger onions, at the outset sow 2–3 seeds per clump in holes 8cm

| Sowing depth | 2cm (¾in) |
| Plant spacing | 2.5cm (1in) for salad onions |
| | 8cm (3in) for large onions |
| Row spacing | 30cm (12in) |

(3in) apart. Healthy clumps can be divided.

**Routine care** Keep weed-free and moist.

**Harvesting** Seedling leaves may be picked after 10–14 weeks. In the second season, harvest the clusters by lifting the plant and splitting off the stems.

**Common problems** As for bulb onions (*see p.91*). Mildew, and rarely rust, may be particularly troublesome. For symptoms and controls, *see* Plant Problems, *pp.246–264*.

**Recommended cultivars**
Varieties seldom available. Welsh onions are closely related and a good substitute.

# Leek

## *Allium porrum*

| Season | Spring | | Summer | | Autumn | | Winter | |
|---|---|---|---|---|---|---|---|---|
| Sow | • | • | • | • | | | | |
| Transplant | • | • | • | • | | | | |
| Harvest | • | • | | | • | • | • | • |

Leeks are a hardy winter crop, grown for their blanched white stem bases, or shanks (*see p.90*), which are harvested from autumn to spring. Cultivars are available that mature early (in late summer and autumn), mid-season (in winter), or late (in spring). Earlies are generally tall, with long, white shanks and pale foliage. Later ones have darker foliage and shorter shanks. From a 3m (10ft) row expect 4–6kg (8½–13lb) of early leeks, or 3–5kg (6½–11lb) of late leeks.

**Site and soil** Leeks do best on a deep, rich soil of a neutral or slightly acid pH (*see p.89*), preferably a light sandy loam. Incorporate plenty of organic matter before sowing or planting. With a high-nitrogen base dressing (*see pp.20–23*), leeks produce a good fibrous root system, which improves soil structure and thus contributes well in crop rotations.

**Sowing and planting**
Sow in early to mid-summer in an outdoor seedbed (*see p.66*) at a minimum of 7°C (44°F).

From mid-summer, when seedlings are 20cm (8in) tall, transplant them (*see pp.90–91*) into their final positions, using a dibber to make deep planting holes. By carefully adjusting sowing times, you can crop the same cultivar earlier or later than the usual period, but quality may not be as good.

| Sowing depth | 2.5cm (1in) |
| Seed spacing | sow thinly |
| Transplanting depth | 15cm (6in) |
| Plant spacing | 15–20cm (6–8in) |
| Row spacing | 30–38cm (12–15in) |

**Routine care** Keep seedbeds and transplanted seedlings free of weeds during the growing period. Once established, water only in very dry spells. Top-dress with a

high-nitrogen fertilizer (*see pp.20–23*) in mid- to late autumn, or in late winter for late crops. If the leeks have not been planted in deep holes (*see pp.90–91*), draw soil up around the stems as far as possible to aid the blanching process.

**Harvesting** Lift leeks as required from autumn onwards. In late winter, you can lift and heel them in until needed, if the same ground is intended for other planting. Leeks are best harvested through winter when the stems are well formed. The plants go to seed in spring, producing spectacular flowers but very tough stems.

**Common problems** Leeks are affected by all allium-related disorders (*see p.91*). Fusarium (*see p.256*) affects leek roots, so they are best raised in modules to give them a good start. Leek rust (*see p.257*), cutworms (*see p.254*), onion maggot (*see p.258*), and onion thrips (*see p.259*) are also significant problems.

**Recommended cultivars**
'Jumbo' – produces thick white stems.
'Rami' – adaptable variety that can be grown for summer, autumn, and winter harvest.

# Pickling onion

## *Allium cepa*

| Season | Spring | | Summer | | Autumn | | Winter | |
|---|---|---|---|---|---|---|---|---|
| Sow | | | | | | • | • | • |
| Harvest | | | • | • | | | | |

These are bulb onion selections (*see p.92*), grown to produce large quantities of very small, tender onions for pickling. Expect 1–1.5kg (2¼–3lb) from a 3m (10ft) row.

**Site and soil** They do best on a fertile, well-drained, alkaline soil, like other alliums (*see p.89*), but will tolerate poorer, drier soils.

**Sowing and planting** Sow seed in drills from late autumn to mid-winter in cool climates. The best density is about 30 plants per 30 sq cm (1 sq ft). Sow in 30cm (12in) rows, or in bands 23cm (9in) wide with 30cm (12in) between bands.

| Sowing depth | 2.5cm (1in) |
| Seed spacing | 5mm (¼in) |
| Row spacing | 30cm (12in) |

**Routine care** Thinning is not needed, since small bulbs are desired. Keep weed-free.

**Harvesting and storing** The onions are ready for harvesting when the foliage dies down, usually in late summer. Lift and dry as for bulb onions (*see p.92*) and store in a cool, dry place (*see p.73*) until ready to pickle.

**Common problems** The usual onion pests and diseases (*see p.91*) may be troublesome. For symptoms and controls, *see* Plant Problems, *pp.246–264*.

**Recommended cultivars**
'Pearl Pickler' – a small, white onion ideal for pickling.

# Shallot

### *Allium cepa* Aggregatum Group

| Season | Spring | Summer | Autumn | Winter |
|---|---|---|---|---|
| Sow | | | | • • • |
| Transplant | | | | • • • |
| Plant sets | | | • • • | |
| Harvest | | • • | | |

This easily grown allium has a distinct flavour, and can be used for both cooking and pickling. The most commonly grown types have a cluster of firm bulbs and yellow or red skins. Shallots are usually planted as bulblets or sets, and need a long growing season. Early in the season, offsets can be pulled off and used raw in salads. Shallots grown from seed produce single bulbs. A 3m (10ft) row produces 60–180 shallots. Shallots are suitable for intercropping (*see p.71*).

**Site and soil** A fertile, well-drained, non-acid soil is best (*see p.89*). For planting sets or bulblets, the soil should be loose (*see p.90*).
**Sowing and planting** Sow seed of shallots in late autumn or early winter, thinning to 5cm (2in) apart. Plant bulblets and sets (*see p.90*) in autumn and winter, as soon as the soil is workable. Small sets are less likely to bolt than large ones. Shallots grown from seed can be used as sets and planted as the next crop. Bulblets can also be used as planting stock.

| Sowing depth | 2.5cm (1in) |
|---|---|
| Seed spacing | 2cm (¾in) |
| Planting depth (sets) | so that just the tips are showing |
| Plant spacing (sets) | 15–20cm (6–8in) |
| Row spacing | 30cm (12in) |

**Routine care** Keep weed-free. If conditions are dry, water in sets and seedlings to give them a quick start and a firm rooting.
**Harvesting and storing** Lift in mid- to late summer when the tops have died down and dry as for bulb onions. Cleaned shallots can be stored in trays or bags in a frost-free place (*see p.73*). If the stock is healthy, save some sets and bulblets for the following year – the best size for seed sets is 2cm (¾in) in diameter.
**Common problems** Shallots are prone to the usual onion problems (*see p.91*), especially downy mildew. For symptoms and controls, *see* Plant Problems, *pp.246–264*.
**Recommended cultivars**
'Golden Shallots' – available as bulbs; each bulb produces 5-10 bulblets.
'Matador' – available as seed; hybrid shallot with golden skin; produces single bulbs.

# Spring onion

### *Allium cepa*

| Season | Spring | Summer | Autumn | Winter |
|---|---|---|---|---|
| Sow | • • • | • • • | • | |
| Harvest | • • | • • | • | |

Spring or salad onions are immature bulb onions (*A. cepa; see p.92*) grown for their small, white shanks and tender, green stem and leaves. Often referred to as scallions, they are usually pulled when about 15cm (6in) tall and eaten raw in salads. Expect 250–300 per 3m (10ft) row. Spring onions are suitable for intercropping (*see p.71*).
**Site and soil** Prepare as for bulb onions (*see p.92*). Soil alkalinity of pH 6.8 or above is needed to achieve best results.
**Sowing and planting** For a continual summer harvest, sow *in situ* in single rows every two weeks from early spring. Higher yields could be obtained in closer rows, but the plants will be more susceptible to downy mildew (see below). Thinning is not usually required.

| Sowing depth | 1–2cm (½–¾in) |
|---|---|
| Seed spacing | 1cm (½in) |
| Row spacing | 30cm (12in) |

**Routine care** Keep watered in dry weather to avoid any check in growth. Drought can cause the plants to become bulbous, especially 'Lisbon' types.
**Harvesting** Pull and use as required after about one month. Spring onions hold well in the garden, becoming larger in leaf and stem. They can be harvested over winter but usually go to seed, forming tough stems by the following spring.
**Common problems** Of the usual onion afflictions (*see p.91*), onion fly can be seriously troublesome, especially in dry weather, as well as onion white rot and downy mildew. For symptoms and controls, *see* Plant Problems, *pp.246–264*.
**Recommended cultivars**
'White Lisbon' – white shanks and bright green tops.
Welsh onions (*Allium fistulosum*) are also grown for use as spring onions.

# Tree *or* Egyptian onion

### *Allium cepa* Proliferum Group

| Season | Spring | Summer | Autumn | Winter |
|---|---|---|---|---|
| Plant | | | • • • | • |
| Harvest | | • • | | |

This easy-to-grow perennial onion is versatile, multiplying at the base to form a cluster of pinkish, sweet-flavoured bulblets. It produces clusters of very small aerial bulbs instead of flowers. These bulblets sprout while still attached to the main plant, developing shoots and further clusters of bulblets to form a multi-layered plant. The stems eventually drop down to the ground under their own weight, where some of the bulblets take root and create new plants. The base bulblets are harvested and used like a small onion in cooking, and are also pickled. No named cultivars are offered.

**Site and soil** This allium needs a sunny situation in fertile, well-drained, alkaline soil.
**Sowing and planting** Plant single bulblets from the basal cluster or plant the aerial bulblets. Both are planted in late autumn or winter, with the pointed top just above the soil surface.

| Planting depth | with just the tip showing |
|---|---|
| Plant spacing | 25cm (10in) |
| Row spacing | 25cm (10in) |

**Routine care** The plants will reproduce readily (*see above*), so may need thinning out if they start to crowd one another.
**Harvesting** Pick the aerial bulblets as they ripen in late summer, before they start to grow. Pull and dry the basal bulblets as for bulb onions. Tree onions store as well as brown onions.
**Common problems** This crop is prey to the same problems as all onions (*see p.91*), but more tolerant of pests.

# Welsh onion

### *Allium fistulosum*

| Season | Spring | Summer | Autumn | Winter |
|---|---|---|---|---|
| Sow | • • • | | | |
| Harvest | • • • • | • • • • | • • • • | • • • • |

The Welsh onion, or ciboule, is a hollow-leaved, robust perennial that grows in clumps 30–45cm (12–18in) tall. The base of the stem is thickened, but does not form a bulb. It is useful as a year-round alternative to spring onions. The leaves, which stay green all year, and tiny bulbs are eaten cooked or raw, often in winter salads. In milder areas, it may be harvested for two years before division of the clump in spring or autumn (*see below*). Seed-raised plants are often hardier than those created by division.
**Site and soil** Welsh onions have the same requirements as bulb onions (*see p.92*).
**Sowing and planting** Sow seeds in spring, and thin to 20cm (8in) apart. For perennial plants, in spring lift the clump, divide it into several pieces, each with healthy leaves and root system, and replant the divisions 20cm (8in) apart.

| Sowing depth | 2.5cm (1in) |
|---|---|
| Seed spacing | sow thinly; thin to 20cm (8in) |
| Row spacing | 23cm (9in) |

**Routine care** Keep well weeded.
**Harvesting** Plants sown in spring should be big enough to start harvesting in summer. Cut single leaves as required, or pull up part or all of the clump.
**Common problems** Prey to the same problems as all onions (*see p.91*), but more tolerant of pests.
**Recommended cultivars**
'Evergreen Long White Bunching' – produces many stems and can be harvested as required.
'Straightleaf' – often grown and used as spring onions.

# Growing legumes

The vegetable legumes include beans such as broad or fava, French or kidney (*see right*), Lima or butter, runner, and yard long snake or asparagus beans, as well as shelling and edible-pod peas. Although the young shoots may be used as green vegetables, legumes are mainly grown for their seeds and seedpods, which are eaten fresh or dried. Some, such as broad beans and peas, are robust crops that resist frost and are well adapted to cool climates. Others, for example French and runner beans, are poorly adapted to cool weather; they grow well through summer in temperate gardens, and in winter in tropical gardens. Snake beans and snow peas also grow very well in the tropics.

### Nitrogen "fixing"

All the legume family (Leguminosae) have nitrogen-fixing root nodules (*see below*), and consequently they need much less nitrogenous fertilizer than many other vegetables. The process of absorbing nitrogen from the air takes energy from peas and beans, so that their yields are proportionately lower than those of other crops; therefore you will need to grow a reasonable number of plants in order to obtain sufficient pickings through the season. On the plus side, however, pea and bean crops are comparatively rich in protein.

### Nitrogen-fixing nodules

*All legumes store, or fix, nitrogen with the help of* Rhizobium *bacteria that live in nodules on their roots. Root residues from legumes are rich in nitrogen and thus they reduce the need for fertilizer.*

Cluster of nodules

Nodule

## Examples of French beans

'Slenderette' (*dwarf*)  'Purple Podded'  'Dolly' (*dwarf*)  'Hunter'  'Borlotto di Fuoco' (*climbing*)

Another benefit of nitrogen fixing in peas and beans is that their foliage makes a valuable addition to a compost heap.

### Choosing a site

Peas and beans are affected by similar pests and diseases (*see pp. 98–100*), and should not be planted in the same soil every year. They are best grown in rotation (*see p. 31*) as a group, usually preceding brassicas, which will benefit from the nitrogen residues in the soil. All legumes grow best in full sun, and the less hardy types demand a warm, sheltered position.

Although broad beans favour clay soil, other legumes perform best on lighter soil. A neutral to mildly alkaline soil (pH 6.5–7) is ideal, although mildly acid soils (not less than pH of 5.5) are usually acceptable. Peas and beans are generally hungry plants, demanding a rich soil. For best results, organic matter should be incorporated throughout the soil, but a traditional trench can be sufficient (*see below*). Adding some extra organic matter will also improve the drainage and soil structure, on heavy clay soils for example, and helps to retain soil moisture – which is very important at flowering time.

## Preparing a bean trench

1 **Where organic matter** is not abundant or the soil is especially poor, a traditional bean trench will supply the nutrients legumes need. Mark out a line and excavate a trench 90cm (3ft) wide and 60cm (2ft) deep. Fork over the soil at the base to loosen it up.

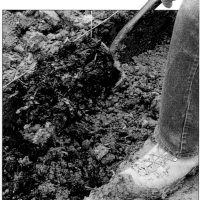

2 **Scatter organic matter,** such as compost or rotted manure, over the bottom of the trench and the dug-out soil. Replace the soil and apply some pelleted poultry manure at a rate of 2 handfuls per m (yd). Leave the soil to settle for at least 2 weeks before planting.

## The need for legume supports

Many peas and beans are tall-growing and require some form of support. Without this, they will sprawl, or get flattened by rain. The benefits of using supports also include easier weeding, watering, and pest control, less weather damage, and more and better pods at harvest time and less bending for the picker.

Common support methods (*see right*) include bamboo canes and twine, canes and netting, and bushy sticks (peasticks). All supports are most easily installed before they are actually needed, and this helps avoid damaging delicate stems when trying to raise fallen crops.

Dwarf cultivars of French and runner beans, peas, broad beans, and leafless peas can grow without supports, but a string along each side of the row is often helpful. Supports are also not needed where climbing cultivars are made to branch by pinching out all the leading growth when the plant is 23cm (9in) tall, followed by further pinching to keep the plant bushy.

## Supports for beans

Climbing runner and French beans will twine around vertical supports as they

## Types of pea and bean supports

**Rows of canes**
*Pairs of canes 15–23cm (6–9in) apart tied together at the top form a good support for runner beans. Secure the top with another cane as a crossbar.*

**Canes and netting**
*For double rows of peas, suspend 30–60cm (12–24in) of chicken wire, or plastic pea and bean netting, from 1.2m (4ft) canes placed at 1.2m (4ft) intervals.*

**Peasticks**
*These are usually prunings, inserted in the soil at 30cm (12in) intervals. As the crops grow, the sticks form a natural-looking support system.*

grow. Double rows or strong wigwams of bamboo canes are ideal for these plants (*see below*). String or twine can be used instead of some of the canes. Train one plant up each string or cane. Mesh supported by tall posts is also suitable for runner beans.

Broad beans are not natural climbers and should be supported by means of strings running between stakes along the bean row. A stake positioned every 1.2m (4ft), with strings running from stake to stake, will hold up the heaviest broad bean crop.

## Supports for peas

Peas climb by means of tendrils. Better yields and easier picking come from supporting peas with netting, thin sticks, or canes and string. These supports should be put in place as soon as the seedlings emerge. Rustic peasticks (*see above*) are renewable forest products that make good pea supports. Insert the sticks so that a continuous "hedge" of twigs is formed. Wire or plastic netting that is supported by stakes is an effective alternative. Peas need a continuous run of netting, possibly with a string on each side to restrain the crop.

## Sowing the crops

Pea and bean seeds are large and fairly expensive. Deep sowing – possibly using a dibber (*see p.69*) – is needed for legume seeds, but in heavy soil this often leads to seeds being placed at a wet, cold, and airless soil level. Wrinkled-seeded cultivars of peas as well as runner and French bean seeds are prone to rot in low soil temperatures. Such seeds have to be sown when the soil warms in mid-spring in cool climates. The seeds are very attractive to mice, so sowing

**Positioning legumes for optimum growth and yield**
*Many peas and beans are tall and need some support. Since they cast shade, a distance of at least half the full height of the crop should be left between them and adjacent crops. Here, runner beans are grown on wigwams of canes about 90cm (3ft) away from marrow plants.*

indoors, in a length of guttering, or in containers under cloches avoids that problem. To increase the chances of success even further, soak the seed for up to 24 hours before sowing, or try pre-germinating the seeds in the same way as for germination testing (*see p.61*). Sow them when they have roots 5mm (¼in) long, spacing them carefully and evenly in the drill, and discarding any that have no roots.

## Sowing in containers

Sowing in punnets or module trays (*see p.65*) is an economical way of raising legumes. Another option is to sow three seeds to a 5cm (2in) or 8cm (3in) pot. Biodegradable pots are suitable for broad beans, which have tap roots that can be easily damaged. Deep pots, such as tube pots (*see p.62*) and root trainers (*see p.108*), are ideal for the long tap roots of runner beans. You should transplant the seedlings in the garden (*see below right*) as soon as the roots hold the potting mix together.

Alternatively, the soil can be warmed, and rain excluded, with cloches (*see p.46*) or some clear film plastic placed over the soil about four weeks before sowing. In warm, moist soil, seed germination is rapid. Cloche and fleece protection for seedlings against cold, wind, rain, and birds is also useful in early to mid-spring.

The harvest period of peas and beans can be extended by using successional

## Sowing pea seeds in a length of guttering

1 **Three-quarters fill** a length of plastic guttering with seed compost and sow the seeds 5cm (2in) apart in 2 staggered rows. Fill with more compost, water, and label. Keep in a bright place under cover at a minimum of 10°C (50°F).

2 **Draw out a** shallow drill outdoors to the depth of the guttering, when the seedlings are 8cm (3in) tall. Slide the entire section of seedlings into the drill, firm well, and water.

sowing (*see p.69*). The plants grow faster in summer than in spring, so later sowings should be more frequently made than early ones. An effective way of deciding when to sow is to use the size of the preceding seedlings as a rough guide (*see individual crops, pp.98–100*).

## Routine care

Legumes are grown in wide rows, and so are vulnerable to weeds. Mulching (*see pp.41–42*) reduces the need for weeding and hoeing, and keeps the soil moist. Use organic mulches, but take care not to cover plant stems with organic matter.

Watering legumes is unnecessary before flowering, unless the it is hot and dry, because it promotes foliage growth at the expense of flowers. However,

plentiful watering during the flowering period greatly increases the intensity of flowering and setting of pods. Beans in particular set better crops if the foliage is wetted during watering. This raises the humidity and enhances pod set.

## Harvesting peas and beans

Garden legumes are unsurpassable in flavour and texture as long as they are consumed very soon after picking. Picking them in the morning, while the pods are cool, and keeping them in the refrigerator help to prolong their shelf life. Because commercially frozen legumes, especially peas, these days taste nearly as good as home-grown ones, some gardeners prefer to concentrate on growing the less common cultivars (*see individual crops, pp.98–100*). To harvest dry peas and beans, treat the pods in the same way as for saving seed (*see below*).

## Saving seeds

Some legumes are self-pollinated, so their seed can be saved with very little risk of cross-pollination, and the resulting plants will be true to type. To save the seed of known self-pollinators, select some early pods and mark them with coloured wool. Let the crop mature, and gather the pods before they split and shed the seed. Alternatively, hang up immature pods to finish ripening. Dry the pods in a cool place (*see p.61*) and shell them; leave the seeds to dry out again, then store them in a dark, cool, dry place. Correctly stored, they should last for several years.

△ **Transplanting climbing beans**
*With their support system already in place, plant out young plants that were sown under cover as soon as they are large enough. Position one plant next to each cane.*

◁ **Pinching out growing tips**
*When the plants reach the top of the canes, pinch out their growing tips in order to stimulate the production of sideshoots.*

# A–Z of legumes

## Asparagus pea

*Lotus tetragonolobus*

| Season | Spring | Summer | Autumn | Winter |
|---|---|---|---|---|
| Sow | • • | | | |
| Transplant | • | | | |
| Harvest | | • • • | | |

This annual is grown for its small, fluted pods. These have a fresh flavour, although they crop lightly and soon become stringy: average yield is 450g per 3m (1lb per 10ft) row. This pea has feathery foliage and red-brown flowers.
**Site and soil** Use an open site in full sun, with light but rich soil.
**Sowing and planting** Sow seed in mid- to late spring, as for peas (*see facing page*).

| Sowing depth | 4cm (1½in) deep in moist soils |
|---|---|
| | 5cm (2in) in dry soils |
| Seed spacing | 25–30cm (10–12in) |
| Row spacing | 38cm (15in) apart |

**Routine care** No support needed, but sticks and canes keep it within bounds (*see p.96*).
**Harvesting** After two months, start picking immature pods, 2.5–5cm (1–2in) long, and continue regularly throughout spring and summer.
**Common problems** As for pea. Birds strip off foliage in some areas, so you may need to provide protection. For symptoms and controls, *see* Plant Problems, *pp. 246–264*.

## Broad bean

*Vicia faba*

| Season | Spring | Summer | Autumn | Winter |
|---|---|---|---|---|
| Sow | | | • • | • • • |
| Transplant | • • | | | |
| Harvest | • • • • | | | |

Broad, or fava, beans are delicious, easy to grow, and very hardy. Although these annuals are usually grown for the immature, green or white seeds or beans, young pods and even the shoot tips can be cooked and eaten. White seeds are reputed to be better flavoured than green ones. Traditional Longpod beans have eight seeds per pod, and Windsors, which have shorter, wider pods, have four large seeds per pod. Modern broad bean cultivars are intermediate in length between Longpods and Windsors, and have shorter stems and small, tender seeds. Broad bean yields average 3kg per 3m (6½lb per 10ft) row. Dwarf cultivars, because they grow only to about 60cm (2ft) – which is half the height of most broad bean cultivars – are especially suitable for growing in containers and small gardens.
**Site and soil** Any moderately fertile, well-drained soil is suitable. Broad beans have a long tap root, so the soil should be deeply dug and well-drained (*see pp. 14–16*). The best yields are usually achieved on relatively heavy soils, but early crops do well on lighter soil if the plants are watered when in flower.
**Sowing and planting** Successional sowing (*see p.69*) will give a constant crop from late winter to early summer; sow the next batch when the preceding seedlings reach 8cm (3in). Dwarf cultivars are best for late harvests. You can sow when your soil is not waterlogged and the temperature is at least 5°C (41°F). In well-drained, sheltered gardens, autumn sowing is possible, although the crop may not fruit until the weather warms. Alternatively, make winter sowings under cover in cold climates, transplanting in early spring.

| Sowing depth | 8cm (3in) |
|---|---|
| Seed spacing | 23cm (9in) |
| Row spacing | 45cm (18in) between single rows |
| | Double rows 23cm (9in) apart, |
| | 60cm (24in) between rows |

**Routine care** Control weeds by hoeing, drawing a little soil around the base of the plants to support and protect them. Stake tall cultivars with stakes and string (*see p.96*). When the lowest blossom has set, pinch out the tops to promote earlier cropping and to remove any aphids that may have appeared on the top shoots. Watering during flowering in dry spells greatly increases the crop.
**Harvesting** Crops mature in three to four months, although autumn-sown crops may take longer. Pick the pods regularly, before they have a chance to get too old – if the part of the seed that attaches it to the pod is brown or black, the pods are too old and the beans will probably be tough. The beans mature in succession, starting from the bottom of the haulm, and several pickings can therefore be taken from each crop.
**Common problems** In warm weather aphids often suck the plant sap, sometimes causing both leaves and stems to look soiled and stunted. Mice (*see p.258*) can damage the seeds. Chocolate spot (*see p.253*) is destructive in wet seasons, especially for overwintered crops.
**Recommended cultivars**
'Big Ben' – large pods on medium-sized plants.
'Coles Dwarf Prolific' – produces good crops on shortish plants.
'Egyptian' – good crop of small pods.
'Exhibition Long Pod' – tall plants producing long pods.

## French bean

*Phaseolus vulgaris*

Heavy cropping, trouble-free French or kidney beans picked fresh from the garden are

| Season | Spring | Summer | Autumn | Winter |
|---|---|---|---|---|
| Sow | • • | • • | | |
| Transplant | • | • | | |
| Harvest | | • • | • • • • | • |

a revelation in flavour. They ripen to "haricot beans" that may be dried and stored for winter use. Half-ripe beans are called "flageolets" and are shelled and eaten like peas. French beans have pods that are round or flattened in cross-section. Kenya beans, sold in supermarkets, are French beans. Although green beans are common, cultivars with yellow, purple, and red- or purple-flecked pods are available, too, making attractive and unusual plants for the ornamental vegetable garden.

Most French beans are dwarf and make a low, bushy annual plant. Climbing French beans, however, can be grown up supports in the same way as runner beans (see p.96). Alternatively, create a wigwam with four to eight 2.5m (8ft) canes and sow three seeds on the inside of each. Dwarf beans mature earlier than climbing ones; but climbing beans may yield more heavily for a longer period and make better use of space in small gardens. The average yield of French beans is 4.5kg per 3m (10lb per 10ft) row.

French beans are self-pollinating, meaning that cultivars will come true to type from home-saved seed.

**Site and soil** Both dwarf and climbing types are sensitive to frost. Sheltered, warm sites are best, but cloche or fleece protection (see pp.45–46) will help elsewhere. Light, fertile, and neutral soils are ideal, but any well-drained soil that has had organic matter added is suitable. French beans may be grown in pots, which can be started off in greenhouses to crop outdoors from early summer onwards.

**Sowing and planting** French beans require at least 12°C (54°F) to germinate. Pre-warming the soil with clear film plastic or cloches for several weeks prior to transplanting can be beneficial.

Leaving room for picking access and inserting supports if appropriate, plant 32–43 seeds per sq m (sq yd), evenly spacing them in single or double rows. The latter provides better yields, and, if they are the dwarf, bushy type, the plants will also suppress the weed growth between the rows.

From late spring to midsummer, sow in succession in open ground, as long as the soil is moist, every few weeks for a continuous supply into autumn. Alternatively, sow climbing bean seed around climbing poles or either side of a climbing frame, in late spring or summer.

| Sowing depth | 5cm (2in) |
|---|---|
| Seed spacing | 5–10cm (2–4in) single row |
| | 15cm (6in) double row |
| Row spacing | 45cm (18in) between single rows |
| | Double rows 23cm (9in) apart, |
| | 45cm (18in) between rows |

**Routine care** Mulching (see pp.41–42 and p.72) improves growth and keeps the pods free from soiling. In the absence of mulch, drawing soil around the plant bases to a depth

of 8–10cm (3–4in) helps to support them and suppress weeds. Numbers of pods and their texture can be improved by watering the soil and the foliage to keep it moist from flowering time onwards.

**Harvesting and storing** Crops take one to two months to mature. Picking every two or three days encourages the production of more beans and prevents any deterioration in quality that may occur once the seeds begin to swell. Pick in the early morning and store in the refrigerator to help retain freshness. Unlike older cultivars, modern ones are free from the string that forms quickly as pods mature. Dwarf beans generally crop heavily for a short period, while climbing beans crop for a much longer period.

**Common problems** Slugs (see p.262) are the most common pests, but birds (see p.251), mice (see p.258), and red spider mite (see p.261) may occur. French beans may suffer from anthracnose (see p.251), but the most common disease is stem and root rot (p.263); avoid it by using a different site each year.

**Recommended cultivars**

DWARF
'Brown Beauty' – old, reliable variety.
'Dolly' – slim baby beans usually served whole.
'Gourmet Delight' – tender, crisp pods produced for a long period.
'Jade' – heavy crop of tender beans.
'Majestic' – butter bean with tender, butter yellow pods.
'Minuet' – heavy crop of small, tender pods.
'Romano' – flat, wide, tasty pods.
'Royal Burgundy' – long, purple pods that turn green when cooked.
'Slenderette' – produces round, slim, tender pods.
'Slenderwax' – butter bean producing heavy crops of butter yellow pods.
'Windsor Long Pod' – good crops of long, flat pods.
CLIMBING
'Blue Lake' – good crops of long, round, tender pods.
'Giant of Stuttgart' – vigorous heavy cropper with tasty, flat pods.
'Purple King' – flat, purple pods that turn green when cooked.
'Tiger' – tasty, flat, purple-flecked pods.

# Lima bean

## *Phaseolus lunatus*

| Season | Spring | Summer | Autumn | Winter |
|---|---|---|---|---|
| Sow | • • | | | |
| Transplant | | • | | |
| Harvest | | | • • | |

These tender annuals or short-lived perennials are grown as dwarf bushes or as climbers. The beans are either used green, in the same way as runner beans, or dried. The sprouted seeds, often called beansprouts, are also edible. There are no cultivars currently available. Grow as for runner bean; they crop best in warm, sheltered

sites and may need protection in cool climates. Minimum temperature needed is 20°C (68°F).

**Harvesting** When crops mature – in three to four months – pick regularly, two or three times per week, so pods do not become over-mature, which will suppress further flowering as the pods will be using up vital energy.

# Pea – shelling

## *Pisum sativum sativum*

| Season | Spring | Summer | Autumn | Winter |
|---|---|---|---|---|
| Sow | | | • • | • • • |
| Transplant | • • • | | | • • |
| Harvest | • • • • | | | |

Annual shelling or garden peas include robust early peas, tiny tasty petit pois, dwarf cultivars good for exposed, windy gardens, and tall cultivars that can be trained up supports to save space. See Peas – snow (p.100) for peas whose whole pod is eaten. For ornamental kitchen gardens, cultivars that have coloured flowers and pods are attractive. Peas are easy to grow in cool weather and, when picked fresh, their flavour is incomparably better than peas from shops. Modern peas have 2–3 pods at each flowering node, compared to the single pod of older peas. Such modern peas are dwarf in habit and more easily supported, and still yield as much as taller cultivars – an average yield being 3kg per 3m (6½lb per 10ft) row.

**Site and soil** Well-drained, neutral to alkaline soil that holds moisture is best. Good soil structure is important and this can be achieved by adding organic matter (see pp.22–23). Open sunny situations are ideal.

**Sowing and planting** Peas are sown so that they flower after the frosts in cool climates. The plants will continue cropping until the weather becomes too hot. Growing peas in afternoon shade extends cropping. Autumn and winter sowings of peas raised in punnets or pots are more likely to succeed than seed sown direct into the soil if it is cold and heavy – temperatures should be at least 5°C (41°F). Birds and mice may also eat seeds sown outdoors. Seeds may be sown in guttering to avoid this (see p.97). Peas sown after mid-spring may succumb to powdery mildew. Sow in succession, when the preceding seedlings are 30cm (12in) tall.

Peas can be sown in single drills or double rows in a wide drill (see p.67) that are easy to hoe, or in beds with around 40 plants per sq m (yd) for optimum yield. However, beds are difficult to harvest and keep weed-free.

| Sowing depth | 4cm (1½in) in moist soils |
|---|---|
| | 5cm (2in) in dry soils |
| Seed spacing | 5cm (2in) in single or double rows |
| | 13cm (5in) in triple rows |
| Row spacing | Equal to plants' eventual height |

**Routine care** Many dwarf, especially leafless, cultivars support themselves, but better yields and easier picking come from using supports (*see p.96*). Regular hoeing and weeding are essential. Watering in dry weather, especially at flowering time, and again as the pods swell, greatly increases the crop.

**Harvesting and storing** Early, dwarf cultivars mature in about 12 weeks, while higher-yielding main crop cultivars may take 14 weeks. Gather peas as soon as they are ready, to encourage the production of more pods. Pick peas shortly before they are needed, and once picked keep them cool, ideally in a refrigerator.

**Common problems** Pea moth gets into the pods spoiling the crop, and is hard to control. Using mouse traps and protecting seedbeds with fleece are the best counter-measures against, respectively, mice (*see p.258*) and birds (*see p.251*). Stem and root rot (*see p.263*) is troublesome where soil is wet and cold. Sowing in protected pots and transplanting peas is the best remedy, but later sowings are usually unaffected. Powdery mildew (*see p.260*) is the worst disease, but usually affects only late crops. Resistant cultivars are available. Pea leaf and pod spot (*see p.259*) is serious but uncommon.

**Recommended cultivars**
'Bounty' – heavy cropper suited to warm climates; powdery mildew resistant.
'Greenfeast' – tall plants that grow on a trellis and produce good crops.
'Kodiak' – dwarf variety resistant to powdery mildew.
'Progress' – dwarf quick-growing plants with large pods.
'Telephone' – space-saving, climbing variety that needs a trellis; produces large pods.
'William Massey' – ('Melbourne Market') dwarf, quick-maturing variety; suits late sowings.

# Peas – snow and snap

*(Pisum sativum vars.)*

| Season | Spring | Summer | Autumn | Winter |
|---|---|---|---|---|
| Sow | • • • • | | • • | |
| Harvest | • • • • | | • • | |

Snow peas or mangetout peas produce thin, flat, edible pods, and snap peas or sugar snap peas have more fleshy, edible pods. Both are tender and delicious in salads or cooked in stir-fry or as a vegetable.

**Site and soil** Snow peas and snap peas have the same requirements as shelling peas. However, snow peas are more tolerant of heat than snap or shelling peas.

**Sowing and planting** Snow peas and snap peas grow best in cool weather but the flowers and pods are damaged by frost. The seed is sown *in situ* in late winter or early autumn in cool climates to avoid frost at flowering. The plants continue to crop while the weather is cool but not hot and not cold. Plants wither with the arrival of hot summer weather.

**Routine care** Provide climbing support for climbing varieties as for shelling peas, and

protect young seedlings from slugs and snails and birds and mice.

**Harvesting** Pick pods when young before the seeds start to swell. Over-mature pods are tough but the peas can be podded.

**Common problems** Snow and snap peas have the same problems as shelling peas.

**Recommended cultivars**
SNOW
'Mammoth Sugar' – vigorous climbing variety with heavy crops of large pods.
'Oregon Giant' – ('Snowman') medium-sized plants with large, flat pods.
'Oregon Sugar Pod' – dwarf plants with sweet, flat pods.
'Viking' – small, sweet, flat pods on medium-sized plants.
'Yakumo' – tall plants with purple flowers and huge pods over a long period.
SNAP
'Sugar Bon' – dwarf plants with sweet, plump pods.
'Sugar Snap Tall' – tall plants grown as climbers with sweet, crunchy pods.

# Runner bean

*Phaseolus coccineus*

| Season | Spring | Summer | Autumn | Winter |
|---|---|---|---|---|
| Sow | • • • • | | | |
| Transplant | | • • | | |
| Harvest | | • • • • | | |

Runner beans are tender perennials, grown as annuals in cool climates. They are climbers growing up to 3m (10ft) tall. Most have red flowers, flat pods, and red speckled seeds, but white-flowered, white-seeded cultivars are widely grown. Runner beans have a stronger flavour than French beans and give a heavier yield: 6kg per 3m (13lb per 10ft) row.

**Site and soil** Runner beans are sensitive to frost and hot wind, and need warm, sheltered conditions where their insect pollinators will be most effective. Deep, fertile soil holding ample water is best. Preparing a trench filled with organic matter (*see p.95*) is a traditional way of ensuring this, although acceptable crops will result from ground prepared by normal digging methods (*see pp.37–40*).

**Sowing and planting** For successful germination, the soil temperature should be at least 12°C (54°F). Heavy, wet soils can be pre-warmed by covering them with clear film plastic or cloches for about four weeks before sowing. Alternatively, raise plants in deep pots (*see p.62*) from mid-spring, planting out in early summer. Protect young plants with fleece or cloches to help them establish. A mid-summer sowing will prolong the harvest into autumn.

Sow runner beans in double rows using sturdy supports, such as 2.5m (8ft) long canes (*see p.96*), ideally with one plant per cane. If canes are in short supply, vertical strings may replace canes, or all of the canes may be replaced by nylon netting. Alternatively, use 6–8 canes to make a wigwam and grow one

plant up each cane. Pinching out the tips of climbers reduces the height. In warm climates, runner beans can be grown as perennials; cut plants back after harvest, mulch with compost, and allow to regrow in spring.

| Sowing depth | 5cm (2in) |
|---|---|
| Seed spacing | 15cm (6in) |
| Row spacing | Climbing beans: double rows 60cm (2ft) apart, 1.5m (5ft) between rows<br>Dwarf beans: as for French bean |

**Routine care** Twist young shoots around the canes to help them start to climb. Pinch out the growing tips (*see p.97*) when shoots reach the top of supports to stop them becoming top-heavy. Watering is vital in dry weather as soon as flower buds appear. Sometimes pods fail to form despite plentiful flowering. Lack of soil and foliage moisture is the usual cause and abundant irrigation the remedy. Cold, windy weather may depress pollinator activity. Warm nights can lead to failure to set pods; the traditional remedy of spraying flowers with water increases humidity and pod set.

**Harvesting** Crops mature in about three months. Pick regularly, 2–3 times a week, to stop pods becoming over-mature, which will suppress further flowering. Similarly, remove any old pods. Saving seed (*see p.97*) is usually worthwhile, but if more than one cultivar is grown nearby the seedlings may not come true to type.

**Common problems** As for French beans (*see pp.98–99*). Runner beans also suffer from poor setting (*see p.258*).

**Recommended cultivars**
'Painted Lady' – old variety with pretty red and white flowers and flat pods.
'Scarlet Runner' – old variety with scarlet flowers and large, flat pods.
'Zenith' – vigorous, adaptable variety with scarlet flowers and large, flat pods.

# Snake bean

*Vigna unguiculata* subsp. *sesquipedalis*

| Season | Spring | Summer | Autumn | Winter |
|---|---|---|---|---|
| Sow | • • | | | |
| Transplant | | • | | |
| Harvest | | | • • | |

Snake, yard long or asparagus beans are tender, tropical plants, growing to 4m (12ft), with narrow pods that can be a metre (yard) long in optimum conditions, where average yields are 560g per 3m (1¼lb per 10ft) row. In a warm site, snake beans can be grown in the same way as runner beans. They suit warm climates and will not tolerate cold soils and chilly nights. Crops take 2–3 months to mature. Pick the pods when 30–45cm (12–18in) long, before they become woody. Seeds are not readily available in cool areas.

# Growing salad crops

The crops described here are mainly salad leaves, but radishes are included since they are grown primarily for use in salads. Apart from the traditional lettuce, salad leaves also include chicory, corn salad, endive, komatsuna, land cress, mibuna and mizuna greens, mustard and cress, rocket, and summer and winter purslane. Salad crops are fast growing – if sown in summer, radishes will mature in two weeks, and lettuces in six weeks. Salads can quickly become coarse and hot-flavoured, and run to seed, however. Sowing small batches in succession (*see p.69*) helps to overcome this problem. Using several cultivars, or crops that take different amounts of time to reach maturity, also helps avoid peaks and troughs in supply.

Leafy salads need little in the way of feeding; a light application of nitrogen fertilizer to the soil before sowing or transplanting should be sufficient.

## Temperature requirements

Leafy salad crops are quite sensitive to temperature, and this affects seed germination – they will not germinate if they are too cold, or even too hot. They grow best in a temperature range of around 10–20°C (50–68°F). Low temperatures of below 5°C (41°F) and slow growth rates can lead to a coarse flavour and texture, and may prevent crops such as lettuces from developing proper hearts. The use of cold frames, cloches, and fleece (*see pp.43–48*) alleviates this problem in cool climates. Some salads, endive, and chicory for example, flower prematurely, or bolt, if exposed to several weeks of low temperatures. These crops cannot be safely sown before summer unless bolt-resistant cultivars are used. Some crops will also bolt if exposed to high temperatures (*see above right*) as they mature.

Most leafy salad plants can be grown all year in temperate gardens but only during winter in the tropics.

## Sowing the crops

Because of the sensitivity of leafy salads to temperature (*see above*), it is usually easier to achieve even germination, especially with early sowings, by sowing

**Salad crops under a floating mulch**
*Horticultural fleece protects crops from frosts or hot sun and also deters flying insects and birds. Lay the fleece so that it floats lightly over the crops, and weigh it down at the sides. Check the crop regularly, and loosen if necessary.*

in spring in temperate gardens (*see p.64*). Germination will depend on the warmth and moistness of the seedbed. Where soils do not readily form a fine tilth, or if they form a cap after heavy rain so that seedlings cannot push through, raising leafy salads in modules or punnets is preferable.

Sowing leafy salads in modules (*see p.65*) also saves space and time. Sow 2–3 seeds per cell, later thinning to the strongest seedling. Some lettuce cultivars need light to germinate; when germination rates are disappointing, try sowing on the surface in module trays, keeping the seeds moist by putting the tray in a clear plastic bag or propagator

**Transplanting radish seedlings**
*For successional batches of small radishes, sprinkle a small quantity of seeds in 8cm (3in) pots at two-weekly intervals. When the roots bind the compost, plant out the entire potful to grow on as a clump.*

**Bolting lettuces**
*Leafy salads, especially non-hearting types of lettuce, quickly bolt and run to seed in hot weather or if short of water. The leaves become bitter and fit only for the compost heap.*

away from direct sun. For radishes, sow 4–5 seeds to a 8cm (3in) pot and plant out the entire clump of seedlings (*see below*), to avoid damaging the roots. Cover early sowings with fleece or cloches (*see pp.45–48*) to avoid problems with low temperatures. In summer, leafy salads germinate better if sown in light shade, such as provided by a fence or tree, and if protected from extremes of dryness and heat. In hot weather, over 25°C (77°F), lettuce seed may become dormant several hours after sowing. Avoid this by sowing in the afternoon so that the critical period falls in the cool of the night. Watering after sowing can also help.

## Thinning seedlings

Leafy salad crops grow quickly, making timely thinning difficult. There are two ways to alleviate this problem. Remove surplus seedlings (*see p.68*) as soon as they can be handled, in three stages: at the first stage, leave just a thumb's width between seedlings; at the second stage, leave half of the intended final spacing; finally, thin to the final spacing. You can use the thinnings in salads. Alternatively, try station sowing (*see p.68*), in which 3–5 seeds are sown together. Thin the seedlings to two strong-growing ones; later, when they have developed into young plants, choose the healthier, sturdier one and remove the other.

## Transplanting

For plants raised in pots and punnets, transplant to their outdoor positions before they become too large. Bare-root transplants from an outdoor seedbed work well only as long as the seedlings are very small. When a newly sown row comes up and there are gaps, fill these in with surplus seedlings thinned out from better populated parts of the row. Care must be taken with the tap roots of lettuces, endive, and chicory when transplanting. Radishes have delicate roots and should not be transplanted bare-root. Naturally, with transplanted seedlings there will be a check in growth, and these plants will mature later than the others. This can be an advantage, however, avoiding the problem of simultaneous maturation.

## Intercropping and catch cropping

Intercropping salad crops with longer-term vegetables (*see pp. 69 and 71*) allows a good return from a given space. A checkerboard planting pattern uses space best, but alternate rows are easier to manage. Lettuces and other leafy salads may be grown with Brussels sprouts and cauliflowers, for example, since they appreciate the same high-nitrogen soil conditions. Radishes and parsnips (*see p. 69*) thrive on low levels of nitrogen. For details, *see individual crops* (see pp. 103–107).

Salads can also be used for a catch crop (*see p. 69*). Grow early leafy salads in an area set aside for purple sprouting

---

## Forcing and blanching chicory

1 **In autumn, lift** chicon types (*see p. 103*) and trim the leaves to 1cm (½in) from the roots. Position upright in a deep box on a layer of moist peat, or peat substitute. Cover with another 23cm (9in) of peat and firm this down. Put the box in a warm, dark place.

2 **Several weeks later,** when they have grown to 15–20cm (6–8in) in length, remove the chicons from the box and cut them away from the roots.

---

broccoli and leeks to be planted out in late summer, for example. Spaces in flower beds can also be used for catch crops of salads.

## Extending the season

Many salads, such as endive, chicory, corn salad, and rocket, can tolerate cold, and if protected (*see pp. 43–48*) can be gathered from early autumn to winter. Chicory chicons may be forced either indoors (*see above*) or outdoors (*see p. 103*) for harvest in winter. Winter radishes and cut-and-come-again leaves (*see below*) may be harvested in winter. In spring, overwintered lettuces, rocket, and land cress will be ready. If over-wintering crops, make sure you choose suitable cultivars and sow at the correct time (*see pp. 103–107*).

## Container growing

Salads can be grown in containers if garden space is limited. Large tubs are best for headed salads, but summer radishes, leafy crops, and cut-and-come-again leaves suit pots or growing boxes – ones that have already supported a cucumber or tomato crop are fine for salads, as their depleted nutrient levels are sufficient for salad crops. Careful watering will be required so as not to let the potting mix dry out.

## Saving seeds

Lettuces are self-pollinating, so that home-saved seed will be true to type, especially if other plants are positioned more than 8m (25ft) away. The seed from rocket, which is a species and not a cultivar, will also come true.

---

# Growing cut-and-come-again salad crops

Most leafy salad crops can be grown to produce several flushes of young, tender leaves for eating. After one cut, the plants regrow to create another crop. Two or three harvests can be made from each sowing. This method is suitable for crops sown either in pots, modules, or a growing bag (*see right*) or outdoors in a seedbed. To cover the whole season, sow successively (*see p. 69*). Leafy vegetables other than salads can be treated in this way:

Amaranth (*see p. 125*)    Kale (*see p. 81*)
Swiss chard (*see p. 128*)  Spinach (*see p. 128*)
Leaf celery (*see p. 122*)   Sorrel (*see p. 145*)
Radish leaves
   (*see p. 106*)

1 **Plant seedlings** of non-hearting salads closely in a growing bag (here oriental greens, land cress, and lettuces). After 3–6 weeks, cut the leaves to 5cm (2in), leaving a stump with enough side-buds to regrow.

2 **After two weeks,** the crops have already begun to regrow from the stumps. In another 1–2 weeks, a fresh crop of salad leaves may be harvested, and another one in a further 3–6 weeks.

# A–Z of salad crops

## Chicory

*Cichorium intybus*

| Season | Spring | Summer | Autumn | Winter |
|---|---|---|---|---|
| Sow | • • • | | • • • | • |
| Transplant | • • • | | | |
| Harvest | • | | • • • | • • • • |

Chicory is relatively cold- and drought-resistant, and makes a handsome plant in the ornamental vegetable garden. When eaten raw in salads, the taste of the leaves can be bitter, although sometimes such bitterness is welcome. Chicory can also be cooked. There are three types of chicory.

Witloof, or Belgian, chicory grows as a rosette of leaves forming a deep root, which when harvested and trimmed can be forced in a warm, dark place to produce white, compact, leafy buds, or chicons (*see p.102 and below*), with the bitterness blanched out.

Red chicory, also known as radicchio, and sugarloaf chicory both form hearts, like those of lettuces. The heart leaves are less bitter than the outer leaves, being naturally blanched or deprived of light. Red and sugarloaf chicory will normally yield 8–9 heads per 3m (10ft) row. A proportion of plants always fails to produce good hearts; older cultivars are especially vulnerable.

**Site and soil**  Chicory prefers an open, sunny site, but will tolerate light shade. It does well on poor soils and needs little fertilizer, making it suitable for organic gardens.

**Sowing and planting**  Sow Witloof chicory in late spring and early summer for forcing (*see below*) in autumn. Sow red and sugarloaf chicories from mid-spring to late summer. Winter sowings in cool climates may bolt (*see p.101*) due to cold and even bolt-resistant cultivars are safest raised in modules in warm conditions, then planted out beneath fleece or cloches. To grow red and sugarloaf chicories as cut-and-come-again crops (*see p.102*), sow in late winter, spring, and from early to late summer.

| Sowing depth | 1cm (½in) |
|---|---|
| Plant spacing | 23cm (9in) for Witloof type |
| | 30cm (1ft) for red, sugarloaf types |
| Row spacing | 30cm (1ft) |

**Routine care**  Witloof chicory produces chicons from roots that are 3.5–5cm (1½–2in) in diameter. To force these *in situ*, cut off the leaves in early autumn, leaving a 5cm (2in) stub. Draw soil over the plants into a 15cm (6in) ridge. The chicons will form under the soil, especially if cloches (*see p.46*) are used to provide extra warmth and rain protection. However, better results are often achieved by forcing indoors (*see p.102*) at a temperature of 10–18°C (50–64°F). Although soil or a similar covering used to be required for well-shaped, compact chicons, modern cultivars (*see below*) need only darkness, such as that provided by an inverted bucket. It is a good idea to keep a stock of roots for forcing in boxes of moist soil or sand until they are needed. Some kinds of red chicory may also be forced to produce small chicons.

Red and sugarloaf chicories need watering in dry spells and feeding with a nitrogen-rich fertilizer if growth flags.

**Harvesting**  Blanched chicons of Witloof chicory will be ready for eating about a month after being covered for forcing. The heads of red and sugarloaf chicory should be gathered after 2–3 months, when they are fully formed and firm. Unlike those of lettuces, the heads are long-lasting (2–4 weeks, depending on the weather) and can be refrigerated or stored in a cool place until needed. After harvesting, the resulting stumps will often sprout another crop of usable leaves, about 2–6 weeks later.

**Common problems**  Slugs (*see p.262*), aphids (*see p.251*), and caterpillars can damage chicory foliage and roots. Tip burn (*see p.263*) is a physiological disorder associated with lack of calcium, and especially troublesome on very dry, light soils.

**Recommended cultivars**

'Bianca di Milano' – forms large heads of tender green leaves, pale inside the head; grow for winter harvest.

'Di Bruxelles' – grown for forcing to produce chicons.

'Greenlof' – tall heads of green with white leaves inside; grown for salads or to force chicons.

'Long Green' – upright with dandelion-like leaves.

'Radicchio Amba' – chioggia-style with tight, round heads of red leaves; grow for summer harvest.

'Red Rib' – upright with dandelion-like leaves with red stems.

'Red Treviso' – leaves turn deep red in cool weather; can be grown for salads or for forcing chicons.

'Redheart' – forms firm hearts of tender, red leaves.

'Witlof' – grown for forcing chicons.

## Corn salad

*Valerianella locusta*

| Season | Spring | Summer | Autumn | Winter |
|---|---|---|---|---|
| Sow/plant | • • • • • | • | | |
| Transplant | • • • | • | | |
| Harvest | • • • | • • • | • • • | • • |

Corn salad provides tasty salad leaves in rosettes with a mild, earthy flavour in autumn and winter. It can be useful in summer salads as well. If sown before midsummer, however, it is liable to run quickly to seed. It is used in supermarket salad packs, often called lamb's lettuce, feldsalat or mache. There are two types: a large-leaved form and a smaller, darker-leaved form. Corn salad matures in 4–6 weeks, and yields 18–20 plants per 3m (10ft) row.

**Site and soil** Any moderately fertile soil in a sunny, open position is suitable. For winter crops in cool climates, protection with cloches, cold frames, or even a fleece tunnel cloche (*see pp. 45–48*) improves quality and reliability. In hot weather, protect plants from hot sun with tall crops or shadecloth.

**Sowing and planting** Either sow in moist soil where the plants are to grow, or in cold climates raise seedlings in punnets or module trays for planting out. Corn salad may also be grown as a cut-and-come-again crop (*see p. 102*).

| Sowing depth | 1cm (½in) |
|---|---|
| Plant spacing | 10cm (4in) |
| Row spacing | 15cm (6in) |

**Routine care** Thin seedlings (*see p. 101*), and use the thinnings for salads. Watering in dry spells is sometimes helpful, but top-dressings of fertilizer are unnecessary.

**Harvesting** After 4–8 weeks, harvest by picking choice leaves or cutting the head from the lower part of the plant, which may resprout for further harvests.

**Common problems** Aphids, slugs and snails are occasionally troublesome. For symptoms and controls, *see* Plant Problems, *p. 251 and p. 263*.

**Recommended cultivars**
'Machelong' – traditional Dutch variety with large, round leaves.
'Verte de Cambrai' - small-leafed variety.

# Endive

## *Cichorium endivia*

| Season | Spring | | Summer | | Autumn | | Winter | |
|---|---|---|---|---|---|---|---|---|
| Sow | | • | • | • | • | • | | |
| Transplant | | | | • | • | | | |
| Harvest | | | | • | • | • | • | • | • |

Endive is similar to lettuce, although it has a bitter taste, and grows as a rosette. The leaves may be curled (frisée type) or broad-leaved (Batavian type). The former are extremely attractive in gardens or salads, but the hardier broad-leaved endive is more reliable. The bitterness can be reduced by excluding light to whiten or blanch the leaves (*see below*), making a refreshing winter salad or cooked vegetable, although sometimes unblanched bitterness is appreciated in salads.

Endives can withstand light frosts, and so remain usable into the winter. They mature over a period of 8 weeks, and will require an additional two weeks to be blanched. Plants should yield 9–10 heads per 3m (10ft) row.

**Site and soil** Endives prefer an open, sunny site and fertile, moisture-retentive soil, with only low levels of nitrogen. Light shade is preferred for summer crops.

**Sowing and planting** When growing endive as a cut-and-come-again salad crop for winter, sow seed in late summer or early autumn. Seed can also be sown in spring for use in salads in spring and early summer. Hot weather can cause bitterness, and crops grown in cool weather have the best flavour. Plants may bolt to seed in hot weather.

| Sowing depth | 1cm (½in) |
|---|---|
| Plant spacing | 23cm (9in) |
| Row spacing | 30–35cm (12–14in) |

**Routine care** Protect new seedlings from slugs and snails, and maintain a moist soil. If growing endive in warm weather, shadecloth will help to reduce bitterness.

**Harvesting** When the heads reach full size, usually three months after sowing, blanch each one by covering the entire plant for about ten days (or 20 days in cold weather), with an inverted, light-proof container such as a pot or bucket, or by laying an inverted dinner plate over the central area. Rots in wet weather can be damaging at this stage; covering the heads with a cloche can help to dry them out. Alternatively, use twine to tie the head into a tight bunch in order to exclude light from the inner leaves. Use the heads as soon as they are blanched, since greenness and bitterness will soon return when they are exposed to light again.

**Common problems** Slugs (*see p. 262*), aphids (*see p. 251*), and caterpillars can damage foliage and roots. Tip burn (*see p. 263*), associated with a lack of calcium, occurs mainly on dry, light soils.

**Recommended cultivars**
'Broadleaf Fullheart' – Batavian type with broad, tender leaves; best grown in winter.
'Green Curled' – compact variety with tender leaves that are bitter when green.
'Tres Fine' – lacy leaves with nutty flavour; quick growing but slow to bolt.

# Komatsuna

## *Brassica rapa* var. *perviridis*

| Season | Spring | | Summer | | Autumn | | Winter | |
|---|---|---|---|---|---|---|---|---|
| Sow | | | | • | • | | | |
| Transplant | | | | | • | | | |
| Harvest | | | | | | • | • | • | • | • | • |

Komatsuna, or mustard spinach, is a diverse group of leafy brassicas with glossy green foliage that may be eaten raw in salads or cooked in the same way as spinach. They will grow into large, robust plants if left to mature fully, but can be harvested earlier, as small plants, if desired. This affects how they are grown (*see below*). The plants mature in 4–12 weeks, and yield 6–9 heads per 3m (10ft) row. Named cultivars are seldom offered.

**Site and soil** Open, sunny sites and fertile soils are best, but light shade is preferred for midsummer crops.

**Sowing and planting** Sow *in situ* in spring and summer or in module trays (*see p. 65*) for transplanting. Thin the seedlings (*see p. 101*) to 10cm (4in) if you desire only small plants, and 45cm (18in) for large ones. Komatsuna may also be grown as a cut-and-come-again crop (*see p. 102*).

| Sowing depth | 1cm (½in) |
|---|---|
| Seed spacing | 2.5cm (1in) |
| Row spacing | 23cm (9in) for small plants |
| | 45cm (18in) for large plants |

**Routine care** Komatsuna will tolerate temperatures as low as −12°C (10°F), and is fairly drought-tolerant, and compared to other mustards it remains mild-flavoured, even in hot weather.

**Harvesting** Pick choice leaves as soon as they are ready. Regrowth will occur, giving a prolonged harvest period.

**Common problems** Slugs (*see p. 262*) may cause minor damage. As a member of the brassica family, this crop might also be affected by a range of problems. These include birds, boron deficiency, bolting, caterpillars, clubroot, cutworm, damping off, downy mildew, frost damage, leaf spot, mealy cabbage aphid, molybdenum deficiency, whitefly, and white blister. Grow in the brassica part of the rotation (*see p. 31*) to avoid clubroot and other soil-borne brassica problems. For symptoms and controls, *see* Plant Problems, *pp. 246–264*.

# Land cress

## *Barbarea verna*

| Season | Spring | | Summer | | Autumn | | Winter | |
|---|---|---|---|---|---|---|---|---|
| Sow | | • | • | • | • | | | | |
| Transplant | | | | | • | • | | |
| Harvest | • | | | • | • | • | • | • | • |

Land, American, or upland cress resembles watercress, with glossy green leaves and a strong, peppery flavour, but it may be grown on dry land. Land cress is robust, making it a useful winter salad. Plants mature in 4–12 weeks, and yield 18–20 heads per 3m (10ft) row. Named cultivars are not offered.

**Site and soil** Any moderately fertile but very moisture-retentive soil, preferably in a sheltered and slightly shaded position, is suitable for growing land cress.

**Sowing and planting** Either sow in moist soil where the plants are to grow in mid-spring to early summer, or raise seedlings in module trays (*see p. 101*) for planting out as soon as seedlings can be handled. Land cress may be grown as a cut-and-come-again crop (*see p. 102*).

| Sowing depth | 1cm (½in) |
|---|---|
| Plant spacing | 15cm (6in) |
| Row spacing | 20cm (8in) |

**Routine care** Thin out the seedlings (*see p.101*); use the thinnings in salads. Generous watering in dry spells is vital to avoid coarse texture and fiery flavour, but top-dressing with fertilizer is unnecessary. For autumn and winter crops in cool climates, protection with cloches, cold frames, or even a fleece tunnel cloche (*see pp.45–48*) improves quality and reliability.

**Harvesting** Harvest by picking choice leaves, leaving the lower part of the plant to resprout for further harvests.

**Common problems** There are few problems but caterpillars (*see p.253*), and slugs and snails (*see p.262*) may occasionally be troublesome.

# Lettuce

## *Lactuca sativa*

| Season | Spring | Summer | Autumn | Winter |
|---|---|---|---|---|
| Sow | • • • | • • • | • • • | • • |
| Transplant | • • | • • • | • • | |
| Harvest | • • | • • • | • • | • |

There are two types of lettuce: those that form hearts or heads, and those that do not. Large, heart-forming lettuces include the cabbage-like butterheads, the crinkled crispheads, and the cos types. Iceberg lettuces are crispheads that develop for another two weeks, forming extremely dense heads. They need large amounts of water and fertilizer, and are much more demanding to grow than other lettuces. Non-hearting or leafy lettuces include the Salad Bowl type and stem lettuces. Leaves of Salad Bowl lettuces can be repeatedly harvested. Stem lettuces are seldom grown today, but yield leaves and a succulent stem that can be eaten like celery. Lettuces tend to mature in a rush, leading to gluts, and frequent sowings of small batches of seed are recommended to ensure an even supply. Packets of mixed cultivars are available; these contain reliable cultivars and are an inexpensive way of growing a variety of lettuces and so staggering the harvest.

Lettuces can be grown throughout the year in temperate Australia. The easiest varieties to grow, particularly in warm weather, are the non-hearting, cut-and-come-again types and cos types, which form an upright head of long, crisp leaves. Cos lettuces are the easiest lettuces to grow in cool weather and they can be harvested through winter in temperate regions. Non-hearting or loose-leaf types come in a variety of leaf colours and shapes, and are most decorative in the garden and in tubs as well as in the salad bowl. Non-hearting lettuces are also the best lettuces to grow in the tropics, where they are grown through the "winter dry" with shade from hot sun where necessary.

Non-hearting lettuces include oak-leaf and frilled and curly leaf varieties in shades of green, red, purple, and flecked. A range of these varieties are included in mixed seed packs and in mixed commercial seedling punnets. These are often called mesclun mixes.

Butterhead lettuces are also available in reddish-brown and green leaf forms. Butterhead varieties form a small head of tender leaves surrounded by loose, tender leaves. They can be harvested as cut-and-come-again lettuces when only a few leaves are required. Crisphead lettuces are difficult to grow well because they require perfect conditions to form a firm head, and they are prone to rotting inside the head, especially in warm weather where they are watered by an overhead sprinkler.

From a spring sowing, butterheads will mature in 8–10 weeks, crispheads and cos in 10–12 weeks, and icebergs in 14 weeks. Non-hearting lettuces yield 18–20 heads per 3m (10ft) row, butterheads 9–12 heads, cos 9–12 heads, and crispheads and iceberg 8–9 heads.

**Site and soil** Open, sunny sites are best, but light shade is acceptable for midsummer crops. Fertile, moisture-retentive soils are needed for best-quality lettuces.

**Sowing and planting** Lettuces intended for an early summer harvest can be sown in a propagator (*see p.101*) from winter to early spring, and planted out in spring. Lettuces for a summer harvest can be sown where they are to crop, from early spring onwards, in a continuous trickle. Thin the resulting seedlings (*see p.101*) to the required spacing, using the thinnings in salad leaves. Alternatively, to save time when thinning and to economize on seed, opt for station sowing the seed (*see p.101*).

Hardy cultivars can be sown *in situ* in late winter, or in mild areas in early autumn, to crop in the winter and spring. Protecting the crop with cloches and cold frames (*see pp.45–48*) will advance the harvest, greatly improve the quality, and make success more likely if the weather is frosty or very wet. Fleece covering (*see p.101*) can be used to protect seedlings from hot sun.

Lettuce seedlings resent root disturbance when transplanted and may soon wilt, especially in summer. Although they can be raised in seed trays or open ground and transplanted as bare-root plants, you will achieve better results by sowing them in module trays (*see p.101*), and transplanting as soon as they can be handled, before they have six leaves. Position the base of the leaves just above soil level. The depth of the seedling is crucial – too deep and it may rot off, too shallow and it will produce a poorly shaped lettuce. Water generously until the transplants are well-established.

Leafy lettuces, such as Salad Bowl types, may also be grown as a cut-and-come-again crop (*see p.102*).

**Routine care** Water in dry spells, especially in the two weeks before the hearts reach full maturity. Feeding is not usually necessary on reasonably fertile soils but, if growth is particularly slow, top-dress occasionally with a nitrogen-rich fertilizer (*see pp.20–23*) at the manufacturer's recommended rate.

| Sowing depth | 1cm (½in) | |
|---|---|---|
| MINI-LETTUCE | | |
| Plant spacing | 15cm (6in) | |
| Row spacing | 23cm (9in) | |
| BUTTERHEAD | | |
| Plant spacing | 25cm (10in) | |
| Row spacing | 30cm (12in) | |
| OTHER TYPES | | |
| Plant spacing | 35cm (14in) | |
| Row spacing | 38cm (15in) | |

**Harvesting** Begin to gather leaves from leafy lettuces, and thinnings from hearting lettuces, as soon as they are usable. When cutting leafy lettuces, leave 2.5cm (1in) of the stem to resprout for later harvests. Cut hearting lettuces as soon as the hearts are mature, in order to prevent rotting and bolting (*see p.101*). Solid, sound hearts may be stored in a refrigerator for several days. Butterhead and non-hearting types of lettuce run to seed much faster than crispheads or cos lettuce.

**Common problems** Cutworms (*see p.254*) may eat the roots. Slugs and snails (*see p.262*), and aphids (*see p.251*) can damage foliage. Fungal rots, or botrytis (*see p.252*), bacterial soft rot (*see p.251*) and downy mildew (*see p.251*) occur in wet weather and with overhead watering, especially in autumn. Mildew and rotting leaves can usually be cut out at harvest, leaving sound heads. Virus diseases can be avoided by using good-quality seed, eliminating aphids, and avoiding repeated cropping on the same piece of ground. Tip burn (*see p.263*) is a physiological disorder associated with lack of calcium, and is especially troublesome on dry, light soils.

**Recommended cultivars**

NON-HEARTING LEAFY LETTUCES
'Cireo' – decorative, frilled, green leaves.
'Freze' – tender, green, crisp leaves; good winter lettuce.
'Green Coral' – decorative, frilly-edged, green leaves.
'Lollo Biondo' – pale green, ruffled leaves.
'Lollo Rossa' – decorative, ruffled, red leaves, pale green at the base.
'Oak-leaf Green' – rosettes of smooth, divided leaves.
'Oak-leaf Italian' – upright, vigorous plant with divided, green leaves.
'Oak-leaf Purple' – smooth, purple, divided leaves.
'Oak-leaf Red' – smooth, reddish-brown, divided leaves.
'Red Coral' – decorative, frilly, red leaves.
'Red Italian' – smooth, brownish-green leaves.
'Red Velvet' – glossy, deep burgundy, broad, crunchy leaves.
BUTTERHEAD LETTUCES
'Buttercrunch' – fan-shaped leaf with small, green heart; good summer lettuce.
'Green Mignonette' – soft, curly, green leaf with small head.
'Red Mignonette' – reddish-brown, curly leaves, green at the base, forming a small heart.
'Sunset' – smooth, red leaves; forms a small heart.

COS LETTUCES

'Cos Verdi' – large, green leaves form a tall heart.
'Freckles' – reddish-brown flecks on pale green leaves and a tall heart.
'Mini Cos' – small, green lettuce forming a small heart.
'Roma Rossa Cos' – tall, red leaves forming a tall heart.
'Ruby Cos' – red-tipped, green leaves and a tall heart.

CRISPHEAD LETTUCES

'Great Lakes' – Iceberg variety with crisp, green leaves and large head; good summer lettuce.
'Green Velvet' – large, solid heart; good winter lettuce.
'Minigreen' – small, tight heads of crisp leaves.
'Webs Wonder' – large, crinkled head; good summer lettuce.
'Yatesdale' – good warm-climate variety with pale green head.

# Miner's lettuce

*Montia perfoliata*

| Season | Spring | Summer | Autumn | Winter |
|---|---|---|---|---|
| Sow | • • • • • | | | |
| Transplant | | • | | |
| Harvest | | • • • • | • • | |

This cool-climate plant, also known as winter purslane or claytonia, has pale, succulent leaves that may be used, together with tender stems and flowers, in salads. Miner's lettuce thrives in poor soils and dry conditions, and frequently self-seeds. It is easily controlled, however, and unlikely to become a nuisance. Plants mature over a period of about ten weeks, and yield the equivalent of 20–24 bunches per 3m (10ft) row. Named cultivars are not offered.

**Site and soil** Choose a well-drained, sunny site, and moderately fertile soil.

**Sowing and planting** Sow in moist soil where the plants are to grow, or raise seedlings in modules (*see p.65*) for planting out in autumn for winter harvest. Plants are usually grown as a cut-and-come-again crop (*see p.102*).

| Sowing depth | 1cm (½in) |
|---|---|
| Plant spacing | 15cm (6in) |
| Row spacing | 23cm (9in) |

**Routine care** Thin seedlings (*see p.101*), using the thinnings for salads. Regular watering or top-dressing with fertilizer are unnecessary.

**Harvesting** When the plants are mature, pick leaves, stems, and flowers, leaving the lower part of the plant in the ground. More leaves will be produced, giving several more harvests. Resprouting of new leaves may take from 2–6 weeks. The thick root is also edible.

**Common problems** Aphids, slugs and snails may occasionally be troublesome. For symptoms and controls, *see* Plant Problems, *p.251 and p.263.*

# Mibuna greens *and* Mizuna greens

*Brassica rapa* and *Brassica rapa* var. *nipposinica*

| Season | Spring | Summer | Autumn | Winter |
|---|---|---|---|---|
| Sow | • • • | • • • | • | |
| Transplant | • • | • • | • | |
| Harvest | | • • | • • • | |

Mibuna and mizuna greens are types of Japanese brassica with rosettes of attractive, glossy green or red foliage and a succulent stem that can either be eaten raw in salads or cooked in the same way as spinach. The leaves have a mild mustard flavour, even when they are mature, and are good for winter harvests and container cultivation. Mibuna greens have a stronger flavour and strap-like leaves, but are less hardy; mizuna greens have feathery leaves.

You can grow mibuna or mizuna greens as small plants that will yield several harvests of young salad leaves. Pick the leaves when they are young and tender, and as required, or leave them to mature into large plants, which are better cooked. Plants will mature in 4–12 weeks, and yield 6–9 heads per 3m (10ft) row. Named cultivars are seldom offered.

**Site and soil** Open, sunny sites and fertile soils are preferred.

**Sowing and planting** Sow seed in spring or summer in punnets or modules (*see p.101*) or in situ in spring. Thin (*see p.101*) to 10cm (4in) apart for small plants and 45cm (18in) for large ones. These greens may be grown as a cut-and-come-again crop (*see p.102*).

| Sowing depth | 1cm (½in) |
|---|---|
| Plant spacing | 10cm (4in) for small plants |
| | 45cm (18in) for large plants |
| Row spacing | 23cm (9in) |

**Routine care** Water in dry spells to keep the soil moist. If plants start to go to seed, cut the foliage right back to above ground level and new foliage will regrow.

**Harvesting** For salads, pick choice young leaves as soon as they are ready. Regrowth will occur 2–8 weeks later (depending on the weather) for a prolonged harvest. Cut large plants when mature.

**Common problems** In common with other crops from the brassica family, these greens are prey to a range of problems, as for komatsuna (*see p.104*). For symptoms and controls, *see* Plant Problems, *pp.246–264.*

# Mustard *and* cress

*Sinapis alba* and *Lepidium sativum*

| Season | Spring | Summer | Autumn | Winter |
|---|---|---|---|---|
| Sow | • • • • | • • • | • • • | • • |
| Harvest | • • • • | • • • | • • • | • • |

Mustard and cress are tasty, fast-growing salad

crops that are especially valuable between mid-autumn and mid-spring. Mustard seeds germinate in 4–5 days, and the seedlings can be cut after 8–12 days. Cress takes about two days longer to germinate than mustard, and can be cut after 10–14 days and added to salads and sandwiches. Named cultivars of mustard and cress are seldom offered. Mustard is often replaced by rape (*Brassica napus* subsp. *oleifera*), which has a stronger flavour. Plain-leaved cress is usually sold; this grows better in winter than curled cress.

**Site and soil** Warm (10–16°C/50–60°F), well-lit windowsills, greenhouses and, in the summer, shade houses (*see pp.45–47*) are best for growing mustard and cress. Trays or pots filled with old potting or growing-bag compost provide ideal conditions. Outdoor crops need shelter and light shade, and they risk contamination from splashed soil.

**Sowing and planting** Seeds must be fresh to germinate quickly and evenly. Seed can be sown throughout the year. Avoid very hot and cold weather. Mustard should be sown two days after cress where mixed crops are wanted. Crops can also be raised on a thick layer of moist kitchen towel (*see p.65*). Scatter the seeds lightly over a fine level surface, gently press them in, lightly water them with tepid water and cover with a damp cloth or a tile until germination has taken place. Mustard and cress may also be grown as a cut-and-come-again crop (*see p.102*).

| Sowing depth | on the surface |
|---|---|
| Seed spacing | almost touching |
| Row spacing | almost touching |

**Routine care** Keep soil or other growing medium moist.

**Harvesting** Cut at the base of the stems with scissors when the seedlings are 4–5cm (1½–2in) tall and the seed leaves or cotyledons are fully developed and green.

**Common problems** Damping off (*see p.254*), where seedling growth is slow or uneven, can ruin the salads. Keeping them warmer and using better-quality seeds can help. Grey mould, or botrytis (*see p.252*), can also be a problem in overly damp conditions.

**Recommended cultivars**
'Perfection Curled Cress' – tasty, tender leaves cut every few weeks.
'White Mustard' – hot and spicy leaves.

# Radish

*Raphanus sativa*

| Season | Spring | Summer | Autumn | Winter |
|---|---|---|---|---|
| Sow | • • • • | • • • | • • | • |
| Transplant | • | | | |
| Harvest | • | • • • | • • • | • • |

There are three types of this fast-growing, crunchy, slightly hot root vegetable. Summer radishes are small, round, cylindrical, or pointed, and are used in salads. Winter radishes are larger, and turnip-like. Summer radishes usually have red, pink, or white skins, but winter radishes may also have black, purple, yellow, or green skins; all usually have white flesh. Small roots are used raw as a salad ingredient, while the larger roots can also be used raw, or can be cooked in the same way as turnips or swedes. Oriental mooli radishes used in stir-fry are grown in the same way as winter radishes. Summer radish plants take 2–8 weeks to mature, yielding a crop of 100–120 radishes per 3m (10ft) row. They can also be grown as a catch crop. In the summer months, maturation rates are more rapid. Winter radish matures in 8–10 weeks, with a yield of ten roots per 3m (10ft) row.

Seedling leaves can be used as cut-and-come-again salads (*see p.102*), while immature seed pods of older plants are also edible.

**Site and soil** Open, sunny sites are best, but light shade is acceptable for midsummer crops. Fertile, moisture-retentive soils are needed for good-quality summer radishes, but winter radishes are more tolerant.

**Sowing and planting** Radishes grow very quickly, soon maturing and becoming fibrous and inedible, so that fortnightly successional sowings are necessary for continuous cropping. Seed is sown *in situ* from spring to autumn for summer radishes, and in summer and early autumn for winter radishes and oriental radishes.

| Sowing depth | 1cm (½in) |
|---|---|
| Plant spacing | 1cm (½in) for summer radish |
| | 23cm (9in) for winter radish |
| Row spacing | 15cm (6in) for summer radish |
| | 30cm (12in) for winter radish |

**Routine care** Adding organic matter before sowing (*see p.68*) will help maintain soil moisture as well as providing adequate nutrients. Water to keep the soil moist; in dry spells, this may mean watering every day. Radishes may also be used for intersowing with parsnips (*see p.69*).

**Harvesting and storing** Use summer radishes as soon as the roots are large enough and before they become "woolly". Winter radishes may be left in the ground until they are needed, and may then reach the same size as turnips or swedes. They may be damaged by frost, however.

To produce edible pods, leave some roots to sprout and flower, and gather the pods while they are still green and crisp, before they get stringy. Radish leaves also make useful greens in the same manner as turnip tops (*see p.88*).

**Common problems** Slugs and snails (*see p.263*) may cause minor damage. Cabbage white butterfly (*see p.253*) can be very destructive, and is best avoided by growing radishes beneath a fleece or insect-proof fine woven mesh (*see p.101*), or by growing only in cool weather. Grow winter radishes in the brassica part of the rotation (*see p.31*) to avoid clubroot (*see p.254*) and other soil-borne brassica problems.

**Recommended cultivars**
SALAD RADISH
'Cherry Belle' – red, oval root and mild, white flesh.
'French Breakfast' – long, scarlet roots, tipped white.
'Mixed Radish' – a mix of purple, red and white varieties.
'Plum Purple' – round, purple root.
'Red Brigade' – hybrid with very red, round roots.
'Red Prince' – round, red root and short leaves.
'White Icicle' – long, white, mild root that stays tender.
WINTER RADISH
'Black Spanish' – black-skinned roots with pungent taste.
'Muncher Bier' – old variety with white skin and pungent taste.
ORIENTAL RADISH (DAIKON)
'Long White' – tapered, white, tasty roots.
'Red Meat' – tasty, round root with green skin and red flesh.
'Summer Hybrid' – large, white roots to 40cm long.

# Rocket

## *Eruca sativa*

| Season | Spring | Summer | Autumn | Winter |
|---|---|---|---|---|
| Sow | • • • | • • • | • • • | |
| Harvest | • • • | • • • | • • • | • |

Rocket, arugula or salad rocket is a tangy member of the cabbage family, whose young leaves add a "mustard" flavour to salads. It is a common ingredient of supermarket salad packs, where it may be called erugala, rucola, or roquette. Rocket is one of the easiest salad vegetables to grow and it can be included in the flower garden as a cut-and-come-again salad plant. Plants usually self-seed and can become a nuisance if all are left to go to seed. Wild (*Diplotaxis* species) and Turkish rocket (*Bunias orientalis*) are almost identical with subtly different, more aromatic, but equally delicious, flavours. They may also be cooked like spinach. The plants mature in 4–10 weeks, and yield the equivalent of 9–10 bunches per 3m (10ft) row.

**Site and soil** Any moderately fertile but moisture-retentive soil, a sheltered and slightly shaded position, is suitable.

**Sowing and planting** Like radishes, rocket soon runs to seed, and repeated sowings are necessary for a constant supply of edible leaves. Sow where the plants are to grow when seedlings from the previous sowing have produced a couple of true leaves, anything from 4–21 days, depending on the weather. Rocket is usually grown as a cut-and-come-again crop (*see p.102*).

| Sowing depth | 1cm (½in) |
|---|---|
| Plant spacing | 15cm (6in) |
| Row spacing | 15cm (6in) |

**Routine care** Thin out the seedlings (*see p.101*) and use the thinnings in salads. Generous watering in dry spells is essential.

**Harvesting** Harvest rocket leaves as soon as they are usable. Frequent cutting will promote tender new growth. The younger the leaves the more tender they are. Old leaves and those on a seedling plant are tough and taste bitter. Remove old plants.

**Common problems** Slugs and snails may cause minor damage. For symptoms and controls, *see* Plant Problems, *p.263*.

**Recommended cultivars** Generally salad rocket is available as the species *Eruca sativa*. However, one cultivar that is offered is 'Cultivata', which has larger leaves than the species.

# Summer purslane

## *Portulaca oleracea*

| Season | Spring | Summer | Autumn | Winter |
|---|---|---|---|---|
| Sow | | • • • | | |
| Harvest | | • | • • • | |

Most Australians consider this plant a weed but it can be grown as a crunchy addition to salads. However, the flavour is bland. There are green- and yellow-leaved forms of this succulent, low-growing plant. The leaves and stems are either eaten raw or lightly cooked or steamed. The green forms are more vigorous, but are less striking in decorative mixed salads than the yellow form. Both forms of summer purslane have a relatively mild flavour and crunchy texture. Plants mature in 4–8 weeks, and produce the equivalent of 20–24 bunches per 3m (10ft) row. Named cultivars are not offered.

**Site and soil** Well-drained soil and a sunny, sheltered site are preferred.

**Sowing and planting** Sow successionally, sowing a new batch of seed when seedlings from the previous sowing have produced a couple of true leaves, for a constant supply of edible leaves. Early sowings should be made under cover (*see p.101*). Summer purslane may also be grown as a cut-and-come-again crop (*see p.102*).

| Sowing depth | 1cm (½in) |
|---|---|
| Plant spacing | 15cm (6in) |
| Row spacing | 15cm (6in) |

**Routine care** Thin out the seedlings when large enough (*see p.101*) and use the thinnings in salads. Generous watering in dry spells is essential to maintain healthy growth.

**Harvesting** Pick the tender young leaves and stems as soon as they are large enough. Regular gathering encourages the production of fresh tender new growth, as long as some leaves are left on the plant after harvesting. Remove any seedheads that develop.

**Common problems** Slugs and snails may occasionally be troublesome. For symptoms and controls, *see* Plant Problems, *p.263*.

# Growing fruiting vegetables

Plants in this group of vegetables, which are grown for their "fruits", range from perhaps the most popular kitchen-garden crop – tomatoes, vine or bush types – to more exotic crops such as okra and tomatillo. Others that are well worth trying are eggplants, sweet and chilli peppers, and sweetcorn.

Fruiting vegetables need a long, hot summer in order for the fruits to ripen fully. This means that it is essential in the early stages to provide some form of protection in cool climates, such as cloches or fleece (*see pp. 44–48*), if the plants are to produce a successful crop.

Fruiting vegetables grow well in tropical gardens through winter. Capsicums and chillis will also grow through the "wet" in some areas.

## Site and soil

Well-drained, light soils that warm up quickly in the spring are best for this group of vegetables. Sowing and harvesting may need to be delayed where the soil is predominantly clay and consequently slow to warm. Adding organic matter (*see pp. 37–40*) will improve the structure of the soil, speeding up both the drainage and warming of the ground. Fruiting vegetables can be very deep-rooting,

and shallow, waterlogged, or compacted soils will limit their growth. In cool climates, try to exploit any warm microclimates in your garden, for example, by planting crops next to a sunny wall (*see right*), in a sheltered corner, or in a raised bed.

You can also help nature along by pre-warming the soil with a clear plastic sheet mulch (*see p. 42*) or a cloche covering from mid-spring, so that you can sow or plant out fruiting vegetables earlier in the season and give them as much time as possible for growth.

## Sowing seeds in a propagator

Many crops in this group, especially eggplants, okra, capsicums, and tomatillo, have small seeds that produce tiny, slow-growing seedlings needing an early start in a greenhouse, or even a windowsill in cool climates. The majority of fruiting vegetables bear fruits over several weeks, eliminating the need for successional sowing.

Sow the seeds thinly in pots of multi-purpose compost, adding sufficient vermiculite or sieved compost to cover the seeds (*see p. 64*). Warm conditions, with a minimum temperature of 16°C (60°F), are needed for successful germination, and this is best provided by a heated propagator (*see p. 63*).

When seedlings emerge, transfer the pots to better-lit conditions, such as a greenhouse or a sunny windowsill in the house. The seedlings will still require

**Using a microclimate**
*When growing tender crops, such as this eggplant, outdoors in a temperate climate, plant them against a sheltered, sunny wall. The wall absorbs heat and radiates it back onto the plant at night, raising the local temperature.*

warmth of at least 18°C (64°F) during the daytime, and 16°C (60°F) minimum at night. Make sure that any windowsill you are using for seedlings does not become cooler than this temperature at any time during the night.

Some crops, such as eggplants and okra, also need humidity, which is easily provided by erecting a plastic tent over the pot of seedlings. Insert a few split canes around the edge of the pot, or bend a length of wire into a hoop and push the ends into the soil at the sides of the pot, and place a clear plastic bag over the canes or wire. Alternatively, you could use a propagator.

When the seedlings are large enough to handle, prick them out (*see p. 64*) into individual 8cm (3in) pots, large module trays, tube pots, or biodegradeable pots (*see p. 62*). The latter are best for plants that resent root disturbance. Feed the seedlings with a balanced liquid fertilizer (*see p. 21*) if growth appears pale, and especially if the lower leaves start to turn yellow.

## Sowing *in situ*

Sweetcorn has much larger seeds that grow quickly, and therefore they can be station sown (*see p. 68*) in the garden in warm areas from mid-spring. For early crops in colder districts, raise

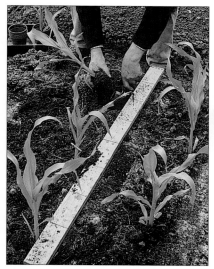

**Planting sweetcorn in a block**
*Sweetcorn relies on the wind for pollination, so plant out seedlings in a block of several short, staggered rows to increase the chances of successful pollination occurring.*

*Sides of each cell are grooved to train roots*

**Root trainers**
*These containers snap together to form long cells – useful for plants that require deep rooting space, such as sweetcorn. They can be opened out easily to remove and transplant the seedling plug without disturbing the roots. Root trainers can be reused many times.*

sweetcorn seedlings in tube pots (*see p.62*) or biodegradable pots, at least 9cm (3½in) in diameter. These will hold the long roots of sweetcorn seedlings in their entirety, and there will be no danger of damaging them at transplanting, which could result in the plant becoming stunted.

For later crops or to extend the growing season, sweetcorn can be sown in succession (*see p.69*). Alternatively, you can grow a selection of cultivars that crop at different times.

## Planting out

The young plants should be ready for transplanting into their final positions, when the roots have fully filled the pot, but before they become overcrowded, usually after about 18 weeks. Harden young plants off (*see p.65*) before planting, by placing them in either a sheltered position or beneath a double layer of fleece for at least a week; in these situations, temperature and humidity levels fall midway between those of the seedling pot and those of the final site. Careful planting is essential to avoid a check in growth,

◁ **Weed mat**
*To minimize weed growth around your crop (here sweetcorn) and help conserve moisture, lay a black woven weed mat on the bed and plant through it.*

△ **Removing tomato sideshoots**
*When growing vine tomatoes, pinch out with your finger and thumb any side-shoots that appear in the angles between the main stem and any of the leaf stems.*

which would curtail the period of cropping and the number of fruits produced. Covering with fleece (*see p.101*) after planting, for two weeks, provides extra warmth and humidity when the plants are at their most delicate. Commercial seedlings available in pots and punnets save time, and

many varieties are available as advanced plants. Tomatoes, capsicum and eggplant are not easy to propagate without a propagator in cool climates, and commercial seedlings are most convenient. However, the range of available varieties of tomato, in particular, is limited.

## Planting sweetcorn in blocks

Plant out sweetcorn seedlings that have been grown in tube pots when the plants are 8cm (3in) tall. Because they are wind-pollinated, it is best to plant them in blocks of at least 12 plants, no closer than 34cm (14in) apart, in a series of short rows (*see facing page*), rather than in single rows. This gives the plants a much better chance of being pollinated successfully, which is necessary for the production of cobs.

## Mulching

Fruiting vegetables grow slowly and can easily be smothered by weeds. Organic mulches (*see above and pp.41–42*) will prevent this happening, and are especially valuable where weeding may be difficult. Before planting, laying a sheet of black plastic, or clear plastic over black, can warm the soil as well as suppressing weeds. Mulching prevents evaporation.

The floppy habit of bush tomatoes leads to fruits lying on the ground, where they are prone to slugs and other problems. Mulching with straw keeps the fruits clean and free from slug damage or rots.

## Providing support for fruiting crops

Because of the weight of their fruits, some fruiting vegetables, such as tomatoes and capsicums, need support. Bamboo canes and twine are often adequate, but for very heavy crops you may need stronger supports such as sawn-timber stakes. The taller the crop, the more substantial the support system should be (*see below*).

**Supporting short crops**
*When lower-growing crops such as capsicums (shown here) begin to form fruits, place 3–5 bamboo canes around each plant and tie in the stems with figure-of-eight loops of twine.*

**Supporting tall crops in a greenhouse**
*Taller-growing crops like vine tomatoes are best trained up single bamboo canes tied into a greenhouse structure for stability. Tie the plants to the canes as they grow.*

## Container growing

Most fruiting vegetables, excluding sweetcorn, grow well in pots of at least 25cm (10in) in diameter. The best position for a container in cool climates is against a warm, sunny wall near the house, where the extra heat and light speed cropping and boost flavour.

Tomatoes are especially suitable for growing in containers, and the bigger the container, the better they grow. Large pots, 35cm (14in) in diameter, filled with compost and potting mix, are suitable without being unwieldy. Vegetables growing in containers dry out quickly, and will require watering at least once a day in hot weather. Pots, and particularly plastic pots, heat when in the sun, causing damage to the roots within. This can be prevented by using concrete tubs or covering the pots with straw mulch. Tomatoes, particularly cherry tomatoes, can be trained to grow on a verandah post or patio rail.

## Common problems

Capsicums, chilli pepper, tomatoes, and occasionally eggplants, suffer blackish, sunken patches at the flower or blossom end of their fruits when calcium supply is insufficient. Inadequate or irregular water is often the cause. Better watering usually prevents blossom end rot (for controls, *see p.252*).

## Routine care

Fruiting vegetables need fertile soil in order to produce a succession of fruits. Before planting them, apply a general fertilizer (*see pp.20–21*) at a rate of 35–70g per sq m (1–2oz per sq yd). Alternatively, use 50–100g per sq m (1½–3oz per sq yd) of an organic food such as dried poultry manure with a 5% nitrogen content (*see pp.22–23*); use double this amount for sweetcorn.

In cool climates, young plants can be protected by covering each seedling with a bottomless plastic bottle or with a plastic shield supported by three stakes. Be sure to remove the covers when the weather warms or the plants will get too hot. As plants start to fruit, a dressing of potash-rich fertilizer is beneficial. Sweetcorn is fertilized with high-nitrogen fertilizer. Water well in dry spells, at a rate of 20 litres per sq m (4 gallons per sq yd). Adequate water supplies are especially necessary during the flowering period, and as fruits swell.

For tall crops, like vine tomatoes, pinch out sideshoots (*see p.109*) to concentrate the plant's energy into fruiting. Tall crops will need staking. For bushy capsicums and eggplants, pinch out the growing tip to encourage the production of sideshoots.

Only remove leaves if they turn yellow or become diseased; otherwise cropping may be reduced. An exception to this rule is tomatoes (*see p.113*).

However, care must be taken when removing tomato leaves that fruit is not exposed to hot sun as this may cause sunburn. If using containers, do not allow pots to dry out. Add a controlled-release fertilizer before planting or apply a balanced liquid fertilizer weekly if growth slows (*see pp.20–21*).

## Harvesting

Most fruiting vegetables are ready for harvest in late summer. Regular picking encourages continuous fruit production. Sever the fruits, with a piece of stalk, using a sharp knife or secateurs.

The fruits of most fruiting vegetables change colour when they are ripe, but it is more difficult to tell when the cobs of sweetcorn are ready for harvesting, so you will need to test them first. The cobs should also be broken off by hand rather than cut (*see below*).

Birds can be particularly troublesome with tomatoes and the plants may need to be covered with bud netting when the fruit ripens.

## Seed saving

Saving seeds of fruiting vegetables such as sweetcorn and capsicums, which cross-pollinate readily, or F1 hybrids, where progeny seldom come true to type, is not worth attempting. It is, however, worth trying with the pulpy seeds of ripe tomatoes (*see p.61*).

# Harvesting cobs of sweetcorn

*Testing for ripeness*

*Picking a ripe cob*

With sweetcorn, it is quite difficult to tell when the cobs are ripe and therefore ready for harvesting. Because of this, cobs are often left on the plant for too long and are overripe when eventually picked.

To ensure that you pick cobs when they are at their most tender, test for ripeness as soon as the tassels turn brown in late summer. Peel back a little of the husk, and insert a thumbnail or fingernail into one of the kernels (*see far left*). If the juice that comes out is milky, the cob is ripe; if the juice is clear, the cob is not yet ripe.

Pick a ripe cob by pulling it sharply downwards with one hand – supporting the rest of the plant with the other – until the cob snaps off (*see left*). Only pick cobs just before they are required; once they are harvested, the sweet flavour is rapidly lost.

# A–Z of fruiting vegetables

## Capsicum *and* chilli

*Capsicum annuum* Longum Group
and *C. annuum* Grossum Group

| Season | Spring | Summer | Autumn | Winter |
|---|---|---|---|---|
| Sow | • • • | | | |
| Transplant | • • • | | | |
| Harvest | | • • • • • | | |

Home-grown capsicums or sweet peppers
have excellent colour, texture, and flavour.
Chilli peppers or chillis are as equally varied
as capsicums and have a hot taste, contained
mainly in the seeds and veins, which is
essential for certain cuisines; some forms are
intended for ornament, with coloured foliage.
Modern F1 hybrids are robust enough to
crop reliably in cool seasons and gardens.
Capsicums are ideal for container and patio
cultivation; they yield 2.75–4.5kg (6–10lb)
per 3m (10ft) row in warm climates. Chillis
are also ideal potted vegetables and the
fruiting plants are most decorative and
compact. Both capsicums and chillis grow
very well in tropical gardens.

**Site and soil** Any fertile, moisture-retentive
soil suits peppers if it drains well and warms
quickly in spring. Light soils are best; pre-
warm heavy soils in cool climates with
cloches or clear plastic film. In the garden, a
sunny, sheltered site is vital.

**Sowing and planting** Sow in a propagator
in temperate regions (*see p.108*) at 18–21°C
(65–70°F). Optimum growing temperatures
for seedlings are 16°C (60°F) at night, 18°C
(64°F) by day. Prick out, then plant out into
borders, pots, or punnets after hardening off
(*see pp.108–109*). Alternatively plant
commercial seedlings.

| Sowing depth | sow thinly, with light covering |
|---|---|
| Plant spacing | 38–45cm (15–18in) |
| Row spacing | 60–75cm (24–36in) |

**Routine care** Provide support for the plants
as they develop (*see p.109*) or their stems can
break under the weight of the crop. If growth
is weak, remove the first flowers and feed
with balanced liquid fertilizer weekly (*see
p.110*). Pinching out the growing tip is not
needed on peppers, and delays cropping. (*See
Mulching, p.109, and Routine care, p.110.*)

**Harvesting and storing** Pick the first fruits
when they are green and the skin is smooth
and glossy, to encourage further cropping.
Later fruits can either be picked green or
allowed to ripen to yellow, orange, or red.
Red capsicums have a sweeter, richer flavour.
Allowing fruits to ripen, however, reduces
cropping by about a quarter.

Chillis may be gathered green or allowed
to ripen, and can be dried (*see p.73*) or
pickled for winter storage. Some ripen yellow
or even white. Black, purple, and violet chillis
ripen to red or purplish-black, depending on
the cultivar. Fruits of capsicums and chillis
will remain in good condition on the plant in
cool, dry weather.

**Common problems** Aphids (*see p.251*),
red spider mite (*p.261*), corn earworm
(*p.254*) and whitefly (*p.264*) are common ,
but biological controls (*see p.52*) are effective.
Botrytis (*see p.252*) rots fruits in cool or wet
weather; speedy removal of diseased material
reduces damage. To avoid soil-borne diseases,
especially verticillium wilt (*see p.263*), grow
on a fresh site every year.

**Recommended cultivars**

CAPSICUMS
'Californian Wonder' – large fruit with sweet,
crunchy flesh.
'Chocolate Beauty' – sweet fruit that turns
from green to brown at maturity.
'Golden Bell' – colourful, large, yellow fruit.
'Jingle Bells' – small plant loaded with small,
sweet, red fruit.
'Palette Mix' – mix of green, orange, yellow,
brown, and purple varieties.
'Sweet Banana' – long, very sweet, yellow
fruit; prolific and early-maturing.

CHILLIS
'Habanero Red' – tall plant producing the
hottest chilli available; needs a warm climate.
'Jalapeno' – moderately hot chilli.
'Long Red Cayenne' – long, narrow,
moderately hot chilli.
'Mitla' – vigorous hybrid; Jalapeno type.
'Thai Hot' – small, round, very hot fruit on
small plants.

# Eggplant

*Solanum melongena*

| Season | Spring | Summer | Autumn | Winter |
|---|---|---|---|---|
| Sow | • • | | | |
| Transplant | | • • | | |
| Harvest | | • • • • | | |

Eggplant, also known as aubergine or
brinjal, are very attractive, slightly spiny
plants of tropical origin, and therefore usually
require heat for propagation in temperate
regions. Yellow-, black-, white-, red-, or
purple-fruited cultivars are available, but for
the kitchen it is best to grow F1 hybrid
black-fruited cultivars. Plants are slow to
establish in cool weather and may take three
months to fruit. They may be grown in
containers on a sunny patio.

**Site and soil** As for capsicum

| Sowing depth | sow thinly, with light covering |
|---|---|
| Plant spacing | 60–75cm (24–30in) |
| Row spacing | 75–90cm (30–36in) |

**Sowing and planting** As for capsicum
**Routine care** Pinch out the growing tip when the plants are about 20cm (8in) tall, and again later if necessary, to encourage bushy plants, which are easier to support (*see p.109*). Small, but numerous fruits result, unless fruits are thinned to one per stem. Water regularly to keep the soil moist. To increase humidity and warmth, grow the plants beneath a tent of fleece. When the fruits begin to swell, feed with a high-potash fertilizer or organic tomato feed. (*See also* Mulching, *p.109*).
**Harvesting** Gather fruits when they develop their full colour, but before they become overripe and pithy. Cut the stem 2.5cm (1in) above the calyx – the joint of the stem and the fruit.
**Common problems** As for capsicum
**Recommended cultivars**
'Black Beauty' – old variety producing large, purple fruit.
'Bonica' – vigorous hybrid that matures well in cool climates.
'Ghost' – elongated, white-skinned variety.
'Early Long Purple' – old variety producing very long fruit.
'Kermit' – compact hybrid producing small, round, green and white fruit.
'Lebanese Bunching' – long, narrow, purple fruit.
'Supreme' – large, oval, purple fruit.
'Turkish Orange' – produces many round orange fruit.

# Okra

*Abelmoschus esculentus*

| Season | Spring | | Summer | | Autumn | | Winter | |
|---|---|---|---|---|---|---|---|---|
| Sow | • | • | | | | | | |
| Transplant | | | • | • | | | | |
| Harvest | | | | • | • | • | | |

Okra or gumbo is a tropical annual related to cotton. Its immature parts have a unique glutinous texture, essential for some cuisines, and are used as a green vegetable. The dried pods can also be used as flavouring. Okra can be grown in the garden in tropical climates but is best grown in a greenhouse in cool climates. Okra yields 1.5kg (3¼lb) per 3m (10ft) row in a greenhouse; for outdoor crops, the yield will be lower.
**Site and soil** As for capsicum.
**Sowing and planting** The seeds are very hard, and a preliminary soaking in warm water for two hours will speed germination. Sow as for capsicum.

| Sowing depth | sow thinly, with light covering |
|---|---|
| Plant spacing | 40–60cm (16–24in) |
| Row spacing | 60–75cm (24–30in) |

**Routine care** Pinch out strong growing tips to encourage bushiness. Provide support. (*See* Mulching, *p.109,* and Routine care, *p.110.*)
**Harvesting** As soon as pods have formed, cut them off with a sharp knife. They quickly become stringy, so regular cutting is essential.
**Common problems** As for capsicum.
**Recommended cultivars**
'Clemson's Spineless' – heavy crop of dark green pods.
'Penta Green' – early variety, suited to cool climates.
'Redskin' – produces red pods.

# Sweetcorn

*Zea mays*

| Season | Spring | | Summer | | Autumn | | Winter | |
|---|---|---|---|---|---|---|---|---|
| Sow | | • | • | • | | | | |
| Transplant | | | • | • | | | | |
| Harvest | | | | • | • | • | | |

Home-grown sweetcorn cobs cooked within minutes of harvest taste superb. The kernels are usually yellow, sometimes white or bicoloured. Improved forms are regularly introduced (older cultivars have poor growing characteristics and insipid flavour). Only one or two cobs are borne per plant; normal yields are 6–9 cobs per sq m (sq yd).

Uniquely for vegetables, sweetcorn (or maize) is a grass with long leaves, the base of which encloses the stem, and is pollinated by wind. Sweetcorn has architectural qualities that make it valuable in ornamental kitchen gardens. The male flowers at the top of the stem are called tassels. They shed pollen, carried on the wind to the "silk", which grows out of the cob containing rows of female flowers. The cob, or fruit, is enclosed in a sheath or husk of leafy bracts.

Sugar-enhanced cultivars have the same amount of sugar as normal sweetcorn, but take longer to go starchy and lose the flavour. Supersweets have a higher sugar content, preferred by most people. They may be frozen for later use. Mini sweetcorns are immature cobs, produced from special cultivars.

Nearby agricultural maize can cross-pollinate sweetcorn, leading to less tasty cobs. Purple and other coloured corn or maize can also pollinate sweetcorn, leading to less flavoursome, parti-coloured cobs. It is therefore best to plant only one variety to ensure best flavour. Sow successive crops a few weeks apart.
**Site and soil** A warm, sunny, sheltered site with light, warm, rich soil is vital (*see p.108*). Cobs may not ripen in shade or windy sites in cool regions. However, corn grows well in tropical gardens through the winter "dry". Maize also grows through the summer "wet".
**Sowing and planting** In cool areas, choose early cultivars, and sow in early summer. Block planting (*see p.109*) will increase the chances of successful pollination, necessary for production of cobs. A soil temperature of at least 10°C (50°F) is essential. Sow 2–3 seeds per station (*see p.108*), using the wider spacing (*see below*) where the soil is of poor quality. Thin to one strong seedling after germination. Seedlings grow best at temperatures of 20–30°C (68–86°F).

The harvest can be extended with successive sowings from early summer. Sweetcorn grows to around 2m (6ft) tall and will shade neighbouring vegetables. It is therefore best grown on the southern side of the garden in temperate regions.

| Sowing depth | 2.5–4cm (1–1½in) |
|---|---|
| Seed/plant spacing | 34–45cm (14–18in) |
| Row spacing | 45–60cm (18–24in) |

**Routine care** Watering will be required in dry weather to ensure good germination and growth. Apply a side dressing of high-nitrogen fertilizer to maintain a healthy green leaf colour. On windy sites, draw up soil around the base of the plants to give stability, or provide a support (*see p.109*). (*See also* Mulching, *p.109,* and Routine care, *p.110.*)
**Harvesting** Test for ripeness as soon as the tassels begin to dry up and turn brown, and if ready break off the cobs (*see p.110*).
**Common problems** The seeds and cobs attract mice and rats (*see p.258*). Corn earworm (*see p.254*) eats into the cobs from the tassel. Poor pollinating conditions may lead to gaps in the rows of ripe kernels. Birds (*see p.251*) may strip crops.
**Recommended cultivars**
'Baby Corn' – produces tiny cobs; picked when immature.
'Early Gem' – quick-maturing, with sweet cobs.
'Golden Bantam' – early variety with golden kernels on large plant.
'Honeysweet Improved' – super-sweet hybrid that ensures sweet cobs; short plants.
'Miracle' – early-season, adaptable variety.
'Petite Hybrid' – hybrid producing up to five baby cobs picked when immature.
'Rosella' – reliable colour and yield.
'Samuri' – super-sweet hybrid with large, sweet cobs.

# Tomatillo

*Physalis ixocarpa*

| Season | Spring | | Summer | | Autumn | | Winter | |
|---|---|---|---|---|---|---|---|---|
| Sow | • | • | | | | | | |
| Transplant | | • | • | | | | | |
| Harvest | | | | • | • | • | | |

The tomatillo, Rendidora, or Mexican husk tomato, is a frost-tender, sprawling plant related to Cape Gooseberry, growing to about 1m (3ft). Its green fruits ripen to yellow, purple, or red, or may stay green. They are used in Mexican cuisine such as salsa and for preserves. The berry is enclosed in a tight-fitting, papery calyx, through which the ripening berry sometimes bursts. Tomatillos yield 1–2kg (2¼–4½lb) per plant. Named cultivars are seldom offered.
**Site and soil** As for capsicum (*see p.111*).
**Sowing and planting** As for capsicum.

| Sowing depth | sow thinly, with light covering |
|---|---|
| Plant spacing | 45cm (18in) |
| Row spacing | 90cm (36in) |

**Harvesting** Many fruits fall before ripe and can be left to ripen on the ground. Full colour indicates ripeness, and green cultivars are ripe when the fruit breaks through the husk.

# Tomato

*Lycopersicon esculentum*

| Season | Spring | Summer | Autumn | Winter |
|---|---|---|---|---|
| Sow | • • | | | • |
| Transplant | | • • | | |
| Harvest | | | • • • • | |

Tomatoes are short-lived, frost-tender perennials grown as annuals. Cultivars have been developed with fruits ranging from currant size, through cherry and plum tomatoes, to the grapefruit-sized beefsteak types. Shapes are spherical, oblong, elongated, or flattened globes, and colours include red, green, yellow, and purple. A fair range of different types may be bought as ready-grown plants in garden centres. There are two main types of tomato plant: vine (or indeterminate) tomatoes and bush (or determinate) tomatoes.

Vine tomatoes are usually grown with the central stem trained up a tall support (*see p.109*), with its sideshoots removed; these cordons will grow to several metres in frost-free conditions. The flowers and consequent fruits are borne on trusses that grow from the main stem. Vine tomatoes are easy to keep within bounds when grown in greenhouses or containers, although if in the latter they will need more attention (*see p.110*). Vine tomatoes require tall stakes when grown in the garden.

Bush tomatoes are much more compact plants with plenty of side branches, and are better for growing in gardens. Flowers appear on the end of each stem. After flowering, the stem ceases to grow, but other stems arise, also bearing flowers, so that a short, bushy plant covered in flowers results.

There are also intermediate or semi-determinate types, which have a habit between the fully bushy and the vine types. They usually require support, but removal of sideshoots is not carried out, the whole plant being loosely tied to the support. Many of the unusual Mediterranean and other less commonly grown cultivars have a semi-indeterminate habit, with some stems ending in flowers and others trailing without end. These unruly plants need careful judgement in curbing the straggling shoots and preserving the flowering ones.

Grafted tomato plants are available from garden centres. These varieties are grafted onto a vigorous wild rootstock to promote vigorous growth. Grafted tomatoes are tied to a tall stake or trained as a climber on a trellis.

Tomato yields vary from variety to variety and with growth habit. Vine tomatoes yield 1.8–4kg (4–9lb) per plant in the garden or 2.7–5kg (6–11lb) in an unheated greenhouse. Bush and semi-indeterminate tomatoes should yield 4kg (9lb) per plant in the garden. However, yields are affected by growing conditions and disease. Cool weather and high humidity can result in poor crops, and disease problems and insufficient moisture and nutrition also reduce yields.

**Site and soil** Any fertile, nutrient-rich, well-drained soil is suitable, if plenty of organic matter has been incorporated in the top 30cm (12in). If necessary, before planting add a general-purpose fertilizer at a rate of 105g per sq m (3oz per sq yd) or pelleted poultry manure at 150g per sq m (4oz per sq yd). Tomatoes produce good crops in temperate gardens when planted in a warm, sheltered site such as against a north wall. In tropical gardens, tomatoes grow best through the winter, although some varieties do better than others. Cherry tomatoes are the most adaptable.

**Sowing and planting** Sow thinly in pots of multi-purpose potting mix, adding enough vermiculite or sieved compost to cover the seeds (*see p.108*). Alternatively, sow two seeds per pot, later selecting the strongest seedling. Warm conditions (15–30°C/59–86°F) are needed for germination, best provided by a heated propagator (*see p.63*). When seedlings emerge, transfer pots to better-lit conditions, such as a greenhouse or sunny windowsill.

After germination, seedlings should be grown at 21–27°C (70–81°F). When the seedlings can be handled, prick into individual 5–8cm (2–3in) pots, large modules or, better, biodegradable pots; feed with balanced liquid fertilizer after 2–3 weeks or if growth appears discoloured. Plant out after roots have filled the pot and the first flower buds appear. Commercial seedlings save time and can be planted directly into the garden. Advanced grafted plants crop earliest.

| Sowing depth | 2cm (¾in) |
|---|---|
| Final plant spacing | vine: 38–45cm (15–18in)<br>bush: 30–90cm (12–36in), depending on vigour |
| Row spacing | vine: 90cm (36in) single or staggered double rows<br>bush: 90cm (36in) |

**Routine care** Cover bush tomatoes in cool climates with fleece or cloches, and support if needed (*see p.109*). Support vine tomatoes, removing sideshoots (*see p.109*).

Water all types generously in dry spells, especially container plants. Overfeeding and overwatering reduce flavour and may lead to disease. If leaves become pale and are shed, weekly feeding with potassium-rich fertilizer, such as tomato feed, until foliage colour improves, will boost plant health and cropping. Mulch with organic matter. Removing leaves beneath the lowest ripening truss helps air circulation and reduces disease; don't touch leaves higher up or fruits may

burn in hot sun, or will be poorly flavoured.

**Harvesting** Ideally allow fruits to ripen on the vine, and pick them when they have developed their full colour and flavour. At the end of the season either pick remaining green fruits and leave them in a warm place to ripen or pull up the entire vine and hang it upside down indoors. Cover bush types in cool climates with cloches to finish ripening.

**Common problems** Tomatoes share several diseases and soil pests with potatoes. They suffer mainly from whitefly (*see p.264*), birds (*p.251*) and occasionally from aphids (*see p.251*), caterpillars (*see p.253*), and red spider mite (*see p.261*). The plants are affected by a number of virus diseases, such as mosaic (*see p.258*), yellow top, purple top, and spotted wilt (*p.263*). Fungal leaf spot, including target spot, is particularly troublesome in humid conditions (*p.263*). Fruit can be damaged by bugs (*p.252*) and corn earworm (*p.254*). Tomato stem borer occasionally tunnel into stems at the soil surface. Fruit fly (*p.255*) are a problem, laying eggs in fruit in fruit-fly areas. Magnesium deficiency is occasionally a problem (*see p.257*). To avoid soil-borne diseases, use containers or growing bags.

**Recommended cultivars**

TALL

'Apollo Improved' – hybrid with round fruit and good yields; early- to mid-season.

'Black Krim' – tasty, black fruit.

'Burnley Surecrop' – shortish plant with heavy crops; early-season.

'College Challenge' – tasty, round fruit; prolific mid-season.

'Firestorm' – hybrid resistant to wilt virus; round, red fruit.

'Grosse Lisse' – reliable yields; produces large fruit; late-season.

'Kelstar' – good cool-climate variety.

'Moneymaker' – vigorous plants with smooth, tasty fruit.

'Mortgage Lifter' – solid, tasty fruit; mid- to late-season.

'Oxheart' – large, fleshy fruit; best in warm areas.

'Rouge de Marmande' – flattish, creased fruit; early-season.

'Sunrise' – hybrid producing masses of sweet, orange, cherry-sized fruit; mid-season.

'Sweet 100' – hybrid producing cherry-sized tomatoes over a long period.

'Tigerella' – orange-striped fruit.

'Tommy toe' – vigorous plant producing walnut-sized fruit for a long period.

'Vivean' – hybrid that grows vigorously with tasty, round fruit.

BUSH

'KY1' – vigorous, small plants and prolific fruit; early-season.

'Mr Stripey' – green-striped fruit over a long period.

'Roma' – egg-shaped fruit resistant to wilt; good for preserves.

'Tiny Tim' – small bush producing small fruit; good for pots.

# Growing cucurbits

Included in the cucurbit, or gourd, family (Cucurbitaceae) are cucumbers, zucchini, melons, pumpkins, squashes, and marrows. These are all tropical annuals that grow well in warm weather, and the leaves and flowers are attractive as well as the fruits. The fruits are either eaten raw or cooked, or used in preserves. The young leaves and shoots are sometimes consumed as greens and the seeds as snacks, and even the flowers are occasionally eaten (*see individual crops, pp. 117–119*, for details of which parts of any crop are edible). The closely related ornamental gourds may be harmful if eaten. If allowed to sprawl, marrows or squashes can take up quite a lot of space; training them vertically overcomes this problem.

## Sowing cucurbit crops

The large, flat seeds of cucurbits usually produce fast-growing seedlings, but germination requires soil temperatures of 13–30°C (55–86°F) and some of the crops are slow to mature. Seedlings need similar soil and air temperatures. Frost is fatal to leaves and stems, although ripe fruits may survive low temperatures.

In cool climates, sow seed in late spring in large modules or 8cm (3in) pots, preferably biodegradable ones (*see above right*) so that there is no disturbance to the roots when planting out the seedlings later. Half-fill the pot or module with potting mix, and sow one or two seeds on their sides, rather than upright; this reduces soil resistance as the emerging seed leaves are raised clear of the soil, still encased in the seed coat. If necessary, thin out the weaker seedling after germination. When the remaining seedling reaches the top of the pot, fill in around it with more potting mix (*see above right*) to produce a strong root system.

Alternatively, sow seed *in situ* when the soil warms. Sowings of fast-growing cucurbits can be made in late spring or in early summer in favourable areas, or earlier if the soil is pre-warmed with clear plastic or cloches (*see p. 46*). Sow one to three seeds per station, on their sides; later, thin to the strongest seedling, if applicable. Protect newly sown areas

## Planting out seedlings in biodegradable pots

1 **When seedlings sown** in biodegradable pots reach the top of the pot, fill in with more potting mix to earth up the stem and encourage strong roots.

2 **About 2 weeks** after sowing, when the seedling has 3 or 4 true leaves and the roots are starting to show through the walls of the pot, it is ready for planting out.

3 **Plant the seedling** in its pot after digging out holes at spacings appropriate for the crop; water the holes and pots thoroughly. Plant so the leaves sit just above the soil surface. Mound a little soil around the seedling stem to prevent water from collecting around it and encouraging rot. Water in to settle the soil, and label.

with fleece (*see p. 48*) if necessary.

Cucurbits cross-pollinate readily. It is therefore best to purchase seed in packs, as home-saved seed may not grow true to type where more than one variety is grown in a garden.

## Successional sowing

Because most cucurbit crops produce a succession of fruits, successional sowing (*see p. 69*) is seldom required. The exceptions to this rule are zucchini and cucumbers, where an early spring sowing may need to be supplemented by an early summer sowing in order to produce later supplies.

## Hardening off

Before planting out seedlings raised in a propagator, harden them off (*see p. 65*) with gradually increasing ventilation, or under a double layer of fleece (*see p. 46*).

## Site and soil

All cucurbits prefer a warm, sheltered site. Cucurbits were traditionally grown on ridges or mounds, often heavily

enriched with organic matter. This helps particularly where soil is poor, shallow, and prone to waterlogging. Mounds and ridges require great labour to make and fill with organic matter, however, and are difficult to water adequately. Flat-topped beds, about 1m (3ft) wide and raised by about 15cm (6in), are just as successful, without the drawbacks. Another traditional practice was to prepare 30cm (12in) planting holes, refilled with soil enriched with organic matter. Equally good crops can be more conveniently grown on well-manured flat soil, especially if it is mulched after planting (*see p. 72*).

Planting cucurbits on old compost heaps to utilize the residual fertility can be successful provided that the abundance of nutrients does not lead to leafy, non-flowering growth. More compact cucurbits, such as cucumbers and zucchini, also grow well in pots of at least 25cm (10in) in diameter. Success, however, is dependent on plentiful and frequent watering and feeding (*see* Routine care, *right*).

Cucurbits are best sown for winter harvest in tropical gardens. They are prone to mildew and fruit rot in humid weather, and the vines are best raised up onto an airy trellis.

## Planting out

As soon as the seedlings have three or four true leaves, usually about two weeks after sowing, they are ready for planting out (*see facing page, and right*). Plant to the depth of the seed leaves; this buries some stem and allows more roots to form, which improves early growth. When conditions are dull and wet, however, shallower planting reduces the risk of disease. If in doubt, make a slight mound around the stem to prevent accumulation of water at the collar of the plant, which might cause rotting. The brittle roots and fragile area where the stem joins the roots means that each seedling needs very gentle handling, especially if it is being planted out as a bare-root seedling (*see p.70*).

Cucurbit seedlings benefit from extra warmth and protection after planting out, provided by either a cloche or fleece (*see pp.45–48*), especially if conditions are still chilly. On frosty

nights, protect with hessian sacking or similar cloth.

## Supporting cucurbit crops

The shoots of trailing or climbing cucurbits can be tied into twine, wires, trellis, or bamboo wigwams (*see below*) to save space and protect fruits from wet soil, slugs, disease, and damage. However, they can ramble freely and crops are often heavier if this is allowed.

## Routine care

Protect all early sowings and plantings in cooler areas, with cold frames, cloches, or fleece (*see pp.45–48*).

### Planting out seedlings

*As an alternative to growing seedlings in biodegradable pots (see facing page), sow seed in 8cm (3in) pots or modules and plant out with care when the seedlings have 3 or 4 true leaves. In a bed prepared with organic matter, plant at appropriate intervals – here 'Turk's Turban' squash seedlings are spaced 1m (3ft) apart. Use a hand trowel or a bulb planter to make the holes. Firm, water in, and label.*

Melons and cucumbers will require most protection when young.

Feeding will increase yields, although too much nitrogen should be avoided because it can lead to excessive leaf production at the expense of fruiting. Cucurbits need only small amounts of fertilizer; a suitable dressing is 75–100g per sq m (2–3oz per sq yd) of a general compound fertilizer, or 100–140g per sq m (3–4oz per sq yd) of an organic feed such as dried poultry manure with a 5% nitrogen content (*see pp.20–23*). Halve these amounts for plants growing in fertile, recently manured soil. Regular feeding is vital for container crops. Mulching (*see p.72*) helps to retain soil

# Supporting cucurbit crops

Some cucurbits have a climbing or trailing habit, and therefore need some form of support to prevent the fruits resting on the ground, where they will be susceptible to rotting, as well as the attentions of slugs and snails. Outdoor crops may be supported with bamboo canes and twine, either in a wigwam or row arrangement. A trellis would suit a sheltered spot and allow fruits to hang down. Greenhouse cordon crops can be twined around single strings hanging vertically from the roof. Individual fruits may also be supported with netting attached to the overall support network.

*Outdoor squashes on a fan trellis*

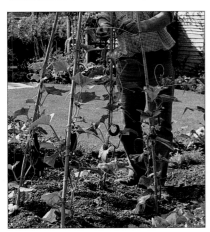

*Tying outdoor cucumbers into cane wigwam*

*Greenhouse cucumber growing up vertical twine*

*Individual melon supported by a net*

moisture, suppress weeds, and keep the fruits clean. Organic mulches feed the crops, but very rich ones, such as mushroom compost, can lead to more leafy growth than fruit.

Frequent, plentiful watering is essential, especially for crops grown in containers. Water after planting and sowing, during flowering and fruit swelling, and in dry spells. A low-level or drip-irrigation system (*see p.54*) can be indispensable. To grow very large fruits such as giant pumpkins as much as 11 litres (2 gallons) per week for each plant may be required, to which liquid fertilizer (*see pp.20–23*) should be added.

## Weed control

The spreading shoots and large leaves of mature cucurbits will suppress weeds by themselves. In the early stages, however, use organic mulches (*see pp.41–42*). Alternatively, prepare the site in early spring and allow the weeds to germinate; before planting, remove them by shallow hoeing or with a contact herbicide. This is known as the stale seedbed technique. If left undisturbed, the soil will remain largely weed-free until the foliage spreads sufficiently to smother the weeds.

## Pollination

Pollination is an essential requirement for most cucurbits to set fruits, and separate male and female flowers are borne on the same plant. The only exception to this are greenhouse cucumbers (*see p.117*). Cucurbits are pollinated by insects, so fleece, frame, or cloche coverings should be opened at flowering time to allow insects access.

When there are too few pollinating insects, or they are insufficiently active, hand-pollination (*see above*) can be carried out by picking a male flower and pressing it lightly onto a female one so that the stigma, in the centre of the female flower, receives pollen from the stamens of the male. Small flowers, such as those of cucumbers and melons, which are easily damaged, are best shaken over the females. Male cucurbit flowers are fertile only for a short time; check that they are ready by brushing a finger over the male flower to detect yellow, powdery pollen. Each

---

# Hand-pollinating cucurbit flowers

**1 Help cucurbit plants to set fruit** by pollinating them by hand, rather than waiting for insects to do it. Pick a fully open male flower – one with no embryonic fruit at the base (*see below*) – and carefully pinch off all the petals to expose the stamens, which bear the powdery yellow pollen.

No fruit below flower

Male flower

Embryonic fruit forming at base of flower

Female flower

**2 Insert the male flower** carefully into a female flower – one that has an embryonic fruit (*see left*) – so that the pollen is transferred from the male stamens onto the stigma of the female flower.

---

fertile male flower has enough pollen for several females.

Repeated pollination on consecutive sunny days is sometimes required for a good "set". Male flowers can predominate during short days early in the season, but the female flowers will prevail later on. Wider spacing between the plants, less shade, later planting, and potassium-rich liquid fertilizers (*see p.20*) can increase female flower numbers. Closer spacing and early

**Protecting ripening fruits**
*If plants are grown unsupported outdoors, place a piece of wood or a brick underneath the ripening fruits (here, a marrow) to raise them off the soil. This will minimize any possibility of soiling or rotting.*

planting out will create a predominance of male flowers.

Cold temperatures cause incomplete pollination, where fruits swell only at the flower end, and shrivel at the other end. Cool weather can also lead to complete failure to set fruit, because pollination fails through lack of insects and impaired pollen germination and development. If pollination occurs but fruitlets fail to develop, it is often because there are more fruits than the plant can support. This will be resolved as the plant grows.

Fruitlets may be thinned to just one per stem, or even one per plant, where large fruits are wanted. This is especially necessary for melons. There is no need to thin cucumbers or zucchini.

## Harvesting and storing

Frequent harvesting of immature zucchini, cucumbers, and melons is essential to prevent poor-quality, over-mature fruits forming. Cut the stalks cleanly with a sharp knife or secateurs. Fruits of marrows, pumpkins, and squashes are ready to harvest when they develop full colour and a hard skin, and ring hollow when tapped. The stem will also start to crack. Fruits for storage should be left to mature on the plants as long as possible. After cutting, cure them in a warm, dry place at 27–32°C (81–90°F) for several days. Store at about 10°C (50°F), with fairly high humidity to prevent shrivelling.

# A–Z of cucurbits

## Cucumber *and* gherkin

### *Cucumis sativus*

| Season | Spring | Summer | Autumn | Winter |
|---|---|---|---|---|
| Sow | • • • • | | | |
| Transplant | | • • • | | |
| Harvest | | | • • • • | |

There are different types of cucumber but the most commonly grown is the green field cucumber, which can be picked as gherkins when immature. Other types include greenhouse cucumbers, which were bred in Europe to fruit without insect pollination; apple cucumbers, which produce round fruit; snake cucumbers, which are popular in Asia and have spiny skins; and small cucumbers that have been developed for picking as gherkins. All grow well through summer in temperate gardens, and through winter in the tropics.

Cucumbers are climbing plants suitable for growing on wigwams, trellis, or wires (*see p.115*), or for trailing along the ground; better-quality fruits will be obtained by using supports, however, and the plants occupy less space. No cucumbers can tolerate frost. They normally yield about 15 fruits per plant.

Modern greenhouse cucumbers are all-female and do not require pollination to set fruit. For these plants, pollination can cause unshapely and bitter-tasting fruits, and should be avoided by growing them well apart from other cucurbits.

All garden cucumbers and gherkins need pollination by insects or by hand (*see p.116*), or no crop will result.

**Site and soil**   For germination, cucumber seeds need a minimum temperature of 20°C (68°F); the optimum growing temperature is 28°C (82°F). Sheltered, warm, sunny conditions are therefore essential for garden cucumbers and gherkins, but black plastic mulches and fleece (*see p.42*) can help warm the soil in cool climates. Plants benefit from the incorporation of organic matter during soil preparation, and mulching (*see p.72*) during the growing period. On heavy soils, it is better to grow cucumbers and gherkins on a flat-topped raised bed (*see p.114*) than a ridge. Cucumbers and gherkins will crop better when protected with cloches, cold frames, or even fleece (*see p.45*), in cold districts.

**Sowing and planting**   In cool climates, sow seed in a propagator in mid-spring, and transplant seedlings into the garden in early summer. Alternatively, sowing direct (*see p.114*) is successful in early summer, especially if soil is pre-warmed with cloches or fleece, or in midsummer for gherkins. Sow three seeds per station, each seed 15cm (6in) apart. Where space is tight, seeds can be sown in a drill (*see p.67*), with the plants later trained up a mesh or trellis fence to make an attractive cucumber hedge.

| Sowing depth | 2.5cm (1in) |
|---|---|
| Plant spacing | 45cm (18in) for drills |
| | 15cm (6in) at stations |
| Row spacing | 60–75cm (24–30in) |

**Routine care**   For supports, use wigwams, trellis, twine, or wires (*see p.115*). Pinch out growing tips of climbers only when they reach the top of the support; plants allowed to trail on the ground crop better and use space more efficiently if growing tips are regularly removed to encourage bushy growth. In cold frames and cloches, train sideshoots to the corners and pinch out the tips again. Water plentifully (*see p.116*); never allow cucumbers to dry out. If growth slows and leaves become pale, use a balanced liquid fertilizer (*see p.21*) as directed by the manufacturer until leaves green up again. Alternatively, use an organic mulch (*see p.41*) to add nutrient, keep fruits clean, reduce water loss, and suppress weeds.

**Harvesting**   Cucumbers and gherkins are best harvested before any yellowing begins, and after the sides become parallel. Avoid picking excessively young fruits, however, as they often taste bitter.

**Common problems**   Powdery mildew (*see p.260*) often occurs in late summer; good cultivation, especially watering and feeding, helps prevent this. Cucumber mosaic virus (*see p.254*) is common and can cause poorly formed fruits; disease-resistant cultivars are sometimes available – remove all diseased plants. Slugs and snails (*see p.262*) can destroy young plants. Red spider mite (*see p.261*) and whitefly (*see p.264*) are very damaging in the greenhouse; biological controls are very effective in these situations. Stem and root rots and bacterial soft rot (*see p.251*) affect stem bases and are associated with overwatered plants and badly drained soil.

**Recommended cultivars**
'Armenian' – long, pale green, ribbed fruit with sweet flavour; suits warm areas.
'Burpless Hybrid' – resists mildew disease and bears easy-to-digest fruit.
'Bush Champion' – compact bush producing large, green fruit over a long period.
'Crystal Salad' – elongated apple type with flecked white skin.
'Green Gem' – mildew-resistant variety producing long, dark green fruit.
'Lebanese' – low-acid, smooth, green fruits that can be eaten without peeling.
'Lemon' – prolific producer of yellow, apple-style cucumbers.
'Long Sweet White' – produces tasty, long, white fruit.
'Revel' – mildew- and virus-resistant variety with dark green fruit.

# Marrow

*Cucurbita pepo*

| Season | Spring | Summer | Autumn | Winter |
|---|---|---|---|---|
| Sow | • • | • | | |
| Transplant | | • • | | |
| Harvest | | | • • • • | |

Marrows, or vegetable marrows, are easy-to-grow, bush or trailing annuals; the fruits are traditional European summer and autumn vegetables that can also be stored for winter use. Marrows are usually elongated and striped, but plain-coloured and rounded types are also available. Vegetable marrows normally yield two large fruits, or 6–8 small ones, per plant.

**Site and soil** Vegetable marrows prefer an open, sunny position and benefit from the addition of plenty of organic matter during soil preparation (*see p.114*). They also do well if grown through a mulch (*see p.116*). Seeds need a minimum soil temperature of 13°C (56°F) to germinate.

**Sowing and planting** For early crops in cool climates, sow in a propagator in mid- to late spring (*see p.114*), and plant out either under cloches or in frames in late spring or in the garden in early summer (*see p.115*). Crops in warm climates can be direct sown, 2–3 seeds per station, in early summer (*see p.114*).

| Sowing depth | 2.5cm (1in) |
|---|---|
| Plant spacing | 90cm (3ft) |
| Row spacing | 90cm (3ft) bush types |
| | 1.2m (4ft) trailing types |

**Routine care** Constant moisture is required especially during the flowering period (*see p.116*). Liquid fertilizer (*see p.21*) can be beneficial if growth slows down, and also during swelling of fruits. If necessary, provide support (*see p.115*) for trailing types. (*See also* Routine care, pp.115–116.)

**Harvesting and storing** For small summer marrows, regular harvesting, when they are at least 15cm (6in) long, encourages further fruiting and increases the yield. For winter storage, let the marrows develop to a full size and acquire a hard, resilient skin. For a perfect finish, turn them occasionally as they ripen in the sun and rest fruits on a piece of wood or a brick rather than allow them to lie on the soil (*see p.116*). Vegetable marrows should be stored in a dry, cool, frost-free place (*see p.116*). A shelf in a garage is ideal but check there are no rats and mice. Also check for rotting fruit regularly.

**Common problems** As they are so closely related, vegetable marrows suffer the same problems as zucchini (*see p.119*).

**Recommended cultivars**
'Long White Bush' – compact plant with white fruit that can be eaten as zucchini when young.
'Rice Marrow' – heavy crop of good-keeping fruit with orange flesh.

# Pumpkin

*Cucurbita maxima, C. moschata, and C. pepo*

| Season | Spring | Summer | Autumn | Winter |
|---|---|---|---|---|
| Sow | • • | • | | |
| Transplant | | • • | | |
| Harvest | | | • • | |

Pumpkins are a valuable, highly ornamental winter vegetable. Most trail to form very large, rambling plants, but some bushy types also exist. Certain types of pumpkin, such as butternuts, are sometimes called winter squash. The seeds of some cultivars may be roasted to eat; the flowers, tendrils, and shoot tips are edible as for zucchini (*see p.117*). Normal yields are one large fruit or 4–6 small fruits per plant.

**Site and soil** An open, sunny site and fertile, well-drained soil are essential (*see p.114*). Seeds require a minimum of 13°C (56°F) to germinate, and the plants grow best at 18–21°C (65–70°F).

**Sowing and planting** A long growing season is required and in cool climates seed is best sown in a propagator (*see p.114*) in mid- to late spring for planting out in late spring and early summer (*see p.115*). Alternatively, station sow in the garden in early summer (*see p.114*). In tropical gardens, seed is sown in autumn for winter cropping.

| Sowing depth | 2.5cm (1in) |
|---|---|
| Plant spacing | 90cm (3ft) bush cultivars |
| | 1.5m (5ft) trailing cultivars |
| Row spacing | 90cm (3ft) bush cultivars |
| | 1.5m (5ft) trailing cultivars |

**Routine care** Trailing types need less water and feeding than other cucurbits as they spread widely, rooting deeply as they go. Bushy plants need normal amounts (*see p.115*), and a mulch (*see p.116*) also helps retain moisture. To save space, you can use short canes to train shoots of trailing types into circles on the ground. Alternatively, grow them up a support (*see p.115*), making sure it is sufficiently sturdy to support large, heavy fruits. Support individual fruits with netting if necessary (*see p.115*). If very large fruits are desired, thin when they are still small fruitlets to only 2–3 per plant.

**Harvesting and storing** Gather fruits when they are fully coloured and have a hollow ring when tapped. Allow the skins to harden in the sun. For storing, use larger, more mature fruits. If carefully cured and stored (*see p.116*), they will keep for several months, sometimes even into early spring.

**Common problems** Powdery mildew (*see p.260*) is the only real threat. The crops might be affected by stem and root rots (*see p.263*), cucumber mosaic virus (*see p.254*), and slugs and snails may attack seedlings (*see p.262*).

**Recommended cultivars**
'Blue Banana' – long, pale grey fruit on large vine; good keeper.
'Buttercup' – medium-sized pumpkin with mottled skin.
'Butternut Hercules' – thick-necked, orange-skinned pumpkin; good keeper.
'Butternut Waltham' – small, tasty, orange-skinned pumpkin; good keeper.
'Dills Atlantic Giant' – huge, orange pumpkin with poor flavour, grown for competition.
'Gold Nugget' – bush pumpkin producing small, hard-skinned, orange fruit on compact plants; good keeper.
'Jap' – soft-skinned, mottled pumpkin, best grown in warm areas.
'Jarradale' – large, grey pumpkin on large vine; good keeper.
'Minikin' – small, tasty pumpkin on large vine; good keeper.
'Queensland Blue' – large, tasty, grey-skinned pumpkin on large vine; good keeper.
'Red Hubbard' – small rounded orange fruit. Keeps well.
'Rouge d'Etampes' – flattish red fruit with excellent flavour.
'Triamble' – tasty, three-lobed, grey pumpkin on large vine; good keeper.
'Turk's Turban' – hard-skinned, decorative, orange pumpkin on large vine; good keeper.

# Sweet melon

*Cucumis melo*

| Season | Spring | Summer | Autumn | Winter |
|---|---|---|---|---|
| Sow | • • | • | | |
| Transplant | | • | | |
| Harvest | | • • • | • | |

Sweet melons are trailing annuals from tropical regions that need plenty of warmth; in temperate areas, they can only be grown successfully if protection is provided. There are three main types of sweet melon: cantaloupe or rockmelon, winter or casaba, and musk. Cantaloupe types have thick, rough, grooved skins, greyish green in colour. Winter melons have yellow, or yellow-and-green-striped, smooth skins, and include honeydew melons. Musk types are usually smaller than the other two types, and have smooth skins, often covered with a network of fine lines, and they smell sweet when ripe. The most commonly grown sweet melons are cantaloupe types. Sweet melons yield 2–4 fruits per plant.

**Site and soil** For uninterrupted growth and good flavour, sweet melons need an especially sunny, warm, and sheltered site, and a rich soil with plenty of organic matter added to it (*see p.114*). A minimum temperature of 16°C (60°F) is required for seed to germinate, and the plants grow best at around 25°C (77°F). In cool, temperate areas, this means growing them in a greenhouse, or protecting them with fleece or cloches (*see pp.45–48*) until the weather is warm.

**Sowing and planting** In cool areas, sow in a propagator (*see p.114*) in mid-spring, and plant out in early summer. When planting, the rootball should only just be covered in soil, since deep planting encourages rotting. In warmer areas, station sow direct in the garden in early summer (*see p.114*).

| Sowing depth | 2.5cm (1in) |
|---|---|
| Plant spacing | 60–100cm (2–3ft) |
| Row spacing | 1m (3ft) |

**Routine care** Constant moisture is required, especially during the flowering period (*see p.116*). If growth flags, apply a liquid fertilizer weekly (*see p.21*). If growing in a greenhouse, train the stems up supports (*see p.115*). After the plants start to run, "stop" the main stems by pinching out the leading shoots. All types of melon are prone to poor fruit set, even when there is a good population of bees about. Therefore do not stop growth until a few fruit have set.

The first fruits to set inhibit further fruit formation. Thin the fruits to two or four per plant when they are 2.5cm (1in) in diameter. Stop any fruit-bearing shoots at 2–3 leaves beyond the fruit to concentrate the plant's energy into the fruits. Support individual greenhouse fruits with netting (*see p.115*).

**Harvesting and storing** When the stalk begins to crack and the fruit develops a sweet scent, the fruit falls off the vine easily. Sweet melons may be stored successfully for several weeks in a refrigerator. Covering fruits with cloches or fleece as cool autumn nights approach will help speed the process of ripening.

**Common problems** Powdery mildew (*see p.260*), cucumber mosaic virus (*see p.254*), stem and root rots (*see p.263*), slugs and snails (*see p.262*), red spider mite (*see p.261*), whitefly (*see p.264*), and aphids (*see p.251*) may all be troublesome.

**Recommended cultivars**
'Banana-shaped' – smooth, yellow fruit with sweet, pinkish flesh.
'Hales Imperial' – firm, orange flesh.
'Honey Dew' – sweet, green flesh but plants are slow growing; suits warm climates.
'Nutmeg' – sweet, greenish-orange flesh that ripens well in cool climates.
'Western Beauty' – large, yellow fruit with orange spots; sweet flesh.

# Watermelon

## *Citrullus lanatus*

| Season | Spring | Summer | Autumn | Winter |
|---|---|---|---|---|
| Sow | • | | | |
| Transplant | | • • | | |
| Harvest | | | • • | |

Watermelons are warm-climate, spreading annual plants. Their stems can grow up to 4m (12ft) in length. The large fruits – up to 60cm (2ft) long – are oblong or rounded, cream or green in colour, striped or mottled, and are eaten raw. Watermelons need a long growing season and plenty of warmth in order to thrive. In cool, temperate regions, a cold frame can give adequate protection for seedlings if sited in a very warm, sunny, sheltered position. New developments include small-fruited, quick-growing cultivars. Watermelons yield one or two fruits per plant.

**Site and soil** Watermelons require similar, conditions to sweet melons (*see above*), but optimum temperatures for growth are higher: 25–30°C (77–85°F).

**Sowing and planting** Sow in a propagator in cool climates in mid-spring (*see p.114*), planting out in late spring to early summer (*see p.115*). Seed can be sown *in situ* in warm climates.

| Sowing depth | 2.5cm (1in) |
|---|---|
| Plant spacing | 60–100cm (2–3ft) |
| Row spacing | 1m (3ft) |

**Routine care** Watermelons are vigorous and require the same watering, feeding, and training as sweet melons (*see above*).

**Harvesting** Gather when the stem dries, and the fruit changes colour, especially if there is a slight yellowing of the pale area that is resting on the ground (*see p.116*). Covering fruits with cloches or fleece as cool autumn nights approach will help speed ripening in cool climates.

**Common problems** Watermelons suffer the same problems as sweet melons (*see above*).

**Recommended cultivars**
'Citron Red Seeded' – large, green jam melon that ripens in cool climates.
'Moon and Stars' – decorative, yellow-spotted, green-skinned fruit.
'Seedless 1600' – hybrid with large, round, seedless fruit; requires a pollinator to set fruit.
'Sugar Baby' – small, green fruit with red flesh; ripens in cool climates.

# Zucchini *and* summer squash

## *Cucurbita pepo*

| Season | Spring | Summer | Autumn | Winter |
|---|---|---|---|---|
| Sow | | • • • | | |
| Transplant | | • • | | |
| Harvest | | | • • • | • |

Zucchini and summer squash are very productive vegetables and one of the most worthy vegetables to grow. Zucchini or courgettes, differ from vegetable marrows (*see p.118*) only in that they produce fruits suitable for harvesting immediately after flowering, although if left they will eventually form marrows. Zucchini are seedless, since they are eaten when young and fresh, and have a firmer texture and a better taste than marrows. They are relatively robust and fast growing, and easy to grow. Some have a trailing habit. Summer squashes are treated in the same way as zucchini. The flowers, especially male ones, are considered a delicacy, stuffed or fried; the tendrils and shoot tips can also be steamed for eating. Zucchini and summer squashes yield 6–12 fruits per plant. They are not suitable for storing.

**Site and soil** Zucchini prefer an open, sunny position, and benefit from the addition of plenty of organic matter during soil preparation (*see p.114*), as well as dressing with a mulch (*see p.116*). Seeds need a minimum of 13°C (56°F) to germinate.

**Sowing and planting** For early crops, sow in a greenhouse in mid- to late spring (*see p.114*), and plant out under cloches or frames in late spring or outdoors in early summer (*see p.115*). Later crops can be direct sown, three seeds per station, outdoors in early summer (*see p.114*). Delay sowing, or planting out, for about two weeks in cooler districts.

| Sowing depth | 2.5cm (1in) |
|---|---|
| Plant spacing | 90cm (36in) |
| Row spacing | 90cm (36in) |
| | 1.2m (4ft) for trailing cultivars |

**Routine care** Water regularly to keep the soil moist, especially during flowering. Feeding (*see p.115*) can help if growth appears too slow. Hand-pollination (*see p.116*) is usually only required for plants grown in cloches and frames. Trailing types may be trained over canes or wires (*see p.115*). For early crops, use cloches or frames (*see p.115*).

**Harvesting** Gather the young fruits when they are about 10cm (4in) long, or when the remnants of the flowers fall off (*see p.116*). If left any longer, the swelling fruits will have less flavour and poor texture, and they will also divert the plant's energy away from the formation of new fruits.

**Common problems** Powdery mildew (*see p.260*) occurs in late summer. Cucumber mosaic virus (*see p.254*) is common, which results in poorly formed fruits, but disease-resistant cultivars are available. Slugs and snails (*see p.262*) can be very destructive to young plants. Red spider mite (*see p.261*) and whitefly (*see p.264*) are especially damaging in cold frames. Stem and root rots (*see p.263*) affect the bases of the stems and are associated with overwatered plants and badly drained soil. Bean seed fly (*see p.251*) can occasionally damage outdoor sowings in early summer.

**Recommended cultivars**
ZUCCHINI
'Blackjack' – hybrid that produces smooth, green fruit over a long period.
'Gold Finger' – hybrid, smooth, golden fruit.
'Gold Rush' – early variety with smooth, golden fruit.
SUMMER SQUASH
'Gem Squash' – vigorous vine producing tasty round, green fruit.
'Golden Crookneck' – vine that produces knobbly yellow fruit with a bent neck.
'Light Green Buttons' – hybrid; bush with prolific crops of pale green button-shaped fruit.
'Spaghetti Squash' – vigorous vine producing long yellow fruit that can be baked whole and the contents eaten like spaghetti.

# Growing stem vegetables

This group includes celeriac, celery, and Florence fennel, all of which have edible fleshy stems and decorative foliage. They are biennials, usually grown as annuals. Celery and fennel are not the easiest crops to grow, but celeriac is much simpler. Celeriac and celery both make useful winter vegetables.

Celery types include modern self-blanching kinds, traditional trench celery, and leaf or cut celery, which is grown for its tender young leaves instead of its stems. Self-blanching types are easier to grow, when the seed is sown in early spring and the seedlings are planted out in mid- to late spring. Commercial seedlings are recommended where propagation conditions are not ideal. Celery cultivars with green, red, or pink stems (*see below*) are also available.

Celeriac and most celery are long-season crops, but leaf celery and fennel are quicker to mature. Leaf celery is frost-hardy and will last through to the following spring in cool climates. Celery and fennel are prone to bolting and running to seed, especially if growth is checked, but some bolt-resistant cultivars are now available.

## Site and soil

All stem vegetables need a fertile, well-drained, moisture-retentive soil, with plenty of organic matter incorporated into it, in an open site. For celery and

**Pink-stemmed celery**
*For an interesting salad, try growing one of the attractive pink- or red-stemmed trench celery cultivars (here 'Blush'). These are usually more cold-tolerant than the white-stemmed types.*

celeriac, acid soils should be limed (*see pp. 18–19*). Self-blanching celery grows either under cover or outside, but is susceptible to frost, and in cool climates should be harvested by mid-autumn unless given some protection. Celery needs high levels of nitrogen, whereas celeriac and fennel prefer low levels.

## Blanching stems

Celery, in particular, needs to be blanched; that is, the plants should be deprived of light so that the stems remain white and more tender to eat. The traditional, laborious method of planting in a trench (hence the name trench celery) and then earthing up the stems is now seldom employed. Self-blanching celery plants should be planted closely in blocks (*see right*) so that their own foliage helps to restrict the availability of light to the stems of the plants in the middle.

The outer plants in a block of self-blanching celery, however, and all trench celery plants, are best blanched with collars (*see above*). In late summer, when the plants are 23–30cm (9–12in) tall, loosely wrap strips – 38cm (15in) long and as wide as the plant is tall – of lightproof paper or cardboard around the stems, and secure with two loops of garden twine. In cool weather, black plastic may also be used, lined with cardboard or paper to prevent the stems sweating, which could cause rotting. In windy areas, tie the twine around a cane to provide support. Leave one-third of the plant exposed to allow it to keep growing, and also make sure that

there is plenty of room for the stem to expand within the collar. If 60cm (2ft) of blanch is required for show purposes, repeat the blanching process 2–3 weeks later. It may be necessary to take off the collars from time to time to check for slugs and snails, since they will flourish in the shelter of the protective sleeves.

## Routine care

To produce tender, non-stringy stems, provide a constant supply of moisture throughout the growing season to swell the stems, but avoid waterlogging. Mulching (*see p. 72*) will help to conserve moisture. Celeriac and celery in cool climates can be protected from frost by a layer of straw placed around the plants. For feeding requirements, *see individual crops, pp. 121–122.*

**Blanching stems**
*For all trench celery plants, and outer plants in a block of self-blanching types, loosely wrap a length of cardboard or paper-lined black plastic around the stems when they are 23–30cm (9–12in) tall. Leave 8–10cm (3–4in) of overlap to allow for plant growth and secure with twine.*

**Planting in a block**
*For celery, especially the self-blanching types, block planting, with the plants positioned 25cm (10in) apart each way, aids the blanching process by excluding some light.*

# A–Z of stem vegetables

## Celeriac

*Apium graveolens* var. *rapaceum*

| Month | Spring | Summer | Autumn | Winter |
|---|---|---|---|---|
| Sow | • • | | | |
| Transplant | | • • • | | |
| Harvest | • • | | • • • | • • |

Celeriac produces a knobbly, swollen "bulb" at the base of the stem, up to 13cm (5in) in diameter (*see illustration, p.34*); the bulb can be cooked or grated raw into winter salads. The leaves can be used like celery and as a flavouring too. It is sometimes described as turnip-rooted celery, having a similar taste to celery. Celeriac is more frost-hardy than self-blanching celery. It is a useful alternative to celery in the winter, because it is less prone to problems. Newer cultivars are being bred to produce smoother stems that are easier to peel. Celeriac yields ten heads, 225–400g (8–12oz) each, per 3m (10ft) row.

**Site and soil** Celeriac needs a rich soil with plenty of organic matter incorporated into it (*see p.120*). It prefers an open site, but will tolerate a limited amount of shade.

**Sowing and planting** For best results, celeriac needs a long, uninterrupted growing season. Seeds are best sown in early to mid-spring in a propagator at 15°C (59°F) either in modules or seed trays, or several seeds to a pot or module (*see pp.64–65*). When large enough to handle, prick out the seedlings into larger modules (*see p.64*), or thin to one per pot or module, and keep above 10°C (50°F). From mid-spring to early summer, plant seedlings in well-spaced rows or blocks (*see p.71*); they need plenty of light and air around them, and if planted too closely will produce poor roots. Better crops are usually achieved if planted out in late spring rather than early summer, so they can establish before the hot, dry weather. Where conditions are ideal, celeriac seed can be sown *in situ*, in spring.

| Sowing depth | on surface |
|---|---|
| Plant spacing | 30cm (12in) |
| Row spacing | 45cm (18in) |

**Routine care** Water well to maintain soil moisture. Apply a mulch to retain moisture (*see p.72*). If the crop is slow growing, or looks pale, top-dress with sulphate of ammonia (*see p.20*) at a rate of 35g per sq m (1oz per sq yd). In midsummer, remove any outer leaves that are splitting away from the stem and yellowing; this should produce stems that are less knobbly.

**Harvesting and storing** Celeriac takes six months to mature. Early cultivars can be harvested from early autumn and later ones up to mid-spring. The stems are ready when they reach 8–13cm (3–5in) in diameter. Lift the stem, trim off the roots, and wash it clean. Twist off the top, unless some of the leaves are to be used in soup. Celeriac is best left in the ground until needed and then used fresh, where the soil is well-drained.

**Common problems** As for celery (*see p.122*).

**Recommended cultivar**
'White Alabaster' – tasty bulbs used fresh in salad or cooked.

## Celery *and* leaf celery

*Apium graveolens* vars.

| Season | Spring | Summer | Autumn | Winter |
|---|---|---|---|---|
| SELF–BLANCHING/GREEN CELERY | | | | |
| Sow | • • • | | | |
| Transplant | • • • | | | |
| Harvest | | • • • • | • • • | |
| TRENCH CELERY | | | | |
| Sow | • • | | | |
| Transplant | | • • | | |
| Harvest | | | • • | |
| LEAF CELERY | | | | |
| Sow | • • • | • | • • | |
| Transplant | • • • | | • • | |
| Harvest | • • • | • • • | • • • | • • |

Celery (*Apium graveolens* var. *dulce*) is grown for its fleshy, blanched stems, up to 25cm (10in) in length, which are eaten raw in salads or cooked as a vegetable or in soups. The inner stems gradually get smaller, but are more tender and better blanched than the outer ones. Celery is difficult to grow well, as it is fussy about soil moisture, fertility, and drainage, as well as growing temperature and humidity. It grows best in cool climates and low humidity with moist, but not wet, soil. There are three main types: self-blanching and green celery; trench celery; and leaf, or cutting, celery, also known as celery herb, smallage and soup celery.

Self-blanching celery cultivars have off-white stalks; these and green celery cultivars are the easiest to grow, but less cold-tolerant and slightly less flavoursome than trench types. Trench celery is a popular crop in Europe, and demands a lot of space in the garden and a fair amount of skill to blanch the stems successfully, whether this is done in the traditional way using trenches and earthing up, or in the more modern way of planting on the flat and using collars (*see p.120*). There are white-, red-, and pink-stemmed cultivars (*see p.120*). Leaf celery is a small, very hardy plant, with fine stems and scented leaves, and it is easy to grow in gardens or in containers. It is useful as a salad herb or flavouring, and stems can be picked as required. When working with celery, beware of celery rash; always keep your hands and arms covered for safety. Self-blanching, green, and trench celery yield 12 heads, 450g (1lb) each, per 3m (10ft) row. Leaf celery yields 15–20 heads per 3m (10ft) row.

**Site and soil**   Celery needs an open site and rich, moisture-retentive, well-drained soil with plenty of organic matter added to it (*see p.120*); it also needs a pH of 6.6–6.8, so you should add lime to acid soils (*see pp.18–19*). For trench celery, in autumn dig a trench 38–45cm (15–18in) wide and 30cm (12in) deep, working in plenty of organic matter. If growing the celery on the flat, fill in the trench to the top; if the celery is to be earthed up, fill to 8–10cm (3–4in) below the surface, leaving the rest of the soil at the side of the trench for earthing up later.

**Sowing and planting**   Always use treated seed in order to avoid seed-borne diseases (*see below*) that can spoil the crop. Celery seed is usually slow to germinate, and commercially grown seedlings are recommended where propagation conditions are not ideal (*see p.62*). For self-blanching celery, sow seed in pots or modules in a propagator (*see p.63*) in early to mid-spring at 15°C (59°F); sow on the surface, since the seed needs light to germinate, and keep it moist. Prick out the seedlings into larger modules when they have one true leaf (*see p.64*). Grow the seedlings at a minimum temperature of at least 10°C (50°F) to avoid bolting. When the plants have 4–6 true leaves, plant them out so that the crown of the plant is at soil level. They can withstand light frosts, but in cool climates, early crops may need covering (*see pp.45–48*). Space the plants about 25cm (10in) apart in a block (*see p.120*). Water in well.

   Sow trench celery as for self-blanching celery. Harden off before transplanting in late spring to early summer in the prepared trench or on the flat in single rows, where blanching collars are to be used; the exact plant spacing depends on the size of stick required. If you need to conserve space, you can use a double row, sited 60–75cm (24–30in) from the next crop.

   For celery herb, sow either in seed trays or pots (*see p.64*) as for self-blanching celery, or preferably as multiblocks (*see p.65*). You can also sow a few multiblocks in late summer to crop in a greenhouse in winter and spring.

| Sowing depth | on surface, or very shallow |
|---|---|
| Plant spacing | self-blanching: 25cm (10in) |
| | trench: 30–45cm (12–18in) |
| | leaf: 13cm (5in) single plants |
| | 20cm (8in) multiblocks |
| Row spacing | self-blanching: 25cm (10in) |
| | trench: 30cm (12in) |
| | leaf: 30cm (12in) |

**Routine care**   Celery requires plenty of moisture, and must grow evenly without any checks to prevent stringiness. Water well and use a mulch to maintain soil moisture (*see p.72*). When the plants are about half their final size, before the leaves touch, top-dress

with sulphate of ammonia (*see p.20*) at a rate of 50g per sq m (1½oz per sq yd), washing any excess off the foliage to avoid scorching. Repeat this, or give a liquid feed (*see p.21*), if the leaves yellow. Earth up trench celery planted in a trench. For trench celery planted on the flat, and for self-blanching celery plants on the outside of a block, wrap collars around the stems (*see p.120*). For celery herb, remove yellow leaves.

**Harvesting and storing**   Celery takes 4–8 months to mature in cool climates. Pick stems as required, or wait until they are crisp but not stringy. It is vital to harvest before the stems deteriorate and the leaves yellow. Water the plants well before harvesting, or the stems will quickly wilt. Dig up the plant, trim off the outer side roots and any small stems; the stick can be stored whole in a refrigerator for over a week. Break individual stems off the main stick as required, and wash and prepare them. If the individual stems are prepared before storing, the cut ends will turn brown. Trench celery is ready in autumn and early winter; harvest in the same way as self-blanching celery. Wash the whole stick before storing. For celery herb, regularly pick leaves from the edges of the plants as needed.

**Common problems**   Slugs and snails (*see p.262*) may be troublesome pests. Diseases that may affect the crop include fungal leaf spots (*see p.257*), stem and root rots (*see p.263*), and bacterial soft rot (*see p.251*).

**Recommended cultivars**

CELERY

'Chinese' – more tender than old English varieties.
'Golden Self-blanching' – compact variety with pale golden leaves and stringless stems.
'Ivory Tower' – a tall self-blanching variety with smooth stems.
'Stringless American' – a green celery that can be blanched or not blanched.
'Tall Utah' – dark green leaves and stringless stems.
'Tendercrisp' – tall, stringless stems; needs a cool climate.
'Ventura' – upright stems on healthy green plants.

LEAF CELERY

'Kintsai' – Easy-to-grow celery with less fleshy stems but strong flavour. Pick as required.

# Florence fennel

*Foeniculum vulgare* var. *azoricum*

| Month | Spring | | | Summer | | | Autumn | | | Winter | | |
|---|---|---|---|---|---|---|---|---|---|---|---|---|
| Sow | | • | • | | | • | | | | | | |
| Transplant | | • | • | | | | | | | | | |
| Harvest | | | | | • | • | | • | • | • | | |

Florence fennel is sometimes called *Foeniculum dulce* but, it is more correctly a tender bulb-forming variety of *Foeniculum vulgare*. Florence fennel produces very handsome, feathery foliage, and makes an

extremely ornamental vegetable for the garden. Succulent, aniseed-flavoured "bulbs", which can be either cooked or eaten raw, develop from the swollen bases of the leaf stalks. The leaves and stalks may also be eaten in salads as can the leaves of the self-seeding herb sweet fennel (*Foeniculum vulgare*). Sweet fennel is a troublesome weed in wasteland and country areas. It does not form a tender bulb but grows as a bamboo-like clump of stems and feathery foliage. The variety 'azoricum', or Florence fennel, does not self-seed like the species. However, plants are extremely prone to bolting, but bolt-resistant cultivars are available. Florence fennel will yield 1.4–2.25kg per 3m (3–5lb per 10ft) row.

**Site and soil**   Florence fennel prefers fertile, well-drained, sandy soil (*see p.120*) that has preferably been well manured for a previous crop (*see pp.22–23*).

**Sowing and planting**   For early crops in cool climates, sow in modules (*see p.62*) in early to mid-spring and plant out when the seedlings have no more than four true leaves, taking care not to disturb the young roots. Even with these precautions, there is still a risk that the crop may bolt. For direct sowings, sow a few seeds at a time, in late spring.

   The seed needs a minimum of 15°C (59°F) in order to germinate. Sow 3–4 seeds per station at 30cm (12in) intervals, and thin to a single, strong-growing seedling when they are large enough to handle. The depth of sowing is critical for success; if the seeds are sown too shallowly the resulting plants are liable to rock in the wind, and they may even twist and break off.

| Sowing depth | 2.5cm (1in) |
|---|---|
| Plant spacing | 30cm (12in) |
| Row spacing | 30cm (12in) |

**Routine care**   Florence fennel needs plenty of moisture throughout the growing period, so mulch (*see p.72*) to help conserve moisture. Feeding is not usually required. If plants start to rock, lightly earth up the stems. When the stems begin to swell, earth up to half-way over the bulb or wrap with cardboard like blanching celery to make it whiter and sweeter.

**Harvesting**   Florence fennel takes at least three months to mature. When the bulbs have reached a good size, harvest them by cutting at ground level so as to leave a stump which will resprout to produce shoots suitable for use in salads. The bulbs may start to elongate, showing that they are running to seed; in this case, harvest them quickly or they will be too tough to use.

**Common problems**   Rhizoctonia, causing plants to rot off either as seedlings or mature bulbs, can be a problem. Practise good crop rotation (*see p.31*) and avoid growing lettuce or radish crops on the same ground. (See also Plant Problems, *p.261*.)

**Recommended cultivars**

Named cultivars are seldom offered.

# Growing leafy vegetables

Leafy vegetables are grown for their tasty and sometimes decorative leaves, which, unlike those of salad crops (*see pp.101–107*), are usually cooked before eating. They grow slowly in cold weather, but many varieties bolt to seed in hot weather. Most leafy vegetables are grown like annuals as short-term leaf crops. Perennial varieties such as New Zealand spinach are pruned at flowering to promote new leaf growth. Flower stems on annual varieties can be removed also to extend leaf harvest. Some leafy vegetables are quite ornamental – silver beet and pak choi have coloured stems and leaf veins that contrast vividly with the green foliage. All yield abundantly and are easy to grow. They fall into two broad groups: spinaches and chards, and oriental brassicas. For western brassicas, such as cabbage and texsel greens, *see pp.76–81*; for salad leaves, *see pp.101–107*.

The spinach and chards group includes amaranths, spinach, Ceylon spinach, New Zealand spinach, and silver beet. Some, such as Ceylon spinach, are tropical or subtropical vines and require high temperatures to grow well; others, like spinach and silver beet, are cool-season, rosette-forming plants that can withstand some degree of frost. They are therefore very useful crops for overwintering, to provide fresh, leafy vegetables from late winter to mid-spring when not many vegetables are available.

Oriental brassicas include Chinese broccoli, Chinese cabbage, flowering greens, mustard greens, spinach mustard, and pak choi. They are quick-maturing plants that are difficult to grow well and respond to the colder weather and dry summers of more temperate climates by bolting (*see above*) or developing very strong flavours. This limits them to sowing in cool climates in late summer for autumn cropping, unless bolt-resistant cultivars are used. However, most varieties tolerate light frost and provide crops in winter and spring. Although usually grown for their young leaves, flowering shoots of oriental brassicas can also be used in salads to add a touch of spiciness.

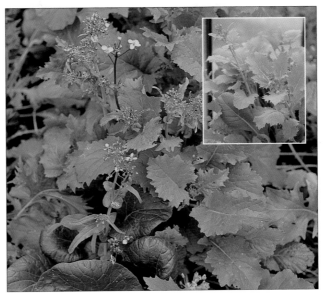

**Bolting crops**
*In summer, or earlier in a greenhouse, oriental brassicas (here mustard greens) may bolt, or run to seed, if they are exposed to excessive cold early in their development, especially in periods of lengthening days. They will also bolt if exposed to excessive warmth or kept too dry. The flowerheads, however, are edible and tasty, and the seeds may be saved unless they derive from a hybrid cultivar.*

## Site and soil

Both spinach and oriental brassicas need very fertile soil that is neutral to slightly alkaline in pH (*see p.18*), with very moist soil; this is best ensured by liberal applications of organic matter when preparing the soil. Freedom from any traces of clubroot (*see p.254*) is also vital for oriental brassicas. Silver beet and New Zealand spinach can be grown on relatively dry soils.

Leafy vegetables grow well through the year in temperate gardens; in the tropics they grow best through winter.

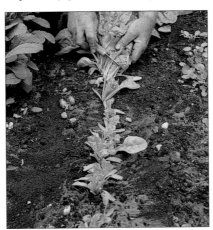

**Cut-and-come-again leaves**
*Some leafy vegetables, such as this silver beet, make good cut-and-come-again crops. When the seedlings are 10–15cm (4–6in) tall, cut them 2.5cm (1in) above ground level.*

## Sowing and planting

Leafy vegetables are best raised from seed sown direct in the garden. If sowing in a propagator, do not sow in trays or pots, since transplanting the bare-root seedlings of leafy vegetables promotes bolting. Plants sown directly in modules or mulch pots (*see p.65*) can be safely transplanted. Leafy vegetables are fast-growing crops, taking 6–10 weeks from sowing to harvest (*see individual crops, pp.125–128*), and they can soon become overmature and unpalatable. It is a good idea, therefore, to make regular successional sowings (*see p.69*); silver beet can be picked over a long period, however, and oriental brassicas may bolt if sown early.

## Seedling crops

Diseases, pests, and bolting can be avoided by growing greens (meaning the foliage of leafy vegetables, rather than spring greens which refers to unhearted spring cabbage, *see p.79*) for use as seedlings or as cut-and-come-again crops (*see left and p.102*). If densely sown, in rows only 10–15cm (4–6in) apart, to obtain one seedling every 1cm (½in), surprisingly large crops of seedling leaves can be taken from small areas – equivalent to 9–12 lettuce heads per 3m (10ft) row. If, when harvesting the first crop, you leave intact the heart leaves in the centres, the seedlings will resprout vigorously to yield another crop. Several harvests of leaves can be taken from late sowings, but early sowings containing oriental brassicas bolt so readily that only one crop is usually possible. The tender leaves are suitable for eating raw in salads or for very light cooking.

Prevent damage from foliage pests by protecting the seedlings with fleece or fine woven mesh (*see p.48*), and also control slugs and snails (*see p.262*). Dead leaves can make subsequent harvests unattractive, so a thorough clean-up after each harvest is essential. Weed control (*see below*) must also be scrupulous, to avoid weed leaves being gathered with the edible leaves.

## Maximizing your crops

Leafy vegetables are quick growing, and their leaves can be gathered while the plants are still small. They are therefore useful for growing as catch crops (*see p.69*) and for intercropping (*see p.71*). Spinach, mustard greens, and silver beet all tolerate light shade, and will fit neatly between tall, widely spaced crops such as sweetcorn.

## Winter crops

Silver beet sown in late summer in cool climates will grow all winter to provide fresh greens until plants go to seed in summer. In warm areas it will also grow well through winter but high humidity can cause rotting. In both cases, protect from slugs and snails, and

birds. The leaves may be harvested even if they do not fully mature.

## Container growing

Leafy vegetables, especially seedling crops, because they are fast growing and shallow-rooted, are suitable for growing in containers (*see above*), using multi-purpose potting mix. This material is sterile and so free of weeds and diseases, ideal where clubroot is present and to minimize weeding. By growing them in containers, fresh vegetables can be raised on balconies, near the back door, or in greenhouses in winter. Silver beet is a particularly rewarding crop to grow in containers, and the coloured varieties are most decorative. The quality of the crops grown in containers is, however, dependent on correct and regular watering and feeding (*see below*).

**Using containers**
*Some leafy vegetable crops, like this silver beet 'Rainbow', can be grown in containers such as troughs to create a decorative display, as well as producing an edible crop. Use a compost that is rich in organic matter, and keep it moist at all times. Regular feeding will also be necessary.*

## Routine care

The best way to control weeds with leafy vegetables is to give them a weed-free start, using a pre-weeded seedbed (*see p.66*). Remove any further weeds by hoeing between the rows as necessary.

Apply a base fertilizer before sowing (*see individual crops, pp.125–128*), unless the soil has been enriched with organic matter. For cut-and-come-again leaves, apply a compound fertilizer at a rate of 35g per sq m (1oz per sq yd) or pelleted poultry manure at 50g per sq m (1½oz per sq yd). Some crops may require another top-dressing of nitrogenous fertilizer (*see individual crops, pp.125–128*).

Water frequently to keep the top 20cm (8in) of soil moist. Lack of water, even if brief, can lead to slow growth, loss of texture, peppery flavours, and bolting in all crops. If keeping your containers well watered is difficult in spells of hot weather, or at holiday times, move them into a shaded area to avoid damage to the plants. All varieties grow best with shade from afternoon sun in hot climates.

## Harvesting

Once mature, the leaves quickly become coarse in texture and flavour, and the stems become fibrous, so commence picking or cutting the leaves and shoots as soon as they reach the desired size, and continue until the plants flower (*see left*). They are best harvested in the cool of the morning or evening, and stored in a refrigerator to avoid wilting. If an entire plant is cut at an early stage as a cut-and-come-again crop, leaving a stump, it should provide another crop.

**Harvesting amaranths**
*Gather young shoots and leaves, cutting them with a sharp knife, when the plants are about 25cm (10in) tall. Keep harvesting until the plants produce flowers and growth ceases.*

**Harvesting spinach**
*You can start to pick the outer leaves about 6–10 weeks after sowing. Alternatively, use a sharp knife to sever the whole plant 2.5cm (1in) above ground level; it will then resprout.*

# A–Z of leafy vegetables

## Amaranth

### *Amaranthus* species

| Month | Spring | Summer | Autumn | Winter |
|---|---|---|---|---|
| Sow | • • | | | |
| Transplant | | • | | |
| Harvest | | • • • • • | | |

Amaranths, which are also known as African or Indian spinach, are rapidly growing annuals, typically reaching 60cm (2ft) tall, whose leaves can be used in salads or cooked in the same way as spinach. They have a sharp, spinach-like flavour. *Amaranthus cruentus* is the most commonly grown cultivar, and has light green, oval leaves. *A. caudatus*, widely grown as an ornamental plant, has bright red, tassel-like flowers and pale green leaves. *A. tricolor*, or Chinese spinach, has greenish-white flowers and green, yellow, or red leaves. Amaranths grow well in warm weather and are not fussy about soil or site; however, they will appreciate a very sunny, sheltered position in cool climates. Amaranths yield 7.25kg per 3m (16lb per 10ft) row.

**Site and soil** Amaranths prefer a moderately deep, fertile, well-drained, acid to neutral soil, in a sunny, sheltered position. If necessary, apply a base dressing as for spinach (*see p.128*) before sowing.

**Sowing and planting** When the soil is warm enough in cool climates in late spring, sow thinly *in situ*. Thin as soon as the seedlings can be handled (*see p.68*), and remove alternate plants when they are large enough to harvest. In warm areas, seed can be sown *in situ* all year. Water when young, but plants tolerate dryness when well established.

| Sowing depth | 2cm (¾in) |
|---|---|
| Seed spacing | sow thinly; thin to 8cm (3in) |
| Plant spacing | 15cm (6in) |
| Row spacing | 30cm (12in) |

**Routine care** Water and top-dress as for spinach (*see p.128*). Pinch out the growing tip when 20cm (8in) tall to promote bushiness.

**Harvesting** Amaranths mature in 10–12 weeks. Start to gather young shoots and leaves when the plants are 25cm (10in) tall (*see p.124*). Continue to harvest until the plants flower and growth ceases. Amaranths often set abundant seed.

**Common problems** Powdery mildew and aphids occasionally occur. For symptoms and controls, *see* Plant Problems, *p.260 and p.251.*

**Recommended cultivars**
'Amaranth Spinach' (*Amaranthus tricolor*) – produces red-centred, green leaves.
'Grain Amaranth' (*Amaranthus hypochondriacus*) – leaves are nutritious and eaten fresh in salads or cooked; grain is high in protein.
'Leaf Amaranth' (*Amaranthus gangeticus*) – fast-growing annual producing red leaves.

## Ceylon *or* Malabar spinach

### *Basella* species

| Month | Spring | Summer | Autumn | Winter |
|---|---|---|---|---|
| Sow | • • | | | |
| Transplant | | • • | | |
| Harvest | | • • • • | | |

Also known as Malabar nightshade, creeping spinach, or basella, these plants are very popular leafy greens in the tropics, and are used as a spinach substitute. They are green- (*Basella alba*) or red-leaved (*B. rubra*), trailing perennials that can become rampant where conditions are favourable. They are useful as climbers. Ceylon spinach yields 3kg per 3m (6½lb per 10ft) row. Named cultivars are not available.

**Site and soil** A fertile, well-drained, but moisture-retentive soil with a good organic matter content (*see p.123*) and a pH of 6–7.5 (*see p.18*) in a sunny, sheltered site is best. Ceylon spinach needs temperatures of 25–30°C (77–86°F) to thrive. If necessary, apply a base dressing as for spinach (*see p.128*) before planting.

**Sowing and planting** Sow seed in a propagator in cool climates in spring, and plant out in early summer. Seed can be sown *in situ* in warm climates. Plants may be raised from stem cuttings, that are 10–15cm (4–6in) long, rooted in small pots and transplanted as for seedlings.

| Sowing depth | 2.5cm (1in) |
|---|---|
| Plant spacing | 10–15cm (4–6in) |
| Row spacing | 30cm (12in) |

**Routine care** Top-dress with a nitrogen-rich fertilizer (*see pp.20–23*), and water regularly to keep the soil moist. Train plants up vertical netting supports to save space, or across netting stretched horizontally just above the level of the crop when it begins to need support – 30–45cm (12–18in) above the ground – to keep the leaves off the ground and thus clean. Pinch out the growing tips when shoots are about 30cm (12in) long, and remove any flowers to keep plants bushy and producing young foliage. Control excessive growth where conditions are favourable. Plants can become rampant weeds.

**Harvesting** Ceylon spinach usually reaches maturity in 10–12 weeks. Gather the fresh young sideshoots when they are 15cm (6in) long. Frequent picking will encourage more shoots to be produced. The seed is worth saving (*see p.61*), but remember that it may not always come true.

**Common problems** This crop is usually trouble-free.

# Chinese broccoli

*Brassica oleraceae* var. *alboglabra*

| Month | Spring | Summer | Autumn | Winter |
|---|---|---|---|---|
| Sow | • | • • • | | |
| Transplant | | • | | |
| Harvest | | • • | • • • | • |

Chinese broccoli, kailaan, broccolini, or Chinese kale, is an oriental brassica (*see p.123*) with succulent, pleasant-tasting, leafy, flowering shoots reminiscent in flavour of purple-sprouting broccoli or broccoli sideshoots, but more tangy. The shoots of Chinese broccoli are green, with white or yellow flowers. The plants are similar to hybrid broccoli, and hybrids have also been developed between the two. Chinese broccoli is tolerant of hot and cold weather. It yields 9–12 bunches per 3m (10ft) row.

**Site and soil** A deep, fertile, moisture-retentive soil with plenty of organic matter (*see p.123*) in a sheltered, sunny site is best. If necessary, apply a base dressing as for spinach (*see p.128*) before sowing or planting out.

**Sowing and planting** Sow in early summer *in situ* and thin (*see p.68*) to the final spacing, or raise seedlings in spring singly in module trays (*see p.65*) and transplant as soon as the rootball can be handled without breaking up; modules, composts, and growing conditions will all influence this timing. Plant seedlings 20cm (8in) apart. To avoid bolting (*see p.123*), if sowing before midsummer, use bolt-resistant cultivars.

| Sowing depth | 2cm (¾in) |
|---|---|
| Plant spacing | 30cm (12in) |
| Row spacing | 30cm (12in) |

**Routine care** Water regularly, thoroughly wetting the top 20cm (8in) of soil. Feeding is not usually necessary.

**Harvesting** Chinese broccoli takes about eight weeks to mature. Cut the mature shoots just before the flowers open, starting with the central one and moving onto the sideshoots. Peel the stems, and use the tender inner flesh. They will not be as large as broccoli shoots, but the tender new shoots continue to grow over a long period and can be harvested as required.

**Common problems** Oriental brassicas are prone to many of the problems suffered by western brassicas, especially cabbage white butterfly and clubroot. Other pests may include whitefly, mealy cabbage aphid, birds, cutworm, and, to a lesser extent, slugs and snails. Diseases may include powdery and downy mildew, and sometimes bacterial leaf spot. Occasionally boron or molybdenum deficiency may also affect the crop. For symptoms and controls, *see* Plant Problems, *pp.246–264*.

**Recommended cultivars**
'Green Lance' – tall hybrid that is fast growing and bears white flowers; tips are picked before the flowers open.

# Chinese cabbage

*Brassica rapa* var. *pekinensis*

| Month | Spring | Summer | Autumn | Winter |
|---|---|---|---|---|
| Sow | • • • | • • | | |
| Transplant | | • • | • | |
| Harvest | | | • • • | • • |

Chinese cabbage, or Chinese leaves, is an oriental brassica (*see p.123*) with dense heads and a crisp, mild cabbage flavour, suitable for light cooking, stir-fry or salads. Flowering shoots are extremely palatable. The head may be barrel-shaped or elongated; the leaves are usually pale green, with white veins and broad, flat ribs. They are very fast growing, and bolt to seed readily if growing conditions are not ideal. Non-hearting cultivars, known as loose-headed cabbage, have darker leaves and a stronger cabbage flavour. Chinese cabbage normally yields 9–12 heads per 3m (10ft) row.

**Site and soil** A deep, fertile, moisture-retentive soil, with plenty of organic matter added, in a sheltered, sunny site is best (*see p.123*). Feed as for spinach (*see p.128*), but double the rate of application if the soil is not very fertile and top-dress with nitrogenous fertilizer (*see p.20*) if growth appears to slow. Early and late sowings in cool climates will benefit from cloche or fleece protection (*see pp.45–48*).

**Sowing and planting** Late summer sowings are less likely to bolt in cool climates and may be station sown *in situ* (*see p.68*), but spring sowings are risky because the lengthening days exacerbate the inclination to bolt. For spring sowings in cool climates, raise seedlings of bolt-resistant cultivars singly in module trays (*see p.65*), in a propagator, and transplant as soon as they can be handled. Seed can also be sown *in situ* if conditions are ideal. Sow seed at any time of the year in warm climates. If planting commercial seedlings, take care that roots are not disturbed or seedlings may bolt.

| Sowing depth | 2cm (¾in) |
|---|---|
| Plant spacing | 30cm (12in) |
| Row spacing | 45cm (18in) |

**Routine care** The roots are shallow, so water little and often, never letting the soil dry out fully. Wet the top 20cm (8in) of soil, adding a nitrogen-rich fertilizer (*see pp.20–23*) before watering if growth slows down. Protect spring-sown crops after planting with fleece or cloches if cold weather threatens.

**Harvesting and storing** Chinese cabbage matures in 7–10 weeks. Cut the heads just above soil level when they feel solid. They can be used fresh, or stored in a refrigerator for six weeks or more. Harvest the leaves of plants that have bolted as loose greens. If a 2.5cm (1in) stump is left when cutting the head, it will resprout to produce more leaves after 2–4 weeks, and may be harvested again several times. Late-sown seedlings are useful as cut-and-come-again crops (*see p.123*) that can be harvested after about two weeks.

**Common problems** As for Chinese broccoli (*see left*); except for resistant cultivars, it is very susceptible to clubroot (*see p.77 and p.254*).

**Recommended cultivars**
'Michihili' – open-pollinated type with tall, tender heads.
'Two Seasons hybrid' – bolt- and rot-resistant hybrid that can be sown in spring as well as summer/autumn; firm, tall heads.
'Wong Bok hybrid' – large, barrel-shaped heads that resist running to seed.

# Flowering cabbage

*Brassica campestris* subsp. *chinensis* var. *utilis*

| Month | Spring | Summer | Autumn | Winter |
|---|---|---|---|---|
| Sow | • • | • | • | |
| Transplant | | • | • | |
| Harvest | | | • • • | • • |

Also known as Chinese flowering cabbage, Chinese greens or choy sum, these oriental brassicas (*see p.123*) are flowering versions of pak choi (*see p.127*), and are used like Chinese broccoli (*see left*). They have a tender, red or green, leafy stalk bearing unopened flowers, and possess a mild, peppery, cabbage flavour that needs light cooking. They are best grown in late summer for harvesting in autumn in cool climates, as earlier sowings will bolt (*see p.123*). Bolted stems are usable, but only for a brief period. The flowering shoots will become overmature quickly in hot weather. Flowering greens normally yield 9–12 bunches per 3m (10ft) row.

**Site and soil** A deep, fertile, moisture-retentive soil, with plenty of organic matter added, in a sheltered, sunny site is best (*see p.123*). If necessary, apply a base dressing as for spinach (*see p.128*), for both normal and cut-and-come-again crops, before sowing.

**Sowing and planting** Late summer sowings in cool climates will not usually bolt and may be station sown *in situ* (*see p.68*), but early sowings are risky because the lengthening days exacerbate the tendency to bolt. Sowing seed at 20–25°C (68–77°F) and then growing on the seedlings at 18–25°C (64–77°F) prevents bolting. For spring and early-summer sowings in cool climates, raise seedlings of bolt-resistant cultivars singly in module trays (*see p.65*), in warmth, and transplant as soon as they can be handled.

| Sowing depth | 2cm (¾in) |
|---|---|
| Plant spacing | 15cm (6in) |
| Row spacing | 45cm (18in) |

**Routine care** The roots of flowering greens are quite shallow, and should therefore be watered little and often, never letting the soil dry out fully. Wet the top 20cm (8in) of soil, adding a nitrogen-rich fertilizer (*see pp.20–23*) before watering if growth appears to slow. If cold weather threatens, protect spring-sown crops after planting with fleece or cloches.

**Harvesting** Flowering greens take about eight weeks to mature. Flowering stems should be cut then, but outer leaves may be picked earlier. Pick while the stalk is tender and the flower buds are closed. Storage is not possible, and they are best used fresh. Regrowth from stumps can be used for greens, and these make good cut-and-come-again crops, (*see p.123*).

**Common problems** As for Chinese broccoli (*see facing page*).

**Recommended cultivars**
'Bouquet hybrid' – also called Rape flower, as the flowers can be used as cut flowers; as a vegetable, stems are picked when young, when buds are immature.

# Mustard greens *and* spinach mustard

*Brassica juncea* and
*B. rapa* subsp. *perviridis*

| Month | Spring | Summer | Autumn | Winter |
|---|---|---|---|---|
| Sow | | • • • • | | |
| Transplant | | • • | | |
| Harvest | | • • | • • • | |

Mustard greens (*Brassica juncea*) are a varied group of oriental brassicas (*see p.123*) with a tangy, peppery, cabbage flavour that becomes more fiery as they run to seed. The flowering shoots can be extremely hot when eaten fresh but are mild when cooked. Leaves may be green, red, or purple, with smooth or blistered surfaces and straight or jagged edges. Rich in vitamins and minerals, mustard greens are nutritionally among the most valuable of vegetables. Spinach mustard (*Brassica rapa* subsp. *perviridis*) is similar, but more closely related to Chinese cabbage (*see p.126*). Mustard greens and spinach mustard yield 1.5kg per sq m (3¼lb per sq yd).

**Site and soil** A deep, fertile, moisture-retentive soil, with plenty of organic matter added, in a sheltered, sunny site is best (*see p.123*). If necessary, apply a base dressing as for spinach (*see p.128*) before sowing.

**Sowing and planting** Late summer sowings will not usually bolt in cool climates, and may be station sown *in situ* (*see p.68*). Early sowings are risky since lengthening days exacerbate the inclination to bolt. Sowing seed at 20–25°C (68–77°F) and growing seedlings at 18–25°C (64–77°F) will prevent bolting even if sowing in spring. For early sowings, therefore, raise seedlings of bolt-resistant cultivars singly in module trays (*see p.65*), in a propagator in late summer for autumn/winter; transplant as soon as they can be handled.

| Sowing depth | 1cm (½in) |
|---|---|
| Plant spacing | 15–30cm (6–12in) |
| Row spacing | 45cm (18in) |

**Routine care** The roots are shallow, and should therefore be watered little and often, never letting the soil dry out fully. Wet the top

20cm (8in) of soil, adding a nitrogen-rich fertilizer (*see pp.20–23*) before watering if growth slows down. Protect spring-sown crops after planting if cold weather threatens.

**Harvesting** Mustard greens and spinach mustard take 6–8 weeks to mature, after which you can cut selected leaves as required. The plants will stand in good condition for several weeks, allowing a prolonged harvest, and regrowth from cut stumps will yield further harvests. They may also be used as cut-and-come-again seedling crops (*see p.123*), usually ready after about two weeks. The seed is worth saving (*see p.61*).

**Common problems** As for Chinese broccoli (*see facing page*).

**Recommended cultivars**
'Green Wave' – open, upright plant with ruffled leaves.
'Mustard Green Giant' – quick-maturing plant with mild flavour.
'Mustard Red Giant' – a red-leafed form of the above.

# New Zealand spinach

*Tetragonia tetragonioides*

| Month | Spring | Summer | Autumn | Winter |
|---|---|---|---|---|
| Sow | • • • | • • | | |
| Transplant | • | | | |
| Harvest | • • • | • • • | • • • | |

New Zealand spinach, or Warragul greens, is a robust, trailing perennial native to Australia. It has a stronger, more acidic flavour than spinach. It has spiky, triangular leaves, about 5cm (2in) long, and trails for up to 1.2m (4ft), sometimes reaching heights of 60cm (2ft). Its young shoots and leaves are used like spinach (*see p.128*). It is slow to bolt, grows quickly, and is fairly tasty. It is an attractive groundcover plant, needing little care, and is suitable for containers, hanging baskets, or the ornamental kitchen garden. It yields 6kg per 3m (13lb per 10ft) row.
Named cultivars are not offered.

**Site and soil** Sunny, sheltered sites are best. Although fertile, moisture-retentive soil (*see p.123*) is ideal, New Zealand spinach can survive on poorer soils and with much less water than spinach or silver beet, and requires no fertilizer on fertile ground of good organic matter content. If necessary, however, apply a base dressing as for spinach (*see p.128*), before sowing or planting out.

**Sowing and planting** Soak the elongated, woody fruits, containing seeds, for 24 hours before sowing, to break down the hard seed coats and speed up germination. Sow singly in module trays (*see p.65*) in mid-spring, and transplant as soon as they can be handled, or station sow (*see p.68*) in the garden, in late spring or early summer. Allow for wide growth when planting.

| Sowing depth | 2.5cm (1in) |
|---|---|
| Plant spacing | 45cm (18in) |
| Row spacing | 45cm (18in) |

**Routine care** Keep weed-free, and water only in the driest spells.

**Harvesting and storing** Shoots and leaves are usually ready to pick about four weeks after sowing, depending on conditions; those from spring sowings may take longer. It is best used fresh, but may also be frozen. Regular picking promotes fresh growth. Young plants may be cut near ground level; the stumps will regrow (*see p.124*). The seed is worth saving (*see p.61*).

**Common problems** This crop is usually trouble-free, but may suffer from downy mildew (*see p.255*) and from birds eating the seedlings (*see p.251*).

# Pak choi

*Brassica rapa* var. *chinensis*

| Month | Spring | Summer | Autumn | Winter |
|---|---|---|---|---|
| Sow | • • • | • | | |
| Transplant | | • • | | |
| Harvest | | • • | • • • | |

Pak choi, or celery mustard, is an oriental brassica (*see p.123*) with a handsome head of paddle-shaped leaves with crunchy, wide midribs. Light cooking in stir-fry will preserve its refreshing, delicate texture and flavour; it can also be eaten raw in salads. Flowering shoots are very palatable. Like Chinese cabbage, it is an excellent crop for late summer, including catch crops (*see p.69*), but will bolt (*see p.123*) if exposed to dryness. Pak choi grows speedily in early autumn in cool climates, and can be harvested through winter. It yields 9–12 heads per 3m (10ft) row.

**Site and soil** A deep, fertile, moisture-retentive soil, with plenty of organic matter added, in a sheltered, sunny site is best (*see p.123*). If necessary, apply a base dressing as for spinach (*see p.128*) before sowing or planting.

**Sowing and planting** Late summer sowings will not usually bolt and may be station sown *in situ* (*see p.68*), but early sowings are risky because the lengthening days exacerbate the inclination to bolt. Sowing at 20–25°C (68–77°F) and growing seedlings at 18–25°C (64–77°F) will prevent bolting even when sowing in spring. For early sowings, therefore, raise seedlings of bolt-resistant cultivars singly in module trays (*see p.65*), in a propagator, in mid- to late spring and transplant as soon as they can be handled. Take care that roots are not disturbed when transplanting seedlings, or plants may bolt to seed. Pak choi can be sown for most of the year.

| Sowing depth | 2cm (⅔in) |
|---|---|
| Plant spacing | 10cm (4in) |
| Row spacing | 45cm (18in) |

**Routine care** The roots are shallow, and should therefore be watered little and often, never letting the soil dry out fully. Wet the top 20cm (8in) of soil, adding a nitrogen-rich fertilizer (*see pp.20–23*) before watering if growth slows. Protect spring-sown crops with fleece or cloches if cold weather threatens.

**Harvesting** Pak choi takes about eight weeks to mature. Pick leaves whenever needed from the seedling stage onwards, or wait for the tight leaves to fully grow. Use the leaves while they are fresh; they wilt quickly if stored. Like Chinese cabbage, the stumps will repeatedly resprout (*see p.124*), providing several pickings of useful greens over 4–8 weeks. Pak choi is usually grown as a cut-and-come-again crop (*see p.123*), ready to harvest after about two weeks.

**Common problems** As for Chinese broccoli (*see p.126*).

**Recommended cultivars**
'Joi Choi hybrid' – quick-growing hybrid that resists running to seed.
'Kwong Moon' – fast-growing with tall, white stems.
'Pak Choi Green' – glossy, pale green leaves.
'Shanghai' – small variety suited to bunching.

# Silver beet *and* spinach beet

*Beta vulgaris* subsp. *cicla* var. *flavescens*

| Month | Spring | Summer | Autumn | Winter |
|---|---|---|---|---|
| Sow | • • | | • • | |
| Transplant | • • | | • • | • |
| Harvest | | • • • • | • • • • | • • |

Silver beet and spinach beet are botanically similar to beetroot (*see p.85*), but have edible leaves and insignificant roots. Their foliage grows to 1m (3ft) and is used as an alternative to spinach. Although less flavoursome and a little more coarse than spinach, these leaves are much easier to grow, more cold-tolerant, and much less susceptible to bolting. Silver beet leaves have prominent midribs which may be cooked separately as an alternative to seakale (*see p.135*). Spinach beet is smaller than silver beet. Silver beet and spinach beet make useful cut-and-come-again crops (*see p.123*), ready to harvest after about two weeks. Their bold leaves, which often have brightly coloured – pink, red, yellow, or green – veins and stems, are highly valued as an ornamental vegetable, and they are also suitable for growing in containers (*see p.124*). Silver beet and spinach beet normally yield 6kg per 3m (13lb per 10ft) row.

**Site and soil** A sunny, sheltered site with fertile, well-drained, moisture-retentive soil (*see p.123*), with added organic matter, is best. The pH is neutral to slightly alkaline, so acid soils may need liming (*see pp.18–19*). Unless the soil has been enriched with plenty of organic matter,

apply a base dressing of compound fertilizer at a rate of 210g per sq m (6oz per sq yd) or pelleted poultry manure at 270g per sq m (8oz per sq yd).

**Sowing and planting** Silver beet and spinach beet are raised from multigerm seeds (*see p.60*), which are each actually a cluster of seeds. Sow thinly, thinning (*see p.68*) to 10cm (4in) apart when the plants can be handled; then remove alternate plants when they are large enough to use. Mid- to late-summer sowings in cool climates, for harvest in autumn, winter, and spring when few other vegetable crops are available, are the most useful. Plants go to seed in early summer.

| Sowing depth | 2cm (¾in) |
|---|---|
| Seed spacing | sow thinly; thin to 8cm (3in) |
| Plant spacing | 15cm (6in) |
| Row spacing | 30cm (12in) |

**Routine care** Water in dry spells. Top-dress with a nitrogen-rich fertilizer (*see p.20–21*) if growth appears to slow down.

**Harvesting** Silver beet and spinach beet usually take 6–8 weeks to mature, but late-summer sowings will mature throughout the winter. Pick tender, young, blemish-free leaves as soon as they are large enough, and continue to pick regularly to promote fresh, new growth of new tender leaves. Mature plants may be left to stand until the leaves are needed, but they become more coarse and unappetizing, and vulnerable to pest damage, until they bolt.

**Common problems** Fungal leaf spot can disfigure older leaves, but the young, tender foliage is seldom affected. For symptoms and controls, *see* Plant Problems, *p.257*.

**Recommended cultivars**
'Fordhook Giant' – popular variety with large, green leaves.
'Lucullus' – pale green, tender leaves.
'Perpetual Spinach Beet' – leaves smaller and smoother than silver beet; shorter plants with long harvest period.
'Rainbow' – vigorous plants with colourful red, yellow, and pink leaf stems and veins.
'Slowbolt' – slow-to-bolt variety with tasty leaves.

# Spinach

*Spinacia oleracea*

| Month | Spring | Summer | Autumn | Winter |
|---|---|---|---|---|
| Sow | | • • • • | | |
| Transplant | | • | | |
| Harvest | • • • | • • • • | • | |

True spinach is a cool-climate annual, with flat, wrinkled leaves (like Savoy cabbage), or semi-wrinkled. The leaves have a very distinctive texture and flavour, and are cooked or eaten raw in salads when young. Spinach is usually harvested as a cut-and-come-again crop (*see p.123*), or used as a catch crop (*see p.69*). The seeds may be prickly or round. Spinach is not the easiest crop to grow, but

the leaves are more tender than silver beet. It normally yields around 6kg per 3m (13lb per 10ft) row. Oriental spinach is a new form of the same species as true spinach. It differs from true spinach in having darker leaves and very long stalks. It is fast growing, and best suited to late-summer and autumn production. Seed is less commonly sold than ordinary spinach.

**Site and soil** Any fertile, moisture-holding soil (*see p.123*) is suitable. Unless the soil is enriched with organic matter, apply a base dressing of compound fertilizer at a rate of 100g per sq m (3oz per sq yd) or pelleted poultry manure at 135g per sq m (4oz per sq yd). Sunny or, in summer, partially shaded sites are best. For cut-and-come-again crops, use compound fertilizer at a rate of 35g per sq m (1oz per sq yd) or pelleted poultry manure at 50g per sq m (1½oz per sq yd).

**Sowing and planting** Sow thinly *in situ* in succession every three weeks (*see p.69*) in late summer for autumn or winter use, or in early spring for spring or early summer use in cool climates. Thin (*see p.68*) the seedlings first to 8cm (3in) as soon as they can be handled, and then remove alternate plants when they are big enough to use. Alternatively, you can station sow (*see p.68*). Wide drills (*see p.67*) are best for cut-and-come-again crops. For autumn and winter crops, sow seed during late summer and early autumn. For spring and summer crops, sow seed in early spring. Plants may run to seed as the days lengthen in early summer. Spinach is not as easy to grow as silver beet but the flavour is superior.

| Sowing depth | 2.5cm (1in) |
|---|---|
| Seed spacing | sow thinly; thin to 10cm (4in) |
| Plant spacing | 20cm (8in) |
| Row spacing | 45cm (18in) |

**Routine care** Water freely to avoid bolting. Top-dress with a nitrogen-rich fertilizer (*see pp.20–23*) if growth appears to slow down.

**Harvesting and storing** Spinach takes 10–12 weeks to mature. Cut individual leaves of mature plants as required, or sever the whole plant about 2.5cm (1in) above ground level, leaving it to resprout for further harvests (*see p.124*). The shoots and leaves may be frozen. Spinach also makes an easy cut-and-come-again seedling crop (*see p.123*), ready to harvest after about two weeks.

**Common problems** Downy mildew (*see p.255*) can be damaging, but resistant cultivars are available, and allowing 50 per cent more space between plants also helps. Birds (*see p.251*) are partial to spinach seedlings; netting (*see p.52*) is the remedy.

**Recommended cultivars**
'Amsterdam' – traditional Dutch variety with large leaves; good in cool weather.
'Sonata' – bolt-resistant in warm weather; spear-shaped leaves.
'Viking' – good warm-weather variety with large leaves.
'Winter Bloomsdale' – large leaves; can be sown in spring in cool climates, in autumn in cool or warm climates.

# Growing perennial vegetables

Perennial vegetables can make unusual, attractive, and interesting additions to the vegetable garden. They are long-term crops and in cool climates, most types die down in autumn, remain dormant through winter and resprout in spring. The perennial group encompasses asparagus, cardoons, Chinese artichokes, globe artichokes, Jerusalem artichokes, chokos, rhubarb – which is normally eaten as a dessert – and yams and seakale. Mushrooms are also included within the perennial vegetable grouping. The edible parts of perennial vegetables range from the young leaves, shoots, stems, and the flower buds to underground tubers. Asparagus is widely popular for its delicious young shoots, known as spears, and is best suited to continuous long-term production.

Chokos grow on perennial vines that look similar to and are as prickly as cucumber vines. However, in warm climates they are perennial and can crop over a long period. In cool climates the plants usually die out during winter and are then replanted in the spring.

This group of vegetables tends to need less intensive care than other groups, because they are hardy and more robust. Most may be grown and harvested for 3–4 years, while asparagus is more long-lived, cropping for 15–20 years. Once they cease to be productive they may be propagated or rejuvenated by the methods described below, so bear in mind that they will semi-permanently occupy a lot of space, which may be a drawback if you have only a small garden.

Rhubarb when well grown can occupy more than 1sq m (3ft x 3ft) and globe artichoke, cardoon and Jerusalem artichokes can grow to 2m high (6ft) when in flower. The position of these plants in the garden is therefore important. Be sure to plant these tall perennial vegetables where they will not shade or smother smaller vegetables.

## Ornamental crops

Apart from the benefit of their edible produce, these plants often have foliage, flowers, or architectural forms that make them worth growing for their ornamental value alone. The stems of rhubarb glow bright pink or scarlet; globe artichokes and cardoons have fern-like silver leaves and large, thistle-like flowerheads; and asparagus and seakale both possess delicate, ferny foliage. Such features can liven up what might otherwise be a rather dull vegetable patch.

These crops can be used for their decorative qualities in a potager (*see pp. 27–28*) or as special feature plants in herbaceous or mixed borders. On the practical side, Jerusalem artichokes provide height at the back of a border, and may even be used as a windbreak to protect other, more vulnerable plants from the elements.

## Site and soil

Before you plant perennial vegetables you will need to think very carefully about where to site them, since these long-term crops could prevent light reaching other, fast-maturing plants. As with most vegetables, an open, sunny site is best, with a deep, rich soil that has free drainage but good moisture retention. The ground must be very well prepared before planting; dig over the entire plot thoroughly (*see pp. 37–40*) and incorporate a good deal of organic matter (*see pp. 22–23*). After planting, add a good layer of organic mulch (*see pp. 41–42*) around the base of the stems to retain moisture and suppress weeds.

## Routine care

Because perennial vegetables are long-term crops, routine care involves regular weeding to remove competition for water and soil nutrients, keeping the plants healthy and strong by removing old foliage, and mulching annually with organic matter (*see below*). The crops will also need regular watering and feeding, and some may require support in order to crop well (for individual crop needs, *see pp. 133–135*).

## Mulching perennial vegetables

1 **In mid- to late autumn,** cut off the dead stems at the base, and pick off any dead or dying foliage (here globe artichoke).

2 **Clear away any debris,** and fork over the soil to loosen it. This aerates the soil and also enables moisture to pass through any old mulch and into the soil.

3 **Cover the soil** around the plant with a 5–8cm (2–3in) layer of well-rotted manure or compost, extending to about 45cm (18in) from the base of the plants. Use a plank to define a neat edge.

## Propagation

Unlike most other groups of vegetables, which are usually grown from seed, perennial vegetables are usually cropped for several years until they reach full maturity, and then they are propagated by cuttings or division to produce new, vigorous, healthy plants. Perennial vegetables can also be increased from bought or home-saved seed (*see p. 61*), but this method is much slower and the results are more variable.

The propagation method used (*see pp. 130–131*) depends on the crop. Globe artichokes, cardoons and chokos can be propagated by seed or by dividing offsets. Dividing rootstocks is suitable for both rhubarb and asparagus – although seed raising is preferable for the latter. Divide offsets to propagate globe artichokes and cardoons; replant healthy tubers for Chinese and Jerusalem artichokes; and take root cuttings for seakale.

## Division of rootstocks

The rootstock, or crown, of a perennial consists of the part of a mature plant at ground level from which both the stems and roots grow. This may be lifted when the plant is dormant, usually in late winter, or just as the buds begin to break in early spring. It is then divided into several, smaller pieces, each with buds and roots of their own, which are

---

## Dividing mature rootstocks

Asparagus and rhubarb may be propagated by dividing their mature rootstocks into sections, or "sets", each with a healthy bud and roots, that will grow into a new plant. This is best done in late winter or early spring. With asparagus (*right*), lift the rootstock and prise it apart with your thumbs; if necessary, use a sharp knife to complete the job. With rhubarb (*below*), use a spade to cut through the rootstock. Replant the sections to grow on.

1 **Gently uncover the top** of the rhubarb rootstock to expose the buds. Look for a side section with at least 1 healthy bud. With a spade, chop down through the rootstock to separate the section.

2 **The new section** may be divided further; each set must have 1 good bud and be as large as a small melon. Replant the sets with the bud just above the soil surface.

---

then replanted to form new, complete plants. For this procedure to be successful, you need healthy rootstocks or the divisions may not grow or crop very well. Weak or unhealthy rootstocks should be discarded. It is best to take the divisions from around the edges of

### Dividing tubers
*Before planting, in spring, Jerusalem artichoke tubers that are larger than a hen's egg should be cut into sections, at the joints, with a sharp knife. Each section should have a number of healthy buds, which should be uppermost when planted.*

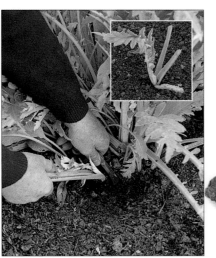

**Dividing globe artichoke offsets**
*In spring, choose a healthy sideshoot with 2–3 leaves. Using a sharp knife, cut down into the rootstock of the parent plant to separate the offset. Take care to preserve any roots, and trim off old stems to just above the leaves.*

Cut tubers at joints

the rootstock, discarding the old, woody central part. This method works well for asparagus and rhubarb when plants are at least 3–4 years old (*see facing page*).

For asparagus, carefully lift the entire rootstock with a fork, and shake off any excess soil. Separate it into two or more sections, or "sets", using your hands or a sharp knife. With rhubarb, use a spade either to cut through the crown while it is still in the ground, lifting the sections individually, or to dig around and lift the entire rootstock before cutting it into sections, each of which should have at least one healthy bud.

Tease out the roots, and cut away any old ones that are damaged or diseased with a sharp knife, to prevent rot from setting in later. Take care not to damage the buds or roots, and never allow the roots to dry out before replanting.

For asparagus, dig a trench 30cm (12in) wide and 20cm (8in) deep. Work in well-rotted manure and top up with 5cm (2in) of soil. Then make a 10cm (4in) ridge along the centre. Plant the divisions 30cm

(12in) apart on top of the ridge, carefully spreading the roots so that they sit evenly on the soil below. Cover with soil to leave just the bud tips visible. Mulch the divisions with 5cm (2in) of manure to keep them moist; the resulting plants can be harvested two years later.

For rhubarb, plant the divisions in holes with the main bud just above the surface; planting too deeply, especially in heavy soil, can cause rotting of the rootstock around the bud. Firm in the soil around the rootstock, but leave it loose on top to allow the rain to penetrate. Mulch (*see p. 129*), leaving a space just around the rootstock to allow the shoots to be produced and to discourage slugs and snails from reaching the buds.

## Division of offsets
Offsets are tiny plantlets produced naturally by the parent plant at the side of the rootstock. These may be detached and replanted to form new plants. Offsets can be taken from established plants that were produced in the same way, so they will all be true to type. This method of propagation is suitable for cardoons and globe artichokes. It is best carried out in cool climates in the spring when the new shoots are actively growing. Wait until the young shoots around the edge of

the plant have started rooting into the soil, as this makes establishment of the new plant much quicker and easier.

In spring, select from the outside of a mature plant a young, healthy shoot with 2–3 leaves (*see facing page*). Scrape away the soil with a trowel so that you can see the roots and the point where the offset is attached to the parent plant. Using a clean, sharp knife, cut the offset away from the parent plant, together with a piece of root. Also if it is possible keep any new roots just starting on the offset. Fill in the hole at the side of the parent plant and leave it to grow. Trim off any of the old stalks around the base of the offset to avoid rotting. Remove all but one of the leaves to reduce unwanted moisture loss through the process of transpiration – the evaporation of water from the leaves once it has carried nutrients from the roots.

To replant, space the offsets 60cm (24in) apart in rows 75cm (30in) apart. Place each offset in a planting hole, fill in around it with soil, and carefully firm it in. The offset should be planted deeply and firmly enough to remain upright. Do not bury the growing point, or it will rot, wither, and die. Water in and cover with fleece (*see p. 48*) to keep the offset moist, warm, and protected from any desiccating winds.

## Division of tubers
Chinese and Jerusalem artichokes and yams are normally raised from tubers that are simply replanted. Because the tubers of Jerusalem artichokes grow much larger than those of Chinese artichokes, however, they may require dividing into smaller sections (*see facing page*) before replanting (*see p. 135*). Tubers are harvested in autumn and stored for replanting.

## Root cuttings
Seakale is seldom grown as a vegetable in Australia. Although it is best known for its large, glorious leaves in the flower garden, the best way to propagate seakale is to use root cuttings, taken from established plants. Seakale is difficult to grow unless conditions are cool and moist and well drained. Where plants are well established in the late autumn to early winter, dig the rootstock out of the ground and select a number of roots of about pencil thickness from around the side of the rootstock and cut them from the parent plant. Stand the root cuttings in a box of moist sand in a cool, frost-free shed. The cuttings in the box should be covered just enough to leave the tips sticking out and to keep the roots moist. Store until early spring when buds start to develop at the top of the cuttings and plant in prepared soil.

# How to grow asparagus

**1** **Asparagus is a delicious, easy-to-grow perennial vegetable**, and it is harvested when few other fresh vegetables are available. Asparagus plants are bought as dormant crowns during winter. The best soil is a well-drained sandy loam to which well-rotted manure has been added. The crowns are spaced 40cm (16in) apart in the bottom of a trench. Spread the roots out in the trench and cover with a thin layer of soil. As the spears emerge through the soil in early spring, gradually fill in the trench. No spears should be cut the first year because this weakens the plant. However in the second year the first spears can be cut below the soil surface with a knife.

**2** **At the end of spring,** leave the spears to grow. By late summer the plants will be tall and ferny and in autumn the fronds begin to dry and brown. At this stage the fronds are pruned off at ground level and the plants are fertilized with manure and compost.

## Obtaining an early harvest

In most regions, rhubarb plants remain in full leaf all year. However, where winter temperatures are low, the plants will usually die down and regrow in spring. Some perennial vegetables, such as rhubarb and seakale, may be induced in cool climates to sprout earlier than they normally would by a process known as forcing. The purpose is to bring the plant back into production soon after winter dormancy. This also makes for sweeter-tasting and more tender crops. You will need to use rhubarb plants that have been in the ground for at least two seasons; if they are forced too early, the plants can suffer and will only recover slowly when they are left to grow on.

## Forcing outdoors

Between late autumn and midwinter, when rhubarb plants have died back, clear away the old leaves, which may be rotting, and thus excluding all light from the crown by covering it up. For this you could use a traditional forcing jar (*see above right*) with a removable lid, which can be opened up so that you can check on progress.

Alternatively, you could also use an upturned box, bucket, or large flowerpot. Cover the drainage hole with a stone or cloth to keep out the light. The cover needs to be at least

**Using a forcing jar to produce an early crop**
*Crops such as seakale and rhubarb may be forced for early cropping. Place a forcing jar, or upturned box or pot, over the emerging stems to exclude light. Remove the cover once the leaves reach the top to reveal blanched stems (above right).*

38cm (15in) high, and the stems will be ready to harvest in 1–2 months.

## Harvesting

Lift tubers of Chinese or Jerusalem artichokes with a fork (*see far left*), and cut globe artichokes just before they open (*see below*). For details of harvesting other perennial crops, *see pp. 133–135*. These vegetables are best eaten fresh.

## Growing mushrooms

Mushrooms are easy to grow in cool climates by either making a growing box and "planting" commercial spawn or by purchasing a mushroom growing kit or "farm". The variety of mushroom commonly grown in Australia are button mushrooms (*Agaricus bisporus*) which is a close relative of the field mushroom. Other types of fungi can be grown when the particular spores are available but growing conditions differ according to the type of fungi.

Mushrooms require an even cool temperature. Growing boxes or bags should be positioned in a shaded, sheltered, cool position, usually in a garage situation or cellar. The part of the mushroom that we eat is the fruiting body or cap of the fungus.

Mushroom spores are like microscopic seeds and when "planted" in a favourable growing compost, the spores germinate and produce a network of microscopic "roots" called mycelium. Fruiting bodies form on the mycelium and emerge on the surface of the compost as tiny white pinheads which quickly enlarge to form button mushrooms and then mature to flat mushrooms. Spores are shed from the gills on the underside of mature mushroom caps and under ideal conditions these will produce a new crop of mushrooms.

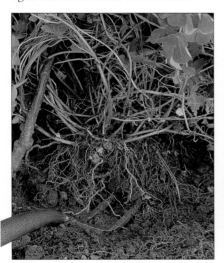

**Harvesting Jerusalem artichokes**
*When the foliage has begun to yellow, the tubers are ready to harvest. Lift the plant with a fork, taking care not to damage any of the tubers. Remove all tubers by the end of the season since this plant can become invasive.*

**Harvesting globe artichokes**
*When the largest head on the plant is plump and its scales are green, soft and just about to open out, cut off the head with a sharp knife. Allow any other heads to grow on to the same size before harvesting them.*

# A–Z of perennial vegetables

## Asparagus

*Asparagus officinalis*

| Season | Spring | Summer | Autumn | Winter |
|---|---|---|---|---|
| Sow/plant | • | | | • • |
| Transplant | | • | | |
| Harvest | • • • | | | • • |

Asparagus grows best in temperate climates. Howver, plants will yield small crops when grown in the tropics. It is grown for its delicately flavoured young shoots, or spears. Most modern plants are all-male F1 cultivars which are much more vigorous than older, open-pollinated cultivars, and have the advantage of not producing seed which can germinate haphazardly in the surrounding beds. Female cultivars do not reproduce true to type and are of poorer vigour. Once established, plants should crop for 15–20 years, yielding 9–12 spears per crown.

**Site and soil** Asparagus needs a soil with good drainage and a pH of 6.3–7.5 to thrive; it can be grown in heavy soils in traditional raised beds (*see pp.32–33*) or in light, sandy soils on the flat. Avoid frost pockets because the spears are tender and may be damaged by spring frosts; asparagus also needs some shelter from winds (*see pp.12–13*). Always use fresh ground to avoid disease problems building up from previous asparagus crops. Dig the soil deeply, or even double dig it (*see p.39*), adding plenty of organic matter.

**Sowing and planting** Asparagus can be raised from seed, or young plants can be purchased. Asparagus seed is best sown singly into modules (*see p.65*) and transplanted in early summer, at spacings shown below. The seedlings often find it difficult to establish in hot, dry weather. Alternatively, sow in an open seedbed (*see p.66*) in early spring. Thin to 15cm (6in) apart (*see p.68*).

To save time, most asparagus is planted, rather than sown. One-year-old crowns planted in winter establish best: you can divide your own rootstocks (*see p.130*), but there is much to be said for buying in crowns of a good stock. If dividing your own stock, the parent should be a healthy plant that is at least 3–4 years old, preferably an F1 hybrid, all-male cultivar. A male plant would have produced no female flowers or berries on the fern during the previous summer. Make sure to remove seedlings if they occur.

The crowns can be planted in single rows on raised beds, but double rows are best in flat beds. To plant a row, dig a trench 30cm (12in) wide and 20cm (8in) deep. Work in well-rotted manure to the base, cover with 5cm (2in) soil, then make a 10cm (4in) high ridge along the centre of the trench. Place the crowns on the ridge, 30cm (12in) apart. Spread the roots evenly and fill in with soil as they

grow so that the bud tips are just visible. Mulch the crowns with 5cm (2in) of well-rotted manure to keep them moist. Leave 45cm (18in) between double rows and stagger the plants. Allow for paths 90cm (3ft) in width between the beds.

| Sowing depth | 2.5cm (1in) |
|---|---|
| Plant spacing | 15cm (6in) |
| Row spacing | 30cm (12in) |

**Routine care** Keep asparagus beds free of weeds and mulched (*see p.129*) to avoid soil compaction and bent spears and to retain moisture. Top-dress with a general fertilizer (*see pp.20–23*) in early spring and repeat when cutting has finished. Be careful not to overfeed because excess nitrogen makes for soft fern growth and can reduce yields.

Support the ferny top-growth with canes and twine in exposed sites to avoid it breaking off in the wind and damaging the crown. Remove any seedlings as they occur and any female plants to avoid seedlings in future years. When the foliage has died and yellowed in autumn, cut it down to 2.5cm (1in) above the ground.

**Harvesting** Normally asparagus spears are not harvested until the plants have been in the ground for two years, to allow for good crops in future years. In the third year, harvest from early spring for six weeks, and in subsequent years for eight weeks. Use an asparagus knife – which has a forked blade for cutting spears singly or a long bladed knife – and carefully cut the spears 2.5cm (1in) below the soil when they are 13–18cm (5–7in) tall. To avoid wastage, you will need to harvest every 2–3 days in warm weather or every 5–7 days in cold weather.

**Common problems** The main pests to affect the crop are slugs and snails (*see p.262*), which can be very damaging to young spears. Look out for are root rots (*see p.255*).

**Recommended cultivars**
'Connover's Colossal' ♀ – available as seed; old variety.
'Mary Washington 500' – available as seeds and crowns; old reliable variety.
'UC 157' – available as seed and crowns, vigorous hybrid that crops earlier with large spears.

## Cardoon

*Cynara cardunculus*

| Season | Spring | Summer | Autumn | Winter |
|---|---|---|---|---|
| Sow | • • | | | |
| Transplant | | • • | | |
| Harvest | | | • • • | |

Although similar to globe artichokes in appearance, cardoons are grown for their celery-like leaf stalks, which are blanched just before harvesting. Cardoon flowers are smaller than those of globe artichoke but the large leaves are popular in floral arrangements. In Australia cardoon is usually grown for visual reasons rather than as a vegetable. Care should be taken to ensure the plants do not self seed and become weeds. Cultivations requirements of cardoon are similar to globe artichokes.

# Chinese artichoke

*Stachys affinis*

| Season | Spring | Summer | Autumn | Winter |
|---|---|---|---|---|
| Plant | • | | | |
| Harvest | | | | • • • |

Chinese artichoke, or Japanese artichoke, or knotroot, is an erect perennial with slender white tubers that are cooked or pickled. Tubers for planting are not readily available in Australia. They are planted as offsets like Jerusalem artichokes or raised from seed.

# Choko

*Sechium edule*

| Season | Spring | Summer | Autumn | Winter |
|---|---|---|---|---|
| Sow/Plant | • • | • | | |
| Harvest | | • • | • • • | • |

Choko, also called chayote and Mexican marrow, is a tropical perennial vine related to cucumbers. The pale, green fruit is shaped like an avocado pear and can be prickly or smooth depending on variety. It contains one seed. The vine grows vigorously, usually trained to a trellis, and it flowers for months in warm weather producing both male and female flowers. Vines die down in cool weather.

**Site and soil** Chokos grow best in a sunny, warm sheltered site. The soil needs to be well-drained to prevent root rot during dormancy. A good quantity of well-rotted manure or compost is dug in to the soil before planting as plants are gross feeders.

**Sowing and planting** A mature choko fruit is kept until the seed inside has started to shoot. The fruit is planted on its side about 10cm (4in) deep in spring or early summer in cool climates or any time in warm climates. The vine will fruit in the first season but crops will increase in subsequent years.

**Routine Care** Fertilize with a complete fertilizer during groweth and water frequently during dry weather. Plants die down when cold weather arrives and the vine is cut back to the crown. In very cold winters the crown should be mulched with straw to protect from frost.

**Harvesting** Cut the fruit from the vine when they are mature but not over mature or the flesh will be fibrous. Chokos are cooked like pumpkin. The tuberous roots are also edible. In cool climates, plants fruit in summer

and again in autumn and in warm climates fruit may be produced all year round.

**Recommended cultivars**
'Green Spine' – suits warm and cool climates; fruit are prickly
'Spineless American' – best in warm climates; fruit are smooth skinned.

# Globe artichoke

*Cynara scolymus*

| Season | Spring | Summer | Autumn | Winter |
|---|---|---|---|---|
| Sow/plant | • • | | | • |
| Transplant | | • • | | |
| Harvest | | • • | • • • | • |

The globe artichoke is a very decorative plant, with silvery foliage and large, thistle-like green or purple flowerheads. It grows best in cool climates and reaches 60–90cm (2–3ft) tall, with a mature spread of 90cm (3ft). Each plant has a few flower stalks with several small flower buds below the large terminal bud. The sepals of the flower bud, and the base of larger buds, are edible. The plants will crop for 3–4 years.

**Site and soil** This crop requires shelter from winds, and hot sun, but must not be shaded by trees. If there are tree roots nearby, beware of honey fungus (*see p. 256*), which can spread to the woody parts of globe artichokes. Avoid planting in frosty sites. Globe artichokes need a rich, well-drained soil that is not too light, because they cannot tolerate soil drying out in summer. You will need to prepare the site well (*see pp. 37–40*) to produce tender buds and incorporate plenty of organic matter into the soil to improve moisture retention.

**Sowing and planting** Globe artichokes are usually raised from offsets planted in spring so that the offspring are true to type. Select a healthy parent plant and take offsets (*see pp. 130–131*), preferably with roots. Plant the offsets in rows, just deep enough to stay upright. Water after planting to settle the soil, then cover with fleece to keep the offsets moist, and protected from desiccating winds. Aim to replant one-third of the plot each year for regular cropping.

If you cannot obtain offsets, sow seed (*see pp. 62–65*) in a propagator in late winter at 15°C (59°F). Prick out seedlings into 10cm (4in) pots and grow on until you have good-sized plants to transplant in spring. Seed can also be station-sown (*see p. 68*) in the garden in early spring and the seedlings thinned. When plants grown from seed are well-established, select the ones that produce good artichokes for eating and use offsets from these to grow more plants (*see above*).

| Planting depth | 5cm (2in) |
|---|---|
| Plant spacing | 75cm (30in) |
| Row spacing | 90cm (3ft) |

**Routine care** Mulch (*see p. 129*) the crop to control weeds and keep the soil moist.

Remove the first head promptly to allow the plants to gain vigour. If large heads are required, reduce the number of stems to three per plant and apply a high-potash liquid feed (*see pp. 20–21*). A moist fertile soil is needed to produce tender buds. Plant stress produces tough, fibrous buds.

**Harvesting** The smaller artichoke flowers can be removed (*see p. 132*) when they reach 4cm (1½in) in diameter, to encourage the terminal bud to grow to a good size. These small buds can be eaten, but they are not as tasty as mature ones. Artichokes are ready for harvesting when the heads are plump and the scales still soft and green and just about to open. If there are no secondary heads left, snap the stem off at the base; if there are secondary heads on the stem, cut off the terminal bud together with a short length of stem. This stimulates secondary shoots; encourage this by top-dressing with a general fertilizer and watering (*see p. 72*).

**Common problems** As for cardoon.

**Recommended cultivars**
'Green Globe' – large buds are produced a 1m (3ft) tall plants.
'Imperial Star' – similar to 'Green Globe'.
'Purple Globe' – produces large purple buds.

# Jerusalem artichoke

*Helianthus tuberosus*

| Season | Spring | Summer | Autumn | Winter |
|---|---|---|---|---|
| Plant | • • • | | | • |
| Harvest | | | • • • • | • |

This close relative of the sunflower is grown for its tubers, which are usually cooked but occasionally eaten raw. The plants can grow 3m (10ft) or more in height topped with colourful yellow daisy flowers in summer. They may be used as a screen or windbreak if planted 30cm (12in) apart in rows 2–3 deep; allow 90cm (3ft) between the rows. They are very vigorous, and should yield 10–12 tubers per plant.

**Site and soil** Jerusalem artichokes will grow on a wide range of soils, including heavy ones, in either sunny or shady positions.

**Planting** Plant tubers, either bought from a mail order seed supplier, a greengrocer or saved from your own stock, that are no bigger than a hen's egg, dividing them if necessary (*see pp. 130–131*). Check first that they are showing no signs of disease.

| Planting depth | 10–15cm (4–6in) |
|---|---|
| Tuber spacing | 30cm (12in) |
| Row spacing | 30cm (12in) |

**Routine care** Earth up the stems to stabilize them when they are 30cm (12in) tall, by drawing soil up to a depth of 15cm (6in). In midsummer, remove the flowerheads and cut back the stems to 1.5–2m (5–6ft) so the plants' energy is concentrated into the tubers. Keep the plants moist to get better-shaped tubers, and provide supports (*see p.72*). When the leaves begin to yellow in autumn, cut back the stems to 8cm (3in) above ground level. Lay them over the plant to keep the soil warm and ease lifting of the tubers in frosty weather.

**Harvesting**  Harvest the tubers as required (*see p.132*), making sure to remove every one, however small, by the end of the season, since any part left could grow and become invasive.

**Common problems**  Sclerotinia, a fungal rot (*see p.262*), may damage stems up to 30cm (12in) above soil level. Slugs and snails (*see p.262*) attack both tubers and foliage. Root aphid (*see p.261*) is a less common problem.

**Recommended cultivars**
'Elongated' – produces masses of cream tubers.
'Round' – tall plants with rounded cream tubers.

# Mushrooms

*Agaricus bisporus*

Mushrooms are a delicious, edible fungi used like vegetables, fresh in salads or cooked in a range of dishes. They can be grown at home in cool climates or in warmer areas where a cool cellar is available. Mushrooms are grown from spores 'planted' in compost and they can be used at any stage of maturity. However, the more mature the caps, the stronger the flavour (see p.135).

**Site and soil**  Mushrooms are grown in compost that is prepared from well-composted straw and manure. The ideal pH of the compost is between 7.5 and 8.5 so lime is normally added to the compost to reduce the acidity. The compost must be free of 'wild' fungi spores and diseases. It should be kept moist at all times but not wet. The ideal temperature is between 15–21°C. The compost should be situated where it is free from draughts in either complete darkness or semi-darkness. Mushrooms are usually grown in a cool garage or cellar.

**Planting**  Spores sometimes called 'spawn', can be purchased in sealed containers for planting 2cm (1in) deep in a box of rich compost. The compost is kept moist and when the mycelium colonize the compost, a fluffy white substance covers the surface. The compost should be covered with a 2–3cm (1in) layer of peat moss. The first pinhead mushrooms will emerge through this covering within 3–5 weeks. Spores are released from mature mushrooms and may produce another crop. Mushroom growing kits or farms available from garden centres during the cooler months of the years and these come complete with spores, sterilized compost and growing instructions.

**Harvest**  Mushrooms are harvested from button stage onwards by holding the caps and twisting so that the stem comes freely from the compost. The stem is trimmed and the hole in the compost is covered with peat moss. Mushrooms are used fresh or they can be kept for a week in a paper bag in the refrigerator.

# Rhubarb

*Rheum* x *hybridum*, syn. *R. cultorum*

| Season | Spring | | | Summer | | | Autumn | | | Winter | | |
|---|---|---|---|---|---|---|---|---|---|---|---|---|
| Sow/plant | • | • | | | | | | • | • | • | • | • |
| Transplant | • | • | • | | | | | | | | | |
| Harvest | | | • | • | • | • | • | | | | | |

Rhubarb is a robust frost-hardy perennial with pink, red, and greenish leafstalks that are used as a dessert, often in pies and crumbles. Plants are easy to grow in cool climates where stalks can be harvested for most of the year. It is suitable for forcing (*see p.132*). Plants should yield 4.5–13.5kg per 3m (10–30lb per 10ft) row. The flavour varies in sweetness depending on the age of the stems.

**Site and soil**  Choose an open site with moist but free-draining soil, since rhubarb does not like to be waterlogged in winter; raised beds are best in high rainfall gardens.

**Sowing and planting**  Rhubarb does not always come true from seed, so to obtain the best results it is advisable to divide rootstocks into "sets" (*see p.130*) and replant these. This may be done at any time from mid-autumn to early spring. If seed is used, it is best sown in modules (*see p.65*) in late winter and planted out in late spring, or sown thinly in a seedbed (*see p.66*) and thinned to 15cm (6in) apart (*see p.68*). Plant sets a minimum of 75cm (30in) apart; the ideal is 90cm (3ft). Different cultivars have different chilling requirements, but most varieties available can be grown without frost periods in winter.

| Sowing depth | 2.5cm (1in) |
|---|---|
| Seed spacing | sow thinly; thin to 15cm (6in) |
| Plant spacing | 75–90cm (30–36in) |
| Row spacing | 30cm (12in) |

**Routine care**  Rhubarb must be kept free of weeds. Apply a mulch (*see p.129*) to hold in moisture, but do not bury the crown as it will rot. Prevent neighbouring crowns smothering each other by removing yellowing leaves. Top-dress with sulphate ammonia in summer to feed the crown. Water regularly to keep it moist and actively growing until autumn.

**Harvesting**  Do not harvest until plants are established and leave at least half of the stems to keep the plant in active growth. If stripped completely, it will take longer to recover. Take hold of the stalk to be pulled, which should be at least 23–30cm (9–12in) long, and push your thumb between the stalk and the next one, easing it out of the ground to avoid snapping off or pulling out another stalk which is not ready. Do not pull too late in the season, as the leaves have to feed the crown buds for the following year. Harvest forced stems as soon as they are ready (*see p.132*). The most flavoursome stems are pinkish in colour. The leaves are poisonous and it is best to cut off the green part of stems and only use the parts that are pinkish in colour.

**Common problems**  Aphids (*see p.251*), slugs and snails (*see p.262*), crown rot (*see p.254*), honey fungus (*see p.256*), and viruses (*see p.264*) may cause problems.

**Recommended cultivars**
'Wandin Winter' – vigorous plant that grows well all year.

# Seakale

*Crambe maritima*

| Season | Spring | | Summer | Autumn | Winter | |
|---|---|---|---|---|---|---|
| Sow/plant | • | • | | | | • |
| Transplant | | | • | | | |
| Harvest | • | • | • | | | |

Seakale is a cool climate perennial often grown in the flower garden. It is also grown for its uniquely flavoured stems, which are eaten raw. The young flowerheads and very young leaves can also be eaten raw, and the leaf midribs cooked. An established plant can be 90cm (3ft) in diameter with stems up to 60cm (2ft) tall. Seakale is difficult to grow in Australia. It is generally propagated by seed or long root cuttings, which are inserted into deep, moist sand (*see p.131*).

# Yams

*Oxalis tuberosa*

Yams, New Zealand yams or Oka in South America, are a frost-tender perennial plant grown as an annual. Yams produce smooth, fleshy, pink tubers that are grown like potatoes and cooked like potatoes but they grow to large finger-size and the flavour is more like sweet potato.

**Site and soil**  Yams tolerate hot, dry conditions but the best tubers are produced in moist, fertile, well-drained soil in a sunny sheltered site. Prepare the soil with compost or well-rotted manure and enrich with complete fertilizer if soil is poor.

**Planting**  Seed tubers are available from specialist mail order seed suppliers. When established, home-grown tubers can be saved for planting. Plant tubers in spring when the risk of frost is past in cool climates, or in autumn in warm climates. Tubers are planted 10cm (4in) deep with 30cm (1ft) between plants. No named cultivars are available.

**Routine care**  Keep soil moist and well weeded. Side dress with complete fertilizer when plants are in full growth. Mound soil up around plants or mulch deeply to keep tubers well covered.

**Harvesting**  Yams take up to six months to mature. When plants die down, dig tubers and put them to 'ripen' in a dry position for two weeks in full light to remove the bitterness before storing.

# CULINARY HERBS

JUST AS FRESH-PICKED HERBS in the kitchen add
zest and colour to dishes, so herb plants have
decorative qualities that enhance both the
ornamental and kitchen garden. Many are
attractive, with the bonus of flowers and aromatic
foliage. Statuesque, feathery herbs such as dill and
fennel deserve a place in any border; sun-loving,
creeping herbs such as thymes are ideal for
softening the edges of paths and paving. Pots
spilling over with mints, sweet marjoram and
tender basil clustered by the kitchen door give a
cottage-garden feel to any plot, but herbs have a
place in formal design too. A neatly trimmed bay
tree in a decorative container would make a
perfect focal point in a pattern of beds neatly
edged with parsley or rows of chives.
Herbs, among the easiest edible plants to grow
and to propagate, can be available to pick fresh,
with a flavour beyond compare, all year round.
They bring with them a rich tradition of varied
use in the home that is fascinating to explore.

# Growing culinary herbs

In general use, the word "herb" refers to a range of annual, biennial, perennial, and shrubby plants that are grown for culinary or medicinal use. Culinary herbs are sometimes called pot herbs. The word also has a more specific botanical usage, where it means any non-woody plant; strictly, a plant without persistent above-ground parts, most commonly a perennial.

## Growing culinary herbs

Almost all the plants that we grow in a culinary herb garden (*see pp. 141–145 for those covered here*) produce aromatic oils in their leaves, stems, and in some cases in their seeds. This group of herbs includes basil, marjoram, mint, sage, and thyme, which are all members of the nettle family, the Lamiaceae. Chervil, coriander, dill, fennel, and parsley, other popular herbs, are umbellifers belonging to the Apiaceae, as do carrots and

parsnips, and producing attractive, flat heads of small flowers. All of these are not only useful as culinary herbs, but also decorative: there are many with attractive leaf and flower variations. A few herbs, including sweet Cicely and horseradish, are valued for the culinary use of their roots.

One advantage of growing herbs is that they are much less demanding than most vegetable crops. Although the annual herbs need raising from seed each year, most germinate easily. Growing culinary herbs is made even easier by the wide availability of seed and plants now on offer. Establish just a few herbs to begin with, choosing the plants that are most frequently used, for example basil, chives, fennel, mint, parsley, and thyme. Experiment with other kinds of herbs and their cultivars as the garden and your experience develop.

## Where to grow herbs

Herbs are usually required in limited quantity, and kitchen needs can easily be met by a few plants in a small garden in the open ground or in containers.

A herb garden need not take up much space. Select a site that receives plenty of sunshine, because most culinary herbs originate in warm climates. Ensure that the site is well-drained, and avoid areas where there has been heavy dressing of organic matter, since rich soil is likely to promote the growth of lush foliage, which may produce less intense flavours than if plants are grown in poorer conditions.

Shrubby herbs require very well-drained soil; in high-rainfall areas they are best grown in containers or between paving stones. Leafy herbs are also best grown in containers in tropical gardens.

Provide shelter (*see pp. 12–13*) from wind around the herb garden: this will

## Planting a herb trough

1 **Half-fill** a 15cm (6in) deep trough with compost. Plant annual herbs (here parsley) raised from seed. Lift and divide perennial herbs and plant the best piece.

2 **Confine a plant** with spreading roots, such as mint, by potting it first in a small plastic pot. Sit the pot in the trough so the rim is level with that of the trough.

3 **Before planting chives** in the trough, trim the leaves back to about 15cm (6in) to promote fresh growth. Cut back any straggly top-growth on other herbs.

4 **Take care** to leave enough space between plants to allow them to grow for some time. Fill in with compost to within 2.5cm (1in) of the rim; firm well.

5 **Position** the planted trough to receive morning sun, or on a kitchen windowsill, and keep it well watered. Harvest the herbs as required.

create a warmer microclimate and raise soil temperature. Herbs such as lavender and rosemary can be grown as low protective hedges to create this shelter. Plant herbs in close proximity to the kitchen door if at all possible, because the shortest walk encourages the most frequent use, especially in poor weather.

## Growing herbs in containers

It is also possible to grow a few herbs in a trough (*see facing page*) or a large pot on any paved area. A particular advantage of container growing is that the plants may be taken under cover to avoid hot, drying sun or to keep up their growth through winter.

Choose a large container with a diameter of at least 30cm (12in) for herb growing. Terracotta or concrete pots are more stable and attractive than plastic, and strawberry pots planted with herbs make fine garden features.

It is essential for container growing (*see pp.35–36*) to ensure that enough water is available at all times, but avoid waterlogging, especially for herbs. Make the potting mix as light-textured as possible by adding 20 per cent grit by volume to garden soil or a proprietary potting mix, and ensure that the container has plenty of drainage holes.

## Herbs as decorative plantings

The ornamental qualities of herbs – from the neat flowerheads of chives and the variegated leaves of some sages to the shapes of trained bay trees and the graceful leaves of fennel – mean that many can be included in decorative borders. Large herbs, especially those that do not need much sun, such as angelica (*Angelica archangelica*), chervil, and lovage, mix well in an informal shaded garden. Formal schemes can be created by planting herbs in patterns such as the traditional knot gardens. Thyme is especially suitable, similarly chamomile (*Chamaemelum nobile*), marjoram, and sage: all of these have golden foliage forms, and sage and thyme have other colourful cultivars. A popular scheme is to plant a herb garden in the shape of a cartwheel, with each section planted with a single species. Quite small areas between paving stones can be similarly planted, perhaps to brighten up the backyard area close to the house.

**Confining mint**
*Mint will spread invasively in the open ground: planting it in a pot sunk into the ground keeps it within bounds. Some gardeners claim that the distinctive flavours of different mints merge if the roots mix, and pots prevent this.*

## Preparing a herb garden

Making a herb garden in the open ground requires the same preparation as a kitchen garden, including clearing weeds (*see pp.49–50*) and ensuring free drainage (*see p.16*) and suitable levels of lime (*see pp.18–19*). Do not, however, incorporate organic matter. On heavier soils, dig in gravel to improve aeration and drainage. Plant herbs in spring, and keep young plants well watered in the time immediately after planting (*see pp.70–71 for more on planting out*).

The majority of perennial herbs can be bought container-grown. To plant these out, first water the container well. Dig the planting hole a little larger than the pot, and fork over the soil at the bottom to encourage rooting. Each

herb should be planted to the same depth as it was in the pot, and firmed in well. Plants that spread by invasive underground parts – in particular, horseradish and mint – should be grown within a barrier, such as a large plant pot or bottomless bucket sunk into the ground, and often replanted.

It is worth considering laying down landscape fabric over the area to be planted and covering it with medium-sized pebble mulch (*see p.34*), which serves both to anchor and conceal the fabric. Pull back the pebbles at the planting stations and make cross-cuts in the fabric: plant the herbs firmly through the cuts before replacing the pebble mulch. This method will suppress weed growth, maintain a suitable soil temperature in summer and winter, and also conserve soil moisture.

It is important to ensure that the soil is thoroughly watered before covering it, and from time to time check that the soil remains adequately moist – it may be worth laying irrigation hoses (*see pp.54*) under the fabric at the outset.

## Routine care

Keep herb plants productive by regular trimming: if not trimmed, some will become straggly, unattractive, and woody, producing fewer new shoots suitable for culinary use. Inspect herb plants regularly, and deal with weeds (*see pp.49–50*) and pests or diseases (*see pp.51–52*) as necessary.

**Pinching out bushy herbs**
*Bay, rosemary, and (as here) sage can be kept compact by frequent trimming of new growth. Pinch out between thumb and forefinger the top 2 or 3 leaves at the growing tips.*

**Cutting herbs for drying**
*Regular harvesting throughout the growing season keeps herbs compact and productive. Choose unblemished stems about 15cm (6in) long and dry them for winter use.*

Keep an eye on those plants that may become troublesome weeds through self-seeding, for example borage and fennel (*see p. 143*). Removing the flowerheads before they set seed can reduce or prevent self-seeding. Periodic renewal by propagation (*see below*) will keep the herbs vigorous and productive.

## Propagating herbs

Most of the culinary herb plants can be propagated at home. Many herbs, especially those grown as annuals, can be raised from seed (*see individual crops, pp. 142–145*). Shrubby herbs, such as rosemary, can be propagated by cuttings; those with creeping roots, like mint, by root cuttings; and others, such as sweet Cicely, by division (*see below*). Some of these methods require practice.

You will also need a protected area (*see pp. 43–48*) in which to start off both cuttings and seed-raised herbs (*see pp. 60–65*). If only small numbers of perennial herbs are needed, it may be worth simply buying container-grown plants, widely available in nurseries or garden centres.

## Maintaining supplies

Steady supplies of herbs can be kept up through the growing season by ensuring that the plants do not suffer excessive drought and by trimming the plants regularly (*see p. 139*). Fresh supplies of many annual herbs can be extended by making successional sowings later in the growing season (*see p. 69*). The main growing season of leafy herbs, such as parsley, can be extended by shading the plants with shadecloth (*see p. 46*) for protection from the hot summer sun.

Cutting and preserving herbs ensures continuing supplies through winter in cool climates, although with some loss of the original intensity of aroma or flavour. Air drying in a warm, dark cupboard, by hanging herbs in bunches or laying them out on trays, is well tried, and the slow process preserves quality of flavour better than rapid microwave drying.

Freezing is possible in many cases: either freeze in sealed plastic bags or fill compartments of an ice-cube tray with chopped herbs and top up with water before freezing it. The ice cubes can be added to food during cooking or the herbs used after thawing the ice cubes in a kitchen sieve. Herbs can also be used to make flavoured oil or vinegar: steep for a couple of weeks in a warm place, shaking regularly, then strain off the liquid into a clean bottle.

## Widening your range

Almost all of the herbs mentioned here are included in the following list of those that are most commonly grown. The potential choice is much wider, however, and there are many other plants not necessarily thought of as herbs that nonetheless have interesting culinary uses.

Some ornamental garden plants rate equally as culinary or medicinal herbs, including marigold (*Calendula officinalis*), and heartsease (*Viola tricolor*), used for the attractive colour of the petals, which brighten rice and soups; lavender (*Lavandula angustifolia*), the flowers of which may be added to jams; bergamot (*Monarda didyma*), used for the orange flavour of its leaves in teas and the flowers in salads.

# How to propagate culinary herbs

▷ **Growing from seed**
*Frost-tender annual herbs, like these young purple-leaved and green-leaved basils, are best raised from seed sown in modules and started in a propagator in cool climates. Plant them out in early summer, either into beds or into containers.*

▽ **Taking softwood cuttings**
*Trim the base of each piece (here lemon balm) to just below a leaf joint to create an 8–10cm (3–4in) cutting. Remove all leaves below the top 2 or 3. Insert the cuttings into a mix of equal parts peat moss and grit or perlite.*

*Softwood cuttings are taken from tips of new shoots*

△ **Dividing shrubby perennial herbs**
*Lift a vigorous, mature plant (here thyme) in late spring. Shake off as much loose soil as possible and remove any dead or damaged parts. Using clean, sharp secateurs, divide the plant into smaller pieces, each with strong roots and top-growth; replant immediately.*

◁ **Taking root or rhizome cuttings**
*Divide roots (here mint) into 4–8cm (1½–3in) sections with at least one growth bud. Make a straight cut at the top end and an angled cut at the other. Insert vertically, angled end down, in a propagating mix, to root in 2–3 weeks.*

# Visual index of culinary herbs

Use this index to locate details of individual herb crops.

*Allium schoenoprasum* p.144
**Onion chives**

*Anethum graveolens* p.143
**Dill**

*Anthriscus cerefolium* p.142
**Chervil**

*Armoracia rusticana* p.143
**Horseradish**

*Artemisia dracunculus* p.145
**Tarragon**

*Coriandrum sativum* p.142
**Coriander**

*Cymbopogon citratus* p.143
**Lemon grass**

*Foeniculum vulgare* p.143
**Fennel**

*Laurus nobilis* p.142
**Bay**

*Levisticum officinale* p.144
**Lovage**

*Melissa officinalis* p.143
**Lemon balm**

*Mentha* species p.144
**Mint**

*Myrrhis odorata* p.145
**Sweet Cicely**

*Ocimum basilicum* p.142
**Basil**

*Origanum* species p.144
**Marjoram, oregano**

*Petroselinum crispum* p.144
**Parsley**

*Rosmarinus officinalis* p.144
**Rosemary**

*Salvia officinalis* p.145
**Sage**

*Satureja* species p.145
**Savory**

*Thymus* species p.145
**Thyme**

**OTHER HERBS**
*Allium tuberosum* .......................... p.143
**Chinese, garlic chives**
*Chenopodium bonus-henricus* ........... p.143
**Good King Henry**
*Polygonum odoratum* ..................... p.143
**Hot mint**
*Rumex* species ........................... p.145
**French sorrel**

# A–Z of culinary herbs

## Basil

### *Ocimum basilicum*

This is a strongly aromatic herb with leaves producing a clove-like flavour commonly used in culinary dishes, especially with tomatoes. Common or sweet basil has oval, bright green leaves and whorls of small, white flowers from summer. It originates in tropical Asia, so should be grown as a summer annual in cool climates. Basil belongs to the Lamiaceae family, along with mint and sage (*see pp.144–145*).

**Cultivation** Grow in a sheltered, reliably warm position in full sun: basil does well in the vegetable garden or a tub. Sow seed in a propagator (*see pp.62–65*) in early to mid-spring, and harden off young potted-on plants for setting out 30cm (1ft) apart when risk of cold weather is past. Alternatively, plant commercial seedlings in early summer. Pinch out the growing tips continually as the plants develop (*see p.139*) to promote a bushy habit.

**Harvesting and storage** For best preserved flavour, basil is made into pesto, or leaves can be stored in oil.

**Forms and cultivars** There are many forms including bush, compact, and low-growing kinds, and a wide range of leaf forms and aromas, such as 'Cinnamon'. Those with coloured leaves, such as 'Purple Ruffles', are decorative, but are less intensely flavoured.

## Bay

### *Laurus nobilis*

The tough, aromatic leaves of bay are used variously in cooking, in particular, as a basic ingredient of bouquet garni. Bay originates from the Mediterranean region. It is a suckering, evergreen tree, naturally growing to at least 5m (15ft) tall. Cream flowers are borne in clusters in spring.

**Cultivation** Bay is drought-tolerant; the leaves are susceptible to infestations of scale. While new plants are slow to grow, bay grows more vigorously in subsequent years. It can be trimmed to form a dense hedge, or planted as a garden tree, or grown in a large pot. It is necessary to trim potted plants. They can be made into decorative shapes such as cones, pyramids, or as standard mop-heads. Position containers in a sunny place sheltered from strong winds. Propagation from ripe heel cuttings, layers, or seed is slow: it may be best to buy a well-grown plant. Grow bay in a fertile, loam-based compost, and water and feed container-grown plants regularly.

**Harvesting and storage** Bay leaves are best used fresh, but can be dried (*see p.140*).

**Forms and cultivars** There are leaf shape and colour variants, but do not confuse sweet bay – also called bay tree, bay laurel, or true laurel – with cherry laurel (*Prunus laurocerasus*) or the Portuguese laurel (*P. lusitanica*), both of which are inedible.

## Chervil

### *Anthriscus cerefolium*

Chervil is used in cooking, particularly as an ingredient of *fines herbes*, for its delicate aniseed flavour. A shade-loving annual growing up to 60cm (2ft), it is decorative, but its tendency to self-seed prolifically can become a nuisance in moist soil. The leaves have some resemblance to parsley (*see p.144*), to which chervil is related.

**Cultivation** This herb does best in partial shade in light, but moisture-retentive and relatively rich, soil: it tends to bolt and run to seed in full sun and dry soil. Sow chervil direct (*see pp.66–69*) in early to mid-spring; plants can also be successfully raised in modules (*see p.62*). Germination may take three weeks, and established seedlings should be thinned to 15cm (6in) apart.

A repeat sowing in late summer will provide plants for use over the autumn and winter. Water thoroughly in dry spells, and remove some of the flowerheads, leaving only a proportion of them to self-seed.

**Harvesting and storage** Chervil grows quite fast, and young leaves can be harvested only nine weeks after sowing. Pick young outer leaves for the best flavour, especially for use as a salad garnish or in egg dishes. Chervil leaves are better frozen than dried (*see p.140*).

## Coriander

### *Coriandrum sativum*

Grown for the distinctive flavour of its lower, lobed leaves and seeds, used especially in oriental dishes, coriander is also sometimes used as a cut-and-come-again salad (*see p.102*). A hardy annual relative of parsley (*see p.144*), it grows up to 45cm (18in) tall in the flowering phase, with heads of small, white flowers.

**Cultivation** Grow in well-drained soil, but keep seedlings moist or they may bolt. Plants grown for leaves can be grown in partial shade; for seeds, choose a sunny site. Coriander leaf, or cilantro, grows best in cool weather, and bolts to seed quickly in hot weather. Coriander grows well in tropical gardens. Sow in succession from early spring to late summer *in situ* (*see pp.66–69*) in rows 30cm (12in) apart, and thin to 15cm (6in) stations. Leaves for winter use can be obtained from autumn sowings. Coriander self-seeds in favourable conditions.

**Harvesting and storage** Pick leaves when young and use fresh or frozen (*see p.140*). Seeds can be gathered when ripe and dried and stored.

# Dill

*Anethum graveolens*

Dill is grown for the mild, distinctive flavour of its leaves, used in a range of dishes from soups to salads. Seeds are added to pickling vinegars. It is a decorative annual, up to 1.2m (4ft), with flat heads of yellow flowers, much resembling fennel, to which it is related.

**Cultivation** Dill does best in moist, fertile soil, otherwise plants bolt early in hot weather. Do not grow dill near fennel, since the plants will hybridize, losing their distinctive flavours. Sow seed *in situ* (*see pp.66–69*), because dill is not amenable to being transplanted. Make successional sowings from spring through to midsummer. Plants self-seed in favourable conditions.

**Harvesting and storage** Pick young leaves before flowering; they can be dried, but are best fresh. Harvest seeds as they turn brown.

# Fennel

*Foeniculum vulgare*

Fennel, or sweet fennel, self-seeds widely and is not recommended where it may become an environmental weed. The foliage is used for flavouring fish, and the peeled stems and seeds as a flavouring for salads, and meat and fish dishes. Fennel is a drought-tolerant perennial with attractive, fine, feathery, green or bronze foliage on stems up to 1.5m (5ft) tall, bearing flat-headed clusters of yellow flowers. This herb is closely related to the more tender Florence fennel, *Foeniculum vulgare* var. *azoricum*, which is an annual vegetable grown for its swollen, aniseed-flavoured leaf-stem bases (*see p.122*).

**Harvesting and storage** Pick leaves and stems throughout the growing season. Unripe seeds can be used fresh, ripe seeds dried.

# Garlic chives

*Allium tuberosum*

The leaves of garlic, or Chinese, chives are cut as for onion chives (*see p.144*), but they can be blanched for a milder flavour. The plant is robust with a rhizomatous stem, flat, garlic-flavoured leaves up to 50cm (20in) tall, and white flowers.

**Cultivation** As for onion chives (*see p.144*). Leaves can be blanched by placing an upturned container over young developing shoots to exclude light.

**Harvesting** As for onion chives (*see p.144*). Harvest blanched leaves after 4–6 weeks once they are pale and yellowed.

# Good King Henry

*Chenopodium bonus-henricus*

Cultivated for its asparagus-flavoured shoots and young leaves, which add interest to salads, Good King Henry is a herbaceous perennial, growing up to 75cm (30in) tall.

**Cultivation** Best-quality shoots are produced on moist, fertile sites, and Good King Henry does well in relatively shady positions. Sow seed during spring in a propagator (*see pp.62–65*) or *in situ* (*see pp.66–69*), for planting out or thinning to 38cm (15in) stations. Established plants can also be propagated by division in spring (*see p.140*).

**Harvesting** New shoots can be harvested for eating fresh from the second year by severing them just below the soil surface. Leaves are picked when young and tender.

# Horseradish

*Armoracia rusticana*

The white-fleshed and pungent roots of horseradish are used to make a hot-flavoured sauce traditionally served with roast beef, and also in coleslaw. It is a herbaceous perennial, closely related to the brassicas (*see pp.76–81*) with basal, bright green leaves. The roots are strong, fleshy or woody, and branching. They establish tenaciously, and it can become an invasive weed if not carefully controlled. Horseradish has a long history as a medicinal and culinary herb. The plant is dormant in winter.

**Cultivation** Horseradish will spread widely in favourable conditions and is best planted in a back corner of the garden. Plants grow best in a rich, well-drained soil in sun or partial shade. Horseradish can be raised from seed, but the best propagation method is to drop 15cm (6in) root cuttings in spring into dibbled holes spaced 60cm (2ft) apart. Horseradish will grow whichever way up the root pieces are put in the ground.

**Harvesting and storage** Lift the plant to harvest its roots in autumn.

# Hot mint

*Polygonum odoratum*

The leaves of hot mint, or Vietnamese mint, are used in Asian cooking. They have a distinctive but strong, pungent flavour. The plant is a wide-spreading perennial and looks similar to mint (*Mentha* species) but the leaf has a brown marking and it bears sprays of small, pink flowers. Hot mint is closely related to knotweed.

**Cultivation** Hot mint thrives in warm, damp conditions and can become invasive. Plant spread can be contained by growing plants in a tub. Root growth is shallow so the container need not be deep. When growth becomes straggly, cut the plant back to ground level to promote fresh foliage. Plants may die down in winter in cool climates.

**Harvesting** Hot mint is picked fresh as required. It can be harvested all year in warm climates.

# Lemon balm

*Melissa officinalis*

Grown for its lemon-scented leaves, which are used in a range of dishes and tea infusions, lemon balm is a frost-hardy perennial that can grow up to 1.5m (5ft) in suitable conditions.

**Cultivation** Lemon balm is quite vigorous; it will grow in a range of soil types and is tolerant of drought and shade. Propagate by sowing seed *in situ* in spring (*see pp.66–69*), by taking softwood cuttings (*see p.140*) in spring, or by dividing clumps in the spring or autumn (*see p.140*).

**Harvesting and storage** Lemon balm should be regularly cut back (*see p.139*) in order to maintain leaves with a strong aroma and prevent the plant from becoming straggly. The leaves can be dried.

**Forms and cultivars** A yellow-leaved type is available. Do not confuse lemon balm with lemon verbena (*Aloysia triphylla*), an attractive, semi-deciduous shrub that in its natural surroundings can reach a height of 3m (10ft).

# Lemon grass

*Cymbopogon citratus*

A strongly lemon-scented, frost-tender perennial grass, this is used extensively as a grated or chopped food flavouring in Asian cuisine. Lemon grass produces strong, often cane-like stems, and is capable of reaching over 1.5m (5ft) in favourable conditions. The leaves are blue-green in colour and the flowers are attractive, although these are not often produced in cultivation. All parts of the plant are lemon-scented.

**Cultivation** Lemon grass originates in warm temperate regions, and needs a moderately humid atmosphere and a minimum temperature of 55°F (13°C). In cool climates, this means growing it in large containers of fertile, moisture-retaining compost in a protected environment (*see pp.43–48*). Propagate by division. Bought stems with a little root left on them may root if potted up and stood on a heated propagating tray.

**Harvesting and storage** Cut stems at ground level at any time and use the lower 8–10cm (3–4in) of the stems.

# Lovage

*Levisticum officinale*

Lovage leaves and shoots are pungent celery- or yeast-flavoured. They are added sparingly to salads and used to flavour soups and stock, savoury and sweet dishes, cold drinks, and herb teas.

Blanched shoots can be eaten as a vegetable, and the roots are edible as a cooked vegetable or used raw in salads.

A lush, leafy, herbaceous perennial, lovage is capable of growing to the considerable height of at least 2m (6ft) in favourable conditions. The leaves are divided, and clusters of pale green to yellow flowers are borne in flat heads in midsummer.
**Cultivation** Grow in sun or partial shade in rich, deep, moist soil. Propagate by seed sown *in situ* (*see pp.66–69*) in late spring or collect self-sown plants. Clumps can be divided in spring (*see p.140*).
**Harvesting and storage** Young shoots are blanched by earthing up, rather like trench celery (*see pp.120–121*) as they develop in spring. Leaves are best picked before flowering.

# Marjoram *and* oregano

*Origanum* species

Four species of *Origanum* are grown for their distinctly flavoured leaves: a short-lived sweet marjoram (*O. marjorana*) and perennial sweet marjoram (*O. x applii*), a more vigorous plant, have white flowers and more delicately flavoured leaves than oregano.

The best oregano for culinary purposes is Greek or White oregano (*O. vulgare* ssp. *viride*), which is taller and more vigorous, with strong-flavoured leaves and white flowers. Wild oregano (*O. vulgare*) is a ground-hugging perennial with pink flowers and poor flavour.
**Cultivation** These herbs do best on fertile soil in a sunny position, and all but *O. marjorana* are drought-tolerant plants. Propagate perennial marjoram and Greek oregano from softwood cuttings or by division (*see p.140*) and keep the plants trimmed, cutting dead stems hard back.

Sweet marjoram, *O. marjorana*, is raised from spring-sown seed.
**Harvesting and storage** Pick marjoram leaves just before the flower buds open and use fresh, frozen, or dried (*see p.140*). Oregano has the best flavour when it has been dried.
**Forms and cultivars** There are numerous forms of *Origanum*, many making attractive garden plants because of their leaf or flower colours.

# Mint

*Mentha* species

The culinary use of mint is long established: leaves are chopped to use in sauces, added to salads and drinks, cooked with vegetables, or used whole as garnishes. The mints comprise a large group of creeping perennials, with many and varied forms, all characterized by highly aromatic foliage and pinkish flowers.
**Cultivation** Mints have an invasive habit and they can be troublesome weeds if allowed to become established among other plants or in pathways. It is possible to restrict its growth by planting it in a sunken container (*see p.139*) or within some other form of physical barrier. Another method is to plant mint near a tap so that growth is confined to the moist area close to the tap.

Propagate by division in spring or autumn, taking rooted shoots or planting 5cm (2in) long pieces of rhizome horizontally so they lie 5cm (2in) deep and 25cm (10in) apart. Mint is prone to mint rust (*see p.258*) on older foliage. Control is easy by cutting the plant back hard. The new growth should be free from disease. Spearmint is most susceptible.
**Harvesting and storage** Pick leaves throughout the growing season and use them fresh. For storage, freezing is more successful than drying (*see p.140*).
**Forms and cultivars** Commonly grown mints include spearmint (*Mentha spicata*) and peppermint (*M.* x *piperita*); winter mint or common mint (*M. cordifolia*) has the best flavour, and foliage persists during cool weather. There are many other kinds that are attractive for their range of aromas, leaf forms, and variegation.

# Onion chives

*Allium schoenoprasum*

Onion chives are grown for their distinctive flavour when finely chopped as a garnish for a wide range of prepared dishes, especially salads. A perennial member of the onion family, they have the general appearance of salad onions, but are clump-forming, usually up to 25cm (10in) tall. They bear attractive mauve flowerheads in summer, which may also be used as a salad garnish but more importantly make the plants very decorative additions to the garden. Onion chives have a tubular leaf and a more delicate flavour than garlic chives (*Allium tuberosum*), which are a taller plant with narrow, flat leaves, and larger, white flowers. Garlic chives are a more robust plant and grow well in the tropics.
**Cultivation** Choose a situation in full sun and keep the plants well watered. Sow seed in plugs or larger modules (*see pp.62–65*) at 18°C (64°F) in early or mid-spring, and plant out as an edging plant to the herb or vegetable garden. Trim plants back hard

regularly and lift and divide clumps (*see p.140*) in the autumn every three years. Chives die back during a cold winter.
**Harvesting** Remove the flowers and harvest regularly for a supply of young leaves, cutting the leaves close to ground level. Chives are best used fresh.

# Parsley

*Petroselinum crispum*

Parsley foliage is used chopped as a flavouring and a garnish in a wide range of hot and cold dishes. It is a biennial herb, which is usually grown as an annual. Most selections grow up to 30cm (12in) in the leafy first-year stage, though some flat-leafed forms may exceed 60cm (2ft), according to growing conditions and site. Flat heads of small, yellow flowers are borne in the second season, and the plants will self-seed in favourable places.
**Cultivation** Parsley does best on fertile, moisture-retentive soil, and in warm temperatures prefers partly shaded or sunny sites. The most reliable method of raising early plants is to sow in plugs or larger modules in a propagator (*see pp.62–65*). Parsley is slow to germinate and may take several weeks to appear if sown *in situ*. Set out plants with the minimum of root disturbance at 23cm (9in) stations. Plants develop quite slowly and the soil must be kept moist.

Successional sowings can be made in the garden (*see pp.66–69*) in drills 1cm (½in) deep in rows 45cm (18in) apart. Thin the seedlings to 23cm (9in) spacings. This system works well for sowings made from summer onwards. Be sure that the seed is sown into moist soil.

Remove flowerheads to prolong the useful life of the plants. Parsley foliage dies back in winter in cool climates. In shallow or poorly drained soils, plants are best grown in a container that is deep enough to accommodate the tap root. Parsley may rot in very humid weather, and in the tropics plants are grown in containers through winter.
**Harvesting and storage** Cut single leaves or bunches low down on the stems with scissors. Parsley leaves can be frozen (*see p.140*) for out-of-season use.
**Forms and cultivars** There are two main sorts. Plain-leaved cultivars of the French and Italian types are the easiest to establish and grow, and are more strongly flavoured than the decorative cut and curled leafed types, of which there are many cultivars. Selections range from pale to dark green in colour.

# Rosemary

*Rosmarinus officinalis*

The highly aromatic leaves of rosemary are a traditional flavouring for cooked meats. An evergreen shrub related to mint and sage, it has short, needle-like leaves densely packed on long branches, and pale blue, sometimes white flowers borne in winter and spring. Rosemary is prone to root rot in poorly drained soil, causing branches or whole plants to die. A gritty, sharply drained soil is best.

**Cultivation** Rosemary bushes are attractive as specimens in the shrub border or as low, semi-formal hedges. One or more plants can be grown in a large container (*see p.138*) and kept trimmed with secateurs; in this form, the plants enjoy the good drainage and warm sun if positioned in a sunny courtyard. Rosemary can be propagated from seed, but softwood cuttings (*see p.140*), as well as cuttings taken from semi-ripened shoots, root easily and the plants establish well on suitable sites. Keep young plants pinched to maintain a bushy habit (*see p.139*), and aim to prune regularly and moderately.

**Harvesting and storage** Pick leaves and flowering shoots as required and use them fresh, frozen, or dried (*see p.140*).

**Forms and cultivars** There are spreading and upright forms. The shrub may grow up to 1m (3ft) high but can be contained by hard pruning, which it tolerates well. The most vigorous and long-flowering form is 'Blue Lagoon', which makes a good container plant or hedge in any soil.

# Sage

*Salvia officinalis*

Sage leaves are used in meat stuffings, and can also be added to salads. A shrubby perennial, sage grows up to 60cm (2ft) tall, with tough, grey-green, highly aromatic leaves, and bears spikes of attractive blue flowers in summer.

**Cultivation** Sage grows best in full sun on well-drained, light soils. It can be propagated by seed sown in a propagator (*see pp.62–65*) in spring or by softwood cuttings in summer or more mature shoots with a "heel", a small piece of the previous year's wood at the base, in early autumn (*see p.140*). Plants establish best from planting out in spring, spaced 45–60cm (18–24in) apart. Pruning after flowering helps maintain shape and encourage new growth, but aim to renew plants every three or four years.

**Harvesting and storage** Leaves can be picked for use fresh or dried (*see p.140*) for winter use. It is best to pick leaves before flowering if drying them for storage.

**Forms and cultivars** The numerous cultivars with coloured and variegated leaves are excellent border plants, but generally less hardy than the common sage.

# Savory

*Satureja* species

There are three main types of this strongly flavoured herb, often used like sage but

especially added to cooked broad beans, salads, and soups. Upright winter savory (*Satureja montana*) is a shrubby perennial, which grows to 50cm (20in), with small, grey-green leaves. Prostrate winter savoury (*S. repens*) is a winter-dormant creeping herb with showy, white flowers. Summer savory (*S. hortensis*) is a smaller annual with softer, less intensely flavoured leaves. All three bear whorls of white to pink or purple flowers in summer.

**Cultivation** Savory thrives on light, well-drained soil in a sunny position and can also be grown in containers. Propagate winter savory by seed sown in spring, by division in spring, or by taking softwood cuttings in summer or heel cuttings in early autumn (*see p.140*). Summer savory should be raised from seed in spring. The plants will grow to approximately 30cm (12in), and should be cut back after flowering in order to encourage new growth.

**Harvesting** Pick the leaves during the growing season and use fresh.

# Sorrel

*Rumex scutatus*

The young leaves of French sorrel are added to soups, sauces, soft cheeses, and egg dishes for their fresh, tart flavour. French sorrel, also called buckler leaf, is an upright perennial with tender, shield-shaped leaves.

**Cultivation** French sorrel grows well in moist soil in sun or partial shade. Propagate sorrel by sowing seed *in situ* (*see pp.66–69*) in mid-spring or by dividing the plants (*see p.140*) in spring or autumn.

**Harvesting** Pick the leaves before flowering in summer and use fresh; remove the flowers as they appear to prevent bolting.

# Sweet Cicely

*Myrrhis odorata*

The leaves and seeds of sweet Cicely are sweetly aromatic, with an aniseed flavour, and are used in salads and fruit dishes. The thick taproot is edible as a cooked vegetable. A hardy, herbaceous perennial, it requires space to accommodate its large stature, as it grows up to 1.5m (5ft) tall in moist, rich soil. It is a handsome plant over a long season, especially for a woodland garden, and has fern-like foliage and bears flat heads of white flowers in summer.

**Cultivation** Sweet Cicely should be grown in rich, moist soil in sun or partial shade. Raise it from fresh seed sown in the autumn (*see pp.66–69*), or by division or root cuttings (*see p.140*). Self-seeding is common where conditions are favourable. Sweet Cicely responds well to periodic cutting down during the growing season.

**Harvesting and storage** Pick leaves throughout the growing season and use fresh

or frozen (*see p.140*). Pick unripe seeds for use fresh. Lift the roots in autumn and use fresh.

# Tarragon

*Artemisia dracunculus*

The leaves of tarragon are strongly aromatic and are chopped for use in salads, and in fish and chicken dishes, particularly as a flavouring for sauces. It is one of the large group of wormwoods, which belong to the daisy family, and is a herbaceous perennial available in two forms. French tarragon (*Artemisia dracunculus*) grows to 75cm (30in) and is variably hardy compared to the more robust Russian tarragon (*A. dracunculus dracunculoides*), which is not so well-flavoured and grows about twice as tall. French tarragon has glossy leaves with a subtle anise flavour, and Russian tarragon has greyish-green, coarse-flavoured leaves.

**Cultivation** The tarragons succeed on fertile, well-drained soil, especially in a sheltered, sunny site. French tarragon does not reliably set seed in cool summers but spreads by rhizomes that may be divided in spring, or softwood cuttings can be taken (*see p.140*) in midsummer. Russian tarragon is propagated by sowing seed under cover in spring (*see p.140*).

**Harvesting and storage** Harvest leaves or whole stems throughout the growing season for use fresh, frozen, or dried (*see p.140*).

# Thyme

*Thymus* species

Thyme is a popular culinary herb, used in a wide range of dishes. An ornamental, low-growing perennial or subshrub, it has small leaves and bears tubular, two-lipped flowers in shades of pink or purple.

**Cultivation** Thymes prefer well-drained, sunny sites, and thrive if grown beside rocks or paving. Propagate every two or three years to avoid straggly plants, by sowing outdoors (*see pp.66–69*) in late spring or early summer, or by dividing clumps and using the parts furthest from the centre (*see p.140*). Thymes should be trimmed after flowering (*see p.139*) to maintain a good flush of growth and to contain their size.

**Harvesting and storage** Pick sprigs as required and use fresh, frozen, or dried (*see p.140*).

**Forms and cultivars** *Thymus vulgaris* is most commonly grown for the kitchen; it develops a semi-shrubby habit up to 30cm (12in) tall and gives a strong flavour. Westmoreland or Turkey thyme (*T.* 'Westmoreland') is an excellent leafy form with good flavour, as is lemon-scented thyme (*T.* x *citriodorus*), which has rounded, glossy, green leaves. There are decorative variegated forms but these are less robust plants.

# FRUIT

IN RECENT TIMES, the work of researchers, plant breeders, and specialist growers has encouraged gardeners to be innovative in fruit cultivation, to adopt new techniques and develop old ones – growing traditionally large trees such as apples and pears in patio pots, for example, or pushing back the boundaries of hardiness with tender crops. Despite the undoubted value of modern techniques, fruit growing still appeals to the senses in ways that bring us closer to nature – the beauty of the plants both in fruit and in blossom, the buzz of pollinating insects about their work, the sun's warmth ripening the crops, the scents and flavours of fresh-picked produce.

One of the pleasures – and sometimes problems – of fruit growing is the fact that many wild creatures are as attracted to fruits as we are. These visitors remind us that to be fruitful, in every sense of the word, a garden must be full of all forms of life. A balanced approach must be sought that protects crops from pests while encouraging "garden friends" to help control problems.

# Visual index of fruit

Use this index to locate details of individual fruit crops.

*Actinidia deliciosa*    p.235
**Kiwi fruit, Chinese gooseberry**

*Ananas comosus*    p.236
**Pineapple**

*Citrus* species    p.235
**Citrus**

*Corylus avellana* and *C. maxima*    p.203
**Hazelnut**

*Cydonia oblonga*    p.200
**Quince**

*Ficus carica*    p.197
**Fig**

*Fragaria x ananassa*    p.211
**Strawberry**

*Juglans regia*    p.204
**Walnut**

*Malus domestica*    p.174
**Apple**

*Mespilus germanica*    p.201
**Medlar**

*Morus* species    p.202
**Mulberry**

*Olea europaea*    p.236
**Olive**

*Diospyros kaki*    p.237
**Persimmon**

*Passiflora* species    p.235
**Passionfruit**

*Prunus armeniaca*    p.196
**Apricot**

*Prunus avium, P. cerasus*    p.189, p.191
**Sweet and acid cherry**

*Prunus domestica, P. insititia*    p.185
**Plum and damson**

*Prunus dulcis*    p.205
**Almond**

*Prunus persica*    p.193
**Peach and nectarine**

*Pyrus communis* var. *sativa*    p.181
**Pear**

*Ribes nigrum*    p.223
**Blackcurrant**

*Ribes rubrum*    p.221
**Redcurrant**

*Ribes rubrum*    p.221
**Whitecurrant**

*Ribes uva-crispa*    p.219
**Gooseberry**

*Rubus fruticosus* and *Rubus* hybrids    p.215
**Blackberry and hybrid berries**

*Rubus idaeus*    p.215
**Raspberry**

*Vaccinium corymbosum*    p.225
**Blueberry**

*Vaccinium macrocarpon*    p.226
**Cranberry**

*Vitis vinifera, V. labrusca*    p.227
**Grape vine**

# GROWING TREE FRUITS

# Planning

Tree fruits are those that naturally grow as trees, including apples, pears, plums, cherries, peaches, nectarines, apricots, figs, quince, medlars, and mulberries. As well as producing their fresh, succulent fruits, these trees often have spectacular spring blossom. The shape and size of the tree is affected by the rootstock (*see p.153*) and cultivar being grown, and the way in which it is pruned. Many may be trained to grow in the restricted but ornamental forms of cordons, espaliers, and fans, all of which take up less space than the bush form. Included among the tree fruits are several nuts: cobnuts, filberts, and almonds are all suitable for an average-sized garden. Walnuts reach a great height; consider them only for very large gardens.

## Using tree fruits in the garden

By choosing cultivars carefully and restricting their size, you can grow quite a range of tree fruits in a small space. For instance, a useful quantity of fruit can be gained from ten apple cordons, five pear cordons, three plum pyramids, and a cherry fan. Spacings depend on rootstocks chosen. Yields vary widely according to cultivar, soil, climate, and site (*see individual crops, pp.174–205*).

If growing a number of trees, plant them in rows to reduce shading, with the largest trees to the south. Grow the same fruits together to aid pollination and management. To save space, or for decorative effect, fruit can be trained on fences, walls, arches, and pergolas. The choice of cultivar depends on preference, although mid- and late-season apples and pears can be stored, whereas earlier ripening cultivars must be used soon after picking. For a limited space, use high-quality dessert cultivars – they can also be cooked.

## Choosing a site

For healthy growth, flowering, and pollination (*see pp.156–157*), and ripening of fruit and wood, grow tree fruits on a warm, sunny site, sheltered

### Forms of young fruit trees
*In the first growing season after grafting, a fruit tree will form a main vertical stem, and sometimes a few short side branches. A tree with a single stem is a maiden whip. If it has side branches after one year, it is a feathered maiden. A two-year-old feathered tree should have several well-placed branches.*

Strong vertical main stem

Graft point, or union

Rootstock

*Maiden whip*

Vigorous central stem

Particularly upright shoots will need to be pruned out

Most branches well-spaced with wide angle to central stem

Lower branches likely to need removal

*Feathered maiden*

from strong winds. Spring frosts at flowering can be devastating, so choose a site on a gentle slope so the cold air will flow away from the trees. Avoid frost pockets (*see p.11*) or, if this is not possible, protect the trees (*see individual crops, pp.174–205*).

Deciduous fruit trees can be grown in all cool to temperate climatic zones of Australia. Open grown trees may need protection against temperature extremes (severe heat or cold) or against frost, strong winds, or hail. Protection against damage from birds, wallabies, kangaroos, or possums may also be required. Increasingly, orchards large and small are being netted. Close planting using dwarfing rootstock, less severe pruning systems, or espalier training are options for easily managed orchards.

## Suitable soils

Soil requirements vary for different tree fruits, including nuts (*see individual crops,*

*pp.174–205*). A well-drained soil, preferably 60cm (2ft) or more deep, is desirable, although thinner soils are tolerated by most tree fruits. On thinner soils, trees will be stressed from water shortage and less stable in wind. The ideal soil is a deep, medium loam and, for most tree fruits, a slightly acid to neutral pH (*see p.18*). Tree fruits are long-term crops, so the more you improve the soil before planting (*see pp.37–40*), the better start they have.

## Soil water levels

Tree fruits have searching roots that need a constant supply of water and nutrients, so both light and heavy soils (*see pp.14–15*) should be thoroughly cultivated prior to planting. Working in plenty of organic matter, such as well-rotted manure or compost, will improve the drainage on heavy soils and the moisture-retention on light soils.

The surface drainage of heavy clay soils can be improved by working in a

2.5–5cm (1–2in) layer of coarse grit to the top 15cm (6in) of soil, but this is laborious. All improvements must be done over the entire planting area — if only the planting hole is treated in this way, it may create a sump in which moisture from the surrounding soil collects. If waterlogging is severe, the installation of a drainage system may be necessary (*see p.16*) or you could resort to growing fruit trees in containers.

All types of soil will need watering, but free-draining, shallow soils with 30cm (12in) or less of topsoil, especially in dry areas, require more frequent irrigation (*see p.160*).

After planting, an annual mulch (*see p.161*) around the trees in late winter or in early spring will continue to improve the soil's moisture-holding capacity.

## The importance of soil pH

If the soil pH differs very much from pH 6.5, which tree fruits prefer, it will need to be corrected. The pH of acidic soils can be increased by adding lime (*see pp.18–19*), and the pH of alkaline soils can be lowered by digging in organic matter. It is best to apply a little and repeat a few months later if needed. Check the pH every few years. Do not place lime around any trees that are intolerant of lime or of alkaline soils.

## Types of tree to buy

Trees establish best if planted in their final positions when young; a more mature tree will usually be overtaken by a younger sapling within a few years. Choose one- or two-year-old trees for most tree forms (*see p.152*). For fan- and espalier-trained trees, part-trained trees, about three years old, are best.

If possible, buy a feathered maiden (*see p.149*), which has a main stem with a number of side branches. These are particularly good for training as bush, spindlebush, pyramid, and cordon trees. Maiden whips (*see p.149*) can be trained into all forms, but take a year longer than feathered maidens. Some cultivars, such as 'Blenheim Orange' apples, do not branch easily in the first year, and so are available only as whips.

Trees are available as either bare-root or container-grown. Bare-root trees are lifted and sold with the roots wrapped,

---

## Good and bad rootballs

When buying a container-grown fruit tree, don't be afraid to knock off the pot and inspect the rootball thoroughly. If the plant is in good planting condition, you should be able to see larger, anchoring roots growing out of the centre and holding together the compost without forming a thick mat. Finer, pale, feeding roots should also be visible. Avoid plants with roots that do not appear to be established in their pot, where the soil falls away from the rootball. At the other extreme, avoid pot-bound specimens with matted roots growing around the sides of the rootball and even out of the top or base of the pot. These roots are unlikely to spread and establish well when planted.

**Good rootball**
*Some healthy, fibrous roots visible, holding compost together*

**Pot-bound rootball**
*Roots coiling around outside of root ball, forming thick, matted layer*

---

but bare of soil, and there is a much better selection of these. Plant them between late autumn and early spring. Container-grown trees can be planted all year, but need more attention to watering if they are planted in spring and summer (*see above*).

Reputable garden centres and mail-order nurseries are good sources of fruit trees. In a garden centre the range may not be wide, but you can inspect plants before buying. For mail-order, you need to order in good time, since trees are despatched from late autumn, and be prepared to unpack and check over the trees when they arrive.

## Heeling in

Trees should be planted only when the soil is not waterlogged. If the conditions are unfavourable or you are not ready to plant, the trees will need protecting. The aerial part of the tree is frost-hardy, but the roots must not be exposed to frost or allowed to dry out. Find a suitable area of ground to heel in bare-root trees and keep their roots moist. If you cannot heel them in the ground, cover the roots with moist compost or straw, and store in a cool but frost-free place. Insulate pots of container-grown trees in severe cold weather.

◁ **Heeling in trees**
*Dig a trench deep enough to cover the roots. Place the trees (here feathered maiden pears) at an angle along one side of the trench so they do not touch. Fill in the trench with soil to cover the roots; firm gently.*

▷ **Small orchard**
*A productive orchard can be created in a small space, if planned with care. Here, small forms such as apple cordons have been used to obtain a variety of cultivars in a cottage garden.*

# Tree fruit forms

Fruit trees can be trained to grow in a range of different forms. Combined with different rootstocks (*see facing page*), which influence their final size, they can be trained to suit a variety of situations, for both large and small gardens, and for growing in containers.

Before choosing a form for your trees, consider the space available, the type of fruits to be grown, the site, and the amount of fruit required. Tree forms can be divided into unrestricted forms, which are generally pruned in winter, and restricted forms, which are

generally pruned in summer. Restricted forms tend to be earlier into cropping and are more productive per area than the unrestricted forms. In small garden areas, for later ripening cultivars, or for fruits that require warm conditions to crop reliably – such as peaches, nectarines, apricots, sweet cherries, late dessert plums, and figs – the fruits benefit from being grown in a restricted form against a trellis, wall or fence.

Apples and pears are the most versatile of the tree fruits, with a great range of forms possible, including the

elaborate restricted forms that were traditionally used in walled kitchen gardens. Other fruits cannot be trained into such a range of forms, usually due to their fruiting habit or vigour, but there is still a selection suitable for training against freestanding post–and–wire supports. For pruning details on each form, *see pp.166–173.*

Gardeners wanting a selection of fruit over a long period could try multiple grafting of different cultivars onto one tree. Every major structural limb could be made to grow a different cultivar.

## Common tree fruit forms

### Bush
*The bush is an unrestricted, open-centred tree with a clear stem of 75cm (30in) before the branches start. All tree fruits can be trained as bush trees, and the final size of the tree will depend upon the type of fruit and the rootstock onto which it is grafted (see facing page). This form is most suitable for fruits that grow well in the open, such as apples, pears, plums, and quinces. Standards and half-standards are trained as for bush trees, but are grown on more vigorous rootstocks and have a longer clear stem – 1.35m (4½ft) for a half-standard and 2m (6ft) for a standard; they are suitable only for large gardens.*

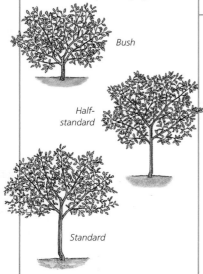

*Bush*

*Half-standard*

*Standard*

### Cordon
*These are restricted forms trained as a single stem, or several stems (a multiple cordon), and suitable for apples, pears, and some plums. The stems can be trained at a 45-degree, oblique angle, horizontally, or vertically, and are closely spaced, so many trees can be grown in a small area. Summer pruning is needed to control their vigour and encourage cropping close to the stem. Cordons are useful on walls or fences, but also flourish on post-and-wire structures or over arches. One of the most productive forms, and easy for a beginner, they come into cropping early in their lives.*

*Cordon*

*Multiple cordon*

### Espalier (multiple-T)
*Most suitable for apples and pears, espaliers consist of a central stem with horizontal arms about 45cm (18in) apart. They can be grown on freestanding posts and wires or a wall or fence. Although productive, they take longer to reach maturity than cordons. A highly ornamental restricted form, espaliers are an attractive way of dividing a garden.*

### Centre-leader trees
*These take two forms: the pyramid and the spindlebush. Each has a central stem and is cone-shaped, with branches starting at 60cm (2ft) from the ground. The slightly neater pyramid is used for many fruits; the spindlebush only for apples and pears. Centre-leader trees are restricted forms, that come into cropping early in the life of the tree. There is good light distribution to all parts, and they cast less shade than a bush tree. They are usually small, from 2m (6ft) to 2.4m (8ft) tall, depending on the rootstock. The spindlebush is best for more vigorous cultivars.*

*Pyramid*

*Spindlebush*

### Fan
*In this restricted form, the branches radiate out on either side of the low, central stem and are attached to wires. Fans can be trained on freestanding posts and wires or a fence and can be used for almost all fruits. They are particularly useful for peaches, nectarines, apricots, and figs, which benefit from the shelter of a wall or fence.*

# Rootstocks

Almost all tree fruits are propagated by grafting, in which a bud or shoot from one tree is joined onto the rootstock – or root system – of another tree to produce one plant. Therefore the rootstock of the tree is different from the fruiting part of the tree. This method of propagating fruit trees has been practised since ancient times and current techniques are little different from those carried out by the ancient Romans and Greeks.

There are a number of advantages to be gained from propagating a fruit tree in this way. Fruits grown from seed do not usually come true, and the majority of seedlings are inferior to the parent. Trees grown from seed also take many years before flowering and fruiting – seven to ten years for apples – and have first to go through a juvenile phase. Most tree fruits do not root easily from cuttings, so grafting is a more reliable method of reproducing a particular cultivar. Trees on their own roots have differing and unpredictable amounts of vigour, and tend to be very vigorous, maturing into large trees that are unsuitable for many garden situations.

Rootstocks are usually classified by the effect they have on vigour, and they help to determine the final size of the tree, although they may also confer other qualities, such as disease resistance, onto the whole plant.

## Propagating rootstock material
Rootstocks can be propagated by a variety of techniques, but the most common is the stool bed method. This

**The rootstock grafting point**
*The point at which the rootstock and scion join should be visible on all grafted fruit trees as a bump near the base of the stem. This point should never be buried, since the scion may root, negating the effect of the rootstock.*

involves cutting down the rootstocks to ground level in late winter. They will produce a number of shoots during the growing season and these are earthed up gradually as they grow. The earthing up encourages the shoots to develop new roots at their bases. Each rooted shoot can then be severed during the following winter and planted out in rows in a nursery bed ready for grafting. This method is mainly used by professional growers to produce large numbers of rootstocks, but can be undertaken by the enthusiastic amateur. For information on grafting methods, *see pp. 154–155.*

## The qualities of rootstocks
The general trend in fruit growing has been towards producing smaller, more manageable trees and, to this end, research stations have concentrated on selecting and breeding more dwarfing rootstocks. This benefits commercial and garden growers, since small trees on dwarfing rootstocks come into fruit bearing earlier in their life and are generally more productive. There is a greater choice of rootstocks available for apples than for other fruits. It has proved difficult to find suitable dwarfing rootstocks for plums and cherries.

When buying a tree, you need to find out what rootstock it is grafted onto and the eventual size that can be expected. This can only be a general guide since mature tree heights vary according to soil, site, and cultivar. Some rootstocks are more suitable for training different forms (*see individual crops, pp. 174–205 for specific guidelines; see also the table below*).

| ROOTSTOCKS FOR TRAINING APPLE TREE FORMS | |
|---|---|
| **Apple form** | **Rootstock** |
| **Pyramid and spindlebush** | M27, M9, M26, or MM106 |
| **Cordon** | M27, M9, or M26 |
| **Espalier (multiple-T)** | M26, MM106, or M111 |
| **Fan** | M26, MM106, or M111, depending on size required and soil |

## How rootstocks affect tree size

The following chart gives an indication of the way in which different rootstocks can affect the mature size of a tree (here apple). There are a great many rootstocks available commercially worldwide, selected according to local soil conditions, climate, pest and disease resistance, and other such factors.

6 — 18

m — ft

M27   M9   M26   MM106   MM111   M25

# Grafting tree fruits

"Grafting" is a term that covers a number of methods of joining a rootstock – or root system – and a scion – or bud – both of which have been selected for desirable characteristics. It is a fairly challenging method of propagation, requiring attention to detail, strict hygiene, and fast working, so that the plant material does not dry out during the process.

However, for the keen fruit gardener, grafting can be a very satisfying way of producing new trees, and it is particularly useful when you wish to propagate a tree not easily obtained from a nursery, such as an unknown garden cultivar or a seedling that you have raised. Most fruit trees can be propagated by grafting. Some trees, such as hazelnuts, are easily propagated from suckers and make medium-sized trees on their own roots.

Grafting involves making a matching cut on both scion and rootstock –

different methods involve different cuts – and placing the cambium layer of each together. The cambium is the tissue between the bark and the pithy or woody centre of a stem, and it is capable of producing new stem cells. Because this tissue is delicate, once exposed by cutting it is vulnerable to bacteria and fungi. Keep grafting knives (*see p.57*) sterile and sharp to avoid infections. A tree from which you are propagating should be disease-free and growing well if good offspring are to be produced.

## Choosing a grafting method

The two simplest methods of grafting, with the highest success rates, are chip-budding and whip-and-tongue grafting. For both methods, rootstocks are needed. You can grow these yourself (*see p.153*), or buy them from a specialist nursery. If you are using several, plant them out in the dormant season 45cm (18in) apart in rows 1m (3ft) apart.

Chip-budding (*see box, below*) is usually carried out in mid- to late summer, and can be done the summer after the rootstocks have been planted. Whip-and-tongue grafting (*see box, facing page*) usually takes place in late winter to early spring, and can be done the year after the rootstocks have been planted.

## Aftercare of grafted trees

After grafting, ensure the graft does not dry out, and remove the tape once callus tissue has formed. As chip-budded shoots grow out, the new growth may need staking, especially on pears and plums. Once whip-and-tongue grafts have united, choose one shoot from the scion and tie it to a cane during the growing season. Remove any other shoots on the scion or on the rootstock when they are 8–10cm (3–4in) long.

For both methods, the resulting maiden trees can be lifted and planted out in the following dormant season.

## Chip-budding a tree fruit

1 **Collect scions** (here the apple 'Laxton's Superb') for budding in mid- to late summer. Choose well-ripened shoots of the current season's growth from the sunny side of the tree canopy, and cut lengths of 25cm (10in) or more.

2 **Remove the leaves** from the ripened part of the scion, or budstick, using a clean, sharp grafting knife. Leave 4mm (⅛in) long leaf stalks (petioles), but pick off any small sub-leaves (stipules).

3 **Prepare buds** from the scion at the site of the rootstock so that no time is lost between taking the bud and grafting it to the stock, minimizing the risk of it drying out. To remove a bud, first make a cut about 2cm (¾in) below a bud. The cut, known as a toe cut, should be about 3mm (⅛in) deep, and angled downwards at about 20°.

4 **Make a second cut** 3.5cm (1½in) above the first. Slice behind the bud and down to meet the first cut. Remove the bud chip (*see inset*), holding it by the bud so that you do not touch the cambium layer, which might infect it with bacteria or natural oil from your hand and so impair bonding of the graft tissues. Work quickly to minimize any moisture loss.

5 **Choose a smooth section** of the stock (here MM106) at 15–30cm (6–12in) above ground level. Make a toe cut just above a node or joint at the same angle and depth as that on the bud.

6 **Hold the bud** against the rootstock to judge where to start the second cut, then slice out a sliver of bark above the toe cut to match that on the bud (*see inset*).

7 **Position the bud** so that its base sits on the lip of the rootstock cut. Check there is good contact between the cambium layers of the scion and stock on at least 1 side. Move the bud to line up with the stock cambium on 1 side only, if necessary.

8 **Bind the bud** firmly to the rootstock by wrapping the entire area with 2.5cm (1in) wide plastic grafting tape. Make sure that the graft is completely covered so that it cannot dry out.

9 **Secure the binding** with a knot. Leave the tape in place for 4–6 weeks until a callus has formed around the bud, then cut the knot and unwrap the tape.

10 **In early spring** of the following year, cut off the rootstock just above the bud, using a sloping cut. The bud should then grow out and become a strong shoot.

1

# Side graft whip and tongue grafting method

1 **Collect scions** for grafting in midwinter. Cut some strong, hardwood shoots of the previous season's growth, about 23cm (9in) long, and keep them in a moist plastic bag in a refrigerator. Prepare the graft in early spring when the rootstock is coming into growth. Choose a healthy bud on the scion, and remove a sliver of wood 3cm (1¼in) long on the opposite side of the stem, with the bud half-way down the cut. Then create a tongue (*see inset*) by cutting into the exposed wood to a depth of 1cm (½in).

2 **Cut back the rootstock** to 15–30cm (6–12in) from the ground, making a gently sloping cut just above a smooth area of stem. On the high side of the sloping cut, remove a sliver on the stock to match that on the scion, and create a matching tongue (*see inset*).

3 **Gently fit the tongue** of the scion into that on the stock (*see inset*). If the scion is narrower than the stock, make sure the edges align on at least 1 side, and that the cambium layers fit snugly together.

4 **Bind the scion and stock** together firmly using 2.5cm (1in) wide grafting tape. On thin rootstocks the tape may cover the cut on the top of the rootstock, otherwise paint all exposed surfaces with grafting wax to prevent moisture loss. After 6–8 weeks, the graft should have formed a callus and the tape can be carefully removed.

# Pollination

Almost all of the fruit trees need to be pollinated to produce fruits. Some species of fig are the exception, producing fruit without fertilization taking place. Pollination involves the transfer of pollen from the anthers (one of the male parts of the flower) to the stigmas (one of the female parts of the flower). Then, under favourable conditions, fertilization will take place. It is vital to understand the pollination needs of the cultivars you wish to grow to ensure a good fruit crop.

## How pollination occurs

Flower structure and the method of pollination can vary. Most fruit trees have flowers that contain both the female parts – stigma, style, and ovary – and male parts – anther and filament, known collectively as the stamen. Within this group, some are self-fertile, that is, the flowers can be pollinated with the tree's own pollen. Often, however, pollen is not released at the same time as the stigmas are receptive, so pollen needs to be transferred from one tree to another.

Completely self-fertile tree fruits include most peaches and apricots, some plums and cherries, and a very few apples. Self-fertile cultivars usually crop more reliably if grown with a pollinator. No pears are truly self-fertile, but some bear seedless (parthenocarpic) fruits if not pollinated.

Some trees, even if their flowers have male and female parts, still need to be cross-pollinated. This involves a transfer of pollen from the flowers of one cultivar to those of a different cultivar of the same fruit that happens to be flowering at the same time. Most apple cultivars require cross-pollination with another cultivar to set a good crop.

Some fruit trees have separate male and female flowers on the same plant – these are known as monoecious plants. They include many of the nuts. Many of these are self-fertile trees, but they crop better if cross-pollinated, since the male and female flowers do not always open at the same time on the same tree.

A few fruit species have male and female flowers on separate plants – these are known as dioecious plants.

## The structure of a flower

This is an apple flower containing male and female reproductive parts. Most tree fruit flowers conform to this structure. Once a flower is pollinated, by insects or by wind, and fertilized, the seeds develop in the ovary, contained within the receptacle, and a fruit starts to form. This occurs in different ways. Apples and pears, for example, are formed of the expanded receptacle of the flower, whereas the flesh of apricots and peaches is formed of the swollen ovary wall.

**Style** *Pollen tube grows down style to fuse with female nucleus in ovary*

**Anther** *Carries pollen grains*

**Stigma** *One of female parts, on which pollen grains germinate*

**Petal** *Attracts pollinators and offers landing platform*

**Stamen** *Male part composed of filament and anther*

**Filament** *Stem of stamen*

**Pedicel** *Flower stalk*

**Receptacle** *Ovary, where seed develops after pollination, lies inside*

They include kiwi fruits. This means that, for pollination to occur, both male and female plants must be grown.

## Pollination compatibility

For cultivation, tree fruit cultivars are grouped into those that flower at about the same time (*see individual crops, pp. 174–205*). Most cultivars that flower at the same time are compatible with one another, although there are some exceptions, including some apples, pears, and a number of sweet cherries.

Most cultivars are diploids (with two sets of chromosomes) or, in a very few cases, tetraploids (with four sets of chromosomes); diploids and tetraploids will pollinate each other. The triploid cultivars, such as those found in some apples and pears, have three sets of chromosomes and are ineffective pollinators, needing to be grown with two other diploid cultivars that will pollinate one another and the triploid.

Some cultivars, particularly of pears, are male-sterile, producing little or no pollen, so are ineffective as pollinators.

## Conditions for pollination

Flower pollination and the subsequent fertilization occur only if the conditions at flowering time are favourable. Pollination takes place in various ways. Many fruits, including apples, pears, and plums, are insect-pollinated, by such pollinators as bumblebees, solitary bees, and honey bees. These insects are necessary for self-fertile plants as well as self-infertile ones to transfer pollen from one flower to another.

Wind-pollinated plants include cobnuts and filberts, and walnuts, all of which are monoecious. The male catkins on these plants produce lots of pollen to ensure successful pollination.

For pollination by both insects and wind, the site is very important, since wind speeds and temperatures can vary over a short distance. A sunny, sheltered site can be several degrees warmer than another site just a few metres away. Insect-pollinated plants need conditions that are warm and calm enough for pollinating insects to fly. Wind-pollinated plants need a fair degree of shelter, too. Conditions may be suitable for pollination on only a few occasions during the blossoming of early-flowering fruits such as peaches, apricots, plums, and pears. Fortunately, under favourable conditions, adequate pollination can take place in just a few days. Once pollination has taken place, fertilization will occur only if the air temperatures are warm enough for pollen tube growth to take place.

To improve chances of pollination, it may be necessary to provide an extra windbreak or hedges (*see pp. 12–13*). It is an advantage if honey bees are kept nearby, and it is possible to increase the numbers of wild pollinating insects, including solitary bees and bumblebees. This can involve leaving part of the garden with longer grass, and leaving some areas unweeded.

For solitary bees it is also possible to obtain bee nesting boxes. Providing nectar-rich plants throughout the year will maintain a good insect population. These include numerous native and traditional flowering plants. Plant species, rather than cultivars, tend to be more successful, and soft fruits, including redcurrants and cane fruits, also attract insects.

### Avoiding frost damage

One of the greatest barriers to achieving pollination, fertilization, and

**Multi-grafting**
*The branches of old and young trees can be cut right back in winter and several cultivars can be grafted onto the one tree.*

**Grafting**
*Plum tree cut back ready for grafting. The tree stump can be grafted into in spring or winter when cut down or, alternatively, new shoots can be allowed to grow for grafting or budding during the summer period.*

subsequent crops of fruit is frost. Most fruit trees are fully winter-hardy, but the developing buds, flowers, and fruitlets are very susceptible to frosts. Frost damage occurs at different temperatures, depending on the stage of development of the buds, flowers, and fruitlets (*see box, below left*). Temperatures at which this damage occurs differ with the fruit type and cultivar, some being much more resistant than others.

Fortunately, in a garden situation,

some frost protection can be provided. When planting, try to avoid frost pockets (*see p. 11*). Trees grown against walls or fences are the most easily protected. On nights when frost is forecast, a cover of double layers of horticultural fleece, shade netting, or hessian (or similar) can be rolled down to cover the tree. Support the cover with bamboo canes (or taut wires) so that it does not touch the tree. Secure this against the wind. Roll up the cover during the day to allow access by pollinating insects.

### Pollination alternative

One way to overcome pollination problems is to graft several cultivars onto the one tree (or buy a multi-grafted tree) so that pollen release is spread over a longer period. An additional advantage is that different cultivars will ripen at different times, spreading the harvest period as well and meaning that tree-ripened fruit is available for several months. Old or young trees can be cut back in winter so that grafting can be done.

### FROST DAMAGE TO APPLES

This table shows the temperatures at which frost damage occurs at various stages of growth in apple trees. It illustrates the general point that the later the stage of development, the more susceptible the tree.

| Stage of development | Temperature where damage occurs |
| --- | --- |
| Green cluster of buds | −3.5°C (26°F) |
| Pink (closed) bud | −3.0°C (27°F) |
| Full (open) bloom | −2.0°C (28°F) |
| Petal fall | −2.5°C (27°F) |
| Fruitlets forming | −1.0°C (30°F) |

### POOR POLLINATION

If trees flower well but do not bear fruit, poor pollination is likely to be the cause. Sometimes unpollinated flowers produce fruitlets, which will develop for a while and then drop off; this is particularly common with cherries and plums. There are several reasons for poor pollination:
- the absence of a suitable pollinating cultivar nearby
- unfavourable conditions for pollinating insects to fly, for example cool, wet, or windy weather
- frost at, or following, flowering time.

# Planting tree fruits

For the future development of the tree, it is important to plant correctly. For closely planted trees, prepare the entire area (*see pp.149–150*), ensuring that it is free of perennial weeds (*see pp.49–50*). It is best to do this at least two weeks before planting to allow it to settle. This is particularly crucial on soils that need improving, such as heavy clay or thin, sandy soils. For widely spaced trees, each planting hole can be prepared separately. Do this just before planting since, if a planting hole is left open for a while, it can fill with water or dry out, depending on the weather, or the sides become too solid for roots to penetrate.

Planting both bare-root and container-grown tree fruits is best done when the trees are dormant, between late autumn and early spring. Planting trees in late autumn is preferable if the soil is still warm because this allows some root growth before the winter. If the soil is waterlogged, however, delay planting until conditions improve (*see p.150*). Bare-root trees must be planted while dormant, while container-grown trees can in fact be planted all year round if necessary. If they are planted during spring and summer, they will need more attention to watering and may get off to a slower start.

## Staking freestanding trees

All freestanding trees require staking, at least initially. The stake supports the tree until the roots have developed enough to anchor it. For trees on semi-vigorous and vigorous rootstocks, the stake can be removed after one or two years, but trees on dwarfing and semi-dwarfing rootstocks need a permanent stake.

A softwood stake that has been pressure-treated or has been soaked with wood preservative should last for at least five years. Wear gloves when handling newly treated stakes. The length of stake and its angle depends on the type of tree you are planting.

## Planting a bare-root tree

1 **Dig a hole** wide enough to spread out the roots and deep enough so that the tree will be at the same depth as it was in the nursery. Check the depth with a spade or cane across the hole – the nursery soil mark is darker than the trunk above. If the planting area has not been prepared, add well-rotted manure or compost to the soil you have removed, plus a slow-release fertilizer, such as bonemeal.

2 **Remove the tree** and drive a sturdy stake about 60cm (2ft) into the soil.

3 **Place the tree** in the hole and refill the hole with soil a spadeful at a time, raising and lowering the tree as you fill so the soil settles around the roots.

4 **Firm down the soil** in the hole with your foot half-way through filling and again when you have finished, but avoid over-firming or stamping.

5 **Attach the tree** to the stake with a tie. Loop the tie around the tree and through the buffer, then fasten it and nail it to the stake.

6 **Mulch around the stem** of the tree with a 5–8cm (2–3in) layer of well-rotted compost or manure in a 45cm (18in) band around the tree, but do not let it touch the trunk.

Upright stakes should be driven in before planting, angled ones afterwards. Angled stakes are very useful for container-grown trees since they can be inserted clear of the rootball.

Pyramid and spindlebush trees on dwarfing and semi-dwarfing rootstocks will need permanent upright stakes 2.5m (8ft) long that are driven 60cm (2ft) into the ground. Bush, standard, and half-standard trees require short stakes, either about 1.2m (4ft) long and inserted vertically with 60cm (2ft) of the stake below ground, or 1.5m (5ft) long, driven at a 45° angle into the soil.

## Choosing tree ties

A tie should form a buffer between the stake and the tree – ideally with a gap of about 8cm (3in) – and should be easily adjustable or removable to allow for the growth of the stem.

There are two types of tree tie available. Use a short nail to secure the tie to the stake so it does not slip down. Check regularly that the tie does not constrict the trunk. Soft plastic tubing is widely used commercially. It is tied in a figure-of-eight knot, with the knot against the stake and fixed to it with a nail. These ties stretch so do not constrict readily, and are particularly useful where a number of ties are required. A chain-lock tie comes in the form of a plastic chain in different grades. Fasten the tie around the stake, then cross back through to form a buffer, fastening it on the tree. Check and adjust regularly since these ties can soon become constricting.

## Planting freestanding trees

The same basic method of planting can be followed for freestanding bare-root (*see facing page*) or container-grown trees. Water them well before planting. With container-grown trees, dig a hole a little larger than the rootball; you do not need to shake the rootball as you firm it. If container-grown trees are pot-bound, any thick, thong-like roots should be cut back and the other roots teased out to encourage them to spread.

When planting, always make sure that the graft union is well clear of the soil. This is to prevent the scion rooting: if the graft union is buried, the scion itself may root, and so the tree will in effect be growing on its own roots, negating

## Planting cordons against a fence or trellis

1 **Fix 3 horizontal wires** to the fence at 60cm (2ft) intervals, starting at 60cm (2ft) from the ground. Tie bamboo canes to the wires so that they are 75cm (30in) apart and angled at 45°.

2 **Dig out a semi-circular hole** at the base of each cane 15–23cm (6–9in) from the fence. Place the tree in the hole at an oblique angle. Ensure the graft union is above soil level and that the scion is uppermost, growing away from the cane; this discourages the scion from rooting. Fill in and firm the soil.

3 **Tie the stem** of the tree to the cane at intervals, using soft twine in a figure-of-eight knot.

the effect of the rootstock (*see p.153*).

If using a proprietary slow-release fertilizer to mix with the soil from the hole, always apply it in accordance with the manufacturer's instructions. On clay soils, fork gently around the edge of the hole after planting to break up any compacted or smeared soil.

## Planting trees to be trained

For trees to be trained as cordons, fans, and espaliers, whether they are against freestanding posts and wires or fixed to a wall or fence, supporting wires should be fixed in position before planting (*see p.162*). For all tree forms planted against a wall or fence (*see above*), plant the tree 15–23cm (6–9in) from the fence so that the roots can benefit from rainwater out of the shadow of the wall or fence. With bare-root specimens, spread out the roots and cut back those growing towards the wall or fence. Those planted by freestanding posts and wires can be planted just in front of the wires. Where a row of cordons is being planted, it is often easier to take out a trench rather than single holes. The trench size

depends on the size of the trees' root systems, but a trench 60cm (2ft) wide and 45cm (18in) deep is generally adequate.

## Mulching a newly planted tree

The mulch that you apply after planting conserves moisture and improves the organic matter content. If it is allowed to touch the tree stem, it could lead to diseases such as collar rot, canker (*see p.253*), or scion rotting. On very fertile soils, an alternative to organic matter is a sheet mulch of black film plastic or landscape fabric. To put this in place, cut a square of the sheet at least 30cm (1ft) larger on each side than the area of ground to be covered – so to cover an area of 120 x 120cm (4 x 4ft), cut a 150 x 150cm (5 x 5ft) piece of sheet. Cut a slit to the centre of the square from half-way along one side, to allow the sheet to fit around the tree. Place it around the trunk and secure by pushing the edges into slit trenches. Check the sheet is tight to the soil, and firm in.

# General care

Once you have planted your fruit trees, they need as close to ideal conditions as possible to grow well and produce good crops. This involves carrying out various routine tasks to meet their needs for water and nutrients, and making regular checks to ensure that the fruits develop without overcrowding, and that they are not attacked by pests or diseases.

## Timing of watering

The demands for water vary according to the tree's stage of growth and to the rainfall in a growing season. The most critical times for watering are after planting in the spring, and from early summer, as the fruitlets are developing, until they are ripe. From midsummer, water is also needed for the production of fruit buds for the following year. If the tree suffers drought stress at this time it may fail to flower the following year and so become biennial bearing. When this happens, a tree fruits heavily in alternate years, bearing little or no fruit in the years in-between.

Additional water applied as irrigation is required during prolonged dry spells, particularly on shallow and light soils. Even in a generally wet year there may be dry periods when irrigation is helpful. Water loss from plants and soil is greatest in early to midsummer when

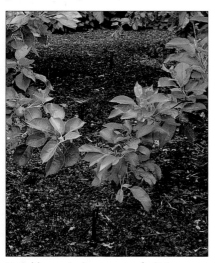

**Sprinkler watering among fruit trees**
*These apple spindlebushes planted in rows are being watered by mini-sprinklers attached to hoses. The sprinklers can be adjusted so that the spray covers the soil between the trees.*

## Thinning blossom and fruitlets

**Blossom thinning**
*On trees prone to biennial bearing, about a week or 10 days after flowering remove alternate blossom clusters. Use scissors or pinch out each blossom at the stem, leaving the leaves below undamaged.*

**Thinning fruitlets**
*Remove misshapen, damaged, or poorly positioned fruits first to leave large, healthy, well-shaped fruits. On plums (shown here), thin the fruitlets by picking to leave a single fruitlet every 5–8cm (2–3in).*

trees are in active growth, temperatures are highest, and sunshine hours greatest, but aim to water trees all through early summer and early autumn if there is a lack of water. Apply 5cm (2in) of water over the rooting area every two weeks – about 50 litres/sq m (11 gallons/sq yd). The rooting area extends to the perimeter of the tree canopy.

## Watering methods

Apply water economically and reduce water loss wherever possible. Ideally, irrigate at night when evaporation and consequent wastage is at its lowest. Surface mulches over the rooting area (*see facing page*) can be very effective in reducing water loss.

Drip irrigation from purpose-made hoses is a good method, particularly if trees are grown in rows or trained on walls or fences. There are several types available (*see p.54*), some of which leak along their length, while others have drippers at intervals and give out water at a controlled rate. Drip irrigation operates at low pressures, so pipes and outlets need to lie close to the trees.

Where trees are more widely spaced, low-level sprinklers are useful because the spray can be adjusted to fit the tree spacing. Both systems can be set up to

work at intervals using timers if needed. If you water manually using a watering can or hose, water thoroughly every two weeks rather than little and often.

## Blossom and fruit thinning

In favourable conditions, fruit trees set more fruit than is ideal. Overcropping results in small, low-quality fruit, poor growth, and stress on the tree. This sometimes causes biennial bearing since the tree is unable to produce flower buds for the next year. In extreme cases overcropping can cause the tree to die.

To counteract biennial bearing where this is known to be a problem, thin the blossoms (*see above*), either removing alternate clusters, or removing most in a cluster. Some gardeners remove blossom from alternate trees in alternate years to overcome this problem. Others use chemical sprays to burn flowers. Blossom removal on very young trees is not recommended.

Fruit thinning should be done as a routine task in early to midsummer to leave the fruits at the optimum spacing (*see individual crops, pp.174–205*). The earlier the thinning, the better the increase in fruit size, since thinning when cell division is still taking place in the early stages of fruit formation has the greatest effect. Many trees drop some fruit naturally but further thinning is usually required (*see facing page*). It is the amount and spacing of the fruit left on the tree that matters, not how many fruits you remove. Depending on how many fruits set in a season, you may not need to thin; in heavy cropping years, you will need to remove several times the number left on the tree.

## Feeding tree fruits

All plants need a supply of nutrients (*see p.17*) to grow and fruit well. Fruits vary in their nutrient needs (*see individual crops, pp.174–205*). Some, such as stone fruits, pears, and culinary apples, require more nitrogen than others for growth, while most fruit trees have a fairly high demand for potassium – vital in fruit bud and fruit development.

Magnesium is often important since some fruits – especially vines, apples, peaches, and raspberries – are prone to magnesium deficiency (*see p.257*), particularly on thin, free-draining soils.

The major nutrients can be applied as inorganic or organic fertilizer and as mulches (*see below*), although the latter provide limited feed value. To correct magnesium deficiency, use magnesium sulphate, also sold as Epsom salts. You can apply this direct to the soil or, for a more rapid response, in solution to leaves at a rate of 20g/litre (½oz/pint). Adding a proprietary wetting agent improves the effectiveness of spraying. To avoid leaf scorch, do not spray in bright, sunny conditions.

## Mulching and weed control

There are two basic types of mulch: organic and inorganic (*see pp.41–42*). Organic mulches are useful on most soils to maintain a good level of organic matter in the soil, helping to keep the soil free-draining and improving its moisture and nutrient retention. A thick layer will also help with weed control. Inorganic mulches are excellent for weed control, although they may lead to a depletion of organic matter in the soil in the long term. On thin, dry soils, inorganic sheet mulches work best with drip irrigation (*see p.54*) beneath them.

Growth and cropping suffer if there is strong competition for water and nutrients. Weeds and grass compete if they are too close to a fruit tree, as do ornamental plants and vegetables. Trees on dwarfing rootstocks are particularly susceptible to competition. Mulching is one of the best ways of weed control; for other methods, *see pp.49–50*.

Trees on semi-vigorous rootstocks can be grown in grass, but they need a weed-free area of 60cm–1m (2–3ft) and, for the first four years, an annual mulch 5–8cm (2–3in) deep to a radius of about 45cm (18in). Trees on dwarfing and semi-dwarfing rootstocks grow best in clear ground. A surface mulch of organic matter is beneficial. Those grown against supports should have a weed-free strip of 60cm (2ft) along the fence or wall or on either side of freestanding posts and wires.

## Protecting your crop

Kangaroos, wallabies, possums, and rabbits can kill or damage young trees by girdling the tree: this is when a ring of bark is eaten around the tree, killing it by preventing moisture and nutrients from travelling up and down the trunk. Young shoots can also be eaten. If possums, kangaroos, wallabies, or rabbits are present, the ideal solution is to fence off the whole garden to exclude them.

To be rabbit-proof, wire fencing of a 2.5cm (1in) mesh needs to be buried vertically 30cm (12in) deep with 30cm (12in) laid horizontally to form an L-shape underground. It should extend above ground by 90–120cm (3–4ft). If this is not possible, a guard around each tree is effective. There are several types: a plastic or galvanized metal mesh guard is best as it allows air circulation. Close-fitting, wrap-around plastic guards are available, but are less satisfactory since they produce damp conditions around the stem, which can encourage canker infection, and they may cut into and restrict the stem. After four or five years, the stem and bark become thick enough to be of no interest to rabbits.

To protect against animal damage, taller wire fencing is needed, of 2m (6ft) or over. Where the area cannot be fenced, only half-standard or standard trees are suitable for growing because the branches will be above browsing height.

## Protection against birds

As tree fruits ripen, they need protection from birds (*see also p.251*). Trees on dwarfing rootstocks and those grown against a support can have a net draped over them, with a cane structure to keep it off the fruits. For an area of fruit trees, a fruit cage can be made, 2–2.2m (6–7ft) high or higher, with a structure of wooden posts and draped netting. Apples, pears, and plums are susceptible to birds attacking fruit buds, so need protection in winter and early spring.

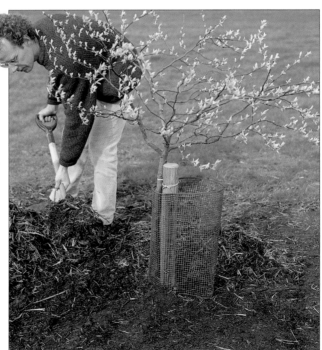

**Mulching and rabbit protection**
*Each spring, spread a layer of mulch around each tree. Use well-rotted manure, compost, or bark chippings about 5–8cm (2–3in) deep and extending around the tree as far as the canopy. Here, a plastic mesh rabbit guard attached to the stake keeps the mulch away from the trunk. If the mulch should lie against the trunk, it may create damp conditions, increasing the risk of disease infection and of the scion rooting.*

# Pruning and training principles

Pruning is the cutting away of growth to keep a plant healthy, and influence its shape, size, flowering, and fruiting. Training encourages a plant to grow in a specific shape and direction, often so it is more productive. When a fruit tree is young, it needs formative pruning to create a healthy branch framework of the shape needed to carry crops in the future. When mature, it usually needs routine pruning so that it bears regular crops of good fruit of a good size. At all stages, pruning is not as complex as it may at first seem. It is crucial to understand the basic principles to get the best possible crop from your tree. Bush and pyramid forms need pruning but little training. Spindlebushes require more pruning and training than the bush and pyramid, but not as much as the restricted forms. Cordons, espaliers, and fans need both pruning and training.

## Supports for different tree forms

Freestanding forms require staking (*see pp.158–159*). Restricted tree forms need to be trained onto horizontal

wires. The wires can be attached to a wall or fence or between freestanding posts. The support framework and wires need to be erected before planting so that you can start training the newly planted tree at once. Use galvanized wire for the supports. For fan-trained trees the wires should be 14-gauge, or 1.2mm (1/16in) in diameter, and spaced 15cm (6in) apart horizontally; for espaliers use 12-gauge, or 2.5mm (1/8in) in diameter, wires that are spaced 45cm (18in) apart; and for cordons, which are about 2m (6ft) tall, you need three 12-gauge wires spaced 60cm (2ft) apart.

### Attaching support wires
*To fix horizontal wires to a brick or stone wall, use eye bolts secured to the wall with expanding bolts. Insert the expanding bolt into a drilled hole and then screw it in to trigger the outer casing to expand to fit the hole tightly. Fix the wires to straining bolts slotted through the eye bolts.*

Eye bolt in casing

Bolt casing

Eye bolt

There are a number of ways of fixing wires to fences or walls. Space the fixings about 2m (6ft) apart along the fence or wall. They need to be held 4–10cm (1½–4in) away from the surface to allow air to circulate. A useful method for walls is to use expansion bolts screwed into the wall and straining bolts fixed through these. Alternatively, screw 10–15cm (4–6in) vine eyes into plugs in the wall or directly into a wooden fence. Fit straining bolts to the vine eyes at one end to adjust the wire tension. Always take care when straining wires: use safety goggles as eye protection, and avoid overstraining the wires since this may cause them to snap.

If a number of closely spaced wires are needed for fan-trained trees, wires can be stapled directly to wooden posts or fixed to wooden battens in walls. Since there are more wires used, straining bolts should not be needed.

## Making a freestanding support
Support frameworks can be of timber or metal posts and must be substantial to withstand the strain put on them by mature trees. The height depends on the tree form chosen and is commonly 2–2.2m (6–7ft). Space posts up to 4m (12ft) apart; the spacing between the posts needs to be at least half the width of the mature tree. At either end, strengthen the post by using a diagonal strut at 45 degrees, and fix it firmly two-thirds of the way up the stake.

If you are using timber posts as uprights, ensure that they have been treated with preservative and are at least 8cm (3in) in diameter. The bases should be sunk at least 45–60cm (18–24in)

## Recognizing the parts of a fruit tree

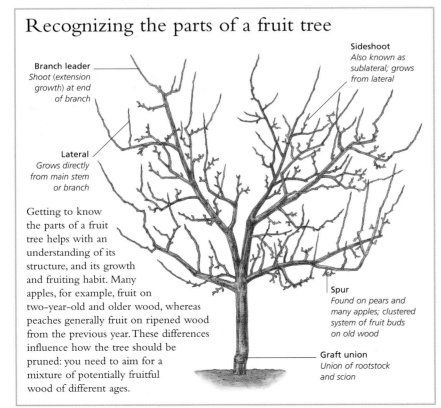

**Branch leader**
*Shoot (extension growth) at end of branch*

**Sideshoot**
*Also known as sublateral; grows from lateral*

**Lateral**
*Grows directly from main stem or branch*

Getting to know the parts of a fruit tree helps with an understanding of its structure, and its growth and fruiting habit. Many apples, for example, fruit on two-year-old and older wood, whereas peaches generally fruit on ripened wood from the previous year. These differences influence how the tree should be pruned: you need to aim for a mixture of potentially fruitful wood of different ages.

**Spur**
*Found on pears and many apples; clustered system of fruit buds on old wood*

**Graft union**
*Union of rootstock and scion*

# Making a good pruning cut

Base of cut is not below level of bud

Correct cut

Rainwater can roll off away from bud

Exposed large surface heals slowly

Over-large, sloping cut

Base of cut below bud weakens it as it grows

Flat surface allows water to collect

Cut too far from bud

Stub above bud will die back

Rough cut

Wood has been crushed and will be prone to disease

When pruning, it is important to make cuts correctly to avoid damaging or impairing growth or introducing disease. The cut needs to be in the appropriate place in relation to a healthy bud or to the branch, and it should be clean to promote swift healing. Always use clean, sharp cutting tools.

◁ **Good and bad pruning cuts**
*A correct cut is made just above a bud, sloping at a gentle angle away from it. This allows the bud to grow away strongly to form a new shoot. Cutting too close to, or too far from, the bud allows disease to enter the wound.*

Branch collar

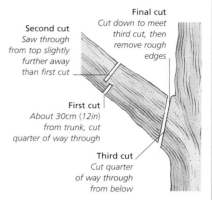

Final cut
Cut down to meet third cut, then remove rough edges

Second cut
Saw through from top slightly further away than first cut

First cut
About 30cm (12in) from trunk, cut quarter of way through

Third cut
Cut quarter of way through from below

△ **Removing a large branch**
*When removing a big branch, it is vital to cut it away in sections to prevent the wood splitting or tearing under its own weight. Leave the branch collar intact to aid healing.*

◁ **Branch collar**
*When removing a branch at the point of origin, look for a slight ridge at the base of the branch, known as the collar. Cutting back to this allows the wound to heal naturally. If the branch is cut flush with the stem, it will wound the framework of the tree. Leaving a larger snag beyond the collar causes dieback and often a cavity.*

into the ground or into metal post supports. Galvanized angle iron is ideal for metal uprights; these need to be sunk to a similar depth.

For metal or timber posts, fix the wires to a straining bolt through one end post, thread them through holes drilled in intermediate posts, and fix them to the other end post.

## Checking tree supports
Permanent ties on freestanding trees on dwarfing or semi-dwarfing rootstocks, or on restricted forms, should hold the tree in position without constricting it, and provide a buffer against the stake or wire. Neither stake nor wire should rub against the tree in case it damages the bark, providing an easy entry point for disease. Check all ties and stakes in spring and during the growing season, adjusting or replacing them as needed.

## Pruning tools
Your tools should be kept clean and sharp to make the best pruning cuts. You need secateurs for basic pruning of

shoots, loppers for larger growth, and a pruning saw for larger branches (*see also p.57*). Pruning saws are either straight-bladed or have a curved blade – called a Grecian blade – and are much easier to use in a tight space than other saws.

## Aims of pruning
Basically, pruning is carried out to keep the structure of the tree strong and open, allowing light penetration and air circulation. This promotes the growth and ripening of new shoots and fruits, and helps to reduce pests and diseases.

Pruning also aims to remove dead, diseased, and damaged wood to protect the health of the tree. Any dead and damaged or broken wood may attract disease, and wood that has already become diseased may infect the rest of the tree. Any affected branches should be cut back to healthy material, but if the infection has affected only one-third or less of the circumference of the branch, and the branch is essential to the structure, it is possible to treat it by cutting away the diseased area to

healthy tissue with a sharp knife; disinfect the knife after use.

Stone fruits are often affected by bacterial canker (*see p.253*). Affected branches should always be removed by cutting them back, either to the point of origin of the branch or to a suitable side branch at least 30cm (12in) below the infection.

Any crowded and crossing branches should be removed to maintain the open shape of the tree. If branches start to rub against one another, they may chafe the bark, causing wounds through which disease may enter. Cutting equipment must be sterilized after use on infected trees to help prevent diseases spreading.

Selective pruning produces a supply of new wood to replace the old wood that has been removed. It also controls the height and spread of the tree, and maintains it in the required form and in satisfactory vigour. Vigour is also greatly affected by training (*see p.164*). Finally, pruning aims to promote the formation of fruit buds (*see p.164*), taking account of the tree's fruiting habit.

# Removing crossing, broken, and diseased wood

△ **Diseased branch**
*This tree has canker, which will affect the entire branch above the infection. Remove the branch back to its point of origin to prevent the canker from spreading into the tree.*

△ **Crossing branches**
*Where two branches are crossing, choose the one that is best placed – that is, growing outwards away from the centre of the tree – and remove the other by cutting it back to the base where it joins the main framework.*

▷ **Broken branch**
*A branch may be broken by chafing with another branch, by its own weight, or by high winds. Whether it snaps off or is still attached, the wound is vulnerable, and so the branch needs to be removed back to the branch collar.*

To achieve a balance between growth and cropping, it is vital to understand how trees respond to different pruning intensities. Pruning too hard results in vigorous growth and light crops of large, poor-quality fruits, which do not store well. Underpruning or lack of pruning results in poor growth and large crops of small, poor-quality fruits that are mainly borne at the top of the tree. Any fruit lower down will tend to suffer more from pests and diseases. Underpruning or neglect can also lead to biennial bearing (*see p.160; see also* Pruning to a bud, *facing page*).

## Aims of training
Horizontal growth tends to be less vigorous but more productive than upright growth, with more fruit buds, and so more fruit, being produced on horizontal branches. Much of the training of fruit trees is intended to maximize horizontal and low-angled growth, and several trained forms, such as the espalier, have been developed with this in mind. On the spindlebush (*see pp.169–170*), branches are tied

down for the same reason. Training, along with pruning in many cases, also aims to make the management of the tree easier, with fruits more exposed to sunlight and accessible for picking.

## When to prune?
Pruning times vary according to the form and the type of fruit being grown (*see individual crops, pp.174–205*). In general, apples and pears are pruned in summer or winter, according to the tree form being grown, whereas stone fruits should be pruned only in spring or summer, when risk of infection from silver leaf and bacterial canker is lowest. Pruning in winter or early spring promotes new, vegetative growth, while summer pruning produces little growth.

## Recognizing fruit buds
There are two types of bud found on a fruit tree: fruit buds and vegetative buds. Vegetative buds, also known as growth buds, produce non-fruiting growth. Fruit buds, or flower buds, are larger than vegetative buds because they contain embryonic flowers.

**Different types of buds**
*This pear shoot clearly shows one-year-old vegetative buds, and two- and three-year-old fruit buds. The age of the wood can be seen by the growth from the previous pruning cuts.*

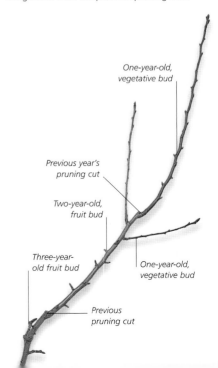

One-year-old, vegetative bud

Previous year's pruning cut

Two-year-old, fruit bud

Three-year-old fruit bud

One-year-old, vegetative bud

Previous pruning cut

A good supply of fruit buds is crucial to the fruiting of any tree, so that the tree has enough to produce good crops. On the other hand, if the tree has too many fruit buds, the resulting crop may be too heavy and will strain the tree physically, possibly breaking branches. An overly abundant crop will also divert energy from the development of fruit buds for the following year.

Fruit buds of apples and pears contain a vegetative bud as well as a flower; the vegetative bud produces a shoot from directly behind the flower, known as a bourse shoot. Due to their natural habit and careful pruning, some apples and pears develop short, woody fruit bud systems, or fruiting spurs.

*Prunus* species (plums, acid and sweet cherries, peaches, nectarines, apricots, and almonds) have separate fruit and vegetative buds. These are found either as single, separate buds or, more often, as double or triple buds, with both fruit and vegetative buds grouped together. The fruit buds tend to be plumper and rounder, while the vegetative buds are more pointed in shape.

## Pruning to a bud
In general, always prune to a vegetative bud. For apples and pears, if this is not possible, you can prune to a fruit bud since there is a vegetative bud behind it. For stone fruits, it is simpler to look for a double or triple bud since you can be more certain of having distinguished a vegetative bud from a fruit bud.

The fruit buds on young shoots are generally of better quality and will produce better fruit than those on old wood. One-year-old shoots often do not produce fruit buds to fruit the following year, although this depends on the fruiting habit of the tree. Those that do fruit on wood produced the previous year include tip-bearing apples (*see p. 175*) and pears (*see p. 182*), as well as peaches (*see pp. 193–195*) and acid cherries (*see pp. 191–192*).

On trees that bear fruit mainly on two-year-old or older wood, such as spur-bearing apples and pears, and plums, it is still important to retain as many one-year-old shoots as possible when pruning since these will bear fruit in the future. In this way you will ensure a good supply of fruiting wood.

*Shoot lacks fruit buds*

*Very vigorous new growth*

*Single extending shoot*

*Fruiting spur*

*Light prune*          *Heavy prune*

### Responses to pruning
*In the shoot on the left, light pruning has produced some extension growth and fruiting spurs on the two-year-old wood. In the example on the right, harder pruning has resulted in vigorous, branching growth, but no more fruit buds.*

## Degrees of pruning
One-year-old shoots respond differently to varying levels of pruning. Unpruned, they produce some growth at the tip – extension growth – and fruit buds, but do not branch much. Light pruning results in a little extension growth, some branching, and fruit buds. Moderate pruning causes more extension growth, strong branching, and some fruit buds. Hard pruning produces vigorous growth, little branching, and no fruit buds. If you decide to remove a one-year-old shoot, remove it at the base without leaving a stub, otherwise the stub will produce strong, new growth.

In general, the harder you prune, the more vigorous is the resulting growth because the tree is trying to restore the balance between the root system and

the aerial parts of the tree. Growth is needed for replacement wood and new fruit buds, but not too much; you need to decide the type of growth you want before choosing how hard to prune.

## Pruning aftercare
Many fruit trees are treated routinely with a wound paint to seal wounds after pruning. Various paints are available for wound dressing. These come in the form of aerosols, spread-on paints or waxes. For stone fruits with cuts over 1cm (½in), seal each wound with a proprietary wound paint immediately after pruning. This helps stop infection from silver leaf or bacterial canker, both of which may enter through the newly exposed wood of pruning cuts.

# Spur thinning
The many apple and pear cultivars that bear their fruits on knobbly fruiting spurs will need spur thinning from time to time, when the spurs become congested. Overcrowding of fruit buds on the spurs prevents fruits from developing to their full size and the spurs may be more disease-prone if they touch. To thin an overcrowded spur system, use secateurs to remove any old, weak, or very congested spurs altogether. Thin out the growth on the remaining spur systems until only strong spurs bearing plenty of fruit buds remain.

*Before thinning*          *After thinning*

# Pruning different tree forms

To create the tree form that you would like, whether it is a freestanding tree such as a bush or pyramid, or a restricted form, such as a cordon or fan, it is necessary to start the appropriate pruning and training soon after planting the tree. Formative pruning is first needed to produce a tree of the desired shape. This pruning is fairly severe to produce strong growth and a good branch framework that can carry future crops. As the tree matures, the pruning becomes lighter to encourage cropping rather than growth. The early years are crucial, for a lack of careful formative pruning can result in a mature tree that is difficult to manage.

This section lays down the principles for pruning all the basic shapes of fruit trees at the formative and mature stages. Most pruning is undertaken in the winter while the tree is dormant. Any differences in timing, and pruning and training techniques, are covered in individual crop entries (*see pp. 174–205*).

## Formative pruning of a bush, half-standard, and standard tree

For trees grown in the open, the most common form is the open-centre tree. This can be a bush, a dwarf bush, a half-standard, or a standard (*see p. 152*). The pruning is similar for all of these forms, the difference being the height of the stem before the branches start.

The bush form described below is suitable for trees on all but the most vigorous rootstocks. Prune apples and pears immediately after planting in the dormant season and prune stone fruits in mid-spring.

In the first year the pruning depends on the type of maiden (one-year-old) tree obtained. A maiden whip, which is a single stem with no branches, will take a year longer to develop than a feathered maiden, which has a single stem with a number of side branches arising from it, allowing quicker formation of the basic bush shape. During the growing season, little is needed in the way of additional formative pruning; simply remove any badly placed, unwanted shoots. The aim of formative pruning is to build and extend the basic branch framework of the bush. A maiden whip should start fruiting in the fourth summer, and a feathered maiden in the third.

To train a standard or half-standard, you will need to grow on the main vertical stem for a season or two to reach the desired stem height of 1.35m (4½ft) for a half-standard, and 2m (6ft) for a standard. Retain the sideshoots until the main stem is the correct height, then train as for a bush.

## Formative pruning of a bush

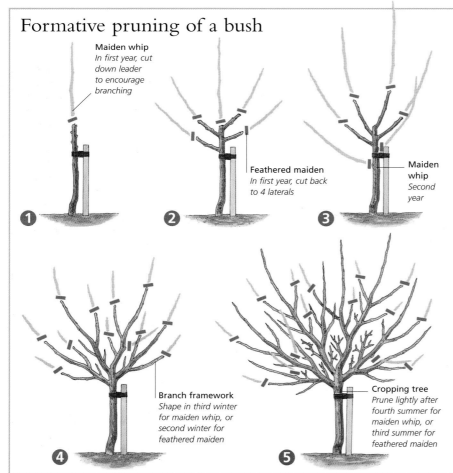

**Maiden whip**
*In first year, cut down leader to encourage branching*

**❶**

**Feathered maiden**
*In first year, cut back to 4 laterals*

**❷**

**Maiden whip**
*Second year*

**❸**

**Branch framework**
*Shape in third winter for maiden whip, or second winter for feathered maiden*

**❹**

**Cropping tree**
*Prune lightly after fourth summer for maiden whip, or third summer for feathered maiden*

**❺**

**1** **Starting with a maiden whip,** prune to a bud at about 75cm (30in) from ground level. Ensure there are at least 4 consecutive plump buds beneath it.

**2** **Starting with a feathered maiden,** choose a wide-angled lateral at about 75cm (30in) from ground level with 3 or 4 well-spaced laterals (feathers) directly below it. Remove the central stem above your chosen lateral. Shorten the 3 or 4 laterals below the cut, by about two-thirds of their length, to buds facing in the required direction – an upward-facing bud if the shoot is near to horizontal, and an outward bud if the shoot is near to vertical. Sideways-facing buds can also be chosen. Remove any low laterals not needed for the basic framework.

If a feathered tree has only 1 or 2 sideshoots, remove them and then treat the tree as for a maiden whip.

**3** **In the second winter** for a maiden whip, between 3 and 6 strong shoots should have been produced. Select the best 3 or 4 to form the primary branches. The top 1 or 2 shoots are often nearly vertical so it is better to cut these back to a lower shoot that forms a wide angle to the stem – this wide angle will make the branch stronger. Shorten each selected branch by about two-thirds to a bud

## Pruning and training an established bush

After the fourth year, annual pruning becomes lighter. There are several ways to treat the mature tree according to the fruit type and its fruiting habit. Fruit trees can be broadly divided into three groups for pruning purposes, based on the age of wood on which they fruit. Most apples and pears fruit on spurs borne on older wood; they require spur pruning once they are mature to encourage new spurs to form year by year and keep trees productive.

Tip-bearing apples and pears, as well as peaches, nectarines, and acid cherries, fruit on growth made the previous year. Apples and pears, as the name implies, fruit just at the tips of the new growth. All need renewal pruning to encourage a steady supply of new wood, while maintaining a strong framework.

Plums, sweet cherries, and apricots fruit at the base of the previous year's wood as well as on older wood, and do not respond well to annual pruning once mature; however, regulative summer pruning will sometimes be required to keep a balanced canopy.

Winter pruning stimulates growth – the harder the pruning, the stronger the growth. The aim is to achieve a balance between cropping and growth. A young tree making strong growth is pruned lightly, while a tree producing weak, drooping growth is pruned hard, until its vigour improves (*see box, below*). For spur bearers, the amount of pruning depends on the vigour of the tree.

Renewal pruning, for tip-bearing apples and pears, and for stone fruits, is lighter than spur pruning, focusing on keeping an open tree shape, and making new fruiting shoots (*see box, below*).

As the tree becomes older, whatever its fruiting habit, it is necessary to carry out regulative pruning. Remove any crossing, crowding, dead, and diseased branches (*see p.164*). Keep the centre open but not bare of fruiting wood, removing some large branches, but leaving fruiting spurs and laterals. If the tree is becoming too large, reduce its height and spread by cutting back to a lower placed branch or replacement branch that is growing in the required direction, which should be at least one-third of the diameter of the piece being removed. On spur bearers, thin out spur systems as they become overcrowded (*see p.165*).

For more detail on pruning specific fruits, *see individual crops, pp.174–205.*

### Overvigorous bush trees

Summer pruning is not usually carried out on bush trees, but it can be effective in controlling overvigorous trees, since pruning when the tree is in leaf restricts growth. Prune well-ripened laterals longer than 30cm (12in), cutting them to a bud at about 15cm (6in). This will encourage fruit bud formation on the remaining shoots and allow better light penetration and air circulation through

facing in the required direction. Remove any shoots that are below the desired framework back to the stem.

**4** **By the third winter** for a maiden whip, or the second for a feathered maiden, the branch framework will be well-developed. Pruning should be lighter at this stage. Shorten each branch leader by one-third to a suitably placed bud. Select 1 or 2 further shoots per branch to form secondary branches, and shorten these by one-third. Any other shoots can be either shortened to about 4 buds to form spurs, or removed if they are badly placed. Remove shoots growing into the centre and cut back to the stem any shoots below the framework junction.

**5** **By the fourth summer** – or the third for a feathered maiden – the tree will probably have started cropping, and so lighter pruning is required during the following winter. The framework will still need to be extended, however. To do this, select a further leader from each branch and secondary branch and shorten by about one-third of its new growth. Leave shoots of 23cm (9in) or less unpruned if there is space, and shorten longer shoots to 4–6 buds to continue spur formation. Remove any badly placed shoots altogether.

## Pruning an established bush

◁ **Spur pruning**
*Shorten each branch leader by one-third of the previous year's growth to a bud facing in the required direction. This should produce branching and new spurs along the leader. If the leader is very vigorous, do not prune it, or at most, lightly tip prune it. Leave laterals under 15cm (6in) unpruned, and remove those over 30cm (12in). Prune the remaining laterals to about 6 buds.*

Prune laterals to encourage spurs to form

**Renewal pruning** ▷
*Remove unproductive or crowded branches. On apple and pear tip bearers, tip prune the branch leaders, without removing too many fruit buds. Leave laterals less than 30cm (12in) long unpruned, and shorten other laterals to produce more shoots, or remove them altogether. Remove low-growing shoots.*

Cut out older, fruited wood

Tip prune only branch leaders of apple and pear tip bearers

the tree. Start pruning in late summer as shoots ripen, and continue into early autumn as the remaining laterals lengthen and become woody.

A vigorous tree pruned in this way will require minimal subsequent winter pruning which would only stimulate growth. If necessary remove branches to keep the centre of the tree open.

## Renovating a neglected bush

A regularly pruned tree is easier to manage and will maintain a balance between cropping and growth, producing regular crops with fruit of a good size. A tree neglected for several years is likely to suffer from a lack of light and air circulation, leading to weak growth; there will be few fruits in the lower part of the tree, and a build-up of pests and diseases. There may also be a number of very tall branches, taking the best fruit out of easy reach.

Before attempting renovation, weigh up whether it is really worthwhile. If the tree is very diseased, with diseased and dead branches, it may not be worth keeping. If it is very large it may be too difficult to restore and require the help of a tree surgeon. If a fruit tree is dominating the garden or is heavily shaded by nearby trees and buildings, it might be easier to remove it and replace it with a number of trees on dwarfing rootstocks, which would be easier to manage and more productive. You may just wish to leave the tree untouched as a feature of the garden but, if it is generally sound with a good original framework, renovation should be possible.

There are two types of neglected tree – the overvigorous, large, and crowded one, and the starved, stunted tree – and two different approaches to pruning are required. For large, overvigorous trees, thin the canopy over a couple of years (*see below*). Do not remove more than one-third of branches in one year. If needed, delay pruning of some until the third year, when you can remove more water shoots (strong, upright shoots with few buds) that will have arisen and more crossing branches. In the third year, you may start routine pruning.

Starved and stunted trees usually have a mass of weak fruiting spurs and little or no young growth. The cropping and fruit quality is usually poor. To improve matters, thin out all of the spurs by about a half and remove any dead or diseased branches. This will stimulate some growth to replace worn-out branches and create new spurs and new, healthy fruit buds.

## Feeding a neglected bush

The soil surrounding a neglected tree may be depleted of nutrients. This will compound the problems of poor growth, poor leaf quality, and weak fruit buds. Such trees will need feeding annually after renovation; use a balanced feed containing trace elements at a rate of 70g/sq m (2oz/sq yd). After three or four years, change to a fertilizer generally recommended for the crop (*see individual crops, pp.174–205*).

---

# Renovation pruning a large neglected bush

With overvigorous, large, and crowded trees it may be necessary to spread the renovation over two or three years. This is because hard pruning in one go can result in even more vigorous growth at the expense of fruit. Flowers will fail to set and shoots will grow out in their place. It is then often difficult to get the tree to settle down into fruiting again. By spreading out the pruning, the imbalance in growth and cropping will not be as great.

**1 Before renovation,** the tree is a mass of twiggy growth, a mixture of healthy and diseased wood that allows for little air circulation within the canopy.

**2 In the first year,** remove any dead, diseased, or broken branches. Also remove some other branches to improve light penetration and air circulation. It is important to remove any crowding in the centre of the tree and to ensure that you create a balanced shape. When removing branches, prune back either to the point of origin or to a branch at least one-third of the diameter of the piece being removed. Do not remove old fruiting spurs or laterals at this stage, even if they are of poor quality, as they may produce some flowers and fruit and so control the tree's vigour.

**3 In the second year,** strong vertical shoots (water shoots) may be produced around large cuts. Leave some unpruned if a new branch is required, otherwise remove them at their base. They can be removed in mid- to late summer or in the dormant season for apples and pears, or spring for stone fruits. In the dormant season, reduce the height if required, cutting back to a smaller branch at least one-third of the diameter of the one being removed, and cut out any crowding and crossing branches.

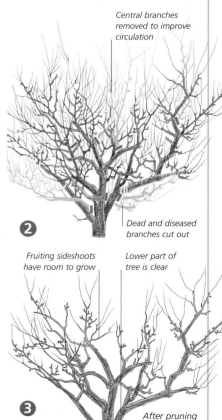

❶ *Twiggy, vertical shoots crowd centre of tree*

*Too many branches obscure basic framework*

❷ *Central branches removed to improve circulation*

*Dead and diseased branches cut out*

❸ *Fruiting sideshoots have room to grow*

*Lower part of tree is clear*

*After pruning*

# Formative pruning of a spindlebush

**1** **In the first winter,** starting with a feathered maiden tree, choose 4 evenly spaced laterals about 60cm (2ft) from the base. Remove any laterals below the chosen 4; leave any shorter laterals above these. Prune the leader to a bud at about 10cm (4in) above the topmost lateral. Do not prune the laterals if they appear strong, but if they are growing weakly, prune each to a downward-facing bud.

**2** **In the first summer,** if the laterals are making vigorous growth, tie them down to about 20 degrees from horizontal in late summer; otherwise leave them to grow naturally.

**3** **From the second summer,** tie down any new laterals arising from the main stem or existing branches if they are not already growing at a low angle. Remove at their bases any strong vertical shoots that are spoiling the overall shape of the tree.

**4** **In the fourth winter,** if any of the upper branches start to grow too wide, spoiling the tree's conical shape, prune them back to a weak, low-angled lateral. Also, shorten lower branches if they are competing with nearby trees. Remove or thin congested branches or shoots to keep light and air circulating.

Ensure main stem is firmly staked

Prune weaker shoots to encourage growth

Remove low-growing shoots

**1**

Cut out at the base vigorous uprights that cannot be trained horizontally

Tie leader to stake as it grows

Ties of soft string secured to wire hoops or metal pegs

**2**

Remove strong vertical shoots

Check existing ties are not chafing

Tie in new horizontal growth

**3**

Remove older, fruited branches

Thin growth by removing some spurs

**4**

## Formative pruning of a spindlebush

The spindlebush is a conical form with a central leader and staggered tiers of productive, almost horizontal branches. This form, which needs a permanent, tall stake (*see p.159*), is suitable for pears and apples. For formative pruning of a feathered maiden, see above. If you are starting with a maiden whip, prune it to a bud at 75cm (30in) in the first winter. The following summer, tie in the leader to the stake and, if needed, tie down the laterals that have developed (*see p.170*) to train them about 20 degrees above horizontal. From then on, treat as for a newly planted feathered maiden.

In the first two or three winters, prune the leader by one-third of its new growth – less if it is very vigorous, more if it is not. Cut it to above a bud, on the opposite side to the previous winter's cut, to form an upright central leader and to promote laterals below. Remove any shoots below the lowest tier and any upright, poorly placed shoots. If it is growing well, the tree should start to bear fruit in the second summer (or the third summer for a maiden whip). Thin the fruit (*see p.160*) to avoid the tree being overloaded. By the third summer, the tree should be cropping and reach its full height of 2–2.2m (6–7ft). Continue tying down branches as necessary and removing any strong vertical shoots as before.

## Pruning an established spindlebush

By the fourth winter, the tree should have developed its mature cone shape, with a wide tier of lower branches and shorter upper branches. From now on, the aim of pruning is to keep the cone shape so that light reaches all parts.

Prune an established spindlebush on a renewal basis in winter to give a supply of young wood that will maintain the tree's vigour and replace older branches. The branches in the upper part of the tree are not permanent. After three or four years, cut out a proportion as they

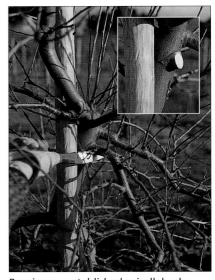

**Pruning an established spindlebush**
*In winter, prune out older growths. Cut out the old stems back to the main central leader, using a cut at a 45-degree angle to the trunk – a Dutch cut. This leaves a stub (see inset) of about 2.5cm (1in) to stimulate a new shoot to grow from the dormant bud beneath it.*

become too long and make the tree's shape unbalanced. Treat fruiting laterals from the lower branches in the same way. If the laterals are crowded, remove them entirely or leave an angled stub to encourage a new replacement lateral. In winter or late summer, remove strong shoots that are competing with the leader, and any growing vertically from the branches. In late summer or spring, continue tying down new shoots.

Do not allow the leader to become too tall (over 2.2m/7ft) or dominant. If necessary, replace a dominant leader by cutting back to a weaker lateral and tying this up in its place. If the leader is crooked, it is an advantage: non-vertical growth tends to be less vigorous.

## Tying down spindlebush branches

There are several ways to tie down the branches so that they grow horizontally. Use strong but fairly soft string, such as three-ply twine. Avoid tying the string tightly around the branch – use a loop instead. Tie lower branches to pegs in the ground or to a nail low down on the stake. Upper branches can be tied down to the lower branches. Remove the strings once the branches have set in position, usually after a few weeks.

An alternative for one-year-old branches is to lower them by attaching a weight to a clothes peg or a loop of wire at the end of the string.

## Formative pruning of a pyramid and dwarf pyramid

The pyramid form, which requires a permanent stake (*see p.159*), consists of a central leader with branches radiating from it to form a cone shape. Economical with space, its shape allows the sun to reach fruits on the upper and lower parts of the tree. It is particularly popular for plums because the pruning can be carried out in the spring and summer, but it is also good for apples, pears, sweet and acid cherries, peaches, and apricots. The method shown here is for plums, sweet cherries, and apricots. Pruning differs slightly for the other fruits due to their fruiting habits (*see individual crops, pp.174–184, 191–195*). A dwarf pyramid is trained as for a pyramid, but is on a more dwarfing rootstock, available for apples and pears.

Formative pruning aims to establish the basic tree shape and a spreading, outward habit. If possible, start with a well-feathered maiden (*see box, below*). If you are starting with an unfeathered maiden, prune to a bud at about 90cm (3ft) and follow the instructions for a feathered maiden from the next spring.

## Pruning an established pyramid

It is important to maintain the pyramid shape of the tree. Any vigorous vertical shoots will become dominant and shade the more horizontal, fruiting branches and so should be removed in summer.

---

# Pruning a pyramid

**1** **In early to mid-spring** following planting, cut back to a bud at 10–20cm (4–8in) above the topmost feather. Remove any feathers below about 45cm (18in) from the ground. Cut the remaining feathers to a bud at about half their length. For strong feathers choose a downward-facing bud, and for weak feathers an upward-facing bud.

**2** **In the first summer,** tie in the central leader to the stake. In mid- to late summer, when the young shoots have stopped growing, prune the current season's growth of branch leaders back to above a downward-facing bud at about 20cm (8in). Cut back laterals growing from the branches to about 15cm (6in), preferably to a downward-facing bud. Repeat until established.

**3** **In early to mid-spring** of the following years until the tree is established, cut back the central leader by two-thirds of the previous summer's growth to a bud on the opposite side to the previous year's pruning.

**4** **Once the full height** has been reached (this depends on the tree and its rootstock), towards the end of each summer when growth has stopped, prune any shoots at the top of the pyramid to about 2.5cm (1in). At the same time, prune the current season's growth on branch leaders to about 20cm (8in) to a downward-facing bud. Cut back laterals arising from the branches to about 15cm (6in), also to a downward-facing bud.

Permanent 2m (6ft) stake

Use secure, padded ties

Cut to downward-facing bud for outward growth

Cut or pinch out any low laterals growing from the main stem

Cut leader on opposite side to previous year's cut for straight stem

Keep growth short at top of pyramid

Check that ties are not chafing – loosen as needed

Cut out inward-growing shoots

Cut out any unhealthy shoots

Remove some older, crowded branches

# Summer pruning of restricted tree fruit forms

Summer pruning, also known as the modified Lorette system, is undertaken on the restricted forms – cordons, espaliers, and fans – for apples and pears. It restricts growth, maintains the tree's shape, and encourages the formation of fruiting spurs. Timing is important. Pruning needs to be carried out as the growth slows down in late summer, and may need to be done gradually over a few weeks. At this time the shoots start to form terminal buds and the stems are becoming woody. The exact timing varies with each season and between different areas. It is earlier in warm, dry, sunny conditions, and later in cool, wet areas and seasons. If pruning is carried out at the correct time, some of the remaining buds will become fruit buds – these are produced from late summer to early autumn. If summer pruning is carried out too early, weak leafy growth will be produced at the expense of fruit buds. If this happens, cut the weak new growth back to one leaf in early to mid-autumn.

1 **First look for** any of the current season's laterals that are more than 23cm (9in) long. If the lateral is growing from another lateral or spur, cut it back to 1 leaf or about 2.5cm (1in) above the basal cluster – the basal cluster is the small group of leaves where the new season's growth starts.

2 **If the lateral is growing** directly from a main branch, cut it back to 3 leaves or 5–8cm (2–3in) above the basal cluster.

3 **Leave unpruned** until early autumn any shoots that are not well ripened or that are less than 23cm (9in) long. After pruning (*see the right side of this 'Ashmead's Kernel' apple fan*), the form of the tree will be restored, allowing the light to reach the developing fruits and ripen the remaining wood for the next year.

As the tree matures, you may need to remove or shorten branches that start to spoil its shape. Do this in mid-spring, cutting back to the point of origin or a suitable branch at least one-third of the diameter of the piece being removed.

## Formative pruning of an oblique cordon

The oblique cordon consists of a single stem trained at an angle, with fruiting branches and spurs. It is very productive and the quickest form to fruit, usually producing some fruit in the second summer, and is suitable for apples, pears, and plums. It is also possible to grow apples and pears as vertical or multiple cordons (*for details, see p.176 and p.182*).

The best tree to obtain for training is a feathered maiden or a two-year-old part-trained cordon. Otherwise, start with a maiden whip. For instructions on planting, *see p.159*. If you are starting with a feathered maiden or part-trained cordon of apple or pear, *see p.172*.

If you are starting with a maiden whip, lightly cut back the tip of the leader to an upward-facing bud to promote sideshoots, then prune as for a feathered maiden from the following winter. In the first spring for a feathered maiden (or second for a whip), remove any blossom to prevent the tree fruiting too early and allow it to establish well. After the initial winter pruning, no further pruning in winter is needed until the tree is well established. For variations for plum cordons, *see p.186*.

## Pruning an established oblique cordon

Summer pruning is needed annually to restrict new growth, while winter pruning is needed from time to time to thin any crowding and congestion (*see p.172*). For pruning established plum cordons, *see p.186*.

## Formative pruning of a multiple-T espalier

An espalier is a symmetrical form with pairs of branches extending horizontally at about 45cm (18in) intervals from a central, vertical trunk. This form is good for apples, pears, and mulberries.

Start with a maiden whip and, during the first winter, prune the stem at 45cm (18in) from the ground where there are four healthy buds below. This height should roughly correspond with the level of the first wire (*see p.162*). Insert a vertical cane to the height of the top wire, and tie the stem to it. Fix two short canes to the wires at 45 degrees on either side. From the first summer on, or if you have bought a part-trained espalier, follow the instructions on p.172.

## Pruning an established espalier

When the tree has enough tiers to reach the top of the wires, remove the leader in summer after you have started to train the final tier. This allows you to keep it as an insurance until the shoots have been trained in on either side, and allows them to develop at a wider angle to the stem. Over the next few years, continue to train in the leaders of the tiers of the branches until they have reached the required length, leaving the extension growth unpruned. Prune the rest of the laterals and any new shoots on the basic summer pruning system (*see box, above*).

As the espalier matures, it may be necessary to carry out some spur thinning in winter (*see p.165*). Full cropping will not be reached until all the tiers of the espalier are formed.

# Pruning an oblique cordon

**1 Following planting,** prune back any laterals longer than 10cm (4in) to 3 buds. Leave the leader and any shorter laterals unpruned.

**2 From the first summer onwards,** the main pruning takes place in the summer, following the basic summer pruning for restricted forms (*see p. 171*). Tie the leader into the cane as it develops during the summer, leaving it unpruned.

**3 Each summer,** follow the basic summer pruning guidelines, tying in the leader to the cane until it has reached the required length – this is usually about 2m (6ft) from the ground, which is the height of the top wire. If space allows, lower the cordon to 35–40 degrees to provide a greater length and so a greater crop. When the leader has reached its final length, prune it back and treat subsequent growth as for other laterals.

**4 Winter pruning** may be necessary after a few years. Thin out and reduce crowded spur systems (*see also p. 165*) over a period of several years since winter pruning stimulates growth.

Leader is tied in and left unpruned

Pruning laterals encourages spur formation

Tree is angled at about 45 degrees on planting

If graft union faces upwards, scion is less likely to root

New laterals from existing lateral pruned to 1 leaf above basal cluster

New laterals from main stem pruned to 3 leaves above basal cluster

New laterals pruned to 3 leaves above basal cluster

Thin spurs to leave healthy, well-spaced fruit buds

Completely remove or thin old, congested spur

Laterals from spur pruned to 1 leaf above basal cluster

Shoots are woody at base before being pruned

# Pruning a multiple-T espalier

**1 In the first summer,** select 3 strong shoots and, as they develop, tie one to each cane. Remove any others. In early autumn, lower the shoots and canes on either side so that they are horizontal, and tie them to the wires.

**2 In the second winter,** look for 4 healthy buds at the level of the second wire, and prune the leader just above the topmost of these. Fix a cane to the wires on either side at 45 degrees, ready for the next tier. Repeat each winter until all the tiers are formed.

**3 In the second summer,** tie in 2 shoots to produce the next tier, and tie the central leader to the vertical cane. Prune any sideshoots on the first tier or main stem on the basic summer pruning system (*see p. 171*) in late summer when the shoots are mature. In the autumn, the shoots trained at 45 degrees can be lowered to the horizontal. Repeat this process of training in and lowering the arms each summer until all the tiers are formed, pruning the existing arms on the basic summer pruning system.

If other shoots grow, prune to 2 or 3 leaves

Lower shoots tied to canes in early autumn

Prune leader to bud just above wire with 3 good buds below it

Tip prune weaker growth for vigour

Lower shoots tied to canes in early autumn

Prune shoots from main stem to 3 leaves from basal cluster

Tie in leaders as they develop

**Mature apple espalier**
*This 'Ellison's Orange' apple is 40 years old and continues to crop well on its established espalier framework.*

# Formative pruning of a fan

**1 Starting with a maiden whip,** prune in winter to a bud at 38–45cm (15–18in) with 3 or more consecutive healthy buds beneath it. Fix 2 canes to the wires, one on either side, at 45 degrees. In the growing season, train in a shoot on either side, fixing it to the cane. Once these are growing well, remove any other shoots. Often the topmost shoot needs to be removed as it is near vertical.

**2 Starting with a feathered maiden,** cut the tree back in winter to 2 sideshoots at 38–45cm (15–18in). Shorten these by two-thirds to an upward-facing bud. In the growing season, treat the tree as a second-year maiden whip.

**3 In the second year** for the maiden whip, prune back the 2 shoots by about two-thirds of their length to an upward-facing bud in winter. During the growing season, train in the new growth, attaching it to the cane. Choose 2 equally spaced shoots on the upper side and 1 on the lower side of each branch and tie these to canes fixed to the wires.

**4 In the third year** for the maiden whip (second year for a feathered maiden), cut back the 4 shoots on each side by one-third of their length to an upward-facing bud. During the growing season, tie in leaders from each branch to the canes. Select more shoots from each branch to extend the framework as space allows. Rub out shoots growing inwards.

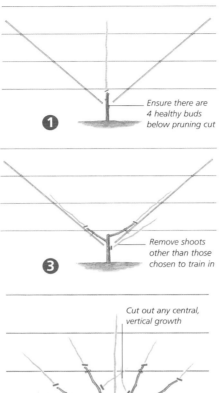

❶ Ensure there are 4 healthy buds below pruning cut

❸ Remove shoots other than those chosen to train in

Cut out any central, vertical growth

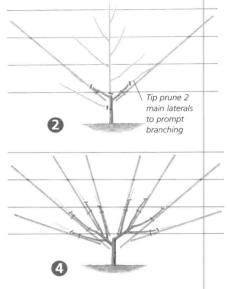

❷ Tip prune 2 main laterals to prompt branching

❹

◁ **Pruning a part-trained fan**
Choose a tree with a well-balanced framework (usually 2 or 3 main branches on each side). If there is a strong shoot in the centre, cut this out after planting. At the same time, remove any unwanted shoots on each side or any growing directly away from the wires to leave an equal number of shoots on each side (between 2 and 4). Shorten these by one-third to an upward-facing bud. During the growing season, prune as for step 4, above.

## Formative pruning of a fan

A fan tree has a short vertical stem and two main arms that bear a network of permanent ribs and sideshoots spread out evenly on each side. There is no central leader as this vertical growth would tend to dominate the rest of the tree. This form is suitable for all tree fruits including almonds, although the timing and details of pruning will vary according to the specific fruit (*see individual crops, pp.174–205*). Basic formative pruning, essential for a well-balanced framework, is the same for all.

Fans can be developed from a maiden whip, feathered maiden, or from a part-trained fan obtained from a nursery. In all cases, follow the instructions given above. When choosing a feathered maiden, make sure it has two suitably placed shoots opposite one another to form the first two branches of the fan.

## Pruning an established fan

From the fourth year onwards for a maiden whip, or from the third if pruning a feathered tree, you should aim to extend the branch framework while keeping a strong, balanced shape. How you should treat individual shoots varies according to the fruit type being trained (*see individual crops, pp.174–205*).

## Renovation of fans, espaliers, and cordons

If the basic summer pruning (*see p.171*) of restricted forms is neglected for only a few years, trees can soon lose their shape, developing branches that are unbalanced and detract from the vigour of fruiting branches. Renovation may not be worthwhile if the form is lost, except in the case of figs (*see p.198*). If the tree is healthy and the original shape still clear, it can be restored.

Renovation will take one to three years, depending on how overgrown the tree is. In the winter, for apples and pears, or spring for stone fruits, cut back any branches not needed for the framework to the point of origin or to a spur near the base. Cut back all the growth at the top of the tree to bring it down to the level it should be. Thin any congested spurs (*see p.165*). If there is a lot to do, spread the pruning over three years to avoid producing too much vigorous growth; remove every other unwanted branch in the first year and the rest in the second and third. If the top tier of an espalier has become dominant, remove it and train a new tier in its place (*see formative pruning, pp.171–172*). In the summer after pruning, start to prune new shoots as for routine summer pruning (*see p.171*) and continue in subsequent years to restrict growth.

# TREE FRUIT CROPS

# Apple

Apples (*Malus domestica*) are the most versatile of the tree fruits. A wide range of dessert and culinary cultivars ripens in different seasons, offering fruit from midsummer to mid-spring, provided that they are correctly stored.

Apples originated in Central Asia, and so are adapted to cold winters and can be grown in the open in most areas. There are cultivars suited to most sites and soils. A sunny, sheltered site is best, with shelter if needed (*see pp. 12–13*). Planting in a frost pocket (*see p. 11*) should be avoided. Most apples tolerate a range of soils if they are well-drained with a pH of about 6.5. Poorly drained and shallow soils, and soils of unsuitable pH (*see p. 18*) can be improved.

## Choosing a tree form

Apples can be grown in a diverse range of tree forms on a wide choice of rootstocks. Some forms are more suited to one of the two types of fruiting habit (*see facing page*) and this might influence your choice of apple cultivar. Suitable freestanding forms are the standard, half-standard, bush, spindlebush, and pyramid. The bush suits both tip and spur bearers, whereas a spur bearer is the best choice for the spindlebush and pyramid forms. The latter both need permanent staking (*see pp. 158–159*).

Apples also thrive in the restricted cordon, espalier, and fan forms, all grown on a wire framework, either with freestanding posts and wires or against a

**Classic apple**
*There is a great range of apple cultivars to choose from, including old favourites such as this crisp 'Cox's Orange Pippin', widely grown since the mid-nineteenth century.*

wall or fence (*see p. 162*). Because fruits are borne on spurs along the stems of cordons, espaliers, and fans, a spur bearer is again the best choice for these forms. Cultivars for multiple-T espaliers may be available part-trained (usually with two tiers), which saves two years of pruning and training. However, the choice of rootstocks and cultivars is limited, and part-trained trees are more expensive than maidens. Part-trained fans are available, but it is more likely that you will have to buy a maiden tree.

Standard and half-standard trees are suitable for larger gardens and orchards. They make tall trees, which are more difficult to prune and pick. For most sites, a bush is a better choice. The spindlebush is a useful form for small gardens and container growing. The pyramid and dwarf pyramid forms are also ideal for the small garden, casting less shade than a bush tree, and producing well-coloured fruits.

Of the restricted forms, the cordon allows a range of cultivars to be grown, even where space is limited. Espaliers and fans are both decorative and suitable for the average garden. Some apple cultivars are sold as Ballerina trees. These are genetically bred to have compact, columnar growth (*see p. 177*) so they can grow in small spaces.

## Choosing a rootstock

The rootstock you choose, combined with the tree form, will have a decisive effect on the final size of the apple tree. It is essential to choose one that is appropriate for the space you have available and the amount of fruit you wish to grow (*see chart below, and p. 153*).

The very dwarfing rootstock M27 is ideal for vigorous cultivars, particularly triploids (*see p. 156*). It is less suitable for very weak cultivars, such as 'Sunset'.

| SPACINGS FOR APPLE TREE FORMS AND ROOTSTOCKS | | | | | | | | |
|---|---|---|---|---|---|---|---|---|
| Type of rootstock and vigour | Standard | Half-standard | Bush | Spindlebush | Pyramid | Cordon | Multiple-T espalier | Fan |
| M27 very dwarfing | – | – | 1.2–1.8m | 1.5–1.8m | 1.2–1.5m | 75cm | – | – |
| M9 dwarfing | – | – | 1.8–3m | 1.8–2.1m | 1.5–1.8m | 75cm | – | – |
| M26 semi-dwarfing | – | – | 2.4–3.6m | 1.8–2.25m | 1.8–2.1m | 75cm | 3.0–3.6m | 3–3.6m |
| MM106 semi-vigorous | – | 3.6–5.5m | 3.6–5.5m | 2.4–3.0m | 2.1–2.4m | – | 3.6–4.5m | 3.6–4.5m |
| MM111 semi-vigorous | 4.5–6.5m | 4.5–6.5m | 4.5–6.5m | – | – | – | 4.5–5.5m | 4.5–5.5m |
| M25 vigorous | 6–9m | 6–9m | – | – | – | – | – | – |

Horizontal cordons (*see p. 176*) need to be on an M27 rootstock. Trees on M27 need good soil, no competition from weeds or other plants, and permanent support (*see pp. 158–159 and p. 162*).

Trees on the dwarfing rootstock M9 also need permanent support and must have no competition from weeds or other plants. M9 is a good choice for spindlebushes, pyramids, and cordons on good soil, and for vigorous cultivars.

M26 is a semi-dwarfing rootstock, reliable for most conditions. It is ideal for bushes, spindlebushes, in the ground or in a container, as well as for dwarf pyramids, cordons, and small espaliers up to three tiers. Freestanding trees on M26 need staking for one or two years.

The semi-vigorous MM106 is widely used, especially for bush trees, multiple-T espaliers, and fans. Freestanding trees on MM106 need staking for a year or two. Ballerina trees are sold on MM106 rootstocks. MM111 is useful for half-standards, bush trees, and espaliers, particularly on poorer soils. M25 is very vigorous and is not used to any great extent in Australia. Trees on this rootstock are large even on poorer soils, and slow to start fruiting.

## Pollination

Apples flower in mid- to late spring, depending on the season and cultivar. This is not early compared with other tree fruits, but they are vulnerable to damage by late spring frosts. In frost-prone areas, choose late-flowering cultivars (*see chart, p. 180*) or those with some resistance to frost (*see chart, p. 179*).

Almost all apples are, to some extent, self-infertile and so will not set a good crop with their own pollen. They crop more consistently when pollinated by compatible cultivars. There are some exceptions, which are self-fertile and will fruit despite flowering after all other common cultivars.

Most apples are diploid (*see p. 156*), and need another pollinator to set a good crop. Some are triploid (*see p. 156*) and must be planted with at least two compatible diploid cultivars to ensure successful pollination.

Apple cultivars are grouped according to the time at which they flower. For good pollination, choose cultivars from the same group if possible (*see p. 180*), although those from adjacent groups will also serve as pollinators. Some cultivars are cross-infertile, generally because they are closely related, such as 'Cox's Orange Pippin' with 'Kidd's Orange Red', 'Holstein', or 'Suntan'; and 'Mutsu' with 'Golden Delicious'.

Sports (natural mutations) of cultivars, such as colour sports, russet sports, and the self-fertile clone of 'Cox's Orange Pippin', usually flower at the same time as the cultivar from which they originated. Trees grown in neighbouring gardens and ornamental *Malus* trees can act as pollinators if they flower at a suitable time.

## Planting

The best time to plant apples is in the dormant season (*see pp. 158–159*). Prepare the stakes and wires (*see p. 162*) required for the form you have chosen before planting. Bare-root plants will usually establish well. You can also plant container-grown apples, but before you buy, check that they are not pot-bound.

## Pruning and training

The fruiting habit of the cultivar (*see below*) dictates which pruning methods are needed for the mature tree. It is important to prune correctly in order to avoid removing the following year's fruit buds. If pruning an unknown cultivar, you can identify its fruiting habit by looking at where the fruit buds (*see p. 164*) arise. Partial tip bearers may demand a combination of pruning methods to obtain the best crop. Most pruning is carried out in winter while the tree is dormant. Summer pruning is done on restricted forms.

Some forms, such as standards, half-standards and bush trees, may be pruned as described on pp. 166–168. Some details of pruning a mature apple

## Fruiting habits of apples

Apples generally fall into different groups according to their cropping pattern. Note that some of the following cultivars are not available in Australia.

**Spur bearers:** 'Arthur Turner', 'Ashmead's Kernel', 'Beauty of Bath', 'Charles Ross', 'Cox's Orange Pippin', 'Edward VII', 'Ellison's Orange', 'Howgate Wonder', 'James Grieve', 'Lane's Prince Albert', 'Lord Derby', 'Reverend W. Wilks', 'Ribston Pippin'

**Tip and partial tip bearers:**
'Bramley's Seedling',
'Cornish Gilliflower',
'Discovery',
'Irish Peach',
'Kerry Pippin',
'Worcester
Pearmain'

**Tip bearer**
*Tip bearers bear fruits at the tip of each shoot. Partial tip bearers produce some spurs as well as fruit buds at the shoot tips. Both types of tip bearer are best grown as bush trees.*

**Spur bearer**
*Spur-bearing apples bear their blossoms and fruits on sideshoots, or spurs, along the main branches. This habit is more convenient for all forms, but is especially useful for pyramids, cordons, and multiple-T espaliers.*

bush will depend on the fruiting habit of the tree (*see right*). The pruning of spindlebush apples (*see pp. 169–170*) is carried out in the dormant season to promote vigour, and in the summer to restrict growth. For pruning of apple oblique cordons and espaliers, *see pp. 171–172*. For formative pruning of a fan, *see p. 173*. Once a fan is established, shoots that are not needed to extend the framework are pruned using the summer pruning system (*see p. 171*).

## Pruning an apple pyramid and dwarf pyramid

Once the basic framework is formed, pyramids are summer pruned to control vigour and maintain a compact shape. A dwarf pyramid, grafted on a dwarfing rootstock, is pruned similarly. Pruning apple pyramids differs slightly from the basic pruning method (*see pp. 170–171*) and in the timing, with additional formative pruning being done in the winter while the tree is dormant. If possible, start with a feathered maiden.

In the first winter, shorten the main stem to a bud at 60cm (2ft). Shorten any sideshoots over 15cm (6in) long to a bud at 13cm (5in), and remove any that are less than 45cm (18in) from the ground. In the first summer, tie the developing leader to the stake. In the second winter, shorten the leader to 20–25cm (8–10in) of the previous season's growth, to a bud facing in the opposite direction to that chosen in the first winter. Shorten branch leaders and laterals to 15–20cm (6–8in) to a downward- or outward-facing bud.

From the second summer, start summer pruning (*see p. 171*), but prune branch leaders to 5–6 leaves above a basal cluster and a downward-facing bud. In subsequent winters, shorten the central leader to 20–25cm (8–10in) of the previous season's growth until the

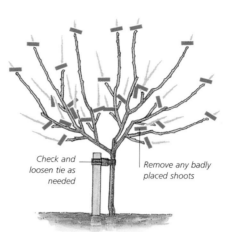

*Check and loosen tie as needed*

*Remove any badly placed shoots*

**Pruning an established bush (spur bearer)**
*In winter, shorten the branch leaders by a quarter to one-third of the season's growth. Prune the sideshoots to 4–6 buds. This pruning should stimulate formation of fruiting spurs from the sideshoots.*

full height of 2–2.2m (6–7ft) is reached. On a mature tree, pruning is done in the summer. You may need to do some winter spur thinning (*see p. 165*) or remove branches that spoil the shape.

## Pruning a horizontal apple cordon

The horizontal cordon is trained into a single wire suspended 45cm (18in) from the ground and secured to posts, so that the tree forms a low barrier, hence the name "stepover". For a continuous boundary, trees are usually spaced 1.5–2m (5–6ft) apart, with support posts that are 3–4m (10–12ft) apart.

To start training, select a very young, weak maiden whip that is flexible enough to bend over. Plant the whip next to a support post, or a stout cane if it is in-between posts, and tie the tree to it. In the spring after planting,

**Pruning an established bush (tip bearer)**
*In winter, cut out some of the older branches that have fruited for several years to make space for younger ones. Cut the branch to where it meets an outward-facing young shoot or back to the trunk to stimulate a dormant bud.*

carefully bend the tree until it is horizontal, and tie it into the wire at several points. From the first summer, when the tree should have developed several sideshoots, prune as for an oblique cordon (*see pp. 171–172*). During the summer leave the leader unpruned and prune any other shoots on the summer pruning system (*see p. 171*). Tie the leader extension growth to the wire in early autumn. Repeat this until the leader has reached the required length, then treat it as any other shoot when following the summer pruning system.

## Pruning a vertical apple cordon

This form, sometimes also called a minarette, can consist of one, two, or several stems (three is not advisable as the central stem tends to become dominant). To obtain a single-stemmed cordon, plant a maiden tree next to a vertical stake that is 2.5m (8ft) long and has been driven 60cm (2ft) into the ground. Prune the tree as for an oblique cordon (*see pp. 171–172*), except that the leader should be pruned by one-third of the new growth each year until it reaches its mature height of 2–2.5m (6–8ft). This pruning method stimulates the production of laterals and fruiting spurs.

**Horizontal apple cordon (stepover)**
*This highly decorative tree form makes an unusual and productive edging to a path or bed. It requires summer and winter pruning to maintain its restricted form and ensure a good supply of fruit.*

For a multiple cordon with two stems, plant a maiden whip against wires as for an oblique cordon (*see p.159*), but place it vertically. Prune to about 45cm (18in) from the ground in winter. In the first summer, train one shoot on each side at about 45 degrees, then lower these to the horizontal in autumn. In the second winter, prune both branches to about 40cm (16in). In the second summer, tie the leaders of both branches to vertical canes and start to train both leaders as for a single vertical cordon.

For a multiple cordon with more than two stems, in the second summer choose two shoots at the end of each branch. Train one of each pair of shoots upright, and one at 45 degrees. In the following autumn, lower the shoots from 45 degrees to the horizontal, and proceed as for a two-stemmed cordon.

### Training a cordon over an arch
This is an ornamental and effective way of training a cordon. At first it is trained as a vertical cordon, with the stem going up the side of the arch. Once the cordon reaches the curve, it is trained as an oblique cordon. Summer pruning restricts it and maintains its shape.

### Pruning a Ballerina tree
If any sideshoots are produced on the Ballerina, use the summer pruning system (*see p.171*). Once the required height of 2–2.5m (6–8ft) has been reached, remove the leader. Thin out the spurs (*see p.165*) in winter.

### Feeding
Apples usually benefit from an annual application of potassium and nitrogen. Apply sulphate of potash in late winter at 35g/sq m (1oz/sq yd). Top-dress with nitrogen at the same rate in early spring, using calcium ammonium nitrate on acid soils or sulphate of ammonia on alkaline soils. For trees in grass, and for culinary apples, you will need to increase the rate of nitrogen; if the leaves are pale rather than mid- or dark green, double the application. A compound of 1:1:2 N:P:K can be used at 70g/sq m (2oz/sq yd) instead of straight fertilizer.

Every third year, apply phosphorus in the form of super phosphate at 70g/sq m (2oz/sq yd) in late winter. Sprinkle the fertilizers over the tree's rooting area; that is, to just beyond the branch canopy. You will need to moderate these quantities if a mulch such as well-rotted manure or compost is used, or if the trees are growing vigorously.

Trees can also be fertilized with organic and rock mineral fertilizers. Apples can suffer from magnesium deficiency – which appears as a yellowing between the leaf veins in early summer. Correct by spraying magnesium sulphate (*see p.161*), giving two further sprays at 14-day intervals. If this problem occurs regularly, apply magnesium sulphate to the soil at 70g/sq m (2oz/sq yd) in mid-spring.

### Mulching
Apply an organic mulch to young trees for the first three or four years, and then annually for trees on dwarfing rootstocks on thin soils. Apply in spring while the soil is moist, at a depth of 5–8cm (2–3in) over a radius of 45cm (18in), keeping it clear of the stem (*see p.161*). For closely planted trees on dwarfing rootstocks, mulch the area with a 2.5–5cm (1–2in) layer of a light organic material, such as chipped bark or straw. On fertile soils with a high organic matter content, sheet mulches (*see p.42*) are a useful alternative to organic ones. Like organic mulches, they should cover a 45cm (18in) radius.

### Watering
Apples grow best in a moist, freely drained soil. Newly planted and closely planted trees, and restricted forms grown on dwarfing rootstocks can quickly become short of moisture in drought conditions. Water in prolonged dry periods in spring and summer and also while the fruits are swelling in midsummer. Water can be supplied in several ways (*see pp.53–54*). For rows of trees, such as cordons, drip irrigation hoses are particularly efficient.

### Fruit thinning
Given favourable conditions at their flowering time, most apple trees set a lot of fruit, but a heavy crop of small, poor-quality fruits can lead to biennial bearing with the tree unable to produce fruit buds for the following year. Most apple cultivars shed some of their fruitlets in early summer. However, if there is a heavy set, most require further thinning, particularly young trees that are still extending their framework.

Start thinning (*see p.160*) in early to midsummer with the earliest ripening cultivars. The earlier the thinning, the greater the increase in fruit size. Remove the king fruit – this is the central fruit of a cluster; it tends to be misshapen and have a short stalk.

**Ballerina apples**
*A Ballerina tree is bred to grow in a vertical, columnar shape with compact, fruiting spurs and few long sideshoots. It requires little summer pruning.*

Vigorous trees are likely to bear more fruit than weakly growing ones. Use the following as a general guide. Thin dessert apples to one or two fruits every 10–15cm (4–6in), and culinary apples to one fruit every 15–23cm (6–9in). Dwarf trees growing on M27 and M9 rootstocks should usually be thinned to one fruit per cluster.

## Harvesting apples

Apple yields vary according to the form in which trees are grown, the cultivar, rootstock, and growing conditions. For an apple bush tree, you may expect an average of 27–55kg (60–120lb) per tree, for an apple spindlebush or pyramid 13.5–22.5kg (30–50lb), for a single cordon 2.25–4.5kg (5–10lb), for an espalier 13.5–18kg (30–40lb), and for a fan 5.5–13.5kg (12–30lb).

If left on the tree to ripen, most apples can be eaten straight from the tree, but many cultivars benefit from storage before they are eaten. Correct timing for mid- and late-season apples is important. Pick too early and they

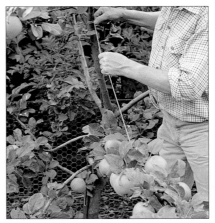

**Supporting fruit-laden branches**
*Where branches are particularly heavily laden, tie string around the centre of the branch and secure the other end to a temporary cane through the middle of the tree or to the trunk.*

will not have developed their full flavour and may shrivel in store. Pick too late, and they will not store well. The time of ripening varies with season and site, and is partly affected by the rootstock. Pick apples only when they

are ready (*see facing page*), and avoid bruising them. You will need to pick several times: the well-coloured apples on the sunniest side of the tree first and those towards the centre last. Some signs that fruits are ripe are that they may change colour, or there may be some first windfalls, or the pips turn from white to straw-coloured to brown – although some early apples are eaten before the pips turn brown. Harvest apples carefully. Line a bucket with soft paper, straw, or hay, or use a special picking bucket (*see below*).

## Storing apples

Storage conditions are important, but need not be sophisticated. Apples require a cool, dark, frost-free, and rodent-proof place with some humidity. There should be some air circulation: too much can cause shrivelling, while too little can deprive apples of oxygen. An ideal temperature is 2.5–4.5°C (36–38°F); make sure it does not exceed 7°C (45°F). Cellars, sheds, and unused garages are suitable, unless the apples could be tainted by chemical fumes, such as those of paint. Lofts and attics are usually unsuitable due to temperature fluctuations.

Store undamaged fruit with stalks (*see left*), keeping cultivars apart because they ripen at different rates. Remove rotting and overripe fruits regularly.

## Common problems

Apples suffer from a range of pests, diseases, and disorders, but some cultivars have good resistance to the more common problems. Pests that may affect apples include codling moth (*see p.254*), aphids (*see p.251*) and woolly aphid (*see p.264*), birds (*see p.251*), capsid bug (*see p.253*), caterpillars (*see p.253*), and red spider mite (*see p.261*). Frost can cause damage (*see p.255*). Apples may also be affected by the following diseases and disorders: apple scab (*p.251*), apple powdery mildew (*see p.251*), brown rot (*see p.252*), iron deficiency (*see p.256*), replant disease (*p.261*), and bitter pit (*see p.252*). Organic methods that can be used to help control pests and diseases include mulch mowing, mulching with grass clippings, and removing fallen leaves and fruit.

# Harvesting and storing apples

1 **To test** whether an apple is ripe, lift it in the palm of the hand and give it a slight twist (never pull it as this can bruise it). If it is ripe it should part easily from the spur.

2 **Place the apples** as you pick them into a padded picking bucket, taking care not to drop them or cause bruising in any other way.

**Lined fruit bucket**
*Soft liner chute can be unfastened to empty fruits through base*

3 **To store apples,** use either moulded liners used by grocers (*far right*, with 'Pixie' apples) or a plastic or wooden crate with slats (*right*, with 'Blenheim Orange' apples). Ensure that the container is clean and the apples are not touching – rots spread quickly from one to another if the fruits touch.

| APPLE CULTIVARS OLD AND NEW (NOTE: Some are not available in Australia) | | | | |
|---|---|---|---|---|
| Cultivar (T) *Triploid* | Pollination group | Picking time | Storage time (months) | Characteristics |
| **DESSERT APPLES** | | | | |
| 'Discovery' ♀ | 3 | Late summer | – | Good flavour, crisp, juicy, and sweet. Fairly compact, with some scab and mildew resistance. Partial tip bearer. |
| 'George Cave' | 2 | Late summer | – | Good flavour, juicy, soft. Reliable, moderate vigour, hardy. Spur bearer. |
| 'Laxton's Epicure' ♀ | 3 | Late summer | – | Aromatic flavour. Hardy, may overcrop, prone to canker. Spur bearer. |
| 'Egremont Russet' ♀ | 2 | Early autumn | 3 | Excellent, nutty, russet flavour. Reliable. Spur bearer. |
| 'Ellison's Orange' ♀ | 4 | Early autumn | 1 | Aniseed flavour. Hardy, reliable. Good scab resistance, canker prone, can be biennial if not thinned. Some frost resistance. Spur bearer. |
| 'Greensleeves' ♀ | 3 | Early autumn | 1 | Crisp, juicy, good flavour. Heavy crops, reliable. Spur bearer. |
| 'Laxton's Fortune' ♀ | 3 | Early autumn | 1 | Excellent flavour, crisp, aromatic. Good scab resistance, but canker prone, can be biennial if fruit not thinned. Spur bearer. |
| 'Lord Lambourne' ♀ | 2 | Early autumn | 1–2 | Sweet flavour. Hardy, reliable, some scab resistance. Partial tip bearer. |
| 'Sunset' ♀ | 3 | Early autumn | 3 | Excellent, Cox-like flavour. Compact, reliable. Spur bearer. |
| 'Worcester Pearmain' ♀ | 3 | Early autumn | 1 | Sweet, chewy, good flavour. Hardy, reliable cropping, mildew-resistant, but prone to scab. Tip bearer. |
| 'Cox's Orange Pippin' | 3 | Early–mid-autumn | 3–4 | Excellent, juicy, aromatic. Prone to scab, canker, and mildew. Not suitable for cooler areas. Choose the self-fertile clone. Spur bearer. |
| 'Kidd's Orange Red' ♀ | 3 | Early–mid-autumn | 3–4 | Excellent, rich, aromatic flavour. Reliable, hardy, needs thinning to maintain good fruit size. Spur bearer. |
| 'Ashmead's Kernel' ♀ | 4 | Mid-autumn | 4–5 | Excellent, firm, aromatic, russet flavour. Light to moderate cropping, flowers prone to frost damage. Spur bearer. |
| 'Falstaff' ♀ | 3 | Mid-autumn | 3–4 | Sweet, crisp, juicy. Hardy, reliable crops. Some frost resistance. Spur bearer. |
| 'Jonagold' ♀ (T) | 3 | Mid-autumn | 4–5 | Good flavour, juicy. Reliable cropping, fairly vigorous. Spur bearer. |
| 'Orleans Reinette' | 4 | Mid-autumn | 3–4 | Nutty flavour. Vigorous. Fruits shrivel easily in storage. Spur bearer. |
| 'Pixie' ♀ | 4 | Mid-autumn | 5–6 | Juicy, aromatic. Heavy crops, reliable. Some frost resistance. Spur bearer. |
| 'Winston' ♀ | 4 | Mid-autumn | 4–6 | Firm, good flavour. Fairly vigorous, reliable. Spur bearer. |
| 'Winter Gem' | 3 | Mid-autumn | 4–5 | Good, rich flavour, firm, juicy. Fairly reliable. Spur bearer. |
| 'Idared' ♀ | 2 | Mid–late autumn | 6–7 | Firm, crisp, juicy, with fair flavour. Moderate vigour. Spur bearer. |
| **CULINARY (COOKING) APPLES** | | | | |
| 'Emneth Early' ♀ | 3 | Midsummer | – | Good flavour, breaks down in cooking. Compact, heavy cropping, needs thinning to prevent biennial bearing. Spur bearer. |
| 'Grenadier' ♀ | 3 | Late summer | 1 | Sharp flavour. Reliable, hardy, some scab and frost resistance. Spur bearer. |
| 'Golden Noble' ♀ | 4 | Early autumn | 2–3 | Excellent flavour, breaks down in cooking. Reliable, quite vigorous. Partial tip bearer. |
| 'Blenheim Orange' ♀ (T) | 3 | Mid-autumn | 3–4 | Excellent dual-purpose, rich flavour, stays in slices when cooked. Very vigorous, best on dwarfing rootstock, can be biennial. Partial tip bearer. |
| 'Bramley's Seedling' ♀ (T) | 3 | Mid-autumn | 4–5 | Excellent, acid flavour. Very vigorous, best on dwarfing and semi-dwarfing rootstock. Blossom susceptible to frost. Partial tip bearer. |
| 'Dummellor's Seedling' ♀ | 4 | Mid-autumn | 4–6 | Good, acid flavour, breaks down in cooking. Fairly hardy. Spur bearer. |
| 'Howgate Wonder' | 4 | Mid-autumn | 4–6 | Fair flavour. Good and reliable cropping, hardy, large fruits. Spur bearer. |
| 'Lane's Prince Albert' ♀ | 3 | Mid-autumn | 4–6 | Acid, stays intact. Hardy, reliable, susceptible to mildew. Spur bearer. |
| 'Edward VII' ♀ | 6 | Mid–late autumn | 5–7 | Good, acid flavour. Reliable, some scab and frost resistance. Spur bearer. |

## APPLE POLLINATION GROUPS (NOTE: Some heritage cultivars are not available in Australia)

(B) *Biennial bearer*
(T) *Triploid*

### GROUP 1: VERY EARLY
'Gravenstein' (T)
'Lord Suffield'
'Manks Codlin' (B)
'Red Astrachan'
'Stark Earliest' ('Scarlet Pimpernel')
'Vista-bella' (B)

### GROUP 2: EARLY
'Adams's Pearmain' (B)
'Alkmene' ✿
'Baker's Delicious'
'Beauty of Bath'
'Ben's Red' (B)
'Bismarck' (B)
'Bolero' ('Tuscan')
'Cheddar Cross'
'Christmas Pearmain' (B)
'Devonshire Quarrenden' (B)
'Egremont Russet' ✿
'George Cave'
'George Neal'
'Golden Spire'
'Idared' ✿
'Irish Peach'
'Kerry Pippin'
'Keswick Codling' (B)
'Lord Lambourne' ✿
'Margil'
'McIntosh Red'
'Melba' (B)
'Michaelmas Red'
'Norfolk Beauty'
'Owen Thomas'
'Reverend W. Wilks' (B)
'Ribston Pippin' ✿ (T)
'Ross Nonpareil'
'Saint Edmund's Pippin' ✿
'Striped Beefing'
'Warner's King' ✿ (T)
'Washington' (T)
'White Transparent'

### GROUP 3: MID-SEASON
'Acme'
'Alexander'
'Allington Pippin'
'Arthur Turner' ✿
'Barnack Orange'
'Baumann's Reinette' (B)
'Belle de Boskoop' ✿ (T)
'Belle de Pontoise'
'Blenheim Orange' ✿ (TB)
'Bountiful'
'Bramley's Seedling' ✿ (T)
'Brownlees Russet'
'Charles Ross' ✿
'Cox's Orange Pippin'
'Delbarestivale' ('Delcorf')
'Discovery' ✿
'Duchess's Favourite'
'Elstar' ✿
'Emneth Early' ✿ (B)
'Exeter Cross'
'Falstaff' ✿
'Fiesta' ✿
'Gavin'
'Granny Smith'
'Greensleeves' ✿
'Grenadier' ✿
'Hambling's Seedling'
'Holstein' (T)
'Hormead Pearmain'
'James Grieve' ✿
'Jerseymac'
'John Standish'
'Jonagold' ✿ (T)
'Jonathan'
'Jupiter' ✿ (T)
'Katja' ('Katy')
'Kidd's Orange Red' ✿
'King of Tompkins County' (T)
'King Russet' ✿
'Lane's Prince Albert' ✿
'Langley Pippin'
'Laxton's Epicure' ✿
'Laxton's Fortune' ✿ (B)
'Loddington' ('Stone's')
'Lord Grosvenor'
'Lord Hindlip'
'Malling Kent'
'Mère de Ménage'
'Meridian'
'Merton Knave'
'Merton Russet'
'Merton Worcester'
'Miller's Seedling' (B)
'Mutsu' ('Crispin') (T)
'Norfolk Royal'
'Peasgood's Nonsuch' ✿
'Polka' (Trajan) (B)
'Queen'
'Red Devil'
'Red Victoria' (B)
'Redsleeves'
'Reinette du Canada' (T)
'Rival' (B)
'Rosemary Russet' ✿
'Rubinette'
'Saint Cecilia'
'Saint Everard'
'Scotch Dumpling'
'Spartan'
'Stirling Castle'
'Sturmer Pippin'
'S.T. Wright'
'Sunset' ✿
'Taunton Cross'
'Tom Putt'
'Tydeman's Early Worcester'
'Wagener' (B)
'Waltz' ('Telamon')
'Wealthy'
'Winter Gem'
'Worcester Pearmain' ✿
'Wyken Pippin'

### GROUP 4: MID-SEASON
'Annie Elizabeth'
'Ashmead's Kernel' ✿
'Autumn Pearmain'
'Barnack Beauty'
'Cellini'
'Chivers Delight'
'Claygate Pearmain' ✿
'Cornish Aromatic'
'Cornish Gilliflower'
'Cox's Pomona'
'D'Arcy Spice'
'Delicious'
'Duke of Devonshire'
'Dummellor's Seedling' ✿
'Ellison's Orange' ✿
'Encore'
'Gala'
'George Carpenter'
'Gladstone' (B)

'Gloster '69'
'Golden Delicious' ✿
'Golden Noble' ✿
'Hawthornden'
'Herring's Pippin'
'Howgate Wonder'
'Ingrid Marie'
'Jester'
'Joybells'
'King's Acre Pippin'
'Lady Henniker'
'Lady Sudeley'
'Laxton's Superb' (B)
'Lord Burghley'
'Lord Derby'
'Mannington's Pearmain'
'Monarch' (B)
'Newtown Pippin' (B)
'Orleans Reinette'
'Pixie' ✿
'Roundway Magnum Bonum'
'Saturn'
'Sir John Thornycroft'
'Sweet Society'
'Tydeman's Late Orange'
'Winston' ✿
'Woolbrook Russet'

### GROUP 5: LATE
'Coronation' (B)
'Gascoyne's Scarlet '(T)
'Heusgen's Golden Reinette'
'King of the Pippins' ✿ (B)
'Mother' ✿ ('American Mother')
'Newton Wonder'
'Reinette Rouge Etoilée'
'Royal Jubilee'
'Suntan' ✿ (T)
'William Crump'
'Woolbrook Pippin' (B)

### GROUP 6: LATE
'Bess Pool'
'Court Pendu Plat'
'Edward VII' ✿
'Laxton's Royalty'

### GROUP 7: VERY LATE
'Crawley Beauty'

'Adams's Pearmain'   'Blenheim Orange'   'Lane's Prince Albert'   'Malling Kent'   'Winter Gem'   'Claygate Pearmain'   'Pixie'

# Pear

Fully ripe pears (cultivars of *Pyrus communis*) are possibly the most delicious of tree fruits. They need more warmth and sunlight than apples to fruit well; they also flower early so are more at risk from late spring frosts. Pears therefore need a warm, sheltered site. In Australia, pear trees are easily grown in the open and most gardeners choose to prune to an open vase shape or to an espalier design. You may also need extra windbreaks (*see pp. 12–13*).

Pears will tolerate a range of soils providing they are well drained, fairly moisture-retentive, and of reasonable depth – about 45–60cm (18–24in). The ideal pH is 6.5. They do not grow well in thin, calcareous soils, such as those over chalk, because the lack of moisture and the high pH cause lime-induced chlorosis (*see p. 253*). On these, and other thin soils, incorporate plenty of organic matter before planting.

**Pear espalier**
*Restricted forms, such as this multiple T espalier of 'Doyenné du Comice', are particularly suitable for growing pears in warm, sheltered locations. Highly trained forms such as this also make the tree more decorative.*

## Choosing a tree form
Pears can be trained in a wide range of forms (*see p. 152*): as half-standards, bushes, spindlebushes, pyramids, vase, cordons, espaliers, and fans. Generally, half-standards are not a good choice: they form large trees that are difficult to protect to ensure reliable cropping, and are often too big for the average garden. The few tip bearers (*see p. 175*), including 'Joséphine de Malines', are best grown as bush trees. The restricted forms are particularly successful for pears because they readily form fruiting spurs and benefit from the shelter of a warm wall or fence.

## Choosing a rootstock
Pears are usually grafted onto quince rootstocks; these are more dwarfing and earlier into cropping than pear rootstocks, although some promising pear stocks that have a more dwarfing effect are currently being developed.

Quince C rootstock is semi-dwarfing and trees grown on it are early to come into bearing. It is good for fertile soils and is particularly useful for cordons and for more vigorous cultivars. Trees grafted on Quince C will require permanent support.

Quince A is a good rootstock for all conditions and is slightly more vigorous than Quince C. Trees on Quince A will normally need staking for the first two years only. The chart below details how the rootstocks affect spacing for different tree forms.

Not all pear cultivars are compatible with quince rootstocks; they need to be double grafted or double budded using a cultivar compatible with both the quince and pear cultivar as a bridge, or interstock, between the two. It involves whip-and-tongue grafting or chip-budding (*see pp. 154–155*) the interstock cultivar onto the quince stock in one year and grafting or budding the chosen pear cultivar as a scion onto the inter-stock in the next year. This will already have been done on trees that have been nursery raised.

## Pollination
Pears flower in early to mid-spring and so are at risk of frost damage at this time. Avoid planting in a frost pocket (*see p. 11*), but, if this is not possible, choose late-flowering cultivars. When trees are young, a tree guard or shelter will give protection from wind and frost as well as from animals. Shelters used in conjunction with mulch around the root system will also reduce evaporation and conserve moisture.

All pears need pollen from a second cultivar to produce a satisfactory crop. Most pears are diploid but some are triploid (*see p. 156*); a triploid requires a diploid to pollinate it and a second diploid to pollinate the first one. Pear cultivars are grouped according to the

| SPACINGS FOR PEAR TREE FORMS AND ROOTSTOCKS | | | | | | | |
|---|---|---|---|---|---|---|---|
| Type of rootstock and vigour | Half-standard | Bush | Spindlebush | Pyramid | Cordon | Espalier | Fan |
| Quince C semi-dwarfing | – | 2.4–3.6m | 1.8–2.25m | 1.5–1.8m | 75cm | 3–3.6m | 3–3.6m |
| Quince A semi-vigorous | 3.6–5.5m | 3.6–5.5m | 2.25–3m | – | 75cm | 3.6–4.5m | 3.6–4.5m |

time at which they flower (*see chart, p.184*). To ensure good pollination, choose cultivars from the same group, if possible. Cultivars from adjacent groups will however also provide some cross-pollination.

Some cultivars, including 'Beurré Bedford', 'Bristol Cross', and 'Marguérite Marrillat', produce little viable pollen, so are ineffective pollinators. 'Conference' is not self-fertile, but may produce seedless (parthenocarpic) fruits without being pollinated. (*See also box, right.*)

## Planting

Before planting, prepare the stakes and wires (*see p.162*) for the form you have chosen. Plant (*see pp.158–159*) in the dormant season because pears start into growth in early spring or even late winter. Bare-root plants usually establish well. Container-grown plants grow away well if they are not pot-bound.

## Pruning and training

Most pears are pruned as spur bearers, but the few cultivars that are tip bearers require a modified pruning technique. Pears can be pruned harder than apples if needed but may produce excessive growth. Pear espaliers are pruned in the usual way (*see pp.171–172*), but

### Pruning a pear pyramid

*In late summer, prune back the sideshoots to reveal the branch leaders and maintain the basic pyramid shape of the tree (here 'Conference').*

*Select sideshoots over 23cm (9in) long and cut to 1 leaf above a basal cluster if they are growing from an existing spur, or 3 leaves above a basal cluster if they are growing from the main stem.*

*Cut branch leaders back to a downward- or an outward-facing bud 5–6 leaves above the basal cluster (see right).*

### INCOMPATIBILITY OF PEAR CULTIVARS

Various cultivars flower at different times and this is usually the basis for classification into pollination groups. However, some pears, although they flower at the same time as other cultivars, will not cross pollinate. Genetic make-up of different species also influences pollination ability. The Asian pear group will not, for example, generally pollinate European pear cultivars although there are rare exceptions. The Asian pear cultivar *'Nijisseiki'* will cross pollinate with some European pears such as *'Beurre Bosc'* and *'Williams'* and the European pear *'Williams'* will cross pollinate with *'Nijisseiki'*.

other forms require different degrees of pruning.

## Pruning a half-standard or bush pear tree

For formative and established pruning of pear half-standards and bushes, *see pp.166–167*. Pears tend to be upright in habit so if branch leaders start to crowd the centre, you should replace them by pruning each to an outward-facing lateral. Remove the stakes of trees on semi-vigorous rootstocks after two or three years of pruning. On a mature tree, in winter, thin spur systems (*see p.165*), and, from time to time, thin

out crossing branches (*see p.164*) by cutting back to a suitable replacement branch.

## Pruning a pear spindlebush

For formative and established pruning, *see pp.169–170*. The only modification for pears is that branches should be tied down to 20–30 degrees above the horizontal, not any lower, otherwise fruiting suffers. Pears produce better fruit on compact spurs, which are less subject to wind damage and bruising from other branches. Shorten laterals not required for the framework to 4–6 buds in winter to encourage more spurs to grow.

## Pruning a pear pyramid and dwarf pyramid

Pruning a pear pyramid is done in the same way as for apples (*see pp.175–176*), using the basic system (*see pp.170–171*) with a few adaptations of technique and timing. Once established, the pyramids are maintained by routine summer pruning (*see p.171 and below left*).

## Pruning a pear cordon

For formative and established pruning, *see pp.171–172*. In summer, follow the summer pruning system (*see p.171*). Pears can also be trained as vertical cordons and over arches in the same way as for apples (*see pp.176–177*). However, they cannot be trained as horizontal cordons, since there are no suitable dwarfing rootstocks for pears.

## Pruning a pear fan

For formative pruning, *see p.173*. For pruning and training an established pear fan in winter, *see facing page*. For summer pruning, *see p.171*.

## Feeding and mulching

Under most conditions pears benefit from an annual application of potassium and nitrogen and an application of phosphorus every three years. Follow the guidelines given under apples for feeding and mulching (*see p.177*), although pears may require an additional nitrogen fertilizer.

## Watering

Pears benefit from plenty of moisture during the growing season and do not tolerate dry conditions well. Water during dry periods in summer. This can be done by several methods (*see pp.53–54*), including drip hoses, which are ideal for rows of trees.

## Fruit thinning

Pear fruits should be thinned out (*see p.160*) to gain good-sized fruits and to reduce the risk of branches breaking or the tree becoming overstressed. Thin in early to midsummer, starting with the earliest ripening cultivars; the earlier the thinning, the greater is the increase in fruit size. As a general guide, thin the fruits on vigorous trees to two fruits per cluster 10–15cm (4–6in) apart.      For compact forms such as cordons, thin to one fruit per cluster 10–15cm (4–6in) apart. It may be necessary to support heavily laden branches (*see p.178*).

## Harvesting pears

Pear yields will vary according to the season and site, the form of the tree, the cultivar, and the rootstock. In general, the more vigorous the tree, the heavier the crop. For a pear bush, you can expect an average yield per tree of 18–45.5kg (40–100lb), for a spindlebush or pyramid 9–18kg (20–40lb), for a single cordon 1.75–3.5kg (4–8lb), for an espalier 9–13.5kg (20–30lb), and

for a fan 5.5–13.5kg (12–30lb). It is particularly important with pears to take care in picking and storing the fruit to prolong the season of use. Pears need to be picked while they are still firm, before they are fully ripe. When it is time to pick there should be a slight colour change, to a lighter green in most cases. Test late cultivars by lifting the fruit in the palm of the hand and giving it a slight twist. If it is ready it should part easily from the spur. Early and mid-season pears may shrivel in storage if picked too early or become rotten at the core if left on the tree for too long. To test an early or mid-season pear for readiness, bite into the pear; if it is hard but sweet it is ready, if it is hard but starchy it is not yet ready.

## Storing pears

Early and mid-season pears require storing for 1–3 weeks before they are ready to eat. Some late-season pears can be stored until mid-spring in relatively simple conditions.

Store pears in a cool, dark, rodent-proof place with some humidity. An ideal temperature is 0–4.5°C (32–40°F); do not allow the temperature to exceed 7°C (45°F). There should be some air circulation, but not too much as this can cause shrivelling in storage. Cellars,

sheds, and garages can be suitable; lofts and attics are usually unsuitable due to fluctuations in temperature and dry air.

Store undamaged fruits in shallow trays with the fruits separated – rot spreads quickly if fruits touch. Check regularly to remove rotting fruits.

## Common problems

Pear trees suffer from fewer pests and diseases than apple trees, but may be affected by: birds (*see p.251*), codling moth (*see p.254*), pear and cherry slugworm (*see p.259*), pear leaf blister mite (*see p.259*), caterpillars (*see p.253*), and aphids (*see p.251*).

Pears can also be affected by the following diseases and disorders: pear scab (*see p.251*), brown rot (*see p.252*), replant diseases (*see p.261*), and especially on light, sandy soils, boron deficiency (*see p.252*).

Fortunately, there are organic controls available for most of the pests and diseases that affect pear trees. Pruning methods can assist pest and disease control by opening the tree to sunshine and facilitating air movement around the tree. Pruning to the open vase shape can reduce tree size and provide an open tree (*see 4 below* which shows the beginning of vase-shaped, multi-branched pruning system).

# Pruning an established pear fan

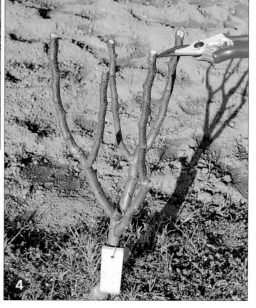

1 **While the fan is dormant** in winter, thin out the complex and overcrowded growth to maintain the balanced shape of the fan and encourage even fruiting the following year. At this time of year, it is easier to see the basic framework of the fan.

2 **Cut back** overly long shoots to a strong, outward-facing spur.

3 **Prune spurs** that have too many branches to a point with only 1-2

branches. This simplifies the spur so that it produces fewer flowers and fruits, but of better quality, and allows light and air circulation.

4 **Take out any wood** showing signs of disease, or that is bare or dead-looking. Remove the affected section back to a spur or shoot showing healthy buds. If the shoots are more than about 1cm (⅛in) thick, use a pruning saw for a smooth cut.

## RECOMMENDED PEAR CULTIVARS

| Cultivar | Picking time | Characteristics |
|---|---|---|
| EUROPEAN PEARS | | |
| 'Beurre Bosc' | Mid-season | Medium to large fruit with coarse, juicy, yellow/white flesh. Skin russetted. |
| 'Josephine' | Late season | Small roundish fruit with smooth, juicy, white flesh. Skin yellow/green. |
| 'Packham's Triumph' | Mid-season | Medium to large fruit with white, smooth-textured flesh. Yellow skin. |
| 'Sensation' | Early season | Medium to large fruit with creamy white, juicy flesh. Skin red-blushed. |
| 'Winter Cole' | Late season | Small fruit with crisp white and juicy flesh. Skin green/yellow and russetted. |
| 'Williams' | Early season | Medium to large fruit with white smooth-textured flesh. Juicy. Skin golden yellow when ripe. |
| 'Winter Nelis' | Late season | Small fruit with yellowish flesh. Smooth texture and juicy. Skin brown russetted. |
| ASIAN PEARS | | |
| 'Hosui' | Mid-season | Medium to large fruit with white/cream, crisp, juicy flesh. Skin mottled light brown. |
| 'Kosui' | Mid-season | Medium roundish fruit with crisp and juicy flesh. Skin golden/bronze. |
| 'Nijisseiki' | Mid-season | Round fruit with creamy white flesh. Juicy and crisp. Skin yellow green. |
| 'Shinsui' | Mid-season | Flat and round fruit with creamy flesh. Very sweet with grainy texture. Skin golden brown and russetted. |

## PEAR POLLINATION GROUPS

| EUROPEAN PEARS | | ASIAN PEARS | |
|---|---|---|---|
| Cultivar | Pollinators | Cultivar | Pollinators |
| 'Beurre Bosc' | 'Nijisseiki', 'Williams', 'Winter Nelis', 'Sensation' | 'Hosui' | 'Shinsui', 'Nijisseiki' |
| 'Josephine' | 'Packham's Triumph', 'Winter Nelis', 'Winter Cole' | 'Kosui' | 'Hosui', 'Nijisseiki' |
| 'Packham's Triumph' | 'Josephine', 'Winter Nelis' | 'Nijisseiki' | 'Hosui', 'Shinsui', 'Williams', 'Kosui' |
| 'Sensation' | 'Beurre Bosc', 'Nijisseiki', 'Winter Nelis' | 'Shinsui' | 'Hosui', 'Nijisseiki' |
| 'Winter Cole' | 'Williams', 'Beurre Bosc', 'Sensation' | | |
| 'Williams' | 'Beurre Bosc', 'Nijisseiki', 'Winter Nelis' | | |
| 'Winter Nelis' | 'Packham's Triumph', 'Josephine' | | |

# Plum

Plums form a group of stone fruits, which includes gages, and damsons, and bullaces (*Prunus insititia*), and cherry plums or myrobalans (*Prunus cerasifera*). They originate mainly from northern Asia and from southern Russia. Plums (including prunes and cultivars of *Prunus domestica*) and gages are the most widely grown; all have similar cultivation needs.

A warm, sunny, sheltered site is best for plums; improve upon the available shelter if necessary (*see pp. 12–13*). They flower early so, if possible, avoid planting in a frost pocket (*see p. 11*). Plums can be grown as freestanding trees in the open in sheltered areas, or trained as cordons or fans against a warm wall or fence. Plums tolerate a range of soils provided that they are well drained, but prefer a heavy clay loam at least 60cm (2ft) deep with a pH of 6–6.5.

## Choosing a tree form

There are several tree forms in which plums can be grown, but not as great a range as for apples and pears. Of the freestanding forms, the pyramid is the best choice since it is economical with space, easily managed with summer pruning, and the low-angled branches are less subject to branch breakage than those of bush trees. The bush form is also suitable for plums, but most Australian gardeners grow open vase-shaped trees, with some being left unpruned after the tree has been trained to between six and ten major limbs.

Of the trained forms, the fan is the most successful. It is particularly suitable for growing well-flavoured plums and

**Ripe damsons**
*The damson is a less commonly grown form of plum. It is too tart to be eaten raw, but when cooked, makes delicious jams, fruit cheeses, and sauces. The older cultivars have the most intense flavours, but modern cultivars produce larger fruits. Damsons thrive on alkaline soils.*

gages, which can benefit from the improved microclimate of a warm wall or fence. Usually a good range of cultivars may be bought as part-trained fans. You could also use a maiden tree.

Plums are less suitable for training as cordons than are apples and pears, due to the lack of a suitably dwarfing rootstock. However, some of the more compact cultivars can be grown as cordons on Pixy rootstocks (*see chart, below*).

## Choosing a rootstock

A relatively limited range of rootstocks is available for plums, with no truly dwarfing rootstock. Pixy, which is semi-dwarfing, is a good rootstock for garden

cultivation; trees come into cropping fairly early in their life, and seldom produce suckers. It is suited to bushes, pyramids, fans, and for less vigorous cultivars grown as cordons. On a Pixy rootstock, a plum pyramid will reach 2–2.2m (6–7ft) in height, and fans will reach a minimum height of 2m (6ft).

St Julien A is semi-vigorous. It is a reliable rootstock and is suitable for half-standard, bush, pyramid, and fan forms. On St Julien A, a pyramid reaches 2.2–2.7m (7–9ft) high, and a fan reaches a minimum of 2.2m (7ft). Plums can be grafted onto various rootstocks including Myrobalan (*see chart, below left*), Marianna plum, peach, and apricot. 'Marianna' rootstock is used in heavy clay soils and produces medium-sized trees but does not sucker heavily.

## Pollination

Plums usually flower in early to mid-spring and so are at risk of damage from frosts during this time. In areas prone to spring frosts, choose late-flowering cultivars (*see chart, p. 188*) and be prepared to use some frost protection. A large number of plums are self-fertile, so if you wish to grow

| SPACINGS FOR PLUM TREE FORMS AND ROOTSTOCKS | | | | | | |
|---|---|---|---|---|---|---|
| Type of rootstock and vigour | Standard | Half-standard | Bush | Pyramid | Cordon | Fan |
| Pixy semi-dwarfing | – | – | 2.4–3.6m | 2.4–3m | 75cm–1m | 3.6–4.5m |
| Myrobalan | – | – | 4–5m | – | – | – |
| St Julien A semi-vigorous | – | 3.6–4.5m | 3.6–4.5m | 3–3.6m | – | 4.5–5.5m |
| 'Marianna' | – | – | 5m | – | – | – |

only one tree, choose one of these. All cultivars benefit from cross-pollination. Plum cultivars are grouped according to the time at which they flower (*see chart, p. 188*). In order to be sure of good pollination, choose cultivars from the same group, if possible, although those from adjacent groups will give some cross-pollination. A few cultivars are not compatible with each other (*see box, below*).

## Planting

Plant plum trees during the dormant season (*see pp. 158–159*) before they start into growth in late winter or early spring. Bare-root plants usually establish better than container-grown ones, although the latter will grow well as long as they are not pot-bound.

## Pruning and training

Pruning is usually carried out in spring or summer. Never prune stone fruits in the dormant season, or in mid- or late autumn. Pruning cuts at these times expose the plant to the risk of infection by silver leaf (*see p. 262*) and bacterial canker (*see p. 253*). To guard against these potentially serious problems, take care to observe good hygiene when pruning and use wound paint on all large cuts immediately. Plums fruit on a mixture of one- and two-year-old wood and older shoots. Plum pyramids may be pruned in the standard way (*see p. 170*), but other forms have more particular pruning requirements.

**Pruning an established plum**
*As the tree matures, you will need to thin out crowded spur systems, either before flowering or at petal fall. Cut back each old spur to a strong bud.*

## Pruning a standard, half-standard, or bush plum

Formative pruning of standard, half-standard, and bush trees is as described on pp. 166–167. The main distinction, as with other stone fruits, is that formative pruning is carried out in mid-spring.

After formative pruning, little regular pruning should be carried out, because pruning cuts can lead to infection from disease. As the branches become more crowded, some thinning out may be necessary, but not too much since a plum tolerates a more crowded head than apples or pears. Do this in spring or summer after flowering, removing dead and broken, and weak and spindly branches back to their point of origin or to a suitable replacement.

## Pruning an oblique plum cordon

The pruning method for plum cordons differs slightly from the method employed for apples and pears. If possible, start with a feathered maiden tree. In the mid-spring following planting, shorten any sideshoots back to about three buds. Shorten the leader, beyond the topmost feather, by about half. If you are starting with an unfeathered maiden, you should also shorten the leader by about half. The following summer, tie in the leader to the cane. Pinch out sideshoots at six leaves of the new growth, usually in

midsummer, and any regrowth later in the season, to just one leaf. In late summer, further shorten the sideshoots that were pinched back to six leaves, by cutting them down to three leaves in order to encourage the formation of compact, fruiting spurs.

In mid-spring of the second year, shorten the leader by about one-third of its new growth to a bud. Repeat this until the cordon has reached the top of the wires. If space allows, you can then lower the leader to about 35 degrees and allow it to grow further. Once at its final length, treat the leader as any other lateral, pinching it back and pruning it further in summer.

## Pruning a plum fan

For formative pruning, follow the standard method (*see p. 173*). From the second summer for a maiden tree, or the first summer if a part-trained tree is being grown, regular summer pruning will also be needed to produce compact fruiting spurs. In early summer, thin out to 10cm (4in) apart any shoots that are not required to extend the framework, or those growing from spurs on the framework; at the same time, pinch these shoots back to six leaves. If there is any regrowth on these shoots, pinch it out to one leaf. After picking, shorten to three leaves the laterals previously pinched to six leaves in order to maintain the compact spurs.

Prune an established fan in spring, either after the buds break and before flowering, or when the petals fall, to take out any unhealthy material. Cut out any dead, diseased, or damaged shoots, as well as any badly placed shoots that are growing towards the support or the centre of the fan, and thin out spurs (*see above, left*). In the summer, prune and train the fan to keep its shape well defined (*see above, facing page*).

## Feeding and mulching

Plums need a steady supply of nutrients for healthy growth. In late winter apply sulphate of potash at 20g/sq m (½oz/sq yd). In early spring, apply a nitrogen fertilizer, such as sulphate of ammonia, at 70g/sq m (2oz/sq yd). Every third year, in late winter, top-dress with superphosphate at 70g/sq m (2oz/sq yd). Alternatively, apply a compound

---

### INCOMPATIBILITY OF PLUM CULTIVARS

There are two recognized incompatibility groups for plums. Cultivars in these groups are all self- and cross-infertile, so they will not pollinate themselves or each other.

INCOMPATIBILITY GROUP **1**
'Coe's Golden Drop'
'Jefferson'

INCOMPATIBILITY GROUP **2**
'President'

# Pruning an established plum fan in summer

**1** **In early summer,** tie healthy laterals into the support wires to fill in gaps in the fan shape. Use garden twine tied in a loose figure-of-eight knot to avoid chafing.

**2** **Pinch back sideshoots** that are not going to be part of the framework to 6 leaves. If the shoots have more than 9–10 leaves, you may have to cut them with secateurs because they will be getting woody. After fruiting in late summer, shorten these pruned shoots again to 3 leaves.

**3** **Look for any unhealthy** or badly placed shoots and cut them out at the base. Here an unproductive shoot bare of leaves is pruned back to a junction with a healthier shoot.

**Established plum fan after summer pruning**
*In addition to routine summer pruning as outlined above, keep shoots at the top of the fan pinched back to 3 leaves, and cut them again to 1 leaf after fruiting. This allows the tree to direct its energies into ripening fruit.*

fertilizer (*see p.20*) annually in late winter at 70g/sq yd (2oz/sq m). Plums will also benefit from an annual mulching with an organic mulch, (*see p.161*) in early spring.

## Watering

Plums will need more watering than apples. Water especially during prolonged dry periods in spring and summer (*see p.160*). In early to midsummer, keep plums well watered as the fruit is swelling and continue until harvesting if dry conditions persist. Irrigation can be supplied to plums by several methods (*see pp.53–54*); for rows of trees, drip hoses are particularly efficient.

## Fruit thinning

It is particularly important to thin the fruitlets on plums – if any overladen branches break, the trees can be infected by silver leaf or bacterial canker. Begin thinning in early summer when the first fruitlets fall naturally (*see p.160*). You may also need to support heavily laden branches by tying them temporarily to a central stake or a sturdy cane (*see also p.178*).

## Harvesting and storing plums

Plum yields differ according to the form in which they are grown, the cultivar and rootstock, and the growing conditions. For a plum bush, you might expect an average yield of 13.5–27kg (30–60lb) per tree, for a pyramid about 13.5–22.5kg (30–50lb), for an oblique cordon 3.5–6.75kg (8–15lb), and for a plum fan 6.75–11.25kg (15–25lb).

Plums develop their best flavour if they are left to ripen on the tree. If they feel soft when gently squeezed, they are ripe. A tree will generally need picking over several times. Fruit to be used for preserving may be picked slightly early. Plums can be stored in a refrigerator for a short while before use.

## Common problems

Plums are subject to a number of pests and diseases: silver leaf (*see p.262*), bacterial canker (*see p.253*), brown rot (*see p.252*), caterpillars (*see p.253*), frost damage (*see p.255*), several species of aphid (*see p.251*), red spider mite (*see p.261*), and birds (*see p.251*).

**Espalier plum**
*Prune plum 'd'Agen', four years old and being trained as a loose, open, fan shape in a fully netted orchard.*

## RECOMMENDED PLUM CULTIVARS

| Cultivar | Picking time | Characteristics |
|---|---|---|
| **EUROPEAN PLUMS** | | |
| 'Angelina' | Mid-season | Medium fruit with very sweet, firm yellow flesh. Skin purple with bloom. |
| 'Coe's Golden Drop' | Late season | Flesh green/yellow. Very sweet, medium-sized fruit. Yellow skin. |
| 'd'Agen' (prune) | Late season | Small, very sweet with firm yellow flesh. Skin red/purple with bloom. |
| 'Damson' | Late season | Very small, sweet but tart with yellow flesh. Skin purple with bloom. |
| 'Green Gage' | Mid-late season | Medium fruit with green/yellow flesh, very sweet honey flavour. Skin green/yellow. |
| 'King Billy' | Mid-late season | Medium fruit with pale green to yellow flesh. Acidic. Dark purple bloomed skin. |
| 'President' | Late season | Large sweet fruit with yellow flesh. Skin purple with blue bloom. |
| 'Robe de Sergeant' (prune) | Mid-season | Medium sized, very sweet fruit with yellow flesh. Skin blue/purple with bloom. |
| 'Sugar Plum' (prune) | Late season | Small, very sweet fruit with deep yellow flesh. Red to purple skin with bloom. |
| **JAPANESE PLUMS** | | |
| 'Donsworth' (blood plum) | Early-mid-season | Large sweet fruit with light red flesh. Skin maroon over green with bloom. |
| 'Flavourbeaut' | Late season | Medium fruit with yellow/pink flesh. Sweet/acid. Light to bright crimson skin over yellow. |
| 'Friar' | Late season | Medium to large fruit with light yellow flesh. Mild sweet flavour. Dark purple black skin. |
| 'Mariposa' (blood plum) | Mid-season | Medium to large fruit with dark red, sweet flesh. Dark maroon skin. |
| 'Narrabeen' | Mid-season | Freestone. Large fruit with creamy white, sweet flesh. Skin pink red over yellow. |
| 'Salad' | Mid-season | Acid sweet, coarse yellow flesh. Medium fruit with skin deep red over yellow. |
| 'Santa Rosa' | Early season | Medium fruit with yellow/pink flesh. Sweet acid. Skin bright red. |
| 'Satsuma' (blood plum) | Mid-season | Medium fruit with red flesh. Sweet and tasty. Mottled dark red skin with bloom. |

## PLUM POLLINATION GROUPS

| EUROPEAN PLUMS | | JAPANESE PLUMS | |
|---|---|---|---|
| **Cultivar** | **Pollinators** | **Cultivar** | **Pollinators** |
| 'Angelina' 'President', 'King Billy' | | 'Donsworth' (blood plum) | 'Mariposa', 'Santa Rosa'. 'Narrabeen' |
| 'Coe's Golden Drop' | 'Green Gage', 'Damson', 'Robe de Sergeant' | 'Flavourbeaut' | 'Friar', 'Santa Rosa' |
| 'd'Agen' (prune) | 'Robe de Sergeant' - partially self-fertile | 'Friar' (partially self-fertile) | 'Santa Rosa' |
| 'Damson' | Self-pollinator or self-fertile | 'Mariposa' (blood plum) | 'Satsuma', 'Santa Rosa','Narrabeen' |
| 'Green Gage' | 'Coe's Golden Drop', 'Damson', 'Robe de Sergeant' | 'Narrabeen' | 'Santa Rosa', 'Salad', 'Satsuma', 'Mariposa' |
| 'King Billy' | 'Angelina', 'President' | 'Salad' | 'Narrabeen', 'Santa Rosa' |
| 'President' | 'Angelina', 'King Billy' | | |
| 'Robe de Sergeant' (prune) | 'Green Gage', 'Damson', 'Coe's Golden Drop' | 'Santa Rosa' | 'Mariposa','Salad', 'Narrabeen', 'Donsworth' |
| 'Sugar Plum' (prune) | 'Damson', 'Robe de Sergeant' - partially self-fertile | 'Satsuma' (blood plum) | 'Santa Rosa' |

# Sweet and duke cherry

The sweet cherry is a cultivated form of the wild cherry (gean or mazzard), *Prunus avium*. The duke cherry is thought to be a hybrid of *P. avium* and *P. cerasus* (acid cherry), and is cultivated in the same way as the sweet cherry.

Cherries flower fairly early (usually in mid-spring), so are at risk from spring frosts and poor pollinating conditions at flowering time. A warm, sheltered site is best. Cherry trees can be grown in the open in Australia, close planted or trained to a trellis system. Avoid planting in a frost pocket (*see p. 11*). Cherries tolerate a fairly wide range of soils. Good drainage is important and soils should be at least 60cm (2ft), preferably 90cm (3ft), deep with a pH of 6.5–6.7. Shallow and waterlogged soils are not suitable and need improving, by deep cultivation (*see p. 39*) or drainage (*see p. 16*), if cherries are to be grown.

## Tree forms and rootstocks

Cherries are naturally vigorous and produce large trees. They can be grown as bush or pyramid trees or as fans. Generally, the fan form is the most suitable because it controls the cherry's vigorous nature and can be most easily protected against frost and birds.

There are few rootstocks available for cherries. Most widely used is the semi-vigorous Colt, which is reliable and most suitable for fan-trained trees. On a Colt rootstock, a fan requires a space 5–5.5m (15–18ft) wide and 2.5m (8ft) high. There are no proven dwarfing or semi-dwarfing rootstocks, but pruning trees early to produce 30–40 main branches will have the effect of dwarfing the tree to make it more manageable. Space bush trees 2.7m (9ft) apart and pyramids 2.5m (8ft) apart. Fans need a space 3.6m (12ft) wide and 2m (6ft) high.

## Pollination

Be prepared to protect trees at flowering time if frosts threaten (*see right*). Sweet cherry pollination is complex, and by far the best choice for garden cultivation are cultivars that are self-fertile (particularly if there is space for only one tree). Other

**Cherry in blossom**
*Sweet cherries need warm, sheltered conditions when flowering to achieve pollination and a good set of fruit.*

cultivars are not only self-infertile, they are also incompatible with some others that flower at the same time. Sweet cherry cultivars are grouped by the time at which they flower (*see chart, p. 190*). A cultivar will be pollinated by another from the same pollination group or adjacent groups, provided that they are not in the same incompatibility group.

## Planting

Plant cherries in the dormant season (*see pp. 158–159*). Dig in plenty of well-rotted organic matter beforehand. Bare-root plants usually establish better than container-grown ones, although the latter should grow well if they are not pot-bound. Prepare the stakes and wires (*see p. 162*) for the form you have chosen before planting.

## Pruning and training

Sweet cherries fruit on one- and two-year-old wood and on spurs of older wood. Never prune in the dormant season due to the risk of infection from silver leaf (*see p. 262*) or bacterial canker (*see p. 253*). For pruning a young bush, *see pp. 166–167*; for an established bush, *see p. 186*, and for a pyramid, *see p. 170*.

## Pruning a sweet cherry fan

As well as carrying out the basic formative pruning for a fan (*see p. 173*), you should follow the guidelines for

## Protecting cherry blossom from frost

1 **To protect the blossoms** and fruits of a trained fan (here 'Stella') from frost, cover it with a "tent" of fine netting overnight. Drape the netting over a crossbar of 25 x 25mm (1 x 1in) timber wired onto the support wire above the fan. Use 3 canes as struts to hold the netting clear of the plant.

2 **Weigh down** the edge of the netting by wrapping the end around 2 or 3 bamboo canes. Secure with thin garden wire by feeding the end of the wire in and out of the net as if stitching with a needle.

3 **Uncover the fan** during the day to allow access by pollinating insects. Hold the rolled-up netting at the top of the plant by securing it to the crossbar with twine or, as here, with small tree ties.

plums (*see pp.186–187*) regarding formative summer pruning and pruning of an established fan. A cherry fan will quickly fill its space, and it is important to shorten the new growth produced each year by about half to stimulate the production of sideshoots and spurs, otherwise bare wood can develop.

## Feeding and mulching
Sweet cherries are naturally vigorous with fairly high nutrient needs. In late winter, apply a compound fertilizer (*see p.21*) at 110g/sq m (4oz/sq yd) over the rooting area. For mulching, *see p.161*.

## Watering and protection
Cherries grow best in a moist but freely drained soil. They benefit from an even supply of water in the growing season, which may demand extra watering in dry periods (*see p.160*), especially on shallow soils. Irrigation can be supplied by several methods (*see pp.53–54*).

Fruit splitting is one of the main causes of fruit loss. It can occur through alternate dry and wet soils as the fruits are swelling. The most common cause, particularly as the fruit reaches maturity, is rain or overhead irrigation falling on the fruit. Once the fruits begin to ripen, the skins stop growing and any absorbed moisture will swell the flesh and split the skins. So, once the cherries form but before they ripen, protect them with a raincover (*see above*). Use a similar method to protect blossom from frost and fruits from birds (*see p.192*).

**Erecting a raincover**
*To protect the ripening fruits, place a length of clear plastic, 2.5m (8ft) wide, over the top of the plant (here 'Stella'). Hold it in place with vertical guy ropes of thin cord tied to pegs. To attach the cord to the plastic, wrap a golf ball or cane ball in the plastic at the edge and knot the end of the cord around it (see inset). This prevents the plastic from tearing. Do not cover the sides to avoid scorching the fruits or creating excessively humid conditions.*

## Harvesting and storing
An average yield for a sweet cherry bush might be 13.5–45.5kg (30–100lb), for a pyramid 13.5–27kg (30–60lb), and for a fan 5.5–15.75kg (12–35lb). Pick cherries when they are fully ripe. Once harvested (*see below*), they are best eaten within a few days. Alternatively, they can be stored if cleaned and frozen as soon as they are picked.

## Common problems
Birds (*see p.251*) are a serious pest and eat fruits and buds. Other problems include aphids (*p.251*), fruit fly (*p.256*), pear and cherry slugworm (*p.259*), bacterial canker (*p.253*), brown rot (*p.252*), frost damage (*p.255*), silver leaf (*p.262*), scorch (*p.262*), and magnesium deficiency (*p.257*).

### RECOMMENDED SWEET CHERRY CULTIVARS

| Cultivar | Description |
| --- | --- |
| 'Bedford' | Juicy, round cherry with good flavour. Dark red in colour. Pollinators: 'Burgsdorf', 'Ron's Seedling', 'Flavorite'. |
| 'Bing' | Roundish, very dark red cherry. Firm and with good flavour. Pollinators: 'Stella', 'Blackboy', 'Van', 'William's Favourite'. |
| 'Blackboy' | Firm, roundish, dark red fruit with good flavour. |
| 'Burgsdorf' | Squarish, red to dark red fruit with red flesh and good flavour. |
| 'Flavorite' | Heart-shaped, dark red fruit. Juicy with excellent flavour. |
| 'Lambert' | Rounded, very dark red fruit. Juicy and with excellent flavour. |
| 'Moss Early' | Sweet and firm heart-shaped red fruit. |
| 'Napoleon' | Round to heart-shaped yellow-red fruit. Sweet and firm. |
| 'Rainier' | Large rounded yellow fruit. Sweet and firm. |
| 'Ron's Seedling' | Large heart-shaped and almost black fruit. Firm with good flavour. |
| 'Sam' | Very dark red fruit. Firm and juicy with good flavour |
| 'St Margaret' | Heart-shaped, very dark red fruit. Firm and juicy with good flavour. |
| 'Starkrimson' | Large, heart-shaped crimson red fruit. Firm and with good flavour. |
| 'Stella' | Red to dark red heart-shaped fruit. Firm and juicy with good flavour. |
| 'Sunburst' | Very large round to heart-shaped red fruit. Firm and with good flavour. |
| 'Van' | Heart-shaped bright red fruit. Firm and juicy with sweet flavour. |
| 'William's Favourite' | Large, oblong, dark red to black fruit. Acid sweet and juicy. |

**Harvesting cherries**
*When the cherries (here 'Stella') are ripe, cut the stalks with scissors or secateurs. Take care to hold the stalk to avoid the fruit falling and bruising. A tree will usually need picking over 2 or 3 times as the fruit ripens.*

# Acid cherry

Acid (or sour) cherries are derived from *Prunus cerasus*. The fruits are generally too acid to eat raw, but are full of flavour and cook and preserve well. Being less vigorous than sweet cherries, acid cherries are well suited to gardens. They also have different pruning needs.

In general, acid cherries crop reliably. They are, however, susceptible to frost at flowering, although less so than sweet cherries, and do not need full sun. Trees can be grown in the open garden and pruned to an open vase or multi-branched bush form. They tolerate a range of soils as long as they are well drained and moisture-retentive, with a pH of 6.5–6.7. The soil needs to be at least 45cm (18in) deep; shallow or waterlogged soils will need improving, by deep cultivation (*see p.39*), or drainage (*see p.16*).

## Tree forms and rootstocks

Acid cherries bear most of their fruit on wood made the previous year. Because of this, they need to be grown as tree forms which are maintained by replacement pruning. These forms are the bush, pyramid, and fan. The pyramid casts less shade than the bush, and is easier to net against birds. Bushes need spacing 3.5–5m (11–15ft) apart and pyramids 3–3.5m (10–11ft). Fans need a space 3.5–5m (11–15ft) wide and 2–2.2m (6–7ft) high. Acid cherries are not large trees, so the semi-vigorous rootstock Colt is suitable for all forms.

'Morello' cherry
*This acid cherry has been trained on wires as a fan and still fruits well after 20 years. A fan makes a highly attractive structural form in the garden, allows the fruits to ripen well, and gives easy access to the tree at harvest time.*

## Pollination

Acid cherries generally flower in mid- to late spring. Be prepared to protect trees at flowering time if frosts threaten (*see p.189*). They are self-fertile, so there is no problem with pollination and, in most cases, only one tree is required to provide a satisfactory crop.

## Planting

Plant cherry trees during the dormant season (*see pp.158–159*) before they start into growth. Dig in plenty of well-rotted organic matter before planting, especially on shallow soils, to improve moisture-retentiveness. Bare-root plants usually establish better than container-grown ones, although the latter should grow well as long as they are not pot-bound. Prepare the stakes and wires (*see p.162*) required for the tree form you have chosen before planting.

## Pruning and training

As for other stone fruits, acid cherries are susceptible to silver leaf (*see p.262*) and bacterial canker (*see p.253*) if pruned in winter. To avoid these problems, always prune in early spring and summer. Since the tree fruits on the previous season's wood, pruning aims to remove some fruited wood and promote new, vigorous wood, while maintaining the structure of the tree.

## Pruning an acid cherry bush

Formative pruning of a bush is undertaken in early to mid-spring (*see*

---

## Pruning an established acid cherry fan in early summer

Thin the new shoots along the ribs of the fan (here a 'Morello') to 5–10cm (2–4in) apart. Aim to keep shoots near the base of those that are bearing this year's fruits. The shoots you retain will form the fruiting wood for next year. Tie these new shoots into the supports. Shorten to 2 leaves any shoots growing directly outwards from the fan. This thinning allows the fruits and new shoots to ripen well without being crowded.

*Thinning new shoots*

**Established fan framework**
*After pruning, the fan should be balanced and free of crowded, crossing shoots. For each shoot* *that is bearing fruit, there should be 1 or 2 new shoots that will replace it in the next season.*

*pp.166–167*). After the first four or five years, prune it after fruiting, as for the cropping tree (*see* Pruning an established bush, *p.167*), in late summer to early autumn. Cut out a quarter of the older wood to young shoots to stimulate production of more new wood. As the tree matures, take sections of three- and four-year-old wood back to young shoots. If the tree is unpruned or pruned lightly, it will eventually crop only around the edge.

## Pruning an acid cherry pyramid
Starting with a feathered maiden in early to mid-spring, cut the leader to 10cm (4in) above the topmost feather or sideshoot. Remove any feathers below 45cm (18in). Shorten remaining sideshoots by half to a downward-facing bud. In the first summer, tie the leader to the stake. In the second spring, shorten the leader by half of the new growth to a bud on the opposite side to the previous pruning cut. Shorten other one-year-old shoots by half. Tie the leader to the stake in summer. In the third spring, prune the leader by half, but leave laterals unpruned; repeat the process with the leader until it gains its full height of 2–2.5m (6–8ft). Pruning is not needed in the third summer.

From the fourth summer, prune after picking. Remove some sections of older wood, cutting back to young shoots and maintaining the pyramid shape. As the

**Protecting fruits from birds**
*In midsummer, erect a fine net over wall-trained trees. Use 2.5m (8ft) canes as struts over which to drape the net. Insert them 60cm (2ft) clear of the base and tie at the top with twine. The net should not touch the fruits.*

## Pruning an established fan after fruiting
In late summer, after fruiting, thin out the fan (here 'Morello') and train in shoots that will fruit next year. Cut back shoots that have fruited this season to leave a replacement shoot of new growth, which will fruit next year. Then cut out any badly placed shoots, including any that are growing outwards from the fan or towards the wall or fence. Also remove shoots that have grown beyond the boundaries of the fan, cutting back to a lower-placed shoot. Tie in the remaining shoots to the supports with twine in a figure-of-eight knot.

*Removing fruited wood*

*Established fan before pruning*

*Established fan after pruning*

tree matures, you may need to cut back some three- and four-year-old wood to replacement shoots. Once the tree is at its full height, cut back shoots at the top to two buds in late summer.

## Pruning an acid cherry fan
After formative pruning (*see p.173*) and once the fan framework is established, thin shoots (*see p.191*) in late spring to early summer, and remove fruited wood in late summer (*see above*). As the fan becomes older, remove three- and four-year-old sections of the framework back to young replacement shoots. If this replacement pruning is not carried out, the fan will fruit only at the periphery.

## Routine care
To produce strong replacement shoots, acid cherries need more nitrogen than many other fruits. In late winter, apply sulphate of potash at 35g/sq m (1oz/sq yd) over the rooting area. In the early spring, apply 70g/sq m (2oz/sq yd) of sulphate of ammonia. Every third year in late winter, apply 70g/sq m (2oz/sq yd) of superphosphate. Mulch to help keep soil fertile and moist (*see p.161*).

Water during dry periods in spring and summer; this is especially important on shallow soils. Irrigation can be applied in several ways (*see pp.53–54*). Drip hoses are useful as they allow for regular, even application of water. If the soil dries out and then becomes wet, fruits may split as they ripen. Protect them with a raincover (*see p.190*).

## Harvesting acid cherries
An average acid cherry bush or pyramid may yield 13.5–18kg (30–40lb) of fruit, and a fan 5.5–15.75kg (12–35lb). Harvest fruits when they are fully ripe, cutting them off by the stalks. You may need to pick over a tree twice.

## Common problems
Acid cherries suffer the same problems as sweet cherries (*see p.190*). Protect ripening fruits against birds (*see left*).

### RECOMMENDED CULTIVAR
'Morello' ♀ *Self-fertile cultivar; harvest the fruits in late summer and in early autumn. This is a very old cultivar of excellent flavour.*

# Peach and nectarine

Peaches (*Prunus persica*) and nectarines (*P. persica* var. *nectarina*) originate from China. They have similar cultivation needs, so throughout this text all details on peaches apply also to nectarines. The trees are fully winter-hardy but flower early – usually in early spring or even late winter – and so the blossom is at risk from frost damage and poor conditions. However, it is possible to grow peaches successfully in a warm site. Provide extra shelter (*see pp. 12–13*) if needed. There are many cultivars of peach and nectarine available in Australia, including some suitable for tropical areas.

There are two types of peaches: the conventional cultivars, which grow fairly vigorously and naturally produce a medium-sized tree, and genetically dwarf compact peaches, which are sometimes known as patio peaches.

Conventional peach and nectarine cultivars will grow in a range of soils as long as they are welldrained, moisture-retentive, and at least 45cm (18in) deep, with a pH of about 6.5. Thin soils over chalk are not suitable unless improved with plenty of organic matter (*see p. 22*).

Compact cultivars are most successful grown in containers in a warm situation such as a sheltered patio. They flower early, but are susceptible to peach leaf curl (*see p. 259*).

## Tree forms and rootstocks
The type of peach cultivar you choose will dictate the tree form in which it can be grown. The conventional peach cultivars can be grown as bushes, vase shapes, pyramids, and fans, but the fan-trained tree is the form that is generally successful. Fan-trained trees need a space of 3.5–5m (11–15ft) wide, and 2–2.5m (6–8ft) high. Bushes and pyramids will produce fruit outdoors. There are few rootstocks for conventional peach cultivars. The most common is the semi-vigorous St Julien A. Peaches can also be raised as seedlings to obtain ungrafted trees (*see p. 195*).

Compact peaches produce extremely short-jointed, neat growth suitable for growing as vase-shaped bush trees.

**Protecting flower buds from frost**
*Wall-trained trees (here 'Hale's Early') need protection in early spring from frosts: cover them with fleece or shade netting from just before bud break to protect the buds. When the flowers open, roll up the fleece during the day to allow access by pollinating insects.*

## Pollination
Peaches and nectarine cultivars are self-fertile, so it is possible to obtain a crop from just one tree. They are pollinated by insects, but since they flower very early there are often few pollinating insects around.

Since both the flowers and fruitlets are very vulnerable to frost damage, be prepared to protect them against frost. Alternatively, a plastic raincover in place to avoid peach leaf curl (*see p. 195*) gives 1–2°C (2–3.5°F) of frost protection and will improve the ambient temperatures, which will also be an aid to pollination.

## Planting
Plant (*see pp. 158–159*) in the dormant season, preferably in late autumn, since peaches start to grow in early spring. Bare-root plants usually establish well. Container-grown plants grow away well as long as they are not pot-bound. Before planting, prepare stakes and wires (*see p. 162*) for the form you have chosen. For planting in a pot, use a loam-based compost. Start a young tree in a 15–20cm (6–8in) diameter pot.

## Pruning and training
Peaches fruit on young wood formed in the previous season, as do acid cherries, and so they also require replacement pruning to produce a supply of new wood each year. When you are pruning to produce a new shoot, it is important to prune to a growth bud, rather than a fruit bud, so you need to recognize the two types (*see below*). If necessary, prune to a triple bud and remove the two side fruit buds. As for all stone fruits, prune peaches in spring and summer to avoid infection from silver leaf (*see p. 262*) and bacterial canker (*see p. 253*).

For conventional peach and nectarine cultivars, prune the bush and pyramid forms as you would for acid cherries (*see pp. 191–192*). Compact cultivars grow slowly and need little or no pruning, apart from the removal of dead or diseased wood when necessary. Peaches and nectarines are easily trained as open vase-shaped trees. Two-thirds of all new growth must be removed each winter to facilitate constant cropping. In small gardens, several cultivars can be grafted onto the one tree. This can be done in winter. Alternatively, bud grafting into new growth laterals can be done during the summer period.

### Pruning a peach or nectarine fan
Formative pruning of a peach fan is undertaken following the basic method (*see p. 173*), with some extra pruning in early summer (*see overleaf*). Peaches usually grow quite vigorously at first, so it is vital to train shoots early on into position. Remove all vertical or near-vertical shoots in the centre as these will tend to dominate

Single growth bud

Growth bud in triple bud

Fruit bud in triple bud

Fruit bud in triple bud

### Recognizing peach buds
*Peaches, as well as other* Prunus *tree fruits, have separate fruit and growth buds, but some are found together as double and triple buds. The growth buds can be distinguished because they are pointed, while fruit buds are round.*

at the expense of the rest of the fan. In the third summer, a few fruits appear along the ribs of the fan, but the first real crop will be in the fourth summer.

On an established peach fan, routine pruning is in spring (*see box, below*) and summer, after fruiting. The aim is to choose a replacement shoot for each fruiting shoot and then to train it in alongside the fruiting shoot – a shoot higher up is also kept as a reserve. Keep the replacement shoots tied in flat so that plenty of light reaches the fan and also because they are difficult to bend flat later in the summer when growth becomes woodier. Other shoots can be kept pinched to one leaf to feed the fruits. Tie in any shoots required to extend the framework if it has not yet reached its full size. If shoots outgrow the available space, pinch them back.

After picking in midsummer to late autumn, cut back the fruiting laterals to the replacement shoots unless there is room to extend the lateral. Cut out any dead or diseased wood to a healthy shoot. If a rib has developed a lot of bare wood, cut the section back to a replacement shoot. If replacement pruning is not carried out, the tree will eventually fruit only around the edges.

## Routine care

Peaches require annual feeding to produce large, good-quality fruits and replacement shoots and fruit buds for the next year's crop. In late winter, apply a general compound fertilizer (*see p.20*) at 100g/sq m (3oz/sq yd) over the rooting area – beneath the canopy of the tree or along the length of a fan-trained tree. Wall-trained trees benefit from an additional liquid feed with a high-potash fertilizer, such as tomato fertilizer, at about 5 litres (1 gallon) per tree every 10–14 days from fruitlet stage until the fruits are full size. All forms grow better with a mulch (*see p.161*).

Peaches need plenty of moisture in the growing season. Do not allow them to become dry, since this can cause checks to growth and the problem of splitting (*see p.262*). The most effective method of maintaining moisture levels for peaches and nectarines is to use drip irrigation (*see pp.53–54*).

Feed container-grown, compact peach cultivars with a liquid feed or slow-release fertilizer during the growing season. Top-dress annually with

---

# Pruning a peach or nectarine fan

**1 Starting with a feathered maiden,** choose a strong lateral on either side at 25–30cm (10–12in) from soil level to form the main arms. In early spring, prune each one to about 38cm (15in) and an upward-facing bud, and tie them to canes attached to the wires. Remove the leader above these laterals; cut back any shoots below. In summer, select shoots to tie in to form the framework – 2 on the top of each arm and 1 below. Pinch back all other shoots to 1 leaf. The next spring, prune main shoots by a quarter of the last year's growth.

**2 In early summer,** keep tying in shoots as they grow. Remove any growing into the support and below the 2 main arms; cut those growing outwards to 2 leaves.

**3 In early summer** of the following year, thin laterals arising from the framework branches to 10–15cm (4–6in) apart. Remove any shoots growing directly towards the wall; stop laterals growing straight out and any other surplus shoots at 2 leaves. Tie in the retained laterals to fruit the next year.

**4 On an established fan** in spring, choose a replacement shoot near the base of each fruiting shoot, and a second reserve one further up the lateral; tie them in. Pinch out all other shoots at 1 leaf.

*Cane at about 40° to wires*

*Prune low shoots to 1 bud*

**❶**

*Fix canes to wires, then tie in new shoots*

**❷** *Remove vertical shoots*

*Cutting outward-growing shoot to 2 leaves*

*Continue to tie in new framework shoots*

*Sideshoot kept to replace fruited shoot*

*Remove inward-growing and crossing shoots*

**❸** *Shorten surplus and overlapping laterals to 2 leaves*

**❹** *Surplus shoots pinched to 1 leaf*

fresh potting compost and repot into a larger container every other year. Once a tree has reached the maximum suitable pot size – 40cm (16in) diameter – repot it into the same pot, removing and replacing any loose compost and cutting away pot-bound roots.

## Fruit thinning

Fruit thinning is important to obtain good-sized peaches (*see right*) and avoid overstressing the tree. Thin nectarines to about 15cm (6in) apart.

## Harvesting and storing peaches and nectarines

Peaches are variable in their fruiting, but in favourable conditions a peach or nectarine bush may yield an average of 13.5–27kg (30–60lb) and a peach or nectarine fan 5.5–11.25kg (12–25lb).

Harvest peaches when they are ripe or almost ripe. To test for ripeness, check for a colour change of the background green colour to yellow-orange. If the flesh is soft, it is ready and the fruit should part easily from the tree. Place the fruits in containers lined with soft material so that they are not touching each other. Some will be ready to eat immediately, while some will require a day or two to ripen fully.

## Raising peaches from seed

Peaches are one of the few fruits that can be grown successfully from seed.

### Thinning peach fruits

*Thin in 2 stages. First, when the fruitlets are about the size of a hazelnut, thin to single fruits 10cm (4in) apart, removing misshapen fruits and those next to the wall or in other places where they have no room to swell. When the fruits are the size of walnuts, thin to 20–25cm (8–10in) apart.*

*After thinning, healthy fruits have room to grow*

The seedlings do not grow true from seed, but they are usually similar or inferior to the peach from which they are raised – and only occasionally better. Seedlings generally take about four or five years to bear fruit.

To be sure of success, select several stones. Clean them and leave them in the sun to dry for a few days. The stones require a period of cold before germination can take place, so store them over the winter in a mixture of 50:50 sharp sand and peat in a 25cm (10in) pot. Plunge the pot in soil in a shady part of the garden, cover it with a fine wire mesh to deter rodents, and keep the sand and peat mixture moist. Protect the stones with a layer of straw or similar material.

In late winter, sow the stones singly in 14cm (5½in) pots of a loam-based compost. Place on a sunny windowsill or, ideally, on a propagating bench with bottom heat of 15–20°C (59–68°F). As each seedling grows, tie it into a vertical cane. In late spring, place the pots outside, preferably plunged in soil. The next winter, plant out the best seedling in its permanent position. It is best not to keep it in a container unless you want to grow it in one permanently. A seedling tree can be trained in the same forms as a grafted tree (*see p.193*).

## Common problems

Peaches are affected by a variety of problems. The most troublesome disease is peach leaf curl (*see p.259*). Other problems include aphids (*see p.251*), red spider mite (*see p.261*), brown scale (*see p.252*), bacterial canker (*see p.253*), silver leaf (*see p.262*), brown rot (*see p.252*), replant disease (*see p.261*), and splitting (*see p.262*).

**Raincover for a wall-trained peach**
*Use a raincover from early winter to late spring to keep buds dry, avoid peach leaf curl, and give frost protection. Make a wooden frame with clear plastic sheeting to cover the fan, leaving the ends and base open for air circulation.*

## A SELECTION OF PEACH AND NECTARINE CULTIVARS

| Cultivar | Picking time | Characteristics |
| --- | --- | --- |
| **PEACHES** | | |
| 'Anzac' | Early summer | White flesh, freestone. Cream and green skin with red blush. Juicy and tasty. |
| 'Elberta' | Midsummer | Yellow flesh, freestone. Yellow skin with red blush. Good flavour. |
| 'Golden Queen' | Late summer | Yellow flesh, clingstone. Orange skin. Very tasty. |
| **NECTARINES** | | |
| 'Independence' | Midsummer | Yellow flesh, freestone. Skin with red blush over yellow-gold. Good flavour. |
| 'Goldmine' | Midsummer | White flesh, freestone. Skin red over yellow/green. Very tasty. |
| 'Fantasia' | Late summer | Yellow flesh, clingstone. Skin shiny red blush over yellow. Very tasty. |
| **DWARF NECTARINE CULTIVARS** | | |
| 'Dwarf Nectarine' | Late summer | Yellow flesh. Skin with red blush over yellow. Good flavour. |

# Apricot

Apricots (*Prunus armeniaca*) originate from China and Central Asia. They are fully winter-hardy but flower early – generally in early winter to mid-spring. Apricots will grow on a range of soils providing the soils are well drained, fairly moisture-retentive, and at least 45cm (18in) deep with a pH of 6.5–7.5. On light, sandy soils (*see p.22*), add plenty of organic matter to improve moisture-retention.

## Tree forms and rootstocks

Apricots can be grown as bushes in a vase shape or pyramids in favourable, warm, sheltered positions. A pyramid is also suitable for growing in a container. Apricots grow particularly well in the dry, inland areas of temperate Australia. They can be grown in the open or trained on a fence or trellis. A very practical tree form is as a fan against a wall or fence. Fan-trained trees need a space 3.5–5m (11–15ft) wide and 2–2.5m (6–8ft) high. The most often used rootstock is the semi-vigorous St Julien A.

## Pollination

Apricots are self-fertile and so just one tree is required for fruits. The blossom is pollinated by insects, but some flowers open at a time when there are often few pollinating insects around. The flowers and fruitlets are very vulnerable to frost damage: be prepared to protect against frost.

## Planting

Plant in the dormant season (*see pp.158–159*), preferably in autumn, as apricots may start to grow away in late winter. Bare-root plants usually establish well. Container-grown plants also grow away well if not pot-bound. Before planting, prepare the stakes and wires (*see p.162*) for the form you have chosen.

## Pruning and training

Apricots fruit on one- and two-year-old wood, and on older fruiting spurs. As for all stone fruits, prune in spring and summer to avoid infection from silver leaf (*see p.262*) and bacterial canker (*see p.253*). For formative pruning of a

**Spur pruned apricot**
*Traditionally spur-pruned open vase shaped apricot that has had most of the previous season's growth removed. Most spur growth is retained.*

bush, *see pp.166–167*; for established pruning, *see Plum, p.186*. For pruning of an apricot pyramid, *see p.170*.

## Pruning an apricot fan

Carry out formative pruning for the basic framework (*see p.173*) in late winter or early spring as the tree starts early into growth. In addition, follow the guidelines for plums (*see pp.186–187*) for formative summer pruning and pruning an established fan.

## Routine care

In late winter, apply sulphate of potash at 35g/sq m (1oz/sq yd) over the rooting area (to just beyond the extent of the branches). In early spring, apply calcium ammonium nitrate at 20g/sq m (½oz/sq yd). Every third year, apply super phosphate at 70g/sq m (2oz/sq yd) in late winter. Apply a mulch (*see p.161*) after the fertilizer in spring. Give extra water in dry periods in spring and summer. For wall-trained apricots, drip irrigation (*see pp.53–54*) is very useful.

## Fruit thinning

Apricots often set enough fruit to need thinning. If a heavy crop is set, thin (*see p.160*) in late spring or early summer, when fruits are the size of hazelnuts, to 5–8cm (2–3in) apart.

**Trellis trained apricots**
*Apricots can be trained to espalier systems. Shown here are close-planted, central leader, fan-shaped trees at flowering stage.*

## Harvesting and storing

Harvest apricots when they are fully ripe and soft; they should part easily from the spur. Use them as soon as possible after picking, storing them briefly if necessary in a cool place.

## Common problems

Apricots suffer from a few pests and diseases, including brown scale (*see p.252*), dieback (*see p.254–255*), silver leaf (*see p.262*), and bacterial canker (*see p.253*). Birds (*see p.251*) can attack the ripening fruit, and so netting may be necessary (*see p.192*).

### RECOMMENDED CULTIVARS

The available cultivars are generally similar in reliability. The following are in order of season of ripening.

**'Early Moorpark'** *Mid–late summer. Juicy, fine-textured, orange flesh.*

**'Goldrich'** *Large fruit of deep orange colour. Firm flesh. Leave fruit on the tree as fruit colour early before maturity.*

**'Hunter'** *Grown for drying. Late ripening cultivar that crops heavily.*

**'Moorpark'** ♀ *Late summer–early autumn. Old cultivar with orange, red-flushed fruits.*

**'Trevatt'** *Medium–very sweet, roundish yellow fruit. Sometimes an orange blush.*

*Fig* 197

# Fig

Figs (*Ficus carica*) have long been grown in the Mediterranean region, where there are warm, sunny conditions, low rainfall, and few frosts. These are the garden conditions in which figs grow best. If it is to fruit well in cooler areas, it is essential to grow a tree in a warm, sunny position. A fig can be fan-trained against a wall, fence, or in a greenhouse; a house wall is ideal for providing some extra warmth all year. Figs thrive in containers. It is possible to grow a fig as a freestanding half-standard or bush in most parts of Australia.

Figs can be grown on a range of soils providing they are well drained. Light and shallow soils, including thin soils over chalk, are suitable but extremely fertile soils tend to induce too much growth.

## Choosing a tree form
The best form for growing a fig outside is as an unpruned freestanding tree or as a fan-trained tree. Each fig tree needs a space about 3.5m (11ft) wide and 2–2.5m (6–8ft) high. Grow it as a bush in a very sheltered spot or in a pot. You can choose the height of stem before the branches start – a convenient stem height is generally 60–90cm (2–3ft) in open ground. In containers, figs can be grown as a multi-stemmed bushes (*see p.199*) or as standards with a clear stem of 60–90cm (2–3ft).

Figs are grown on their own roots and propagated from hardwood cuttings (*see p.199*). Unfortunately, there are no rootstocks to control their vigour, and they grow very vigorously (7m x 10m (21 x 30ft)) on fertile soils where there is plenty of rainfall.

## Pollination
Most fig cultivars that are cultivated in cool temperate regions develop parthenocarpic fruits – that is, seedless fruits produced without fertilization. Therefore no pollination is necessary. Figs are unusual among tree fruits because the flower is enclosed within what becomes the fruit and so is never visible; the fig simply grows in size.

## Planting and root restriction
Figs are available as container-grown plants. Choose a young plant that is not pot-bound – take it out of the pot and inspect it before buying. Plant in late spring. Figs are both salt- and drought- tolerant so are a good choice for dry areas.

When planting a fig in open ground it is a good idea to restrict the root run; this will keep the tree compact and enable it to fruit well rather than putting all its energies into producing new growth. The size of the rooting area will determine the ultimate size of tree.

For a fan-trained tree 2–2.5m (6–8ft) tall and 3.5m (11ft) wide, a rooting volume of about 0.15 cubic metres (5 cubic feet) is needed. This can be provided by making an open-bottomed box with paving slabs, bricks, or heavy-duty hard plastic sunk into the soil (*see below*). For a freestanding tree, make the open-bottomed box with four sides instead of three. Other ways to provide root restriction include planting a fig in a narrow border between a wall and a concrete path, or planting it in a hole set in a paved area.

Growing figs in containers will automatically provide root restriction. Generally, containers of 30–40cm (12–16in) in diameter are most suitable; a larger pot can be used, but will be too heavy to lift. Ensure good drainage. Use a loam-based potting compost.

## Pruning and training
Although figs fruit freely in a warm climate, in cooler areas usually only one crop per year is produced. Figs develop in the axils of the leaves of the young shoots and, provided that they are not subjected to frost, overwinter as embryo figs about the size of peas. These fig embryos will ripen in midsummer to early autumn of the following year (*see p.198*). In warm areas a second crop will develop in one season and ripen

## Constructing a planting pit

1 **For a fan, construct a pit** about 45cm (18in) deep against a wall and line it with three 60 x 60cm (24 x 24in) paving slabs. The tops of the slabs should stand proud of the surface by at least 5cm (2in) so that roots cannot not stray along the soil surface. Fill the bottom 15–20cm (6–8in) with large crocks or rubble to discourage any large roots from growing through.

2 **Fill the pit with soil** enriched with compost, or with loam-based potting compost plus a slow- or controlled-release fertilizer, leaving a watering rim of 2.5cm (1in). Plant a young fig (here 'Brown Turkey') in the centre, leaning it towards the training wires; fill with more compost.

3 **Firm in the plant** and cut back the stem to a bud facing to one side 45cm (18in) from the ground. Water and label.

from early to mid autumn. However, if this second crop does not ripen, it should be removed in late autumn.

Figs should be pruned twice a year. In early to mid-spring, after the danger of frost has passed, cut them back to regulate the shape. In summer, pinch out the shoot tips *(see right)*; this will encourage the formation of a new supply of embryo figs for the next year, and allow light to reach ripening fruits.

## Pruning a half-standard fig or a fig bush

Formative pruning of a half-standard or bush is similar to that for other tree fruits *(see pp. 166–167)*, with the pruning being done in early spring. For spring pruning of an established bush, *see box, below*; it may not be necessary to remove large, bare branches every year, but just as needed. In early summer each year, pinch or cut out the growing tips of all the shoots once they have five leaves *(see above right)*. For pruning a container-grown fig, *see facing page*.

## Pruning a fig fan

Formative training and pruning of a fan is as for other tree fruits *(see p. 173)*, and

Embryo figs for next year's crop develop in leaf axils

This year's secondary fruit

Overwintered fruit now ripening

Pinch soft shoot firmly with fingertips

**Development of fig fruits**
*Figs at 3 stages of development are visible on this shoot. At the base is a ripening fruit that has overwintered from last year. Above it are 2 figs formed this spring that may ripen in favourable conditions. Near the tip are embryo figs that may overwinter and ripen next year.*

**Summer pruning**
*In order to produce compact, short-jointed shoots with plenty of embryo figs, pinch or cut out the tips of the shoots when they have formed 5 leaves in early summer. This allows time for the shoots that grow out to ripen and produce embryo figs in the autumn.*

is done in early spring after the worst of the frosts. If the tree has two or more sideshoots, choose two well-placed shoots and prune them back by only one-third of their length to an upward-facing bud, and remove the rest.

For pruning an established fan in spring, *see box, below*. In midsummer, continue to tie in the developing shoots to the wires so that they are exposed to the full sun and ripen well.

## Renovating a neglected fig

If a fig tree has been neglected for a

number of years, most of the fruit will be borne on young shoots around the edge of the tree, with bare sections in the centre. For a neglected bush tree, remove a proportion of the older, bare branches in mid-spring back to a stub of about 5cm (2in). If there are quite a few old branches to remove, spread the pruning over two or three years to avoid stimulating excessive new growth in the fig. As new shoots grow, select the strongest and best-placed for a balanced tree, and prune out the other shoots.

## Pruning an established fig tree in spring

**Pruning an established fig bush**
*In mid-spring, cut back branches that have become long and bare to a stub of about 5cm (2in) to stimulate new shoots from the base. Remove shoots that are crowded and crossing the centre.*

Balanced, open, crown after pruning

Keep base of trunk clear

**1 Take out about a quarter** of the oldest and most congested stems, cutting them to a stub of 5–8cm (2–3in) at the base to encourage new, vigorous growth. Use a pruning saw for a clean cut.

**2 In late spring**, before bud break, look for any badly placed shoots that are growing into or away from the fence, or, as here, are crossing other branches. Remove them and tie in the remaining new shoots.

*Fig* **199**

For a fan-trained tree, also prune in mid-spring. Start by removing branches growing directly out from the wall or fence, cutting back to their point of origin. Thin out crowded branches by cutting back to a stub of about 5cm (2in). Again, if there is a large number of branches to remove, spread the pruning over two or three years.

With both forms, remove any suckers (vigorous shoots) arising from the base. These will spoil the shape of the tree, taking strength from the other shoots.

## Routine care
In early spring each year, apply a top-dressing of a high-potash (1:1:2 N:P:K) compound fertilizer (*see pp. 20–21*) at a rate of about 70g/sq m (2oz/sq yd). During the summer, feed the fig with a high-potash liquid fertilizer, such as a tomato feed.

Figs require regular watering during the spring and summer because the root restriction, and the required good drainage, increase the risk of the roots drying out.

## Care of figs in containers
Feed trees in containers every week during spring and summer with a liquid feed. Alternate between a high-potash fertilizer, such as a tomato feed, and a more balanced feed. Water all year as required and do not allow the compost to dry out completely.

Every two years, the fig is likely to need repotting in the dormant season. Remove the tree carefully from its pot, knock off any loose compost, and cut away with secateurs any thick, thong-like roots. Repot with some fresh loam-based potting compost into the same container or into a slightly larger container.

## Protection of crop
Figs are very attractive to wildlife, particularly birds and flying foxes. Although netting the trees is an option this is difficult for very large trees. Pruning trees severely will facilitate the use of netting on a built structure around the tree. Fig trees will fruit well even when pruned heavily.

## Propagation
Figs can be propagated by hardwood cuttings in autumn. Take cuttings at

**Pruning a container-grown fig**
*As an alternative to the bush with a short stem, a fig in a container can be grown with several stems. Cut a two- or three-year-old fig to soil level, then select up to 10 good shoots that grow from the base. Remove 3 or 4 stems each year to keep a new supply of shoots. Summer prune by pinching shoots to 5 leaves.*

least 30cm (12in) long from the ripe, current season's growth, and trim off the leaves and any soft growth from the tip to make woody cuttings of about 23cm (9in) long, each with a straight cut at the base and an angled cut above a bud at the top. Insert the cuttings in a trench 15cm (6in) deep, spacing them 10–15cm (4–6in) apart. They should root within several months; leave them to develop to the end of the following growing season and then transplant to their final positions.

## Harvesting figs
Fig yields vary quite widely according to the tree size and the growing conditions. Harvest figs when they are fully ripe and soft. When ready to pick,

**Freestanding fig trees**
*Fig trees grown in the open can reach 10m or more. Regular pruning by simply thinning branches and branchlets every 3–5 years is all that is required to keep trees healthy. This tree in Victoria has just been pruned.*

they hang downwards and splits begin to appear in the skin, especially at the stalk end. A drop of nectar may exude from the eye of the fig. Pick fruit by holding the stalk and breaking it away from the shoot. Figs are best eaten soon after picking.

## Common problems
The following pests and diseases may affect figs: brown scale (*see p. 252*), and red spider mite (*see p. 261*), particularly under glass or in a warm situation outside, birds (*see p. 251*).

| RECOMMENDED FIG CULTIVARS | | |
|---|---|---|
| Cultivar | Picking time | Characteristics |
| 'Black Genoa' | Early summer & late autumn | Large purple-green fruit, excellent flavour. Used fresh, for jam or drying. |
| 'Brown Turkey' ♀ | Mid-season | Brown fruits, sweet, dark red flesh. Excellent outside. |
| 'Preston Prolific' | Early summer & late autumn | Round/conical brown and yellow fruit with good flavour. Used fresh, for jam or drying. |
| 'White Adriatic' | Early summer & late autumn | Large yellow-green conical fruit. Used fresh, for jam or drying. |
| 'White Genoa' | Early summer & late autumn | Large, roundish, pale green fruit. Used fresh, for jam or drying. |

# Quince

The true quince (*Cydonia oblonga*) is a relative of the pear, and originated in central to south-western Asia. It is often confused with the shrubby ornamental *Chaenomeles* species, which are also edible. Those are thorny shrubs, whereas the true quince is a thornless, medium-sized tree. Quinces make ornamental and productive trees, with an attractive habit and large, dog-rose-like flowers. Ripe fruit is eaten raw, and is used for cooking and preserving.

Quinces need a warm, well-drained site. Some heritage quince cultivars are available from specialist suppliers. They tolerate a range of soils, but grow best in a deep, moisture-retentive soil. The trees grow well beside streams or ponds, but not in soil prone to waterlogging.

## Tree forms and rootstocks
The most suitable forms for quinces are the half-standard and bush tree. Restricted forms are not suitable.

Quinces can be established on their own roots but are often grown on the quince rootstocks Quince A and C. Quince A is semi-vigorous, producing a half-standard tree 3.5–4.5m (11–15ft) in height and spread. Quince C is semi-dwarfing and will produce a bush tree 3–3.5m (10–11ft) in height and spread.

## Pollination
Quinces are self-fertile and are insect-pollinated, so only one tree needs to be grown to produce a crop.

## Planting
Plant in the dormant season, (*see pp. 158–159*). Bare-root plants usually establish well, as do container-grown plants if they are not pot-bound. It is worth obtaining a two-year-old bush tree with the first branches already formed.

## Pruning a quince half-standard or bush tree
Quinces fruit mostly on the tips of the shoots made the previous year, and produce few fruiting spurs. Prune in the dormant season between late autumn and early spring. Formative pruning is undertaken as on pp. 166–167; this pruning is vital as quinces have a rather

## Pruning an established quince tree

*Before pruning*

*After pruning*

Before pruning (*see far left*), the quince displays typical, haphazard growth, with shoots growing in any direction, creating a crowded canopy. Winter pruning is needed to thin out the canopy and to improve light penetration and air circulation.

Remove no more than a quarter of the oldest branches by cutting them back to the point of origin, or to a shoot that is one-third of the diameter of the branch being removed. Cut off crowded branches (*see above*), very vigorous shoots, and branches showing little growth.

The canopy after pruning (*see bottom left*) is more open, with a neater outline and plenty of fruit-bearing laterals.

irregular growth habit and need a good basic framework. For the cropping tree, prune every winter (*see above*). This pruning is generally fairly light, but make sure you remove any vigorous shoots that may spoil the tree shape.

## Routine care
Quinces benefit from regular feeding. In late winter, apply sulphate of potash at 20g/sq m (½oz/sq yd) over the rooting area, and sulphate of ammonia at 35–70g/sq m (1–2oz/sq yd) in early spring. Every third year, apply super phosphate at 70g/sq m (2oz/sq yd).

For the first four years after planting, and every year for trees on dry soils, mulch well (*see p. 161*). Give extra water during dry spells in spring and summer.

## Harvesting and storing
Quince yields are very variable. Harvest the fruits when they are fully ripe, golden-coloured, and aromatic, usually in mid- to late autumn. Store undamaged fruits in a cool, dark, frost-free place on shallow trays so the fruits do not touch. They are highly aromatic

so avoid storing them with apples or pears, otherwise the apples and pears may taste of quince.

## Common problems
Although quinces are troubled by some of the same pests as apples and pears, these are seldom significant. They might, however, suffer from a few diseases: quince fleck (*see p. 261*), brown rot (*see p. 252*), and powdery mildew (*see p. 260*).

### RECOMMENDED CULTIVARS

**'Champion'** *Produces good crop of large, rounded fruits.*

**'Smyrna'** *Very large aromatic quince. Heavy cropper. Tender.*

**'Portugal' (syn. 'Lusitanica')** *Vigorous and less hardy than the other cultivars, but has the best-flavoured fruits.*

**'Vranja Nenodovic' (syn. 'Berezki De Vranja')** ♀ *Pear-shaped, aromatic fruits of very good flavour. Crops early.*

# Medlar

The medlar (*Mespilus germanica*) is an attractive ornamental, as well as fruiting, tree. It is related to the hawthorn and to the quince. A deciduous native of southeastern Europe and central Asia, it has been naturalized throughout much of Europe. Its spreading habit makes it a graceful addition to the garden, while it also has large, leathery leaves that have good autumn colour, and simple, white rose-like flowers in mid- to late spring.

The fruits can be used after picking for making a pleasantly flavoured jelly. Alternatively, they can be eaten raw if left until they reach the point of decomposing in the process known as "bletting" (*see below*).

Medlars thrive in a warm, sheltered site in sun or partial shade and are tolerant of a range of soils provided that they are well-drained.

## Tree forms and rootstocks

Due to the spreading habit of medlars, the standard, half-standard, or bush are the only suitable tree forms. Space each tree about 5–6m (15–20ft) from surrounding plants to allow it to fulfil its natural habit without restriction.

Medlars can be grafted on quince or hawthorn rootstocks. Quince rootstocks are generally the better choice, offering greater stability. Of these rootstocks, the semi-vigorous Quince A is most suitable. These will produce a standard or half-standard tree 4–6m (12–20ft) in height and spread.

## Pollination

Medlars are self-fertile and pollinated by insects, so only one tree needs to be grown to produce a crop.

## Planting

Plant in the dormant season (*see pp.158–159*). Bare-root plants usually establish well. Container-grown plants also grow away well if they are not pot-bound. If possible, obtain a part-trained standard or half-standard tree and tie it in to a low stake at planting. If you are starting with a maiden tree, plant it next to a tall stake – with about 2m (6ft) out of the ground for a standard and 1.5m (5ft) for a half-standard – and tie it in to the stake to ensure a straight stem.

**Ripening fruits of the medlar tree ready to harvest**
*The brown, distinctive medlar fruits are about 2.5–5cm (1–2in) across when ready to pick. They should be left on the tree into autumn to develop their flavour until they are fully mature. They will then part easily from the spur when lifted gently in the hand.*

## Pruning a medlar standard or half-standard tree

With a ready-trained standard or half-standard, for the first three or four years after planting, prune the branch leaders by about one-third of the previous summer's growth to an outward-facing bud. Leave any short shoots unpruned and remove any poorly placed or crowded branches in winter if needed. For a maiden tree, grow on the main stem, tying it in, until it reaches the required height. Remove low branches and train the remaining ones as above. On a mature tree, winter prune only to keep an open framework, removing any crowded, diseased, or dead branches.

## Routine care

In late winter each year, apply a general compound fertilizer (*see p.20*) at about 70g/sq m (2oz/sq yd) over the rooting area. Mulch (*see p.161*) with organic matter, such as well-rotted manure, compost, or bark, for the first three or four years. Water well in dry periods in spring and summer. Medlars should be able to grow well without a lot of irrigation.

## Harvesting and storing

Pick medlars in mid-autumn (*see above*) in dry conditions, and dip the stalks in a strong salt solution to prevent them rotting. Store them eye downwards and not touching, on trays in a cool, dark, place. Bletting, when the flesh softens and turns brown, will take two to three weeks. The medlars will then be ready to eat.

## Common problems

Medlars are rarely troubled significantly by pests or diseases.

### RECOMMENDED CULTIVARS

**'Dutch'** *Spreading habit and fairly large fruits.*
**'Nottingham'** *More upright habit than 'Dutch'. Fruits fairly small with best flavour.*

# Mulberry

The mulberry species most frequently cultivated for fruit is the black mulberry (*Morus nigra*). Native to western Asia and grown throughout Europe, it is a long-lived and decorative tree. The white mulberry (*Morus alba*) is used to feed silk worms, but has inferior fruit.

Mulberries grow best in sheltered, warm sites. They are tolerant of a range of soils, provided that they are well drained with a pH of 5.5–7, but prefer a fertile, moisture-retentive soil.

## Tree forms and rootstocks

Mulberries in the open are best grown as, a vase, standard or half-standard trees. They are fairly slow growing, taking five years or so to start cropping. Eventually they make substantial trees, needing 5–10m (15–30ft) for their natural shape to develop, and so are suitable only for very large gardens, unless constantly pruned. In cool areas, they benefit from training as an espalier, where they need a space 4.5m (15ft) wide and 2.5m (8ft) high.

Mulberries are usually grown on their own roots or grafted onto seedling rootstocks. There are no dwarfing rootstocks available.

## Pollination

Mulberries are self-fertile. They flower relatively late, so tend to escape the effects of frosts.

## Planting

Plant in the dormant season (*see pp.158–159*). Bare-root plants usually establish well. Container-grown plants also grow away well if they are not pot-bound. For a standard or half-standard tree, try to buy a part-trained tree to obtain a well-formed tree more quickly.

## Pruning a mulberry standard or half-standard tree

Prune mulberries when they are fully dormant: cutting in the growing season results in bleeding from the wounds. In the winter after planting, remove any shoots that spoil the shape, and any on the stem below the framework branches. Repeat in early to midwinter each year, removing any poorly placed shoots for a good framework. Once the

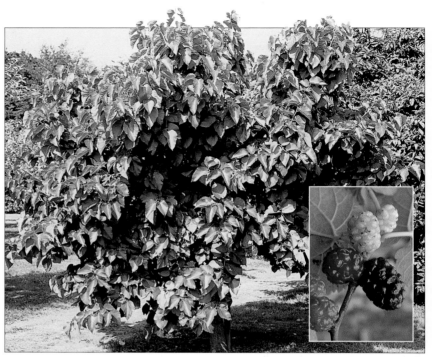

**Mature mulberry tree and fruit**
*Once established, the mulberry soon develops a gnarled appearance and somewhat irregular shape. As long as the branches are well spaced, this adds to its decorative value in the garden. Pick fruits (see inset) when they have turned black and are fully ripe.*

tree is established, little pruning is needed; simply remove any crossing, crowding, dead, or broken branches.

## Pruning a mulberry espalier

Formative pruning of an espalier is undertaken (*see pp.171–172*) in early to midwinter. Once the tree is established, prune lateral shoots arising from the stem and branches of the espalier in late summer, when the growth has slowed down, shortening them to three or four leaves to produce fruiting spurs.

## Routine care

In late winter each year apply a general compound fertilizer (*see p.20*) at 70g/ sq m (2oz/sq yd) over the rooting area. Apply a mulch of organic matter such as well-rotted manure, compost, or bark in spring (*see p.161*). Give extra water during dry periods in the spring and summer for the first 3–4 years after planting; after that mulberries should grow with minimal irrigation.

The branches of mature trees may become brittle. If necessary, provide support by driving a forked stake into

the ground and resting the branch on cushioned sacking in the fork.

## Harvesting mulberries

Mulberry yields are very variable. The fruits mature over a few weeks in mid- to late summer, and are almost black when ripe, parting easily from the spur. For preserving, use slightly underripe fruits. Take care when harvesting as the juice stains clothes easily. For large trees spread a cloth beneath the tree to catch fruits, then gently shake the branches.

## Common problems

Mulberries are seldom troubled by pests and diseases. However, birds (*see p.251*) will take the fruits.

### RECOMMENDED CULTIVARS

Choose from these named clonal selections rather than unnamed seedlings.

**'Black English'** *Red/black berries, sweet acid taste. Long fruit.*

**'Hick's Fancy'** *Red juicy berries. Sweet but acidic.*

# Hazelnuts

There are two forms of hazelnut, both similar in appearance, and hybrids between the two. The cobnut (*Corylus avellana*) has a short husk with the nut protruding, while the filbert (*Corylus maxima*) has a long husk, which covers the nut. Cobnuts and filberts grow best in full sun or light shade; they will grow, but not crop well, in heavy shade.

Choose a sheltered site, avoiding frost pockets (*see p.11*). The trees are tolerant of a range of soils provided that they are well drained and have a pH of 6.7–7.5. Light, sandy soils are preferable, since on very fertile soils the trees tend to produce too much growth.

## Tree forms and rootstocks
The most suitable tree form is an open-centred bush grown on a trunk of 30–45cm (12–18in). Space bushes about 4.5m (15ft) apart. Due to this wide spacing, and the fact that more than one tree is needed for pollination (*see below*), these trees are not suitable for a small garden unless multi-grafted trees are used.

## Pollination
Cobnuts and filberts are monoecious, that is, they have separate male and female flowers on the same tree (*see below*). The flowers are fairly hardy but appear early, often in late winter to early spring, so may be affected by frost.

Bracts

**Female flower**
*Flowers are about 8mm (⅓in) long, with red styles protruding from end*

**Male flower**
*Ripe catkins are yellowish-brown when shedding pollen*

### Successful pollination
*Flowers are wind-pollinated; pollen drifts from catkins to female flowers, so it helps to plant a group of trees in square formation.*

Although cobnuts and filberts are self-fertile, pollen is not always produced when the female flowers are receptive, so you need to grow more than one cultivar for good wind pollination.

## Planting
Plant in the dormant season (*see pp.158–159*). Bare-root plants usually establish well. Container-grown plants also grow well unless pot-bound. If possible, obtain a part-trained bush. In a very sheltered situation, staking may not be needed; otherwise secure to a short stake for the first two or three years.

## Pruning a cobnut or filbert bush
Formative pruning (*see pp.166–167*) is done in the winter following planting. With cobnuts and filberts, about eight branches can be retained. Once the tree is established, prune twice a year.

Summer pruning is known as "brutting" (*see above*). In spring, when pollen is being shed (the movement aids pollination), shorten branch leaders by about half to an outward-facing bud. Shorten strong laterals brutted (*see above*) the previous summer to three or four buds, or remove them if they are very vigorous. Leave weak laterals unpruned. If the tree becomes too tall – above 3–3.5m (10–11ft) – cut the leader back to a lower replacement lateral. Remove any branches crowding the centre. As the tree matures, remove overlong side branches, cutting back to a stub of about 2.5cm (1in); the branch will regrow from this. Remove any suckers at the base in the growing season.

### Brutted cobnut shoots
*In late summer, stop strong laterals 30cm (12in) or more in length half-way along by snapping them without completely breaking them off, and leave them hanging down. This encourages fruit buds to form and reduces vigour.*

## Routine care
In late winter each year, apply a general compound fertilizer (*see p.20*) at 70g/sq m (2oz/ sq yd). For the first 3–4 years, mulch in spring (*see p.161*) and water during dry spells in spring and summer.

## Harvesting and storing cobnuts and filberts
Yields are very variable for cobnuts and filberts. Harvest in early autumn when husks start to turn yellow, but before they start to drop. Nuts harvested too early do not store well and those left too long may be eaten by animals. Dry the nuts in the sun, and remove the husks when dry. Store in a cool, rodent-proof place in containers that allow some air circulation, such as slatted trays or suspended net bags.

## Common problems
Powdery mildew (*see p.260*) may be troublesome.

### RECOMMENDED CULTIVARS

#### COBNUTS
**'Cosford Cob'** *Sweet nuts with a thin shell. Reliable and a good pollinator.*
**'Pearson's Prolific'** *Round nut of good flavour. A compact tree producing a lot of catkins, and a good pollinator.*

#### FILBERTS
**'Butler'** *Heavy cropping with large nuts.*
**'Gunslebert'** *Heavy cropping with medium-sized nuts of strong flavour.*
**'Kentish Cob'** *Very good flavour and fine-textured nuts. Hardy and reliable.*

# Walnut

The species cultivated for its edible nuts is the Persian or English walnut (*Juglans regia*), native to Iran, Central Asia, and China. The North American black walnut (*Juglans nigra*) is more vigorous and the nuts are of poorer quality.

Walnuts make very handsome, but substantial trees of 18–20m (60–70ft) in height and spread. Slow-growing at first, they reach 10m (30ft) in the first 20 years. Although there are some more compact cultivars available, they still are suitable only for very large gardens.

Walnut trees are fully winter-hardy, but the early growth is susceptible to spring frosts. They grow best in deep, well-drained, moisture-retentive soil with a pH of 6.5 to 7, and will tolerate some alkalinity.

## Tree forms and rootstocks
Grow walnut cultivars freestanding, unpruned, or as centre-leader standards. They are usually grown on a seedling rootstock of *J. regia* or *J. nigra*. Plant only grafted, named cultivars since seedlings take a long time to come into bearing and usually offer inferior nuts.

## Pollination
Walnuts are monoecious – with male and female flowers on the same tree – and pollinated by wind. Most cultivars are self-fertile, but the male flowers often open before the females, so good crops are assured if there is at least one other cultivar growing no more than

**Harvesting walnuts**
*For storing, gather the nuts when their hulls crack to release the nuts from the shell (as here), and they start to fall. For pickling, harvest before the shell and hull harden.*

80m (280ft) away for cross-pollination. Spring frosts may damage flowers and young shoots, causing poor cropping.

## Planting
Plant in late autumn or winter (*see pp. 158–159*). Choose young plants, 3–4 years old, and part-trained as standards. Avoid pot-bound specimens as walnuts have a long taproot. Tie into

a short stake 45–60cm (18–24in) above ground. It is essential to site a walnut 12–18m (40–60ft) in a large garden, well away from other plantings. Walnuts secrete chemicals into the soil that may inhibit growth of some plants, so it is best not to grow other plants in their rooting area.

## Pruning and training a walnut centre-leader standard
Prune walnuts as little as possible as they bleed sap easily. Mid-autumn, when risk of bleeding is least, is best. For formative pruning, *see box, below.* A mature tree needs minimal pruning: remove crossing or broken branches.

## Routine care
On poor soil, broadcast a balanced compound feed (*see p. 20*) at 70g/sq m (2oz/sq yd) in early spring beneath the canopy area. After planting and for the first 3–4 years, mulch (*see p. 161*) and water in dry conditions.

## Harvesting and storing
Walnut yields are erratic. Harvest in autumn (*see left*). To store nuts, clean the shells before they discolour – wear gloves as the sap stains easily – and dry, preferably in sun. Store in a slatted box in cool, airy conditions such as a shed.

## Common problems
Walnuts are fairly problem-free, apart from walnut leaf blight (*see p. 264*). Birds (*see p. 251*) may take the nuts.

## Formative pruning
The centre-leader tree shape is basically pyramidal, although due to the walnut's spreading habit, it will become rounder with age. The aim in formative pruning is to promote a central, vertical leader from which all the main framework branches will grow. First, remove any competing leaders and vertical shoots that might spoil the shape. Then remove all laterals on the lower third of the stem to leave several wide-angled branches that start to form the crown of the tree. Continue in subsequent years to remove vertical shoots and maintain the crown.

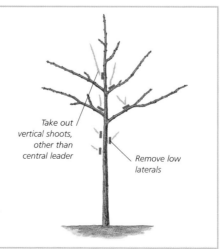

Take out vertical shoots, other than central leader

Remove low laterals

# Almond

The sweet almond (*Prunus dulcis*), which is cultivated for its edible nuts, is closely related to the peach and nectarine (*see pp. 193–195*). It originated in central Asia and the eastern Mediterranean. Bitter almonds and many almond seedlings have a high concentration of hydrocyanic acid in their nuts, and so are grown only as ornamental trees.

Almonds have very similar cultivation requirements to peaches. They need a favourable spring and warm, sunny conditions throughout summer and early autumn to produce and ripen good crops. Because they flower in early spring – often even earlier than peaches – they are vulnerable to frost damage in spring. Consequently they do not crop reliably in a cool climate. However, in areas with long, hot summers or in sheltered positions, they are well worth growing for their ornamental value, with the bonus of nut crops in most years.

Choose a sunny spot sheltered from cold winds (*see pp. 12–13*), and avoid frost pockets (*see p. 11*). Almonds can be grown on a range of soils provided that they are well drained, ideally with a pH of approximately 6.5.

## Tree forms and rootstocks
The three most successful forms for growing almonds are the bush, vase, and the fan. All forms also have excellent ornamental value in the garden, and the fan is particularly useful in a less favourable situation, where the tree can be trained against a warm wall or fence. Space bushes 4.5–6m (15–20ft) apart. A fan requires a space 3.5–4.5m (11–15ft) wide and 2–2.5m (6–8ft) high when mature.

Almonds can be grown on St Julien A rootstock, which will produce a

**Maturing almonds**
*Almond trees look very similar to peach trees, but need particularly warm conditions to set and ripen their crop reliably. Unlike peaches, the crop does not need thinning.*

medium-sized tree. Seedling peach or almond rootstocks can also be used, but tend to produce a larger tree.

## Pollination
Almond cultivars are either self-fertile or partly self-fertile and crop better if they are cross-pollinated. They flower in early spring when pollinating insects are not always active but during most years pollination and fruiting will occur provided it is not a very wet spring.

## Planting
Plant in the dormant season (*see pp. 158–159*), preferably in late autumn, since almonds come into growth early. Bare-root plants usually establish well. Container-grown plants also grow away well if not pot-bound. Before planting, prepare the stakes and wires (*see p. 162*) for the form you have chosen.

## Pruning and training
Almonds fruit on young wood made the previous season in the same way as peaches and nectarines, and so will need replacement pruning to produce a supply of new wood each year. Prune them in spring and summer to avoid infection from silver leaf (*see p. 262*) and bacterial canker (*see p. 253*).

For formative pruning of an almond bush, *see pp. 166–167*. For established pruning, follow the method for acid cherries (*see pp. 191–192*). For formative pruning of a fan, *see p. 173*. To prune an established almond fan, follow the method for peaches (*see pp. 193–194*).

## Routine care
Follow the guidelines under peaches (*see pp. 194–195*).

## Harvesting and storing
Almonds start cropping after three or four years, although their yields are unpredictable. When they are ready to harvest, the hulls will crack open and they will fall to the ground. When this starts to happen, pick the remainder and clean them (*see below*). Store them in cool, airy conditions such as in a rodent-proof shed or garage.

## Common problems
Almonds suffer from similar problems to peaches and nectarines (*see p. 195*).

**Cleaning almond fruits**
*Remove the almonds by peeling away the soft husks. Clean them, and dry thoroughly, preferably in the sun, before placing them in a slatted tray or box for storing.*

### RECOMMENDED CULTIVARS
**'All in One'** *Self-pollinating. Soft shell and sweet kernels.*
**'Chellaston'** *Long, narrow nuts with good-flavoured kernels. Soft shell.*
**'IXL'** *Paper shell and tasty kernel. Broad, rounded shape.*
**'Ne Plus Ultra'** *Firm to soft shell and plump kernels with good taste.*

# GROWING SOFT FRUITS

# Planning

Soft fruits include cane fruits, such as raspberries, blackberries, and hybrid berries; bush fruits, for example red-, white-, and blackcurrants, gooseberries, blueberries, cranberries, and strawberries, which are herbaceous perennials. Of these, strawberries bear fruit the soonest after planting, in just under a year. Most cane fruits crop from the second year after planting; autumn-fruiting raspberries may crop in the same year. For bush fruits, speed of cropping depends on the age of the plant and its fruiting habit. Black-currants and blueberries bear fruit on the current or last season's wood, so may fruit within a year of planting.

### Soft fruits in the garden

Soft fruits are highly rewarding. Not only are they at their most flavoursome when eaten straight from the plant, but they are also the most versatile of all the fruits in terms of how they are grown in the garden. They can be positioned in a separate area, possibly in a netted cage to fend off the birds (*see p.209*). An area of 10 x 20m (30 x 70ft) would yield enough fruit for a family of four.

Alternatively they can be mixed with other plants in the ornamental garden to exploit their attractive features: some strawberry cultivars have white and pink flowers, or variegated leaves, while blackberries and hybrid berries have a long, slender habit that makes them

**Potted strawberries**
*With their dainty flowers, pendent scarlet fruits, and shapely foliage, strawberries look particularly attractive in pots. They appreciate*

ideal for climbing up a fence or arch. This informal approach may also have the benefit of companion planting, since the mix of plants attracts a wider range of beneficial insects.

Growing soft fruits in containers increases opportunities in the garden and, with greenhouse protection, can extend the season from the usual outdoor span of early summer to mid-autumn to mid-spring to early winter. Suitable containers include hanging baskets, patio pots, and growing bags.

*the free drainage and the fruits remain free of soil splash and slug damage, although they need extra watering.*

### Good soil for soft fruits

For details about different soil types, *see p.14*. The ideal soil for soft fruits is a fertile, well-drained loam about 45cm (18in) deep. Heavy soils require careful management to create a warmer soil with improved drainage. Blackcurrants and blackberries are more tolerant than other soft fruits of wet sites, but still prefer good drainage. Sandy soils will need improvement to increase retention of moisture and nutrients. The addition of organic matter, in the form of garden compost, farmyard manure, or green manures, has the potential to improve most soils. For details on preparing your soil, *see pp.37–40 and p.208*.

### Soil-borne problems

Replant diseases (*see also p.261*) may occur when replanting fruit beds, particularly in a mature garden. Caused by soil-borne fungi, the symptoms are stunted growth of successive plantings of the same plant group. Replacing the topsoil overcomes the problem, but it is expensive and hard work. Choosing a vigorous cultivar and planting into a

**Hanging garden**
*Make use of hanging baskets to grow strawberries. Plant about 4 or 5 to a 40cm (16in) basket in potting compost, and add water-retaining gel and slow-release fertilizer granules to help the plants thrive.*

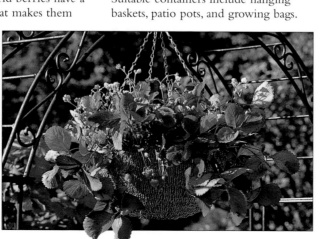

black plastic sheet mulch (*see p. 208*) will help mitigate the disease's effects.

Avoid planting strawberries after strawberries or potatoes for at least five years to minimize the possibility of verticillium wilt (*see p. 263*), which is also a soil-borne disease. Soil drench formulations containing beneficial micro-organisms are available to redress the balance and revive a "sick soil". Growing soft fruit in containers (*see p. 208*) avoids all of these problems.

## Nutrition and pH levels

The levels of nutrients in the soil and its acidity or alkalinity affect the growth and productivity of soft fruits. It is worth testing your soil nutrient and pH levels before planting (*see p. 17 and p. 18*) and monitoring these levels at intervals to avoid under- or overfeeding, both of which can adversely affect crops.

Strawberry crop sites may need to be sampled annually, whereas the woody, longer-living cane and bush fruits may need sampling every three years if the soil was prepared well before planting. Periods of heavy rain and overwet soil conditions, especially when plants are dormant, cause particular nutrients, like nitrogen, to leach out of the soil.

Most soft fruits perform best at a slightly acidic pH 6.2–6.7. Blueberries are an exception, preferring the more acidic pH 4–5.5. An alkaline soil above pH 7 causes manganese and iron to be unavailable to plants and a resulting chlorosis of the leaves will show (*see p. 253*). This is especially visible in raspberries. Dieback of sideshoots on cane and bush fruits is another symptom. A very acidic soil will cause some minor nutrients to be too readily available at levels toxic to many plants.

## Choosing a site

A garden fence or wall or a sheltered sunny position provides the warmest and sunniest aspect for soft fruits, although care needs to be taken that on hotter, drier days the foliage does not burn. The sun ripens growth, especially cane- and bush-fruit wood, encourages healthy flower buds, and gives ripe, flavoursome fruits. Hybrid berries and blackberries tolerate partial shade.

Frost is particularly damaging to soft fruits when they are in blossom as the low temperatures can kill the flowers,

causing the loss of the crop. If it is not possible to avoid planting in a frost pocket (*see p. 11*), choose more frost-tolerant crops, or later-flowering cultivars. Cane fruits flower later than bush fruits and many strawberries, so are less susceptible to loss of fruit due to frost, *see p. 209*.

## Providing shelter

Soft fruits need shelter (*see pp. 12–13*) to prevent strong winds from damaging new growth, flowers, and fruits. Shelter will also increase the local temperature slightly, encouraging pollinating and other beneficial insects, and providing a more favourable environment that leads to less disease, and improved ripening of fruit and stems.

Artificial windbreaks of plastic mesh may be preferred to hedges or used as a temporary measure on the leeward side of a young natural windbreak while it is still growing to maturity.

## Altitude and rainfall

Soft fruits can be grown at altitudes of up to 180m (600ft), although they will need sufficient shelter from the stronger winds at such heights. At high altitudes, the temperatures are generally lower and the growing season shorter.

Water is essential for plant growth, including the swelling of the fruit as it

ripens, but excessive rainfall – 900mm (3ft) or over per year – will cause nutrients to be lost from the soil and plants, diseases such as botrytis (*see p. 252*) to proliferate, and some physical damage, which could also be the entry point for disease infections.

If you live in an area of high rainfall, you may decide to plant soft fruits in a greenhouse or polytunnel, which must be provided with shade and adequate ventilation in summer and winter. Chemical fungicides control diseases encouraged by wet. Some cultivars have some resistance to botrytis diseases.

## Planning the layout

Once you have found a suitable site for soft fruit, plan the positioning of the plants. This will help you to judge how many plants you can fit in, and ensure that taller plants will not shade others (*see pp. 29–30*). A square or rectangular plot will be easier to net against birds. Strawberries are best planted in a bed or area of their own for three or four years before replacing. They can also be included with vegetables so that they can be replanted regularly along with the vegetable rotation. Select cultivars that fruit in succession to extend the season and avoid a glut. Of the soft fruits, only blueberries need another cultivar as a pollinator.

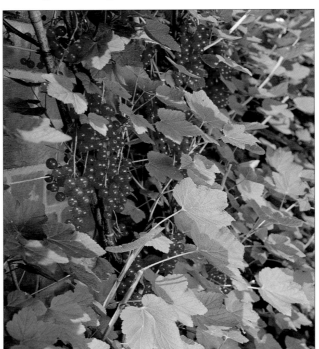

### Wall fruit

*All the cane fruits and most bush fruits, such as these delicious redcurrants 'Jonkheer van Tets', can be trained against a wall or fence. This is an economical use of space in the garden, ensuring that the fruits receive as much sun as possible to ripen them. Plants grown in this way are also easier to net against birds, as well as to harvest.*

# Planting soft fruits

To ensure sound establishment, a good crop of fruits, and to maintain healthy plants, it is important to prepare the soil properly before planting (*see pp.37–40*). Growing soft fruits in containers can provide fruit in the short term if long-term soil preparation is needed.

## Preparing the soil

When you are planting an area with soft fruits, prepare the whole patch rather than individual planting holes. Unless you are following the "no-dig" system (*see p.39*), start by digging over the area, removing any perennial weeds.

Incorporate organic matter before planting to provide a good medium in which the roots can establish. Add additional fertilizer as an insurance to top up nutrient levels. New gardens may need up to one barrowload of organic matter per 3sq m (3sq yd), 35g/sq m (1oz/sq yd) of sulphate of potash, and 15g/sq m (½oz/sq yd) of superphosphate.

There are a number of ways in which to improve less-than-perfect soils (*see pp.22–26*). On heavy soils, mounding the soil up to 20cm (8in) for planting can improve drainage and soil warming and reduce the root rots caused by the *Phytophthora* fungus (*see p.259–260*). On shallow soils, mounding will improve the local soil depth.

**Planting a bare-root plant**
*In winter, when the plant is dormant, prepare a planting hole large enough to accommodate the roots. Use a cane across the hole to check that the planting level will match the nursery soil mark on the stem once it is firmed in. Hold the plant at this level while you fill in with soil.*

## Planting a container-grown plant

**1** **Using a black plastic sheet mulch** will help to warm the soil and suppress weeds. Rake a 10cm (4in) deep bed to a mounded surface. Cut a piece of plastic about 30cm (12in) wider than the bed. With a spade, push the edges of the plastic into a slit trench around the bed.

**2** **Mark out** the planting holes at the correct spacing. Use a garden knife to cut cross-slits at each planting site.

**3** **Dig a hole** large enough to take the rootball. Place the plant (here a bush gooseberry) in the hole, checking that it is at the same depth as it was in its pot. Fill in with soil and firm it in well. Water the plant thoroughly through the planting slits.

If you are planting in a raised bed, add bulky organic matter and, in a heavy soil, plenty of grit. To prepare growing bags, plump them up, cut out the holes required, and water them if they are dry. For containers, use a mixture of peat-based potting mix or peat substitute and soil-based potting mix. Mix coarse bark and grit into the lower levels of large containers to increase drainage. Adding a slow-release fertilizer will provide optimum nutrition.

## Choosing and planting soft fruits

Start with vigorous, healthy plants from a reliable source. Many soft fruits have certification schemes in which the fruits have been inspected and certified as free of pests and diseases. Plants are supplied with bare roots or in containers. Bare-root plants are usually less costly but can be planted only when dormant – from late autumn to early spring. Autumn is preferable, if the soil is still warm, to promote root establishment. Bare-root strawberry plants (runners) can be planted all the year round (*see p.212*), as can container-grown plants.

It is best to plant bare-root plants as soon as you buy or receive them. If this is not possible, store them with the roots in moist peat or peat substitute in a plastic bag on a concrete floor in an unheated building, or heel them in the garden by digging a shallow trench, placing the roots in the trench, and covering with well-firmed soil. Before planting, soak the roots in water for two hours. Adding a biostimulant, such as seaweed extract, will give faster and improved root growth. As you plant, shake the soil progressively around the roots to avoid any air holes. Firm in each plant carefully, water it thoroughly and then mulch with organic matter.

Container-grown soft fruits should grow away well even in the summer, provided they do not dry out. Rootballs in peat-based composts dry out more than the surrounding soil; to counteract this, plant them slightly deeper to cover the rootball, and apply a mulch. For planting in containers, *see p.36*.

Plant most soft fruits at the depth of their nursery soil mark – plant cane fruits and blackcurrants more deeply.

# General care

Although good soil preparation is the basis for healthy, sound soft fruit plants, a simple programme of routine care will ensure that your plants remain at their optimum health.

### Watering

Watering is essential to the wellbeing of soft fruits, especially at planting and as fruits swell. Avoid overwatering mature fruit plants, which causes the fruit to rot more readily as it ripens, and reduces the taste and sweetness. It can also result in poor root activity and nutrient loss from the soil.

### Feeding

The organic matter incorporated before planting needs to be topped up annually with mulches (*see pp. 41–42*), usually in early to mid-spring when the soil temperature has started to rise. Hay, which has been shown to break down more readily and release more nutrients than straw, is particularly beneficial.

Green manures (*see p. 23*), such as grazing rye, white clover, vetch, and mustard, can be sown around newly planted soft fruit in late summer to avoid creating too much competition. Their flowers will attract beneficial insects, both pollinators and predators, but cut them before they set seed.

Apply any additional dressings of fertilizers (*see pp. 20–23*) needed to maintain soil fertility sparingly in order to avoid wastage and pollution of water courses. Use nitrogen and potassium annually in spring or early summer, and phosphorus occasionally in spring. Soil analysis (*see p. 17*) is advisable to monitor the soil pH and potassium and phosphorus levels. Growing bags will require liquid feeds after four weeks of growth. To other containers, add a slow-release fertilizer in spring, according to the instructions on the packaging.

### Weed control

Remove perennial weeds as soon as they become apparent; if left, they will compete with soft fruits for moisture, nutrients, and light, and, since they can prevent air movement around the plant canopy, they may cause damp-related

△ **Protection from birds**
*Fruit cages for bird protection are available in kit form or you can make a system of sturdy stakes wired together and drape netting over them. Secure netting to the soil with pegs.*

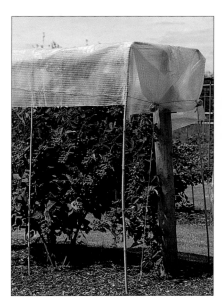

◁ **Protection from rain**
*A simple raincover, such as plastic sheeting, will protect ripe fruit from being ruined and can extend the fruiting period from late summer into autumn.*

diseases to arise. Annual weeds also compete with the crop for nutrients and water. In an organic system, weeds can be kept under control by mulch mowing, or by using old carpet or layers of newspapers layered and covered with mulch. Trees and shrubs can be mulched heavily each year.

### Frost protection

To protect flowers and young fruits against frost damage, you may be able to cover soft fruit bushes with hessian or fleece. Since they are low-growing, strawberries can be covered with fleece or cloches, with the addition of some newspaper if the frost is severe. Move container-grown fruits under cover.

### Soft fruit problems

If proper care is taken over preparation of the site, over planting, training and pruning, and routine care, the incidence of pests and diseases will be reduced. Overfeeding with nitrogen will cause soft growth that attracts sucking insects such as aphids (*see p. 251*).

If problems do occur, choose an appropriate method of control – either chemical methods or exploiting natural predators with use of biological controls (*see p. 52*). Always follow the supplier's instructions with care.

Soft fruits are particularly prone to attack from birds, which are attracted by the colour and smell of ripening and over ripe fruit, and eat soft fruit as a source of water as well as food. The most effective way to protect ripening fruit is a fruit cage. This may also be needed in winter when birds eat the following year's fruit buds.

Fruit cages can be bought in kit form in all shapes and sizes. For the most basic cage, you can erect corner posts and put flower pots or plastic bottles over the tops of the posts to support the netting. A fine woven mesh will keep out insect pests (and any beneficial insects), but roll the netting up at the sides at flowering time so pollinators can enter.

Netting draped over plants is less expensive than a fruit cage, but needs to be removed to give access to pick the fruit and, unless it is very well-secured, birds will find their way in. Noisy bird scarers can be effective, but may irritate you and the neighbours. A line that hums in a slight wind can be strung across the garden, emitting sound that disturbs birds, but other animals, including pets, will also be affected. Container-grown soft fruits can be brought under cover for protection as their fruits ripen.

For other problems that may be likely to affect soft fruits, *see individual crops, pp. 211–226*.

## Pruning soft fruits

Soft fruits require dead, diseased, and damaged growth to be removed to maintain health and vigour. Pruning at planting reduces the need for water until the roots are established. Pruning also encourages productivity. Crown thinning of strawberries (*see p.213*) and spur pruning (*see below right*) of gooseberries improve air circulation as well as flower quality and fruit size by regulating the numbers of flower buds. Fruit size is not an important consideration when growing for home.

Pruning is also vital for creating and maintaining the shape of woody soft fruits. On a basic level, the removal of crowded and crossing branches ensures that the plant has a balanced shape. Replacement pruning to produce new growth can also break the life cycle of some diseases, like American gooseberry mildew (*see p.251*) on gooseberries and blackcurrants, and coral spot (*see p.254*) on red- and whitecurrants. Some bush fruits, such as gooseberries and red- and whitecurrants, may also be pruned and trained into cordon or fan shapes to make use of a wall or fence, for ease of fruit picking and management, and for a more decorative effect.

Since cane fruits (except autumn-fruiting raspberries) produce their fruits on the previous year's wood, they need annual pruning to remove the fruited wood. Strawberries also need routine pruning in the form of removal of their runners as they appear (*see below*).

*Use a figure-of-eight knot to tie new shoots to the support to prevent the stems rubbing directly against the wires.*

**Train in new growth**
*Carefully lower new shoots to train into supports*

**Cut out fruited wood**
*Using angled cuts, remove fruited wood just above ground level*

### Pruning and training blackberries and hybrid berries

*This basic method shows how the new season's shoots are trained in vertically at the centre of the plant. Once the previous season's shoots have fruited, they can be cut out. The new season's shoots can be lowered and tied in to the support wires as replacements when growth restarts in spring. There are several other ways of training cane fruits (see p.217).*

## Training and support systems

Training goes hand in hand with pruning. It is needed to form the basic shape of woody soft fruit plants, and, for those grown against supports – such as cane fruits, and fan- and cordon-trained bush fruits – it is the means of maintaining the plant shape.

Cane fruits are traditionally trained on a freestanding post-and-wire support system to avoid breakage of the canes and to keep fruit off the soil. There are several ways of erecting the posts and horizontal galvanized wires according to preference and the number of plants being grown (*see p.216*). Wires can also be attached to fences and walls using hooks. Allow up to 10cm (4in) between the wires and the supporting structure so that air can circulate.

The use of wooden trellis, pergolas, and arches will show off cane fruits to good effect in the ornamental garden. Planting cane fruits by a single post and training them around it will use less space, but demands careful training to keep the canes within bounds.

Bush fruits, such as blackcurrants and blueberries, are usually grown as stooled plants, meaning that new stems grow from below ground to maintain vigour. These need no training. Gooseberries, redcurrants, and whitecurrants are generally trained as a bush form on a short stem, or leg, to reduce vigour. Where they are trained as fans or cordons, they require a system of wire supports on posts or against a fence.

### Pruning strawberries
*Rooted runners affect the size and quality of fruit on the parent plant by competing for water, light, and nutrients. Remove the runners before they have rooted by cutting or pinching them out close to the parent plant.*

**Prune main shoot**
*Remove about one-third of previous season's growth to encourage branching*

**Shorten sideshoots**
*Cut each sideshoot back to few buds from main shoot*

### Spur pruning bush fruits
*When forming a permanent framework of fruiting branches on a red- or whitecurrant or gooseberry bush, aim to produce a system of short, fruiting spurs on the main shoot by reducing long sideshoots in winter.*

# SOFT FRUIT CROPS

# Strawberry

Strawberries are renowned for their succulent and sweetly flavoursome fruits. They can be enjoyed for up to ten months of the year, from early spring to early winter, by planting a variety of cultivars and judicious use of containers and protective covers.

The cultivated strawberry, *Fragaria x ananassa* (pineapple strawberry), is the result of a cross between the Chilean strawberry *Fragaria chiloensis* and the North American meadow strawberry *Fragaria virginiana* (first reported in 1766). Breeders have since created a vast range of more productive, better tasting, and larger-fruited cultivars. Strawberries are commonly grown in temperate regions as a hardy herbaceous perennial that may crop for up to four years. In warmer regions, they are often grown as annuals where they produce very high yields of quality fruit over an extended season.

Cultivars are grouped according to their season of fruiting. "Summer bearers" produce flower buds in the

*Strawberries are one plant that responds extremely well to hydroponic systems. A small hydroponic system is easy to construct; piping and troughs are easy to assemble as is the necessary header tank and small pump.*

short days of late summer and early autumn; "perpetual" (remontant) types usually form flower buds in the longer days of summer. Alpine strawberries (*see p.214*) are a selection of the wild strawberry *F. vesca* subsp. *alpina*. They make an attractive ornamental edging for the border, and the fruits, although small, are fragrant and sweet.

Strawberry plants are inexpensive, compact, and versatile. Planting them direct into garden soil, either in flat or raised beds, allows unrestricted root growth, which benefits perennial crops. Strawberry beds usually last for three or four years with the plants in good health and cropping well before they need replanting. Strawberry plants can also be incorporated with the vegetable rotation and replanted annually. Raised beds can improve drainage on heavy soils, increase rooting depth on stony ground, and, if covered with a sheet mulch (*see box, right*), can be used to extend the growing season.

Another way of extending the season is to grow strawberries in containers, such as hanging baskets, windowboxes, tubs, and growing bags. As well as being free of soil-borne problems, container

plants can be raised up off the ground for easier maintenance and picking, placed under cover to protect them from the weather, and moved around the garden as you wish.

## WHICH SHEET MULCH?

- **Plastic sheet mulches** control annual, and most perennial, weeds and allow early soil preparation for planting. All plastic mulches need to be laid as tight to the soil as possible throughout the life of the crop to avoid surface puddles forming and encouraging rotten fruit. Laying the sheet in warm weather helps to keep it tight.
- **Black plastic** warms the soil, helping to bring forward cropping, but may become too hot in summer and cook the fruits.
- **Coloured plastics** generally stay cool by transmitting heat into the soil and can bring forward cropping by up to four days.
- **White plastic** and other reflective plastics keep soil cooler so delay the start of fruiting, but increase light levels in the crop's canopy, helping photosynthesis and fruit ripening. Research has shown that aphid numbers and consequent virus infections have been considerably reduced where reflective mulches have been used.

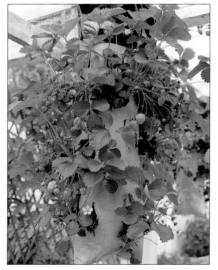

**Hanging strawberry planter**
*Suspended from a firm support, a standard growing bag can be used as a hanging planter for strawberries. Place the growing bag in a sunny location outdoors, or keep it under cover to obtain early fruits.*

## Planting strawberries in a flat bed

**1 Mark out a planting row** with a garden line in well-prepared and levelled ground. Measure out planting holes for each strawberry plant at 30–38cm (12–15in) intervals.

**2 Plant a runner** at each of the marked points. Avoid constricting or bending the roots, trimming any over-long roots to no less than 10cm (4in) if necessary.

**3 Ensure that the crown** of each plant is level with the surface. Fill in the hole and firm in with your fingers. Test whether the plant is sufficiently firm by gently pulling at a leaf.

**4 Water the row** of runners thoroughly to settle the soil around the roots. After planting, keep all the plants well watered, especially while they are starting to produce new leaves.

With their pretty flowers, sometimes variegated foliage, and red and white fruits, strawberries are too versatile to be confined to the fruit patch. Try white-flowered cultivars with trailing Arctic raspberries for a productive and colourful container.

### Preparing strawberry beds

Strawberries thrive in a free-draining, fertile loam, so prepare the soil well before planting (*see p.208*). Develop good soil structure for root growth and free drainage, discouraging soil-borne diseases that thrive in waterlogged conditions. For the best growth and fruit flavours, avoid planting in shade.

**Planting through a sheet mulch**
*To plant through a plastic sheet mulch, spread the sheeting taut over a mounded bed that is 10–20cm (4–6in) deep and 1.2m (4ft) wide. Cut cross-slits in 2 rows at 30–38cm (12–15in) staggered intervals. Plant each strawberry at least as deep as it was in its pot. Firm; water.*

Mix in plenty of well-rotted organic matter on clay and sandy soils. Dig out perennial weeds or treat them with a systemic chemical weedkiller well before planting, when they are in active growth.

When growing strawberries through a sheet mulch on a raised bed, keep the plastic taut so that it is effective in warming the soil. Prepare the soil underneath to a fine tilth to ensure a snug fit, and mound it so that water will run off the plastic. Plastic mulches conserve existing moisture in the soil, but the plants will soon fill the planting holes and prevent the penetration of sufficient water to the roots. They will need additional watering during hot, dry weather and when the fruits are swelling, so you will need to install a watering system. This could be through plant pots sunk through the plastic into the raised bed or via a low-pressure watering system underneath the plastic.

### Planting

Traditionally, bare-root strawberry runners are planted in beds. Buy in new plants from a certified source for successful crops.

Late-summer plantings of summer bearers establish well and fruit in the following year; autumn and spring plantings should have their first flush of flowers removed so the plants crop well in their second year. Perpetuals are best

planted in autumn or spring. Cold-stored runners, frozen at −2°C (28°F) after lifting from nurseries, are available for planting out from late spring to midsummer. If watered with a fine spray until established, they should crop well in 60 days. They revert to the usual season of fruiting in the second year.

When planting bare-root runners in flat beds, first rake over the bed, then plant as shown above. Alternatively, plant in a raised bed through a sheet mulch (*see left*). It is easier in both cases to insert plants with a special planting fork, using the fork to straighten out the roots in the soil. Ensure that the crown is at soil level with its top uncovered so that it does not rot.

In containers, use a loam-based potting mix or add water-retentive granules to a soilless potting mix to reduce the need for watering. Installing an automatic low-pressure watering system or a reservoir and wick system can also help, but beware of overwatering.

### Routine care

Keep plants well watered after planting until they produce new leaves; during dry spells and as the fruit is ripening to improve crop yields; and in early autumn for summer bearers to ensure a healthy supply of flower buds for the following year. Once the fruits have formed, avoid watering plants overhead, especially late in the day, in case the damp encourages botrytis (*see p.252*) and slugs (*see p.262*) on the fruits.

Fruiting plants often need liquid feed through the watering system. Using tomato feeds with a high potash content during the growing season will markedly improve flower quality and the flavour and colour of the fruit. Those in growing bags will need a balanced liquid feed after four weeks of growth and until flowering. From then until the end of harvest use a tomato feed, then revert to the balanced feed.

The use of sheet mulches and of containers will keep plants neat, giving good flower and fruit quality. Where the runners that arise naturally from strawberry plants root, they compete for water, nutrients, and light. Unless they are needed for propagation (*see p.214*), remove them as they appear (*see p.210*).

In early spring, tidy plants to make way for new leaves (*see right*). Crown numbers will increase as the plants get older and may need to be thinned out at the same time (*see right*).

## Protecting the crop
Protective coverings can be used to extend the fruiting period and protect ripening fruit from the weather and birds. Covering outdoor plants in the early spring with a tunnel cloche (*see pp.46–47*), at least 45cm (18in) wide and 30cm (12in) high, or a fleece (*see p.48*) will encourage flowering and

## Tidying and thinning strawberry plants

1 **Tidy up** strawberry plants in early autumn. Some gardeners burn the strawberry patch, others run a mower over the old plants, but it is most effectively done by hand. Pinch out or cut off all dead, damaged, or diseased leaves and old runners and fruits to eliminate any pests and diseases.

2 **Thin out crown numbers** as the plants get older. A crown is formed by a cluster of leaves arising from a growing point at the base of the plant. Pull off the smaller crowns at the base to leave 3 or 4 crowns per plant. This will concentrate the plant's energies into producing good-sized fruits.

hence fruiting about seven days earlier. The fleece can be laid over the plants or, for added frost protection, raised on wire hoops. Lift the covering during the day at flowering to allow access by pollinating insects. Similar protection in early autumn will shield late fruit from the effects of rain and cold.

The developing fruits will also need protection. To protect the crop from birds, drape a fruit net on posts about 1.2m (4ft) high over the crop. Wire netting can also be used if animals are proving to be a problem. You also need

to keep individual fruits clean of soil. Sheet mulches will prevent soil splash on raised beds. Crops on the flat need to be protected by a mulch of straw or bracken, or a strawberry mat (*see below*). Straw can be a source of botrytis (*see p.252*) and home to slugs when wet, and should therefore be removed in the autumn.

Covering some strawberry plants in late winter with a 20–30cm (8–12in) deep layer of straw (secured with netting if exposed), or an opaque white plastic sheet, will delay flowering by seven days by trapping cold in the soil. This will slightly extend the fruiting season. Remove the covering in late spring so the plants can resume normal growth.

### Container-grown strawberries
To extend the fruiting season further, move plants in containers into a frost-free greenhouse or conservatory in late winter. Heating it to a minimum of 10°C (50°F) will bring forward the time of flowering, but air temperatures should not exceed 16°C (61°F) until flowering to avoid flower blindness (when flowers do not form). Increase the temperature to 16°C (61°F) at flowering to enhance the flowers' ability to pollinate and set fruit. If pollinating insects are in short supply, you may prefer to hand-pollinate. You can hand-pollinate by using a paintbrush or a

## Protecting the fruits

**Using a straw mulch**
*Tuck clean straw under developing fruits to protect them from soil splash. On black plastic sheet mulches, this also prevents the fruits from being scorched.*

**Using strawberry mats**
*These fibre mats are often easier to buy and use than straw, and last longer. Put a mat around each plant. Use in early autumn to protect late fruits from rain and cold weather.*

hair dryer to redistribute the pollen between the flowers. After fruit set, maintain a temperature of 17°C (63°F) and ventilate at 20°C (68°F) until harvest.

To enhance growth of new leaves and of flower buds for the following year, continue watering and feeding until early autumn and, for perpetuals, until the end of harvest. Allow all plants to experience the winter cold; most need a spell at cold temperatures to break plant dormancy and stimulate flowers and growth in the new season.

Strawberries are well suited to hydroponic systems where the roots of the plants lie in an aerated flowing water and nutrient mix. A simple system can be made using a bucket, drainage system, header tank, and a small water pump.

## Propagation

Strawberries are fairly easy to propagate by transplanting rooted runners into pots. Choose only those from the previous year's certified plants that are free from aphids (which carry viruses). If you use runners from an older crop, there is no guarantee they will be free from disease, especially viruses.

## Harvesting and storing strawberries

Bare-root runners, if planted in late summer, and runners propagated in pots and planted in early spring, will fruit in the new season. Expect to pick 450g (1lb) or more of fruit per plant from healthy plants. Picking when daytime temperatures are high gives juicy, sweet-flavoured fruits. Harvest fruits when they are fully coloured and eat them as soon as possible, otherwise they may continue to ripen after picking.

To store strawberries, pick them when the fruit has a white tip and is slightly unripe, cool them quickly, and keep for a few days at 2–4°C (36–39°F). Strawberries can be frozen but not many cultivars remain intact and look appetizing after they have been thawed out.

## Common problems

Monitor for pests and diseases all year round, especially in the greenhouse. Particular problems that may affect strawberries are viruses and botrytis. Strawberry viruses (*see p.263*) can be minimized by planting only plants that have been certified virus-free and by controlling aphids (*see p.251*).

To avoid botrytis (*see p.252*), maintain dry foliage and good ventilation around the plants. Remove any overripe fruits.

Other likely problems include birds (*see p.209 and p.251*), and verticillium wilt (*see p.263*).

If red spider mite (including the glasshouse species) is a problem, buy in natural predators (*see p.261*). Avoid wet mulches if slugs and snails (*p.262*) are present, and encourage natural predators.

To avoid powdery mildew (*p.260*), which affects protected crops and perpetuals, maintain good ventilation and watering.

### ALPINE STRAWBERRIES

These attractive and fragrant miniature strawberries are best grown from seed and replanted every two years or so. Once the seeds have germinated, prick them out. Harden off both autumn and spring sowings to plant out in late spring. Allow 30cm (12in) between plants and 75cm (30in) between rows. Harvest the ripe fruits in the evening, crush them, add sugar, and leave overnight to develop their full flavour.

▷ **Dainty crop**
*Alpine strawberries are quite hardy and will happily seed themselves around the garden. The tiny fruits are not as sweet as those of garden cultivars, but nonetheless are a useful crop. The plants form a good ground cover in a potager garden.*

◁ **Raising from seed**
*Collect seeds from dried alpine strawberries, removing them by rolling the fruits between thumb and fingers (see left). Keep in a paper packet in a cool, dry place. Sow the seed in autumn or spring in seed compost, covered with sharp sand. Keep shaded at 18–24°C (65–75°F).*

# Raspberry, blackberry, and hybrid berries

Cane fruits are so called because they flower and fruit on sideshoots of long, vigorous canes. These fruits include raspberries (*Rubus idaeus*), blackberries (*R. fruticosus*), and many hybrid berries. The hybrids include loganberries, boysenberries, and tayberries, among others, and result from crosses between species within the *Rubus* genus. Some are less vigorous than blackberries, while others are thornless – both qualities making them ideal for the fruit or ornamental garden. They have the same cultivation needs as blackberries.

Raspberries have a life expectancy of up to ten years, while blackberries may remain productive for 15 years. Most cane fruits flower and fruit on canes produced in the previous year; autumn-fruiting cultivars fruit on canes grown in the same year. Raspberries produce upright growth – with the exception of the Artic raspberry, which has trailing canes ideal for ground cover. Hybrid berries and blackberries have longer growth, requiring more attention to training and support to keep them off the soil. Cane fruits are a useful addition to the fruit garden since they

---

## Types of cane fruit berry

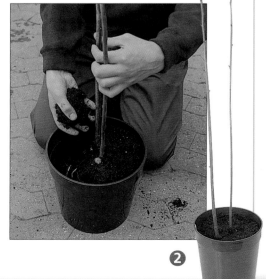

| Raspberry | Blackberry | Loganberry | Boysenberry | Tayberry |

---

flower later than most other fruits and so usually avoid frost damage. Fruiting is from midsummer to early autumn. With some protection from frosts and cold, autumn-fruiting raspberries can fruit into early winter, and if summer-fruiting cane fruits are potted up and placed in a glasshouse in midwinter, they can be forced, with gentle heat, to produce fruit by mid-spring (*see below*). It is feasible for the amateur to produce these succulent fruits for eight or nine months of the year. The fruits also store well when frozen.

Cane fruits like full sun but blackberries tolerate partial shade, particularly where the summer temperatures are high. Shelter from wind (*see pp. 12–13*) is important to reduce damage to fruiting canes.

### Preparing the site

Plant quality, good soil drainage, and depth of planting are critical for the success of cane fruits. To prepare the soil, start by digging the whole area (*see pp. 37–40*) and removing weeds. Incorporate organic matter such as well-rotted manure or compost. A soil analysis (*see p. 17*) will indicate whether more fertilizer, particularly phosphate and potash, needs to be added.

Raspberries, in particular, require good drainage (*see p. 16*). On heavy soils, cane fruits can be planted in a raised bed to improve drainage, soil warming, and rooting depth. Autumn-fruiting raspberries need a warm, sunny position to ripen before the first frosts.

Think at this stage about what kind of support structure you would like to use (*see p. 216*), although erection of the support system can wait until the autumn following planting. Cane fruits are traditionally planted in rows with freestanding supports to prevent wind damage; it is also possible to train them on horizontal wires against a wall or fence. Raspberries are usually planted to form continuous rows of canes, while, for ease of training, blackberries and hybrids are planted and maintained as individual plants.

Planting and training in a spiral around a single, stout post (less vigorous cultivars, for example the

---

## Potting early raspberry canes

**1** **In midwinter**, lift unpruned canes and trim off any dead or damaged wood. Check that each plant has at least 1 good bud on the roots and a good root system. Pot 2 or 3 canes into a 10 litre (10in) pot, using a light, free-draining potting mix. Fill around the roots with potting mix, ensuring the rootball is about 5–8cm (2–3in) below soil level, firm well, and water in.

**2** **Cut the canes** to a bud at about 1.2m (4ft). Grow under protection for a crop in mid-spring. For pollination and fruit set, either introduce insects or use a hair dryer on a cool setting to redistribute pollen at flowering.

**2**

thornless loganberry are best for this) or vertically up an arch (*see below*) are other space-saving options that add an interesting feature to the garden, making the most of the plants' decorative features. For example, the blackberry 'Oregon Thornless' has attractively cut leaves with good autumn colour.

## Choosing plants

Choose plants from a certified source so that they are vigorous, free of pests and diseases, and of a named cultivar. Each new plant should have a stem of pencil thickness, or 7–10mm (¼–½in), with a fibrous root system showing at least one white bud. This bud should produce a new cane soon after planting.

Raspberries may be bought bare root or container-grown; blackberries and hybrid berries are usually bought as container-grown plants. Plant bare-root raspberry canes in late autumn or early in winter. If soil conditions are poor, with waterlogging, delay planting to late winter or early spring. Container-grown plants can be planted at any time of the year.

## Planting raspberries

When planting, space raspberry plants 35–45cm (14–18in) apart along the row. The space between rows depends on the vigour of the cultivar; allow 1.5–2m (5–6ft) for summer-fruiting cultivars. A row of autumn-fruiting raspberries needs to be at least 2m (6ft) away from other fruits; the wider row is to produce enough fruit at each picking since autumn-fruiting raspberries crop less abundantly than others.

To encourage new canes to emerge and grow to their optimum height, plant raspberries no deeper than 5–8cm (2–3in); use the soil mark on the stem as a guide. On bare-root plants, cut any long roots back to 20cm (8in) before planting to promote new root growth, and spread the roots horizontally. After firming in, cut the cane to 30cm (12in) from soil level; leave the cane unpruned on container-grown plants since the root system is already well established.

Raspberries can also be planted in containers for early fruits (*see p.215*), or to overcome poor soil conditions, such as drainage. The pots can be brought in from the risk of frost when in flower.

## Planting blackberries and hybrid berries

Prepare the ground (*see pp.37–40*). It is simplest to erect the supports before planting since the canes will require support in their first summer. Spacing for blackberries and hybrid berries varies widely. A moderately vigorous cultivar needs 2.5–3.5m (8–11ft) between plants. A particularly vigorous blackberry cultivar may need up to 4.5m (13ft) to allow enough space to

---

# Supports for summer-fruiting raspberries, blackberries, and hybrids

These systems are all ideal for summer-fruiting raspberries, while the stool system is best for blackberries and hybrid berries. All cane fruits can be grown over an arch to form a compact and decorative feature. Of the row systems, the hedgerow system takes the least space and produces the highest yield. The stool system is the easiest to manage, with good light and air and access for weed control. For supports, use preservative-treated posts 75mm (3in) in diameter and 2.5m (8ft) long (75cm/30in driven into the soil) at the ends of rows, plus intermediate posts up to 10m (30ft) apart if needed. Use galvanized 12-gauge or 3.5mm (⅛in) thick wires.

*Wires 60cm (2ft) apart vertically*
*Double wire*
*Strut helps to take strain of wires and weight of canes*
*Tips of canes should be cut off in early spring*
*String at intervals of 45cm (18in)*

### Hedgerow system
*After fruiting, cut out unwanted canes and tie in new canes 10cm (4in) apart to the 2 sets of wires. Prune the tops of the canes to 15cm (6in) above the top wire in early spring or, for a higher yield, twist them in.*

### Double post-and-wire system
*Tie strings between 2 wires to create a support "net" for new canes. Use a second tier of wires and string for strong cultivars. The fruit canes are not tied in, so this method is not suitable for windy sites.*

*Structure requires more space than others*
*Cross wire helps to brace 2 parallel wires*
*Rows of posts 90cm (3ft) apart*
*Stooled plant*
*Wires 60cm (2ft) apart vertically for raspberries, 45cm (18in) apart for blackberries*
*Canes firmly tied to support with string*

### Scandinavian system
*Wrap new canes around 1 of the 2 parallel wires and tie them in to form a V-shaped row. The following year's canes will grow up through the centre of the fruiting canes, allowing you clear access for picking the fruit.*

### Stool system
*Remove all but 6 or 7 canes per plant, and tie these to the wires in a fan shape to give improved ventilation and light levels. Prune the tops of canes to 15cm (6in) above the top wire or loop them over and tie in (see also p.210).*

### Training over an arch
*Train new canes over the arch and tie them in with garden twine. There should be no need to trim the cane tops. With this system, it may be difficult to separate fruiting and non-fruiting canes, so picking may be less easy.*

**Looping canes over wires**
*When training in the new raspberry canes that remain after the fruited canes have been removed, loop over the long, pliable canes and tie them in with a figure-of-eight knot to the top wire. This keeps them secure against winter winds. Tip prune any weaker canes.*

train the much longer canes. Plant the canes so that the rootball is covered with about 8cm (3in) of soil.

## Training cane fruits
Careful training is essential for healthy, productive cane fruits. It helps to protect the canes from wind damage, and separates the new from the fruiting canes, making harvesting and pruning easier and decreasing the risk of diseases passing from old to new canes. Training also allows sufficient light and air to circulate around the canes, discouraging pests and diseases.

There are several training systems from which to choose (*see facing page*); you need to consider the space available and the vigour of the cultivar.

Since blackberries and hybrid berries tend to be more vigorous than raspberries, they require more training. There are several training systems that leave room for new canes that will bear next year's crop to grow upwards and be kept separate from currently fruiting canes. A basic fan shape (*see p.210*) is good for less vigorous cultivars; new canes grow up through the centre. Fruiting canes can also be trained in one direction along the wires to leave space for training the new canes in the opposite direction. Vigorous cultivars with pliable canes can be woven in

horizontal wave shapes and attached to the wires to save space; again, the new canes grow up through the middle. Wear gloves to handle cultivars with thorns. Thornless cultivars are more amenable to work with and safer when grown over a structure such as an arch.

Raspberries can also be woven, or looped over (*see above*) for the winter. Tip prune the canes in spring to about 15cm (6in) above the topmost wire. Autumn-fruiting raspberries do not need such elaborate supports because their canes are cut down over the winter. A post-and-single-string system along either side of the row should support canes with ripening fruit and stop them flopping over.

## Pruning cane fruits
Pruning is important to remove fruited canes and promote new cane growth from the roots. If left, the old canes can be a source of pests and diseases; also, they can suffer from windrock, where the wind causes the rocking cane to create a hole at soil level that fills with water, causing the roots to die.

Canes of summer-fruiting raspberries flower and fruit in their second year. Cut off those that have fruited at soil level in early to mid-autumn. Select new canes of pencil thickness and thicker and tie or train them into the supports. Remove thin canes and any that do not reach the lowest support wire or are growing more than 20cm (8in) away from the centre of the row.

Gardeners who do not want to go to the trouble of pruning and training raspberries can leave the canes unpruned. Cutting the fruiting canes at various lengths will allow the canes to support themselves once new growth begins in spring. For such a self-supporting system, it is best to grow the raspberries in a thick "block" up to 1m (3ft) wide.

Since autumn-fruiting raspberries flower and fruit on canes produced in the same season, all the canes need to be cut off at soil level in late winter. To extend the fruiting period into early winter, immediately remove fruited canes to encourage replacements. Alternatively, for an extra, late spring crop of fruit in the new year, cut off the fruited tips of the canes in late winter.

Prune blackberries and hybrids as for summer-fruiting raspberries, but leave new canes tied together with soft string attached to the wires to protect them

**Cutting back canes after fruiting**
*Prune fruited canes to ground level after fruiting, leaving no stubs to harbour rot. With summer-fruiting raspberries, blackberries, and hybrid berries, take care to avoid damaging the new season's canes. Select the best of these to keep and train in, and prune out the others. For autumn-fruiting raspberries, prune out all of the canes.*

over winter. Untie them and retrain them to replace the old canes in spring just before they start into growth.

## Routine care

Watering is particularly beneficial as the fruit starts to change colour, and will markedly improve the size and weight of fruit. Water the soil to avoid wetting the fruit and new canes which could provide a possible site for diseases.

Hoeing off weeds may damage surface roots, so use mulches instead. Apply organic mulches in early spring. A black sheet mulch (*see p.208*) will smother weeds and emerging new canes, allowing only stronger and better quality growth through the planting holes. Top-dress annually in spring with a balanced compound fertilizer (*see p.20*) from the second year onwards.

Control numbers of new canes in the growing season to keep the crop within bounds and to produce fewer but better quality canes for the following year. Summer-fruiting raspberries grown as rows need ten canes per metre (3ft) of row, and stool systems 7–10 canes per stool. The more vigorous blackberries and hybrids can retain up to 24 canes per stool and still fruit well. Remove unwanted new canes by pulling them or digging them out, or cut them off at soil level. Autumn-fruiting canes do not need to be thinned.

To protect flowers and the soft new cane from frost, drape hessian or fleece over a support structure. Ventilate well during the day. When fruits start to change colour, exclude birds (*see p.209*).

## Propagation

Cane fruits can be propagated by lifting new canes along with their rootballs, cutting them away from the main row of canes, and replanting. Shoot tips of blackberries and hybrid berries root naturally when in contact with the soil. They can be cut away once rooted and replanted. If necessary, pin down shoot ends to encourage rooting. Choose only newly planted, disease-free stock from which to propagate.

## Harvesting and storing cane fruits

Summer cultivars will ripen for picking by midsummer, typically yielding

**Picking cane fruits**
*Pick blackberries (left) and hybrid berries complete with core, or plug, and stalk; the core is edible and helps the fruit to keep its shape. Pick raspberries for eating and storing by gripping each fruit between the fingertips and, with a gentle squeeze, pulling it from the core.*

*Raspberry without core*

*Blackberry with core*

2–3kg (4lb 8oz–6lb 12oz) per metre (3ft) of row. Autumn-fruiting raspberries yield up to 1kg (2lb 4oz) per metre (3ft) of row and ripen from late summer to the first frosts. Rain causes fruits to rot and shortens the fruiting period, so a raincover (*see p.209*) will ensure good fruit and may extend fruiting into early winter. Yields from blackberries and hybrids can reach 6.75–9kg per 3m (15–20lb per 10ft) row.

The best time to eat the berries is freshly picked on a warm evening. Pick the fruit every two or three days to prevent any overripe fruit from rotting and spreading disease.

Fruit can be put into bags to avoid desiccation and it can be kept in a fridge for two or three days. It can be frozen for eating and processing when thawed.

## Common problems

Cane spot (*see p.253*) and fungal leaf spots (*see p.257*) may affect raspberries; resistant cultivars are available. Raspberries may also suffer from raspberry cane blight (*p.217 and p.261*), birds (*see p.251*) on early raspberries, and raspberry viruses (*see p.261*). Other problems on cane fruits are: botrytis (*see p.252*), and chlorosis (*see p.253*). Rusts (*p.262*) are unlikely to be serious. Red spider mite (*see p.261*) may affect plants in warm, sheltered sites.

---

## RECOMMENDED CANE FRUIT CULTIVARS

### RASPBERRY

**'Canby'** *Early to mid-season, small berries, thornless canes.*

**'Glen Clova'** *Very early cropper, fruit susceptible to rot, short storage period.*

**'Fairview'** *Late-season cropper, medium-large fruit, tall canes and low sucker production.*

**'Meeker'** *Late-season, medium-sized berries with medium yield.*

**'Neika'** *Old cultivar, early to mid-season. Good crops of medium-sized berries.*

**'Willamette'** *Mid-season cropper, large berries, tall canes.*

### BLACKBERRY

**'Lawtonberry'** *Sturdy, with upright canes; suckers profusely. Sweet fruit, heavy bearer.*

**'Smoothstem'** *Very vigorous, no thorns and very few canes. Fruit sour until very ripe.*

### HYBRID BERRIES

**Boysenberry** *Thornless. Large purplish fruit.*
**Loganberry 'LY 59' ♀** *Thorns. Medium vigour. Long, acidic fruit.*
**Loganberry 'LY 654' ♀** *Thornless.*
**Marionberry** *Dark red berries with distinctive flavour. Soft when ripe.*
**Silvanberry** *Early ripening. Large crops of sweet, black fruit.*
**Tayberry ♀** *Early, heavy crops. Thorns.*
**Youngberry** *Vigorous. Thorny and thornless cultivars available. Blackish purple, flavoursome fruit. (Note that thornless cultivars have less flavour.)*

# Gooseberry

Up to 3000 gooseberry cultivars (*Ribes uva-crispa*) have been recorded since the 1700s and there are currently up to 150 in cultivation. New cultivars overcome some of the hazards of growing gooseberries, such as mildew and leaf spot, and the fierce spines. The berries are the earliest soft fruits of the year, and may be red, green, or yellow and are suitable for both cooking and eating fresh as a dessert. The natural growth habit varies from upright to pendent (weeping), depending on the cultivar.

Gooseberries are amenable to various forms of training. A gooseberry is most often grown as a bush on a short "trunk" that raises the level of the branches to make fruit picking and care easier. It can also be grown as a standard on a longer trunk, or trained on a free-standing support or against a wall as a single- or multi-stemmed cordon, or fan. On posts and wires in the open, cordons and fans are dramatic features when the sun shines through them.

A standard plant allows the site to be used more efficiently since strawberries, bedding plants, and vegetables can be planted underneath. For a standard, choose a vigorous cultivar, or, if you want to grow a less vigorous one, buy it grafted onto a rootstock of *Ribes aureum*.

## Planting gooseberries

1 **Dig a hole** large enough for the rootball. Position it so that the soil mark on the stem is level with the surface.

2 **Fill with soil,** firm, and water. Make sure there is 10–20cm (4–8in) of trunk clear below the branches. If planting in autumn or winter, do not prune until spring. If planting in early spring, as here, select 5 main stems; prune to 15–23cm (6–8in). Remove surplus stems.

Gooseberries need good drainage; they tolerate slightly alkaline soils and some shade. Since they flower very early in the year, do not plant them in a frost pocket (*see p.11*). Shelter (*see pp.12–13*) is also needed to protect the brittle new shoots from wind. Gooseberries flourish in containers, a good option where garden soil is poorly drained. Plants in containers brought under cover in late winter will start into growth earlier and crop in the late spring.

### Preparing the site

Prepare soil by digging in a 2.5–5cm (1–2in) layer of well-rotted organic matter. Double dig heavy, poorly drained soils (*see p.39*). Before planting, take a soil sample to check pH and nutrient levels (*see p.17*). Incorporate compound granular fertilizer into the top 15–20cm (4–8in) where required.

### Planting

Gooseberry bushes can be bought as bare-root or container-grown plants. Choose plants with 10–20cm (4–8in) of clear stem (trunk) above the roots, and at least four or five young branches. Bushes grown as standards are also available to purchase ready-trained and, where necessary, pre-grafted.

Plant bare-root bushes between autumn and early spring. Container-grown plants can be planted all year round, but need plentiful watering to help the bushes establish. For improved weed control and moisture retention, lay a plastic sheet mulch and plant the gooseberries through slits in the plastic (*see p.208*). Since gooseberries are a long-term crop, lasting up to ten years, the plastic needs to be thick or covered with a layer of bark chippings or gravel.

Plant bushes 1.2–1.5m (4–5ft) apart. Space single-stemmed cordons 30–40cm (12–16in) apart; for a multi-stemmed cordon, allow an extra 30cm (12in) for each additional arm. Space plants to be fan-trained 1.5m (5ft) apart. For standards, stake at planting with a sturdy stake tall enough to reach

*One-year-old, fruiting wood*

*Two-year-old wood*

*Current season's growth, which will fruit in following year*

**The fruiting habit of gooseberries**
*Gooseberries fruit on one-year-old wood and older spurs. Spur pruning encourages fruiting spurs. Renewal pruning (see p.220) removes older wood for a balanced shape.*

# Renewal pruning an established bush

The primary aim of renewal pruning an established bush is to maintain eight to ten well-spaced branches. The balanced shape allows light and air to penetrate, especially during summer, to encourage new growth and prevent the onset of diseases such as botrytis (*see p.252*) and American gooseberry mildew (*see p.251*). It also makes it easier to pick the fruit.

Prune in early spring to allow the identification and removal of wood that may not have any buds or is dead due to disease. Remove also shoots where the buds look wispy and have not fully closed over winter due to mildew. Additional pruning in summer improves the air circulation, reducing the risk of fungus disease, and produces fewer but larger fruits. Cut back new shoots arising from the main shoots by half in midsummer. If you wish, you can cut the same stems back to two healthy buds in early spring.

△ **Removing old branches**
*Use loppers to remove a proportion of old, unproductive branches, cutting them back to their base.*

**Remove crossing branches**
*Take out branches that cross centre, restricting light and air*

**Keep trunk clear**
*Remove any shoots growing less than 10cm (4in) from ground*

◁ **Creating a balanced shape**
*Aim to remove no more than one-third of branches, including crowded, crossing, weak, and damaged ones.*

---

the top of the stem at its final height. For details about how to prepare a container, *see p.208*.

## Pruning and training gooseberries

Tailor your pruning cuts to the habit of the cultivar. Cut to an outward-facing bud on an upright cultivar, and to an upward-facing bud on a pendent one.

When pruning a bush after planting (*see p.219*), aim to obtain a vase-shaped bush of four or five evenly spaced branches. Leaving pruning until spring enables the removal of any winter damage, and ensures the good healing of cuts. Prune a two-year-old bush in spring, cutting back the new growth at the end of each branch by half. Cut out any new shoots that are surplus to the permanent framework, and those that are crowding or crossing the centre.

Once the bush is established you can prune it in one of two ways. Renewal pruning (*see above*) aims to encourage new, well-spaced shoot growth, while spur pruning (*see p.210*) is a much more detailed method concentrating on the production of fruiting spurs.

To train a standard, take the strongest vertical stem and tie it to the planting stake. Shorten other shoots to one bud.

When the main stem is 60cm–1.2m (2–4ft) tall, cut off the tip. Next year, select 4–5 evenly spaced shoots near the top of the stem, remove all others, then train as for a bush. Train cordons and fans as for redcurrants (*see pp.221–222*).

## Routine care and propagation

Water in dry periods, especially as fruits swell, using 25–50 litres/sq m (5.5–11 gallons/sq yd) each time. Gooseberries are prone to potassium deficiency. Add sulphate of potash at 15g/sq m (½oz/sq yd) in late winter, with a balanced fertilizer. Mulch against weeds in early to mid-spring with a well-rotted manure or compost. A healthy bush will produce fewer suckers – shoots at ground level – than one under stress. Pull off any suckers with a gloved hand; cutting them off will encourage more suckers to grow the following year.

Bring container-grown plants in flower under cover for frost protection. All gooseberries need netting (*see p.209*) against birds that feed on dormant flower buds, and blackbirds, which feed on ripening fruit.

To propagate gooseberries, take hardwood cuttings from healthy wood as for blackcurrants (*see p.224*), making the cuttings about 30cm (12in) long.

## Harvesting gooseberries

A mature bush should yield 3.5–4.5kg (7–10lb). A single cordon bears up to 1kg (2lb 4oz). Protected plants ripen fruit by late spring and fruit until early summer. For early fruits for cooking on outdoor plants, thin alternate fruits when they are 12mm (½in) long in early summer. Leave the others to ripen for harvesting later in the summer. Pick fruit with a short stalk, otherwise the skin may tear when pulled off its stalk.

## Common problems

Problems include American gooseberry mildew (*see p.251*), botrytis (*see p.252*), fungal leaf spot (*see p.257*), aphids (*see p.251*), birds (*see p.251*), caterpillars (*p.253*), and gooseberry dieback (*see p.256*).

### RECOMMENDED CULTIVARS

'**Careless**' ♀ *Green culinary cultivar with earliest fruits. Reliable cropping.*
'**Crown Bob**' *Yellow berry turning a deep claret at maturity. Fruit large and slightly hairy.*
'**Leveller**' ♀ *Yellow dessert cultivar with excellent flavour. Needs good soil.*
'**Roaring Lion**' *Acidic, red-coloured fruit. Pick when fruits turn from green to red.*

# Redcurrant and whitecurrant

These deciduous shrubs (*Ribes rubrum*) form attractive ornamental plants, especially when the fruits are ripening. Redcurrant cultivars, old and new, display incredible shades of scarlet as the fruit ripens, while whitecurrants are pure white through cream to almost yellow when ripe. The fruits are borne in dense trusses, known as "strigs". The strigs show considerable differences in length and fruit size, and can be used for table decoration, as well as in summer puddings, jellies, and sauces.

Red- and whitecurrants fruit at the base of the previous year's shoots, and on spurs on older wood. They can be grown in bush form on a short trunk, or as single- or multi-stemmed cordons and fans where space is restricted or for their interesting shapes. Growing under cover results in fruits about two weeks earlier than unprotected bushes.

Choose a sunny site with shelter (*see pp. 12–13*) from strong winds. Avoid frost pockets (*see p. 11*). Partial shade is tolerated and plants can be trained against a fence or wall; the fruits will be later and have less flavour than those from plants in the sun. A well-drained, fertile soil is needed, with a slightly acid or neutral pH (*see p. 18*).

## Preparing the site and planting

Soil preparation, planting, and spacing, is as for gooseberries (*see pp. 219–220*). Improve poor drainage (*see p. 16*) in particular, since red- and whitecurrants do not tolerate waterlogging.

Buy healthy bushes from a reliable source. A one-year-old plant is the least expensive option; two- and three-year-old trained bushes are also available.

Cordons and fans require a support system of horizontal wires, attached to freestanding posts or to a wall or fence. Position the first wire at 60cm (2ft) above soil level, and fix subsequent ones at 60cm (2ft) intervals. On planting, tie the stems and required branches to canes attached to the support wires. For preparing a container, *see p. 208*.

## Pruning and training

Pruning of red- and whitecurrants mainly takes place in early spring. Always cut carefully to a healthy bud to promote quick healing, because these plants are particularly prone to botrytis (*see p. 252*) and the subsequent coral spot (*see p. 254*). In summer it is possible to snap off the new season's growth, and this seems to cause fewer dieback problems than cutting them off. Prune bushes as for gooseberries (*see p. 220*).

## Pruning a redcurrant or whitecurrant cordon

For pruning and training a single cordon, *see below*. A double cordon has two vertical main shoots in a "U" shape. To start training a double cordon, look for two strong shoots that are

---

## Pruning redcurrant cordons

1 **In early spring** following planting a one-year-old plant, cut the main vertical stem back by half of the previous year's growth. Cut other shoots back to 1 bud.

2 **In the summer** after planting, shorten the new growth on the shoots. This concentrates the plant's growth on strengthening the main stem rather than on extending the shoots. If the shoots have developed sideshoots, cut or pinch these to 1 leaf. Repeat this pruning each summer.

3 **In early spring** in subsequent years, keep pruning the new growth on the main vertical stem by a quarter of the previous year's growth, or by half if growth is weak. Cut to a bud on the opposite side to the previous year's cut to keep the growth straight. Once the cordon is at the desired height, cut to 1 bud of new growth each year in early summer. Prune the shoots from the main stem and any other sideshoots to build up fruiting spur systems.

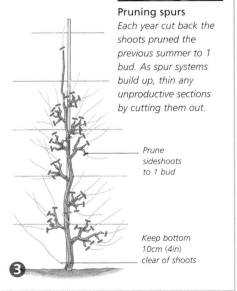

**Pruning spurs**
*Each year cut back the shoots pruned the previous summer to 1 bud. As spur systems build up, thin any unproductive sections by cutting them out.*

*Tie in new growth to cane*

*Top of original cutting; growth above was made previous year*

*Shoots cut to 1 bud*

**Shorten new shoots**
*When the shoots pruned the previous winter have about 8 leaves, shorten them to 5 leaves, either by breaking them off or pruning the shoots.*

*Prune sideshoots to 1 bud*

*Keep bottom 10cm (4in) clear of shoots*

**1** **2** **3**

nearly opposite each other. Cut back the central shoot to just above the higher of these two. Trim to two leaves any shoots below the chosen two, and remove them altogether in summer. Tie the two shoots to canes fixed to the wires at an angle of 30°. When each shoot tip is 30cm (12in) from the main leg, train the new growth vertically up canes attached to the wires. From then on, treat each vertical arm as a single cordon (*see p.221*). Keep each arm cut to the same height to avoid one growing more dominant than the other.

For a triple cordon, which has a central vertical stem plus one on either side, start by selecting three well-positioned shoots. Train the central one as for a single cordon (*see p.221*), and the shoots on either side as for a double cordon. Keep the middle vertical shoot cut to the same height as the other two so that it does not become dominant. As the three vertical arms develop, prune each as for a single cordon.

## Pruning and training a red- or whitecurrant fan

To train a fan, select up to five strong lateral shoots after planting. Prune out the central vertical stem above the topmost lateral. Train the laterals on either side of the main stem on canes at 45° attached to support wires. Cut each back by half. In summer, select several well-spaced sideshoots on each shoot and train in to form permanent ribs to the fan. Keep the shape balanced, and remove over vigorous shoots.

In the second spring, shorten shoots and ribs by half and sideshoots to one bud. Fill in gaps by training in more

**Fan-trained redcurrant**
*With a fan you are aiming for several well-spaced shoots with permanent sideshoots to fill the available space and provide an even covering. Five main shoots are usually trained, but the number is often determined by the vigour of the new growth, with extra shoots trained to divert excessive vigour. A wall or fence will provide extra shelter for the fan, so that pollination and netting are easier, and the fruit should ripen more quickly.*

shoots in the following summer for an even framework of shoots of the same length. Prune each permanent shoot as for a cordon (*see p.221*), ensuring that the tips of the main shoots are cut to the same height to stop the middle, vertical stems becoming dominant.

## Routine care and propagation

In late winter apply 15g/sq m (½oz/sq yd) of sulphate of potash or wood ash. On light sandy or poor soils, apply a balanced compound fertilizer (*see p.20*) at the same time. In early to mid-spring, as the soil starts to warm up, put down a 2.5–5cm (1–2in) thick organic mulch (*see p.41*). In dry conditions, water the soil beforehand, using 25–50 litres/sq m (5.5–11 gallons/sq yd). Mulch under the plant as far as the furthest tips of the branches. Water with similar amounts of water in summer as fruits start to swell and ripen.

Remove perennial weeds when the soil is moist or treat them with a systemic chemical weedkiller directed away from the crop. Pull off any suckers

by hand. Net the bushes against birds (*see p.209*) as the fruits change colour.

To propagate red- and whitecurrants, take hardwood cuttings about 30cm (12in) long from healthy wood, as for blackcurrants (*see p.224*).

## Harvesting red- or whitecurrants

Plants grown under protection can be ready for picking in early summer. Those grown outside will be ready from mid- to late summer. A mature bush may yield 4–5kg (9–11lb) and a single cordon up to 1kg (2lb 4oz) of fruit.

Most cultivars are thin-skinned and it is difficult to pick individual fruits without squashing and tearing them. Instead, use scissors to sever the entire strig from the bush.

## Common problems

Aphid infestation (*p.251*) is seen as red blistered foliage on young shoots. Other problems include birds (*p.251*), botrytis (*p.252*), mostly on fruits, coral spot (*p.254*), fungal leaf spots (*p.257*).

**Redcurrant in flower**
*The flowers on this redcurrant are displayed to their best advantage since the plant is trained as a fan. The contrast between the boldly shaped leaves and delicate flowers is one of the more ornamental features of this plant.*

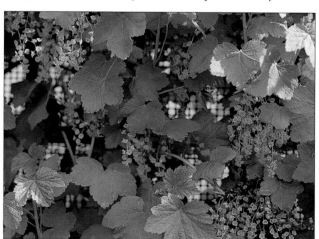

## RECOMMENDED CULTIVARS

'Fay's Prolific'  *Large, deep-red berries.*
'Jonkheer van Tets' ♀  *Very heavy, early crop of large, red berries.*
'La Versaillaise'  *Mid-season, heavy crops of large berries.*
'Red Dutch'  *Good crops of red berries.*
'Ruby Castle'  *New introduction. Mid-season crop.*
'White Grape' ♀  *Strong, upright growth. Good flavour.*

# Blackcurrant

Easy to grow and very productive, blackcurrants (*Ribes nigrum*) produce delicious clusters, or "strigs", of fruits that are full of vitamin C. They form large, rather straggly bushes that can reach up to 2m (6ft) in height and spread. Their flowers are insignificant but, particularly after rain, the foliage of these deciduous shrubs has a wonderful scent. Jostaberries, hybrids of blackcurrants and gooseberries, are cultivated as for blackcurrants. Jostaberries are very strong and vigorous plants that can produce new shoots of over 1m (3ft) in length in one season. The plants can be trained as a bush form with many branches, but are also well suited to training as an espalier against a wall, trellis, or fence. The mature fruit look a little like large blackcurrants and are quite delicious.

Blackcurrants fruit best on strong, young shoots produced the previous summer and, to a lesser extent, on two-year-old and older wood. They are usually grown as stooled, or multi-stemmed, bushes with plenty of new growth from soil level being stimulated

*Young wood has smooth, brown bark, and fruits in following year*

*Two-year-old and older wood has grey, peeling bark*

*Stalks that carried strigs of fruit may be visible on two-year-old wood*

### Stages of growth
*Aim to keep as much of the smooth, young wood as you can when pruning. Some of the older, peeling wood is cut out, although it will fruit a second time and may bear new shoots.*

## Planting depth for blackcurrants

△ **Judging the planting depth**
*Use a length of wood across the planting hole to check the planting level. This container-grown bush is being planted 5cm (2in) deeper than it was in its pot.*

▷ **Planting a bare-root bush**
*Make a hole large enough to spread the roots and deep enough to cover the stems to 5cm (2in) above the nursery soil mark, to encourage the basal buds to shoot.*

*Basal buds*

**Planting level**
*Cover roots and stems with soil to this point*

**Basal buds**
*Plant should have at least 3 or 4 healthy buds at base of stems*

by annual hard pruning. Very vigorous cultivars can be grown on a short trunk, as for gooseberries (*see p. 220*) and redcurrants, to control their growth in restricted spaces, and to provide an attractive, goblet-shaped bush.

Blackcurrants tolerate a wide range of soils, including slightly alkaline ones, but the soil needs to be highly fertile and moisture-retentive. Being heavy feeders, they demand plenty of organic matter to give sufficient nutrients and to hold an adequate supply of water. Slightly impeded drainage is tolerated, but they prefer a site that is free from frost and sheltered from cold, damaging winds (*see pp. 12–13*).

An alternative growing method is to plant blackcurrants in containers so that they can be brought under cover to protect them against cold winds at flowering, ensuring good pollination and fruit set. They can also be kept under cover from winter to early summer to bring forward cropping.

### Planting
Prepare the soil well by removing perennial weeds (*see p. 49*) and digging in a 5cm (2in) layer of well-rotted

compost or farmyard manure.

Most plants obtainable from plant nurseries in Australia have been produced from virus-free stock material. It is advisable to buy a certified plant to avoid viruses, to which blackcurrants are particularly prone. Plant bare-root plants from autumn to spring, preferably in autumn. Container-grown plants can be planted at any time, but need copious watering to aid establishment in summer.

It is crucial to plant both bare-root and container-grown blackcurrants at about 5cm (2in) lower than the nursery soil mark. This stimulates the plant's natural habit of producing vigorous new shoots from the base; these young shoots are vital to ensure a productive, stooled bush (*see above*). Space plants 1.5–2m (5–6ft) apart. For planting in containers, *see p. 208*.

### Pruning and training blackcurrants
When planting a bare-root blackcurrant in winter or spring, cut all shoots back to two buds 2.5cm (1in) above soil level to help the roots

# Pruning a blackcurrant bush in winter

◁ **Cutting to the base**
*Remove a quarter of stems to within 2.5cm (1in) of soil level to generate young growth. Cut out weak and crowded branches and those drooping towards the soil. Retain a mixture of one-year-old and older wood, both of which can be recognized by their colour (see p.223).*

◁ **Before pruning**
*The centre of this bush is crowded, allowing little light and air to circulate between the stems, and so encouraging disease and making ripening slower.*

▷ **After pruning**
*This pruned bush has a balanced shape, with unproductive older wood removed, and the remaining stems thinned.*

establish. If the bush is planted earlier, in autumn, the roots should establish before winter and you can leave half of the shoots unpruned to yield a small crop in the following summer. In general, do not prune container-grown plants after planting; however, if they are planted in the summer and regular watering cannot be guaranteed, prune them as for autumn bare-root plantings so that new growth is initially concentrated in the roots.

Prune established blackcurrant bushes in winter, as shown above. Overgrown and neglected bushes can be renovated by cutting down all of the branches to soil level in autumn, and applying a mulch (*see below*) to provide nutrients for the roots. The subsequent new growth should be thinned to leave 8–12 vigorous, young shoots.

## Routine care
Apply a balanced compound fertilizer in early spring, plus extra nitrogen at a rate of 25g/sq m (¾oz/sq yd). Spread a thick mulch of mushroom or garden compost, or well-rotted manure, around plants every spring to provide required nutrients and to suppress weeds.

Blackcurrants need a minimum of 50 litres/sq m (11 gallons/sq yd) at each watering. Frequency of watering will depend on the weather conditions and temperature, but it is particularly essential during dry spells and as the fruits start to swell and colour. To avoid disease infections, attempt to keep the base of the bush dry by watering carefully onto the soil or laying down a

low-pressure watering system (*see p.54*). Birds like to feed on ripe fruit, so it is essential to net blackcurrants (*see p.209*) as fruits ripen.

Repot blackcurrant bushes planted in containers every two or three years. As the plant grows larger and heavier, it may be worth putting the pot on a base with castors so that it is easy to move under cover for protection against frost or for protected cropping.

## Propagation
Prunings from newly planted certified plants can be used to propagate more blackcurrants; avoid using long-established plants that may carry disease. Make each cutting 20cm (8in) long, using a straight cut below a bud at the base, and an angled cut above a bud at the top, removing the soft tip of the shoot. Push the hardwood cutting into the soil or into potting mix in a container. The cuttings should root readily and produce several shoots to make a stooled bush.

## Harvesting
Fruit will ripen from midsummer through to early autumn. Protected crops will ripen about two weeks earlier than those grown outside. Expect to pick at least 4.5 kg (10lb) of fruit per bush when established.

Older cultivars have fruits that ripen at different times along the strig. Pick these fruits individually, taking care not to damage them, or they will not store well. When grown under bird netting, currants can be left on the bushes until

the whole bunch is ripe. It is easy then to pick the whole bunch with fingers or scissors.

## Common problems
Possible problems include aphids (*see p.251*), big bud mite (*see p.251*), American gooseberry mildew (*see p.251*), birds (*see p.251*), blackcurrant gall midge (*see p.252*), botrytis (*see p.252*), which mostly affects the fruits, and reversion disease, transmitted by big bud mites (*see p.251*). Fungal leaf spots (*see p.257*) may occur but are seldom serious.

### RECOMMENDED CULTIVARS
Cultivars in a rough sequence of ripening are:
'Magnus'
'Tough Champion'
'Baldwin'
'Super Champion'
'Boskoop Giant'
'Hatton Black'
'Hickmans'
'Goliath'
Jostaberry *This hybrid between a blackcurrant and a gooseberry is resistant to mildew, leaf spots, and big bud mites; has blackcurrant-type fruits, but twice the size. Thornless and very vigorous.*

# Blueberry

American highbush blueberries (*Vaccinium corymbosum*) are branching, deciduous shrubs that provide interest for much of the year, with their white bell-shaped flowers, dusty blue fruits, and spectacular autumn colour. Some cultivars reach 2m (6ft). Blueberries need a light, free-draining, acid soil of pH 4–5.5. They prefer sun or partial shade and are relatively frost-hardy. Provide shelter (*see pp. 12–13*) from cold winds. For regular, heavier crops, plant more than one cultivar because they are only partially self-fertile. Blueberries may be planted as freestanding bushes, as part of a hedge, or in a container.

## Planting

Soil pH (*see p. 18*) is critical, so prepare for planting well in advance. Neutral to alkaline soil can be acidified, but this is laborious and hard to maintain. To lower the pH of alkaline soil, add peat, sulphur (as flowers of sulphur), and sawdust individually or as a mix. Peat can be added to the planting hole prior to planting; dig in the other additives a year before planting. Application rates depend on soil type and pH. Sawdust needs nitrogen to decompose, so reduces the amount in the soil. Add sulphate of ammonia at 15g/sq m (½oz/sq yd) annually to counteract this.

Alternatives to acidifying soil are to use a raised bed or container. A raised bed, 15–20cm (6–8in) high and 1.5m (5ft) wide, aids drainage on badly drained soils and can be filled with peat-based compost. Peat substitute may have a high pH, so add flowers of sulphur to lower it. In pots, use an ericaceous compost with grit added.

Container-grown blueberries often establish more quickly than bare-root ones. Plant from autumn to spring (*see p. 208*). Space bushes 1.5m (5ft) apart. If planting in a container, start with a 2 litre (3½ pint) pot and pot on in later years.

## Pruning and training blueberries

Prune after leaf drop. Follow the method for blackcurrants (*see pp. 223–224*), pruning at soil level to encourage strong, new shoots.

Cut one or two unproductive branches to soil level each year, ideally in autumn to early spring when buds are obvious.

## Routine care

After pruning, apply a balanced compound fertilizer plus extra nitrogen (sulphate of ammonia) at 15g/sq m (½oz/sq yd). To maintain a low pH and suppress weeds, mulch (*see p. 41*) in mid-spring with a 8–15cm (3–6in) layer of acidic material, such as bark, old pine needles, or peat. If chlorosis (*see p. 253*) shows in the leaves, top-dress soil with flowers of sulphur to lower the pH.

Blueberries need copious amounts of water, preferably rainwater, which is acidic. Apply 50 litres/sq m (11 gallons/sq yd) at each watering. Do not use lime in the soil or around blueberry plants, as they are intolerant of alkaline conditions. Raised beds demand more water. During flowering, either provide frost and wind protection in the form of fleece or plastic sheeting, or bring plants in containers under cover.

Repot blueberries in containers every two years in autumn. The largest size you should need is a 50 litre (11 gallon) pot for a bush about 1.5m (5ft) tall.

▽ **Maximizing the crop**
*Fruit buds are considerably fatter than growth buds. When pruning, learn to recognize and retain branches bearing more fruit buds since they are likely to crop more heavily. Prune out branches with a larger proportion of growth buds so that the plant's energies go into producing fruit, not foliage.*

*Growth bud*

*Fruit bud*

## Propagation

Take 10–15cm (4–6in) cuttings of soft, healthy growth in midsummer. Trim off the lower leaves. Insert the cuttings into pots of one part peat and three parts coarse sand and place in a propagator. Once they have rooted, transplant into pots, harden them off, and give a high-potash feed every ten days. Plant in their final positions after about a year.

## Harvesting blueberries

Harvest from late summer to early autumn. A bush will yield 2.25–5kg (5–11lb). Pick berries by gentle pulling.

## Common problems

Birds (*see p. 251*), botrytis (*p. 252*), and chlorosis (*p. 253*) may cause problems.

### RECOMMENDED CULTIVARS

**'Bluecrop'** *Large, pale berries; high-yielding.*
**'Blue Rose'** *Largish fruit with full flavour when ripe. Berries store well.*
**'Jenny'** *Sweet, smallish fruit with excellent flavour.*
**'Northland'** *Small to medium berries with excellent flavour.*

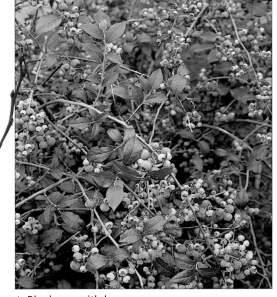

△ **Blueberry with heavy crop**
*Borne on large, attractive bushes, blueberries are delicious eaten fresh, and keep well even in the freezer. When cooked, they make deliciously aromatic muffins and jam.*

# Cranberry

An evergreen, straggling, low-growing shrub, the cranberry (*Vaccinium macrocarpon*) likes boggy soil conditions and so is well suited to poorly drained gardens. Its wiry stems root along the ground, enabling the plant to spread readily. It needs soil with a low pH to grow and fruit well, and prefers a sunny, fairly cool site. In addition to the red fruits, widely used for cranberry sauce, the bush provides good autumn colour.

**Fruiting cranberry**
*Wild cranberries grow naturally in moorland and boggy areas and those under cultivation require similarly acidic and moist growing conditions in order to fruit well.*

## Planting
Cranberries are usually grown in a sunken bed to maintain moist conditions, and a soil with a pH of 4–5.5 (*see below*). Only container-grown plants are available for planting. Plant at any time of year after saturating the bed with water, or prepare the bed before winter and plant in the spring.

## Pruning and training cranberries
Cranberries need pruning to thin the stems and keep plants within bounds. Start once a plant covers the surface of the bed. In autumn after harvesting, trim the bed edges to remove straggly stems. In early spring, prune to prevent overcrowding. Cut out excess stems at soil level to leave a single layer across the ground. Hedging shears can be used to trim top-growth, but a more detailed pruning is needed every three years.

## Routine care and propagation
Maintain the moisture content of the bed with copious amounts of water in early to midsummer, using rainwater if possible to keep pH low. Apply a 2.5cm (1in) layer of coarse, acidic sand every three years after pruning to the bed surface to encourage the stems to root, promoting plant vigour and fruit yield. Maintain a low soil pH as for blueberries (*see p.225*). Cranberries can be propagated by layering: shoots will root naturally and can then be detached from the parent plant and replanted.

## Harvesting cranberries
The first cranberries will be ready to pick in early autumn, but it is easier to wait until the majority of the fruit is ripe. The yield may be as much as 0.5–0.75kg/sq m (1lb–1lb 8oz/sq yd). Either pick individual fruits by hand or, with fingers spread, gently "comb" the fruits off the stems. Store cranberries dry for up to three weeks at room temperature or three months in a refrigerator at 2–4°C (36–39°F). Fruit will freeze for longer storage.

## Common problems
No problems affect cranberries except possibly chlorosis (*see p.253*) on alkaline soils, and birds (*see p.251*).

## Making a cranberry bed

Dig out the soil to a spade blade's depth and about 1m (3ft) square. Line the pit with a sheet of fine proprietary plastic mesh to maintain water to a high level, but allow drainage of excess moisture. If the soil is particularly heavy and poor-draining, dig the pit to 30cm (12in) deep, and lay a drainage pipe leading to a sump or ditch. Cover the pipe with a 8–10cm (3–4in) deep layer of coarse, acidic aggregate and place a sheet of fine plastic mesh over the aggregate to prevent the topsoil from blocking the drainage of excess water. Fill the remaining hole with a mix of two parts peat and one part soil, avoiding heavy garden soil, which will not mix well, and alkaline soil. Alternatively, use 100 per cent peat or ericaceous compost; peat substitutes can be used with flowers of sulphur to lower the pH. Finally, cover with a 2.5cm (1in) layer of coarse, acidic sand to act as a mulch and so reduce the drying out of the bed. The mulch also controls weeds and encourages the rooting of the stems as they grow. Water the bed regularly with rainwater.

Heavy soil
Ericaceous compost or peat
Slotted drainage pipe, 5cm (2in) diameter
Cranberry
2.5cm (1in) sand
Plastic mesh liner
10cm (4in) aggregate

## RECOMMENDED CULTIVARS
'Bergman'
'Early Black'
'Franklin'
'Howes'
'Stevens'

# GRAPE VINES

# Planning

Grape vines have been cultivated for thousands of years both for their sweet fruits, known as dessert grapes, and for wine-making. They probably arose in Asia Minor and the Caucasus region, and spread to Mediterranean countries and North Africa. In cooler climates than these, their outdoor cultivation is less reliable, but provided that cultivars are carefully chosen and conditions are suitable they may be grown successfully (*see pp.231–232*). Grape vines grow and crop best in regions with warm, frost-free and fairly dry conditions in spring, late summer, and autumn. If you are doubtful of providing the necessary conditions outside, it is best to grow vines under cover (*see pp.228–230*).

Vines may easily be propagated from hardwood cuttings and grown on their own root systems; however, in countries where the root pest *Daktulosphaira vitifolii* is present, it is necessary to grow them on resistant rootstocks (*see below*).

## Grapevines in the garden
The grape vine is a vigorous climbing plant that produces fruit on one-year-old shoots, and therefore needs careful annual pruning. It will bleed sap profusely if pruned in early spring, so it is essential to complete all major pruning of vines while they are dormant in late winter. There are several good methods of training vines for optimum cropping, of which the cordon, guyot, and standard forms are the most suitable for garden or greenhouse cultivation.

## Single and multiple cordons
The cordon, sometimes known as the rod-and-spur system, is one of the most versatile forms of training grape vines, and is widely used under cover; it is also suitable for growing vines on walls, fences, and pergolas, or in rows on freestanding posts and wires.

A single cordon (*see p.228*) consists of one permanent stem that produces

**Grapes grown under cover**
*Many greenhouses and conservatories are suitable for growing grape vines, provided that they are well ventilated. In a small conservatory, you can grow the vines as a cordon along the central ridge; in large greenhouses, it is possible to train them up one or both sides towards the ridge. Both methods require a system of stakes and wires in order to support the fruiting sideshoots (see pp.228–229).*

a series of fruiting sideshoots, or laterals, spaced about 23–30cm (9–12in) apart along it, and supported on horizontal wires. The main stem can be as long as can be accommodated in the space, but 2–3.6m (6–12ft) is usual. Single cordons may be grown vertically or at an angle if under cover, or vertically and then horizontally on an outdoor pergola. Multiple cordons (*see p.229*) consist of two rods – a double cordon – or several vertical rods, 1–1.2m (3–4ft) apart, produced from two horizontal stems. Horizontal branches can also be developed, about 60cm (2ft) apart, from the rods. These are suitable for a range of outdoor situations, such as house walls, pergolas, and arches.

## The guyot system
Widely used in vineyards, this system (*see p.232*) creates fruiting arms that are replaced each year. A single guyot has one arm, and a double guyot has two. Single guyots should be spaced about 1m (3ft) apart and double guyots about

1.5m (5ft) apart. They are trained on support systems of posts and wires.

## Standard vines
Standard vines have a clear, tall main stem, which must be well staked, with a group of spurs at the top (*see p.230*). They are suitable for container-grown vines, and for those grown under cover in areas that are too small for a cordon.

## Rootstocks
In the world's great wine regions, the European vine, *Vitis vinifera*, is grafted onto rootstocks of American vines such as *V. labrusca*, which are resistant to the devastating insect pest, *Daktulosphaira vitifolii* (*see p.233*). Only in countries such as Chile, where it is absent, or where there is no major wine industry, as in the UK, is *V. vinifera* grown commercially on its own roots. Some vineyards in Australia still grow vines on their own roots but grafted plants are used wherever possible. Grafted plants are readily available from plant nurseries or from specialist suppliers.

# Grape vines under cover

In cool climates, the large-berried table, or dessert, grapes must be grown under cover, in a greenhouse, conservatory, or even a porch. In particularly cool areas, and for late-ripening cultivars, some additional heat (*see p.44*) in spring and sometimes autumn may be required. Vines under cover are usually grown as cordons, but they can also be grown as standards in containers if space is tight. To fruit successfully, grape vines need a cool period in winter: if they are grown in a greenhouse or conservatory that is heated throughout winter, they must be container-grown so that they can be moved outside for a few weeks.

## Planting grapes under cover

Vines to be grown in a greenhouse can be planted from early autumn to early spring. Planting them outside and training the rod inside the greenhouse makes watering and feeding easier. Those planted inside in a border, however, have the advantage of starting earlier into growth, as the soil warms up earlier, but need good preparation of the border soil, with plenty of added manure, and regular watering. Over time, the roots will spread outside.

## Creating a single cordon

Single cordons require a support system of tautly stretched horizontal wires (*see p.162, p.231*) that are 23–30cm (9–12in) apart. Formative pruning (*see below*) will

## Formative pruning of a single cordon vine

**1** **Year 1, early winter:** after planting a strong, healthy vine, whether indoors or outdoors, use a pair of sharp secateurs to cut down the leading shoot to a strong bud on well-ripened wood, about 30cm (12in) above the level of the soil.

*Pinch back laterals between finger and thumb*

**2** **Year 1, summer:** tie in the new leading shoot to a cane, and allow it to grow unhindered. Pinch back the main sideshoots, or laterals, to 5–6 leaves. Pinch any sideshoots that the laterals themselves have produced back to 1 leaf.

*Cut back sideshoots to 1–2 strong buds*

**3** **Year 2, winter:** after the leaves have fallen, cut back the new growth of the leading shoot by a half to two-thirds of its length, leaving only brown, ripened wood. Prune back all the laterals and sideshoots to 1 or 2 strong-looking buds.

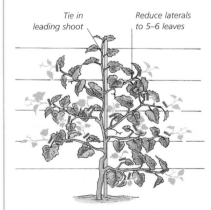

*Tie in leading shoot*   *Reduce laterals to 5–6 leaves*

**4** **Year 2, summer:** tie in the leading shoot, and pinch back the laterals to 5–6 leaves and any sublaterals to 1 leaf. Remove any flower trusses, unless the vine is growing very well, in which case allow just 1 to develop into a bunch of grapes.

*Carefully prune back all laterals to 1–2 strong, healthy buds*

**5** **Year 3, winter:** as in the previous winter, prune back the leading shoot to well-ripened wood, and the laterals to 1 or 2 strong-looking buds. On the leading shoot, the bud should face in the opposite direction to the one chosen a year earlier.

**6** **Year 3, spring:** from each spur, the point where the laterals join the main stem, 3–4 shoots will have formed. Thin these out at the base to 1–2 strong shoots. A second one may be useful as a replacement if the first fails to develop.

take several years, but is well worth the effort. After the third year, repeat the pruning cycle for the established cordon until the grape vine has reached the required length (*see below*). Then, gradually increase the number of flower trusses allowed to develop into bunches of grapes on the established cordon until one bunch per spur is obtained.

### Creating a multiple cordon
In the first summer, train a strong, healthy vine as a single stem, as for a single cordon (*see facing page*). Early in the first winter, prune the stem back to a bud about 38–45cm (15–18in) above the ground. In the following summer, select one shoot on each side and tie it to a cane angled at 45 degrees. In early winter, lower these to the horizontal and prune back to a bud at about 60cm (2ft) from the central stem. If you want only a double cordon, in the following summer train the endmost shoots up to a cane in the same way as for a single cordon. Prune back the laterals along the horizontal stem to five leaves, in order to develop fruiting laterals. To obtain a larger multiple cordon, train the endmost shoot at a 45-degree angle to continue it, and train the adjacent shoot vertically. Repeat this process until the required number of arms has been started. The arms themselves are extended in the same way as described for a single cordon (*see facing page*).

### Care of mature multiple cordons
Prune established multiple cordons as for a single cordon (*see below*), with the rods 1–1.2m (3–4ft) apart. Horizontal arms to be developed from the rods should be spaced 50–60cm (20–24in) apart. To encourage new shoots, bend the stems over (*see bottom*).

## Pruning an established single cordon vine

Established single cordon grape vines require regular attention to pruning and training in order to keep them producing healthy new growth and cropping well.

1 **In summer,** select 1 lateral from each spur, and also a reserve shoot, and remove all the other shoots. Prune the laterals at 5–6 leaves past a flower truss, allowing 1 bunch of grapes to develop per lateral, and cut sublaterals back to 1 leaf. Pinch out all other flower trusses.

2 **In winter,** shorten the laterals to 2 buds. If spurs are becoming over long, shorten to the replacement lateral; the spurs should be 23–30cm (9–12in) apart. Thin out congested, over large spurs, using a pruning saw for a clean cut.

In early spring, cut back the leading shoot to a bud below the top wire, untie it, and bend it down to the horizontal carefully. Tie it into a wire. This encourages shoots to break along the lower part of the main stem. When the buds start to break, retie the leader in a vertical position.

Tie in shoots after pruning

Pinch back sideshoots to 1 leaf

Pinch out flower trusses

Lower leading shoot

Use a pruning saw to thin out congested spurs

Prune laterals with sharp secateurs

## Training an established multiple cordon vine

1 **To encourage production** of new shoots all along the multiple cordon stems, untie them from their supports in early spring. Carefully bend the stems over to the horizontal so that the top is arched downwards, and tie them into the wires. Buds will break at regular intervals along the stems (*see inset*).

2 **Once the buds have opened** all along the stems, and started to grow out strongly, untie the stems and gently ease them back into a vertical position.

# Creating a standard vine

Standard vines have a stem 1–1.2m (3–4ft) tall with spurs at the top. For the first 1–2 years, allow laterals to develop on the stem. In the third winter, remove these to leave just the top spurs. Tie the stem to a cane so that the laterals can be supported with string when carrying grapes. Let 5–6 laterals develop at the top; prune these to 5 leaves and sub-laterals to 1 leaf. In the first cropping year, allow 1 bunch only; thereafter allow 1 bunch per lateral. In early winter, prune the laterals to 2 buds.

*Thin out old spurs on mature plants if they are congested*

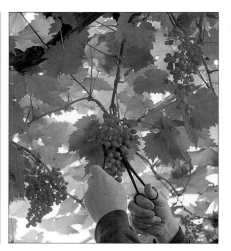

### Thinning grapes
*Once bunches of berries have formed, thinning the grapes will enable the others to grow large and juicy. Prop the bunch with a forked twig, and use sharp, fine scissors to snip out about one-third of the berries evenly throughout the bunch. Start at the top sprig or shoulder, and work your way down the bunch.*

## Routine care of indoor vines

Grape vines rooted under cover and in containers need additional nutrients and will benefit from liquid feeds of a high-potash fertilizer (*see pp.20–23*) from about one month after growth starts until the fruits start to ripen. If they are making poor growth, use a more balanced or high-nitrogen liquid feed.

Vines grown in the greenhouse border or in containers require regular watering during the growing season. Those that have their roots outside the greenhouse, however, will need little additional water.

Apply a 5–8cm (2–3in) layer of mulch, such as well-rotted manure, garden compost, or bark (*see pp.41–42*), to a radius of 45cm (18in) around each vine each year in late winter. Do not let the mulch touch the stem.

In early to midwinter, carefully remove any loose bark (*see below*) to expose any pests. If there are any present, such as mealybug (*see p.257*) or brown scale (*see p.253*), spray the vine with a winter wash.

### Scraping off old bark
*To reduce problems with pests such as mealybugs, which shelter in crevices, after winter pruning remove most of the outer layers of old, loose bark from the vine stems. Use a sharp knife. This will expose any lurking pests, which can then be easily eradicated.*

## Temperature requirements

Most vines will grow well in unheated greenhouses or conservatories, but in areas with a short growing season, or where late-ripening vines are being grown, it may be necessary to provide extra heat. A good time to start is in late winter, when a minimum night temperature of 4–7°C (39–45°F) is beneficial. It is very important to ventilate the plants, however, if daytime temperatures reach about 19°C (66°F).

Container-grown grape vines in greenhouses or conservatories that are constantly heated in winter should be moved outside into temperatures below 5°C (40°F) for 4–6 weeks in order for them to experience the period of chilling necessary to initiate flowering.

## Pollination of grape vines

Some vines will set fruit under cover without any additional pollination. Most benefit, however, if you tap the rods around midday on warm days during flowering. If they do not set well, then gently stroking the bunches with cupped hands will transfer pollen from the stamens to the stigmas and so assist pollination. Keep the atmosphere fairly dry during flowering, and do not water from above.

## Thinning dessert grapes

This is necessary in order to produce berries of a good size and to allow air movement between the berries and so prevent the development of grey mould, or botrytis. Thin with scissors when the berries are small (*see above*), using a small forked stick to support the bunch: touching grapes with fingers damages

the bloom on the surface of the berries and can lead to infection. First remove any berries that are crowding the centre of the bunch, and then thin those on the outside. Avoid over-thinning the top sprigs, or shoulders, of the bunches; aim for a balanced shape.

## Harvesting dessert grapes

Dessert grapes should be harvested when fully ripe (*see below*). To avoid touching them with your fingers, which might cause damage, cut the bunch off together with a piece of the lateral stem above it, to use as a handle. It is best to harvest just one bunch at a time, as they ripen, since the grapes will only keep for a few days once harvested.

### Harvesting dessert grapes
*The grapes are ripe when the skin of the fruits becomes translucent. To avoid damaging the bloom of the grapes, hold the stem above the bunch, and cut it 4–5cm (1½–2in) either side of the bunch to form a handle (see inset).*

# Grape vines outdoors

A warm, sunny slope, wall, or fence, preferably below an altitude of about 120m (400ft), is best for growing grape vines outdoors. Vines are tolerant of a wide range of soils, provided that they are at least 30cm (12in) deep and well drained. They have deep and extensive root systems, and are thus capable of withstanding drought. The ideal pH is 6.5–7 (*see p.18*). They may suffer lime-induced chlorosis on thin soils over chalk (*see* Iron deficiency, *p.256*); a high-potash feed can remedy this. It is vital to choose cultivars that are suitable for cultivation in the open; these will usually be white wine grapes (*see p.233*).

Vines can be planted outdoors in the dormant season between late autumn and early spring. However, container-grown vines, are best purchased and planted in late spring when they have started to grow and all danger of air frosts has passed. Vines outdoors may be grown as cordons (*see pp.228–229*) or on the guyot system.

## The guyot system

This is the most widely used vineyard form of training vines, and it is also an excellent form for garden cultivation, particularly for wine grapes. The vines are pruned on a replacement system (*see p.232*) as either single or double guyots (with one or two fruiting arms). This usually results in good-quality fruit buds each year, and a fine crop of grapes. Vines should be planted 1m (3ft) apart for a single guyot and, for a double guyot, 1.5m (4ft) apart. If you intend to grow more than one row of vines, orient the rows north–south and space them 1.5–2m (5–6ft) apart.

## Creating a support system

Guyot vines require a support system of posts and wires, using 2mm-gauge (1⁄16in) galvanized wire. This should consist of treated posts spaced 4–5m (12–15ft) apart, depending on the spacing of the plants, with two single lower wires at 40cm (16in) and 55cm (22in) from the ground. There should also be three sets of double wires at 90cm (3ft), 1.2m (4ft), and 1.5m (5ft). Use straining bolts to attach the wires to the end posts, running them through

cup-hooks on the intermediate posts so that they can be removed easily for winter pruning. The end posts require support struts, as described for tree fruit supports (*see pp.162–163*). Guyot vines grown against walls or fences need only single rather than double wires, since the shoots will be trained between the wires and the wall or fence.

## Guyot training

To create a double guyot vine, follow the formative pruning steps outlined on p.232. For a single guyot, the training is the same except that only two shoots are used, and then one arm only is selected. In the first cropping year – the first year that the arms are tied in place – retain only one or two bunches on each arm to avoid overly stressing the vine. In the second cropping year, retain two or three bunches per arm. In the third cropping year, if the grape vine is growing strongly, retain all the bunches.

Established guyot vines should be pruned every year (*see p.232*). As the use of a three-bud "stub" leads to the framework gradually getting higher, occasionally select a lower-placed shoot as a stub, so that the vine can be cut back to this in the following year.

## Routine care of outdoor vines

In late winter, feed with a general compound fertilizer (*see pp.20–23*) at a rate of approximately 70g per sq m (2½oz per sq yd) and sulphate of potash at about 15g per sq m (½oz per sq yd). Mulch with a 5–8cm (2–3in) layer of well-rotted manure, garden compost, or bark mulch, spread over a radius of 45cm (18in) for the first 4–5 years, and every year for wall-trained vines. The mulch should not touch the stem.

Established vines require little or no watering, but newly planted vines need irrigation during dry periods in spring and summer. Foliage should be thinned out in late summer (*see below*).

## Harvesting vine grapes

For wine-making, grapes must contain the maximum amount of sugar; the sugar levels can be determined using specialist instruments, but a good guide is to taste the grapes as they approach ripeness and harvest when they are very sweet. Green grapes usually turn more translucent and slightly yellow when ripe. Cut them off where the stalk joins the cropping lateral. Grapes are best eaten fresh, but should keep for a little while if stored in a cool place.

**Thinning the foliage of outdoor grape vines**
*In late summer, as the fruits (here the black wine grape 'Rondo') are ripening, thin out the foliage to allow the sun to reach the fruits.*

*Using sharp secateurs, cut out at the base any leaves that are shading the fruits. Try to avoid touching the grapes while you are working.*

# Formative pruning of a double guyot vine

1 **On planting in winter,** insert a stake and tie it into the horizontal wires. Prune the vine back to 15cm (6in) above the soil, with at least 2 strong buds.

2 **Year 1, summer:** tie the leading shoot to the stake with soft twine. Cut sideshoots back to 5 leaves, and remove strong, upright shoots and low shoots.

3 **Year 2, winter:** cut the leading shoot back to just above 3 strong buds that are below the lowest set of wires.

4 **Year 2, spring and summer:** as the vine grows, choose 3 strong shoots, pruning back any others, and train them upwards, tying them into the central support (*see right*). Tuck the sideshoots from the 3 main shoots into the parallel wires to grow horizontally; their leaves will feed and strengthen the vine. Throughout the summer, rub or pull off any other shoots at the base of the vine (*see inset*).

5 **Year 3, winter:** tie 2 of the 3 sideshoots to the bottom wires on each side in a shallow arc to form the guyot's arms. If either breaks off, use the third unpruned shoot to replace it. If not, prune this shoot to 3–4 good buds (*see far right*).

6 **Year 3, summer:** guide shoots from each arm vertically through the pairs of wires. Pinch out their tips when they reach the top; pinch any sideshoots they produce back to 1 leaf. Let 3 shoots grow from the central stub, also pinching back their sideshoots. These 3 shoots are reserved to form next year's fruiting arms.

7 **Year 4, winter:** untie and cut off the guyot's arms completely. As in step 5, bend 2 of the central, reserved shoots to the horizontal and tie them into the 2 bottom wires. If the third is not needed as a reserve, prune it back to 3–4 buds.

# Pruning an established guyot vine

In summer, as in step 6 above, train evenly spaced sideshoots upwards from the guyot's arms, tucking them between the double wires. These shoots will flower and fruit. Tie in and reserve 3 strong shoots from the central "stubs" as before. Remove any flowers produced by these shoots. Prune all vertically trained shoots back to 10–15cm (4–6in) above the top wire when necessary, and pinch or cut back any sideshoots they produce to one leaf. Remove any shoots on the clear trunk. In early winter, as in step 7 above, cut back the fruited arms and tie in the replacement shoots.

*Pinching sublaterals on the 3 reserved shoots*

*Summer pruning of shoot tips and sideshoots*

## RECOMMENDED GRAPE VINE CULTIVARS

### DESSERT GRAPES

Dessert grapes are the only ones suitable for growing under cover, and they are classified in three groups: sweetwater, muscat, and vinous. Sweetwater are earliest to mature and easiest to grow in unheated greenhouses. Muscat grapes have the finest flavour and ripen later. They can be grown in unheated greenhouses in milder areas, but benefit from added heat.

**'Chasselas'** ♀ *Early, small, white, sweetwater grape; can be grown outside in warm areas.*
**'Foster's Seedling'** ♀ *Early-cropping, white, sweetwater grape.*
**'Muscat Hamburg'** ♀ *Earliest to crop of the muscats, a good-flavoured, black grape.*
**'Muscat of Alexandria'** ♀ *Late-ripening, white, muscat grape; one of the best-flavoured, but often needs additional heat in spring and autumn to ripen well.*
**'Schiava Grossa'** (syn. **'Black Hamburgh'**) ♀ *Mid-season, black, sweetwater grape.*

### WINE GRAPES

**'Cabernet Franc'** *Vigorous vine with slight tolerance for salinity. Red wine with a distinctive flavour.*
**'Cabernet Sauvignon'** *Vigorous vine with small, tight fruit bunches. Excellent red wine.*

*Suitable for cool and warm regions.*
**'Chardonnay'** *Vigorous vine, suitable for cool areas, with early-ripening fruit. Distinctively flavoured white wine.*
**'Chenin Blanc'** *Vigorous vine with medium compact grape bunches. Can be grown without irrigation to produce sweet white wine.*
**'Grenache'** *Medium-vigorous vine with short, stumpy bunches of grapes, often used for rose wines or combined with other cultivars. Heat-tolerant.*
**'Malbec'** *Vigorous, spreading vine. Bunches well filled with small grapes. Soft, pleasant red wine often combined with other cultivars.*
**'Merlot'** *Vigorous, highly productive vine but susceptible to salinity. Excellent red wine, often mixed with other cultivars.*
**'Pinot Noir'** *Several clones of this medium-vigorous vine are available. Tight, compact bunches. Suited to cool regions, where wines are highly regarded.*
**'Reisling'** *Medium-vigorous vine with small, compact bunches of small grapes that turn golden. White wine with distinctive flavour.*
**'Ruby Cabernet'** *Vigorous vine suitable for hot, dry areas. Bunches are loose, grapes medium-sized and dark-coloured. Excellent red wine.*

**'Sauvignon Blanc'** *Vigorous, upright growth with small, compact bunches of greenish-yellow grapes. Wines from cool areas have distinctive flavour.*
**'Semillon'** *Moderately vigorous. Conical, compact bunches of small greenish grapes. Produces a dry white wine.*
**'Shiraz'** *Medium vigour. Long, cylindrical bunches of small oval grapes. Excellent wine, often mixed.*
**'Traminer'** *Very vigorous. Small tight bunches of pink to red grapes. Grow in cool areas to produce a good wine.*
**'Verdelho'** *Moderately vigorous. Small loose bunches of greenish-yellow grapes. Used to produce table wines with varietal characteristics.*

'Muscat of Alexandria', white muscat grapes

## COMMON PROBLEMS OF GRAPE VINES

In warm climates, where vines are widely grown outdoors, they may succumb to a number of common problems. In cooler areas, vines grown outside suffer from few pests other than birds taking the fruits, but they can be affected by certain diseases and disorders. Vines grown under cover are more susceptible to all types of problem. For more details, *see* Plant Problems, *pp.246–262*.

### PESTS

**Birds** *As fruits ripen, net vines both outside and across the doors and ventilators of greenhouses, to protect them from birds.*
**Brown scale** *Usually only a problem under cover, but sometimes also for wall-trained vines (see p.252).*
***Daktulosphaira vitifolii* (syn. *Phylloxera vastatrix*)** *This pest can cause serious problems. A voracious root feeder, it causes severe stunting; leaf galls may form and the vine may die. This pest multiplies rapidly and is impossible to eradicate using conventional pesticides.*

*The solution in is grafting onto resistant rootstocks (see p.227).*
**Mealybug** *Only a serious problem for vines under cover (see p.257).*
**Red spider mite** *Often a problem under cover, but rarely outside (see p.261).*
**Vine weevil** *Adults attack the foliage, but it is the grubs in the soil that can seriously harm a vine (see p.264).*
**Wasps** *May affect early-ripening cultivars. Use traps, or protect fruits with muslin bags or sections of nylon tights (see p.264).*

### DISEASES

**Downy mildew** *Seldom affects vines in cooler areas (see p.255).*
**Botrytis** *Also known as grey mould, this is a common problem both outside and under cover, but regular pruning and fruit thinning reduces the risk (see p.252).*
**Powdery mildew** *Affects leaves and fruits, and can be a problem both outside and under cover (see p.260).*

### CULTURAL DISORDERS

**Magnesium deficiency** *May occur both outside and under cover, but is easily controlled (see p.257).*
**Oedema** *May occur on vines under cover when conditions are too moist, usually through lack of ventilation. Do not remove the affected parts as this will exacerbate the problem (see p.258).*
**Scald and scorch** *Can be a problem with vines under cover, when grapes and leaves near glass suffer as a result of lack of ventilation. Remove affected parts and improve air circulation (see p.262).*
**Spray damage** *Vines are very susceptible to damage from hormonal weedkillers, causing twisted and distorted growth. Leaves may be distorted and cupped or they may be thin and stringy with little green. Sometimes just fumes of spray can be enough to poison plants. Do not spray near vines or store chemicals near them.*

# GROWING OTHER FRUITS

## Citrus

### *Citrus* species

Many citrus species are grown for their fruits, including oranges, grapefruits, lemons, and limes. Calamondins (x *Citrofortunella microcarpa*), and kumquats (*Fortunella japonica* and *F. margarita*), are also classified as citrus fruits.

Citrus trees are evergreen and can reach 3–10m (10–30ft) tall, with a spread of 5–8m (15–25ft). In warm climates, flowers and fruits are borne year-round, often appearing on the tree at the same time.

It is usual to grow grafted citrus trees, and the chosen rootstock will affect the degree of pruning needed.

Most citrus will survive brief spells at 0°C (32°F), but will fruit freely only in relatively frost-free climates that have hot summers and an average winter minimum of 15°C (59°F). Citrus become dormant at 13°C (55°F) and to bear ripe fruit, need a minimum of 14°C (55°F) for six months after flowering. Fruit ripens 9–11 months after pollination. Most are self-fertile, so no pollinator is required. The higher the temperature, the better the flavour of the fruit.

**Site and planting**  Citrus tolerate a range of soils, but prefer fertile, well-drained, slightly acid conditions (pH 6–6.5). Plant in spring into prepared sites. Citrus trees can be grown in all states of Australia but usually require some form of irrigation. In cooler regions, citrus need to be sheltered from cold winds,

hot winds and early and late frosts. Fences can be erected around them, windbreaks planted or the citrus trees can be planted among other shrubs and trees that provide shelter.

**Pruning and training**  Citrus may be trained as a standard (*see below*) in a container. Prune between late winter and early spring. Citrus will, however, generally respond well to pruning at any time, especially in warm or tropical climate areas. Young citrus trees are usually trimmed to a bush shape at first planting to encourage new growth, but are not regularly pruned, as with most deciduous fruit trees. If trees are pruned harshly, the bark of exposed limbs should be painted with a white water-based paint to prevent sunburn. Most gardeners only prune citrus trees if they are sick, become injured or diseased, are too wide spread, or if they grow too bushy, shading the centre of the tree. Citrus trees can be grown as thin-foliaged espalier shapes on a trellis, against a wall, as hedges or spreading specimen trees. Many gardeners grow citrus as standards in pots and prune the top foliage area into topiary shapes.

**Fertiliser requirements**  Citrus trees are shallow-rooted plants that naturally live on rotting organic matter provided by mulches and forest litter. They are hungry plants and require a balanced fertilizer regime that includes all the basic foods: nitrogen; phosphorous; and potassium; as well as minor nutrients such as boron; copper; manganese; magnesium; and zinc. In some nutrient-deficient soils and in highly alkaline or

severely acidic soils, nutrient deficiency symptoms will show, mostly as varying yellowish patterns on citrus leaves. Generally, citrus trees require plant food in autumn, during spring growth and subsequent growth periods. Nitrogen can be applied in autumn, but more nitrogen may be needed during the year as trees begin new growth phases. Other major nutrients (phosphorous and potassium) can also be applied during autumn. As an alternative to individual fertilizer applications, a general complete fertilizer may be given to the trees. This will contain all the major and most of the minor nutrients (trace elements). Organic fertilizers can also be used. Mature citrus trees may require up to 5kg of fertilizer per year or about 20–30kg of an organic fertilizer to maintain good cropping and growth. Leaf analysis will show whether a plant needs more food and if it is lacking certain nutrients. If it is evident that there are minor nutrient deficiencies, foliar applications of the appropriate trace elements can be made.

**Routine care for citrus in pots**  Water well and give a high-nitrogen, medium-potassium liquid feed monthly during the growing season; use a fertilizer that includes trace elements (*see p.20*). Prevent citrus from drying out, as drought causes fruit drop. Remove suckers from the rootstock, at their points of origin. Repot citrus in containers every third or fourth year in early spring.

**Harvesting and storage**  Harvest the fruits when ripe, using secateurs to cut them with a

## Training a citrus standard

Use figure-of-eight knot to tie vertical stem to stake

Remove one-third of length of each sideshoot

Allow leaves to remain on stem – these will fall naturally

Cut out sideshoots that were pruned previously

Remove any sideshoots from main stem that are below desired stem height

**1**  **When planting,** tie in the main vertical stem, or leader, to a stake, and shorten any sideshoots by one-third.

**2**  **Once the main stem** has grown to more than the final required height of the trunk, prune it back to a healthy bud. Do not prune any new sideshoots, since these will help to thicken the trunk, but remove any sideshoots that were shortened in the previous year.

**3**  **When 3 or 4 well-spaced sideshoots** have developed above the desired trunk height, remove all shoots below these to leave a clear trunk and the beginnings of the permanent head of the standard. Prune the 3 or 4 remaining shoots by 3–5 leaves. In subsequent seasons, prune as for a bush tree (*see above*) to gain a rounded, balanced shape.

short stem. Undamaged fruits can be stored for several weeks at 4–6°C (38–42°F) in well ventilated conditions.

**Propagation** For named cultivars, T-budding is the usual propagation method. This is similar to chip-budding (*see p. 154*), but instead of grafting a "chip" onto the rootstock, a bud is grafted. Make a T-shaped cut through the bark of the rootstock about 23cm (9in) above ground level. Prepare a bud of the cultivar to be grafted by choosing a section of ripe, new growth and slicing out a bud with a gentle scooping cut. Insert the bud into the T-shaped cut, and bind the area with plastic tape so the graft cannot dry out. Remove the tape after 4–6 weeks. When the budded shoot is 2.5cm (1in) long, cut off the rootstock top-growth just above it.

Citrus can also be raised from seed. Although many citrus do produce offspring that are similar to the parent, seed-raised plants can take six years or more to begin fruiting, and there is always a risk of inferior quality fruit. It is better to buy in named cultivars from a reputable supplier.

**Common problems** Citrus may be affected by mealybugs (*p. 257*), red spider mite (*p. 261*), scale insect (*p. 262*), and whitefly (*p. 264*). Crown rot (*p. 254*), root-knot eelworm (*p. 262*), fruit fly (*p. 255*), and thrips (*p. 263*) are sometimes troublesome. Viruses (*p. 264*), spread by aphids, cause loss of vigour, smaller fruits, and pitting on fruits. Spray aphids.

**Recommended citrus cultivars**
x *Citrofortunella microcarpa* ♀ – calamondin; small, ornamental fruit, good for preserves.
*C. aurantiifolia* 'Tahiti', *syn.* 'Persian' – lime; the most cold-tolerant, with fairly sweet fruit.
*C. aurantium* 'Chinotto' – sour orange; compact, free-flowering, bitter flavour.
*C. limon* 'Eureka' – lemon; few-seeded, very acid, medium-sized fruit.
*C. x meyeri* 'Meyer' – the hardiest and most compact lemon; small, rounded, acid fruit.
*C. x paradisi* 'Marsh' – grapefruit; free-flowering with seedless, white-fleshed fruit.
*C. reticulata* 'Dancy' – mandarin orange; compact with small, sweet, juicy fruit.
*C. sinensis* 'Washington' – sweet orange; sweet, juicy, seedless navel orange.
*C. x tangelo* 'Minneola' – tangelo; aromatic, with sweet, tangy flesh.

# Kiwi fruit

*Actinidia deliciosa*

Kiwi fruits, or Chinese gooseberries, are rampant, twining, deciduous plants that grow up to 9m (28ft) in length; they require sturdy, permanent supports and a great deal of space.

Kiwi fruits need temperatures of 5–25°C (40–77°F) to fruit well, although they will survive temperatures down to −8°C (18°F) when dormant. Protection from wind is vital (*see pp. 12–13*). They should be grown against a fence, trellis or wall in cool temperate areas.

## Summer pruning kiwi fruit

In early to midsummer, look for sideshoots that have developed fruitlets at the base. Use secateurs to cut back each shoot to 5 leaves above the fruitlets, making the cut just above a leaf. This will divert energy from producing foliage to the swelling fruits. After fruiting, cut the sideshoots back to 2 buds beyond the last fruit. This method of pruning will build up a productive system of fruiting spurs.

Plastic screening may be used for additional protection in cold areas.

**Site and planting** Choose deep, well-aerated soil rich in organic matter and with a pH of 6–7. Add a general-purpose fertilizer at a rate of 50–110g (2–4oz) per plant. Erect post-and-wire support with horizontal wires at 30cm (12in) intervals. Plant in winter, allowing 4–5m (12–15ft) between plants.

For successful pollination, plant both male (non-fruiting) and female plants; one male will pollinate up to eight or nine females.

**Pruning and training** The most practical way to grow a kiwi fruit in domestic gardens is as an espalier (*see p. 152*). After planting, tie in the leading shoot as it grows to a cane attached vertically to the wires. Train in a pair of shoots along each horizontal wire, pinching out the tips when they fill the allotted space; these will form the permanent fruiting framework. The fruits are borne on one-year-old wood. Allow sideshoots to develop at 50cm (20in) intervals, pinching them out to leave five leaves. These should bear fruit the following year; for summer pruning, *see above*. Every three years or so, cut sideshoots back to dormant buds near the main horizontal shoot to encourage new sideshoots.

**Routine care** Apply a thick mulch in spring (*see pp. 41–42*) and a general-purpose fertilizer rich in phosphate and potassium. Water well to keep moist throughout the growing season.

**Harvesting and storage** About three or four years after planting, the vines should start to bear fruit. Harvest the fruits as they start to soften. Store laid out in trays in single layers. Wrapped in kitchen film at near-freezing temperatures, they keep for 4–6 weeks.

**Propagation** Take softwood cuttings, about 10–15cm (4–6in) long, in spring, selecting healthy, unripened wood. Trim leaves off the lower third of each cutting and insert in a pot of cuttings potting mix with bottom heat (*see p. 62*). Once rooted, pot up into larger pots before hardening off and planting out.

Alternatively, take some hardwood cuttings in winter. Trim to 20–30cm (8–12in) long, and insert them in sandy compost. Once rooted, transplant to their final positions. Selected cultivars may be grafted by means of T-budding (*see* Citrus, *left*) or whip-and-tongue grafting (*see p. 155*).

**Common problems** Kiwi fruit are seldom prone to significant pest or disease attack.

**Recommended cultivars**
'Bruno' – female; large, elongated, dark brown fruits, with bristly hairs and sweet flavour.
'Hayward' – female; large, oval, pale brown fruits, softly hairy with good, sweet flavour.
'Tomuri' – male; good pollinator.

# Passionfruit

*Passiflora* species

Vigorous climbers, passionfruit bear yellow or purple fruits on the current year's growth. The species usually grown for their fruit are

**Purple passionfruit**
*Passionfruit vines can be grown successfully in all states of Australia. Vines produce equally well if they are pruned or left unpruned.*

the yellow-fruited *P. edulis* f. *flavicarpa* and the purple-fruited *P. edulis*. Both require a winter minimum temperature of 10°C (50°F). When in growth, purple-fruited variants do best above 20°C (68°F), while those with yellow fruits need temperatures above 24°C (75°F). Both need moderate humidity to fruit well.

**Site and planting**  Passionfruits thrive in full sun, and grow well on fences, trellis frames or as regularly pruned espalier shapes. They tolerate a range of soil types as long as there is good drainage – add well-rotted organic matter and sharp sand to the planting hole, along with a general-purpose fertilizer. For containers (*see pp. 35–36*), use a fertile potting mix with a high organic content and add a general-purpose fertilizer; choose a container over 35cm (14in) in diameter.

Prepare a support in the form of a trellis or wires on a wall (*see p. 162*). Plant in spring, and space the plants about 3m (10ft) apart.

You may need to pollinate by hand (*see p. 157*) and fruit set will be poor where temperatures fall below 16°C (61°F). For good health and productivity, replace the plants every five or six years.

**Pruning and training**  Select and train two main stems up and then along the top of the support. These stems will produce sideshoots every year that hang down and bear fruit. Tip prune these to keep them clear of the ground. If the main stems are reluctant to flower, pinch out the tips.

Every year after fruiting, prune back the hanging sideshoots to about 20cm (8in) or two buds; fruited shoots will not fruit again.

**Routine care**  For plants grown in beds, apply a general-purpose fertilizer with a medium- to high-nitrogen content every three or four months, from spring onwards. Keep plants mulched (*see pp. 41–42*) and well-watered. In pots, use a liquid feed or general-purpose fertilizer (*see pp. 20–23*) every four weeks during the growing season.

**Harvesting and storage**  The best quality fruits are obtained when left on the plant until fully coloured and slightly shrivelled. They can, however, be ripened off the plant if picked as they begin to change colour.

Fruits may be stored for up to 21 days at a temperature of 6–7°C (43–45°F) and 85–90 per cent humidity.

**Propagation**  To grow passionfruit from seed, extract the seeds from ripe fruits and allow them to ferment in their own pulp for a few days, then wash and dry them. Sow into a proprietary seed compost and cover lightly. Germinate at a temperature of 20–25°C (68–77°F). When the seedlings are 20–35cm (8–14in) tall, transplant to their final position.

Propagation by cuttings is not advised as older plants succumb to passion vine woodiness virus and it is likely that cuttings will also be infected. Root with bottom heat (*see p. 62*) on a mist bench, or mist them regularly until the cuttings have rooted.

Chip-budding (*see p. 154*) can also be used to propagate passionfruit.

**Common problems**  Passionfruit may be affected by aphids (*see p. 251*), fruit fly (*p. 255*), red spider mite (*p. 261*), and scale insect (*p. 262*).

**Recommended cultivars**
'Crackerjack' – free-flowering, with large, aromatic, deep purple to black fruits. 'Golden Nuggett' – free-flowering, with sweet, golden yellow fruit.

# Pineapples in pots

*Ananas comosus*

Pineapples are succulent perennials, of the bromeliad family, that originate in tropical climates. To produce fruit, pineapples need high levels of light, moderately high humidity, and temperatures of 18–30°C (64–86°F). Plants usually fruit at about three years of age. Pineapples grown in containers are more easily managed, but will produce smaller fruits than those grown in beds.

**Site and planting**  Pineapples prefer a sandy medium loam with a pH of 5–6.5 (*see p. 18*), although they will tolerate a range of soil conditions. In spring, plant suckers or "slips" in prepared beds, about 30cm (12in) apart, with 60cm (24in) between rows, or at 50cm (20in) apart each way. Alternatively, use 30cm (12in) diameter pots filled with potting mix with a high organic content. Provide maximum light, a temperature of

**Propagating from a crown shoot**
*Increase your stock by removing the crown shoot of a ripe pineapple with 1cm (½in) of the fruit attached; do not cut through the base of the shoot. Insert into a pot of potting mix.*

at least 20°C (68°F) and humidity of about 70 per cent. Bottom heat improves growth. Pineapples are very sensitive to draughts, so avoid exposure to them at all times. You could create a microclimate around the plants in the greenhouse using a film plastic "tent".

**Routine care**  Water regularly, particularly when young, and provide a thick organic mulch (*see pp. 41–42*) on beds to help retain moisture. Apply a high-nitrogen, medium-potassium liquid feed every three or four weeks during the growing season.

**Harvesting and storage**  Each plant will produce a single fruit. When fruits begin to turn yellow, cut through the stem below each fruit, leaving a small stalk attached. The fruits can be stored at 8°C (46°F) with 90 per cent humidity for about three weeks.

**Propagation**  Suckers grow from the leaf axils, stem bases, or below the fruit. Cut off the sucker with a sharp knife, dip the cut surfaces in fungicide, and leave to dry for several days. Trim off the lower leaves and insert into sandy potting mixture to root.

Take crown shoots as cuttings (*see below*), keeping them at a temperature of 18–21°C (64–70°F). Once the suckers or crown roots have rooted, pot them into 15cm (6in) pots.

**Common problems**  Mealybugs (*see p. 257*), root-knot eelworm (*p. 262*), scale insect (*p. 262*), red spider mite (*p. 261*), and thrips (*p. 263*) may affect pineapples. In overly wet conditions, *Phytophthora* heart-rot (*see p. 259*) may become a problem.

**Recommended cultivars**
If propagating from crowns of shop-bought pineapples, 'Queen', imported from Kenya or Malaysia, is sweet, well-flavoured and ripens quickly. 'Smooth Cayenne', grown in Hawaii and the Azores, has smooth, spineless leaves and juicy, highly flavoured fruit.

# Olive

*Olea europea*

Olives are slow-growing, evergreen trees, reaching a height of 9–12m (28–40ft) and a spread of 7–9m (22–28ft) in optimum conditions. They thrive in Mediterranean regions with an ideal temperature range of 5–25°C (41–77°F). Trees remain productive for decades, developing gnarled bark and a twisted habit. To set and ripen fruits, trees need long, hot summers followed by cool winters. Although moderately cold-hardy, even mature trees will sustain damage if temperatures fall below −10°C (14°F).

In cool climates, olives can be grown in pots (*see pp. 35–36*). They may be grown outdoors in sheltered gardens.

**Site and planting**  Select a well-drained site with soil of medium to low fertility. Alkaline soils (*see p. 18*), up to pH 8.5, are suitable. Provide shelter (*see pp. 12–13*) from wind. A warm site is essential in cool temperate climates. Choose either rooted cuttings or budded plants, and stake firmly on planting. Space them 7–12m (22–40ft) apart. Olives are wind-pollinated and most cultivars are self-fertile, but you may need to plant two or more plants in cooler climates to improve pollination and fruiting.

**Pruning and training** Prune olives in early spring. Take out the main vertical shoot when it is about 1.5m (5ft) tall, selecting three or four strong branches below the shoot to form a permanent framework. Keep the stem clear of shoots below the framework shoots. Routine pruning consists of removing older branches to promote new growth (fruits are borne on one-year-old wood) and to maintain an open centre to the tree. To restrict the size of a pot-grown olive, tip prune the main branches, cutting back to a good replacement shoot each year.

**Routine care** Apply a general-purpose fertilizer with medium to high nitrogen levels two or three times a year. Water regularly while trees establish, and mulch with organic material. Keep plants in containers moist during the growing season and apply a liquid feed every three or four weeks. Olives need a period of winter chilling to initiate flowers.

**Harvesting and storage** An olive in the open may start to fruit three or four years after planting. Timing of harvesting depends on what the olives are to be used for. Olives to be used for fermenting are picked when they are ripe but green; these fruits are processed to remove their bitterness. Those that are used as table olives are picked when they are black and firm, then packed in salt until dehydrated, and subsequently stored in olive oil or brine.

**Propagation** Olives are usually propagated by stem cuttings. Take hardwood cuttings in winter, removing sections of one- or two-year-old wood about 30cm (12in) long. Treat the base with a hormone rooting product, then insert the cutting to half its depth in a pot of propagating mix. Rooting should take about 30 days at a temperature between 13–21°C (55–70°F).

**Mature olive tree**
*Olive trees are very long-lived; the pretty creamy white flowers appear in midsummer, followed by fruits in autumn.*

## Persimmon fruit

**1** **Many persimmon cultivars** are available. Of particular interest to the home gardener are the non-astringent cultivars such as 'Vanilla', here. They can be picked and eaten straight from the tree like an apple.

**2** **Persimmons are rarely attacked** by pests or infected with diseases but during very hot weather the fruit can become sunburned as shown above. Ripe fruit may be attacked by birds (as also shown above).

Transplant into larger pots to grow on. Semi-ripe cuttings, 10–15cm (4–6in) long, can be taken in summer.

T-budding (*see* Citrus, *p.235*) can be used to graft cultivars onto vigorous olive seedling rootstocks or, for a dwarfing influence, onto *Osmanthus* stock.

**Common problems** Olive scab (*see p.251*), root-knot eelworm (*see p.261*), scale insect (*p.262*), and verticillium wilt (*p.263*) may all affect olives grown in the open. Under cover, common problems may include fruit fly (*see p.255*), red spider mite (*p.261*), thrips (*p.263*), and whitefly (*p.264*).

**Recommended cultivars**
'El Greco' – large fruit with small stones.
'Mission' – free-fruiting and cold-resistant.

# Persimmon

### *Diospyros kaki*

*Diospyros kaki* is the botanical name of the fruit known as oriental persimmon now grown widely, particularly in Japan and China, its place of origin. Persimmons are deciduous trees that, in the wild, grow to 10m (30ft) or more but cultivars suitable for home gardens generally grow into small bushy trees. The fruit is bright orange, of variable shape, with orange flesh. There are astringent and non-astringent cultivars available.

**Site and planting** Persimmons are versatile plants and will grow in most cool and temperate climate areas but will also grow in semitropical zones. The persimmon tree develops colourful autumn foliage and is often valued for this fact alone. Some cultivars require two trees for cross-pollination. Most selected cultivars are partially fertile but will produce better crops if another pollinator is present. An alternative to purchasing two trees is to graft a different cultivar onto one of the branches of one tree. Persimmons will grow in almost any soil providing it is well drained. They have fairly brittle branches and need protection from wind. If well supported they can be grown as espaliers trained on a trellis.

**Routine care** Persimmons are easy to look after as all they need is a little fertilizer, weed control around the tree base, some water, and very little pruning. .

**Harvesting and storage** With astringent cultivars, fruit is harvested then ripened or left until ripened and soft on the tree. Astringent fruits can be placed into the freezer to get rid of the astringent taste or left until very soft and squishy. Non-astringent cultivars can be picked from the tree and eaten straight away. Fruit is usually ready for harvest during autumn-winter.

**Propagation** Persimmons are usually propagated by budding or grafting onto selected or seedling rootstocks.

**Common problems** Persimmons do not have many pests or diseases but birds can can make it necessary to net plants. Exposed fruit may become sunburned.

**Recommended cultivars** A selection of available cultivars includes: 'Dia Dai Maru' – non-astringent flat/square fruit, eaten straight from tree ; 'Fuyu' – non-astringent cultivar with flat/round fruit, also eaten straight from tree; 'Hyakumo' – astringent, large, round fruit, requires cross-pollination; 'Nightingale' – astringent, large, conical fruit; 'Tanenashi' with astringent, large, heart-shaped fruit, self-fertile; and 'Vanilla' a delicious non-astringent flat/round cultivar that is not readily available.

# Avocado

*Persea americana*

The avocado is one of the best-known tropical fruits. The plant originates from the highland areas of Mexico, Tropical America and Central America, but many selections of seedling trees have since been brought into cultivation.

**Site and planting** Avocado trees will grow in a range of well-drained soil types, but prefer sandy soils. The trees grow well in the tropics and some of the more cold-tolerant cultivars will grow as far south as Tasmania where commercial plantings are being trialled. Young plants are very sensitive to frost, especially during the initial 4–5 years of formative growth. They do not like draughty cold winds or, in warmer climates, hot winds, so the plants need shelter from wind. The best position is a sheltered place receiving plenty of sunshine.

The pollination of the avocado is one of the true wonders of nature. Most cultivars are self-pollinating but the flowers change sex. One day there may be all female flowers on the tree; next day they may have changed to male. Sometimes, though, there is no overlap so flowers do not get pollinated. Growing two or more cultivars helps to ensure fruit set.

**Routine care** Avocado trees need to be looked after. They should be planted into a well-prepared hole that has some blood and bone or pelletized organic fertilizer at the base covered slightly with soil so that roots don't come in contact with the fertilizer. An alternative on heavier soils is to build a large mound to plant the tree into. The tree should be staked and the roots watered with a liquid seaweed product. Protect young trees from frost and strong winds with a shelter for 4–5 years. Trees grow easily from seed but may not begin fruiting for up to 16 years.

Avocado trees need little pruning unless they are growing in a lopsided way. If they become too vigorous then some trimming may be done. They can also be cut to a stump and grafted if needed.

Avocado trees require moisture but not too much, so mulch during summer. Mulch will also act as a weed control measure. Feed while young with organic fertilizers such as fowl manure (this actually suppresses root rot organisms). Thinning of fruit is not necessary.

**Harvesting and storage** The fruit remain hard until removed from the tree so it is usually difficult to judge maturity. Some cultivars such as 'Hass' alter skin colour at maturity, others lose the fruit bloom. Sometimes the fruit stalk turns yellow. The best bet is to pick one fruit and let it ripen indoors. If it ripens without shrivelling then it's time to pick the fruit. It's not essential to pick all fruit at the one time; it's not unusual to see a tree in flower with the previous year's fruits still hanging on the tree.

**Propagation** Avocado plants are usually

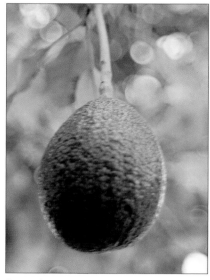

Avocado

*Close-up of seedling avocado fruit. Lumpy skin shows parentage is related to Hass cultivar.*

grafted onto seedling rootstocks or selected rootstocks free of sun blotch virus and resistant to *Phytopthora cinnamoni* root rot, a fungus that kills many plants grown in wet soils. Buy grafted plants unless you particularly want to grow your own from seed.

**Common problems** Few pests and diseases affect avocado fruit and trees so they are very easy to grow organically. Even the Queensland fruit fly does no harm to hard-skinned cultivars; it may lay eggs in the fruit but they do not hatch into maggots. It is important, though, to buy virus-free plants grafted onto *Phytopthora*-resistant rootstocks. Fruits may develop a stem end rot late in the season but preventative copper sprays will control this. Having a few damaged fruit may be preferable to using copper sprays.

**Recommended cultivars** There are many avocado cultivars available, some developed in Australia. Those available include the following:

'Bacon': a cold-tolerant cultivar with smooth texture and smooth skin; mild flavour, not recommended for fruit fly areas.

'Endral': good flavour, thick-skinned, pear-shaped fruit.

'Fuerte': a small to medium pear-shaped fruit with great flavour and a thick green skin. Often sets tiny fruit without seed which are sold as "cocktail" avocados. Slightly cold tolerant.

'Hass': very small fruit with bubbly lumpy skin but one of the best-tasting avocadoes. Suitable for cool climates.

'Hazzard': very large elongated fruit type. Great flavour suited to semitropical and tropical zones only.

'Pinkerton': medium-sized fruit round or pear shaped. Good flavour and high oil content, small seeded.

'Ricon': a large seeded fruit with medium flavour. The tree is cold tolerant.

'Reed': slightly cold tolerant, round "cannon ball"-type fruits with thick skin. Prolific bearer and reasonably well flavoured.

'Sharwill': medium-sized good-flavoured fruit that is thick and rough skinned. Slightly cold tolerant.

'Sheppard': small to medium fruit with a thick green skin that peels easily. Smooth-textured flesh of good flavour.

'Zutano': oval pear-shaped with thin glossy skin. Tree is very cold tolerant but not suited to areas where fruit fly is a problem.

# Banana

*Musa* species

Bananas are grown in nearly every country with tropical to semitropical climatic areas; vast areas are planted with bananas in NSW and Queensland in Australia. Although there are many different species and hundreds of cultivars such as large-fruited cooking types and red skin coloured bananas growing in places such as Papua New Guinea, there are only a few types grown commercially in Australia.

Wild bananas (*Musa* species), and the related Abyssinian banana (*Ensete ventricosum*) have seeded fruits with hardly any flesh or pulp. The most common commercially grown banana, the 'Cavendish' cultivar, is, however, seedless; seeds do start to form but are aborted (the tiny black specks in the fruit) allowing the banana skin to fill completely with edible pulp. A few of the smaller 'Lady Finger' and

Bananas

*Typical cover used by banana growers to protect bananas and to help them ripen.*

'Sugar' bananas are also grown commercially.

**Site and planting** There are restrictions on growing bananas in both Queensland and NSW. A permit must be obtained from the relevant Department of Agriculture and planting material must be clean, soil-free and from a registered plant nursery. The 'Lady Finger' is the only one permitted to be grown in the home garden in Queensland as it is more resistant to some pests and diseases. In NSW, a weed-free zone of 2m (6.2ft) around the plant stem, must be maintained by law.

Banana plants are shallow rooted, producing a mass of fibrous roots that need feeding regularly. Plants grow a palm-like stem with a crown of wide, large, soft leaves; each plant produces a huge flower stem, fruits and then dies, relying on sucker growth for continued propagation. The plants thrive on organic manures and thick mulches; they require moisture but detest waterlogged conditions. Plants will grow in the tropics, semitropics and even as far south as Melbourne if placed in a sunny, wind-sheltered, frost-free position. Banana palms grow in a large range of soils provided that the soils are well drained and fertile.

**Routine care** All older leaves should be cut and removed from plants as they age and the whole plant can be cut to ground level after it has fruited and begun to die.

New banana plants are grown from selected healthy suckers that grow around the base of the plant. It is advisable to prune out any unwanted sucker growth to prevent the build-up of pests or diseases and then select one or two suckers for fruiting the following year.

Plants must be examined regularly for pests or diseases and to judge when fruit is ready for picking. Most growers place an open-ended blue plastic sheath around the banana bunch as soon as the tiny fruit begin to form for protection and to assist the ripening of the bunch. Rogue suckers should be removed and a weed-free root area around the banana plant must be maintained.

**Harvesting and storage** Commercially grown 'Cavendish' bananas (whole bunches) are picked when mature but still green, cool stored and then gas ripened or picked when the skins start to change colour. 'Lady Finger' or 'Sugar' bananas need to be picked when near ripe and do not store for long periods. Bananas left to ripen on the plant in warm areas are subject to attack by fruit fly and fruit bats.

**Propagation** Bananas are propagated from selected suckers and some species from seed.

**Common problems** Banana plants suffer from a few pests and diseases, some of which may grow uncontrolled if not checked. Among the most virulent are Panama disease cause by the fungus *Fusarium oxysporum*; its symptoms are death of older leaves followed by gradual death of the whole plant and staining in any cut tissue in the root system. The other main disease is Bunchy top virus: symptoms include poor yields, narrow leaves, deformed fruits, and dark streaks and spots on the leaf. The disease is spread by sucking insects. Another pest is the banana weevil borer; its white larvae (grubs) invade root systems. Fruit flies will attack ripe fruits: control measures include planting pests and disease-free plants. Detailed information on methods of control of pests and diseases is available from departments of agriculture.

**Recommended cultivars** 'Dwarf Red Dacca', 'Lady Finger', 'Sugar', 'Williams'.

# Guava

## *Psidium* species

Guavas are evergeen, although when grown in cooler areas some leaf fall may occur. There are about 140 species of these tropical shrubs or small trees, many of which provide edible fruits. Very few of the total number of wild species have been selected for gardens or commerce. *Psidium guajava* is the most common guava and it is the one grown commercially to make jams, preserves, and sauces. It has a tremendous variation in fruit form, taste, acidity, and sweetness when grown from seed. Some of the commercial red-fleshed coloured cultivars, for instance, taste rather bland but are very useful for processing. The fruit flavour and sugar content of this species is adversely affected if low temperatures are experienced when the fruit is ripening.

**Site and planting** The guava is very adaptable to most soil types and can withstand some salinity and drought conditions when mature. In general, *Psidium* species need shelter from cold and hot winds, and must be grown in a frost-free situation. They need moisture during the growth and fruiting period and respond well to feeding with a complete fertilizer.

In the tropics, guava plants may produce fruit year round but in cooler areas they usually have one fruiting season with flowering commencing in spring.

**Routine care** Guava plants need regular fertilizer application and perform well with organic fertilizers, watering, pruning, and shelter from winds.

It is an advantage to prune these plants lightly leaving all small twigs. These produce many new growth shoots instead of just a few and this will lead to better cropping.

**Harvesting and storage** Guava are usually picked from the plant as they ripen or just as they are changing to the mature colour. The fruit will only store for a few days, but can be cool-stored for about one week in a refrigerator if needed.

**Propagation** Guavas seed readily in warm climates and seedling plants from undermature plants can be selected or seed can be collected and propagated. Guavas can be propagated using cuttings, and by grafting.

**Common problems** Fruit fly is the main insect problem so baiting or covering plants with insect-proof netting or protective paper fruit bags is needed. Scale insects and mealybugs can be a problem and anthracnose fungal disease will occur in unseasonal wet weather conditions.

**Recommended cultivars**
*P. cattleianum* (Strawberry Guava) with small black/purple coloured fruits and a slight strawberry/acidic flavour is easily grown in the tropics and in southern regions; *P. lucidium* (Yellow Cherry Guava) which produces perhaps the sweetest fruits of all guavas, small and yellow coloured; and *P. quajava* (various names).

**Guava**
*Immature developing guava fruit. With some cultivars the skin turns yellowish at maturity while others maintain their green colour.*

**Cherry Guava**
*Near ripe fruit and leaves of cherry guava. Fruit becomes more purple red when ripe and the flesh softens.*

# Lychee

### *Litchi chinensis*

The fruits are full of vitamins, minerals and natural sugars. The lychee originates from China and it is thought that the plant was introduced into Australia during the early 1800s. Serious commercial production did not start until the 1980s, so it is a relatively new commercial crop in Australia.

An evergreen tree that can, on maturity, reach 10-15m (30-45ft) but dwarf forms are available. It has masses of small, rounded, bubbly fruit with a hard brittle red/pink "shell" that encloses almost translucent flesh around one seed.

**Site and planting** This is one of the truly tropical fruits although it has been grown further south when given protection in a greenhouse. Lychee trees can grow in many soil types but must have acid soils to do well. The trees are intolerant of lime, and like organic fertilizer given little and often rather than as an oversupply all at once. Too much fertilizer will result in shoot growth instead of fruit production. Lychees must be given shelter from winds and too much sun may cause sunburn.

**Routine care** These trees must have good drainage and wind protection and need soil moisture during fruit set to harvest. Ideally, the trees should have cool, dry autumns and winters with hot summers to initiate good crops. It will be necessary to net trees to avoid damage from fruit bats and other animals.

Usually the plants are trained to have multiple branches and are pruned regularly each year just after harvest to promote new shoots for the following flowering season.

**Harvesting and storage** Fruit can be harvested when it has developed a full red/pink colour and the flesh is sweet to taste. At this stage the fruit feels soft when squeezed. The harvest period usually extends to 2-3 weeks in early summer but will be later in cooler regions. New cultivars are being introduced to give a longer harvest period. Individual fruits are picked with a small stalk attached and can be cool-stored at 2-7°C (36-49F) for about one week. The fruits can be frozen but they lose all the outside colour; this is not important as the red "shell" is peeled from fruits before use.

**Propagation** Lychees are mostly propagated by "marcotting". This is the removal of a section of bark from a selected small branch. The area is then packed with peat moss or another material, then wrapped with plastic, aluminium foil, or similar materials to promote roots from the wound area. Once roots have formed, the branch is cut from the tree. Grafting is also done but is not as efficient.

**Common problems** The lychee is attacked by many pests that need to be controlled. Erinose mites create a furry brown growth on the underside of leaves; bats eat fruit as do birds. The macadamia stem girdler and nut borer are often evident. Fruit-sucking insects and those that eat flowers or pollen are also often a pest.

**Recommended cultivars** Some good cropping cultivars are 'Bosworth,' 'Salanthial' and 'Wai Chee', all of which have done well in subtropical climates. Among other cultivars available are: 'Bengal', 'Gee Kee', 'Kwai May Pink' (*syn.* 'Bosworth' but often sold as a separate cultivar). There are many more cultivars being tested especially for Australian conditions.

# Macadamia nut

### *Macadamia integrifolia*

The macadamia is one of the very few fruit/nut-producing trees of Australian origin that has been extensively planted commercially, although it is interesting to note that this nut was first developed commercially in Hawaii. The first nuts from macadamia trees were collected in 1843 by the explorer Leichhardt but the tree was not named until 1858 by Ferdinand von Meuller who collected his own samples. Macadamia nut trees were planted in Hawaii during 1892 and research work selecting cultivars began about 40 years later. Interest in planting the nuts in Australia did not begin until the 1950s when Hawaiian cultivars were imported for trials. There are more trials being done now with selected Australian seedlings and hybrids to select better cultivars.

The trees have whorled leaves around the stem and produce clusters of large marble-shaped fruit (nuts) with a hard, shiny, often rough shell and a kernel that is delicious when roasted. Macadamia nuts are believed to

**Macadamia**
*Macadamia nuts collected from seedling tree grown in a home garden in Melbourne, Victoria. The nuts are tasty even though the shells are very thick.*

be good for people with high cholesterol with some research suggesting that 40g (1oz) of macadamia nuts taken daily may help to reduce cholesterol levels.

**Site and planting** Macadamia trees grow in semitropical areas of Australia but will grow outside that range in a large range of soils as long as they are well drained. Macadamia nut trees will also grow as far south as Bruny Island in Tasmania where there is one specimen that has as yet failed to set nuts. Evergreen olive-green leafed macadamia trees make great garden plants.

Trees can be grown from seed; these trees will always grow nuts at some stage although they may take from 5-8 years to crop. Some seedling cultivars produce nuts with extremely hard, thick shells.

**Routine care** Macadamia trees can be grown organically with the help of predator insects, and acceptable organic spray materials and by using organic fertilizers. The main focus of routine care should be on orchard management, tree health, fertilizer applications, pruning, and weed control to achieve good crops. Before starting to grow macadamia trees organically it will pay to obtain a soil analysis to check for any major or minor nutrients deficiencies in your particular soil. Larger crops are often obtained when, for instance, zinc foliar sprays are applied in areas where zinc is deficient in the soil.

Macadamia trees do not usually need pruning but can be if pruned if necessary. Some commercial producers grow the trees as hedges, pruning them regularly.

**Propagation** Macadamia trees have traditionally been grown from seed, but large-nutted, thinner-shelled cultivars are propagated by budding and grafting onto selected rootstocks or by taking cuttings. The grafts that have been used on macadamia include whip grafts, side-wedge grafts, and bark grafts for larger limbs or reworked trees. Seed grafting is also used. The germinating seedling has its soft shoot removed. The short stem that remains is cut downwards forming a cleft and is grafted using tiny scion shoots. Air layering can produce plants and patch budding is also used on selected rootstocks. The rootstock and donor plants (scion material) must be at a stage where the bark slips away easily.

**Common problems** Macadamia trees have several native insects that have adapted to the plant and are attacked at times by many more. There are, however, only a few species that can cause problems: the fruit-spotting bug, macadamia nut borer, and scale insects (*see p.262*). Diseases are husk spot, phytophthora, and armillaria.

**Recommended cultivars** Many trees are grown from seed. Some newly selected grafted commercial cultivars (with numbered names that refer to original row plantings) are also becoming available and include A263, Daddow, A4, A16, A38, 849.

# Mango

## Mangifera indica

Thought to be native to the Burmese, Indian and Malaysian regions of the world, mango trees have been grown for thousands of years. Seeds of mangoes were introduced to northern Queensland about a hundred years after European settlement. Since then, Australia has developed its own distinctive mango (a selection of an introduced seedling) called 'Kensington Pride' or the 'Bowen Mango' and this is still widely grown today. A relatively new Australian cultivar developed from a 'Kent' x 'Kensington Pride' cross is the 'R2E2' cultivar.

The mango tree is self-fertile and has huge massed flower heads containing thousands of individual flowers. These are often produced at the ends of branches, so that when fruit forms it is highly visible hanging outside the tree foliage.

**Site and planting** Mango trees will grow in most soils, including quite poor soils, provided that not too much fertilizer is applied as it promotes vegetative growth and little fruiting wood. Trees can withstand slight waterlogging at times but are fussy about when they receive moisture. Water or rain is needed in summer after the trees set fruit, but plants require a dry winter to initiate flowering, a dry spring to reduce fungal infections, and a dry period when fruit start ripening. Very young trees are susceptible to frosts.

**Routine care** Trees are often grown as street trees or backyard trees for shade in the tropics. Most gardeners reduce or stop watering for three months before flowering, but trees need plenty of water during summer. A little organic fertilizer should be given to plants every year: fruiting trees can be given fertilizer during the fruiting period and again in late summer. Mulch can be applied around the roots and protection from winds and frost should be given to very young plants.

Mango trees, if left to grow naturally, can become huge so most gardeners prune hard initially to produce 5-10 main branches then prune hard again next season. Some commercial growers prune directly after harvest to keep trees open and small in size.

**Harvesting and storage** Different cultivars mature at different times during the summer period. Either wait for the fruit skin to turn yellow or check maturity by selecting one fruit and cutting through to the seed: if the flesh is yellowish near the seed then fruits are close to maturity and can be picked and cool-stored if needed. Fruits must be clipped from the tree, leaving a short stem.

**Propagation** Mangoes are propagated from seed and also grafted onto selected seedling rootstocks. Selected cultivars grafted to dwarfing rootstock or one of the dwarf cultivars available can be purchased. Plants can be grown from seed but will take several years

**Mango**
*Mangoes are popular fresh fruit eaten straight from a tree. Grafted trees provide fruit three years after grafting.*

to fruit. There are two problems with growing from seed: the tree can grow to 40m (120ft) tall; and seedling variation of some cultivars may result in a plant with strongly turpentine tasting fruits which are not very palatable. Seedling trees take up to ten years to produce fruits, grafted plants only 3-4 years.

**Common problems** Fruit fly will invade ripening fruits, so baiting and spraying for this pest is mandatory (see p.255). Various scale insects may cause problems. The mango tip borer can bore into tip growth and the mango weevil can be found inside the seed of ripened fruit. The fungus anthracnose causes black spots on ripening fruits leaves or flowers and can cause serious damage, but in years of little rainfall the problem may not be a concern (see p.251). Bordeaux sprays and white oil sprays will help control some pests and diseases, as will pruning to allow air flow through the tree canopy.

**Recommended cultivars** 'Ah Toy Long', 'Apricot', 'Banana', 'Bombay Green', 'Bowen Special', 'Brooks', 'Crimson Blush', 'Fazli', 'Florigon', 'Glenn Kent', 'Irwin', 'Isas', 'Keitt', 'Kensington Pride', 'Mackay', 'Nam Dok Mai', 'Ono', 'Palmer', 'Peach', 'R2E2', 'Sensation', 'Strawberry', 'Tommy Atkins', 'Valencia Pride', and 'Zilate'.

# Papaya

## Carica papaya

The delicious papaya, commonly known in Australia as the pawpaw, is a frost-tender, single trunk, herbaceous plant growing to 2–10m (30ft). It prefers a tropical to subtropical climate to grow well and produce sweet fruits. The plant is palm-like in that it grows a bare trunk. Its giant palmate leaves form a rounded crown, the lower ones falling off as the tree grows. The leaves have very long stalks (petioles).

The female flowers form and produce rounded or elongated melon-like fruits that have a hollow centre, usually filled with small black seeds. The fruit often hang downward

along the trunk. Pawpaws grown from seed can produce male or female plants but some produce both flowers on the one plant.

There are many forms including those that produce red-fleshed fruit instead of the usual yellow/orange-fleshed cultivars. Juice and seeds from pawpaw fruit contain the enzyme papain which can be used to tenderize meat, and pawpaw flesh has therapeutic qualities. The green fruit can be used as a vegetable and the seeds are spicy.

Other plants within this family, notably the babaco (C. pentagona) with long narrow lemon tasting fruits and mountain pawpaw (C. pubescens) with very small rounded fruits, are suitable for cooler climates.

**Site and planting** Pawpaws require a frost free zone and good fertile, rich soils that are free draining. Organic fertilizers are preferred and mulching around each plant is recommended.

**Routine care** A little water often is needed to keep plants growing well and mulching the root system will conserve moisture. Excess seedlings need to be removed. Little pruning is needed but tall plants can be cut back to a serviceable level of 1-2m (3-6ft).

**Harvesting and storage** The fruit's skin is green, turning to a yellow when ripe. Fruits can be used green in salads or as a vegetable or picked just before ripening and allowed to ripen off the plant. Care must be taken to avoid the sap from skin and stems as it is an irritant.

**Propagation** Pawpaws are propagated from seed and, because the sex of the trees is not known until flowering begins, 3-5 seeds are grown in the one place where the tree is to stand and the plants thinned at a later date as they begin to flower.

**Common problems** There are a few pests and diseases that affect these plants such as fruit fly, mites, powdery mildew, and various post-harvest fruit rots, but most can be controlled organically and by using good hygiene and selecting superior seedlings.

**Recommended cultivars** 'Bisexual Yellow', 'Red/Orange Bisexual Paw Paw'.

**Papaya**
*Seedling trees can have male or female flowers on one tree and some have both.*

# Average crop yields

Use this chart to help plan your crops. All quantities are approximate, and will vary from year to year, depending on season, spacing, stage of harvesting, age of fruit trees and bushes, and specific growing conditions of vegetables. They are provided here as a quick-reference guide when deciding how much of each crop to plant. For more detail, *see individual crop entries, pp. 74–135 and 174–237.* Culinary herbs are harvested continuously, so are not included here.

## AVERAGE VEGETABLE YIELDS

| Crop | Yield | Crop | Yield |
|---|---|---|---|
| Amaranth | 7.25kg per 3m (16lb per 10ft) row | Mibuna and Mizuna greens | 6–9 heads per 3m (10ft) row |
| Asparagus | 9–12 spears per crown | Miners purslane | 20–24 bunches per 3m (10ft) row |
| Asparagus pea | 450g per 3m (1lb per 10ft) row | Mustard greens | 1.5kg per sq m (3–4lb per sq yd) |
| Bean, broad | 3kg per 3m (6½lb per 10ft) row | Mushrooms | 1–2kg per 3m (2¼–4½lb per 30cm$^2$(ft$^2$) |
| Bean, French or kidney | 4.5kg per 3m (10lb per 10ft) row | Mustard spinach | 6–9 heads per 3m (10ft) row |
| Bean, lima or butter | 560g per 3m (1¼lb per 10ft) row | New Zealand spinach | 6kg per 3m (13lb per 10ft) row |
| Bean, runner | 6kg per 3m (13lb per 10ft) row | Okra | 1.5kg per 3m (3¼lb per 10ft) row |
| Bean, snake | 3–4kg per 3m (½–8½lb per 10ft) row | Onion, bulb | 60 small, 30 large onions (1–3kg/2¼–6½lb) per 3m (10ft) row |
| Beetroot | 30 450g–1kg beetroot per 3m (1–2lb per10ft) row | Onion, Japanese bunching | 250–300, or 40–50 large, per 3m (10ft) row |
| Broccoli | 110–225g (4–8oz) per plant | Onion, pickling | 1–1.5kg per 3m (2¼–3lb per 10ft) row |
| Brussels sprout | 60–70 sprouts per plant | Onion, spring | 250–300 per 3m (10ft) row |
| Cabbage, Chinese | 9–12 heads per 3m (10ft) row | Pak choi | 9–12 heads per 3m (10ft) row |
| Cabbage, spring or winter | 6–8 450g–900g (1–2lb) heads per 3m (10ft) row | Parsnip | 4kg per 3m (9lb per 10ft) row |
| Cabbage, summer or autumn | 6–8 cabbages, 450–900g (1–2lb) each, per 3m (10ft) row | Pea (shelling) | 3kg per 3m (6½lb per 10ft) row |
| Capsicum | 2.75–4.5kg per 3m (6–10lb per 10ft) row | Pea (snow) | 2.5kg per 3m (10ft) row |
| Cardoon | 3–6 heads per 3m (10ft) row | Potato | early: 4.5kg per 3m (10lb per 10ft) row; maincrop: 10kg per 3m (22lb per 10ft) row |
| Carrot | 3kg per 3m (6lb per 10ft) row | Pumpkin | 1 large or 4–6 small fruits per plant |
| Cauliflower | 5–6 (or up to 20 mini) curds per 3m (10ft) row | Radish, summer | 100–120 per 3m (10ft) row |
| Celeriac | 10 heads, 225–400g (8–12oz) each, per 3m (10ft) row | Radish, winter | 20 per 3m (10ft) row |
| Celery | 12 heads, 450g (1lb) each, per 3m (10ft) row | Rhubarb | 4.5–13.5kg per 3m (10–30lb per 10ft) row |
| Celery herb | 15–20 heads per 3m (10ft) row | Rocket or erugala | 9–12 bunches per 3m (10ft) row |
| Ceylon or Malabar spinach | 3kg per 3m (6½lb per 10ft) row | Salsify | 1.5kg per 3m (3lb per 10ft) row |
| Chicory | 8–9 heads per 3m (10ft) row | Scorzonera | 1.5kg per 3m (3lb per 10ft) row |
| Chilli pepper | 3–4.5kg per 3m (6½–10lb per 10ft) row | Seakale | 6–8 stems per plant |
| Chinese broccoli | 9–12 bunches per 3m (10ft) row | Shallot | 60–180 shallots per 3m (10ft) row |
| Corn salad or lamb's lettuce | 18–20 heads per 3m (10ft) row | Silver beet or spinach beet | 6kg per 3m (13lb per 10ft) row |
| Cucumber | 10–25 fruits per plant | Spinach | 6kg per 3m (13lb per 10ft) row |
| Endive | 9–12 heads per 3m (10ft) row | Sprouting broccoli | 1.5kg per 3m (3–4lb per 10ft) row |
| Eggplant or aubergine | 3–4.5kg per 3m (6½–10lb per 10ft) row | Summer purslane | 20–24 bunches per 3m (10ft) row |
| Florence fennel | 1.4–2.25kg per 3m (3–5lb per 10ft) row | Summer squash | 15–25 small fruits per plant |
| Flowering cabbage or choy sum | 9–12 bunches per 3m (10ft) row | Swede | 6kg per 3m (13lb per 10ft) row |
| Garlic | 25–35 bulbs per 3m (10ft) row | Sweet melon | 2–4 fruits per plant |
| Gherkin | 20–30 fruits per plant | Sweet potato | 3–6kg per 3m (6–12lb per 10ft) row |
| Globe artichoke | 6–15 large, 24–60 small, per 3m (10ft) row | Sweetcorn | 9–18 cobs per sq m (sq yd) |
| Hamburg parsley | 3kg per 3m (6½lb per 10ft) row | Texsel greens (salad crop) | 6–9kg per 3m (13–20lb per 10ft) row |
| Jerusalem artichoke | 10–12 tubers per plant | Tomatillo | 1–2kg (2¼–4½lb) per plant |
| Kale or curly kale | 1.8–2.25kg per 3m (4–5lb per 10ft) row | Tomato, bush | 4kg (9lb) per plant |
| Kohlrabi | 2.5kg per 3m (4–6lb per 10ft) row | Tomato, vine | 3–6kg (6.5–13lb) per plant |
| Land cress | 18–20 heads per 3m (10ft) row | Tomato, vine greenhouse, unheated | 4–8kg (9–18lb) per plant |
| Leek | early: 4-6kg per 3m (8½–13lb per 10ft) row; late: 3–5kg per 3m (6½–11lb per 10ft) row | Turnip | 30 500–750g (1–1½lb) turnips, or 48 multiblock (baby) turnips, per 3m (10ft) row |
| Lettuce, butterhead | 10–15 heads per 3m (10ft) row | Turnip tops | 500g (1lb) per 3m (10ft) row |
| Lettuce, cos | 10–15 heads per 3m (10ft) row | Watermelon | 1–2 fruits per plant |
| Lettuce, crisphead | 8–9 heads per 3m (10ft) row | Zucchini or courgette | 10–15 fruits per plant; 6kg per 3m (10lb per 10ft) row |
| Lettuce, iceberg | 8–9 heads per 3m (10ft) row | | |
| Marrow | 2 large or 6–8 small fruits per plant | | |

## AVERAGE FRUIT YIELDS

| Crop | Yield | Crop | Yield |
|---|---|---|---|
| Acid or sour cherry, bush | 13.5kg–18kg (30–40lb) per tree | Nectarine, fan | 5.5–11.25kg (12–25lb) per tree |
| Acid or sour cherry, fan | 5.5–15.75kg (12–35lb) per tree | Peach, bush | 13.5–27kg (30–60lb) per tree |
| Almond | Erratic cropping | Peach, fan | 5.5–11.25kg (12–25lb) per tree |
| Apple, bush | 27–55kg (60–120lb) per tree | Pear, bush | 18–45.5kg (40–100lb) per tree |
| Apple, dwarf/spindle/pyramid | 13.5–22.5kg (30–50lb) per tree | Pear, dwarf/spindle/pyramid | 9–18kg (20–40lb) per tree |
| Apple, espalier | 13.5–18kg (30–40lb) per tree | Pear, espalier | 9–13.5kg (20–30lb) per tree |
| Apple, fan | 5.5–13.5kg (12–30lb) per tree | Pear, fan | 5.5–13.5kg (12–30lb) per tree |
| Apple, single cordon | 2.25–4.5kg (5–10lb) per tree | Pear, single cordon | 1.75–3.5kg (4–8lb) per tree |
| Apricot, bush | 13.5–45.5kg (30–100lb) per tree | Plum, bush | 13.5–27kg (30–60lb) per tree |
| Apricot, fan | 5.5–15.75kg (12–35lb) per tree | Plum, fan | 6.75–11.25kg (15–25lb) per tree |
| Blackberry | 6.75–9kg per 3m (15–20lb per 10ft) row | Plum, pyramid | 13.5–22.5kg (30–50lb) per tree |
| Blackcurrant | 4.5kg (10lb) per bush | Plum, single cordon | 3.5–6.75kg (8–15lb) per tree |
| Blueberry | 2.25–5kg (5–11lb) per bush | Quince, bush | 25–45.5kg (55–100lb) from a mature tree |
| Cobnut and filbert | 5–15.75kg (11–35lb) from a mature bush | Raspberry, summer-fruiting | 6.75–9kg per 3m (15–20lb per 10ft) row |
| Cranberry | 0.5–0.75kg per sq m (1–1.5lb per sq yd) | Redcurrant | 4–5kg (9–11lb) per bush |
| Fig | 2.25–9kg (5–20lb) from a mature fan | Strawberry | 450g (1lb) per plant |
| Gooseberry | 3.5–4.5 kg (7–10lb) per bush | Sweet or duke cherry, bush | 13.5–45.5kg (30–100lb) per tree |
| Grape | 2.25–3.5kg (5–8lb) or 8–10 bunches from a mature single cordon or single guyot | Sweet or duke cherry, fan | 5.5–15.75kg (12–35lb) per tree |
| Medlar | 13.5–27kg (30–60lb) from a mature standard | Sweet or duke cherry, pyramid | 13.5–27kg (30-60lb) per tree |
| Mulberry | Erratic cropping | Walnut | Erratic cropping |
| Nectarine, bush | 13.5–27kg (30–60lb) per tree | Whitecurrant | 4–5kg (9–11lb) per bush |

# Seasonal tasks

Use this chart as a handy reminder of seasonal tasks to do in the kitchen garden. As a distillation of advice from text throughout the book, it aims to aid forward planning, but bear in mind that timings of operations vary considerably as climatic conditions differ from region to region. Sowing dates, for example, will be later at more southerly latitudes and higher altitudes. Allow also for seasonal fluctuations, such as cold springs, hot summers, and mild winters.

## SEASONAL TASKS PLANNER FOR TEMPERATE GARDENS

### VEGETABLES AND HERBS

#### Early spring

- **Sow in propogator seed of broccoli, broad beans,** celery, capsicum and chilli peppers, eggplant, pumpkins, basil, and tomatoes.
- **Direct sow seed of beetroot,** carrots, leeks, lettuce, parsnip, peas, salad greens, snow peas, silver beet, spinach, salad and spring onions, turnips, and parsley.
- **Plant seedlings of lettuce,** beetroot, cabbage, cauliflower, broccoli, spinach, silver beet, and salad onions.
- **Plant tubers of potato** and Jerusalem artichoke tubers and onion sets.
- **Erect supports** for peas.
- **Harvest beetroot,** broccoli, cabbage, cauliflower, broad beans, carrots, leeks, parsnips, spinach, silver beet, winter lettuces, Brussels sprouts, and asparagus.

### FRUIT

#### Early spring

- **Finish planting** and pruning fruit trees and bushes.
- **Prune flowering cobnuts** and filberts if pollen is being shed.
- **Mulch young trees,** fruit bushes, raspberries, and other cane fruits, and apply fertilizers that are appropriate to the fruit in question.
- **Control weeds** in all fruit beds, preferably by hand pulling – to avoid potential root damage by hoeing.
- **Prune espaliered peaches,** nectarines, and apricots.
- **Where mildew has been a problem,** spray gooseberries just before the flowers open and continue at fortnightly intervals. Check integrity of netting covers to ensure continued protection against birds, which eat the buds.
- **Aid pollination** on vines under protection (glass).
- **Check blackberries,** loganberries, and tayberries, and tie canes into wires as necessary.
- **Plant strawberry runners** in prepared ground, and mulch.
- **Tidy up** strawberry beds, removing dead, damaged, and diseased leaves and old runners.
- **Cover established flowering strawberries** with cloches or fleece for earlier fruits; lift during the day for pollinating insects to do their work.

## SEASONAL TASKS PLANNER

| VEGETABLES AND HERBS | FRUIT |
|---|---|

### Mid-spring

- Sow in propagator seed of eggplant, sweet melons, capsicum and chilli pepppers, cucumbers, pumpkins, tomatoes, basil, zucchini, and summer squash.
- Direct sow seed of beetroot, carrots, leeks, lettuce, parsley, parsnip, radish, salad greens, silver beet, spinach, spring onions, turnips, zucchini, and summer squash.
- Plant seedlings of lettuce, beetroot, broccoli, celery, globe artichoke, Florence fennel, parsley, spinach, silver beet, salad onions, early tomatoes.
- Plant out tubers of potatoes, and Jerusalem and onion sets.
- Weed young vegetables and herbs and protect from slugs and snails.
- Continue earthing up potatoes.
- Re-pot or top-dress perrenial plants in containers.
- Harvest beetroot, broccoli, cabbage, cauliflower, broad beans, carrots, leeks, parsnip, rhubarb, salad greens, spinach, silver beet, lettuces, Brussels sprouts, and asparagus.

### Late spring

- Direct sow seed of annual herbs, sweet corn, French beans, runner beans, lettuce, pumpkin, radish, salad greens, zucchini, and summer squash.
- Plant seedlings of eggplant, lettuce, beetroot, cucumber, Florence fennel, parsley, pumpkin, spinach, silver beet, salad onions, capsicum and chilli peppers , sweet melons, tomatoes, and basil.
- Weed young vegetables and herbs and protect from slugs and snails.
- Thin seedlings of carrot, parsnip, leek, beetroot, and lettuce.
- Erect supports for runner beans.
- Finish earthing up potatoes; weed and mulch all vegetables.
- Remove leek, parsley, carrot, parsnip, beetroot, and other crops that have gone to seed.
- Harvest asparagus, broad beans, broccoli, Brussels sprouts, cabbages, peas, cauliflower, lettuce, salad greens, snow peas, spring onions, and rhubarb.

### Early summer

- Sow in propagator seed of of Brussels sprouts.
- Direct sow seed of annual herbs, cucumber, sweet corn, French beans, runner beans, lettuce, radish, salad greens, carrot, parsnip, swedes and turnips, beetroot, leek, spring onions.
- Plant seedlings of eggplant, capsicum and chilli peppers, lettuce, basil, salad greens, tomatoes.
- Thin seedlings of carrot, parsnip, leek, beetroot, and lettuce.
- Fertilize summer vegetables and perennial vegetables such as asparagus.
- Pull and dry garlic.
- Watch for cabbage white butterfly on all brassicas.
- Water all vegetables well and mulch around plants with straw.
- Tie tomato plants to stakes.
- Harvest broccoli, cabbages, cauliflower, globe artichokes, lettuce, peas, snow peas, spring onions, French beans, potatoes, zucchini and summer squash, and rhubarb.

### Midsummer

- Direct sow seed of coriander, sweet corn, French beans, runner beans, lettuce, radish, swedes and turnips, salad greens, spring onions, and a second crop of zucchini and summer squash.
- Plant seedlings of celery, lettuce, Brussels sprouts, leek.
- Thin lettuce seedlings.
- Tie tomato plants to stakes.
- Continue watering all vegetables and provide shade protection for leafy vegetables and young seedlings if sun is too hot.
- Pull and dry bulb onions and shallots.
- Remove vegetables, such as broccoli and spinach, that have gone to seed and peas that have withered.
- Harvest baby carrots, lettuce, spring onions, French beans, runner beans, globe artichokes, potatoes, sweet corn, zucchini and summer squash, tomatoes, cucumber, capsicum and chilli peppers.

### Late summer

- Direct sow seed of lettuce, salad greens, coriander, parsley, peas, snow peas, swedes and turnips, spinach and silver beet.
- Plant seedlings of broccoli, celery, coriander, cabbage, cauliflower, parsley, spinach, silver beet, lettuce, salad greens.
- Harvest herbs for drying and deadhead perennial herbs.

### Mid-spring

- Finish planting raspberries, if not done in late autumn.
- Check nets, stakes, and ties.
- Prune young stone fruit trees, and branch leaders on trained trees and plum pyramids.

### Late spring

- Pull out any new young raspberry canes that emerge a long way from the original rows.
- Water as necessary, especially espaliered trees.
- Continue to weed strawberries, and put straw around the plants, together with a sprinkling of slug pellets if slugs are known to be a problem.
- Put netting over developing soft fruit.
- Begin to tie in selected shoots to extend framework of espaliered peaches, nectarines, apricots, and plums, and thin out badly placed new shoots.
- Prune espaliered cherries.

### Early summer

- Check and water all fruit trees and bushes in dry periods.
- Pick strawberries, raspberries, currants, and gooseberries regularly.
- Begin to train and tie in new shoots of blackberries and hybrid berries.
- Remove strawberry runners unless needed to make new plants.
- Begin routine thinning of tree fruits.
- Tie in framework shoots on espaliered plums and sweet cherries, shorten the remainder, and pinch or prune out any going in the wrong direction.
- Tie in selected shoots of espaliered peaches and nectarines, and thin the fruit if necessary.
- Protect ripening fruits of espaliered cherries from rain and birds.

### Midsummer

- Continue to train in the canes of blackberries and hybrid berries.
- After fruiting, cut the leaves off strawberry plants, remove the straw, and weed between the rows. Water if dry.
- Finish thinning tree fruits that have not thinned themselves naturally.
- Continue to train and tie in tree fruit growing as espaliers.
- Support branches of plum trees that are very heavily laden, if necessary.

### Late summer

- Begin summer pruning of espaliered apples and pears.
- Plant out well-rooted runners in new strawberry beds.
- After summer-fruiting raspberries fruit, cut out old canes; tie in new ones.
- Prune damsons and plums, if necessary, when they have fruited and cut out any damaged branches.

## SEASONAL TASKS PLANNER

| VEGETABLES AND HERBS | FRUIT |
|---|---|

### VEGETABLES AND HERBS

#### Late summer (*cont.*)

- **Tie** tomatoes to stakes.
- **Watch for cabbage white butterfly** on all brassicas.
- **Remove finished plants** such as beans, zucchini and summer squash, and sweet corn.
- **Harvest eggplant,** carrots, lettuce, spring onions, French beans, runner beans, globe artichokes, potatoes, sweet corn, zucchini and summer squash, tomatoes, cucumber, capsicum and chili peppers.

#### Early autumn

- **Direct sow** seed of winter lettuce, salad greens, coriander, peas, snow peas.
- **Plant seedlings** of coriander, silver beet, spinach, winter lettuce, broccoli, cabbage, and cauliflower .
- **Maintain** soil moisture and remove weeds.
- **Divide** perennial herbs.
- **Remove** finished plants such as beans, tomato, zucchini and summer squash, and sweet corn.
- **Harvest** eggplant, carrots, lettuce, parsnips, spring onions, French beans, runner beans, peas, snow peas, globe artichokes, potatoes, sweet corn, zucchini and summer squash, tomatoes, cucumber, capsicum and chilli peppers.

#### Mid-autumn

- **Sow** in a propagator seed of bulb onions.
- **Direct sow** seed of bulb onions and broad beans.
- **Plant** seedlings of winter lettuce, coriander, cabbage, cauliflower, and plant bulbs of garlic and shallots, and tree onions.
- **Dig** potatoes, dry and store.
- **Remove** finished plants such as beans, tomato, zucchini and summer squash, and sweet corn.
- **Harvest** eggplant, carrots, chokos lettuce, parsnips, spring onions, globe artichokes, Jerusalem artichoks, potatoes, tomatoes, peas and snow peas, capsicum and chilli peppers, parsley, and coriander.

#### Late autumn

- **Direct sow** seed of broad beans.
- **Plant** bulbs of garlic, shallots and tree onions and seedlings of bulb onions.
- **Harvest pumpkins** before any frost damages the skin. Leave to cure in the sun before storing.
- **Remove finished plants** such as  basil, beans, tomato, zucchini and summer squash, and sweet corn.
- **Cut asparagus fronds** to the ground and mulch the bed with compost or manure and seaweed.
- **Harvest Brussels sprouts,** potatoes, spinach, silver beet, winter lettuces, peas and snow peas, beetroot, carrot, parsnip, parsley, and coriander.

#### Early winter

- **Plant seedlings** of bulb onions.
- **Weed all vegetables** to expose the soil to the sun.
- **Check that stored** pumpkins, potatoes, and onions are in good condition.
- **Dig, dry and store** all potatoes and Jerusalem artichokes if soil is too moist. Keep tubers remaining in the ground covered with dry soil or straw.
- **Harvest** Brussels sprouts, spinach, silver beet, winter lettuces, beetroot, carrot, parsnip, parsley, turnip, swede, and coriander.

#### Midwinter

- **Plant seedlings** of salad onions and crowns of asparagus and rhubarb.
- **Order vegetable seed** for the coming season.
- **Trim and divide** if desired, rhubarb and globe artichoke plants.
- **Harvest Brussels sprouts,** spinach, silver beet, winter lettuces, beetroot, carrot, parsnip, turnip, sweede, parsley, and coriander.

#### Late winter

- **Sow** in a propagator seed of broccoli, cabbage, cauliflower, lettuce, spinach and silver beet.
- **Plant seedlings** of salad onions, broccoli, cabbage, cauliflower, globe artichoke, and Florence fennel.
- **Prepare soil** in potato bed.
- **Set out seed potatoes** in the light to encourage strong shoots.
- **Harvest Brussels sprouts,** spinach, silver beet, winter lettuces, beetroot, carrot, parsnip, turnip, swede, parsley, and coriander.

### FRUIT

#### Late summer (*cont.*)

- **Summer prune** peaches and nectarines after fruiting.
- **Prune fan-trained cherries,** cut out wood which has borne fruit, after fruiting, and secure new shoots by tying in.

#### Early autumn

- **After fruiting,** cut out at base old canes of blackberries and other hybrid berries, and tie in new canes.
- **Weed thoroughly** around fruit trees growing in grass.
- **Cut off and burn** any mildewed top-growth on gooseberries.
- **Order new** fruit trees and bushes.
- **Finish summer pruning** of espaliered apples and pears, if not done already.
- **Shorten shoots and cut out** wood which has borne fruit on espalier-trained cherries, after fruiting, if not done already, and secure new shoots by tying in.

#### Mid-autumn

- **Harvest and store** good fruit in cool, frost-free place.
- **Take cuttings,** if necessary, from gooseberry and currant bushes.
- **Prepare ground** for planting new fruit trees and bushes.
- **Tidy up** strawberry plants, removing dead leaves.

#### Late autumn

- **Finish picking** apples and pears and store sound fruit.
- **Begin planting new fruit trees,** bushes, and raspberry canes as soon as possible after leaf fall.
- **Check tree ties** and rabbit guards on fruit trees.

#### Early winter

- **Prepare ground** for spring planting.

#### Midwinter

- **Inspect stored apples** and pears regularly, and take out any fruit that is starting to go rotten.
- **Prune apples** and pears.
- **Continue to plant** fruit trees and bushes if weather permits.
- **Insulate pots** of container-grown fruits in severe weather.
- **Begin spraying** peaches and nectarines against peach leaf curl.

#### Late winter

- **Cover strawberry plants** with cloches for an early crop.
- **Prune cobnuts** and filberts when the catkins are shedding pollen.
- **Continue to plant** fruit trees and bushes, if weather permits.
- **Check tree ties** and rabbit guards on fruit trees.
- **Net apples, pears,** and plums against birds and animals.

# Plant problems

The first lines of defence against plant problems in the kitchen garden are to use sound cultivation techniques, sustain a fertile soil, and practise good hygiene (*see pp. 51–52*). This ensures strong crops with natural resistance to pests, diseases, and cultural disorders. But even a well-managed garden may suffer infestations.

This section forms a handy reference to the most common problems that you may encounter. Unusual problems have been omitted – to include them would be to imply that plants are always beset by legions of pests and diseases, which is seldom the case. Some crops, such as brassicas, attract many problems, while others, like medlars, suffer relatively few.

For ease of reference, pests, diseases, and cultural disorders are listed together alphabetically in the following "A–Z of plant problems" (*pp. 251–264*). Solutions can be accessed in several ways.

A list of the most usual problems is found under the heading "Common problems" in each individual crop entry throughout the book; these direct you to the relevant information in the "A–Z of plant problems". Or you may prefer to use the quick-reference charts (*see pp. 247–249*) to identify a possible problem from signs visible on the plant. For example, if you observe deformed roots on your carrots, look up the "Roots and tubers" column; you will find the most likely culprit listed. A third option – for experienced gardeners – is simply to confirm your suspicions by looking up details directly.

The controls described in the "A–Z of plant problems" include chemical and organic methods, as well as cultural ones that reduce or avoid infection or infestation. The importance of prompt action cannot be underestimated – the earlier you control a problem, the less damage will be sustained by the crop. Untreated disorders may also spread to other crops or become established in the soil, leading to recurring troubles with crops in following years.

## How to use this section

▽ **Symptom identification chart**
*Charts on the following pages list each crop by common name. The most likely problems* *for each crop are in columns that indicate the part of the plant in which symptoms appear.*

| CROP | SYMPTOMS | | |
|---|---|---|---|
| | Roots | Leaves and stems | Fruits and flowers |
| Strawberry | Verticillium wilt Vine weevil | Aphids Powdery mildew Red spider mite Strawberry viruses | Birds Botrytis Mice Powdery mildew Slugs & Snails Sunburn |

**Site of plant symptoms**
*In strawberries, powdery mildew affects leaves, stems, and fruits*

▷ **A-Z listings**
*The "A–Z of plant problems" forms a directory of the pests, diseases, and cultural disorders affecting crops covered in this book. The directory lists all problems in alphabetical order. Each entry discusses crops affected, symptoms, causes, and controls – biological or cultural remedies are given as the preferred option.*

### Cabbage white butterfly

**Crops affected** All brassicas.
**Symptoms** Holes in leaves, young seedlings eaten and green grubs contaminating vegetables at harvest.
**Cause** The white butterfly *(Pieris rapae)* lays her eggs on the leaves of brassicas. The green larvae grow to 30 mm and feed on the leaves and flowerbuds.
**Control** Grow brassicas in cool weather to avoid the grubs. Dust young plants with Derris dust or spray with a caterpillar spray containing the biological control bacteria, Bt.

**Cabbage whitefly:** *see* Whitefly.

**Crops affected**
*Plants listed here include those most affected, as detailed on charts, as well as plants that may act as hosts or suffer little real damage.*

**Cross-reference**
*Alternative names cross-referenced to relevant entry*

## COMMON VEGETABLE PROBLEMS

| CROP | SYMPTOMS | | | CROP | SYMPTOMS | | |
|---|---|---|---|---|---|---|---|
| | Roots and tubers | Leaves and stems | Fruits, pods, and seeds | | Roots and tubers | Leaves and stems | Fruits, pods, and seeds |
| Amaranth | — | Aphids<br>Powdery mildew | — | Eggplant (aubergine) | | Downy mildew<br>Aphids, Red spider mite<br>Verticillium wilt<br>Whitefly | Botrytis<br>Slugs |
| Asparagus | Stem & root rots | Stem & root rots<br>Slugs & Snails | — | Endive | | As for Chicory | |
| Bean, broad | — | Chocolate spot<br>Rust<br>Spotted wilt | Mice | Florence fennel | Rhizoctonia | Slugs | — |
| Bean, French, runner, and Lima | Stem & root rots<br>Fusarium<br>Sclerotinia | Anthracnose<br>Halo blight<br>Leafhoppers<br>Red spider mite<br>Slugs & Snails | Anthracnose<br>Birds<br>Mice<br>Fruit set failure | Flowering greens | | As for Brassicas | |
| | | | | Garlic | | As for Onion | |
| | | | | Globe artichoke | Honey fungus | Slugs & Snails | Petal blight |
| Beetroot | Cutworm | Boron deficiency<br>Damping off<br>Leaf spot (fungal)<br>Manganese deficiency<br>Leafminer | — | Hamburg parsle | | As for Parsnip | |
| | | | | Jerusalem artichoke | Slugs | Sclerotinia<br>Slugs & Snails | — |
| Brassicas | Clubroot<br>Cutworm | Birds<br>Boron deficiency<br>Caterpillars<br>Downy mildew<br>Flea beetle<br>Leaf spot (bacterial)<br>Mealy cabbage aphid<br>Molybdenum deficiency<br>Powdery mildew<br>Slugs & Snails<br>Whitefly | Bolting | Kale | | As for Brassicas | |
| | | | | Kohlrabi | | As for Brassicas | |
| | | | | Komatsuna | | As for Brassicas | |
| | | | | Land cress | | No major problems | |
| | | | | Leek | Cutworm<br>Onion maggot | As for Onion<br>Leek rust | Bolting |
| | | | | Lettuce | Cutworm<br>Wireworm | Aphids<br>Botrytis<br>Downy mildew<br>Slugs & Snails<br>Tip burn<br>Bacterial soft rot | Bolting |
| Broccoli | | As for Brassicas | | Malabar spinach | | No major problems | |
| Brussels sprouts | | As for Brassicas | | Marrow, vegetable | | As for Zucchini | |
| Cabbage | | As for Brassicas | | Melon, sweet | Stem & root rots | Aphids<br>Cucumber mosaic virus<br>Powdery mildew<br>Red spider mite<br>Slugs & Snails<br>Whitefly | — |
| Capsicum and chilli | | Powdery mildew<br>Aphids<br>Botrytis<br>Red spider mite<br>Whitefly | Blossom end rot<br>Corn earworm<br>Bacterial soft rot | | | | |
| | | | | Mibuna greens | | As for Brassicas | |
| | | | | Mint | — | Mint rust | — |
| | | | | Miner's lettuce | | Aphids<br>Slugs | — |
| Cardoon | | Slugs & Snails | Petal blight | Mizuna greens | | As for Brassicas | |
| Carrot | Bacterial soft rot<br>Nematodes | Aphids<br>Downy mildew<br>Powdery mildew | Bolting | Mustard and Cress | — | Botrytis<br>Damping off | — |
| Cauliflower | | As for Brassicas | | Mustard greens | | As for Brassicas | |
| Celeriac | | As for Celery | | New Zealand spinach | | As for Spinach | |
| Celery, leaf celery | Stem & root rots | Leaf spot (fungal)<br>Slugs & Snails<br>Bacterial soft rot | Bolting | Okra | — | Aphids<br>Red spider mite<br>Whitefly | Botrytis |
| Ceylon spinach | | No major problems | | Onion, bulb, Japanese bunching, spring, tree or Egyptian, Welsh, and shallot | Onion maggot | Birds<br>Downy mildew<br>Fusarium<br>Onion neck rot<br>Onion thrips<br>Onion white rot<br>Stem & bulb Nematode<br>Viruses<br>Onion smudge | Bolting |
| Chicory | Slugs | Slugs & Snails<br>Tip burn | — | | | | |
| Chinese artichoke | | Slugs & Snails | | | | | |
| Chinese broccoli | | As for Brassicas | | | | | |
| Chinese cabbage | | As for Brassicas | | | | | |
| Choko | Root rot | Frost | — | Pak choi | | As for Brassicas | |
| Corn salad | — | Aphids<br>Slugs | — | Parsnip | Parsnip canker<br>Bacterial soft rot | Red spider mite<br>Downy mildew<br>Powdery mildew | Bolting |
| Cucumber | Stem & root rots | Cucumber mosaic virus<br>Powdery mildew<br>Red spider mite<br>Slugs & Snails<br>Whitefly | Bitter fruits<br>Poorly formed fruits<br>Fruit set failure | Pea, all types | Stem & root rots | Birds<br>Mice<br>Powdery mildew | Birds<br>Pea leaf and pod spot<br>Mice |
| | | | | Potato | | | |

## COMMON VEGETABLE PROBLEMS

| Crop | Roots and tubers | Leaves and stems | Fruits, pods, and seeds |
|---|---|---|---|
| | Cutworm Potato moth Nematode Potato common scab Potato blight Potato cyst Potato powdery scab Slugs Wireworm | Black leg Frost damage Potato blight Potato viruses Purple top wilt virus Whitefly | — |
| Pumpkin | Stem & root rots | Cucumber mosaic virus Powdery mildew Slugs & Snails | Fruit set failure |
| Radish | Clubroot | Slugs & Snails Flea beetle | Bolting |
| Rhubarb | Honey fungus | Crown rot Slugs & Snails Viruses | — |
| Rocket | — | Flea beetle Slugs & Snails | Bolting |
| Salsify | — | | — |
| Scorzonera | Clubroot | | — |
| Sea kale | — | Flea beetle | Bolting |
| Silverbeet, spinach beet | — | Leaf spot (fungal) Leafminer Leafhopper | Bolting |
| Spinach | | Birds Downy mildew | |
| Spinach mustard | | As for Brassicas | |
| Sprouting broccoli | | As for Brassicas | |
| Squash, summer | | As for Zucchini | |
| Squash, winter | | As for Pumpkin | |
| Sunflower | | Slugs & Snails | Birds Mice |

| Crop | Roots and tubers | Leaves and stems | Fruits, pods, and seeds |
|---|---|---|---|
| Swede | Clubroot | Boron deficiency Downy mildew Flea beetle Mealy cabbage aphid Powdery mildew | — |
| Sweetcorn | — | Birds Mice | Corn earworm Mice, Rats, Birds |
| Sweet potato | Bacterial soft rot | Aphids Red spider mite Whitefly | — |
| Texsel greens | | As for Brassicas | |
| Tomatillo | | No major problems | |
| Tomato | Stem & root rots | Bugs Caterpillars Magnesium deficiency Mosaic virus Leafhoppers Potato blight Purple top wilt virus Russet mite Red spider mite Spotted wilt Target spot Thrips Whitefly | Blossom end rot Tomato blotchy ripening Tomato ghost spot Fruit fly Target spot Sunburn Birds Corn earworm |
| Turnip, turnip tops | Clubroot Cutworm Wireworm Slugs & Snails | Downy mildew Flea beetle Powdery mildew | Bolting |
| Watermelon | | As for melon, sweet | |
| Zucchini (courgette) | | Cucumber mosaic virus Powdery mildew Red spider mite Slugs & Snails Whitefly | Bitter fruits Poorly formed fruits Slugs |

## COMMON FRUIT PROBLEMS

| Crop | Roots | Leaves and stems | Fruits and flowers |
|---|---|---|---|
| Almond | Phytophthora Honey fungus | Anthracnose Aphids Canker (bacterial) Peach leaf curl Red spider mite Silver leaf Scale insect | Frost damage Split stone Anthracnose Shothole |
| Apple | As for almond | Apple scab Apple powdery mildew Canker (fungal) Caterpillars Iron deficiency Red spider mite Replant disease Woolly aphid | Apple scab Birds Bitter pit Blossom wilt Brown rot Codling moth Frost damage Fruit fly Light brown apple moth |
| Apricot (continued over) | As for almond | Brown scale Canker (bacterial) Dieback Silver leaf | Birds Brown rot Freckle Shot-hole |

| Crop | Roots | Leaves and stems | Fruits and flowers |
|---|---|---|---|
| Apricot (cont.) | | Brown rot Shothole | |
| Blackberry | — | Aphids Cane spot Chlorosis Leaf spot (fungal) Raspberry spur blight Rust Viruses | Botrytis |
| Blackcurrant (see also Red- & whitecurrant) | Phytophthora | American gooseberry mildew Aphids Big bud mite Leaf spot (fungal) Viruses | Birds Botrytis |
| Blueberry | Phytophthora | Botrytis Chlorosis | Birds |
| Cherry, acid and sweet (continued over) | As for almond | Aphids Brown rot Canker (bacterial) Magnesium deficiency Cherry aphid | Birds Blossom wilt Brown rot Frost damage |

## COMMON FRUIT PROBLEMS

| CROP | SYMPTOMS | | |
|---|---|---|---|
| | Roots | Leaves and stems | Fruits and flowers |
| Cherry, acid and sweet (*cont.*) | | Leafminer<br>Pear & cherry slug<br>Scorch<br>Silver leaf | Fruit fly<br>Wasps |
| Citrus fruit | Collar rot<br>Crown rot<br>Phytophthora | Mealybugs<br>Red spider mite<br>Scale insect<br>Sooty moulds<br>Thrips<br>Whitefly | Birds<br>Brown rot<br>Bugs<br>Fruit failure<br>Fruit fly, Mites<br>Viruses |
| Cranberry | — | Chlorosis | Birds |
| Fig | — | Brown scale<br>Coral spot<br>Frost damage<br>Red spider mite | Birds<br>Frost damage<br>Wasps |
| Gooseberry | — | American gooseberry mildew<br>Aphids<br>Birds<br>Botrytis<br>Caterpillars<br>Gooseberry dieback<br>Leaf spot (fungal) | Birds<br>Wasps |
| Grape vine | Vine weevil<br>Phylloxera<br>Phytophthora | Brown scale<br>Downy mildew<br>Magnesium deficiency<br>Mealybugs<br>Oedema<br>Powdery mildew<br>Red spider mite<br>Scorching<br>Vine weevil | Birds<br>Botrytis<br>Wasps |
| Hybrid berries | | As for Blackberry | |
| Hazelnut | As for Almond | Powdery mildew<br>Big bud | Birds |
| Kiwi fruit | Phytophthora | Sunburn | Birds |
| Medlar | | No major problems | |
| Mulberry | | Mulberry canker | Birds |
| Olive | Root knot eelworm | Olive scab<br>Red spider mite<br>Scale insect<br>Thrips<br>Verticillium wilt<br>Whitefly | Fruit fly |
| Passion fruit | Phytophthora | Aphids<br>Passionvine hopper<br>Red spider mite<br>Scale insect | Cucumber mosaic virus<br>Fruit fly |
| Peach and nectarine | As for Almond | Aphids<br>Brown scale<br>Brown rot<br>Canker (bacterial)<br>Cherry aphid<br>Peach leaf curl<br>Red spider mite<br>Rust<br>Shothole<br>Silver leaf | Birds<br>Brown rot<br>Frost damage<br>Fruit fly<br>Split stone |
| Pear (*continued over*) | As for Almond | Aphids<br>Pear scab<br>Birds<br>Canker (fungal)<br>Caterpillars<br>Pear leaf blister mite | Birds<br>Blossom wilt<br>Boron deficiency<br>Brown rot<br>Codling moth<br>Frost damage |

| CROP | SYMPTOMS | | |
|---|---|---|---|
| | Roots | Leaves and stems | Fruits and flowers |
| Pear (*cont.*) | | Pear & cherry slug<br>Quince fleck<br>Replant disease<br>Scale | Pear scab<br>Quince fleck<br>Wasps |
| Pineapple | Phytophthora<br>Root knot nematode | Mealybugs<br>Scale insect<br>Red spider mite<br>Thrips | — |
| Plum | — | Birds<br>Brown rot<br>Canker (bacterial)<br>Caterpillars<br>Red spider mite<br>Silver leaf | Brown rot<br>Frost damage |
| Prickly pear | — | Mealybugs | — |
| Quince | As for Almond | Powdery mildew<br>Quince fleck<br>Frost damage | Brown rot<br>Frost damage<br>Quince fleck |
| Raspberry | Phytophthora | Aphids<br>Chlorosis<br>Leaf spot (fungal)<br>Raspberry cane blight<br>Raspberry spur blight<br>Raspberry viruses | Birds<br>Botrytis<br>Sunburn |
| Red- and whitecurrant | — | Aphids<br>Coral spot<br>Leaf spot (fungal) | Birds<br>Botrytis<br>Sunburn |
| Strawberry | Verticillium wilt<br>Vine weevil | Aphids<br>Powdery mildew<br>Red spider mite<br>Strawberry viruses | Birds, Botrytis<br>Mice<br>Powdery mildew<br>Slugs & Snails<br>Sunburn |
| Walnut | As for Almond | Walnut blight | Birds<br>Sunburn<br>Walnut blight |

### Wasps on fruit
*There are some pests and diseases such as these. European wasps, that can afflict a range of crops Here the wasps suck the sweetness from a ripe Nashi pear*

# Most common problems

Use this index to locate details of the most common problems.

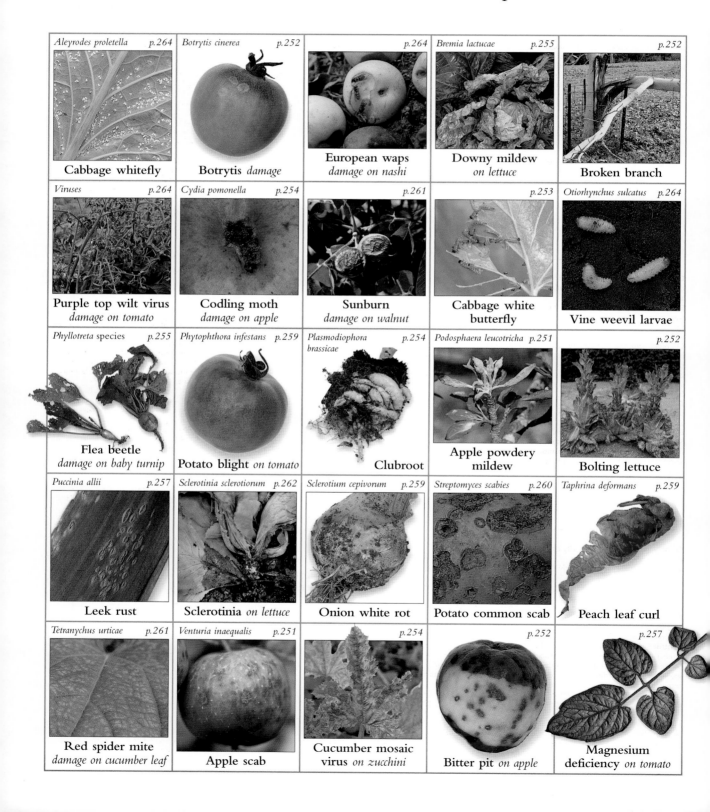

| | | | | |
|---|---|---|---|---|
| *Aleyrodes proletella* p.264 | *Botrytis cinerea* p.252 | p.264 | *Bremia lactucae* p.255 | p.252 |
| **Cabbage whitefly** | **Botrytis** *damage* | **European waps** *damage on nashi* | **Downy mildew** *on lettuce* | **Broken branch** |
| *Viruses* p.264 | *Cydia pomonella* p.254 | p.261 | p.253 | *Otiorhynchus sulcatus* p.264 |
| **Purple top wilt virus** *damage on tomato* | **Codling moth** *damage on apple* | **Sunburn** *damage on walnut* | **Cabbage white butterfly** | **Vine weevil larvae** |
| *Phyllotreta* species p.255 | *Phytophthora infestans* p.259 | *Plasmodiophora brassicae* p.254 | *Podosphaera leucotricha* p.251 | p.252 |
| **Flea beetle** *damage on baby turnip* | **Potato blight** *on tomato* | **Clubroot** | **Apple powdery mildew** | **Bolting lettuce** |
| *Puccinia allii* p.257 | *Sclerotinia sclerotiorum* p.262 | *Sclerotium cepivorum* p.259 | *Streptomyces scabies* p.260 | *Taphrina deformans* p.259 |
| **Leek rust** | **Sclerotinia** *on lettuce* | **Onion white rot** | **Potato common scab** | **Peach leaf curl** |
| *Tetranychus urticae* p.261 | *Venturia inaequalis* p.251 | p.254 | p.252 | p.257 |
| **Red spider mite** *damage on cucumber leaf* | **Apple scab** | **Cucumber mosaic virus** *on zucchini* | **Bitter pit** *on apple* | **Magnesium deficiency** *on tomato* |

# A–Z of plant problems

## American gooseberry mildew

**Crops affected** Blackcurrant and gooseberry.
**Symptoms** Powdery, grey-white fungal growth appears on upper leaf surfaces, stems, and fruits. Young growth may become distorted and die off. Mildew on the skin of fruits turns buff as it ages and can be scraped off. Fruits are unsightly but edible, although they turn brown when cooked.
**Cause** The fungus *Sphaerotheca mors-uvae*, which is encouraged by stagnant air around the branches and by excessive use of nitrogen fertilizers. It overwinters on the branches and in the buds.
**Control** Prune out affected branches as seen; prune to thin growth and improve air circulation. Use a general fertilizer rather than a high-nitrogen one. Grow cultivars with some resistance. Dust with sulphur or spray with a fungicide.

## Anthracnose

**Crops affected** Various, especially French, dwarf, and runner bean, and cucumber, almond, avocado and mango.
**Symptoms** Various fungi cause spots or patches of discolouration on leaves, stems, and on fruit. Affected tissue may die; in severe cases, the whole plant dies back. On bean crops, longitudinal, sunken brown marks appear on stems. Leaf veins may develop red colouration and leaves may brown and die off. Red-brown spots appear on pods, followed in wet weather by pink slimy growths.
**Causes** *Colletotrichum* species are the most common agents; the bean anthracnose fungus, *Colletotrichum lindemuthianum*, is usually seed-borne. Spores are spread by rain or water splash from infected seedlings to nearby plants.
**Control** Remove infected plants on sight; do not save seed. Use resistant cultivars. Chemical control rarely justifiable.

## Ants

**Crops affected** Various, especially citrus trees.
**Symptoms** The Argentine ant, which is about 3mm long, tracks in large numbers along branches and foliage. Other ants can also be found infesting trees.
**Cause** Different species feed on different foods and the Argentine ant commonly seen feeds on honeydew secreted by insects such as aphids and scale.
**Control** Treat the infestation of insects by removing the food source. Ants can also be controlled with insecticide dusts that specify ants and pyrethrum spray. Green ants are used as a biological control on citrus trees in the Northern Territory.

## Aphids

**Crops affected** Few plants are unaffected by aphids; some are host-plant specific.

**Symptoms** Affected plants show varying degrees of reduced growth and leaf distortion. Upper leaf surfaces are often sticky with the honeydew excreted by aphids and this often becomes infested by black sooty mould. The nymphs shed their whitish skins as they grow, which accumulate on leaves below those on which aphids are feeding. Viruses are often spread from one plant to another on aphid mouthparts.
**Cause** Sap-sucking insects, about 2mm (1/12in) long, may be green, grey, pink, black, yellow, or brown, depending on species.
**Control** Organic treatments include pyrethrum, rotenone, and insecticidal soaps. Control overwintering eggs on deciduous fruit trees or bushes withan oil wash in winter. For details of control on specific plants see individual entries. *See also* Cherry aphid, mealy cabbage aphid, woolly aphid.

## Apple powdery mildew

**Crops affected** Apple, and less seriously, pear, quince, and medlar.
**Symptoms** Leaves are covered in powdery white fungal growth (*see p.250*); young leaves may be badly infected from spores that overwintered from the previous year. They become distorted, fail to develop fully, and die prematurely. Stems may show silvery white patches in winter.
**Cause** The fungus *Podosphaera leucotricha* overwinters on apple buds or on stems. Spread and development is rapid in hot summers, especially when dews are heavy. Dry soils also encourage development.
**Control** Keep apples well watered and well mulched to conserve water. Prune out badly affected growth. Keep the crowns of trees open to permit good air circulation. Treat with sulphur dust or spray with a fungicide.

## Apple, pear, *and* olive scabs

**Crops affected** Apple, pear, and olive.
**Symptoms** Black or brown scabby areas on the surface of young fruits (*see p.250*). In severe cases, it may be widespread and cause misshapen, cracked fruits. Brown or olive-green spots appear on the leaves, which may appear blistered. Early leaf fall can occur, reducing the crop the following year. Young shoots are also attacked.
**Causes** The fungus *Venturia inaequalis* on apples and pears, *Venturia pirina* on pears, and *Spilocaea oleagina* on olives. The fungi overwinter on young stems and fallen leaves. Scabs are most prevalent in damp seasons and on trees with crowded branches.
**Control** Gather up and destroy fallen leaves. Prune out cracked or scabby shoots to limit overwintering. Prune regularly to ensure good air flow, and to reduce conditions favourable to fungal growth. Seek cultivars showing resistance. Fungicides that contain mancozeb or carbendazim are effective if sprayed at regular intervals.

## Bacterial blight

**Crops affected** Various, including leeks, peas, and mulberries.
**Symptoms** Brown to black patches on leaves surrounded in yellow and also on young stems and pods.
**Cause** The bacteria *Pseudomonas syrringae* pvs. occurs in wet weather when the soft young growth is vulnerable.
**Control** Reduce humidity by improving air flow and drying of foliage. *See also* Walnut leaf blight.

**Bacterial canker:** *see* Canker.
**Bacterial gummosis:** *see* Canker.

## Bacterial soft rot

**Crops affected** The fleshy parts of many vegetables, including roots and tubers, fleshy shafts, bases and fruit. The crops include carrots, potatoes, crucifers, celery, and lettuces.
**Symptoms** Development of soft, slimy, rotten flesh occurs in growth and storage.
**Cause** The bacteria *Erwinia carotovora* pv. *carotova* affects fleshy parts in damp or humid conditions.
**Control** Do not overwater. Improve airflow around plants in the garden and in storage. Improve soil drainage.

**Bean rust:** *see* Rusts.

## Bean seed fly

**Crops affected** French and runner bean, onions, cucurbits.
**Symptoms** Ragged leaves and damaged stems are seen on newly germinated seedlings; sometimes, seedlings fail to emerge, having been eaten below soil level. Provided that the growing point has not been destroyed, plants will survive although growth will be slow at first and sideshoots may develop.
**Cause** The maggots of *Delia platura*. The adults look like house flies.
**Control** Slow-germinating seed is most vulnerable, so avoid sowing when the soil is cold or wet. Instead, sow in pots or trays and set out after the first true leaves have unfolded. The adult fly is attracted to fresh organic matter, so apply manures in autumn rather than spring. There are no approved insecticides to control this pest.

## Big bud

**Crops affected** A wide range, including vegetables such as tomatoes, potatoes, and lettuce.
**Symptoms** Enlarged or deformed buds and thickened and deformed green stems. Sometimes called "greening".
**Cause** The mycoplasma is spread from plant to plant by the brown leafhopper (*Orosius argentatus*).
**Control** Remove weeds that may be host to the leafhopper.

## Big bud mite

**Crops affected** Blackcurrant.
**Symptoms** Buds are abnormally large and rounded and do not develop into leaves or stems. Each bud contains hundreds of microscopic white mites. The buds become swollen in winter, but desiccated big buds can be found at any time of year. Infestation causes loss of vigour, but, more seriously, the mite can spread reversion disease.
**Cause** A mite, *Cecidophyopsis ribis*. The mites breed in summer and autumn and proliferate inside the buds during winter. At bud burst in early spring, they move on to infest buds that have previously been healthy.
**Control** Removing big buds by hand from lightly infested bushes in winter, well before bud burst, provides a measure of control. Dig up and burn all of the badly affected plants after fruiting and replace them in autumn. The cultivars 'Foxendown' and 'Farleigh' are most resistant. The chemicals that are available to gardeners do not control the mites.

## Birds

**Crops affected** Most soft and tree fruits, onion family, pea, bean, brassicas, spinaches, and sweetcorn.
**Symptoms** Birds may eat flower buds, peck or eat whole fruits, strip leaves off brassicas and peas, eat pea and bean seeds and lettuce seedlings, or pull up any newly planted brassicas and onion sets.
**Causes** Birds are the prime suspect if fruit tree flower buds are eaten; blackbirds, parrots, starlings, and other birds peck holes in fruits and eat small fruits, such as raspberries, whole. Blackbirds are the main culprit in pulling up onion sets, and pigeons cause damage to the foliage of brassicas and peas.
**Control** Small trees and soft fruits can be netted or grown in a fruit cage; on larger trees, protect the best fruit trusses by containing them in bags of muslin or old tights.
For other crops, fine-gauge netting is the only certain way of deterring birds. If you try using such items as scarecrows, humming lines, glitter strips, and model cats or predator birds, you will find that they work only for a while. The birds quickly get used to them, especially if they are hungry and other food sources are scarce.

## Bitter fruits

**Crops affected** Cucumber and gherkin.
**Symptoms** Fruits have a bitter flavour.
**Causes** Pollination of fruit-bearing, female flowers by male flowers, or an excess of nitrogen in the soil.
**Control** Remove all male flowers as they appear (female flowers have tiny, nascent fruit immediately behind the flower) or grow all-female cultivars.
Use a balanced rather than a high-nitrogen fertilizer.

## Bitter pit

**Crops affected** Apple.
**Symptoms** Apple skins speckled with slightly sunken brown spots, usually 1–3mm (¹⁄₁₆–¹⁄₈in) in diameter (see p.250). The flesh tastes slightly bitter. The marks sometimes develop while the fruits are on the tree; more often they develop in storage. Large fruits and those from heavy cropping trees are most susceptible.
**Causes** Calcium deficiency in the fruits. Soil calcium levels may be adequate, but in dry weather the tree cannot take up sufficient calcium – hence the greater susceptibility of large fruits and heavy-cropping trees.
**Control** Use a mulch to retain soil moisture and keep trees well watered. Avoid excessive use of high-nitrogen fertilizers; use balanced fertilizers instead. Spray developing fruits with calcium nitrate solution between early summer and early autumn.

**Blackberry cane spot:** see Cane spot.
**Blackcurrant gall mite:** see Big bud mite.
**Black leg:** see Potato black leg.

## Black spot

**Crops affected** Grapes, strawberries, and other soft fruits in humid weather.
**Symptoms** On grapes – brownish black patches on young stems and flowers and fruit may wither. On strawberries – small black spots on leaves and fruit enlarge.
**Causes** On grapes the fungus *Elsinoe ampelina* and on strawberries *Colletotrichum acutatum*.
**Control** Improve aeration of plants and when irrigating, water the soil rather than the foliage. Also remove diseased material by pruning.

## Blossom end rot

**Crops affected** Tomato and capsicum.
**Symptoms** A sunken patch occurs at the blossom end of developing fruits; the skin at the base becomes leathery, then turns brown or black. Not all fruits in a truss will be affected, nor will all trusses on the same plant necessarily suffer.
**Causes** Calcium deficiency due to dry conditions at the plant roots inhibiting its uptake. Lack of calcium causes cells to collapse and discolour. A very acidic growing medium increases the problem.
**Control** Ensure an adequate and regular water supply. If rot does develop, remove affected fruits and improve irrigation. Small-fruited cultivars and plants grown in open ground or large containers are less susceptible.

## Blossom wilt

**Crops affected** Apple, apricot, cherry, plum, peach, and pear.
**Symptoms** Flower trusses wither shortly after emergence. Dead trusses remain on the tree, forming a source of infection for leaves, which wilt, turn brown, and die, remaining on the branch. Raised, buff-coloured, pinprick-sized fungal pustules appear on infected areas. Localized dieback of stems may occur.
**Causes** The fungus *Monilinia laxa* or, on apple crops, *M. laxa* f. *laxa*. It may overwinter as cankers on affected stems, or as pustules on flowers and foliage. Wind-borne spores spread most rapidly in damp weather.
**Control** Prune out infected flower trusses before infection spreads to the leaves or into the spur. There are no approved chemicals for use by amateur gardeners.

**Blotchy ripening:** see Tomato blotchy ripening.

## Bolting

**Crops affected** Various, including brassicas, the onion family, and spinach.
**Symptoms** Premature production of flowers and seeds, before full development of the crop, or before harvest is complete.
**Causes** Various factors. The most common include exposure to low temperatures at a critical growth stage, often accompanying a cold, late onset of spring, and excessively dry soil conditions during early growth stages.
**Control** Avoid growing early varieties of susceptible vegetables, as these are more prone to bolting. Choose cultivars that are listed as having bolt-resistance.

## Boron deficiency

**Crops affected** Listed below.
**Symptoms** The symptoms vary with the crop affected.
**Beetroot:** Rough, cankered patches on roots, often with secondary rotting at the heart, revealed as the development of brown rings in the inner root tissue and crown. Leaves are small and necrotic.
**Cabbage:** Distorted leaves and hollow areas in the stems.
**Carrot:** Splitting of root, often exposing a greyish central core, and splitting of stems. Yellow and pink discolouration of leaves.
**Cauliflower:** Poor curd development and browning of curds. Roughening of main stems, leaf stalks, and midribs.
**Celery:** Transverse cracks in the outer leaf stalk, followed by reddening of the inner tissues, sometimes with leaf distortion.
**Pear:** Fruits are distorted, with hard brown flecks in the flesh. This may be accompanied by slight shoot dieback.
**Radish:** Dull, split skin with woody flesh.
**Strawberry:** General stunting. Small leaves are puckered and yellowed at tips. Berries are small and pale, typically forming a "waist" close to the calyx. Not a common affliction.
**Swede and turnip:** "Brown heart", which is revealed when the roots are cut across as grey or brown, discoloured areas. These may appear in concentric rings in the lower parts of the root.
**Causes** Boron deficiency often occurs on light soils because this element is readily leached out by high rainfall; it also occurs if soil is limed excessively or when soil is allowed to become very dry.
**Control** For vegetable and strawberry crops, apply 35g of borax per 20sq m (1oz per 175sq ft) of ground before sowing or planting. Mix the borax with fine horticultural sand to make even distribution easier. For pear crops, spray at petal fall with 70g borax in 22 litres of water (2½oz in 5 gallons) together with a wetting agent. Take care when applying borax; it is easy to overdo it.

## Botrytis

**Crops affected** Various.
**Symptoms** Fuzzy, grey, off-white, or grey-brown fungal growth (see p.250) on infected areas (hence the common name, grey mould). This ubiquitous, air-borne fungus lives on dead or living plant material, and can attack most above-ground tissues. It usually gains entry through wounds. Fruits may be infected through open flowers; the fungus remains dormant until fruit ripens. Prior to development of the fungal fruiting stage, tissue becomes discoloured, often turning brown and soft. Growth above the site of infection may deteriorate, leaves may yellow and wilt, and flowers and fruit may die. Infection of petals or fruit can cause colour changes without rotting; petals appear bleached or form pale brown spots (ghost spotting). The fungal resting bodies – small black sclerotia – resist a wide range of adverse conditions, staying dormant until conditions are suitable for their growth.
**Causes** The fungus *Botrytis cinerea*; spores are spread readily by water splash and air currents, and persist from year to year in the soil, or on plant debris, as sclerotia.
**Control** Good hygiene is the first line of defence as control of such a widespread fungus is difficult. Clear away all plant debris promptly. Remove dead and injured plant parts before infection sets in. Remove infected tissues from live plants as soon as seen, cutting back into clean, healthy growth. Carbendazim is approved for treatment of botrytis on blackcurrant, broad bean, gooseberry, raspberry, and strawberry crops.

## Branches breaking

**Crops affected** Most fruit trees.
**Symptoms** Branches split from trunk and broken at crotch.
**Causes** A heavy crop of fruit and poor branch training.
**Control** Train branches to join trunk as close to a right angle as possible as narrow angle crotches form a weak junction. Thin fruit and shorten branches to reduce crop load and provide branch supports.

## Brown rot

**Crops affected** Tree fruits.
**Symptoms** Soft brown areas develop on skins of fruits, the flesh deteriorates, and the rot spreads rapidly to the whole fruit and new shoots may die if the fungal growth surrounds the stem. Raised, creamy white pustules appear on infected areas, in concentric rings. Fruits may become mummified, remaining on the tree, or may fall; in both cases, they will form a source of re-infection.
**Causes** The fungus, *Monilinia fructigena*, on apple crops; *M. laxa* on other host plants. The fungus gains entry via wounds, such as bird pecks, frost cracks, codling moth exit holes, and scab infections; any wound will predispose plants to infection. Spores are spread by birds, insects, rain splash or by direct contact with a source of infection.
**Control** Take all precautions against possible injuries. Control insect pests, net against birds, remove infected and fallen fruits promptly, and prune out mummified fruits, along with a short section of their spur, and destroy by burning. Spray trees at bud swell with a copper-based fungicide. Repeat sprays during fruit development. Use alternative fungicides where problem persists.

## Brown scale

**Crops affected** Many tree and bush fruits, including fig, grape vines, peach and nectarine, pineapple, and apricot.
**Symptoms** Shell-like, convex, brown "lesions", up to 5mm (¼in) long, appear on stems of infested plants. Sooty moulds grow on leaves that are sticky with honeydew. Infestations are most common in warm, sheltered sites; on plants that are trained against warm walls or grown in greenhouses, for example.
**Cause** *Parthenolecanium corni*, a sap-feeding insect, which lays its eggs beneath the scale. There is one generation a year.
**Control** Spray deciduous fruit trees and bushes with winter oil to target overwintering nymphs.

## Brown spot

**Crops affected** Citrus and passionfruit.
**Symptoms** Brown spots on leaves, fruit and young stems. Spots enlarge and may girdle the stem and cause the fruit to drop.
**Cause** Species of the fungus *Alternaria* thrive in warm humid conditions.
**Control** Improve aeration between plants by thinning foliage. Avoid wetting foliage during irrigation. Spray with a copper-based fungicide.

**Bud drop:** see Drought.

## Bugs

**Crops affected** Various fruit and vegetable crops.
**Symptoms** Sap sucking causes dimples in fruit, shrivelling foliage, flowers, and fruit.
**Cause** Bugs generally have a semi-hard shield-shaped body and are smelly when crushed. They include green bugs such as Apple dimpling bug (*Camplyomma livida*), Green vegetable bug (*Nazara viridula*), Spined citrus bug (*Biprorulus bibax*) and Fruitspotting bug (*Amblypelta nitida*), and brown bugs such as Rutherglen bug (*Nysius vinitor*), and multi-coloured bugs such as Harlequin bug (*Dindymus versicolor*).
**Control** Remove habitat such as weeds and debris around the garden. Shake bugs into a container of boiling water.

**Bryobia mite:** *see* Mites.
**Bulbous or blown fruits:** *see* Poorly formed fruits.

# Cabbage moth

**Crops affected** Brassicas, particularly cabbages.
**Symptoms** The small brown moths lay their eggs on leaves and the small green larvae grow to 12mm and eat small holes in the leaves.
**Cause** The moth *(Plutella xylostella)* thrives in hot dry weather.
**Control** Dust young plants with Derris dust or use a caterpillar spray containing the biological control bacteria, Bt. Avoid planting Brassicas during hot weather.

# Cabbage white butterfly

**Crops affected** All brassicas.
**Symptoms** Holes in leaves, young seedlings eaten and green grubs contaminating vegetables at harvest.
**Cause** The white butterfly *(Pieris rapae)* lays her eggs on the leaves of brassicas. The green larvae grow to 30mm and feed on the leaves and flowerbuds.
**Control** Grow brassicas in cool weather to avoid the grubs. Dust young plants with Derris dust or spray with a caterpillar spray containing the biological control bacteria, Bt.

**Cabbage whitefly:** *see* Whitefly.

# Calcium deficiency

**Crops affected** Various.
**Symptoms** Shoots and young leaves often grow poorly, curl, and they generally deteriorate. Symptoms are various, depending on plant and plant part affected.
**Brassicas:** Internal browning of Brussels sprout buttons and cabbage hearts.
**Carrots:** Root cavities.
**Celery:** Blackening of central leaves.
**Lettuce:** Tip burn *(see p.263)*.
**Potato:** Rolled leaves and spindly shoots.
**Causes** Calcium may be deficient in the soil or compost, or be unavailable for uptake by very dry or acidic conditions in the growing medium.
**Control** Keep plants well watered and mulch to retain soil moisture. If possible, lime acid soils to raise the pH.
*See also* Bitter pit, Blossom end rot.

# Cane spot

**Crops affected** Blackberry, raspberry, and hybrid berries.
**Symptoms** Lens-shaped, purple or brown-purple spots that have silver-grey centres appear on the canes, sometimes spreading to leaves and flower stalks. As spots enlarge, canes may split and die.
**Cause** The fungus *Elsinoe veneta*, which is most active in early summer.
**Control** Prune out infected canes as soon as seen. Avoid growing susceptible cultivars. Spray affected plants with an appropriate fungicide.

# Canker

**Crops affected** Tree fruits and nuts.
**Symptoms: Bacterial canker** affects cherry, plum, apricot, peach, and nectarine crops. Clearly defined areas of bark flatten and sink inwards, and amber-coloured resin may ooze from the bark, especially when injured. Buds at the branch tips fail to open and leaves may wither and die back. Leaves on affected limbs may be small and yellowed, and often have holes in them.
**Symptoms: Fungal canker** affects apple, pear, and mulberry crops. Areas of bark sink inwards, usually starting near a bud or wound. Bark becomes discoloured, then shrinks and cracks, forming concentric rings of flaky bark, and there may be swelling around the infected site. As the canker enlarges, it may girdle the shoot, causing dieback of growth above it. Any infected fruits rot before maturity. In summer, the canker may host raised white pustules, and in winter, red fruiting bodies appear.
**Causes** The bacterium *Pseudomonas mors-prunorum* (on plum and sweet cherry) and *P. syringae* (on peach, apricot, cherry, and plum).
Bacterial infections occur most commonly in wet, windy weather in autumn, or in damp conditions in spring, when soft young growth is most vulnerable. Spring infections usually begin on the leaves and spread to the bark. Most bark infections enter through wounds caused by pruning, frost crack, or leaf fall. Summer infection is rare.
Fungal spores are wind-borne and enter through leaf scars, pruning or insect wounds, frost crack, or scab injuries *(see also* Apple and pear scab, *p.251)*.
**Control** Prune out areas affected by bacterial canker in dry weather during the summer.
Spray infected trees with the copper-based fungicides, Bordeaux mixture or copper oxychloride. Spray once at the end of summer, once in early autumn, and again in mid-autumn.
With fungal cankers, prune out entire spurs or branches where possible. On larger branch or trunk infections, carefully pare away all infected material, cutting back to clean healthy tissue. Spray with Bordeaux mixture and treat the wound with a proprietary wound dressing. Dispose of prunings carefully, preferably by burning. Improve cultural conditions, especially poor drainage; wet soils increase susceptibility. Avoid growing apple cultivars known to be vulnerable. Sprays for apple scab and apple powdery mildew give a degree of incidental control.

**Canker of parsnips:** *see* Parsnip canker.

# Caterpillars

**Crops affected** Various.
**Symptoms** Most caterpillars feed on leaves, as with cabbage white butterfly larvae. Ragged holes are left on leaves, and a black frass (excrement) may remain; the culprits are often found on or beneath the leaves. Some attack roots, while others bore into stems, feed inside leaves as leaf miners, or feed on fruits and berries.
**Causes** Caterpillars are the larval stage of moths and butterflies. They vary in size, colour, and hairiness, but are generally long and tubular in form with a distinct head. They have three pairs of jointed legs at the head end and two to five pairs of clasping legs on the abdomen.
**Control** Most caterpillars are easily removed by hand and, as most are night feeders, can be found easily by torchlight. They can be treated with a biological control, the bacterium *Bacillus thuringiensis*, or sprayed with pyrethrum, rotenone when signs of caterpillar feeding are seen.
*See also* Codling moth, Cutworm, Cabbage white butterfly.

**Cherry slug:** *see* Pear and cherry slug.

# Cherry aphid

**Crops affected** All cherries.
**Symptoms** Sap sucking black aphids on the new leaf shoots cause curling of leaves and stunted growth.
**Cause** The cherry specific aphid *Myzus cerasi*. Young aphids are brown and adults are black.
**Control** Prune off affected foliage. Encourage predators such as ladybirds. If infestation persists, spray with a systemic aphid spray after harvest is complete. Oil spray while dormant in winter.

# Chlorosis

**Crops affected** Various.
**Symptoms** Yellowing of leaves primarily, but also other plant tissues. Yellow, red, or orange colouration may also develop. The primary symptom is due to the loss or deterioration of chlorophyll; this green pigment usually masks other natural pigments and its loss reveals them.
**Causes** Most commonly deficiencies of iron and manganese (so-called lime-induced chlorosis), nitrogen, or magnesium. It can also be caused by viruses and unfavourable cultural conditions, such as waterlogging, low temperatures, or weedkiller contamination.
**Control** Take appropriate action to remedy nutrient deficiencies, remove sources of viral contamination, and ameliorate poor cultural conditions.
*See also* Iron deficiency, Magnesium deficiency, Manganese deficiency.

# Chocolate spot

**Crops affected** Broad bean.
**Symptoms** Chocolate-brown spots on upper leaf surfaces, and brown streaks on stems, pods, and flowers. The seed coats may also be affected. Severe infections may kill plants and even mild cases can reduce yield.
**Causes** The fungus *Botrytis fabae*. It is most prevalent when the air is damp and humid. The fungus overwinters on plant remains and may be seed-borne.
**Control** Grow beans in well-drained soil and do not sow seed too early. Space the plants more widely than at the usual recommended spacings – more than 23cm (9in) apart – to permit thorough air circulation around the plants. Maintain good weed control between rows to minimize humidity and any damp air around plants. Avoid the use of high-nitrogen fertilizers, which encourage soft, infection-prone growth; sulphate of potash will help harden tissues slightly.

**Citrus bud mite:** *see* Fruit deformed.

# Citrus gall wasp

**Crops affected** The citrus gall wasp is an Australian native insect that normally attacks citrus-related species such as the desert lime *(Eremocitrus glauca)* and finger lime *(Microcitrus australasia)*. The main trees susceptible to this pest in the home garden are selected lemon tree cultivars, the rough lemon, and grapefruit. Other citrus, including oranges, can be attacked but the insect does not cause as much damage. This insect used to be confined to warm areas of NSW and the semi tropical regions of Queensland but is now widely spread as far south as Melbourne.
**Symptoms** Plants affected by this insect show elongated, flat, or round swellings on the stem or trunk of the plant. As these galls age they become perforated with emergence holes created by the emerging mature wasps. If the full grown galls are cut in half longitudinally two layers of cells are seen. These contain the larvae which are surrounded by soft tissue on which they feed. The swellings are especially prevalent in new seasons' growth when the insect is active and well established.
**Cause** Adult citrus gall wasps, which are only about 2.5mm long, lay eggs inside new growth twigs, stems or leaf ribs and hatching larvae excrete a substance that creates an overabundance of woody tissue that causes the swelling galls to form. The larvae remain inside these galls for over one year before hatching .
**Control** If trees are only lightly infected no real damage to cropping potential of the trees will be noticed, but heavy infestations create a massive number of knobbly galls, some up to 15cms or more in length. Chemical control is possible using a systemic insecticide, however home gardeners interested in the non-chemical option should just prune all galls from the infected trees. It is important to remove all suspect swellings and burn them to prevent insects hatching and continuing their life cycle. This may mean that the tree has to be reduced to a stump, in which case the bark of the stump should be painted with a white water-based paint to prevent the tree trunk becoming sunburned. If the tree is drastically reduced in size heavy applications of fertilizer and adequate watering in spring are recommended to allow the tree to grow back healthily.

# Citrus leaf-miner

**Crops affected** This insect will attack most citrus species and is now widespread even in areas of Victoria where it was unknown only a few years ago. The spread is mainly attributed to movement of infected plants from one area to another.
**Symptoms** The larvae of this insect cause the most distinguishing symptoms: silvery-white wriggly markings on leaf

surfaces. These markings are caused by the death of tissue where the larvae have tunnelled under the leaf surface. Leaves can be distorted by the activity of the larvae and mature larvae tend to pupate inside curled up leaves of the plant.
**Cause** The larvae of a very tiny moth is responsible for this damage to citrus leaves. The moth is about 5mm long and only active during the night. It lays its eggs on new succulent growth shoots so is active during citrus growth flushes, the full cycle from egg to larvae to cocoon to adult taking only a few weeks.
**Control** By discouraging new growth flushes through water use and irrigation, the moth will be controlled to some extent. The leaves can also be sprayed regularly with a fine oil spray to deter this insect and kill the larvae. In small home gardens, removal of infected leaves will give some control and reduce pest numbers.

## Clubroot

**Crops affected** Brassicas, including radish, seakale, swede, and turnip.
**Symptoms** Swollen roots and a distorted root system (*see p.250*) with pale, chlorotic foliage. Plants wilt readily especially in hot weather, even if the soil is moist. Crops are reduced and plants may die.
**Cause** A soil-borne slime mould, *Plasmodiophora brassicae*. It can live in soil for 20 years or more, even without a host. Infection enters through the root hairs, and when the roots disintegrate, they release spores into the soil. The pathogen can be introduced to gardens in soil that adheres to boots, tools, and wheelbarrows, in garden compost or manure, and directly on infected plants. It is most common on soils that are acid and waterlogged.
**Control** Improve drainage and lime the soil. Burn all infected plants promptly, before roots disintegrate. Raise your own rather than buy plants, in 5cm (2in) pots or larger, so their root systems are well established before setting out. Otherwise, buy from a trusted source and check plants thoroughly before planting. Choose resistant cultivars, if available. Maintain good weed control; weeds such as charlock, shepherd's purse, and wild radish are alternative hosts for clubroot. Avoid spreading spores around the garden on boots and tools, and do not transfer potentially infected soil to other parts of the garden. If there is no alternative to growing brassicas on infected soil, dip the roots of young plants in a suitable formulation of thiophanate-methyl before planting them out.

## Codling moth

**Crops affected** Apple and pear.
**Symptoms** In mid- to late summer, fruits are tunnelled by small, brown-headed white caterpillars. By ripening time, the caterpillars have tunnelled to the core and the fruits are inedible; exit holes may be seen at the eye end (opposite stalk) of the fruit (*see p.250*) or elsewhere on the fruit surface.
**Cause** The larvae of the codling moth, *Cydia pomonella*. Females lay their eggs on fruits on warm nights in early to

midsummer. Larvae hatch two weeks later and tunnel into the fruit at the eye end leaving no visible holes. There can be up to three separate hatchings in one year. After feeding, they leave to spin cocoons beneath flakes of bark; most overwinter, but some pupate in late summer to produce a second adult generation in early autumn.
**Control** Pheromone traps attract males, reducing the mating success of females and the incidence of maggoty apples. The timing of chemical treatments is critical, because it is vital to destroy the larvae before they enter the fruit; pheromone traps indicate when adults are active and likely to be laying eggs. Spray in early summer, with treatments at three-week intervals.

**Collar rot:** *see* Phytophthora.

## Copper deficiency

**Crops affected** Various.
**Symptoms** Yellowing of leaves or blue-green discolouration is occasionally followed by dieback (*see below*). Symptoms are rather vague and difficult to distinguish from many other problems.
**Cause** Copper deficiency is uncommon but most likely to occur on acid soils.
**Control** Treatment with a general compound fertilizer (*see p.20*) may help.

## Coral spot

**Crops affected** Currant and fig crops are most susceptible, but many different woody plants can be affected.
**Symptoms** Bright coral-pink or orange raised pustules appear on dead woody stems or branches. They may not arise until the tissue has been dead for several weeks. Dieback occurs, and if the infection spreads down into the crown, the whole plant may die.
**Cause** The fungus *Nectria cinnabarina*. It lives on dead twigs, old pea sticks, logs, and other woody debris, and produces spores throughout the year. They are spread in water splash. Infection gains entry through wounds or dead snags left after pruning and may then colonize living tissue, causing dieback. If the infection is left unchecked, the whole plant may die.
**Control** Prune out the infected tissue promptly, cutting back to healthy, living wood. Remove and burn all of the infected tissue. Maintain good hygiene to ensure all potential sources of infection are removed.

## Corn earworm

**Crops affected** Various, including tomatoes, beans, and sweet corn.
**Symptoms** Holes in fruit caused by a brownish grub about 40mm long. Cobs of corn are damaged at the tips and bean pods and other fruits are holey and contain the grub inside.
**Cause** The grub is the larvae of *Heliothis armiger*.
**Control** It is too late for control when the grub has eaten its way inside the fruit.

## Crown gall

**Crops affected** Various, including apples, stone fruit, grape vines, and nut trees.
**Symptoms** Poor growth, foliage wilts readily due to slight stress, poor yields.
**Cause** The bacteria *Agrobacterium* spp. inhabit the soil and gain entry to plant roots through a wound causing soft lumpy galls and damaging the vascular system.
**Control** In areas prone to crown gall, dip roots of plants before planting in a specially formulated solution containing a non-pathogenic strain of *A. rhizogenes.*

## Crown rot

**Crops affected** Rhubarb, apple, strawberry, and citrus fruits.
**Symptoms** Rotting of tissues at the plant crown, the junction between stem and roots. Rot may spread to stems and foliage and the plant can die.
**Causes** Various soil- and water-borne fungi and bacteria, often in combination (rhubarb). *Phytophthora* species affect fruits. See also Phytophthora.
**Control** Prompt action may save the plant. Remove affected areas by cutting well back into healthy tissue. Keep base of tree trunk free from mulch and irrigation water.
*See also* Phytophthora.

## Cucumber mosaic virus

**Crops affected** Various, including eggplant, but especially cucurbits.
**Symptoms** Plants and leaves are stunted and deformed, and leaves show distinctive yellow mosaic patterning (*see p.250*). Flowering is reduced or non-existent, and plants may die completely. In cucumbers, zucchini, and marrows, the fruits, if produced at all, are small, pitted, and unusually dark green with bright yellow patches; they are also hard and inedible.
**Causes** The cucumber mosaic virus has a very wide host range and can be spread to crop plants on the mouthparts of aphids and other sap-sucking insects.
**Control** Destroy infected plants; there are no chemical controls available. Reduce risk of infection by controlling aphids and clearing weeds, which may be alternative hosts. Do not handle healthy plants after touching infected material without washing hands first.

**Curly leaf:** *see* Peach leaf curl.

## Cutworm

**Crops affected** Root vegetables, brassicas, lettuce, and leek.
**Symptoms** Young plants wilt and die. Examination of the roots reveals that they have been severed just below soil level. Root vegetables may have cavities eaten into them. Creamy brown or greenish-brown caterpillars, up to 4cm (1½in) long, may be found in the soil near affected plants. They may also feed on foliage above soil level at night.
**Causes** Soil-dwelling caterpillars of several moths.

**Control** Cutworms will work their way along crop rows, and sifting the soil near a damaged plant may reveal the culprit. Good weed control reduces the incidence of these pests. Insecticides for use against these pests are no longer available to the amateur gardener.

## Damping off

**Crops affected** All seedlings are vulnerable, including mustard and cress.
**Symptoms** Seedlings flop over, often showing discolouration at the stem base, which may appear water-soaked. The infection spreads rapidly and clumps of seedlings die off; whole trays of seedlings can be killed within a few days. Any ungerminated seeds may fail to appear. Fuzzy, white fungal growth appears on the surface of dead and dying seedlings.
**Causes** Several soil-borne fungi, in particular, *Pythium*, *Phytophthora*, and *Rhizoctonia* species. They proliferate in over-wet compost and in prolonged high temperatures. The most common reason for damping off is sowing seed too thickly, causing overcrowding, and inadequate light. It is also encouraged by poor hygiene. Unsterilized compost, pots, trays, and implements, and non-mains water may all be contaminated with fungal spores.
**Control** Observe strict hygiene; scrub pots, trays, and implements before use. Use only proprietary, sterilized seed composts. Use only tap water for watering. Sow seedlings thinly and make sure that they have good light and are not exposed to high temperatures for longer than is needed for germination. Drench compost with a copper-based fungicide before sowing. Treat seedlings with the same fungicide at intervals throughout their development.

**Deformed growth:** *see* Mites.

## Dieback

**Crops affected** Woody-stemmed crops, such as tree and bush fruits.
**Symptoms** Plant stems die back, usually from the tip, but often from the base, or sometimes part-way up the stem. Dieback rarely affects all stems simultaneously. Dark blotches or sunken patches may develop at the initial point of infection. Leaves wilt, turn yellow, and die. If unchecked, the symptoms spread down the stem, finally to the base or crown, causing death of the whole plant.
**Causes** Various fungi, some of which are wound-invading pathogens, while others can affect formerly healthy stems. Root infection by soil-dwelling pathogens, such as honey fungus (*see p.256*) or phytophthora (*see p.259*), can also cause stem dieback in woody plants. It may also be caused by unfavourable cultural conditions, especially where dieback occurs from the stem tip downwards. These include drought, waterlogging, and poor establishment of newly planted trees and bushes – if watering has been neglected, for example.
**Control** Prune out affected stems back to healthy growth. Improve cultural conditions to increase plant vigour and ensure plenty of replacement shoots.

## Downy mildew

**Crops affected** A wide range.
**Symptoms** Discoloured or yellowed areas appear on upper leaf surfaces, with corresponding slightly fuzzy, pale grey or purplish fungal growth beneath each patch (*see p.250*). As the infection spreads, large areas or even entire leaves die. Downy mildew is most common on young plants and on those in damp environments. It can be difficult to distinguish from powdery mildew (*see p.260*), which is more prevalent in dry conditions.
**Causes** A range of fungi, mostly *Peronospora*, *Bremia*, and *Plasmopara* species. Some are specific to their host: *Peronospora parasitica* on brassicas, *P. destructor* on onion, *P. farinosa* f. *spinaceae* on spinach, *Bremia lactucae* on lettuce, and *Plasmopara viticola* on grape vines.
**Control** Remove any infected leaves as soon as seen. Improve air circulation around plants by maintaining good weed control and planting at wider than usual spacings. Keep greenhouses well ventilated. Avoid overhead watering. Lettuce downy mildew can be controlled with mancozeb.

## Drought

**Crops affected** Various.
**Symptoms** Symptoms vary according to the crop and whether the drought is recurrent, continuous, or occasional. Poor growth and stunting occurs if drought is recurrent or continuous; foliage wilting is the first sign of dry conditions. If prolonged, drought may cause poor flowering, bud or fruit drop, and the formation of small, poor quality fruits. Drought followed by high rainfall or sudden watering may cause splitting of fruits and stems.
**Causes** Inadequate rainfall or watering is the most obvious cause. Occasionally, drought results from root damage that prevents uptake of sufficient water. Plants in containers or with restricted root runs are especially vulnerable, as are those on light, freely draining, sandy or chalky soils.
**Control** Water consistently and regularly to prevent the soil from becoming completely dry. Take all steps to improve the soil's moisture retention by incorporating plentiful organic matter and by mulching.
Protect container-grown plants from the desiccating effects of direct sunlight and consider the use of water-retaining gels or granules in the growing medium.

## Earwigs

**Crops affected** Various fruit and vegetables.
**Symptoms** Holes in flowers, stems, and leaves particularly of lettuces. Adult earwigs creep into split fruit, particularly stone fruit.
**Causes** These brown or black insects (*Forficula* spp.) have a pair of thick curved pincers at the end of their bodies.
**Control** Clean up debris around the garden where they can hide. Make traps for them from crumpled newspaper placed in a container.

## Eelworms

**Crops affected** Various.
**Symptoms** Generally, eelworms cause distortion, discolouration, and death of plants. Many are specific plant parasites, which cause characteristic symptoms in their host plants.
**Causes** Eelworms, or nematodes, are mostly microscopic, worm-like creatures. Not all are pests, many feed on dead tissue, bacteria, fungi, and on other microscopic creatures. Some eelworms are parasitic on garden pests. Slugs and vine weevils, for example, can be controlled in gardens by beneficial eelworms. Pest species may feed internally on their hosts, or are soil-dwelling, attacking root hairs. They are sap-suckers and so may spread virus diseases from plant to plant on their mouthparts.
**Control** Parts of the garden from which virus-infected plants have been removed should not be replanted with the same type of plant, otherwise they may quickly become re-infected by the eelworms. The normal life cycle needs soil moisture to develop, but dormant larvae and eggs in cysts can survive adverse soil conditions for years. Eelworms and their associated viruses are most often spread in gardens on infected plant debris, or in soil on boots, tools, and plant rootballs – maintain good hygiene. There is no effective chemical control available to gardeners for soil-dwelling eelworms.
*See also* Root knot nematode, Stem and bulb eelworm,
Virus vectors.

## Flea beetle

**Crops affected** Potato, avocado, lettuce, brassicas, swede, turnip, seakale, radish, and rocket.
**Symptoms** Small, shiny black beetles, sometimes with yellow-striped wing cases and usually about 2mm (1/12in) long, leap from affected foliage when disturbed. Some species are larger, to 4mm (1/6in), and are metallic blue or yellow-brown in colour. They eat small round holes in the upper leaf surfaces (*see p.250*), seldom penetrating the leaf entirely. Damaged tissues desiccate and turn pale brown. Heavy attacks may kill seedlings and check the growth of established plants.
**Causes** There are many species of flea beetle. Brassicas are most usually affected by *Phyllotreta* species. Adults damage the foliage while the soil-dwelling larvae feed on roots. They are active in mid-spring and late summer.
**Control** Sow when growing conditions are good, so that seedlings can germinate and grow rapidly through the vulnerable seedling stage. Protect seedlings and young plants with horticultural fleece or similar barriers. If necessary, spray with bifenthrin or rotenone; the latter can be used as a dust for seedlings.

**Fleck:** *see* Quince fleckt.

## Freckle

**Crops affected** All stone fruit and apricots and peaches in particular.
**Symptoms** Freckle-like small spots on fruit which may form cracks or fruit may shrivel. Spots may also develop on leaves.
**Cause** The fungal disease, *Fusicladium carpophilum*, prevalent in humid weather.
**Control** Thin branches at pruning to improve airflow and spray with a copper-based fungicide during dormancy and early spring.

## Frost damage (buds *and* flowers)

**Crops affected** Various, especially bush and tree fruits.
**Symptoms** Buds, whether tightly closed or partially open, become discoloured. They usually turn brown and often become soft and squidgy to the touch. Buds on more exposed areas of the plant are the worst affected. Damage may only occur at certain developmental stages of the bud or flower, so on any given plant, some will escape injury. Nevertheless, there will be a subsequent loss of the fruit crop to a greater or lesser degree.
**Causes** Freezing causes extensive cell damage; cells are ruptured as the frozen cell contents expand. This is exacerbated when thawing is rapid. Slightly tender plants and early flowering cultivars are most vulnerable, but late frosts, which often occur unpredictably after the flower buds have opened, can be particularly damaging.
**Control** Choose planting sites carefully. Avoid known frost pockets and sites where plants will receive direct early morning sun, if possible. Protect more tender plants. In cold areas, choose later flowering cultivars.
Seek out local cultivars of tree and bush fruits; these are generally older cultivars that have been selected to suit prevailing climatic conditions and are most likely to be available from specialist local nurseries.

## Frost damage (foliage *and* stems)

**Crops affected** Various leafy crops, including early potato crops.
**Symptoms** Leaves, usually towards the shoot tips, and on other exposed parts of the plant, appear scorched and turn brown or black. Affected parts may wilt, wither, and die, and young stem growth adjacent to frosted leaves may also die back. Occasionally, isolated patches of damage occur on otherwise sound stems.
**Causes** Freezing causes extensive cell damage; cells are ruptured as the frozen cell contents expand. This is exacerbated when thawing is rapid, as it is when crops are exposed to direct early morning sun. Slightly tender plants, overwintering and early crops are most vulnerable, but late spring frosts, which occur unpredictably, can be particularly damaging.
**Control** Choose planting sites carefully, especially for crops known to be easily frost-damaged. Avoid known frost pockets and sites that receive direct morning sun when possible. Protect vulnerable crops, with horticultural fleece or similar. With potatoes, earthing up helps to reduce damage. An autumn dressing of sulphate of potash helps to harden stem growth and may minimize damage to overwintering crops.

## Fruit bats

**Crops affected** Soft fruits, especially tropical fruit.
**Symptoms** Fruit damaged and eaten.
**Cause** These mammals are native to Australia and live in colonies in trees and feed at night. They are found in most tropical and subtropical climates and isolated colonies also live in some southern temperate areas.
**Control** Covering the trees with bird net is the most reliable control. Smelly moth-ball bags in the trees and noisy bird scaring devices have limited deterring effect.

## Fruit deformed

**Crops affected** Various.
**Symptoms** Deformed fruit. Fruit with wrinkles and lumps.
**Cause** Very often the cause of deformed fruit occurs soon after flowering by a tiny sap-sucking insect. This may be thrips in the case of strawberries or citrus bud mite (*Eriophyes sheldoni*) in the case of lemons and oranges.
**Control** Seldom necessary. A spray in late autumn and midwinter with sulphur may reduce the problem.

## Fruit drop

**Crops affected** Various fruit and nuts.
**Symptoms** Immature fruit fall before ripening.
**Cause** Many causes are likely including lack of fertilization if tiny fruit fall after flowering and nuts may be empty inside. Late fruit drop can be due to sunburn which prevents development, or an excessively large fruit set, or it can be due to lack of adequate moisture to sustain the crop load.
**Control** Ensure pollination be growing the right varieties of fruit and nut trees, and ensure there are pollinating insects where flowers are insect-pollinated. Also thin fruit to a sustainable quantity and ensure adequate moisture during fruit development. Regularly apply required fertilizers for adequate nutrition.

## Fruit fly

**Crops affected** Most fruits in fruit fly zones including citrus, passionfruit, peach, plum, olive, and melon.
**Symptoms** Fruit flesh is infested with small white maggots. Adult insects, about 6mm (1/4in) long, have red-orange heads, black bodies marked yellow and white, and mottled wings. They resemble tiny house flies and may be seen on or flying around plants.
**Cause** Many species, including *Ceratitis capitata*. Native of the Mediterranean and subtropical regions, it is a greenhouse pest in cooler climates. It may be introduced on shop-bought fruit or imported plants. The flies breed throughout the year where temperatures permit and are serious fruit pests in warmer parts of the world, but not in cool-temperate climates, such as Tasmania.

**Control** Yellow sticky traps and pheromone traps help reduce populations, the latter by foiling the reproductive success of females by attracting and trapping male flies. Food lure traps attract both sexes of the fly. Chemical treatments should be targeted at adult flies, since once inside fruits, larvae are difficult to reach with sprays. Prevent adult flies from laying eggs by spraying with an approved insecticide at times when the adults are seen to be active.

**Fruit set failure:** *see* Poor fruit setting.

## Fruit size small

**Crops affected** All fruits and nuts.
**Symptoms** Small undersize fruit.
**Cause** Among the many causes is a large fruit set which results in excessively large numbers of fruit. Also poor nutrition and inadequate moisture can also cause small fruit.
**Control** Thin fruit after fruit set to reduce the total number of fruit. Generally the fewer the number of fruit, the larger each will be. Ensure adequate nutrition and moisture.

**Fruit splitting:** *see* Drought, Splitting.
**Fruit spotting bug:** *see* Bugs.
**Fruit tree red spider mite:** *see* Red spider mite.

## Fusarium

**Crops affected** Bulb onion, Welsh onion, and garlic.
**Symptoms** Decay spreads up through the bulbs from the basal plate. Once infected, the plant is effectively dead.
**Cause** The fungus *Fusarium oxysporum* f. sp. *cepae*. Unlike most other strains of *F. oxysporum* (*see below*), this one does not cause wilting. It is more prevalent in warm-temperate climates.
**Control** Remove and burn infected plants promptly to minimize spread.
Do not put them on the compost heap. Practise crop rotation (*see p. 31*).

## Fusarium wilt

**Crops affected** Various, both woody- and soft-stemmed. Pea, melon, and tomato crops are commonly affected.
**Symptoms** Soft stems wilt, in part or in their entirety, while woody-stemmed plants may retain their overall shape, but leaves on affected parts wilt and wither. The decisive symptom is brown or black staining on the internal vascular tissue, which is apparent beneath the bark or at the root core. Plant death is almost inevitable. In cool, damp conditions, fluffy, pale pink, or white fungal growth may be visible on infected tissues.
**Causes** Various strains of the fungus *Fusarium*, most commonly *F. oxysporum,* cause fusarium wilt. The fungi are often host-specific, but all are responsible for blocking the vascular tissues with gum-like substances, which cause wilting in much the same manner as drought. Unlike plants suffering from drought, however, those affected by fusarium wilt

do not recover when watered. The fungus persists in plant debris and is also capable of surviving in the soil, in the absence of a host, for several years.
**Control** Remove infected plants promptly to minimize spread and destroy, preferably by burning. Do not put them on the compost heap. Where practicable, remove soil or compost from the immediate vicinity of the roots. Do not grow the same or closely related plants on the same site again, or for a minimum of five years. There is no chemical cure.

**Ghost spotting:** *see* Tomato ghost spot.

## Gooseberry dieback

**Crops affected** Gooseberry and, less commonly, blackcurrant.
**Symptoms** Dieback of stems. Usually only some stems are affected, but the infection occasionally spreads; if the main stem or base of the plant is affected, the entire bush dies back. In damp weather, fuzzy, grey fungal growth is seen around the damaged areas. Leaves on infected stems yellow, turn brown, and fall prematurely. Any developing fruits will shrivel and die.
**Cause** The fungus *Botrytis cinerea* (*see also* Botrytis, *p. 252*). Spores are spread in air currents and in water splash.
**Control** Prune out infected shoots promptly, removing all wood that shows staining or discolouration; cut back to a bud on healthy wood. Remove any infected fruits, which form a source of further infection. Spray the bush with the fungicide.

**Grape phylloxera:** *see* Phylloxera.

## Grasshoppers

**Crops affected** Grasshoppers are very common in all parts of Australia, including inland areas, the tropical zones and as far south as Tasmania. Grasshoppers, especially, in the unwinged "hopper" stage and the later flying stage can cause lots of damage when they occur in very large numbers. There do not seem to be many plants that will escape rampaging locust or grasshopper swarms that contain perhaps millions of insects because they are so voracious as to eat anything that is green. Grasshoppers have been known to eat all the foliage of grape vines, pear trees, potato plants, young citrus trees, corn plants, and many more fruits and vegetables. Grasshoppers in the "hopper" stage can move through an area making it devoid of all grass, weeds and green plants and are very difficult to stop.
**Symptoms** Grasshoppers in low numbers will eat ragged holes in leaves of plants that they feed upon but when in plague numbers will strip every vestige of green from plants.
**Cause** The most common grasshoppers likely to worry farmers and gardeners are the Australian plague locust (*Chortoicetes terminifera*), the Giant grasshopper (*Valanga irregularis*) and the Spur-throated locust (*Austracris guttulosa*). Grasshoppers lay their eggs in barren dry ground. When the nymphs hatch out they go through several growth stages before becoming a

winged adult. During this time they are voracious eaters and will consume anything they take a fancy to.
**Control** Little can be done to stop plague locusts but they can be sprayed with chemical insecticides if necessary. The only way to protect crops and vegetables is to use insect-proof netting to prevent insects getting at these crops.
The use of chickens or ducks in orchard areas will help control sporadic infestations of grasshoppers to some extent.

**Green vegetable bug:** *see* Bugs.
**Grey mould:** *see* Botrytis.
**Gummosis:** *see* Canker.

## Halo blight

**Crops affected** Dwarf French and runner bean.
**Symptoms** Small, angular spots appear on the foliage. At first they appear water-soaked and they then darken in colour with each spot surrounded by a bright yellow "halo". The leaves begin to turn yellow between the veins and eventually the entire leaf is affected and it dies. Growth and yields can be seriously affected. If stems or pods are infected, they develop grey patches, again with a water-soaked appearance.
**Cause** The bacterium *Pseudomonas phaseolica*, which is spread by water splash and is carried by seeds, which are usually the initial source of infection.
**Control** Pick off infected leaves as soon as they are seen and avoid overhead watering. Remove and burn all affected plants at the end of the season and do not store the seed.

**Harlequin bugs:** *see* Bugs.

## Honey fungus

**Crops affected** Tree and bush fruits, strawberry, rhubarb, and globe artichoke. Most woody plants are susceptible.
**Symptoms** Affected plants begin to die back, leaves may discolour and wilt, or trees may fail to leaf up in spring. Death can be rapid or may be drawn out over several seasons. Fruit trees may set an unusually good crop before dying. The roots and stem or trunk bases develop a white fungal sheet, with a decidedly mushroom-like aroma, between the bark and the woody tissues beneath. Around the root system in the soil, there may be "rhizomorphs", which resemble black or brown bootlaces, or old tree roots. They can be branched and flattened or may be plump and more rounded, varying in diameter from less than a millimetre to several millimetres across. If the black outer rind is stripped off, it may be lined with pink or white fungal growth. The rhizomorphs feed on dead woody material, but may grow through the soil to latch onto living tissues. Rhizomorphs may also be found beneath the bark at the base of the stem or trunk of infected plants. In late summer or autumn, clumps of honey-coloured toadstools may appear. They cluster at the base of the plant, or may form colonies that follow the line of the roots. They are commonly seen infesting old, dead tree stumps. The stipe

or stem of the toadstools usually bears a distinctive creamy white ruff or collar.
**Causes** Various species of the fungus *Armillaria*. These show varying degrees of ability to cause disease, with some being far less virulent than others. Less virulent species tend only to infect the plants that have root wounds or are otherwise stressed.
Without laboratory identification, it can be difficult to differentiate between the species, except on the basis of the damage they cause. Spread occurs either by direct root contact or by rhizomorphs, which can grow at a rate of up to 1m (3ft) per year.
**Control** Keep plants in good health by good cultivation, keeping them well fed, mulched, and watered. Avoid damaging the roots when cultivating the soil around plants. Honey fungus is an opportunistic pathogen that will latch on more easily to plants that are stressed, for example by drought, excessive pruning, or severe pest infestations.
Remove all dead trees from the garden, including their roots, regardless of their cause of death, since dead woody tissues are a prime food source for honey fungus. It is imperative to remove as much of the root system of infected plants as possible; hire a stump grinder if necessary.

## Iron deficiency

**Crops affected** Many, including apple, pear, blueberry, raspberry, and blackberry.
**Symptoms** Leaf yellowing, or chlorosis (*see p. 253*), between the leaf veins, often in combination with brown discolouration that starts at the leaf margins and moves in towards the veins. Young growth is affected earlier and more severely than older growth.
**Causes** Iron deficiency is usually seen in combination with manganese deficiency (*see p. 257*). It is most common in acid-loving plants, such as blueberries, when grown on limy (alkaline) soils; hence the term lime-induced chlorosis. It can also affect other plants that are not noted as being acid-lovers.
A shortage of soil iron is rare, but iron (and manganese) can be rendered unavailable to plants if soils are too alkaline; the mechanism is complex but, in brief, the excess calcium "locks up" the iron in the soil, so that plants cannot absorb it.
**Control** Do not grow acid-loving plants on soils that are not sufficiently acidic. Treat the affected tree, bush, and soft fruits with a chelated compound containing iron, manganese, and other trace elements; these will be in a form that does not become locked up by calcium, and they will be available to plant roots.
Restrict liming on soils that are already alkaline. If soils are very alkaline, consider acidifying the soil by using sulphur or aluminium sulphate and ferrous sulphate before planting.
For acid-loving plants, use an acidic mulch of pine needles or chopped conifer bark; incorporate some in the planting hole before planting. Feed them with a fertilizer formulated for use on acid-loving plants.

**Leaf blight:** of walnuts, *see* Walnut blight.
**Leaf blotch:** of walnuts, *see* Walnut blotch

## Leaf Eating Ladybirds

**Crops affected** These leaf eating ladybirds can be found on plants in the pumpkin family and other plants in the same family (*Solanaceae*) especially rockmelon plants. *H. sparsa vigintisexpuntata*, in particular, is mostly found on potato plants but the two may be present on the one plant.
**Symptoms** Both the hairy larvae of the insect and the beetle adult eat the leaves of plants. The larvae will generally feed on the underside of the leaf and adults on the topmost surface. They eat the surface tissue and leave the veins showing, resulting in the leaves having a papery thin appearance with some dead tissue evident. Sometimes holes are eaten through the leaf leaving the veins intact.
**Cause** Both the Twenty-eight spotted ladybird (*Henosepilachna viginioctopunctata*) and Twenty-six spotted ladybird (*Henosepilachna sparsa vigintisexpuntata*) are responsible for the damage caused. Adults have the typical ladybird beetle shape and are orange in colour. The only observable difference is the number of black spots, one has 28: the other 26. The larvae are unusual, about 10mm long and hairy. The most unusual thing is that the "hairs" are forked and this gives the larvae a distinct appearance. The life cycle is completed in about 5-6 weeks and all stages of the insect, eggs, larvae, pupae and adults may be found on the plant at the same time.
**Control** This insect can be controlled with contact chemicals but in the home garden it is best to pick them off by hand.

## Leafhopper

**Crops affected** Various, including apples, cucumbers, melons, and tomatoes.
**Symptoms** Mottled leaves and an infestation of small greenish insects on the underside of leaves.
**Cause** A few species of leafhoppers invade garden plants. The young are pale and wingless and jump around the undersurface of leaves. The adults can fly. Leafhoppers suck sap and can transmit virus diseases.
**Control** Spray or dust with pyrethrum or rotenone. Repeat sprays may be necessary.

## Leafminer

**Crops affected** A wide range, including citrus, beans, and potatoes.
**Symptoms** Usually meandering white lines on the leaves caused by leafminers tunnelling under the leaf surface. Some leafminers cause lumpy patches on leaves.
**Cause** The larvae of a number of different beetles, wasps, sawflies, and moths attack leaves in this way.
**Control** Very often the plants are not severely damaged by leafminers. Where plants are suffering from leafminer activity, systemic sprays will be required. Remove affected parts; try oil sprays.

## Leaf spots (bacterial)

**Crops affected** Various, including brassicas, cucumber, and mulberry.
**Symptoms** Grey or brown, usually angular or circular necrotic spots appear on leaves, often with a yellow "halo" around them. There are no minute, raised fungal bodies visible, as there are in fungal leaf spots.
**Causes** Various bacteria may be involved. Examples include *Pseudomonas syringae* pv. *maculicola* on brassicas, *P. syringae* pv. *lachrymans* on cucumber, and *P. syringae* pv. *mori* on mulberry. They are most often spread by water splash, or occasionally from stem lesions to leaves (as with bacterial canker, which can cause leaf spots on *Prunus* species). In most cases, the damage is cosmetic, but it can indicate that the plant is under stress or suffering from another, more serious problem.
**Control** Remove infected leaves promptly and avoid overhead watering. There is no chemical treatment.

## Leaf spots (fungal)

**Crops affected** Beetroot, blackberry, celery, currants, Swiss chard, gooseberry, and raspberry.
**Symptoms** Grey or brown, circular necrotic spots appear on leaves; they may join together so that large areas of leaves die. The spots often have concentric rings of discoloured tissue around them and often bear tiny, raised, black or brown fungal fruiting bodies.
**Causes** A wide range of fungi, some of which are host-specific, for example, *Cercospora beticola* on beet leaves. Although entire leaves may die, fungal spots are not very serious, but they may indicate that the plant is suffering from some other, more fundamental problem. *See also* Target spot.
**Control** Remove affected leaves if necessary. At the end of each season, rake up fallen leaves to minimize the numbers of overwintering spores. Fungicides such as mancozeb can be used to control certain leaf spots, but check product labels for details.

## Leek rust

**Crops affected** Leek.
**Symptoms** Outer leaves develop lens-shaped, bright orange, raised fungal pustules, 1–2mm (¹⁄₁₆–¹⁄₁₂in) long. When these erupt, they release conspicuous masses of bright orange spores. The affected leaves turn yellow and die back. The inner leaves are seldom as badly affected.
**Causes** Strains of the fungus *Puccinia allii*. The strains that attack leeks do not attack onions or chives. They are most prevalent in damp conditions and in wet weather.
**Control** Remove and destroy all affected leaves at harvest. Dispose of all debris thoroughly at the end of the season and grow leeks and other onion family members on a fresh site each year. Avoid the use of high-nitrogen fertilizers, which encourage soft, disease-prone growth. At planting time, apply a dressing of sulphate of potash at a rate of 15–20g per sq m (½–¾oz per sq yd); this helps harden tissues and improves resistance. Space plants more widely than usual to improve air circulation and maintain good weed control. Choose leek cultivars with known resistance.

## Light brown apple moth

**Crops affected** Various fruit, including grapes, apples and citrus.
**Symptoms** Holes or eaten surface of leaves and grooves around the stem of young fruit. The larvae are green and about 20mm long and web bunches of grapes or leaves together or roll one into a tunnel.
**Cause** The insect larvae of the light brown apple moth (*Epiphyas postvittana*) are native to Australia and prevalent in cool weather.
**Control** Where damage is severe, the larvae can be sprayed with a caterpillar spray containing the biological control bacteria, Bt..

## Magnesium deficiency

**Crops affected** Apple, lettuce, grape vine, potato, cherry, some brassicas, and tomato.
**Symptoms** Yellowing develops between the leaf veins (interveinal chlorosis) and around the leaf margins, leaving clear green bands immediately adjacent to the veins (*see p.250*). As the green colour is lost, other pigments may be revealed, so instead of yellowing, red, purple, or brown discolouration may occur. Apple crops may be so severely affected as to defoliate. Symptoms are most pronounced towards the end of the season, and the older leaves always show deficiency symptoms first (compare with iron deficiency, *see facing page*). Magnesium is very mobile in the plant and when in short supply it is transferred from older lower leaves to new ones nearer the stem tips.
**Causes** Magnesium deficiency is most common in very acid soils or potting mixes, and after heavy rain or watering, especially on light, sandy soils. When water levels are high, magnesium is readily leached from the soil. The excessive use of high-potash fertilizers or sulphate of potash may exacerbate this deficiency, because high levels of potassium in the soil can render magnesium unavailable to plant roots.
**Control** When liming, consider using magnesian limestone. For more rapid amelioration, apply magnesium as a foliar spray. Apply Epsom salts at a rate of 200g in 10 litres of water (8oz in 2 gallons), adding a wetting agent. Alternatively, apply Epsom salts to the soil at a rate 40g per sq m (1½oz per sq yd).

## Manganese deficiency

**Crops affected** Various, including pea, bean, brassicas, beetroot, parsnip, spinach, and bush and tree fruits.
**Symptoms** Yellowing develops between the leaf veins (interveinal chlorosis) of older leaves, and necrotic brown patches often appear on the yellowed areas. In potato crops, the young foliage may be pale and rolled upwards at leaf margins. Pea and bean seeds may exhibit almost circular brown spots that become visible when the cotyledons are pulled apart.
**Causes** Manganese deficiency, which is most common in acid, peaty soils and on poorly drained, sandy soils. It can be induced by an excess of iron in the soil, but may also occur in tandem with an iron deficiency.
**Control** Avoid overliming susceptible soils. Spray affected plants with a solution of manganese sulphate at the manufacturer's recommended rate. *See also* Chlorosis, Iron deficiency.

## Mealy cabbage aphid

**Crops affected** Brassicas and swede.
**Symptoms** Yellow patches appear on the foliage and flower heads between mid-spring and mid-autumn. Beneath the leaves, there are corresponding dense colonies of grey-white aphids, which are covered in a mealy white wax. During early summer, the aphids infest the shoot tips and the new leaves are distorted when they emerge and they have a pale mottled appearance. If infestations are severe, the shoot tip may be killed and multiple branching occurs as a result.
**Causes** The sap-sucking aphid *Brevicoryne brassicae*.
**Control** Treat with an insecticidal soap, pyrethrum, rotenone. Avoid growing brassicas in warm weather and remove old plants.

## Mealybugs

**Crops affected** Most greenhouse plants, including citrus fruits, grape vine, pineapple.
**Symptoms** Soft-bodied, pale grey or pink insects, up to 4mm (⅛in) long, infest stems, usually in inaccessible places like leaf axils. A fluffy white wax is secreted from the insect bodies and this also conceals their eggs. Excretions of honeydew are host to black sooty mould.
**Causes** There are several species of mealybugs that occur in greenhouses; the most common are *Pseudococcus* and *Planococcus* species.
**Control** A thorough spray with insecticidal soap can be very effective, as can hand-picking if done frequently. Where daytime temperatures are 24°C (75°F) or more, a biological control – the ladybird predator *Cryptolaemus montrouzieri* – can reduce infestations.

## Mice and rats

**Crops affected** Stored fruits, vegetables, and seeds; and in the garden, pea, bean, and sweetcorn are especially vulnerable to nibbling by mice and rats.
**Symptoms** Pea, bean, and sweetcorn seeds and seedlings are removed and eaten. Stored produce is also eaten during autumn and winter, when mice migrate indoors, or raid sheds and outhouses.
**Causes** *Mus* and *Apodemus* species, are the usual suspects.
**Control** Set mouse traps or place bait in places where mice have caused damage. In the garden, put traps under the cover of logs or bricks, away from birds or pets. Humane mouse traps, which trap live animals, are only humane if checked at least twice daily, because these small creatures are killed easily by starvation, stress, dehydration, or heatstroke. The culprits should be released at least 300m (1000ft) away from the capture site.

## Millipedes

**Crops affected** Various.
**Symptoms** Millipedes are generally more nuisance than damaging although some species do attack roots of young seedlings and soft ripe fruit, such as strawberries, in contact with the ground.
**Causes** Millipedes are brown, segmented and long and thin with a hard covering and many legs. They are found in rotting organic matter and curl up when touched. The black Portuguese millipede that often invades buildings does not attack plants.
**Control** Reduce a build-up of organic matter.

## Mint rust

**Crops affected** Mint, marjoram, and savory.
**Symptoms** Leaves and stems are distorted and flecked with yellow; in mint, the stems may be conspicuously contorted as they emerge from the ground in spring. Cupped, orange fungal fruiting bodies develop on the stems and leaves, later turning yellow-orange, then dark brown.
**Cause** The fungus *Puccinia menthae*. This overwinters as resting spores in the soil and within infected rhizomes.
**Control** The easiest means of control is simply to cut off all foliage. Alternatively, dig up and burn plants, and to replace them with new ones in spring. Obtain stock from a reliable source and plant in a completely new site. It is possible to kill the fungus with a flame weeder; burn off the top-growth at the end of the season and scorch the soil. It is difficult to do this safely and reliably and there is a risk of overdoing it and killing the plant entirely.

## Mites

**Crops affected** Various.
**Symptoms** Different mites cause different symptoms. Physical injury to plants includes finely spotted fruit and dried leaves (*see also* red spider mite). Other damage includes deformed growth caused by mites that secrete substances that cause changes in plant growth. This damaage can be enlarged buds or stems and bushy growth and deformed fruit (*see* Fruit deformed.) Some viruses are transmitted by certain species of mites. Leaf infestations usually occur on the underside of leaves.
**Causes** The various mites include Bryobia mite (*Bryobia rubrioculus*) which causes whitish mottling of leaves on fruit trees such as apples, pears, almonds, and plum. Eriophyid mites suck sap causing damage to various fruits and foliage. Tomato russet mites infest tomatoes, eggplants, capsicum, and potatoes and cause browning of the lower leaves and move up the plant. Certain mites can also cause blister-like growths on leaves such as walnut. Mites are barely visible with the naked eye and they thrive in hot, dusty conditions.
**Control** Reduce dust in the orchard. Specific miticides can be used for specific mites where the problem is severe, but control is difficult.

## Mole crickets

**Crops affected** These unusual insects do not readily attack any plant although they may eat very soft plant tissue such as found in germinating vegetable crops. It is mainly their burrowing activity that causes some concern.
**Symptoms** The mole cricket, as the name suggests, is an insect that burrows through the soil and in doing so will dislodge some seedling plants or planted seeds. It leaves the soil surface with uplifted crumbly soil tracks where it has burrowed under the soil surface but does little harm as it is not usually present in such numbers as to cause much damage. It seems as if the conditions have to be right for this insect to be active as ground that shows no mole cricket activity for months and months can suddenly be "ploughed up" overnight.
**Cause** The mole cricket is a cute but ugly, velvety brown insect about 3cm long that has two front legs that are adapted to digging . These are blade-like with flattened serrated edges and very powerful for the size of the insect. They do have wings and can often be seen flying at night when attracted to a light source.
**Control** Individual insects can be removed from an area by hand. There is no real need to harm these insects as they are not a big problem and probably do more good by aerating the soil than they do harm to plants.

## Molybdenum deficiency

**Crops affected** Broccoli and cauliflower.
**Symptoms** Leaves are mottled yellow and stunted, and they may die off. The growing tips are often distorted; this is a typical symptom of molybdenum deficiency, sometimes known as whiptail of brassicas.
**Causes** It is rare that soils are deficient in molybdenum, but acid soils or composts may render this element unavailable. Molybdenum is needed for the assimilation of nitrogen by the plant. Its deficiency causes abnormal cell formation and subsequent check to growth.
**Control** Increase pH of acid soils by liming. Alternatively, drench soil of affected plots with ammonium or sodium molybdate; dissolve 2.5g (⅒oz) in 0.5 litre (1 pint) of water to treat 1 sq m (1 sq yd).

**Mosaic virus:** *see* Viruses.
**Neck rot:** *see* Onion neck rot.
**Nematodes:** *see* Eelworms and Stem and bulb nematode and root knot nematode.

## Nitrogen deficiency

**Crops affected** Various.
**Symptoms** Growth is reduced and leaves are small and yellowed (chlorotic). In some plants, red or purple discoloration of the leaves may occur as chlorophyll levels drop. The oldest, lower leaves are affected first, but if the deficiency is not corrected, all parts of the plant may be affected. Flowering, fruiting, and root or tuber formation are impaired.
**Causes** Most soils can develop nitrogen deficiency, but it is more prevalent on light soils and those with a low organic matter content. Plots that have been heavily cropped are also susceptible. In cool springs, nitrogen deficiency may occur temporarily, but this is usually self-righting as the soil warms up and soil bacteria become active. Soils that have been heavily mulched with wood chips may suffer deficiency because nitrogen is removed from the soil as the lignin in the wood is broken down.
**Control** Make regular applications of composts and well-rotted or matured mulch materials, and apply nitrogen-rich fertilizers. Grow legumes (for example, peas and beans) which are capable of fixing nitrogen by means of bacteria in their root nodules. Leguminous green manures, such as crimson clover (*Trifolium incarnatum*), will also fix nitrogen in the soil.

## Oedema

**Crops affected** Various, but grape vines are particularly vulnerable.
**Symptoms** Raised, wart-like growths appear, most often on the lower leaf surfaces, but sometimes on grapes. They are leaf-coloured at first, but they may become brown and corky. Affected leaves may become distorted, but death is not inevitable.
**Causes** A cultural condition whereby leaves take up more water than is lost by transpiration. Small groups of cells become waterlogged, swelling to form blister-like, pale green, warty growths. If conditions do not improve, the cells rupture and die, turning brown and corky. The condition is most common when humidity is high and the water levels at the roots are excessive.
**Control** Avoid overwatering, improve drainage, and ventilate crops under glass. Space plants more widely than the recommended distances to permit good air circulation. Do not remove affected leaves because this exacerbates the problem.

**Olive scab:** *see* Apple, pear, and olive scabs.
**Onion eelworm:** *see* Stem and bulb nematode.

## Onion maggot

**Crops affected** Onion family: mostly onion, but also leek, shallot, and garlic.
**Symptoms** Young plants collapse in early summer, with the roots eaten by white maggots, up to 8mm (⅜in) long.
**Causes** The maggots are the larval stage of the fly *Delia platina*, which resembles a house fly. There is one generation in early summer and a second in late summer; the latter feeds on roots and burrows into the bulbs, so causing the secondary rots to set in.
**Control** Grow onions from sets; they are less vulnerable than seedlings to attack by first-generation maggots. Growing the plants under horticultural fleece will keep out the egg-laying females. Lift any plants that are infested and destroy them before the maggots move into the soil to pupate. There are no chemical controls available to amateur gardeners, and maggots inside the bulbs would be inaccessible anyway.

## Onion neck rot

**Crops affected** Onion family.
**Symptoms** The bulb scales of infected onions become semi-transparent, pale brown, and soft. The affected areas develop a dense grey fungal growth and begin to dry out, taking on a mummified appearance. Black tiny fruiting bodies (sclerotia), which may be several millimetres long, arise on affected parts and are often clustered around the neck end of the bulb. The rot is often first noticed on stored bulbs.
**Cause** The fungus *Botrytis allii*. It is the most common cause of rot in stored onions. The sclerotia are able to persist in the soil or on onion debris, as a source of re-infection.
**Control** Do not grow onions on the same site for more than two years in succession. Buy seed and sets only from a reputable supplier, as the fungus may be brought in on infected seed or sets. Do not apply fertilizers after midsummer, and avoid the use of high-nitrogen fertilizers, since they induce soft, infection-prone growth.

Keep crops well watered and improve cultural conditions so that firm, well-ripened bulbs are produced.

At harvest time, allow onion necks to flop naturally rather than bending them over to terminate growth; bending can cause wounds that form entry points for disease.

When they are drying off prior to storage, protect onions from rainfall in a covered, open, well-ventilated place. Red- or yellow-bulbed, rather than white onions, are generally more resistant to infection.

## Onion smudge

**Crops affected** White onions
**Symptoms** Spots develop on the bulbs before harvest and become rotten patches in storage.
**Causes** The fungus, *Calletotrichum circinans*, may develop in humid conditions. Spores are spread by wind.
**Control** Discard infected bulbs. Ensure crop rotation and grow brown onion varieties that may be resistant to this disease.

## Onion thrips

**Crops affected** Onion family, including leek. Also lettuces, tomatoes, beans, and cucumbers.
**Symptoms** A fine, white mottling develops on leaves during the summer. Black or pale yellow, narrow-bodied insects, up to 2mm (½in) long, are found on the leaves.
**Causes** The adults and nymphs of a sap-sucking insect, *Thrips tabaci*. Many ornamental plants are alternative hosts. Thrips are most troublesome in hot, dry summers and, while light infestations are tolerable, heavy ones will cause a significant check to growth. Heavy infestations are characterized by the loss of much of the green colour in leaves before late summer.
**Control** Effective treatments include sprays of rotenone or pyrethrum.

## Onion white rot

**Crops affected** Onion family.
**Symptoms** The foliage turns yellow and wilts. The base of the bulb and roots develop fluffy white fungal growth (*see p.250*), which later produces tiny black fruiting bodies (sclerotia). The sclerotia fall off into the soil, where they can persist for seven years or more.
**Cause** A fungus, *Sclerotium cepivorum*.
**Control** Remove and burn infected plants as soon as seen and do not grow members of the onion family on the same site for at least eight years. There is no chemical treatment available.

## Oriental peach moth

**Crops affected** This insect pest mainly infests peach and nectarine trees, although it has been known to attack quinces and ornamental flowering forms of *Prunus* spp. and also apples and pears but this is rare. Warm growing conditions associated with fairly high humidity favour this pest as it needs new soft growth shoots for the larvae to invade.
**Symptoms** These are found first in the new shoots when seemingly healthy new shoots suddenly wilt and bend over. This is because the moth has previously laid eggs on the new shoots or leaves and the larvae as they hatch burrow into stems to eat the soft pithy tissue within. The infected shoots will eventually die and turn black in colour. During summer some fruits may be infected and the most distinguishing evidence of the larvae presence is a gummy hole eaten into the side of the developing fruitlets. There may also be a little frass (insect droppings) around the injury point.
**Cause** The Oriental peach moth is a small moth that grows to only 6mm long with a wing span twice this measure. The moth is mostly active during the night but is sometimes disturbed when limbs are contacted or shaken during daylight hours. The moth can be well camouflaged and cannot easily be seen when it is resting on grey tree bark. as it is a basic grey colour with some whitish bars and patches of white/grey markings on the folded wings.
The moth lays tiny (1 mm) spherical whitish eggs on leaves and plant stems and these hatch into larvae that look like a bit like codling moth larvae. Over wintering eggs hatch around September when new shoots have already grown on the trees. The complete life cycle from egg to larvae to cocoon to adult moth takes just over one month in warm weather conditions.
There may be several hatchings or life cycles during one full season. Any fruits that are damaged when the fruit is near ripe may also be infected with brown rot fungus at the injury point. This sometimes results in significant fruit loss.
**Control** There are chemicals that can be used to control this insect but these chemicals may lead to a build-up of two spotted mites. It is best, therefore, to use other control measures in the home orchard. By inspecting the trees you will be able to determine when the moth is active as any shoots that have been attacked will start to wilt. This is the stage to remove any wilted shoots (before they become blackened) by cutting them off well below the larvae entry point. The collected shoots should be crushed, burnt or destroyed to kill the larvae inside the shoot stems.

## Parsnip canker

**Crops affected** Parsnip.
**Symptoms** Roughened cankers appear on the root, especially at the shoulder. They are usually red-brown, orange-brown, or black.
**Causes** The fungus *Itersonilia pastinacae*. It may spread to the soil from infected leaf spots and often enters through damaged root hairs.
**Control** No control is available. Grow resistant cultivars. Improve soil drainage and avoid or remove all potential sources of root injury. Late sowing at closer than normal spacings produces smaller roots, which appear to be less susceptible to canker.

## Passionvine hopper

**Crops affected** Various but mainly passionfruit, tomatoes, beans.
**Symptoms** When foliage is disturbed, small moth-like insects fly away, young hoppers or nymphs hop and bounce about. Foliage may pale due to sap-sucking.
**Causes** Passionvine hoppers (*Scolypopa australis*). The adults look like a small brown moth with transparent wings and the nymphs are greyish with erect tail part and are most active.
**Control** Seldom is infestation severe. If spraying is required, apply at the nymph stage with a recommended insecticide.

## Pea leaf *and* pod spot

**Crops affected** Pea.
**Symptoms** Sunken brown or yellow spots appear on leaves, stems, flower stems, and pods. These lesions may also bear small, pinprick-sized, fungal fruiting bodies.
**Causes** Various fungi, including *Ascochyta pisi* and *A. pinodes*. They usually attack fully grown peas, but occasionally attack seedlings, usually fatally. It persists from year to year on plant debris and, if seeds are collected from infected pods, the resultant seedlings will succumb too.
**Control** Clear up and burn infected plant material at the end of the season. Do not save seed from infected plants. Sow fresh seed in a new site in spring.

## Peach leaf curl

**Crops affected** Peach, nectarine, and almond.
**Symptoms** Leaves develop pale green puckering and blistering that later turns bright red or purple (*see p.250*); they are affected when or soon after they unfurl in spring. A white powdery layer of spores develops on the leaf surfaces, and the affected leaves fall prematurely. When a second flush of leaves appears later in summer, they are usually healthy. In nectarine crops, the infection may spread to the fruits, causing rough, slightly raised patches; peach fruits are usually unaffected.
**Cause** The fungus *Taphrina deformans*. Growth and cropping is usually only seriously compromised if repeated infections occur over several successive years. The fungus overwinters as spores that lodge in bark cracks and crevices, or in bud scales. It is spread by wind and in water splash.
**Control** Remove affected leaves as soon as seen. Keep trees well fed and watered to promote healthy new growth. Spray with a copper-based fungicide several times from mid- to late winter, but ensure that spraying is complete before blossom burst. Repeat the spraying in autumn before leaf fall.

## Pear *and* cherry slug

**Crops affected** Pear, plum, cherry, quince, and almond.
**Symptoms** Foliage is infested by club-shaped, pale yellow, caterpillar-like larvae, up to 1cm (½in) long, between late spring and mid-autumn. They secrete a slimy black mucilage all over, giving them a slug-like appearance. They feed by grazing off the upper leaf surfaces, skeletonizing them and causing the damaged tissues to become brown and desiccated.
**Cause** The larvae of a sawfly, *Caliroa cerasi*, which produces two or three generations during the summer. The larvae overwinter in cocoons in the soil.
**Control** Most contact insecticides offer good control, if trees are small enough to spray. Spray as soon as larvae are seen with pyrethrum, or rotenone. Alternatively dust with ash or lime.

**Pear fleck:** *see* Quince fleck.

## Pear leaf blister mite

**Crops affected** Pear; apple crops are also affected, but less frequently.
**Symptoms** Young pear leaves develop pink or yellowish-green blisters, or raised blotches that superficially resemble the damage caused by peach leaf curl (*see above*). On expanded leaves, the damage forms broad bands on either side of the midrib; by midsummer, the blisters have turned black. Less than 3mm (⅛in) across, these lesions should not be confused with the larger ones caused by apple and pear scab (*see p.251*).
**Causes** A microscopic mite, *Eriophyes pyri* lives within the leaves. The blisters are the plant's response to chemicals that are secreted by the mites as they feed.
**Control** Although the unsightly lesions give the appearance of ill health, the damage is largely cosmetic and does not seriously affect cropping. None of the insecticides that are available to amateur gardeners gives control, but on lightly infested small trees, affected leaves can be picked off by hand. If done thoroughly, this will reduce populations in subsequent years.

**Pear scab:** *see* Apple, pear, and olive scabs.

## Petal blight

**Crops affected** Cardoon and globe artichoke.
**Symptoms** The flowerheads develop pale brown spots and later the entire head becomes shrivelled and infected by fluffy grey fungal growth. Sometimes, pinprick-sized, black fruiting bodies (sclerotia) are seen on the fungal mass. If infection is extensive, the whole crop may be lost.
**Cause** The grey mould fungus, *Botrytis cinerea*. Spores are spread readily by water splash and air currents, and they persist from year to year in the soil, or on plant debris, as sclerotia.
**Control** Good cultural practice and hygiene are the first lines of defence, since control of such a widespread fungus is difficult. Avoid damp or shaded sites. Keep plants growing well and in good health by regular feeding and watering. Remove any dying buds or flowerheads promptly as soon as they are seen; the fungus will rapidly invade dying or damaged tissues and will spread to previously unaffected ones. Cut back to clean, healthy stems. Clear away all plant debris promptly.
*See also* Botrytis.

## Phylloxera

**Crops affected** Grape vines.
**Symptoms** Stunted growth and yellowing of foliage. Galls on roots.
**Cause** The root-infesting form of the aphid, *Daktulosphaira vitifolii*, forms galls on the roots of vines followed by root rot. Infestations spread readily.
**Control** Ensure that the grape vines are grafted onto resistant rootstock varieties.

## Phytophthora

**Crops affected** Various, including pineapple, apple, and other tree fruits, raspberry, and strawberry.
**Symptoms** Plants begin rotting at the collar between the roots and the stem base. Foliage may be sparse, discoloured, and show signs of dieback. Roots are blackened and the finer roots are killed. Stems may show signs of dieback and the whole plant may be killed. Bark under the main stem or trunk is reddish- or blackish-brown.
**Causes** Various soil- or water-borne fungi of the genus *Phytophthora*; *P. cinnamomi* is the most common and can cause root rot of tree fruits. *P. cactorum* causes fruit rot of apples and collar rot of apples and other fruit trees (*see p. 254*); *P. syringae* also affects several tree fruits in a similar way. *Phytophthora* is also one of the causal agents of damping off (*see p. 254*).
**Control** Maintain good hygiene and water only with mains water. Improve drainage and ventilation. Unfortunately, this fungus thrives in exactly the damp and humid conditions in which pineapple crops are grown. Remove infected plants, along with the soil in the vicinity of the roots. There is no chemical control available to gardeners.
*See also* Root rots and Potato blight.

**Pod spot:** of peas, *see* Pea leaf and pod spot.

## Poor fruit setting

**Crops affected** Many fruit crops: raspberry, strawberry, apple, pear, and other tree fruits and nuts.
**Symptoms** On tree fruits, flowers appear as normal but they then fail to set fruit. On raspberry and strawberry crops, some fruits form incompletely or are distorted.

On raspberries, individual drupelets on the berry may be dried and brown, while other adjacent berries are perfect.
**Causes** There can be several causes. On fruit trees, poor pollination may result from a lack of a compatible pollinator or frost damage (*see p. 255*) at flowering time.

With all fruits, poor pollination may also be a result of a lack of pollinating insects, usually bees, either because there are none in the vicinity, or because wet and windy weather has prevented them from flying.
**Control** When planting fruit trees, check on their pollination requirements and plant accordingly; choose self-pollinating cultivars if they are available. Choose sheltered spots to avoid frost damage; this will also be beneficial for bees. Plant plenty of other flowering plant species to attract pollinating insects. Use any chemical sprays with care, selecting specific pesticides where possible; try to spray at dusk when insects have generally ceased flying. Some tropical fruits and vegetables require high humidity for fruit set and watering the foliage at flowering can be helpful.
*See also* Potassium deficiency.

## Poorly formed fruits

**Crops affected** Cucurbits.
**Symptoms** Fruits are small, pitted, and unusually dark green with bright yellow patches; they are also hard and inedible.
**Cause** Cucumber mosaic virus (*see p.254*). This virus has a wide range of hosts and it can be spread on the mouthparts of aphids and other sap-sucking insects.
**Control** Destroy all of the infected plant as there are no chemical controls available. Reduce the risks of infection by controlling aphids and clear away any weeds around the plants, as they are likely to provide alternative hosts. Do not handle healthy plants after touching any infected material without washing hands thoroughly first.

## Potassium deficiency

**Crops affected** Various.
**Symptoms** The most frequent symptom is poor flowering, often with undersized flowers and a correspondingly poor fruit set. On tomato crops, this is often a factor in blotchy ripening (*see* Tomato blotchy ripening, *p.263*). Leaves may appear scorched at the tip or margins, and show purple-brown spotting beneath.
**Causes** A deficiency of potassium in the soil. This deficiency is most common on light, sandy soils and those with a low clay content.
**Control** Apply rock potash or sulphate of potash in spring and autumn.

## Potato black leg

**Crops affected** Potato.
**Symptoms** Leaves are stunted and yellowed with slightly incurled leaf margins, most noticeably on the uppermost leaves.

The stem base is blackened, slimy, and rotten at ground level. If the stem is cut across, it reveals distinct, discoloured, or black spotting.

The parent tuber is completely rotted and plants may die before a crop is produced.
**Causes** The bacterium *Erwinia carotovora* var. *atroseptica*. It is most prevalent in wet soils and may be introduced on symptomless, but nevertheless infected, seed tubers. When these are planted, affected plants may be seen scattered throughout a crop of healthy, apparently unaffected plants. The bacterium infects the potatoes via any wounds that are made while plants are in the soil, or when seed tubers are being lifted.
**Control** Do not lift potato crops in wet weather, and lift carefully to avoid causing any damage; both factors make infection more likely. Clear away all crop debris, and do not allow heaps of discarded potatoes to stand; they may form a source of infection.

Store only perfectly healthy, undamaged potatoes; infected ones rot in store and the rot will spread to healthy tubers. Avoid growing cultivars known to be susceptible.

## Potato blight

**Crops affected** Potato and tomato.
**Symptoms** Necrotic brown patches appear on the leaves and fruits or tubers (*see p.250*). They are found mainly at the tips and at the margins. As they enlarge, the leaf withers and dies. Slightly fluffy, white fungal growth may appear around the spots, usually beneath the leaves. This is most common in humid conditions or in wet weather. Haulms of infected potatoes develop dark brown patches and then collapse. The skins of infected tubers develop sunken dark patches with red-brown colouration on the flesh beneath. These are dry at first, but they often become foul-smelling and slimy due to secondary infections, which usually rot the entire tuber.
**Cause** The fungus *Phytophthora infestans*. This is the same organism that causes blight on tomatoes. Spores are produced by the leaf lesions and are then spread by rain splash and air currents. They may also wash down to the tubers in rainfall or irrigation water. The fungus becomes active only when there are two consecutive 24-hour periods with a minimum temperature of 10°C (50°F) and a relative humidity of 89 per cent or more for 11 hours in each of the 24-hour periods.
**Control** Reduce the risk of infection spreading to the tubers by earthing them up deeply.

If haulms show symptoms of infection, remove them as soon as they begin to die down.

Spray the foliage with a copper-based fungicide such as Bordeaux mixture or copper oxychloride, or with mancozeb. If the weather conditions are favourable for fungal growth spray as a precaution.

## Potato common scab

**Crops affected** Potato, swede, turnip, radish, and beetroot.
**Symptoms** The tuber develops rough, raised, corky patches on the skin (*see p.250*). The skin ruptures leaving the scabs with ragged edges. Damage may be superficial or may result in cracking or pitting. The flesh is usually undamaged, although there may be some discolouration beneath the scabs.
**Causes** *Streptomyces scabies*, an organism that is related to both fungi and bacteria. It is particularly common on sandy soils that are deficient in organic matter, but it occurs naturally as part of the microflora in most soils. Potatoes planted in plots that were formerly grassland are especially prone to attack. The organism thrives in soils that have been limed, and it is less common on acid soils.
**Control** Do not lime the soil prior to planting potatoes. Improve the organic content of the soil and keep it well watered in dry weather; there is a link between dry soil conditions and the proliferation of this organism. Use acidic materials, such as sulphate of ammonia or superphosphate, to reduce scabbing. Although crops are seldom badly reduced and tubers remain edible, they usually have to be peeled deeply to become palatable. There is no chemical treatment available.

## Potato moth

**Crops affected** Potatoes, tomatoes.
**Symptoms** Tiny larvae cause blisters in the leaves and tunnel stems causing death of the foliage above. They also tunnel into fruit and tubers underground and in storage.
**Cause** Potato moth (*Phthorimaea operculella*) adults fly at night. The maggot-like larvae cause the death of plants and rotting of fruit and tubers.
**Control** Remove host weeds such as nightshade and thornapple. Keep potato tubers well covered with soil. Apply a recommended insecticide when infestations are severe.

## Potato powdery scab

**Crops affected** Potato and tomato.
**Symptoms** Small, scabby patches develop on potato tubers. They are almost circular with a slightly raised margin. When the scabs mature, they burst open to release spores into the soil. There may be cyst-like growths on roots and stolons. In rare instances, a canker form of powdery scab develops causing marked deformations of the tuber, which resemble symptoms of the notifiable, but now very uncommon, potato wart disease. In powdery scab, the tuber protuberances are smooth, not warty, and wart disease never affects the roots.
**Cause** The fungus *Spongospora subterranea*. It is most common in wet seasons and on heavy soils, especially on sites that have grown crops of potatoes for many seasons.
**Control** Dispose of all infected tubers; do not put them on the compost heap because they will spread the disease. Do not grow potatoes for at least three years following an outbreak. Improve soil aeration before planting.

## Potato viruses

**Crops affected** Potato.
**Symptoms** Various, depending on the potato variety, the growing conditions, and the virus or combination of viruses that are involved.

Leaf symptoms include yellow flecking, streaking or mosaicing, dark spotting and leaf distortion, and stiffening and upward rolling of the leaflets.

If home-saved seed potatoes are grown for many years in succession, there is likely to be a gradual decline in the vigour and crop quality due to a build-up of viruses.
**Causes** Several different viruses including potato leaf-rolling virus, tobacco rattle, and potato viruses X and Y.
**Control** None is available. Always grow potatoes on a fresh site, do not save tubers for seed, and buy in certified, virus-free seed potatoes.

## Powdery mildew

**Crops affected** Various.
**Symptoms** Powdery white fungal growth occurs, first on the upper leaf surfaces, then later often spreading to the lower surfaces. Mildew may also affect all other above-ground plant parts, but its location depends on the mildew and plant species that are involved.

Affected leaves and other parts may turn yellow and become distorted; distortion is particularly common when it is young growth that is affected. Fruits that have been affected may split or crack because they cannot expand normally. On leaves, mildew may kill small areas of tissue. These will then die and fall away, giving a shothole effect. Growth may be quite poor and, in extreme cases, dieback or even death may follow the premature leaf fall.
**Causes** Various fungi, including species of *Erysiphe, Microsphaera, Oidium, Phyllactinea, Podosphaera,* and *Uncinula*. These fungi are most prevalent where the soils are dry, but the air around the plants is humid and stagnant.
**Control** Keep plants adequately watered but avoid overhead watering. Remove any affected leaves promptly. Seek out resistant cultivars. Some crops may be sprayed with a suitable fungicide, for example sulphur.

**Premature seeding:** *see* Bolting.
**Purple top wilt virus:** *see* Viruses.

## Quince fleck

**Crops affected** Quince, pears, loquats.
**Symptoms** Many small, irregular red spots appear on the leaves; the spots later turn black and may join together. The leaves then turn yellow before falling prematurely. Sometimes, similar spots occur on the fruits, which may also become quite distorted. Affected shoot tips may develop dieback.
**Cause** The fungus *Diplocarpon mespili*, which overwinters on infected shoots.
**Control** Remove and burn all of the fallen leaves, and prune out any stems that are infected. No suitable fungicides are available to gardeners.

## Rabbits

**Crops affected** A wide range.
**Symptoms** Grazing occurs on all parts of leafy plants, to a height of about 50cm (20in). Tree bark may be gnawed, and if the damage girdles the stem or trunk, the tree dies. Bark feeding occurs at any time of year, but trees are especially at risk when other food sources are scarce. New plantings may also receive special attention; like deer, rabbits are inquisitive feeders.
**Cause** Rabbits, *Oryctolagus cuniculus*.
**Control** Trapping, shooting, and gassing are generally unsuitable techniques in a garden situation. The only reliable way of excluding rabbits is to erect fencing. This must be 1.2–1.4m (4–4½ft) tall, with 30cm (12in) of the netting buried below ground, angled outwards, to deter them from digging through or burrowing beneath. The mesh size must be a maximum of 25mm (1in), otherwise young rabbits can squeeze through. Do not forget to net gates as well, and keep them closed when not in use. Protect trees with individual guards, either netting or spiral tree guards around the base of the trunks. Animal repellent products are not generally reliable, but domestic cats can be very efficient hunters of rabbits.

## Raspberry cane blight

**Crops affected** Raspberry.
**Symptoms** Areas of bark peel away from the canes in summer and autumn and the stems die back, becoming very brittle. Minute, black, fungal fruiting bodies form on dead stems and eject spores.
**Causes** This is a fungal infection, caused by *Leptosphaeria coniothyrium* which enters wounds in the canes. The wounds can result from pruning, or late spring frosts.
**Control** Prune carefully to avoid creating ragged cuts and protect from frost where possible. If blight does occur, cut out affected canes and any discoloured wood from the crown. Spray crowns and any new growth with a copper-based fungicide.

**Raspberry cane spot:** *see* Cane spot.

## Raspberry sawfly

**Crops affected** Raspberries and blackberry-type berry bushes.
**Symptoms** Holes in leaves and tunnelling in canes causing dieback.
**Cause** Raspberry sawfly (*Priophorus morio*) adults lay eggs in the canes or leafstalks. The larvae are yellowish with a brown stripe.
**Control** Spray the larvae under the leaves with a recommended insecticide.

## Raspberry spur blight

**Crops affected** Raspberry, loganberry, blackberry, and hybrid berry crops.
**Symptoms** Buds of new canes develop dark pink–purple patches around them, which enlarge and spread down the canes causing widespread discolouration.

In autumn, canes develop a greyish silver colour and are covered in many pinprick-sized, black fruiting bodies. Infected canes bear very few viable buds in the following spring and, if they survive, produce very few fruits.
**Cause** The fungus *Didymella applanata*. It occurs in most seasons but is especially prevalent in wet weather.
**Control** Avoid high-nitrogen fertilizers, as they will induce soft, more disease-prone growth. Avoid overcrowding, which encourages rapid spread. This is best done by selecting only the strongest canes when pruning. Prune out the affected canes. Spray new growth in spring with a copper-based fungicide.

## Raspberry viruses

**Crops affected** Raspberry.
**Symptoms** Leaves develop yellow patterning, usually in mosaic form, and this is accompanied by various distortions such as, down-curling of the leaves, stunting, and a general failure to thrive. Cropping is often reduced.
**Causes** Various viruses. The most common are raspberry mosaic, curly dwarf, and raspberry yellow dwarf. These viruses may occur alone or in combination.
**Control** Remove and dispose of affected plants promptly. Choose a new site for replacement canes, and do not use the same site again for raspberries. Control any insect vectors, such as aphids; some viruses are also spread by soil-dwelling eelworms.

## Red-legged earth mite

**Crops affected** This mite can attack many crop plants, vegetables, and flowers, and is found on many weed species.
**Symptoms** Red-legged mites have a sucking action drawing sap from plant tissue by puncturing cells. The constant cell puncturing and the resultant death of some tissue gives the plant leaves a whitish speckled appearance. If the mites are present in large numbers they can actually cause the death of young plants or seedlings and inhibit plant growth severely.
**Cause** There are several mite species that can cause similar problems to those caused by the red-legged earth mite but this mite is very distinctive in that it has brilliant coloured red legs. These legs are easily seen with the naked eye even though the mite itself is only about 1 mm long. The mite's body is a dense black colour which enhances the red legs. These mites can sometimes be seen crawling in huge sprawling masses over and around plants or on the soil . The mites are often seen during the autumn–winter period when conditions are most favourable for them.
**Control** Some natural predators can control this mite to some extent and changing weather conditions may kill populations quite suddenly. However, if the mites are present in very large numbers chemical sprays can be used or sulphur spray may be used as an alternative organic approach. Crop and field rotation and fallowing of the soil will also deter this mite.

## Red spider mite

**Crops affected** Many, including tree fruits and vegetable crops.
**Symptoms** Foliage loses its healthy green colour and develops a silvery sheen, becoming increasingly dull and chlorotic. A fine pale mottling is observed on the upper leaf surfaces (*see p.250*) and large numbers of tiny, dark red mites, 1mm (¹⁄₁₆in) long, and their spherical eggs can be seen beneath the leaves. Severe infestations can cause premature leaf fall. In the greenhouse, plant leaves exhibit similar dullness and loss of colour. Close examination of the lower leaf surface, preferably with a x10 hand lens, will reveal spherical eggs and tiny, yellow-green mites with two large dark marks on the back near the head end (sometimes known as two-spotted mites). In autumn and winter, they turn bright orange-red. In heavy infestations, silky white webbing covers the leaves and stems. Leaves dry up and fall prematurely, and only young leaves remain at the stem tips.
**Causes** There are two species of red spider mite. The sap-feeding fruit tree European red spider mite, *Panonychus ulmi*, occurs mostly on fruit trees. The heaviest infestations occur in hot, dry summers. The red spider mite, *Tetranychus urticae*, is the more common culprit. In hot, dry summers, it moves outdoors to attack a wide range of crops.
**Control** The fruit tree red spider mite is not generally a problem on unsprayed trees since predatory mites and other predators provide a degree of natural control. Sprays are often indiscriminate and kill many beneficial insects. Where trees have been routinely sprayed, mite populations build to problem proportions and their overwintering eggs, laid in bark crevices, may be so numerous as to give the bark a distinct red hue. If red spider mite becomes a problem, spray with an insecticidal soap.

Red spider mite breeds rapidly in warm conditions and strains have developed that are resistant to pesticides. Biological control with the predatory mite *Phytoseiulus persimilis* gives good results if introduced before heavy infestations develop. It needs warm daytime conditions in the absence of pesticides to become established. Misting plants with clean water twice daily provides high humidity, which suppresses mite activity. Alternatively, use sprays as for fruit tree red spider mite; several applications will be necessary.

## Replant diseases

**Crops affected** Soft fruits, tree fruits.
**Symptoms** Newly planted trees and bushes fail to thrive and may show signs of dieback. There are no obvious cultural problems, such as drought, waterlogging, or poor planting technique. The problem occurs where new trees are planted on a site previously occupied by the same species.
**Causes** The exact mechanism of replant problems is unclear, but it may involve eelworms, viruses, soil-borne fungi, and nutritional depletion. The last may be a result of infection of roots that renders them incapable of taking up nutrients properly. There is also evidence that some plants' roots exude chemicals

to deter growth of plants of the same species too near to them; a mechanism that, under natural circumstances, would prevent competition.
**Control** Affected plants may recover if moved to a fresh site. The problem is best avoided by not planting on a site where the same species has been grown previously. There is no reliable control. If absolutely necessary, the soil may be removed and replaced with virgin soil. A "cube" of soil, that has a minimum dimension of approximately 45 x 45 x 45cm (18 x 18 x 18in), must be replaced, so this is not a task to be undertaken lightly if many plants are to be replaced. Planting well-established, container-grown plants with a good root system, feeding with a high-nitrogen fertilizer, and watering thoroughly can help minimize the problem. It is essential also to keep the soil in good health by incorporating plenty of well-rotted organic matter.

## Rhizoctonia

**Crops affected** Celery, Florence fennel, potatoes, beans, and many seedlings.
**Symptoms** Plants are stunted, and yellow and dark green-black lesions appear on the stems, roots, fennel bulbs, and at the base of leaf stalks. Sometimes, red-brown streaks are also seen.
**Cause** The fungus *Rhizoctonia solani*. *Rhizoctonia* species are also common causal agents of damping off and stem and root rots (*see pp. 254 and 263*).
**Control** There is no cure. Prevent the spread of the disease by immediate removal of affected plants, along with the soil at their roots. Prevent initial infection by maintaining good hygiene, washing pots, trays, and implements thoroughly before sowing seed. Use only sterilized potting mixes and mains water for irrigation. Sow seedlings thinly and make sure that they have good light and are not exposed to high temperatures for longer than is needed for germination. Drench with a copper-based fungicide before sowing. Treat seedlings with the same fungicide at intervals throughout their development.

## Root knot nematode

**Crops affected** A wide range.
**Symptoms** Plants fail to thrive, display poor foliage colour, and knobbly swellings form on the roots.
**Causes** Microscopic eelworms that live within the roots and cause knobbly swellings (not to be confused with nitrogen-fixing nodules normally found on the roots of legumes). The tissue distortion they cause disrupts the intake of water and nutrients. There are several species, most in the genus *Meloidogyne*.
**Control** Remove affected plants along with the soil around their roots. There is no effective chemical control available to gardeners. In susceptible situations, prevent infection by dipping dormant tree rootstocks in nematode preventative solution before planting and use nematode-resistant rootstock varieties.

**Root rots:** *see* Stem and root rots, Crown rot, Phytophthora, Honey fungus.

## Rusts

**Crops affected** Various.
**Symptoms** Foliage and stems may be affected, depending on the host plant and the rust involved. Spore masses or pustules are usually bright orange or dark brown, but their colour may vary at different times of the year and they frequently begin yellow or orange and turn brown later. They often have several distinct spore stages, commonly known as winter, spring, and summer spores. Affected areas usually discolour and may wither and die.
**Causes** Various fungi, the most common of which are species of *Puccinia* (see p.250), *Uromyces*, *Phragmidium*, *Melampsora*, and *Gymnosporangium*. Some need an alternate host to complete their life cycle, while others are monospecific. All need a moist environment to become infectious, so they are generally more troublesome in damp weather conditions.
**Control** Remove affected leaves. Improve air circulation, and where possible, choose resistant cultivars. Currant and gooseberry crops may be sprayed with Bordeaux mixture. There are no suitable fungicides available to gardeners to control rust on other fruits or vegetables.
See also Leek rust, Mint rust.

**Rutherglen bug:** see Bugs.

## Scale insect

**Crops affected** Various.
**Symptoms** The stems and foliage of many garden and greenhouse plants can be affected. The offending insects secrete a waxy shell or scale over their bodies. They are mobile when young, but once they have found a suitable niche, they settle down and are fixed in place for the rest of their lives. The scales may be grey or brown in colour, and flat or domed in shape. The size, which varies according to species, is 1–6mm (¹⁄₁₆–¹⁄₄in). Some scale insects excrete honeydew, which hosts black sooty moulds. Most species hatch in midsummer, but breeding may occur throughout the year.
**Causes** Scale insects, many species.
**Control** Most scale insects conceal their eggs beneath their own bodies. The newly hatched nymphs are more vulnerable to insecticides, such as insecticidal soap and white oil.
See also Brown scale.

## Sclerotinia

**Crops affected** Various.
**Symptoms** Fruit and stem base infections are the most common, but the majority of above-ground tissues can be affected, becoming brown and slimy as they rot (see p.250). Large quantities of fluffy, cotton-wool-like fungal growth develops, which is scattered with black fruiting bodies (sclerotia). Fruits and tubers may be affected when in store.
**Cause** The fungus *Sclerotinia sclerotiorum*. It is most prevalent in cool, damp conditions and overwinters in the soil. It then produces cup-shaped fungal growths known as apothecia, which contain the spores that are responsible for the following season's infections.

**Control** Remove and burn all affected plants promptly. At the end of each season, dispose of all plant debris. Do not grow susceptible plants on the same site for at least four years following an outbreak of the disease.

## Scorch (stems & leaves)

**Crops affected** Various, but plant crops, such as grape vines, are usually more susceptible.
**Symptoms** Scorched tissue, usually of softer parts like petals or leaves, turns pale brown or bleached. Damaged areas dry out and become crispy. Stems are occasionally scorched, with the area of damage appearing on the exposed side.
**Causes** Hot or bright sun is the most common cause, but cold, dry winds can also be very damaging. With sun scorch, the problem is exacerbated by droplets of moisture on the leaf surfaces, which magnify the sun's rays. Sun scorch of bark is most likely on young, thin-barked trees. Water droplets may also increase low temperature damage if they remain on the leaf surfaces during cold nights, especially in spring and autumn. Accidental contact with weedkillers, either directly or from drifting spray, may also produce similar symptoms, as can the use of inappropriate pesticides. Some plants are very sensitive to certain chemical sprays.
**Control** Water in the early evening so that leaves have a chance to dry off before nightfall and are not exposed to bright sunlight immediately afterwards. Provide adequate shading. Check label recommendations for pesticides to ensure that they are suitable for use on the plant in question.

**Shield bugs:** see Bugs.

## Shot hole

**Crops affected** All stone fruits, particularly almonds and apricots.
**Symptoms** Small brown spots on the leaves fall out leaving holes. Gummy raised spots may form on fruit and on stems.
**Cause** Shot hole (*Stigmina carpophila*) occurs on early flowering varieties of stone fruit in humid conditions.
**Control** Prevent infection with a programme of copper-based sprays through winter and early spring.

## Silver leaf

**Crops affected** Stone fruits, particularly plum and cherry, and also peach, nectarine, almond, apple, and pear.
**Symptoms** Single or several branches develop leaves with a silvery sheen. If affected stems of 2.5cm (1in) diameter or greater are cut across, the inner tissues reveal central brown staining. Other apparently normal limbs may show symptoms at a later date. Affected limbs may die off and fall, or fail to leaf up the following spring. Fruiting bodies, often clustered together and adhering closely to the bark, may form on dead wood.

Their exposed surface is dark purple-grey. These symptoms may be mimicked by other causes, such as bad weather damage, drought, malnutrition, or insect attack.
**Cause** The fungus *Chondrostereum purpureum*. This is a fresh-wound parasite of deciduous trees and shrubs, and pruning cuts or pest attack are the most frequent wounding agents. Spores are produced from fruiting bodies on limbs of infected trees or on fallen timber. It is spread on air currents, in water splash, and on pruning tools. The fungus produces a toxin that causes the upper leaf surface to become detached from the main leaf blade, and air that accumulates between the two layers deflects light, giving a silvered appearance to the leaf. The infection is not carried by the leaves themselves.
**Control** None is available. Mildly affected trees sometimes recover spontaneously. In general, however, the infection spreads through the tree unless affected branches are removed. Cut them off at least 15cm (6in) beyond the point where staining is apparent, cutting back to clean white wood. Infection is least likely to occur during the summer months, so all pruning of susceptible trees should be undertaken in summer. Although it is no longer generally recommended to use wound paints, it is certainly recommended in trees that are susceptible to silver leaf and should be done straight after pruning. Locate any sources of infection, such as fallen timber, and remove and burn them.

Plum and cherry crops are especially prone to infection. The rootstock also influences susceptibility.

## Slugs

**Crops affected** Various.
**Symptoms** A wide range of plants are damaged; soft parts are most susceptible. Irregular holes are eaten in flowers, leaves, and stems. Slugs secrete a slimy, silvery mucilage from their bodies; these silvery deposits, left as trails on affected plants, can be a key sign of both slug and snail damage.
**Causes** Several species of slugs occur in gardens: the grey field slug (*Deroceras reticulatus*), the garden slug (*A. hortensis*). They are ubiquitous and present through the year, continuing to feed whenever temperatures remain above 5°C (40°F). Most are night feeders.
**Control** Slugs can never be eliminated from gardens, so control measures should concentrate on protecting vulnerable plants, especially seedlings and soft-leaved plants, such as lettuce. Non-chemical means of control include hunting by torchlight on mild, damp nights. Slug traps consisting of a jar half-filled with beer sunk into the ground invite slugs to death by drowning. Grapefruit skins, placed open end down, are also attractive traps; the victims can be collected and disposed of in the morning.

The parasitic nematode *Phasmarhabditis hermaphrodita* is a biological control that can be used where soils are moist but well drained, and above a temperature of 5°C (40°F). It is most effective in spring and autumn. The microscopic nematodes penetrate the slugs' bodies when they enter the soil to seek shelter during the day and release a bacterium that causes a fatal disease in infected slugs. Under

suitable conditions, it gives effective reduction in numbers for up to six weeks.

Poisoned baits in the form of slug pellets can harm cats, dogs, and birds, which may consume poisoned slugs, so use with great care. Where pets use the garden, instead of scattering them thinly among plants, place them inside an old drainage pipe beside vulnerable plants, to reduce risks of accidental poisoning of pets. Slug pellets containing metaldehyde cause slugs to secrete an excess of slime and they die of dehydration, but slugs may recover in wet conditions. Aluminium sulphate is less toxic to pets and is mainly active against young slugs; it is best applied in mild, damp weather in spring and autumn.

**Smudge:** see Onion smudge.

## Snails

**Crops affected** Various.
**Symptoms** A wide range of plants are damaged between spring and autumn; soft parts are most susceptible. Flowers, leaves, fruits, and stems are eaten, with irregular holes rasped away. Often their surfaces are grazed off and the tissue beneath becomes desiccated and browned or bleached. This is apparent on the stems of cardoons. Silvery slime trails are left behind. Snails are most active after dark and in wet weather. They are less common on acid soils, which lack the calcium necessary to form their shells.
**Causes** The most common snail pest is the garden snail, *Helix aspersa*.
**Control** As for slugs. Biological control is less effective because snails live above the soil and are less likely to be infected by bacteria-carrying nematodes. Since snails often hibernate communally, significant numbers can be disposed of by strategic placement of suitable hibernation shelters, such as old drainage pipes, chimney pots, or upturned flowerpots. Congregating slugs can be collected *en masse* during the winter months and disposed of.

## Sooty moulds

**Crops affected** Various.
**Symptoms** Black sooty covering that sticks to the surface of leaves and stems.
**Cause** Sooty mould fungi grow in the "honeydew" excreted from aphids and scale insects. It does not invade the leaf tissue but it looks dirty and reduces photosynthesis and plant vigour.
**Control** Control the aphids or scale insects producing the "honeydew". Later wash the mould growth off with water.

**Spider mite:** see Splitting.
**Split stone:** see Red spider mite.

## Splitting

**Crops affected** Various.
**Symptoms** Fruits or stems split, usually longitudinally, sometimes only around the fruit stalk, while the rest of the plant appears perfectly healthy. Earwigs may enter at the wounds. Cracks may dry and heal over, but dieback and rotting may

follow due to secondary infections entering the wounds. Fruits may have an impaired flavour.
**Causes** An erratic supply of water and nutrients, such as calcium deficiency, are the most common causes, along with poor pollination and great fluctuations in temperature, as in frost crack.
**Control** Mulch to conserve soil moisture and keep plants well fed and watered. Hand-pollinate fruit crops. Observe damaged areas for signs of secondary infections and treat as appropriate. Remove damaged fruits – they will rot and form a source of further infection.

## Spotted wilt

**Crops affected** Various, including tomatoes, capsicums, potatoes, lettuces, broad beans and many ornamental plants.
**Symptoms** Brown or sometimes yellow spots or rings on the leaves and dying of new shoots.
**Cause** The virus disease is spread by onion thrips which are most active in hot, dry weather.
**Control** Destroy infected plants and remove weeds, such as nightshade, that may also be infected.

## Stem *and* bulb nematode

**Crops affected** Onion family.
**Symptoms** Young onion plants are abnormally swollen and distorted. The tissues become soft and mealy, and they are readily infected with secondary rots. Plants usually die before reaching maturity; onions may produce bulbs if infested late in the season, but they will rot in store.
**Causes** The microscopic nematode, *Ditylenchus dipsaci*.
**Control** There is no effective chemical control available to gardeners. Remove infested plants as soon as seen. Eelworms are spread in gardens on infested plant debris, or in soil on boots, tools, and plant rootballs, so maintain good hygiene. Buy onion seeds and sets from reputable suppliers to reduce the risk of bringing eelworms into the garden. Crop rotation may reduce infestations; grow crops that are not affected, such as lettuce, swede, turnip, and any of the brassicas.

## Stem and root rots

**Crops affected** Asparagus, celery, tomato, cucurbits, melon, pea, bean, and soft fruits.
**Symptoms** Infections at the stem base cause tissues to darken, atrophy, and soften. The upper parts respond by wilting, discolouring, and dying back. Root rotting may occur at the same time.
**Causes** Various fungi, often those responsible for damping off. Other fungi, including fusarium and verticillium wilts (*see pp.256, 263*) may cause both wilting and foot rot symptoms.
**Control** There is no cure for infected plants. Prevent the spread of the disease by immediate removal of affected plants, along with the soil or compost at their

roots. Maintain impeccable hygiene, washing pots, trays, and implements thoroughly before using them. Use only sterilized potting mixes and mains water for irrigation.

**Stinkbugs:** *see* Bugs.

## Strawberry viruses

**Crops affected** Strawberry.
**Symptoms** Stunting and distortion of the whole plant, with the same symptoms accompanying yellowing in the leaves. Various patterns of discolouration are seen: streak, ring-spot, and mosaic or yellowing of leaf margins. Plants fail to thrive and may not flower or fruit well.
**Causes** Various viruses, the most common being strawberry yellow edge or little leaf virus, arabis mosaic, strawberry ring spot.
**Control** None available. Remove and burn affected plants as soon as symptoms are seen. Control aphids (*see p.251*), which are important virus vectors. Do not grow strawberries on the site again. Do not propagate from infected plants; runners carry infection without always showing symptoms. Always buy certified stocks of strawberry plants; they are guaranteed to be virus-free when they are purchased.

## Sunburn (fruit)

**Crops affected** Various soft fruit and nuts.
**Symptoms** Brown patches on fruit and developing nuts that are exposed to hot sun. Nut kernel desiccates. Berries and vegetable fruits may bleach to white. Sunburn is worse on north and west sides of the plants and on plants that do not have a good covering of leaves.
**Cause** High temperatures and lack of foliage covering developing fruit.
**Control** Shade vulnerable fruit with shadecloth. Do not prune off foliage that may shade developing fruit. Ensure adequate soil moisture.

## Target spot

**Crops affected** Tomatoes, capsicums, eggplant, potatoes.
**Symptoms** Brown to black spots or patches develop on the leaves with rings like a target. Spots may also form on stems, fruit, and tubers.
**Cause** The fungus, *Alternaria solani*, is sometimes called Tomato target spot. It can be troublesome in warm, humid conditions.
**Control** Ensure crop rotation and remove likely host plant weeds such as nightshade. Spray affected plants with a copper-based fungicide.

## Thrips

**Crops affected** Many, including onion, leek, and pea.
**Symptoms** A fine, silvery white discoloration appears on the upper leaf surfaces. The growth of the plant is

checked. Adult thrips may be quite easy to see on the leaves because, unlike most sap-sucking pests, they feed readily on the upper leaf surfaces instead of concealing themselves beneath.
**Causes** Most thrips are narrow-bodied black insects. They are up to 2mm (1/16in) long, and have two pairs of heavily fringed wings. The wings are folded when not in flight so the hairy fringing may not be immediately apparent.

The immature nymphs are wingless and a creamy yellow colour. Some thrips are virus vectors. The most common type to be found on vegetable crops is the onion thrips, *Thrips tabaci*.
**Control** As for onion thrips (*see p.259*).

## Tip burn

**Crops affected** Chicory, lettuce.
**Symptoms** Leaf margins are scorched and brown.
**Causes** Calcium deficiency, botrytis, or bacterial infection. Of these, calcium deficiency is the most usual cause of tip burn.
**Control** As for calcium deficiency (*see p.253*) and botrytis (*see p.252*).

## Tomato blotchy ripening

**Crops affected** Tomato.
**Symptoms** Randomly scattered patches of hard, green or yellow flesh that remain unripened on the fruit. The damage is visible only on the mature fruits, and those on the lower trusses are the most often affected.
**Causes** The disorder is usually associated with some form of malnutrition. A deficiency of potassium (*see p.260*) is the most frequent cause, but dry soil, or a poorly functioning root system, may also play a part.
**Control** Keep plants well fed. In particular, ensure that a high-potash feed (*see p.20*) is used.

## Tomato ghost spot

**Crops affected** Tomato.
**Symptoms** Unripe fruits display rings of discolouration. These may be pale green or yellow. As the fruits begin to ripen, the rings may change colour and become yellow or pale orange.
**Cause** The fungus *Botrytis cinerea*. The fruit are edible; the discolouration is caused by a hypersensitive reaction to the fungal spores. These spores are spread by rain or water splash and on air currents, and the fungus is widespread.
**Control** As the fruits remain edible, and they rarely deteriorate any further, there is no need to treat or remove them from the garden. By practising good hygiene you will help to eliminate the sources of the infection.
*See also* Botrytis.

**Tomato mosaic virus:** *see* Viruses.
**Tomato russet mite:** *see* Mites.
**Tomato spotted wilt:** *see* Spotted wilt.
**Tomato target spot:** *see* Target spot.
**Two-spotted mite:** *see* Red spider mite.

## Vegetable weevil

**Crops affected** Various, particularly vegetables.
**Symptoms** The larvae shelter underground during the day and feed under leaves at night, causing eaten leaves and young stems.
**Cause** Also called Brown vegetable weevil (*Listroderes obliquus or difficilis?*). The larvae are about 12mm long and creamy in colour. They pupate in the ground and emerge as brown beetle-like insects with an elongated weevil-like snout.
**Control** Remove weeds and ensure crop are rotated.

## Verticillium wilt

**Crops affected** Many, including eggplamt, olive, strawberry, apple, pear, plum, cherry, and quince.
**Symptoms** Plant foliage wilts. All or nearly all of the leaves on affected branches or stems show symptoms, but the whole plant is seldom affected simultaneously. Leaves may turn yellow or brown between the veins and then die. Stem death follows shortly after, but it may take several years for large woody plants to succumb totally. Smaller bushes or herbaceous plants, such as strawberries, may be killed within a single season. If the bark is removed from an affected stem, staining can be seen on the vascular tissues beneath; purple-brown or brown streaks run the length of the stem but are more apparent at the stem base. Roots also develop a central core of discoloured tissue.
**Causes** The fungi *Verticillium albo-atrum* and *V. dahliae*. Both are common in plant debris, plant tissues, and soil; the latter species forms fungal resting bodies that persist in the soil. They have a wide host range and many garden weeds can harbour the infections.
**Control** None available. Remove affected plants promptly, along with the soil in the immediate vicinity of the roots. The infection may be spread on pruning tools, so always clean them thoroughly when they have been used on an infected plant. Do not introduce the same species of plant on sites that have previously supported infected plants.

## Vine weevil

**Crops affected** Various.
**Symptoms** Both adults and larvae cause damage. Adults eat irregular notches from the leaf margins between spring and autumn, and although this damage is largely cosmetic, it should alert the gardener to the far greater potential damage caused by the fat, creamy white larvae under the soil. Plants make slow growth, followed by wilting and eventual death. The larvae (*see p.250*) eat plant roots and may sever them completely; they also remove the outer bark from woody stems. Plants grown in containers are particularly at risk.
**Causes** The adults and larvae of the vine weevil, *Otiorhynchus sulcatus*. The adults are active at night between spring and autumn. They are slow moving, dull black weevils, to 1cm (1/2in) long, with

pear-shaped bodies and and antennae that are bent at an angle about half-way along their length. They are capable of laying many hundreds of eggs over a period of several months. The legless, soil-dwelling larvae are up to 1cm (½in) long, with slightly curved bodies.

**Control** Adult vine weevils can be seen by torchlight at night and disposed of. Biological controls include pathogenic nematodes, *Steinernema carpocapsae* or *Heterorhabditis megidis*. Water the nematodes into the potting mix in late summer, while it is warm and moist, but before the grubs are large enough to cause serious damage. Pathogenic nematodes are ineffective in dry, heavy, or cold soils (less than 14°C/57°F).

## Virus vectors

Many viruses that affect plants are spread by certain pests, and these are described as virus vectors. Nearly all of these are sap-feeders and have piercing mouthparts; aphids (*see p.251*) and thrips (*see 263*) are common examples. When they insert their mouthparts into virus-infected plants, they pick up some virus particles and transfer them to new host plants when next they feed. Some soil-dwelling eelworms (*see p.255*) also transmit viruses as they feed on plant roots. This is one of the reasons why it is so important to control pests; some virus vectors feed on a wide range of plants and are capable of transmitting more than 100 viruses. Although they may not cause debilitating damage in themselves, the viruses that they spread often do. Moreover, there are no chemical treatments currently available to control viruses. It is best to destroy virused plants by burning, and new plants of the same type should not be grown on the soil that has harboured them.

## Viruses

**Crops affected** A wide range.
**Symptoms** The most common effects of viruses are stunting and distortion. Distortions may take the form of crinkling, crumpling, curling, or rolling. Leaves and other above-ground parts of plants show various markings, usually yellow or purple, and they take the form of spotting, mottling, mosaic, streaking, or flecking. Virused plants generally crop poorly, if at all, and they often suffer premature death. Some viruses can infect without causing visible symptoms and this is known as latent infection. It is often the case that alternative hosts show no symptoms; cucumber mosaic virus (*see p.254*) for example, may exist in a number of common weeds that act as a source of infection for other plants, even though these plants appear to be perfectly healthy.
**Causes** There are many virus species, the majority of which are sole agents of disease. Some, however, infect plants in combination, and plants that are stressed, for whatever reason, may fall prey to several viruses at once. There are several means of transmission, the most common being sap-sucking insect vectors. Whitefly, aphids, thrips, and leafhoppers are a few examples. Eelworms and fungi can also be virus vectors.

In most cases, viral infection is non-persistent, meaning that the virus cannot survive for long outside its host. An insect can acquire a virus after feeding on a plant, but the virus has a window of only a few seconds or minutes during which it must be passed on to another host, otherwise it dies. Other viruses, however, are persistent. The insect may pass it on for hours after feeding and may even carry the virus for rest of its life.

Viruses can also be transmitted by handling plants; by grafting (so-called graft-transmissible viruses); by handling tubers, bulbs, and corms; and during routine operations such as pruning, disbudding, or pinching out.
**Control** None available. Remove and dispose of affected plants promptly. Wash hands and tools thoroughly after handling infected plants. Do not introduce plants of a similar type onto sites that have previously supported infected plants. Control vectors, and control weeds, which may be alternative hosts. Do not propagate from infected plants. Where possible, choose resistant cultivars and buy plants that are certified as virus-free.

## Walnut blight

**Crops affected** Walnut.
**Symptoms** Black spots on leaves, green fruit and young stems. Fruit infected at flowering will be black inside.
**Cause** The bacterium *Xanthomonas campestris* pv. *juglandis*.
**Control** Spray with copper-based fungicide in spring to prevent blight. Weekly sprays may be necessary in damp weather.

**Walnut blister mite:** *see* Mites.

## Wasps

**Crops affected** Ripe, sugar-rich fruits.
**Symptoms** Soft inner tissues of fruits are eaten out, eventually creating large hollow cavities. On relatively soft-skinned fruits, wasps are capable of initiating damage; on tougher-skinned ones, such as apples and pears, wasps usually enlarge existing damage caused by bird pecks.
**Causes** Various species of social wasp are significant fruit pests: especially European wasp, *Vespula germanica*.
**Control** Protect ripening fruits by enclosing selected fruit trusses inside muslin bags or old nylon tights. If wasp nests can be located, they can be controlled by using an insecticidal dust at the nest entrance at dusk when the wasps have stopped flying for the night.

## Waterlogging

**Crops affected** Any.
**Symptoms** Foliage wilts and yellows; in extreme cases flowers may also wilt. Yellowed leaves fall prematurely. Inspection of the roots may reveal deterioration; the outer skin may peel and can often be stripped easily from the root core.
**Causes** Overwatering, excessive rainfall, or poor drainage may all be implicated, singly or together.

**Control** Attempt to improve soil conditions and avoid overwatering. On heavy soils, make sure that a large area of soil is lightened by the incorporation of large quantities of grit and bulky, well-rotted organic matter before planting. The application of a foliar feed can help to counteract the effects of slight or temporary waterlogging; it stimulates root production to replace those lost.

**Weevil:** *see* Vegetable weevil, Vine weevil.
**Whiptail of brassicas:** *see* Molybdenum deficiency.
**White rot:** *see* Onion white rot.

## Whitefly

**Crops affected** Brassicas, okra, capsicum, sweet potato, tomato, cucurbits, and many other glasshouse fruits and vegetables.
**Symptoms** Small insects, about 2mm (½in) long, fly up when disturbed from beneath the leaves (*see p.250*). Adults have white wings. They lay their eggs beneath the leaves and these hatch into flat, oval, scale-like nymphs. The final nymphal stage is sometimes called a pupa, and is plumper, often with hairs or waxy white secretions on the upper surface. Both nymphs and adults excrete sticky honeydew, which drops onto the leaves and is host to sooty moulds.
**Causes** There are a few important pest species: including the glasshouse whitefly, *Trialeurodes vaporariorum*, which may infest outdoor plants in warm weather. The glasshouse whitefly breeds continuously throughout the year in warm conditions.
**Control** On brassicas, light infestations can be tolerated. Treat heavy infestations with pyrethrum, or insecticidal soap. Several treatments at weekly intervals may be necessary with organic sprays.

Pesticide resistance is a problem with glasshouse whitefly; biological control with a tiny parasitic wasp, *Encarsia formosa*, is often the best remedy under glass. It must be introduced between mid-spring and mid-autumn, when temperatures will be high enough for it. Release the wasp when pest populations are still low; it needs time to breed before it can control whitefly. Sticky yellow traps are effective and useful indicators of rising whitefly populations. Sooty moulds can easily be wiped off tomato and cucumber crops with a damp cloth.

The use of *Encarsia* can be integrated with the use of insecticidal soaps, which do not affect it. Other pesticides are harmful to *Encarsia* and, in any case, may give poor control if a resistant strain is present. Several applications at five-day intervals will be necessary even for susceptible strains.

**Wilt virus:** *see* Spotted wilt.

## Wind damage

**Crops affected** Any.
**Symptoms** Leaves appear scorched, and one side of a plant is often more severely affected than the other. Most damage occurs on the side of the prevailing wind. If winds are salt-laden, the damage is exacerbated and the plant may die back or die completely. Where strong winds are persistent, as they often are in coastal

areas, for example, trees may develop a lop-sided growth habit; this is known as "krumholtz" or wind-training, where they grow away from the prevailing wind.
**Cause** Wind. The effects of wind are made worse if wind tunnels are present (where wind speeds up when funnelled between two walls, for example) or if windbreaks are removed.
**Control** Construct a shelter or plant or erect windbreaks (*see pp.12–13*) to filter the wind. Prune out dead stems to prevent secondary infections setting in.

## Wireworm

**Crops affected** Root vegetables and seedlings, lettuce.
**Symptoms** Seedlings are killed and the stems are severed just below soil level. Potato tubers and carrots are extensively tunnelled in late summer. Slender, orange-brown, worm-like larvae, up to 25mm (1in) long, with three pairs of short legs near the head end may be found in the soil or in the tubers. They have a small but distinctive protuberance at the rear end of the abdomen.
**Causes** The larval stage of click beetles. There are several species, including *Agriotes lineatus, A. obscurus, A. sputator,* and *Athous haemorrhoidalis*. They occur most commonly in plots that have been newly converted from grassland. If the ground is kept in cultivation, they will decline steadily over a three- or four-year period.
**Control** Dig up potato tubers as soon as they mature to reduce damage. There are no chemical controls available to amateur gardeners for the control of wireworms.

## Woolly aphid

**Crops affected** Apple.
**Symptoms** A woolly, white waxy growth occurs on the stems, fruit and the bark of apple trees in late spring and summer. It is secreted by pinkish-brown aphids. They often cluster around old pruning wounds and cracks or splits in the bark. Later in the summer, they migrate to young branches and cause knobbly brown swellings to develop. If these galls split in frosty weather, they can form an entry point for canker (*see p.253*). Woolly aphids feed on woody tissue in the root system all year and above ground in warm weather.
**Cause** A sap-sucking aphid, *Eriosoma lanigerum*. It overwinters as immature nymphs beneath loose bark.
**Control** Spray as soon as seen in spring with bifenthrin. Heavy summer infestations are difficult to control and a systemic insecticide will be required.

# INDEX